HOW TO PREPARE FOR THE
NATIONAL TEACHER EXAMINATIONS

NTE

CORE BATTERY
AND SPECIALTY AREA TESTS

FIFTH EDITION

Albertina Abrams Weinlander, Ph.D.
Professor Emerita of Education
Wittenberg University, Springfield, Ohio

WITH CONTRIBUTIONS BY:

Jerome Notkin
Professor and Teaching Fellow
New College, Hofstra University, Hempstead, New York

Maurice Bleifeld
Principal Emeritus
Martin Van Buren High School, Queens Village, New York

Joseph A. Mascetta
Formerly Chemistry Teacher and Coordinator, Science Department,
Presently Principal
Mount Lebanon High School, Pittsburgh, Pennsylvania

Lester W. Schlumpf
Retired Principal, John Adams High School, Queens, New York
Former Lecturer in Mathematics, Queens College, Queens, New York

Robert Lehrman
Former Teacher and Supervisor of Science, Roslyn High School, Roslyn, New York

William O. Kellogg
Former Head of the History Department, St. Paul's School, Concord, New Hampshire

Edward A. Mainzer
Social Studies Teacher, Roslyn High School, Roslyn, New York

Sheila K. Hollander, Ph.D.
Director of Programs for Teaching Special Needs Populations
Adelphi University, Garden City, New York

John B. Jeffrey, Ed.D.
Superintendent of Schools, Big Rapids, Michigan

Max M. Weinlander, Ph.D.
Retired Psychologist, Veterans Administration, Dayton, Ohio
Former Lecturer in Education, Miami University, Oxford, Ohio
Former Adjunct Professor in Psychology, Wright State University, Dayton, Ohio

BARRON'S

BARRON'S EDUCATIONAL SERIES, INC.

The author is grateful to Dr. Max M. Weinlander, Ph.D. for his encouragement, research and for proofreading the entire manuscript. Many thanks are given to the contributors, ETS, and the libraries, museums, magazines, newspapers, and other sources for the loan of materials.

In addition to those noted in the text, we gratefully acknowledge the following copyright holders for permission to reprint text, photographs, or graphs, as noted.

Page 171: Writing passage from "Cheating: Alive and Flourishing," by Claudia H. Deutsch, April 10, 1988. Copyright © 1988 by The New York Times Company. Reprinted by permission.

Pages 171–172: Writing passage from "Literary Lackluster," by Gilbert Sewall. Reprinted, with permission, from the Spring 1988 issue of the AMERICAN EDUCATOR, the quarterly journal of the American Federation of Teachers.

Page 246: Graph. Copyright © 1988 by The New York Times Company. Reprinted by permission.

Pages 257, 410, 412, 416: Photographs of dancers from HOW TO ENJOY BALLET, by Mary Clarke and Clement Crisp, published by Piatkus Books. Reprinted by permission.

Page 426: Writing passage from MISEDUCATION: PRESCHOOLERS AT RISK by David Elkind. Copyright © 1987 by David Elkind. Reprinted by permission of Alfred A. Knopf, Inc.

Page 362: Bar graph. THE WORLD ALMANAC & BOOK OF FACTS, 1987 edition, copyright © Newspaper Enterprise Association, Inc. 1986, New York, NY 10166.

Page 382: Excerpt from "A Rose for Emily" from the COLLECTED STORIES, by William Faulkner. Reprinted by permission of Random House, Inc.

Answer sheets for Model Tests selected from *A Guide to the NTE Core Battery Tests (Revised)*, 1986.

© Copyright 1992 by Barron's Educational Series, Inc.

Prior editions © Copyright 1988, 1984, 1971, 1968 by Barron's Educational Series, Inc.

All rights reserved.
No part of this book may be reproduced
in any form, by photostat, microfilm, xerography,
or any other means, or incorporated into any
information retrieval system, electronic or
mechanical, without the written permission
of the copyright owner.

All inquiries should be addressed to:
Barron's Educational Series, Inc.
250 Wireless Boulevard
Hauppauge, New York 11788

International Standard Book No. 0-8120-4998-5
Library of Congress Catalog Card No. 92-4993

Library of Congress Cataloging in Publication Data

Weinlander, Albertina Abrams.
    How to prepare for the National teacher examinations, NTE: core battery & most specialty tests/Albertina Abrams Weinlander; with contributions by Jerome Notkin . . . [et al.]. — 5th ed.
    p.   cm.
    ISBN 0-8120-4998-5
    1. National teacher examinations — Study guides.   I. Title.
LB1762.W4 1992
379.1'57 – dc20   92-4993
                                                                                                    CIP

PRINTED IN THE UNITED STATES OF AMERICA

23   100   987654321

CONTENTS

Introduction 1
An Overview of the Tests 1
   Core Battery 1
   Specialty Area Tests 2
   Content Area Performance Assessments 3
Registration 3
   Typical Test Schedule 4
Fees 4
Special Arrangements 4
   For Handicapped Persons 4
   For Monday Testing 4
   For a Special Test Center 4
Preparing for the NTE 5
   Building Your Confidence for Test-Taking 5
Taking the NTE 5
   Test-Taking Strategies 5
   Marking the Answer Sheet 6
   Guessing 6
Scores 6
   Reporting of Scores 7
   Cancellation of Scores 7
   Rescoring Service 8
Test Validity and Reliability 8

Part I   Test of General Knowledge: Description, Review, Practice 9

Social Studies 10
   Preparing for the Social Studies Section 10
   Glossary of Social Studies Terms 11
   Chronological Summary of Some Important Developments in American History 21
   Diagnostic Practice Test 42
Mathematics 49
   Preparing for the Mathematics Section 49
   Strategies for Answering Mathematics Questions 49

iii

CONTENTS

    Review 50
    Diagnostic Practice Test 75
Literature and Fine Arts 79
    Preparing for the Literature and Fine Arts Section 79
    Literature Glossary 79
    Art Glossary 82
    Music Glossary 85
    Diagnostic Practice Test 87
Science 99
    Review 100
    Diagnostic Practice Test 113

Part II Test of Communication Skills: Description, Review, Practice 119

Listening 120
    Strategies for the Listening Section 120
    Developing Listening Skills 120
    Diagnostic Practice Test 122
Reading 128
    Preparing for the Reading Section 128
    Strategies for Answering Reading Questions 129
    Reading Exercise 129
    Diagnostic Practice Test 131
Writing: Multiple-Choice 139
    Preparing for the Multiple-Choice Writing Section 139
    Strategies for Answering the Multiple-Choice Writing Questions 139
    Review 140
    Diagnostic Practice Test 166
Writing: Essay 174
    Review 175
    Essay Writing Hints 175
    Diagnostic Practice Test 179

Part III Test of Professional Knowledge: Description, Review, Practice 181

Teaching Principles and Practices—Topics for Review 182
Bibliography 187

CONTENTS

Worksheets for Applying Principles 188
Diagnostic Practice Test 209

Part IV Model Test 1: Core Battery 239

Test of General Knowledge 243
   Answer Keys and Explanations 274
Test of Communication Skills 287
   Answer Keys and Explanations 307
Test of Professional Knowledge 317
   Answer Keys and Explanations 344

Model Test 2: Core Battery 361

Test of General Knowledge 361
   Answer Keys and Explanations 395
Test of Communication Skills 408
   Answer Keys and Explanations 428
Test of Professional Knowledge 437
   Answer Keys and Explanations 465

Part V Specialty Area Tests 479

Art Education 480
Biology and General Science 485
Business Education 488
Chemistry, Physics, and General Science 491
Early Childhood Education 494
Education in the Elementary School 498
Education of Students with Mental Retardation 503
Educational Leadership: Administration and Supervision 507
English Language and Literature 516
Foreign Language 520
   French 521
   German 524
   Spanish 527
Health Education 530
Home Economics Education 535
Introduction to the Teaching of Reading 538

CONTENTS

Library Media Specialist **541**

Marketing Education **545**

Mathematics **549**

Music Education **551**

Physical Education **555**

Social Studies **559**

Special Education **562**

Speech Communication **566**

Teaching Hearing-Impaired Students **569**

Teaching Visually Handicapped Students **573**

Technology Education **578**

Appendix
State Departments of Education **581**

Introduction

Since 1950, the Educational Testing Service has administered the National Teacher Examinations. These consist of three independent, largely objective, standardized tests, collectively termed the Core Battery, and various Specialty Area tests. The Core Battery tests are given three times a year, typically in October, March, and June. The Specialty Area tests are administered a few weeks later, typically in March, July, and November. In addition special administrations for limited numbers of candidates are given in certain cites and states. For specific information concerning regular and late registration, test dates, and special administrations consult the *NTE Information Bulletin* (see below) for the year in which you expect to take the examinations.

This study guide, *How to Prepare for the National Teacher Examinations*, was written to assist prospective teachers and teachers in the field who plan to take either the Core Battery or both the Core Battery and a Specialty Area examination. This book will help you in a variety of ways. For the Core Battery, it contains review material in the various fields, quizzes and practice tests, and two full-length model tests that in format, difficulty, and content echo today's NTE Core Battery tests. Answers are given for all tests, as well as explanations for the correct choices to questions in the model tests. For most Specialty Area tests, there is a brief description followed by sample questions.

This Introduction contains basic information regarding the tests and their administration. In addition, two publications of the Educational Testing Service are especially helpful. You should obtain or at least examine:

NTE Programs: Descriptive Book for the Core Battery and Specialty Area Tests (Revised), which describes all the tests and gives sample questions for each type.

and you *must* obtain:

NTE Bulletin of Information [for the current year], which contains detailed information on test centers, fees, and registration, including registration forms.

These can be obtained by writing:

NTE Programs
Educational Testing Service
CN 6051
Princeton, NJ 08541-6051

or by telephoning (Monday through Friday):

(609) 771-7395   Princeton, NJ: call 8:30 A.M. to 9:00 P.M. (Eastern time)
(415) 653-5400   Berkeley, CA: call 8:30 A.M. to 4:30 P.M. (Pacific time)

Check the Score Recipient List included in the *NTE Bulletin of Information* to determine whether the school district, state agency, or association to which your scores must be reported is included. If it is not, follow the directions given by the Educational Testing Service.

An Overview of the Tests

CORE BATTERY

The Core Battery consists of three separate tests: The Test of General Knowledge, the Test of Communication Skills, and the Test of Professional Knowledge. With the exception of the essay-writing section in the Test of Communication Skills, all questions are multiple-choice.

Test of General Knowledge

The two-hour Test of General Knowledge consists of four 30-minute sections: (1) Social Studies; (2) Mathematics; (3) Literature and Fine Arts; and (4) Science. (The sections may be given in any order, and the number of questions in a particular section may vary from time to time.) This test is designed for the generally well-educated person, rather than for the specialist in any of the four fields.

INTRODUCTION

Test of Communication Skills

The two-hour Test of Communication Skills consists of four 30-minute sections: (1) Listening; (2) Reading; (3) Writing: multiple-choice; and (4) Writing: essay. The multiple-choice questions in Section 3 measure the candidate's command of standard written English; the emphasis is on the ability to detect errors and to correct faulty constructions.

Test of Professional Knowledge

The two-hour Test of Professional Knowledge consists of four 30-minute sections, only three of which count toward your score. Each section covers the same content and has the same type of questions. The test focuses on two broad areas: (1) the context of teaching and (2) the process of teaching. Included in area 1 are such topics as school law; the rights of the handicapped and the minority student; bilingual instruction; extra-classroom influences on teachers (parents, the community at large, other teachers, special interest groups, the media, etc.); and extra-classroom influences on students (physical and developmental factors, parents, peers, etc.). Area 2 deals with regard to students, parents, fellow teachers, and the general public.

For more detailed information on each of these tests, along with review, practice, and model tests, see Parts I, II, III, and IV of this book.

SPECIALTY AREA TESTS

Each of the 74 Specialty Area tests takes two hours. These tests measure the candidate's knowledge of subject matter and appropriate skills for teaching in the following areas:

Accounting (135 questions)
Agriculture (140 questions)
Agriculture (CA, OR) (148 questions)
Agriculture (PA) (140 questions)
Art (PA) (128 questions)
*Art Education (150 questions)
Audiology (150 questions)
Biology (150 questions)
*Biology and General Science (160 questions)
Business (PA) (80, 77, 80, 76, 73 questions)
*Business Education (160 questions)
Chemistry (120 questions)
*Chemistry, Physics, and General Science (140 questions)
Communication (150 questions)
Composition, Literature, and English Language (150 questions)
Computer Literacy/Data Processing (120 questions)
Cooperative Education (157 questions)
*Early Childhood Education (150 questions)
Earth/Space Science (120 questions)
Economics (105 questions)
*Education in the Elementary School (150 questions)
*Education of Students with Mental Retardation (150 questions)
*Educational Leadership: Administration and Supervision (145 questions)
*English Language and Literature (150 questions)
Environmental Education (140 questions)
Foreign Language Pedagogy (55 questions)
*French (160 questions)
General Science (120 questions)
Geography (135 questions)
*German (160 questions)
Government/Political Science (125 questions)
*Health Education (120 questions)
Health and Physical Education (145 questions)
*Home Economics Education (150 questions)
*Introduction to the Teaching of Reading (150 questions)
Italian (130 questions)
Japanese (130 questions)
Latin (130 questions)
*Library Media Specialist (150 questions)
*Marketing Education (120 questions)
*Mathematics (120 questions)
*Music Education (150 questions)
Office Technology (135 questions)
*Physical Education (150 questions)
Physics (100 questions)
Pre-Kindergarten Education (120 questions)
Psychology (120 questions)
Reading Specialist (150 questions)
Russian (102 questions)
Safety-Driver Education (125 questions)
School Food Service Supervisor (150 questions)
School Guidance and Counseling (140 questions)
School Psychologist (135 questions)
School Social Worker (120 questions)
*Social Studies (150 questions)

INTRODUCTION

Sociology (115 questions)
*Spanish (160 questions)
*Special Education (150 questions)
*Speech Communication (150 questions)
Speech-Language Pathology (150 questions)
Teaching Emotionally Disturbed Students (120 questions)
Teaching English as a Second Language (120 questions)
*Teaching Hearing-Impaired Students (120 questions)
Teaching Learning-Disabled Students (120 questions)
Teaching Minimally Mentally Handicapped Students (120 students)
Teaching Orthopedically Impaired Students (130 students)
Teaching the Physically and Mentally Handicapped (120 questions)
Teaching Speech to the Language Impaired (120 questions)
*Teaching Visually Handicapped Students (120 questions)
*Technology Education (150 questions)
U.S. History (120 questions)
Vocational General Knowledge (110 questions)
World and U.S. History (130 questions)
World Civilization (120 questions)

*A description of these Specialty Area tests with sample questions are included in Part V of this book.

CONTENT AREA PERFORMANCE ASSESSMENTS

While several states require just the National Teacher Examination Specialty Area tests for licensure, other states use both the Specialty Area tests and the Content Area Performance Assessment (CAPA) tests for certification. The CAPA tests are given at selected sites on the same day as the Specialty Area tests. Preregistration for both tests is required (see the current *NTE Bulletin*).

The CAPA examinations do not use multiple-choice questions. The examinee is required to give direct responses through essay and/or short written answers. The CAPA tests cover these five subject areas:

- *The English Language and Literature test* (two essay questions) has the candidate demonstrate an understanding of and the ability to analyze literary passages.
- *The Life Science test* examines four areas: the use of scientific knowledge and conceptualizations, using simple hypotheses to develop demonstrations and experiments, and to interpret relevant data, the ability to explain scientific processes and systems, understanding of and the ability to explain science and technology and their affect on human behavior.
- *The Mathematics test* (four problems) requires knowledge of algebra and geometry, calculus, probability and statistics, and mathematical relationships with quantitative and logical emphasis for problem-solving. (Calculators are permitted.)
- *The Physical Science test* (four questions) assesses the following abilities: using scientific knowledge conceptually, preparing demonstrations and experiments for the classroom and interpreting relevant data, using scientific ideas and information in relation to natural processes and understanding scientific concepts and principles in relation to current science and technology and their effect on human behavior. The questions may be drawn from any two sciences, such as chemistry, geoscience, physics, or related physical science.
- *The Social Science test* (two essay questions) is based on the analysis and interpretation of U.S. and world maps and documents. The test is derived from interdisciplinary fields in the behavioral sciences, economics, geography, U.S. government and political science, and U.S. and world history.

Registration

The *NTE Bulletin of Information*, which you must obtain, contains registration forms for the Core Battery and the Specialty Area tests, together with detailed instructions for filling out these forms. The completed form(s), together with the appropriate fee (see next section), is returned to Educational Testing Service in the special envelope(s) provided in the Bulletin.

Note: You may choose to take one, two, or three tests (the entire Core Battery) on the same date. You cannot take the Core Battery tests and a Specialty Area test on the same day.

You must use a different registration form for each test date. Be sure to accurately indicate your name, address, and other information by filling in the appropriate grids.

INTRODUCTION

TYPICAL TEST SCHEDULE

Core Battery Tests

7:30 A.M.	Report for Test of General Knowledge
10:30 A.M.	Dismissal (approximate)
10:45 A.M.	Report for Test of Communication Skills
1:30 P.M.	Dismissal (approximate)
1:30–2:15 P.M.	Lunch—You may wish to bring your own in case food services near the test center cannot serve large groups in the allotted 45 minutes.
2:15 P.M.	Report for Test of Professional Knowledge
5:00 P.M.	Dismissal (approximate)

Specialty Area Tests

8:00 A.M.	Report to the test center
11:00 A.M.	Dismissal (approximate)

CAPA Tests

11:15 A.M.	Report to the test center
2:00 P.M.	Dismissal (approximate)

Fees

Fees are subject to change without notice. A recent schedule is as follows:

One Core Battery test	$40.00*
Two Core Battery tests, taken on same date	$60.00*
Three Core Battery tests, taken on same date	$80.00*
One Specialty Area test	$60.00*
CAPA Test	$60.00

In addition, various nonrefundable fees are charges for special services (e.g., $15 for late registration).
*Missouri, Nevada, and Ohio examinees pay additional costs.

Special Arrangements

Certain circumstances may make it difficult or impossible for a candidate to take the NTE examination(s) at the regularly scheduled time or place. In that case special arrangements may be requested.

FOR HANDICAPPED PERSONS

If you have a handicap (visual or hearing impairment, or physical or learning disability), and if you are unable to obtain a waiver of the NTE requirement from the school system, institution, or agency to which you are applying, you may request special testing arrangements. You should *not* fill out a registration form, but instead should submit a letter explaining the circumstances. Specify each school system, institution, or agency that requires the test(s) and to which scores should be sent, and the special arrangements needed (e.g., a reader if visually impaired, a seat near the supervisor or written instructions if hearing impaired, a wheelchair if physically disabled). Enclose a physician's report verifying your handicap and describing its extent.

FOR MONDAY TESTING

If your religious convictions prohibit your taking the NTE on Saturday, you may apply for administration of the test on the Monday immediately following the Saturday date. Fill out your registration form in accordance with the special instructions in the *NTE Bulletin of Information* for this situation. Enclose a letter from your minister or rabbi verifying that in your religion the Sabbath is observed on Saturday.

FOR A SPECIAL TEST CENTER

A list of the test centers in each of the 50 states, as well as in the District of Columbia and Puerto Rico, is given in the *NTE Bulletin of Information*. If you live more than 150 miles from the nearest center, you may request to take the test at a supplementary center established for this purpose. Your letter of request should accompany

INTRODUCTION

the completed registration form. In addition to the standard fee for the test(s) you wish to take, you must pay a service fee of $35 for the supplementary center.

Preparing for the NTE

Basically, the Core Battery measures general knowledge with which the well-educated teacher should be familiar, communication skills (listening, reading, and writing), and specific knowledge related to teaching. Each of the Specialty Area tests assesses the skills and in-depth knowledge acquired in preparation for teaching a specific field.

Although there is little value in indiscriminate cramming (the requisite information, skills, and abilities should have been acquired over many years), intelligent preparation will certainly be helpful. The information used on the National Teacher Examinations is derived from the course content of the education curriculum in most teacher education programs of the colleges and universities. It is based on long-term learning with interpretation and application of such information. Reviewing your class notes, old tests, and papers you have written will refresh your memory about relevant information and how it can be used in your field of study and/or for certification as a teacher. Since the validity and reliability of the NTE tests has been verified by authorities in the fields, it is likely that you have already been exposed to this information, particularly if you are a senior or a graduate student. You should spend time on course work with which you have some difficulty, such as writing essays.

The first step in your preparation is to read the description of each test section in Parts I, II, and III of this book. This will give you a good idea of what to expect on the test. After reading the description of a particular section, read (or skim) the review material for that section. Then take the Diagnostic Practice Test and check your answers against the answer key. (You may wish to take the test before looking at the review material, especially if you feel confident of your expertise in that area.) Use the results of the Diagnostic Practice Test to help you pinpoint your weaknesses. Concentrate your preparation on these areas. Look over pertinent course notes, and study the review material in Parts I, II, and III of this book, even if you have already done so. Where necessary, do some outside reading on topics that seem likely to appear on the tests and about which you know little.

After you have reviewed all weak areas, you are ready for Model Test 1. If you have worked conscientiously and intelligently, you should do significantly better than you did on the Diagnostic Practice Tests. Once again, use the answer keys to pinpoint any weaknesses. Finally, take Model Test 2 for further practice.

BUILDING YOUR CONFIDENCE FOR TEST-TAKING

There are several actions you can take to build your confidence before taking the NTE:

1. Take a positive attitude toward the test. It is based on information you have already studied and applied in classroom exercises, tests, or student teaching.
2. Accept the fact that it is an important link in your certification and job placement, but *do not worry about it*.
3. Schedule the test for a time when you are not under high stress from other causes, such as student teaching, finals, or personal activities.
4. Plan to use *Barron's How to Prepare for the National Teacher Examinations* to begin your review several weeks before the test. Your admission card or registration materials from ETS may not be available to you before 30 days of the test date; so begin before that time so you will not feel pressured.
5. Realize that no one is expected to get all the answers correct.
6. When you use this NTE study guide, check the various content areas closely for each subject on the NTE. If there is an area that was not taught in your college, get at least two of the latest books from the library on the topic and review them.
7. Because mind and body affect the performance of the other, rest, good nutrition, and exercise, along with time management, can help you.

Taking the NTE

TEST-TAKING STRATEGIES

The following suggestions will help you to do your best:

1. Get adequate sleep the night before the test(s).
2. Eat your customary breakfast or (preferably) a better one. Even a light meal is better than none.

INTRODUCTION

3. Leave ample time for travel. Allow for such contingencies as a late train or bus or a crowded parking lot.
4. Bring these items with you:
    a. Identification that includes a photograph (e.g., a student ID card, driver's license, or passport).
    b. Your admission ticket or other authorization to take the test.
    c. One copy of your completed Critical Information Form, taken from the NTE Bulletin of Information.
    d. Three or four No. 2 pencils, with points reasonably sharp but not to the extent that they are likely to break.
    e. An eraser that does not smudge.
    f. A watch by which to pace yourself during the examination.
    g. Your lunch, unless you are familiar with the test center and know where you can obtain food during the 45 minutes allotted.
5. Leave these items at home:
    a. All books, including dictionaries.
    b. Slide rules, protractors, compasses, and calculators.
    c. Recorders and cameras.
    d. Papers of any kind.
6. Read each set of directions carefully. Know what you are asked to do before you begin work.
7. Work rapidly but not carelessly. Do not get bogged down on any one question. Remember, all questions carry the same point value. After a reasonable amount of time, guess if it is a Core Battery test, or just go on to the next question if it is a Specialty Area test. In either case, circle the question in your test booklet, so that you can come back to it if you have time.
8. Eliminate as many wrong answers as you can. Deciding between two choices is easier than deciding among five. Even if you have to guess, every answer you eliminate improves your chances of guessing correctly.
9. On Core Battery tests, answer every question. There is no penalty for incorrect answers.
10. Remember that you are allowed to write in the test book. You can and should do your mathematical computations in the booklet. There is no need to try to do them in your head. And if it helps you to doodle while you think, then doodle.
11. Check frequently to make sure that you are answering the questions in the right spots. No machine is going to notice that you made a mistake early in the test, answered question 4 in the space for question 5, and all your subsequent answers are the right answers, but in the wrong spots.
12. Do not be concerned about any unusual pattern of answer choices (e.g., repetition of the same letter or absence of a particular letter) that you may observe as you mark your answer sheet.
13. Specialty Area tests carry no penalty for guessing. Correct answers become your score.

MARKING THE ANSWER SHEET

Since all of the multiple-choice questions are scored by machine, incomplete erasures or light or partial markings can cause you to lose credit. You must:

1. Use a No. 2 (soft) pencil.
2. Select your answer from the row of choices bearing the same number as the question.
3. Mark the space (A, B, etc.) that corresponds to the answer you have chosen as correct.
4. Choose only one answer to each question.
5. Fill in each intended space completely and heavily.
6. If you change your mind, erase your original answer completely.

GUESSING

Core Battery and *Specialty Area* tests: You will receive credit for the total number of questions you answer correctly; you lose no points for wrong answers. Therefore, you should attempt to select the best answer rather than leave the answer blank. If you make a correct guess, you will raise your score.

Scores

With the exception of the essay portion of the Test of Communication Skills, the answer sheets are scored by machine. For this reason it is essential that you (1) use a soft-lead (No. 2) pencil; (2) fill in completely each answer space you choose, and (3) erase completely any answers you later decide to change.

INTRODUCTION

You will receive a score for each test you take. Possible scores on the three Core Battery tests may range from 600 (no questions answered correctly) to 695 (all questions answered correctly) in intervals of one point; the scale for the Specialty Area tests may range from 250 to 990 in increments of 10.

REPORTING OF SCORES

You are entitled to four copies of your score of each test you take: one for yourself and up to three for recipients that you designate. Additional reports will be charged a $15 fee and must be requested by letter (not telephone, fax, or telegram).

For each section of the General Knowledge test and each section of the Communication Skills test, the number and percent of those questions for which you had correct answers will be reported. The scores for the Professional Knowledge test will be reported according to content classifications, the number of questions in each classification, and the number and percent of questions for which you had correct answers. The recipient agencies requesting your test scores will be sent a report showing the number and percent of content questions you answered correctly on each Specialty Area test.

Performance test norms for a minumum of 100 examinees who took the same test at one administration will be provided to the examinee. Within this group of at least 100 examinees, NTE uses three performance classifications with approximations: *low*, 25 percent; *high*, 25 percent; and an *average* or middle group, 50 percent of the examinees. When you receive the NTE report of your scores, an interpretation will be provided. Whenever you take the test, you will have different questions and achieve a different score; therefore, your performance will have a different interpretation for each test.

The Communication Skills test has both multiple-choice questions and an essay question (30 minutes). This essay is read by two readers, each of whom assigns it a score on a 6-point scale. The total score is the sum of the two independent ratings and the combined multiple-choice scores. If the two readers' scores differ by more than one point, a third reader also assigns the essay score; the closest two of the three scores are then added to obtain the final score.

Because the Educational Testing Service does not assign a passing score, it is suggested that each recipient agency use the NTE report as only one of several criteria for certification or job placement. The agency to which you have your test score sent determines how near the top or mean (average) your score should be in relation to your degree, experience, and/or interview for the position you seek. ETS does not send test scores to recipients who have violated the "Guidelines for Proper Use of NTE Tests." NTE test scores are reported for five years only, in order to stay current on measuring and interpreting academic performance.

You will receive a copy of your test scores within ten weeks. In some states your score will be sent automatically from ETS to the state departments of education, thus limiting your scores to only two other recipients. READ CAREFULLY THE CURRENT NTE PROGRAMS BULLETIN OF INFORMATION AND INDICATE THE RECIPIENTS BY THEIR PROPER CODES. BE SURE YOU HAVE USED THE SAME NAME WITH MIDDLE INITIAL FOR EACH REGISTRATION AND ON ALL FORMS AT THE TEST SITE. THIS WILL AVOID ANY DELAY IN RECEIVING YOUR TEST SCORES. ALWAYS FOLLOW ALL INSTRUCTIONS FOR REGISTRATION TIME, FEES, AND TESTING CENTER; ALL ARE SUBJECT TO CHANGE.

CANCELLATION OF SCORES

By the candidate: If you are unhappy after your performance on a test, you may request cancellation of the score. Such a request must be made by sending a letter or telegram within one week after the test is taken or (preferably) by notifying the supervisor before leaving the testing room.

By the NTE Policy Council: Misconduct during the test may result in dismissal from the test center; the answer sheet will not be scored. If, after scoring, doubts are raised about an individual's performance, the Educational Testing Service will investigate and, if necessary, take appropriate action. To avoid any suspicion of misconduct, therefore, do not:

1. give or receive help.
2. use notebooks, papers, calculators, or other aids.
3. remove pages from test books.
4. remove test books or answer sheets from the testing room.
5. attempt to take the test for another person.
6. allow another person to attempt to take the test for you.

INTRODUCTION

7. work on the wrong section of the test.
8. begin before the start of the test.
9. try to enter the room without your identification.

RESCORING SERVICE

Although machine scoring is highly accurate, you may wish to have your score verified by hand-scoring. This service can be secured by *letter* (not telephone, fax, telegram, or mailgram) within 6 months after you take the test(s). Address your request to:

> NTE Programs
> Attention: NTE Score Verification
> CN 6054
> Princeton, NJ 08541-6054

and include the following information to confirm your identity: full name, including former name if different from the one you now bear; sex; mailing address; date of birth; test date; name of test(s) taken; registration number if available; Social Security number (optional). For a fee of $25 per answer sheet, your test(s) will be manually scored.

Test Validity and Reliability

Validity. Is a particular test related directly to the content of existing teacher education programs? The answer is that the tests are developed using the guidelines of authorities on college curricula in the various fields, and that studies have demonstrated substantial agreement between (1) the NTE tests and college curricula in specific states and (2) the NTE tests and the curricula of specific colleges that use the test scores.

It usually takes between two and three years to develop a new test. For the Core Battery a panel of about 30 experts nominated by professional associations set up the framework and specifications for the three tests. After 3,000 individuals review preliminary test specifications, the information is used to determine the final test format. The level of difficulty and comprehensiveness is determined, and pretests are given to 20,000 people in 135 colleges and universities in 44 states. Two teacher panels then review the results and consider test question changes. Advisory committees and other ETS experts agree on the final draft. After the preliminary testing is completed, a sensitivity review is done to determine that no questions are biased, sexist, or racist in content. It is reviewed and a list of correct answers is prepared.

Reliability. Does a particular test measure *consistently* what it is supposed to measure? The answer is that tests are not precise instruments, and therefore the NTE, like other tests, has a degree of error. For a recent administration of the Core Battery tests this standard error of measurement had a range of 4 to 6. For the Specialty Area tests the range is 15 to 40 points. In other words, if you took the examination a second time, your score could vary 15 to 40 points above or below your first score.

Will It Help My Score If I Practice for the Tests?

One of the factors that reduces examinee efficiency is general anxiety about taking any kind of test. Fear may inhibit the recall of information you know. Successful practice with sample-type questions can lead to a more relaxed attitude toward the test, resulting in more careful reading of the questions and fewer mistakes.

You can become familiar with the types of test questions, the content of each test, and the problem-solving required for the NTE by using the tests in this book to practice. Even though the questions on the actual test you take will be different, after practice many people perform better on a test.

The mean scores, validity, and reliability studies refer only to the actual NTE tests. The scores you achieve on sample or practice tests in study guides cannot be compared to NTE means and scaled scores. Practice tests help you determine whether you are having difficulty with certain content areas, the range of your knowledge, and the application of methodology to classroom situations. The multiple-choice questions and essay topics in practice tests will help you increase your concentration and improve your performance under the pressure of time.

To further prepare you for giving your best possible performance on the NTE, you should also review current philosophies of education and changing techniques in the Specialty Areas in which you intend to teach.

Part I
Test of General Knowledge: Description, Review, Practice

The Test of General Knowledge consists of four separately timed sections: Social Studies, Mathematics, Literature and Fine Arts, and Science.

The *Social Studies* section contains 30 questions that cover United States historical and cultural events and movements, characteristics of societies and cultures, relationships between culture and individuals, economic concepts, geography as it pertains to human settlement and culture, and the methodologies of social science.

The *Mathematics* section contains 25 questions on math topics ranging from ratio and proportion to interpreting graphs and charts. The questions are designed to assess cumulative knowledge of mathematics from having studied it through at least one year of high school, and possibly for one year in college.

The *Literature and Fine Arts* section contains 35 questions based on examples taken from literature or photographs of various types of art works, including examples of architecture, theater, and dance. The questions are designed to assess skills in analysis and interpretation.

The *Science* section contains 30 questions designed to measure knowledge and understanding of certain themes that are major areas of scientific interest and current concern. The questions are based on important themes from the biological, physical, and earth sciences.

More detailed descriptions of each of these sections follow, along with appropriate review and practice.

TEST OF GENERAL KNOWLEDGE: DESCRIPTION, REVIEW, PRACTICE

Social Studies

The Social Studies examination consists of 30 questions designed to assess the candidate's level of competency in social studies. The questions measure knowledge and the ability to analyze, synthesize, interpret, and utilize information.

The questions focus on four major topics:
  I. Institutions, culture, and factors that contribute to change, in Europe, Africa, Third World countries, United States
 II. Human behavior as demonstrated by individuals, groups, and institutions, including civil rights, education, prejudices, racial bias, discrimination
III. World cultures, including similarities and differences among people and nations, and basic issues about interrelatedness, survival, advancement
 IV. Knowledge of methodology used in the social sciences and the ability to use it in the classroom to help students in their concept-building and information-processing as they use generalizations, value statements, and information in daily living.

Questions relate to historical events, political systems, cultures and society, and the multiple roles of minorities in the United States. The methodologies for teaching the social studies and interpreting the agents of social change are included. Review information from global and U.S. points of view: major facts, concepts, events, and movements as they are presented in the social sciences—history, sociology, economics, world geography, social psychology, and anthropology.

Preparing for the Social Studies Section

Use the review section that follows to refresh your memory about important names, events, and concepts in social studies. Use the Diagnostic Practice Test later in this section to familiarize yourself with the types of questions that appear on this part of the Test of General Knowledge. The Diagnostic Practice Test will also help you determine whether you need to study further for this part of the exam and which areas of social studies need more of your attention. The two Model Tests in Part IV of this book will provide additional practice if you need it.

The social studies review that follows contains a glossary of social studies terms, names and events, and an outline of important events in U.S. history.

Since the Social Studies section of the Test of General Knowledge does not usually require factual knowledge of minute details of U.S. or world history, we do not suggest that you try to memorize the information contained in this review or in any other review material you may have. Instead, look over the material to familiarize or refamiliarize yourself with events, terms, and concepts related to social studies. Note that most NTE Social Studies questions that require factual knowledge of historical events are on U.S. history as opposed to world history. Therefore, do not spend much time studying historical events that are not related to U.S. history.

SOCIAL STUDIES

Glossary of Social Studies Terms

Acculturation The process of borrowing between cultures, especially on the part of a less developed culture from a more developed culture, resulting in new patterns. Unlike diffusion, it usually refers to borrowings that occur under pressure, such as the introduction of Catholicism into Spanish-conquered Latin America in the 1500s. See Diffusion.

Adaptation The process whereby populations change on an on-going basis in response to alterations in their environments.

Affirmative action Policies designed to incorporate ethnic and racial minorities, including women, into political, economic, and social institutions. First use of the term was in 1961 in an executive order issued by President John F. Kennedy.

Agribusiness Large-scale production, processing and marketing of food and nonfood farm commodities and products. Agribusiness is a major commercial business. California has the largest concentration of agribusiness in the United States.

Animism The religious belief that views inanimate objects such as trees and mountains as possessing supernatural forces. Together with ancestor worship it appears to have been the "first religion" of people all over the world.

Anthropology The social science that studies biological and cultural variations in human populations.

Archeology The branch of anthropology or history that examines the remains of prehistoric cultures, that is, cultures for which there are no remaining written records and which thus can be known only through an examination of their material remains.

Artifact Preserved remains of nonnatural things, that is, things made by human beings, such as tools or housing. See Fossil.

Assimilation The merging of cultural traits from distinct cultural groups.

Balance of payment The system of recording all of the country's economic transactions with the rest of the world during a particular period. The balance of payment is typically divided into subaccounts, such as the capital and current accounts. The current account covers import and export goods; the capital account covers movements of investments. These subaccounts may show a deficit or surplus; the overall balance of payments, however, will not be in surplus or deficit since every dollar spent on foreign items is returned to buy U.S. goods or securities. See also Balance of trade.

Balance of trade The difference over a period of time between the value of a country's imports, such as automobiles and stereos, and its exports of merchandise, such as foodstuffs and computers. When a country exports more than it imports, the balance of trade is in surplus and the country is said to have a favorable balance of trade. However, an unfavorable balance of trade does not necessarily mean the country is in a weak economic condition since a strong economy can often lead to increased imports.

Bankruptcy State of insolvency of an individual or an organization, that is, an inability to pay debts.

Bicameral The organization of the legislative body into two distinct groups of members, selected on different bases, and usually different terms; called the *houses* in English speaking countries, elsewhere they are usually called *chambers*; the lower house is usually selected by broad popular vote (U.S. House of Representatives), the upper may represent political subdivisions within a country (U.S. Senate); although they deliberate and vote separately, both houses must pass most measures to be enacted; a bicameral structure is thought to prevent the passage of poorly considered legislation.

Bilateral Two-sided, as opposed to unilateral, one-sided, or as compared to multilateral, many-sided action or treaty.

Bilateral kinship A type of kinship system in which an individual's descent is traced on both his/her mother's and father's sides. See Matrilineal descent, Patrilineal descent.

Black market The illegal sale of merchandise. For example, during wars, black markets spring up for restricted goods in short supply. In many countries, black markets for foreign exchange exist owing to government restrictions on the prices that will be paid for foreign currencies, such as the U.S. dollar.

Bureaucracy Permanent administrative agencies of government designed to carry out public policy; commonly used in a negative sense to connote unresponsiveness or an unreasoning devotion to rules.

Cabinet Composed of the heads of major administrative departments who, as a group, discuss whatever matters the President decides to bring to their attention; among its members in the U.S. government are the Attorney General and the Secretaries of State, Treasury, Defense, Interior, Agriculture, Commerce, Labor, Transportation, Education, and others.

Capitalism Economic system with four major traits: (1) private ownership of property exists; (2) property and capital provide income for individuals and firms that accumulated and own it; (3) individuals and firms are relatively free to compete with others for their own economic gain; (4) the profit motive, that is, the search for profits, is basic to economic life. Although no nation is an example of a pure capitalist society, the United States is organized primarily along the capitalist lines.

Cash crop A crop produced for sale, as distinguished from a crop used for consumption on the part of the producers.

Caste system A social system incorporating hierarchical groups with differential access to prestige and economic resources. In a caste system one's position in society is usually completely determined at birth and not subject to change. The Hindu religion incorporates a caste system into its beliefs.

Checks and balances An organizational arrangement that enables each of the coordinate branches of government to exercise some degree of control over the others, for example, the power of the chief executive to veto acts of the legislature; this system enables the legislative, executive, and judicial branches to exercise some limited control over the others and thereby protect itself against encroachments on its authority.

Civilization Derived from the Latin word for "city," an advanced socio-cultural system. Such systems are usually characterized by the presence of not only cities, but also of territorially defined borders, symbiotic economies, advances toward the exact and predictive sciences, and public works and monumental architecture.

Class A group of individuals who are similar in their opportunity to obtain economic resources and/or social prestige. In contemporary society class usually relates to one's education and job, and is often broken down as upper class or rich, middle class or white collar jobs, working class or blue collar jobs, and poor. See Social stratification.

Communism In theory, anticapitalist proposals of Karl Marx and his followers that communal ownership of the means of production is preferable; in practice, economic systems in which production facilities are state-owned and production decisions are made by official policy and not directed by market action.

Culture The way of living and ideas people share and transmit from one generation to another.

Democracy Rule by the people; government by the consent of the governed, either directly as in town meetings or indirectly through the election of representatives; based on the principles of individual dignity, majority rule, liberty, equal rights, and equal opportunities.

Depression Economic condition characterized by a severe recession, that is, a severe curtailment in business activity. The Great Depression of the 1930s was marked by unemployment rates near 25% of the labor force. Although political observers frequently assert that opposition policies resulted in a "depression," most economists reserve the use of this term to exceptionally deep recessions.

Desegregation To put an end to separation due to race. Usually accomplished by a judicial order.

Détente A period of time, or a policy, of lessening the tensions between two hostile nations.

Diffusion The process whereby traits belonging to one society or culture become part of another society or culture. Examples of diffusion are numerous in the modern world, including such things as both playing of baseball in Japan and the popularity of Japanese food in the U.S.A.

Disfranchisement The taking away of the right to vote in a public election.

Due process As interpreted by the Supreme Court, the due process clauses of the Fifth and Fourteenth Amendments prohibit the national government and the states from depriving any person of life, liberty, or property by unreasonable, arbitrary, or capricious action.

Easy money State of the money supply when the Federal Reserve allows ample funds to build in the banking system, thereby making loans easier to get. This sort of policy is often said to lead to lower unemployment, higher growth rates of real GNP, and higher inflation rates. Contrast Tight money.

Economic sanctions   Internationally, restriction upon trade and financial dealings that a country imposes upon another for political reasons, usually as punishment for following policies of which sanctioning country disapproves.

Egalitarian society   A type of society in which there are as many positions of prestige in any given age-sex group as there are persons capable of filling them, so that there is no significant social hierarchy. This type of structure is usually found in hunting and gathering groups that wander in search of food and thus accumulate few possessions. See Social stratification, Social structure.

Elastic clause   Article I, Section 8 of the U.S. Constitution, which grants Congress the power "to make all laws which shall be necessary and proper" for carrying out its legislative powers; also referred to as the "necessary and proper" clause.

Emigration   The leaving of one country to reside in another.

Equal protection of the law   Based on the Fourteenth Amendment of the U.S. Constitution, which prohibits arbitrary, unreasonable, and invidious discrimination against individuals or classes of individuals; "no State shall make or enforce any law which shall abridge the privileges or immunities of citizens of the United States; nor shall any State deprive any person of life, liberty, or property, without due process of law; nor deny to any person within its jurisdiction the *equal protection of the laws.*"

Ethnocentrism   The belief that one's own culture and/or cultural group is inherently superior.

Exchange rate   Price at which one country's currency can be converted into another's. The exchange rate between the U.S. dollar and the British pound is different from that between the dollar and the West German mark, for example. Most exchange rates float freely and change slightly each trading day; some rates are fixed and do not change as a result of market forces.

Extended family   A family group consisting of two or more families, or a household containing relatives such as, aunts, uncles, cousins, and grandparents, in addition to the nuclear family. See Monogamy, Nuclear family.

Extradition   The returning of a person suspected of committing a crime from one state or country to another.

Family   The basic unit in society organized around kinship and usually including at least a husband and wife and young offspring. See Extended family, Monogamy, Nuclear family, Polyandry, Polygamy.

Fascism   Doctrine; collection of concepts; and dictatorship by government of a country, often involving hostile nationalistic attitudes, racism, and private economic ownership under rigid government control. A fascist regime is often militarily belligerent.

SOCIAL STUDIES

Favorable trade balance Situation where the value of a nation's exports is in excess of the value of its imports.

Federal Trade Commission (FTC) Federal agency established in 1914 to foster free and fair business competition and prevent monopolies and activities in restraint of trade.

Feudalism A system in which power is held by local lords with vast tracks of land, usually inherited.

Fifteenth Amendment Amendment to the United States Constitution which guarantees all citizens the right to vote regardless of race, color, or previous condition of servitude. It was ratified in 1870.

Fiscal policy Federal taxation, spending, and debt policies designed to level the business cycle, achieve full employment, and keep the inflation rate low. Fiscal policy is set by an action of the Congress and president. Fiscal policy is administered separately from monetary policy, although the goals are the same.

Fossil Preserved remains of living things (plants or animals). See Artifact.

Free market Market in which there is little or no control or interference by government or by any other powerful economic force or entity, such as a monopoly, cartel, or collusive oligopoly.

Geography The science that deals with the earth and life upon it, including the study of both the physical features on the earth's surface and the human activities on that surface.

Geology The science that deals with the history of the earth, especially as recorded in rocks.

Gross national product (GNP) Total value of goods and services produced in an economy over a period of time, usually one year. The GNP is comprised of consumer and government purchases; private, domestic, and foreign investment (purchase of capital goods); and net exports.

Guild An association of merchants or artisans in the same trade. The term is used with reference to craft guilds in medieval Europe, composed of workers in a particular craft, such as goldsmiths or weavers.

Horizontal merger The combination into one business of two companies that sell similar products. For instance, the purchase of J.C. Penney by Sears would be a horizontal merger. Horizontal mergers are often deemed likely to lead to increased market concentration and adverse economic behavior. At the limit, a horizontal merger could produce a monopoly or near monopoly. Therefore, horizontal mergers are usually carefully scrutinized by government agencies, such as the Federal Trade Commission. See Federal Trade Commission, Monopoly, Vertical merger.

Humanism A philosophy that asserts the dignity and worth of man and his capacity for self-realization through reason. It is often spoken of in contrast to belief systems that rely upon supernatural revelation.

TEST OF GENERAL KNOWLEDGE: DESCRIPTION, REVIEW, PRACTICE

Hypothesis   A tentative assumption made in order to test its consequences, often used to label a statement in contrast to facts.

Ideology   A system of beliefs, often with related norms and values.

Immigration   The coming into a country for permanent residence.

Imperialism   Policy of systematic domination and exploitation of a country by another country or an empire. Marxists assert that the United States engages in imperialism because powerful U.S. businesses need to protect their foreign markets.

Implied power   Powers inferred from one or more express grants of authority in the Constitution; powers that exist because the Constitution authorizes Congress to make "all laws which shall be necessary and proper, for carrying into execution the foregoing powers...."

Import quota   An imposed limit upon the quantity of a good or service that may be brought into a country or economy over a period of time. Quotas may be imposed by governments or producers themselves.

Industrial revolution   The period marking the introduction of mass production, improved transportation, technological progress, and the industrial factory system. It first began in Great Britain in the mid-1700s and reached the U.S. by the mid-1800s.

Industrial society   A society that derived most of its wealth and income from factory-type production, as against home or village-based manufacture or agriculture.

Inflation   General rise in the prices of goods and services. Inflation is measured using a price index.

Interest rate   Cost of borrowing funds, or return from saving funds, expressed as a percentage rate per time, usually one year. For instance, the interest rate on a car loan may be 11% per year.

Internationalism   An ideology that emphasizes the unity of the world's peoples, and which deplores restrictive national boundaries and competing national governments.

Isolationism   A foreign policy which discourages alliances and compacts with other nations.

Keynesian economics   Body of macroeconomics thought originated by the British economist John Maynard Keynes (1883-1946), whose landmark book, *The General Theory of Employment, Interest, and Money*, was published in 1935. Keynes believed that active government intervention (monetary policy and particularly fiscal policy) in the marketplace was the only method of ensuring economic growth and stability. He held that insufficient demand causes unemployment and that excessive demand causes inflation. Keynesian economics has had a great influence on the public economic policies of industrial nations, including the United States. See Fiscal policy, Monetary policy.

Kinship system   The pattern of relationships by which people link themselves to others. These links, which vary widely from culture to culture, may or may not involve blood or marriage, but are culturally recognized and often carry obligations. See Bilateral kinship, Matrilineal descent, Patrilineal descent.

Laissez-faire Economic doctrine that minimal interference of government in business and economic affairs is best. Adam Smith's path-breaking book, *The Wealth of Nations* (1776), described this in terms of an "invisible hand" that would provide for the maximum good of all. The laissez-faire period in the U.S. history was ended by the beginning of the twentieth century, when large monopolies were broken up by government action. Keynesian economics advocates a rejection of laissez-faire. The movement toward deregulation of business in recent years is to some extent a return to laissez-faire policies. See Keynesian economics.

Law Norms that carry sanctions enforced by the government or community.

League of Nations International organization created after World War I to promote international peace and security. The refusal of the United States to join the League of Nations harmed its effectiveness. The League of Nations was replaced in 1946 by the United Nations.

Left-wing Individuals or groups whose views are considered liberal or, in extreme cases, radical. The terms "left" and "right" originated in a meeting of the National Assembly in Paris in 1789 in which the more revolutionary members sat on the left of the speaker's rostrum and the less revolutionary on the right.

Lobbyist An individual or agent of an interest group who endeavors to influence the determination of public policy by presenting information to individual legislators, legislative committees, and other public officials or by resorting to other techniques of persuasion.

Locke, John English philosopher and political theorist (1632–1704). Locke's writings on natural individual rights and political systems through the consent of the governed were employed by the founding fathers of the American republic in both the Revolution period and the formation of our own constitutional form of government.

Marxism Political, social, and economic theories of Karl Marx. Applied Marxism, in an economy, results in either a communist economy or a heavily socialist economy.

Matrilineal descent The type of system that traces an individual's descent only through the female lines. See Patrilineal descent.

Monetary policy Federal Reserve decisions about changes in the money supply designed to stablize the economy and smooth the business cycle. It is generally believed that Federal Reserve actions to increase the growth rate of the money supply and/or lower interest rates spur economic growth, lower unemployment, and raise inflation. The reverse occurs when the Federal Reserve lowers the growth rate of the money supply and/or raises interest rates. See Easy money, Tight money.

Monogamy Marriage with only one person at a time. See Polyandry, Polygamy.

Monopoly The control of the production of a good or service by one firm. Monopoly, which is characterized by lack of competition, leads to high prices and a general lack of responsiveness to the desires of consumers. Antitrust laws enacted in the late nineteenth and twentieth centuries have outlawed most of the flagrant monopoly practices in the United States.

Nationalism   The takeover of a private company's assets or operations by a government. The company may or may not be compensated for the loss of its assets. In developing nations, an operation is typically nationalized if the government believes the company is exploiting the host country and/or exploiting too high a proportion of the profits. In developed countries, industries are often nationalized when they need government subsidies to survive, (Also patriotism, loyalty, jingoism).

Neolithic   Of or relating to the latest period of the Stone Age, which started perhaps as early as 8000 B.C. and is characterized by the domestication of animals, the development of agriculture, and the invention of farming tools. The technological developments of the Neolithic period were the key steps in the evolution of village life with its occupational specialization and creation of more complex forms of human activities, including government, science, and religion.

New Deal   Term used by President Franklin D. Roosevelt during his first campaign for election in 1932; used to describe the wide-ranging series of social and economic reforms advocated during the Roosevelt presidency.

Nineteenth Amendment   Provides that the right to vote shall not be denied on account of sex. Known as the women's suffrage amendment to the United States Constitution, it was ratified in 1920.

Norms   Definitions of acceptable and unacceptable behaviors for the members of society. Norms may be formal (laws) or informal (customs).

North Atlantic Treaty Organization (NATO)   A mutual defense alliance formed in 1949 by the United States and Western Europe to protect Western Europe from attack; expanded to include additional countries in the Atlantic area, the alliance has been weakened in recent years by political conflicts.

Nuclear family   A family structure in which the immediate family unit consists of only a married couple and their unmarried children. See Extended family.

Opportunity cost   A fundamental concept in economics. The opportunity cost of an item or action is the value of the next based alternative that had to be sacrificed to pursue the selected item or action.

Parliamentary government   A system of government in which the executive and legislative functions are combined and headed by a Prime Minister and Cabinet, who hold offices as representatives of the majority in the Parliament; to lose a vote of confidence results in resignation of the governing officials and the call for another election.

Patrilineal descent   The type of kinship system that traces an individual's descent only through the male lines. See Matrilineal descent.

Political science   The social science that examines political systems and the process of government.

Polyandry   The marriage of one woman to more than one man at the same time. See Monogamy, Polygamy.

SOCIAL STUDIES

Polygamy   The marriage of one man to more than one woman at the same time. See Monogamy, Polyandry.

Polytheism   The belief in many approximately equal gods.

Primary   An election within a political party to nominate candidates for office or delegates to a convention; voters in a *closed* primary must be members of the particular political party; nonaffiliated voters may also participate in an *open* primary.

Primary source   In historical research, a first-hand account of an event or individual, such as a diary entry, letter, or oral eye-witness account. See Secondary source.

Progressive taxes   Tax system in which those with higher incomes pay taxes at higher rates than those with lower incomes. The U.S. income tax is an example since households with higher incomes generally face higher marginal tax rates than households with lower incomes. Contrast Regressive taxes.

Psychology   The biological and social science which studies human and mental process and behavior.

Real earnings   Wages, salaries, and other earnings, corrected for inflation over time so as to produce a measure of actual change in purchasing power.

Recession   Downturn in economic activity, commonly defined as at least two consecutive quarters of decline in a country's real GNP. A recession bridges the period between a peak and a trough in the business cycle. A severe and long-lasting recession is called a depression. See Depression.

Regressive taxes   Tax system that results in the rich paying a lower percentage of their income as taxes than do the poor. Contrast with Progressive taxes.

Right-wing   Individuals or groups whose views are considered conservative or in extreme cases, reactionary.

Secondary source   In historical research, an account, such as a textbook or scholarly monograph, constructed out of primary sources. See Primary source.

Secular   Relating to worldly things or things that are not regarded as religious, spiritual, or sacred.

Segregation   The policy or practice of separating racial or ethnic groups, particularly blacks from whites in the United States; facilities and practices that were supposedly "separate and equal" came under widespread criticism and protest in the 1960s and sparked a civil rights movement that resulted in a substantial change.

Separate but equal doctrine   First held in the Supreme Court case of *Plessy v. Ferguson*, 163 U.S. 537 (1896) stating that separation of races was permissible if the facilities were of equal quality. Overturned by *Brown v. Board of Education*, 347 U.S. 483 (1954).

Social science   Areas of academic study that consider the nature of human societies and the interrelationships of individuals within societies. Among the social sciences are usually counted anthropology, economics, political science, psychology, and sociology.

TEST OF GENERAL KNOWLEDGE: DESCRIPTION, REVIEW, PRACTICE

Social stratification   A society composed of a number of social levels, usually based primarily on economic measurements, such as upper class, middle class, lower class. See Class, Egalitarian society, Social structure.

Social structure   The network of relationships between individuals and groups by which a particular society is set up. See Egalitarian society, Social stratification.

Socialism   The method of organizing an economy so that the government owns most, if not all, of the nation's capital. The state then runs most, if not all, of the nation's businesses. Contrast Capitalism.

Socialization   The process whereby parents and others pattern the behavior of those new to the culture, usually children, to conform to the standards of the particular culture.

Society   A group of individuals of the same species organized in a cooperative manner. A society possesses at least one and, in some cases, more than one culture.

Sociology   The social science that examines human groups and societies.

Sovereignty   An independent state with supreme authority within its borders; the power of a nation to act without the interference or control by another.

Standard of living   Sum total of amenities, quality, and quantity of goods and services consumed by consuming units within an economy.

State rights   In a federal system of government, these are the rights and powers reserved to the states. (For example, control of intrastate commerce.)

Suffrage   The right to vote in an election; the U.S. Constitution states, in the Fifteenth Amendment, that the right to vote shall not be denied "on account of race, color, or previous servitude"; in the Nineteenth Amendment, shall not be denied on account of sex; and in the Twenty-sixth, shall not be denied to anyone 18 years or older.

Tariff   Federal tax on imports or exports. When the tax is imposed to protect domestic producers from foreign competition, it is called a "protective tariff."

Third world   Nations lacking industrial development, and usually relying heavily upon agriculture. Includes much of Latin America and Africa and parts of Asia.

Thirteenth Amendment   Amendment to the United States Constitution that abolished slavery and involuntary servitude. It was ratified in 1865.

Tight money   When credit is difficult to obtain, usually because of the monetary policy of the Federal Reserve. Tight money is frequently said to lead to higher unemployment, reduced growth in the real GNP, and lower inflation. Contrast Easy money.

Trade deficit or surplus   Excess of imports over exports (for a trade deficit) or of exports over imports (for a trade surplus), resulting in a negative or positive balance of trade. The trade deficit is one part of the current account. Factors influencing the balance of trade include the country's exchange rate, production advantages in key manufacturing areas, and whether the country can produce enough of certain products to completely satisfy the domestic demand for them. See Balance of payments.

SOCIAL STUDIES

Underground economy   Portion of the economy that goes largely undetected by taxing authorities. Transactions usually are barter or in cash and include both illegal activities and activities that would be legal except for their unrecorded nature.

Upwardly mobile   Description of a segment of the population that is attempting to move up on the socioeconomic class scale. Upwardly mobile describes a trend toward higher status in terms of income, material goods, and life-styles. The "Yuppies" are an example of this upwardly mobile trend.

Urbanization   The movement of people from rural areas to the cities, generally associated with industrialization.

Vertical merger   Combination into one business of firms at different stages of production. For instance, the purchase of General Motors of one of its steel suppliers would be a vertical merger. Vertical mergers generally do not pose the major threat of creating a monopoly and so are often easier to consumate than horizontal mergers. Compare Horizontal merger.

Windfall profit   Profit that occurs suddenly as a result of an event not controlled by the person or company profiting by it.

Zero population growth (ZPG)   Forecast of no further increase in the population of the United States. Demographers study fertility rates to determine whether the United States will incur ZPG; economic and business implications are significant.

Chronological Summary of Some Important Developments in American History

COLONIAL AMERICA BEFORE 1763

Reasons for Exploration

Search for a sea route to the Far East
Desire for glory and wealth
Quest for new lands
Adventure

Reasons for Colonization of the New World

Religious freedom
Economic opportunity
Political freedom
Farmland
Social change

Territory of European Colonies in the New World

Spain: All of South America except Brazil, plus Central America, Mexico, Florida, California.
France: All of Canada except the Hudson Bay region, plus the Great Lakes region, the Mississippi Basin, the French West Indies.
Holland: The Hudson River Valley in New York.
England: The eastern coast from New England to Georgia, west to the Appalachian Mountains.

TEST OF GENERAL KNOWLEDGE: DESCRIPTION, REVIEW, PRACTICE

Geography and Its Effect on Settlements

The physical nature of the settled land usually determined the occupation and manner of life of the period.

New England: Rocky soil and long winters prevented extensive farming; wheat, corn, hay, and flax were the main agricultural products; colonists lumbered vast forests and fished off the coast; because of excellent harbors and rivers they developed trade as their chief source of income.

Middle Colonies: Level, fertile, rich land and good rainfall made for abundant farming; wheat, oats, and barley were grown in such quantity that these states were called "bread colonies."

Southern Colonies: Warm climate, long growing season, and fertile lands produced rich crops of cotton, tobacco, rice, and indigo; a good river system provided easy transportation inland; the produce was shipped to England and brought plantation owners large profits and manufactured goods in return.

Some Contributions of Mother Countries to North America

England: Democratic forms of local government; tradition of hard-working, zealous individuals; English language; Puritan religion.

France: Language, culture, and Roman Catholic religion established in Canada and Louisiana and introduced to many Indians west of Appalachians.

Spain: Schools, hospitals, and printing presses established by missionaries; Spanish language in Southwest; teaching of Christianity to Indians.

THE ERA OF THE AMERICAN REVOLUTION—1763–1789

Some Causes of the American Revolution

The Theory of Mercantilism: Held that the colonies existed only for the profit of the mother country; caused discontent among American businessmen and traders.

Navigation Acts: Controlled commerce with England and other countries.

Concept of the Rights of English Subjects: Colonists believed their rights were being denied by Parliament.

Important Events of the Revolutionary Period

First Continental Congress: All colonies except Georgia were represented; pledged to boycott all English goods if England did not settle existing disagreements.

Battle of Concord and Lexington: Minutemen and Massachusetts militia, forewarned by Paul Revere and William Dawes, routed English in first battle of the Revolution.

Second Continental Congress: Met in Philadelphia, attended by all thirteen colonies; made provisions for raising a colonial army, issuing and borrowing money; appointed George Washington as commander-in-chief of army; drafted the *Articles of Confederation,* an agreement among the states outlining the operation of the united government.

Declaration of Independence: Signed by John Hancock, president of the Second Continental Congress, and all the members present, stated the equality of all people, declared

the right of people to rebel when denied life, liberty and the pursuit of happiness by their governments.
Treaty of Paris: England recognized the independence of the colonies and ceded land from Canada to Florida.

Development of the Constitution

The *Articles of Confederation:* America's first Constitution had the following weaknesses:
    Each state, regardless of size, had only one vote.
    Congress could make laws, but there was no executive to enforce them.
    Amendments could be adopted only by unanimous vote.
    There was no national court to settle arguments between states.
    Congress could not regulate commerce between states, collect taxes, or force states to contribute to government needs.
    Congress could only ask states for troops, but could not raise an army.
Constitutional Convention: Convened at Independence Hall, Philadelphia, to revise *Articles of Confederation* but decided to draw up completely new document.

Compromises Reached in Forming the Constitution

The Great Compromise: Resolved the conflict between large and small states by providing equal representation in the Senate and representation based on population in the House of Representatives.
Three-Fifths Compromise: Resolved the conflict between slave and free states by counting five slaves as three people in determining representation.
Commerce Compromise: Resolved the conflict between agricultural and manufacturing states by permitting Congress to tax goods entering but not leaving the country.
Indirect Vote for President: Resolved the conflict between aristocrats and democrats by having president elected by electoral college.

The Great Architects of the Constitution

Known as the Founding Fathers, the men most responsible for its adoption were George Washington, James Madison, Alexander Hamilton, John Jay, Gouvernour Morris, Robert Morris, Benjamin Franklin, and George Mason.

The Three Branches of the Constitutional Government

Authority was vested in three branches which acted as a check on each other:
Legislative: The House of Representatives and the Senate make laws according to the powers granted in Article I Section 8. These powers include making laws concerning such items as money, commerce, courts, war, the armed forces, immigration, and taxation.
Executive: The president, who heads the executive branch, enforces the laws and conducts foreign policy. The president is commander-in-chief of the army.

TEST OF GENERAL KNOWLEDGE: DESCRIPTION, REVIEW, PRACTICE

Judicial: Supreme Court and such lesser federal courts as Congress establishes determine guilt and the constitutionality of laws and the interpretation of the Constitution.

The Bill of Rights

A written guarantee of the people's liberties, these were added to the Constitution as the first ten amendments in 1791. Several states refused to ratify the constitution unless a Bill of Rights was added immediately. The Bill of Rights guaranteed:

Freedom of speech, press, religion.
The right to bear arms.
That people would not be forced to quarter soldiers.
Protection against illegal search.
The right to know reasons for arrest.
The right to a quick trial by a jury of peers.
The right to trial by jury in civil cases involving more than $20.
Protection against cruel and unusual punishment and excessive bail.
That no rights not listed in Constitution should be therefore denied.
That the people and states would retain powers not assigned to the federal government.

THE NEW NATION — 1789–1824

The Establishment of the Federal Government

President Washington developed the concept of a *cabinet* to advise him. Alexander Hamilton, Secretary of the Treasury, supported a *loose interpretation* of the Constitution to give power to the government in Washington. Thomas Jefferson, Secretary of State, supported a *strict interpretation* of the Constitution to give more power to the people and the state governments. These interpretations continue to divide people today. Congress passed laws establishing the framework of the government, including the Judiciary Act of 1789.
Whiskey Rebellion 1794: Washington used state and federal troops to crush a farmers' rebellion in Pennsylvania, giving strength to the federal government.
Washington's Farewell Address 1797: Called for no foreign alliances, two terms for the president and no factions (parties) in political life.
Chief Justice John Marshall: Appointed to the Supreme Court, Marshall led the Court in interpreting the Constitution to give power to the federal government.

JACKSON AND THE WEST — 1824–1850

The Growth of Sectionalism

The Industrial North: As trade and manufacturing became the most important activities of the northern section of the United States, the North developed the following political and economic needs:

A national bank that would guarantee uniform and stable currency.
The end of the sale of cheap lands in the West to workers needed for northern industry.

SOCIAL STUDIES

A high protective tariff to protect native products against foreign competition.

Building of roads and canals to link the West to the East.

The prevention of the spread of slavery to new western territories.

The Slave South: With the invention of Eli Whitney's cotton gin in 1793 unskilled slave labor became increasingly important to plantation owners whose main crop, cotton, produced almost all of southern wealth. The economic and political needs of the South were:

Cheap western lands in which more cotton could be grown.

The extension of slavery to these lands.

Opposition to internal improvements (roads and canals) because they benefited only the North and West.

Opposition to a high tariff since it raised the price of manufactured goods, which they imported from Britain to whom cotton was sold in payment.

The Farming West: Agriculture was the principal activity and chief source of wealth in the West. Its political and economic needs were:

Cheap money accompanied by slow but steady inflation (cheap money means lots of money in circulation even though, as a result, the value of that money in terms of purchasing power is lessened).

Extension of voting rights to all, regardless of property holdings.

Internal improvements (roads and canals) to transport produce to the market.

Sectional Compromises

As each section tried to gain control of the federal government to pass bills advantageous to itself, bitterness between the sections increased and problems could be settled only by compromise. Some of the more important compromises were:

Missouri Compromise (1820): A compromise made to keep the balance between southern slave states and northern free states, so that neither would gain political control of Congress.

Compromise Tariff of 1833: The compromise between the North's push for high tariffs and the South's opposition to raising the tariff. The compromise avoided war.

Compromise of 1850: When California asked for admission in 1850, the balance between the North and South was once again endangered. The Compromise of 1850, called the Omnibus Bill, and also written by Henry Clay, provided that:

The people of Utah and New Mexico would vote to determine whether they should be free or slave states (known as popular or "squatter" sovereignty).

California would be admitted as a free state.

The Fugitive Slave Law would be strengthened.

The slave trade would be prohibited in the District of Columbia.

Important Milestones in Expansion (1787–1853)

Northwest Ordinance of 1787: Adopted by the government under the Articles of Confederation, it made provision for western lands conquered by George Rogers Clark in the Revolution and stated that:

No more than five and no less than three states were to be formed from the territory.

Inhabitants of a territory would be admitted to the Union as an equal state when its population reached 60,000.

Slavery was prohibited in the territory.

Louisiana Purchase: Extending from the Mississippi River to the Rocky Mountains and from Canada to the Gulf of Mexico, this vast territory was purchased from Napoleon for $15 million during Jefferson's administration in 1803.

Florida Purchase: In 1819, the United States purchased the eastern part of Florida from Spain for $5 million.

The Oregon Territory: Originally claimed by Britain, the United States, Spain, and Russia, by 1818, the other two countries ceded rights to the United States and Britain who occupied it jointly. In 1846 a compromise was worked out with Britain and a treaty signed which gave the United States rights to the land south of the 49th parallel.

The Mexican War: In 1845, Texas was admitted to the United States as the 28th state. In 1846, war broke out between the United States and Mexico—Mexico being angered by American annexation of Texas and claims to all land north of the Rio Grande. The United States won a series of battles in Mexico. California was captured.

The Treaty of Guadalupe-Hidalgo: Signed in 1848, provided that New Mexico and Upper California were ceded to the United States. The Rio Grande River was fixed as the southern boundary of Texas. The United States agreed to a payment of $15 million for the territory.

Gadsden Purchase: A small strip of land now incorporated in Arizona and New Mexico purchased from Mexico in 1853 to provide a good southern railroad route to the West.

THE CIVIL WAR AND RECONSTRUCTION—1850–1877

Basic Causes of the Civil War

Economic: The Northern manufacturers needed a high tariff, skilled labor, internal improvements, and a national bank. The Southern planters needed low tariffs, slave labor, state banks, and opposed internal improvements.

Political: The North opposed extension of slavery to new states because it wanted political control of Congress, which made laws. The North believed the Union had created "one nation, indivisible." The South favored extension of slavery to new states because it, too, wanted to control Congress. The South believed that the states which made the Union could unmake it and secede.

Moral: Abolitionists and others felt that slavery was an evil, was against the Declaration of Independence, and must be eliminated. The South defended slavery by claiming it was established by God and quoted Bible passages to prove it.

Start of the War

The Election of 1860: The Republican Party candidate, Abraham Lincoln, ran on a platform that stated:

    Kansas was not to be admitted as a free state.

    Slavery was not to be extended to the territories.

    Free farming land was to be given to those settling in the West.

    A high protective tariff was to be maintained.

Lincoln was elected by the electoral college system, even though he received no more than 40 percent of the votes cast.

Southern Secession: With Lincoln's election, seven states (South Carolina, Texas,

SOCIAL STUDIES

Louisiana, Mississippi, Alabama, Florida, and Georgia) seceded from the Union. They created the Confederate States of America, with Jefferson Davis as president.
Lincoln's Inaugural Address (March 4, 1861): Lincoln refused to accept the dissolution of the Union, and stated that war or peace was in the hands of the South.
Fort Sumter: On April 12, 1861, Southern forces fired on Fort Sumter. Civil war had begun. Virginia, Tennessee, Arkansas, and North Carolina joined the Confederacy.

Results of the Civil War

Northern Business and Industry: It grew and prospered during the war, and replaced Southern agriculture as the principal activity of this country.
Homestead Act (1862): The act provided free land in the West for those who settled on it and developed it. The South had not supported such legislation before the war.
Pacific Railroad Acts (1862 and 1864): Prior to the war southern routes for the railroad were considered. The route approved after secession went from St. Louis to San Francisco. It would tie the industry of the East to raw materials and farm products of the West.
Constitutional: The federal government was proven more powerful than any state government. No state could secede from the Union.
Destruction of the Southern Plantation Economy: Based on slavery, it was destroyed forever. It was replaced by sharecropping.
Wartime Rights of Civilians: The Supreme Court in *ex parte Milligan* upheld the Constitutional rights of a civilian during war time. The case established civilian rule as primary.

Reconstruction

Issue I: Readmission of rebel states to the Union.
Solution: Lincoln's plan was to re-admit states when 10% of the voters pledged loyalty to the United States and agreed to the abolition of slavery. After his assassination, Northern members of Congress, called Radical Republicans, became harsher, passed the *Reconstruction Acts of 1867,* which treated the South as a conquered province. To gain admittance the seceded states had to ratify the 14th Amendment and Northern troops occupied the South until the states met all conditions of re-admission.
Issue II: Guarantee of civil rights to black Americans.
Solution: Southern legislators made black codes which denied the civil rights of blacks. The *Civil Rights Bill of 1866* was aimed at undoing the effects of these codes. The 14th and 15th Amendments were to guarantee these civil rights. None of these actions was successful in protecting civil rights.
Issue III: Government of rebel states.
Solution: Former slaves, but not Confederate leaders, were allowed to vote at state conventions until states were readmitted, after which the states again set their own rules as to who could vote.

Results of Reconstruction

Formation of the Solid South: After 1877, the bloc of southern states voted for the Democratic party on almost all occasions, as a result of the whites' dislike of Radical Republicans. This concept of the Solid South is still a consideration in elections in the 1980s.

TEST OF GENERAL KNOWLEDGE: DESCRIPTION, REVIEW, PRACTICE

13th Amendment: 1865—Abolished slavery in the United States.
14th Amendment: 1868—Black Americans were made citizens of the United States. It guaranteed that no state could deny life, liberty, or property without due process of law.
15th Amendment: 1870—No state can deny the right to vote on account of race, color, or previous condition of servitude.
Ku Klux Klan: It was formed to control ex-slaves and to "keep them in their place" and not allow them to change the basic political and social structure of the South. The Klan grew larger after the troops were recalled from the South by President Hayes (1877), after he was declared the winner of the disputed presidential election of 1876.
New Constitutions of Southern States: They established free public schools for all children, abolished imprisonment for debt, abolished property qualifications for voting and jury duty.
Railways, highways, and national banking system strengthened the federal government.
Prevention of Black Voting (after 1877): To counteract influence of black voters, and to block the 15th Amendment, the South tried to deny them political rights by state measures that limited voting privileges to those:

  Who could pass literacy tests
  Who could pay a poll tax
  Who owned property
  Whose grandfather had voted

THE GROWTH OF INDUSTRIAL AMERICA, POPULISTS AND PROGRESSIVES—1877–1916

The Industrial Revolution

Change from hand manufacturing at home to machine manufacturing in a factory was stimulated by:
Growing trade, especially after the revolutionary war, removed British restrictions on American industry. Markets for exported goods were soon found and the U.S. was also free to import under our own tariff regulations.
Invention of the cotton gin by Eli Whitney in 1793 provided northern textile workers with an abundance of raw material.
Availability of power from swift-running rivers and of abundant natural resources (coal, iron, and lumber).
Napoleonic Wars, War of 1812, and British blockade forced American manufacture to grow, since we could no longer rely on imports.
Building of roads and canals made transportation of raw materials and finished products easier and stimulated manufacturing in industrial centers.
Labor shortage in the Civil War encouraged and increased the use of machinery, as did war needs.

Influence of Geographic Factors on Industrial and Agricultural Development

The United States can be divided into four major geographic areas: the Atlantic coastal plain, the Appalachian highlands, the great central plain, the Cordilleran highlands.
Atlantic Coastal Plain: East of the Appalachian Mountains. First area settled by colonists.

SOCIAL STUDIES

Suitable for growth of manufacturing cities because of:
> Power available from rivers flowing down from Appalachian Mountains.
> Proximity to excellent harbors.

Long, narrow plainland between mountains and Atlantic is excellent for farming.
Appalachian Highlands: From Adirondack Mountains through Allegheny and Cumberland plateaus to central Alabama in the South. Mountain area, originally dense forest, provided protection for colonists during Revolutionary War. It was a great lumbering region later.
Plains area, suitable for farming.
Rich mining areas in mountainous parts of Pennsylvania, West Virginia.
The Great Central Plain: From the Appalachians to the Rockies, and from Canada to Mexico, this is the largest region, comprising almost half of the land in the United States.
Richest agricultural region in the world because of long, fertile plains area.
Lush land for stock grazing from North Dakota to Texas.
Growth of great cities on excellent harbors provided by Great Lakes; growth of cities along the Mississippi River, great North–South waterway route of the country.
Cordilleran Highlands: From Rocky Mountains to Pacific Ocean. Mountainous area rich in lumber and mineral resources.
Valley and lowland area near Pacific, suitable for fertile fruit orchards and farmland.

Results of Early Industrial Revolution

Growth of great cities as people changed their occupation from farming to manufacturing.
Rapid growth of city population, causing slums and increased crime rate.
Bad working conditions shared by many people, leading to development and growth of trade unions.
Trade unions which organized laborers to demand such items as shorter working days, safer working conditions, and insurance to cover injuries.
Greater interest in reform and politics.
Need for political parties to change programs to meet new problems created by industrial change.
Increase of America's productivity and power.
Imperialism, a search for colonies as sources of raw materials and markets for finished products.
Speeding up of transportation, bringing people closer together.
Increased demand for education.
More foods and materials available to a greater number of people.
New giant industries (railroad, oil, steel, etc.).
Transformation in farming techniques.
Increased standard of living of most people.
Rising expectations of people to share in the "good life" produced by material plenty.

Effects of Industrial Revolution on American Life

New Production Methods: Large-scale production in factories produced new techniques of organizing work: *division of labor, assembly line, standardization of parts.*

Business Combines: Until the Civil War, factories were small—but afterward they began growing larger and larger. Individual capitalists were unable to finance these huge projects, and new business forms were created: the *corporation* and the *trust*.

Development of Trade Unions: The early factory system was responsible for many evils such as:

- Use of child labor.
- Low pay and a long working day.
- Unsanitary working conditions.
- Forced purchase at company stores.
- No laws to restrain abuses of employer.

Workers had found as early as 1793 in America that they could best achieve their demands by uniting. Gradually, unions grew. The most important were:

Knights of Labor: Organized in Philadelphia, 1879, by garment workers, aimed at organizing all workers into one large union. Although it reached a membership of 700,000, poor leadership and internal disputes caused its disappearance.

American Federation of Labor (AFL): Founded in 1886, soon replaced Knights of Labor; organized skilled workers according to their trade, or craft. In 1936 the *Committee on Industrial Organization* (CIO) broke away from the AFL to create a union based on all the workers in a particular industry—for example, all workers in the steel industry became members of the Steel Workers Union.

Populists

With the disputed election of 1877 settled in favor of Hayes, the Reconstruction Era ended. The nation's interests turned to issues of economics. As business grew, wealth accumulated in the hands of business people and bankers. Agricultural prices began a decline in 1884, which again intensified farm protests. Section antagonism intensified. Finally in 1892, several years of efforts to unite labor and farmers led to the formation of a third political party—the People's or Populist Party. Holding its first national convention in Omaha, the party produced a platform that proposed significant reforms, including coinage of silver at a 16-1 ratio with gold, a graduated income tax, direct election of senators, a shorter working day and restrictions on immigration.

In 1896 the Populists nominated William Jennings Bryan for president. His campaign, while extensive, focused on the issue of the coinage of silver, which was considered the best way to help the farmers and workers as it would create an inflationary pattern. Bryan lost to William McKinley (Rep.) and with the return of better economic conditions and the Spanish-American War the Populist Party declined.

Progressives

The Progressive Movement grew at the turn of the century largely as a response to problems created in urban areas by industrial growth. The Progressives worked within the established party framework. They achieved a variety of reforms ranging from the Pure Food and Drug Laws (1906) under Theodore Roosevelt to the establishment of the Federal Reserve System (1913) under Woodrow Wilson. Both Roosevelt and Wilson were leaders of the Progressive Movement and illustrate the varied backgrounds of par-

SOCIAL STUDIES

ticipants. The Movement died with the U.S. entry into World War I but not before it had made profound changes in America's business and political life.

Legislation and Supreme Court Decisions Related to Industrial Growth and the Progressive Movement: 1877–1916

Interstate Commerce Act (1877): Set up fair rate schedules for railway freight, prohibiting special rates to trusts and the charging of greater rates for short hauls than for long ones.
Sherman Anti-Trust Act (1890): Aimed at breaking huge trusts into smaller units, it failed because it was not enforced and because some presidential administrations favored big business.
Plessy v. Ferguson (1895): In this Supreme Court decision the court established the principle of separate but equal facilities for blacks. This created a two-tier system of rights for blacks and whites. This decision established the civil rights system of America until the 1950s.
Pure Food and Drug Act (1906): Prohibited sale of impure food and medicine; later false advertising was prohibited.
Department of Labor (1913): To give labor representation in the cabinet.
Federal Reserve Act (1913): Set up a system of Federal Reserve banks under the joint control of the people, government, and the banking industry to regulate and control credit.
Clayton Anti-Trust Act (1914): Prohibited unfair agreements that might diminish competition; established a Federal Trade Commission to investigate charges of unfair competition and prosecute such cases; prohibited competing businesses from having the same men on Boards of Directors.
Conservation of Resources: Under President Theodore Roosevelt, a conservation program to end abuses of our natural resources was begun.

Continued American Expansion

In the post Civil War period, Americans continued to move west and settle the frontier. In 1890, the Census Bureau reported there was no longer a frontier; the country was settled coast to coast. With the "closing of the frontier," a new era began, one in which the growth of cities became the chief focus of America's "expansion."

Factors Behind the Growth of Great Cities

Cities were founded by the earliest colonists. Transportation facilities—harbors, rivers, river fords, and later canal and railroad lines—were important in determining the location of cities. The nearness of raw materials, the availability of a labor supply, and the convenience of cheap transportation also were important factors in city location and growth.

American Expansion Overseas

The Alaska Purchase: Termed "Seward's Folly," Alaska was purchased upon the urging of Secretary of State Seward in 1867 for $7.2 million.

Annexation of Hawaii: In 1889, the native queen was overthrown by a rebellion, and the new government petitioned the United States to annex it. In 1898, Congress approved annexation.

Pacific Islands: In 1867, the United States annexed uninhabited Midway Island as a coaling station.

In 1889, the United States acquired Tutuila, Pago Pago for its valuable harbor.

Spanish-American War: In the 1895 Cuban patriots revolted against harsh Spanish rule and were severely punished; sensational American newspaper stories demanded intervention, as did American business owners who had considerable investments in Cuban sugar and tobacco.

In February 1898, the American battleship *Maine* was mysteriously blown up while in the harbor of Havana; the slogan "Remember the Maine" aroused the American public and in April, Congress declared war on Spain.

An American army was landed in Cuba and soon destroyed Spanish resistance in Santiago; meanwhile, the Spanish fleet was thoroughly beaten.

The Treaty of Paris signed in December 1898, contained the following provisions:
- Puerto Rico, Guam, and the Philippines were ceded to the United States.
- Cuba was granted independence. U.S. was to supervise this independence.
- The United States was paid $20 million for the Philippines.

The Panama Canal Zone: With possessions in the Atlantic and Pacific, the United States needed a short water route between the two oceans.

The U.S. under President Theodore Roosevelt in 1903 offered $10 million and a yearly rental of $250,000 to Colombia for use of land in the province of Panama for a canal but the Colombian government refused.

In November 1903, the Panamanian people rebelled, and with United States support, set up an independent government; 15 days later the new republic accepted the same terms offered to Colombia and gave the United States the right to build a canal and exclusive control of a Canal Zone in perpetuity. The United States paid Colombia $20 million as redress for the loss of Panama and Colombia recognized the independence of Panama.

Virgin Islands: These islands, purchased from Denmark in 1917, provided a defense for the Panama Canal. They provided naval bases on the perimeter of the Caribbean Sea.

WORLD WAR I AND THE INTER-WAR PERIOD—1916–1941

World War I

Causes: Sparked by the assassination of Archduke Ferdinand of Austria-Hungary on June 28, 1914, World War I was really caused by imperialistic and economic rivalry.

Why America Joined: Although President Wilson urged a policy of neutrality, Americans sold arms to the Allies, and in 1917 abandoned its neutral position. The following events caused us to enter the war:

Sinking of Lusitania by German submarines aroused public opinion.

Announcement of unrestricted submarine warfare by the Germans.

Discovery of the *Zimmermann Note* (which demonstrated that Germany planned to urge Mexico to attack the United States).

On April 5, 1917, after Germany continued to sink our ships despite a note of warning, Congress declared war.

America During the War: An army of 4 million men was raised by a draft or Selective Service. Many volunteered. Bond drives helped to pay the huge expense of financing the war. These bonds were called Liberty Bonds.

American naval power broke Germany's blockade of England and helped destroy her fleet of submarines.

2 million American soldiers in Europe, added to the force of the Allies, crushed Germany on land. The American Expeditionary Force (AEF) under General John J. Pershing participated in battles at Belleau Wood, Chateau Thierry, St. Mihiel, and the Argonne Forest.

An armistice was signed on November 11, 1918.

Wilson's 14 Points: Wilson's plan for a peace treaty included 14 points which he hoped would prevent future wars. Some important points were:

Reduction of armaments.

An end to secret treaties.

Freedom of the seas.

An equitable solution to the colonial problem.

Self-determination of peoples.

Establishment of a League of Nations to arbitrate problems among nations peacefully.

Treaty of Versailles: Largely ignoring the Fourteen Points and intending to make Germany powerless to wage war forever, the Allies formulated a treaty which was signed June 28, 1919. Some of its important provisions were:

Surrender of German Territory: Cession of Alsace-Lorraine on the border of France and Germany to France; cession of other territories and colonies to other European allies and Japan. The colonies were to be administered by the various victorious nations under *mandates* of the League of Nations.

A promise by Germany to compensate the Allies for war damages. This compensation was called *reparations*.

Germany allowed *Allied occupation* of the Rhineland (between the Rhine River and the French and Belgian borders).

Germany *admitted her guilt* for starting the war.

The League of Nations: Although the League was Wilson's idea, the U.S. Senate voted not to accept the treaty. The failure of the United States to join and the failure of the League to act effectively in subsequent disputes caused the League to be ineffective in preventing the outbreak of World War II.

The 1920s

In the immediate post-war period there were many problems of adjustment to peace. Jobs were hard to find for many returning veterans. Farm prices were depressed and remained so during the entire period until the New Deal. Industry slowly recovered and there was a boom; but it is now clear that the prosperity was not evenly distributed. There was a great land boom in Florida in which many people lost money and the heavy speculation on the stock market culminated in the crash of October 1929.

TEST OF GENERAL KNOWLEDGE: DESCRIPTION, REVIEW, PRACTICE

The Red Scare of the early 20s was directed against communism. Attorney General Palmer and J. Edgar Hoover made reputations for themselves, but the actual threat to the nation was exaggerated.

The Harding Administration proclaimed a post-war *return to normalcy*. The U.S. turned down the Treaty of Versailles with its League of Nations and returned to *isolationism* as the policy of ignoring Europe was called. The administration ended with several scandals (Teapot Dome) and this discredited the role of the federal government in the nation.

The Great Depression and The New Deal

Although 10 years of prosperity and inflation followed World War I, the United States was engulfed in a depression after that decade of good times. Causes of the depression were:
> *High tariffs* aimed at eliminating European competition from American markets reduced trade and made it impossible to sell U.S. goods abroad.
> *Speculation* in real estate and stocks causing artificial rises in prices.
> *Overproduction and unemployment* caused in part by replacement of workers with machines.
> *War debts* absorbed European purchasing power, lessening foreign trade.
> Issuance of *too much credit* on easy terms caused financial collapses when borrowers were unable to make good.

The *stock market crash* of October 1929 is considered the starting point of the Great Depression. The federal government under President Hoover took little action to correct the economic problems believing the economy would adjust naturally without interference and the states or local charity should help the jobless until the economy again was operating *fully*.

In the *election of 1932* Franklin D. Roosevelt, a Democrat, defeated Herbert Hoover. As a candidate Franklin D. Roosevelt promised action to combat the depression. These ideas were incorporated in the *New Deal:* The various measures taken by *Franklin D. Roosevelt's* administration to combat the depression have been grouped by some historians in the general categories of:

1. *Relief* — direct giving of goods, clothing, shelter and jobs to the unemployed.
2. *Recovery* — laws aimed at curing the sickness of the economy at that moment;
3. *Reform* — long term changes in the economy designed to prevent future depressions.

Some historians reject this classification as some acts fit in more than one category. However, the "3 R's" provide one organizational scheme for categorizing the many New Deal Measures. Examples of each type of legislation would be:
> *Relief: Works Progress Administration (WPA):* The government gave employment to men on projects it initiated.
> *Relief: Civil Works Administration (CWA):* The government provided work projects to employ individuals needing work in the winter of 1933.
> *Recovery: Home Owners Loan Corporation (HOLC):* Government loans to homeowners to prevent loss of their homes to mortgagers.
> *Recovery: Agricultural Adjustment Act (AAA):* Reduced amount of crops planted to create artificial shortage and stimulate prices.

SOCIAL STUDIES

Reform: Tennessee Valley Authority (TVA): Comprehensive development of the interstate Tennessee River Valley with flood control measures and the production of electricity. Opposed by many as government involvement in industry, but approved by the Supreme Court. Electricity produced was vital to the development of the atomic bomb by the U.S. in World War II.

Reform: Reciprocal Tariff Act: Removed barriers to trade by lowering tariffs through reciprocal negotiation.

Reform: National Recovery Administration (NRA): Codes of fair practices including rights of workers drawn up by each industry involved in interstate commerce. The Supreme Court, interpreting the Constitution very strictly, declared this and other New Deal legislation unconstitutional.

Supreme Court Controversy: Roosevelt attempted in 1937, after his overwhelming re-election, to change the composition of the Court. The Congress refused to support his plan and this was the start of less active legislation by Congress. Roosevelt had been upset by the failure of the Court to approve his legislation. With the death of several judges, Roosevelt was able to appoint new judges who supported his legislation and interpreted the Constitution more loosely.

Recession of 1937: In the first few years of the New Deal economic conditions improved in the nation. About 1937 there was another little recession. With the coming of World War II the American economy picked up and the Great Depression quickly receded from view.

Organized Labor: The American Federation of Labor (AFL) had organized only skilled workers. In 1935, the AFL created a Committee for Industrial Organization, headed by John L. Lewis, to organize unskilled and semi-skilled workers. The committee left the AFL in 1936, and in 1938 formed its own labor organization, The Congress of Industrial Organization (CIO). Instead of dividing workers by *craft,* the CIO divided them by *industry.* For example, all workers in the automobile industry, whether skilled or unskilled, became members of the United Automobile Workers. The CIO made quick progress in organizing previously unaffiliated industrial workers in such fields as steel, textile, shipbuilding, and rubber.

WORLD WAR II AND AFTER—1941–1988

World War II

Background

Rise of Fascism: In 1922, Mussolini, leader of Italian Fascists took power. Pursuing a militaristic policy as a solution to Italy's economic problems, he attacked Ethiopia in 1935.
In 1931, Japan led by a military dictatorship, attacked China and annexed Manchuria. In 1937 Japan invaded China.
Germany, under Hitler, who took power in 1933, also embarked on a militaristic program, annexed Austria in 1938, and attacked Poland in 1939. Vicious attacks on Catholics, Jews, and suppression of all who didn't agree with his policies, had already turned the free world against nazism and its leader. Germany, Italy and Japan formed an alliance known as the axis.
When Hitler attacked Poland in September, 1939, France and Britain declared war on Germany to help resist that attack, but they failed. Germany speedily conquered Norway, Denmark, the Netherlands, Belgium, and then France. Great Britain and the

35

Commonwealth together with governments in exile from the conquered countries and the colonies of these countries withstood the air onslaught of the Germans in 1940. Finally in June, 1941, Hitler broke a peace treaty with the Soviet Union and attacked her bringing the Russians into the war on the side of the allies.

American Involvement in the War: Although on the outbreak of war in Europe in 1939, a policy of neutrality was declared by President Roosevelt, it was later repealed and replaced by the Lend-Lease Act which gave the president power to sell or lease war equipment to any country whose defense he deemed important to the preservation of American safety. America became "the arsenal of democracy," and supplied Great Britain with arms after the Fall of France in 1940.

On December 7, 1941, the Japanese air force, in a sneak attack on Pearl Harbor, destroyed a large part of the American fleet which was stationed there. The United States became a participant in World War II when, the next day, Congress declared war on Japan, and three days later, Germany and Italy declared war on the United States.

The War in Europe: In November, 1942, General Eisenhower landed with allied armies in French West Africa and captured Morocco and Algeria. In 1943 Sicily and then Italy were invaded.

The final phase of the war began on June 6, 1944 with the allied invasion of the Normandy Peninsula, in France. Caught between an attack by Russian troops on the east, and allied troops on the west, German resistance crumbled after a final attempt to stop the invasion in the Battle of the Bulge in December, 1944. On May 1, it was announced that Hitler committed suicide, and on May 7, 1945, the Germans surrendered unconditionally.

The Immediate Post-War Period

Demobilization

The problem of demobilizing 12 million servicemen and returning them to civilian life was solved by the *Serviceman's Readjustment Act* of 1944, commonly known as the *G.I. Bill of Rights*. Among its provisions were:
    Government financed job training and education for discharged servicemen.
    Unemployment payments for veterans.
    Loans to veterans for business, farms, and home construction.

With the end of rationing and price control, prices skyrocketed. There was a period of inflation, but a post-war depression, which many people feared, was avoided. No truly satisfactory solution for the problem of inflation was found, and inflationary pressure continued to affect the nation for many years.

The United Nations

Meetings at Bretton Woods in 1943 and at Dumbarton Oaks in 1944 laid the basis for a worldwide organization dedicated to finding peaceful solutions to international problems. On April 25, 1945, delegates from 50 nations met in San Francisco to draw up the charter for a new organization, the United Nations, to replace the League of Nations. The main provisions of the charter were:
    Member nations would not help an aggressor nation.
    They would settle disputes peacefully.
    They would use neither force nor the threat of force.
    They would use the armed might of an international police force to fight
    against aggressors.

SOCIAL STUDIES

The Cold War

At the end of World War II, previously amicable relations between the United States and Russia deteriorated. President Truman, who had become president after the death of Roosevelt in April 1945, reacted quickly, and the basis of U.S. post-World War II foreign policy was set by the end of 1947. The focus was a struggle with the Soviet Union. Their expansion was to be blocked, while the interests of the U.S. and its allies were to be protected. Nuclear weapons held by both sides after 1948 deterred a "hot war" between the superpowers. The antagonisms have remained between the two superpowers although there have been times of improved relations, such as the period of *Detente* under President Nixon and *Glasnost* under President Reagan.

Major Cold War Events

Truman Doctrine (1947): Truman announced the doctrine which pledged aid to the governments of Greece and Turkey, which Truman believed were being threatened by Russian Communist interests. The doctrine was later interpreted to mean the U.S. would oppose the overthrow of any democratic government.
National Security Act (1947): This Act established the National Security Council as an advisory body to the president and the CIA as an information gathering/spying organization.
Marshall Plan (1947): Secretary of State Marshall introduced his European Recovery Program, known as the Marshall Plan, which made provision for U.S. financial assistance to European countries whose failing economies made them targets for communism.
Berlin Blockade (1948): The Russians blocked land access to Berlin and the U.S. responded with an airlift of supplies.
North Atlantic Treaty Alliance (NATO) (1949): The first U.S. peacetime military alliance was designed to block or contain Communist, especially Soviet, expansion. It brought the nations of the North Atlantic and northern Mediterranean together for mutual defense.
Communist Victory in China (1949): After a struggle dating back to the 1920s, the Chinese communists under Mao-Tse Tung defeated the Nationalist forces of Chiang Kai-shek. The Nationalists fled to Taiwan, establishing a government there which was recognized by the U.S. and the U.N. until the Nixon administration as the government of mainland China.
Korean War (1950–1953): Communist North Korea attacked South Korea; the U.S. and other nations under the U.N. flag fought for three years to block aggression. The armistice terms essentially restored the status quo.
Southeast Asia Treaty Organization (SEATO) (1954): Designed to contain Communist, especially Chinese, expansion in Asia.
Fall of Dien Bien Phu and Geneva Conference on Vietnam (1954): After the French lost their important base at Dien Bien Phu to the Vietnamese Communists, the U.S. considered military intervention. Instead at Geneva a peace plan was developed for the region. It was later rejected by Ngo Dinh Diem, premier of South Vietnam.
Hungarian Revolt (1956): Hungary's attempt to throw off Soviet domination was crushed by Soviet arms.
Suez Canal Seized (1956): Responding to Egypt's seizure of the Canal, France, England, and Israel invaded Egypt and were stopped by the U.S. and U.S.S.R. This provided an example of superpower cooperation.
Eisenhower Doctrine (1957): Approved by Congress, this permitted the U.S. to extend

economic and military aid to Near Eastern countries who wanted it because they believed they were threatened by Communists.

Lebanon (1958): U.S. sent troops to keep Communists from seizing power.

U-2 Spy Plane (1960): The Soviets shot down a U.S. spy plane over Soviet territory, which ended a move towards rapprochement.

Cuban Revolution (1961): Castro's guerrilla troops finally seized control of Cuba. Relations with the U.S. rapidly deteriorated. Many Cubans fled to the U.S. and finally the U.S. broke diplomatic relations with Cuba.

Bay of Pigs (1961): Unsuccessful attempt by Cuban refugees backed by U.S. to invade and overthrow Castro's regime in Cuba.

Berlin Wall (1961): East Germans seal off their part of Berlin from the West.

Cuban Missile Crisis (1962): Soviet attempt to set up intermediate range missiles in Cuba blocked by a U.S. blockade and political maneuvering to avoid nuclear war.

Hot Line Agreement (1963): Established direct rapid communication between Moscow and Washington suggesting cooperation was possible between the superpowers.

Limited Nuclear Test Ban Treaty (1963): After many years of bomb testing and unilateral stopping of tests, a treaty was signed banning the testing of nuclear weapons in the atmosphere, in outer space, or under water. Underground tests were permitted.

Dominican Republic Intervention (1965): President Johnson sent U.S. troops into the Dominican Republic to crush a "band of communist conspirators" who the president claimed had gained control of a revolution against an authoritarian president.

Outer Space Treaty (1967): Banned military bases, weapons, and weapons tests in space and established principles for peaceful development of space.

Pueblo Seized (1969): A U.S. intelligence gathering ship was seized by the North Korean government. After a U.S. officer signed a statement accepting guilt for spying, the ship was released.

Nuclear Nonproliferation Treaty (1969): The Treaty banned the spread of nuclear weapons. It approved of access to nuclear energy for peaceful uses.

Nixon's Visit to China (1972): A new era in relations between the U.S. and China was confirmed with President Nixon's visit to the People's Republic of China. Changes had been underway for several years, including the U.S. acceptance in the U.N. of the People's Republic, not Taiwan, as the holder of the Security Council seat.

Moscow Summit (1972): President Nixon visited Moscow and signed several agreements including the ABM (Anti-Ballistic Missile) Treaty. An easing of Cold War tensions was obvious and was given the name Detente by the press.

Yom Kippur War and Shuttle Diplomacy (1974): War erupted again in the Near East in October 1973, which resulted in a costly Israeli victory. Secretary of State Kissinger undertook a series of visits to the Near East ("Shuttle Diplomacy"), which resulted in cease-fire agreements between Israel and Syria. The Soviet Union sought influence in the Near East to balance that of the U.S. and Israel, and tensions remain in the region.

SALT II Agreement (1979): The agreement limited the number of missiles and long-range bombers held by the U.S. and Soviet Union. It was signed at a summit meeting in Geneva, but President Carter asked the Senate to delay ratification after the Soviet Union invaded Afghanistan.

Afghanistan Invasion (1979): The Soviet Union sent troops into Afghanistan to maintain Soviet influence over the government. President Carter responded with a grain embargo, cutting off Soviet food supplies from the U.S.

Anti-Soviet Trade Boycott (1981): President Reagan declared the Soviet Union responsible for repression in Poland and placed limits on trade with the Soviets. This attitude prevailed during the first five years of the Reagan administration, whose policy was based on the president's view of the Soviet Union as an "evil empire."

SOCIAL STUDIES

Arms Negotiation: Limited discussions were held with the Soviet Union throughout the Reagan years. They gained momentum in 1985. After two summit meetings in Switzerland and Iceland, an INF (Intermediate Range Nuclear Forces) Treaty was signed at a summit meeting in Washington suggesting a shift in Cold War attitudes and a return to a detente of the Nixon years.

El Salvador/Nicaragua (1981 ff.): Early in the Reagan years concern was shown for guerrilla movements in El Salvador and their relationship to the Sandinista-controlled government of Nicaragua, which the U.S. viewed as controlled by Soviet and Cuban communists. How to deal with the issue became a major foreign policy concern with many Cold War ramifications. The issue included funding a guerrilla organization (Contras) opposed to the Sandinista government.

Iran-Iraq (Gulf) War (1981 ff.): War broke out between these two oil-producing Muslim nations on the Persian Gulf. Both the U.S. and the Soviet Union have important interests in the region and the conflict added tensions to relations between the superpowers.

Iran Contra Affair (1987): A complex plan to free hostages held in Lebanon by selling arms to Iran and then using the monetary profits to fund the Contras fighting against the Sandinista government of Nicaragua. The plan was developed secretly, and lacked congressional approval.

Vietnam War

Starting in 1945, the U.S. showed an interest in a non-Communist Vietnam. The French were supported in their fight against the Communist Viet Minh. When the French were defeated at Dien Bien Phu in 1954, the U.S. secretly aided South Vietnam in a small way until 1961 when President Kennedy began to increase the aid and make it more open. As war against the North Vietnamese and Viet Cong Communists broke out, the U.S. continued to expand its involvement.

Although President Kennedy insisted it was the Vietnamese's war to "win or lose," he sent in more troops. President Johnson continued the policy and, after a confusing incident in the Gulf of Tonkin involving U.S. naval vessels, he obtained from Congress support to prevent further aggression and protect U.S. forces in the Gulf of Tonkin Resolution. Lyndon Johnson's support for the war put strain on his Great Society program and after his defeat in the New Hampshire primary in 1968, he withdrew from the presidential race. The massacre of civilians by U.S. troops at My Lai in 1969 and the shooting of student demonstrators by the National Guard at Kent State intensified U.S. protests against the war. Nixon desired to end the war but "with honor." Negotiations proved lengthy and difficult and he authorized the invasion of Cambodia in 1970 and in 1972 the bombing of North Vietnam to put pressure on North Vietnam to negotiate. A pullout of U.S. forces was begun with the South Vietnamese gradually taking over responsibility for maintaining their nation. After lengthy negotiations which began in 1969, a settlement was reached in 1973 and the U.S. forces were completely withdrawn.

In 1975 the governments of South Vietnam, Cambodia, and Laos all fell to the Communists. In 1974 President Ford offered clemency to Vietnam War Draft Dodgers and in 1977 President Carter granted a full pardon to Americans who fled to Canada rather than be drafted to fight.

This war, which some Americans see as the first war the U.S. "lost," continues to have profound effect on the nation. Many refugees including the so-called boat people, fled Vietnam and some have found asylum in the U.S. Many veterans had felt the lack of support from the nation and had felt alienated. During the Reagan years some contacts were made with the Communist government of Vietnam but relations remained strained.

TEST OF GENERAL KNOWLEDGE: DESCRIPTION, REVIEW, PRACTICE

The "lessons of Vietnam" are referred to in debates over policy for Central America in the late 1980s but there is disagreement as to what these lessons are—to interfere or not to interfere, to fight against native Communists or not, to subsidize guerrilla warfare in other nations or not.

Presidential Administrations—1952–1992

Dwight D. Eisenhower: Eisenhower's foreign policy was one of Cold War confrontation and brinkmanship. John Foster Dulles served as a forceful Secretary of State. Domestically, after the demise of Joseph McCarthy's "witch hunts" against the domestic threat of communism, the Eisenhower years were quite peaceful. The civil rights movement was stimulated by the *Brown vs. Board of Education* Supreme Court decision on school integration and Eisenhower gave moderate support to the movement. His administration held to a high standard of honesty in government when Sherman Adams, his White House Chief of Staff, was asked to resign after it was revealed he had accepted a vicuna coat as a gift. The most far-reaching domestic legislation of his presidency was the National Highway Act, which set up the interstate highway network.

John F. Kennedy: Elected president by a narrow margin over Richard M. Nixon. He was the first Catholic to win the office and the youngest ruler of a major world power. His administration supplied much polish and glitter, but little substantial domestic legislation. Kennedy's administration appears the most noted for foreign policy developments, among them the Alliance for Progress, the Peace Corps, the Bay of Pigs, the Cuban Missile Crisis, the Space Race, and the extension of the U.S. commitment to Vietnam. Kennedy was assassinated on November 22, 1963 in Dallas, Texas.

Lyndon Johnson: Johnson initiated a *War on Poverty* in an attempt to eradicate poverty in America. In many ways it was an updating and extension of Franklin Roosevelt's New Deal. It began well and included such diverse programs as Head Start and Medicare. His concept of the Great Society was hampered by increased involvement in the war in Vietnam and the need for military expenditures there.

Student unrest in the mid-60s reflected a change in attitude among some young people and culminated in anti-war protests which forced President Johnson to announce he would not run for a second term. The unrest took many forms, including the "Hippie" movement, greater use of illegal drugs, establishment of communes, anti-war demonstrations in Washington and elsewhere, and violence at the Democratic Convention in Chicago in 1968. One hero of the movement, Robert Kennedy, was assassinated in Los Angeles in 1968 while campaigning for the Democratic presidential nomination, removing an important political leader of the movement.

The extension of civil rights was another important aspect of the Kennedy/Johnson years. Supreme Court decisions, Congressional civil rights legislation, and the efforts of many workers and leaders led to a great breakthrough in the extension of rights to blacks. The 1968 assassination of Martin Luther King, Jr., a believer in nonviolent protest, was followed by outbreaks of violence and the movement lost momentum in the Nixon years. The slogan of Black Power inspired many other minority groups to seek power, with the result that Mexican-Americans (Chicanos), Native Americans, homosexuals (Gay Power), and women organized to have an impact on political affairs.

Richard M. Nixon: Elected president in 1968, Nixon promised to "bring the nation together" and end the Vietnam War. He gradually withdrew troops from Vietnam while expanding the war into Cambodia. With his Secretary of State, Henry Kissinger, he ended the war in Vietnam during his second term. There were periodic outbursts of anti-war violence (e.g., Kent State—1970) during his presidency, which led his administration to seek ways to prevent it. Many of their attempts proved to be illegal and under the term *Watergate* were revealed to the American public through newspaper exposes and Grand Jury inquiries. Vice-President Agnew was forced to resign as a result of illegal acts on his part, and finally, through evidence revealed on tape recordings of White House meetings, President Nixon resigned in August 1974. He was the first president to be forced from office.

As the Vietnam War was winding down, the Nixon administration made moves to end the Cold War and to reverse the policies of the previous twenty-five years. Nixon met with Brezhnev, the premier of the Soviet Union, both in Moscow and Washington. He also made a trip to Communist China, opening diplomatic relations with that nation for the first time since the Communists seized control of mainland China in 1949. Nixon's move towards negotiation with the Soviet Union and recognition of the People's Republic of China were the most important developments in foreign policy during his administration.

Gerald R. Ford: President Ford, the first man to come to the presidency by appointment rather than election, served the remaining years of Nixon's term. Ford continued the policy of detente, holding a summit conference in Vladivostok in 1974 and visiting China in 1975. The aftermath of Watergate, including Ford's pardon of Nixon, colored his administration. There was high inflation and Ford introduced his WIN (Whip Inflation Now) policy to combat it with limited success. OPEC (Organization of Petroleum Exporting Countries) and its oil policies affected domestic affairs.

James E. Carter: Jimmy Carter considered himself a "born again" Christian. Elected as an "outsider," President Carter found it difficult to be effective in dealing with the established bureaucracy of Congress and government. His foreign policy focused on the issue of human rights. He desired to streamline the government and make it more efficient. Domestic issues of inflation and energy crises, together with the international crisis of the Iranian Revolution and the seizure of American hostages, clouded his administration. The highlight of the administration of Jimmy Carter was the establishment of the Camp David Peace Accord, which finally brought peace in the Near East between Israel and Egypt, although it did not solve all of the outstanding issues in the area. He also negotiated a new treaty with Panama, eventually giving that nation control over the Panama Canal.

Ronald Reagan: Viewed by many as an extreme conservative Republican, Ronald Reagan overwhelmed Jimmy Carter in the election of 1980. The Republicans gained control of the Senate, and in the first year of his administration, a major reform program was pushed through Congress. It called for reduction of social service benefits, a reduction in taxes, and increased expenditures for military preparedness. A major debate on the need for a balanced budget and military versus social welfare expenditures continued throughout his administration. Supply side economics, the philosophical position behind the Reagan reforms, did not operate as expected and a huge government budget deficit developed. A large trade deficit continued to cloud the economic picture as Reagan's last year in office began. Throughout his administration, decisions were made to remove government regulation of the private sector yet there were strong pressures for the government to interfere in areas of "privacy" as defined by the Supreme Court—for example, prayer in schools and abortion rights.

In 1983, it was learned that Cuba and the USSR were building a major air strip in the little Carribbean country of Grenada. Because of the threat to U.S. security and the danger of the Communist presence to 700 U.S. medical students studying in that country, Reagan launched an invasion of the country by U.S. marines and paratroopers. The president supported aid to the Nicaraguan Contras, which was opposed by Congress, leading to extra-legal funding of the Contras. Mikhail Gorbachev came into power in

1985 and introduced the concept of *Glasnost* (openness). The Reagan years ended with a huge budget deficit and major unresolved economic, social, and environmental problems. The relationship between the United States and the USSR improved.

George Bush: This Republican president took office in 1989 with a Democrat Congress. His domestic policies emphasized no new taxes, improved relations with Congress, new laws on crime and drug cartels, and a national effort to improve education. Manned space flights were resumed with the Columbia shuttle. President Bush continued talks with the Soviet Union focusing on reducing chemical-weapons stockpiles and nuclear missiles. In December, Bush sent U.S. troops to Panama in support of Panamanian insurrection, because of General Manuel Noriega's drug trafficking and election violations. In an effort to escape Communism in East Germany, many people passed through the Berlin Wall to the West. In Romania, Ceausecu was overthrown and executed. In 1990, Communist governments were replaced in Czechoslovakia, Hungary, Poland, and Bulgaria. The Baltic States seceded from the USSR, followed by other republics. In October of that year, East and West Germany were reunited. On January 17, 1991, the United States and 28 U.N. allies launched the Persian Gulf War (Desert Storm), under the command of General Norman Schwarzkopf, with the goal of liberating Kuwait, which Iraq's Saddam Hussein had invaded. Continuous bombings and 100 hours of ground war brought victory, but left Hussein in power. U.S. casualties were considered very low—268. President Bush's high popularity ratings after the war gradually declined, as the economy worsened and the unemployment rate exceeded seven percent. Mikhail Gorbachev, head of the Communist party in the Soviet Union, resigned after a failed coup and Boris Yeltsin, the elected president of Russia, assumed the top post in that country. The dissolution of the USSR and the Communist party was officially proclaimed on December 25, 1991. To stabilize Yeltsin's leadership, avoid civil war, and strengthen democracy, the United States and other nations began a large airlift of food to the newly formed Commonwealth of Independent Republics.

Diagnostic Practice Test—Social Studies

Time—30 minutes

Directions: For each question or incomplete statement below, there are five suggested answers or completions. Select the one that *best* answers the question or completes the statement.

1. Human modes of living differ most according to
   (A) geographic region
   (B) maintenance needs
   (C) psychosocial needs
   (D) climate
   (E) occupation

2. The beginning of economic life stems from
   (A) human wants
   (B) national needs
   (C) political interests
   (D) an abundance of goods
   (E) unlimited productivity

3. The main characteristic that distinguishes modern Western civilization from other civilizations is its
   (A) worldwide dissemination
   (B) narrow orientation
   (C) cultural orientation
   (D) confinement to North and South America
   (E) emphasis on discipline and moral living

SOCIAL STUDIES

4. A very strategic area of world commerce is a small body of water through which one sixth of the world's oil supply is shipped. The nations of the world become nervous whenever a conflict in this region threatens to close the
   (A) Strait of Magellan
   (B) Black Sea
   (C) Straits of Hormuz
   (D) English Channel
   (E) Panama Canal

5. In recent years the number of newspapers and the daily circulations of the remaining ones have declined, mainly because of
   (A) lack of public interest in what is happening
   (B) inflation, which has raised the price of newspapers
   (C) unemployment, which has reduced available money
   (D) the rising illiteracy of the American public
   (E) the popularity of TV news, which has lured away many former newspaper readers

6. Geographically, which of the following is closest to the South Pole?
   (A) The Cape of Good Hope
   (B) The Panama Canal
   (C) The Amazon River
   (D) Cape Horn
   (E) The Strait of Gibraltar

7. You have been assigned to write a description of the campaign to capture Atlanta during the Civil War, using only primary sources. Which of the following would NOT qualify as a primary source?
   (A) An account by a confederate soldier in General Hood's army, in a letter to his mother
   (B) An account by an Atlanta woman who witnessed the siege, in her diary
   (C) An account by General Sherman, in his memoirs
   (D) An account by a reporter, in a contemporary Georgia newspaper
   (E) The account by Margaret Mitchell, in *Gone with the Wind*

8. Below are four documents important in American history:
   I. Northwest Ordinance
   II. Declaration of Independence
   III. Constitutional amendment ending slavery in the United States
   IV. Versailles Treaty

   In which of the following are these documents listed in correct chronological order?
   (A) IV, III, II, I
   (B) III, I, IV, II
   (C) II, I, III, IV
   (D) I, III, II, IV
   (E) III, II, IV, I

9. Which one of the following was the first black to be appointed a Justice of the U.S. Supreme Court?
   (A) Andrew Young
   (B) Ralph Bunche
   (C) Jesse Jackson
   (D) Thurgood Marshall
   (E) Martin Luther King

TEST OF GENERAL KNOWLEDGE: DESCRIPTION, REVIEW, PRACTICE

10. One of the main forces that operated during the twentieth century to upset the existing balance of power in Europe was the
    (A) rapid development of technology
    (B) growing number of new nations
    (C) rise of powerful leaders
    (D) decline of monarchies
    (E) growth of mercantilism

11. A phenomenon of the American political scene is the efforts by various special interest groups to influence legislation in ways that will benefit them. For example, in 1947 the Marshall Plan, under which food and other aid were supplied to war-devastated countries, was under consideration by Congress. It might have been expected (and, indeed, was the case) that passage would be strongly supported by

    (A) The Veterans of Foreign Wars
    (B) The American Farm Bureau Federation
    (C) The Daughters of the American Revolution
    (D) The Florida Junior Chamber of Commerce
    (E) The Brotherhood of Railroad Trainmen

Favorite Son

12. The cartoon above depicts a U.S. presidential candidate supported by
    (A) both national political parties
    (B) one national political party
    (C) a national political party in one state
    (D) independent voters
    (E) mostly men

13. All of the following have been (or were) influential in the civil rights movement in the United States EXCEPT
    (A) Julian Bond
    (B) Jesse Jackson
    (C) Martin Luther King, Jr.
    (D) Booker T. Washington
    (E) Andrew Young

14. In his 1982 State of the Union message President Reagan proposed a "new federalism." Which of the following would be an example of this policy?
    (A) An increase in federal income taxes
    (B) A decrease in the size of the Armed Forces
    (C) A transfer of powers now held by the states to the federal government
    (D) A transfer of social-welfare programs from the federal government to the individual states
    (E) A requirement that the federal budget be balanced

SOCIAL STUDIES

15. By 1971, 26 amendments to the U.S. Constitution had been passed. From 1972 to 1982 a strong effort was made to pass another amendment. What was this proposed amendment called?
    (A) The Equal Rights Amendment
    (B) The District of Columbia Representation Amendment
    (C) The Antigun Amendment
    (D) The Drug Control Amendment
    (E) The Balanced Budget Amendment

16. Every society has both a material and a nonmaterial culture. The nonmaterial culture consists of
    (A) libraries
    (B) tools
    (C) communication systems
    (D) folkways and language
    (E) food, shelter, and clothing

Big City, U.S.A.
Property and School Tax Levies

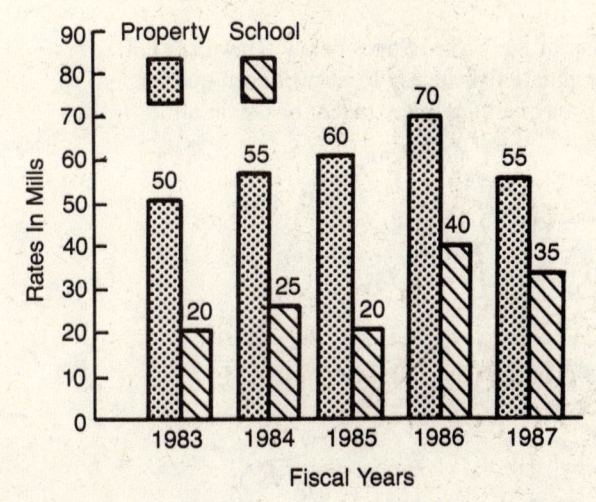

17. Since the establishment of schools in the Northwest Territories, state and local financial support for schools has been a basic concern. States differ in the way financial support is obtained; however, property taxes, with special school levies, continue to provide the main revenue for schools in many districts.

    In the bar graph above, school taxes are shown separately as a proportion of the total property taxes for the fiscal years 1983 through 1987. Which of the following statements about the information in the graph is INCORRECT?

    I. School taxes took the smallest proportion of property tax monies in 1983.
    II. The school taxes in 1983 and 1985 were the same proportion of the property taxes.
    III. The highest proportion of property taxes was applied to school taxes in 1987.
    IV. The school millage rate doubled between 1985 and 1986.

    (A) I only
    (B) I and II only
    (C) III only
    (D) II and III only
    (E) IV only

45

TEST OF GENERAL KNOWLEDGE: DESCRIPTION, REVIEW, PRACTICE

18. The last written words of President Franklin Roosevelt were as follows: "Today we are faced with the pre-eminent fact that, if civilization is to survive, we must cultivate the science of human relationships—the ability of all peoples, of all kinds, to live together and work together, in the same world, at peace." To which of the following present-day concerns is this warning most applicable?
    (A) Worldwide inflation
    (B) Internal revolutions in Central and South American countries
    (C) Apartheid in South Africa and racial discrimination elsewhere
    (D) The nuclear arms race
    (E) The conflict among various religious groups in Lebanon

19. At the turn of the twentieth century most immigrants to the United States settled in East Coast cities because
    (A) they had come from coastal cities in Europe and wanted to live in similar surroundings
    (B) they had no means of transportation to inland rural areas
    (C) they had no money to travel further
    (D) they were unambitious, and it was easier to stay where they landed
    (E) they were assured of financial help from city governments

Questions 20–22 refer to the partial map of the United States below (Hawaii is not included), on which the letters A–E designate five states. To answer each question, choose one of the letters. A letter may be used once, twice, or not at all.

SOCIAL STUDIES

20. Which state has the largest area?

21. Which state has the largest population?

22. In which state is the highest mountain?

23. The process whereby beliefs or practices common to one area of human settlement become part of the life-style of people in another area is called
    (A) socialization
    (B) ethnic association
    (C) cultural diffusion
    (D) deindividualization
    (E) imperialism

24. The economist refers to all things that have utility as
    (A) essentials   (D) resources
    (B) goods   (E) products
    (C) raw materials

25. The term that denotes the feeling held by each culture group that its way of doing things is the best is
    (A) nationalism   (D) heliocentrism
    (B) chauvinism   (E) patriotism
    (C) ethnocentrism

26. The purpose of Affirmative Action is to
    (A) stop loopholes in the draft registration of young men
    (B) provide additional benefits for the unemployed
    (C) correct past educational and employment discrimination against minority groups
    (D) create tax shelters for the poor in America
    (E) register eligible voters in all states

27. Relations between China and the United States could be marred by conflict over
    (A) Hong Kong   (D) Australia
    (B) Guam   (E) India
    (C) Taiwan

28. The first ten amendments to the U.S. Constitution guarantee certain rights. The exercise of these rights is sometimes challenged, however, by persons who feel that their own rights or viewpoints are being threatened. Which of the following headlines best reflects a situation of this kind?
    (A) "Parents Assail Closing of Neighborhood School"
    (B) "Audience Shouts Down Proabortion Speaker"
    (C) "Students Hold Vigil to Protest Nuclear Plant"
    (D) "Town Board Denies Appeal to Change Zoning"
    (E) "School Board Threatens Striking Teachers with Injunction"

29. The Sandinista political party in Nicaragua is supported by which of the following countries?
    (A) Costa Rica   (D) Guatemala
    (B) Cuba   (E) The United States
    (C) Honduras

TEST OF GENERAL KNOWLEDGE: DESCRIPTION, REVIEW, PRACTICE

30. Individual creativity in food production first arose in regions in which crop-growing and animal husbandry were combined. It would seem that creativity was fostered by this system mainly because
- (A) people were required to increase food production
- (B) men and women performed similar food-producing tasks
- (C) animals were used as a source of energy for food production
- (D) child labor was increased in food-preservation activities
- (E) meat was added to the supply of food

Answer Key

1.	A	7.	E	13.	D	19.	C	25.	C
2.	A	8.	C	14.	D	20.	A	26.	C
3.	A	9.	D	15.	A	21.	B	27.	C
4.	C	10.	A	16.	D	22.	A	28.	B
5.	E	11.	B	17.	B	23.	C	29.	B
6.	D	12.	C	18.	D	24.	B	30.	C

Mathematics

The Mathematics section of the Test of General Knowledge consists of 25 questions designed to assess your knowledge of the basic mathematics that you may need to function as a teacher, whether or not you will be teaching mathematics per se. The Mathematics test assesses six basic competencies:

1. Possesses good number sense (understanding of how numbers behave).
2. Can use numbers appropriately to meet various needs.
3. Can recognize mathematical relationships and use them appropriately.
4. Understands the basic elements of measurement—concepts, relationships, systems, units, scales, etc.—and can apply this knowledge correctly.
5. Understands deductive reasoning and can use it appropriately.
6. Can interpret graphic material of various types (graphs, charts, pictographs, diagrams, etc.)

Some of the topics on which you may be asked questions are as follows:

- Quantitative data, charts, graphs, or diagrams
- Comparing and ordering numbers
- Using ratio, proportion, and percent
- Measuring and using scales
- Interpreting formulas and written symbols
- Logical reasoning
- Solving problems in more than one way
- Understanding the metric system
- Identifying equivalent relationships in different forms
- Predicting and extrapolating information from data
- Drawing a valid conclusion from a series of statements
- Interpreting a schematic illustration (flowchart, electrical wiring diagram, etc.)

Preparing for the Mathematics Section

The following pages provide a basic review. If the Diagnostic Practice Test later in this section reveals a serious deficiency in some area, ask a mathematics teacher to recommend additional sources for review and practice. The Model Tests in Part IV of this book will also provide additional practice.

Strategies for Answering Mathematics Questions

1. Use your time wisely. You have 30 minutes to answer 25 questions, therefore, you should allow yourself a minute to a minute and a half for each question. If you find that you are spending as much as two minutes on a question, you must come to some decision about your answer, even if you have to guess. Remember, there is no penalty for guessing on this part of the NTE, so do not leave any questions unanswered. You can, however, circle the question and come back to it later if there is time.
2. Read each question carefully to make sure you answer the question that was asked and not the one you expected to be asked. Incorrect answer choices are often answers to what you might have incorrectly anticipated the question as asking.

TEST OF GENERAL KNOWLEDGE: DESCRIPTION, REVIEW, PRACTICE

3. Take all relevant information into consideration. This goes hand-in-hand with reading the question carefully. But be aware that often some irrelevant information is included in the question; you must determine which information falls into this category as well.
4. Mark up diagrams given in the test booklet, adding information either directly stated in the question or that you can infer from what is stated.
5. Where a diagram is not given, draw your own if it will help.
6. If you are having trouble answering a question involving variables, try substituting numbers for the variables.
7. Try working backwards from the answers if you are stumped. On some questions this tactic is particularly useful.
8. Eliminate answer chices that cannot possibly be correct. For example, if you had to find the area of a portion of a figure and you were given the area of the whole figure, then you would eliminate any answer choice that was equal to or greater than the area of the whole figure.
9. Make sure your answer is reasonable. After you have gone through your computations and chosen an answer, thoughtfully consider whether the answer you have chosen is plausible.

Review

MATHEMATICAL CONCEPTS

Mathematics uses a universal language based on

- Certain undefined terms
- Defined words, symbols, and signs
- Axioms or postulates (assumptions believed to be true; accepted propositions)
- Theorems (rules based on the assumed truth of the axioms)

Inductive and Deductive Reasoning

By observing a number of objects or living things, or by conducting experiments, such as successful space flights, conclusions can be made that are based on performance. This is inductive reasoning, and it has a role in mathematics. If one counterexample to a generalization drawn by induction is found, however, it will disprove the entire proposition. Therefore mathematicians use *deductive reasoning* to proceed from a set of assumptions to an inevitable conclusion. To prove a proposition, a part of a statement or *hypothesis* is accepted; from this hypothesis a logical conclusion is drawn. This conclusion has to be true for all cases on a universal basis. Any mathematician using the same hypothesis will reach the same conclusion.

Example. If the temperature is 95 degrees, then the pavement is hot.
The temperature is 95 degrees.
The pavement is hot.

If we accept as true "If the temperature is 95 degrees, then the pavement is hot" and "The temperature is 95 degrees," then the conclusion is "The pavement is hot."

Example. If $x = 6$, then $x + 3 = 9$.

MATHEMATICS

Statements	Reasons
1. $x = 6$.	Hypothesis
2. $x + 3 = 6 + 3$.	Property of additive equality
3. $x + 3 = 9$.	Addition of $6 + 3$
4. If $x = 6$, then $x + 3 = 9$.	Chain rule.

The Number System

Natural numbers are the counting numbers: 1, 2, 3, 4, 5, ...
Whole numbers are the counting numbers with 0 added: 0, 1, 2, 3, ...
Integers are the positive and negative whole numbers: . . . , −3, −2, −1, 0, 1, 2, 3, ...

A *rational number* is a number that can be expressed as the ratio of two integers: $\frac{3}{4}$, $-\frac{5}{7}$, $\frac{2}{3}$, $\frac{6}{3}$.

A *numeral* is a symbol used to represent a number, such as 12 (Arabic) or XII (Roman).

Example. When the board of education reports the purchase of six new school buses, it indicates the number of buses; the symbol 6 is used to represent that quantity; therefore 6 is a numeral.

Number Values. Each numeral in the representation of a number shows its value by the place in which it is written.

We use 10 numerals to represent all numbers:

$$\begin{array}{cccccccccc} 0 & 1 & 2 & 3 & 4 & 5 & 6 & 7 & 8 & 9 \\ 10 & 11 & 12 & 13 & 14 & 15 & 16 & 17 & 18 & 19 \\ 20 & 21 & 22 & 23 & 24 & 25 & 26 & 27 & 28 & 29 \end{array}$$

Three-digit numbers and all larger numbers repeat the 10 numerals: 100; 1000; 10,000; 100,000; etc.

The Number Line (Signed Numbers)

The number line shows that we have both positive- and negative-place values of numbers:

$$-7 \quad -6 \quad -5 \quad -4 \quad -3 \quad -2 \quad -1 \quad 0 \quad +1 \quad +2 \quad +3 \quad +4 \quad +5 \quad +6 \quad +7$$

This collection of whole numbers created from a set of 10 digits is an infinite *set*, for *there is no last number*. This idea is indicated as 0, 1, 2, 3, 4, 5, 6, 7, 8, 9, 10, ...

Numbers—Properties and Relations

Mathematical System. A mathematical system consists of the following components:

- A set of elements
- One or more operations using the elements of the set
- Properties that concern the set of elements and the operation(s)
- One or more relations, such as equivalence ($6 + 6 = 12$)

Properties are assumptions that are accepted as truths about the way the system works (axioms or postulates), such as $3 + 2 = 2 + 3$.

TEST OF GENERAL KNOWLEDGE: DESCRIPTION, REVIEW, PRACTICE

Decimal Notation. In decimal notation the place value of each digit used in a number system is determined by multiplying it by a power of 10. Thus the decimal system is a *positional system*.

Example. Rational numbers between 0 and 1 are expressed as $\frac{1}{10}, \frac{2}{3}, \frac{1}{4}, \frac{3}{5}, \frac{1}{2}$, etc. To simplify computation, decimal numerals can be substituted for these fractions. The place values of the numerals are maintained by using *decimal points*. The places of the digits to the right of the decimal point have names as follows:

1. $0.1 = \frac{1}{10}$ = one tenth
2. $0.01 = \frac{1}{100}$ = one hundredth
3. $0.001 = \frac{1}{1000}$ = one thousandth
4. $0.0001 = \frac{1}{10,000}$ = one ten-thousandth

Binary Operations. These are called binary from *bi-*, meaning "two"; only two terms can be added or multiplied at a time. We add pairs of addends together and then combine this sum with other addends.

Example: $(6 + 4) + 2$ is first added as $6 + 4 = 10$; then we add $10 + 2 = 12$. Multiplication is also a binary operation, for we multiply $(6 \times 8) \times 2$ as $6 \times 8 = 48$; we then multiply $48 \times 2 = 96$.

Identity Elements. An identity element is one that, when used with a number in addition or multiplication, leaves that number unchanged.

Example: Zero is the identity element for addition: $4 + 0 = 4$; $0 + 2 = 2$. One is the identity element for multiplication: $8 \times 1 = 8$; $1 \times 6 = 6$.

Commutative Property (interchangeable order). The sum or product of two numbers is unchanged regardless of the order in which they are added or multiplied.

Example. In addition: $2 + 4 = 4 + 2$
$6 = 6$
In multiplication: $2 \times 5 = 5 \times 2$
$10 = 10$

To further demonstrate commutative property, we can substitute letters such as a and b for the numerals.
In addition: $a + b = b + a$.
In multiplication: $a \times b = b \times a$.

Associative Property (serial order). As explained above, addition and multiplication are binary operations. In addition, the order in which the terms are totaled does not affect the sum obtained.

Example: $(2 + 3) + 5 = 2 + (3 + 5)$
$5 + 5 = 2 + 8$
$10 = 10$

When a, b, and c represent numbers, then $(a + b) + c = a + (b + c)$.

MATHEMATICS

Example: $(5 \times 8) \times 3 = 5 \times (8 \times 3)$
$40 \times 3 = 5 \times 24$
$120 = 120$

Again, in multiplication we can let a, b, and c represent numbers: $(a \times b) \times c = a \times (b \times c)$, or $(ab)c = a(bc)$.

Distributive Property of Multiplication with Respect to Addition. Multiplication has a distributive property. It states that we can distribute the multiplier to each of the numbers in the multiplicand. The common multiplier can be used to find the product with each of several numbers that are to be added. We then add the separate products and obtain the answer.

Example: $a(b + c) = (a \times b) + (a \times c)$. When we use numbers, we get

$$4 \times (3 + 2) = (4 \times 3) + (4 \times 2)$$
$$4 \times 5 = 12 + 8$$
$$20 = 20$$

The distributive property of numbers indicates that the value expressed by a number represented by several numerals is the sum of the values expressed in the digit positions of the numerals. This is a valuable generalization when multiplying three-digit or larger numbers. For example, 535 can be written as $500 + 30 + 5$. To multiply this expression by 7, it can be distributed as follows:

$$7(500 + 30 + 5) = 3500 + 210 + 35 = 3745$$

or as

$$\begin{array}{r} 535 \\ \times\ 7 \\ \hline 35 \\ 21 \\ 35 \\ \hline 3745 \end{array}$$

Relations. The language of mathematics associates objects with other objects to show that the objects are *similar* or *different* or the *same*. Symbols used to represent these relations include $\geq$ (is greater than or equal to), $<$ (is less than), and $=$ (equals).

Functions. Expressions such as *produced by, depends on,* and *is a function of* show that two elements, qualities, or traits are related and vary one with the other, or are dependent on another one.

Example. The amount of time taken to complete an assignment can be said to be a function of the speed with which the person works.

Ratio and Proportion

Ratio. Many numbers have meaning only when compared to other numbers. A ratio is a comparison between two quantities expressed in the same units. The ratio between

TEST OF GENERAL KNOWLEDGE: DESCRIPTION, REVIEW, PRACTICE

two quantities is determined by dividing one quantity by the other. Thus, in determining the ratio of the sizes of two boxes of the same kind of cereal, one containing 40 ounces and the other 16 ounces, you would compare 40 to 16. This comparison could be shown in four ways: 40:16, 40 ÷ 16, $\frac{40}{16}$, and 40 to 16.

The terms of ratios can be reduced, increased, or simplified, as is done with fractions. In this case the ratio $\frac{40}{16}$ becomes $\frac{10}{4} = \frac{5}{2}$. Five boxes of cereal, each weighing 16 ounces, are equal to two boxes of cereal, each weighing 40 ounces. (There is a difference between the fraction $\frac{5}{2}$ and the ratio $\frac{5}{2}$. The fraction becomes the mixed number $2\frac{1}{2}$; the ratio compares 5 to 2.)

Proportion. Many physical and chemical relationships are expressed as proportions. Four numbers such as 5, 6, 15, and 18 will form a proportion if the ratio of the first two in the order named equals the ratio of the last two in the order named: $\frac{5}{6} = \frac{15}{18}$. In a ratio the first and last terms (5 and 18 in the example) are called the *extremes*; the second and third terms (6 and 15) are the *means*. In any proportion the product of the means equals the product of the extremes:

$$6(15) = 5(18)$$
$$90 = 90$$

Use of algebraic language in proportions. We can solve algebraic problems of proportion by applying the relationship above so that all fractions are removed. If $\frac{a}{b} = \frac{c}{d}$, then, as shown above, $bc = ad$. If we have three numbers in a proportion, we can let the fourth one be x and solve for x. For example, $4:12 = x:48$; we solve by multiplying the means ($12 \times x$, or $12x$) and then multiplying the extremes (4×48):

$$12x = 192$$
$$x = 16 \quad \text{and} \quad 4:12 = 16:48$$

Word Problem. If Jane's car gets 52 miles per 2 gallons of diesel fuel, how many miles will she get on 13 gallons?

We set up a proportion: $52:x = 2:13$

$$\frac{52}{x} = \frac{2}{13}$$
$$2x = 13(52)$$
$$2x = 676$$
$$x = 338$$

Factor. In the word problem above we multiplied two numbers (factors) to get the product. Since we can use both numbers and letters, 2 and x are factors producing a product, $2x$; a and b are factors producing a product, ab.

Exponent. An exponent is a symbol used with a base to tell how many times the base is to be multiplied by itself. For instance, 5^3 symbolizes 5 multiplied or used as a factor three times: $5 \times 5 \times 5 = 125$. In 5^3, 5 is called the base and 3 is called the exponent.

MATHEMATICS

THREE FORMS OF PERCENT PROBLEMS

Finding a percent of a number $\quad (p = rb)$

What is 3% of 123?

Base (b)	Rate (r)	Part (p)
$123	3%	?

$p = 3\% \times \$123 = \$3.69$

Finding what percent one number is of another number $\quad (r = p/b)$

What percent of 200 gallons is 45 gallons?

Base (b)	Rate (r)	Part (p)
200 gal.	?	45 gal.

$r = \dfrac{45}{200} = 22.5\%$

Finding the whole when a given percent is known $\quad (b = p/r)$

A salesman gets a commission of 6½% on all sales. His commission in August was $335. What were his sales?

Base (b)	Rate (r)	Part (p)
?	6½%	$335

$b = \dfrac{\$335}{6.5\%} = \$5153.85$

Meaning of Metric System Prefixes

mega- = 1,000,000 (millions)

kilo- = 1,000 (thousands)

hecto- = 100 (hundreds)

deca- = 10 (tens)

deci- = 0.1 (tenths)

centi- = 0.01 (hundredths)

milli- = 0.001 (thousandths)

micro- = 0.000001 (millionths)

base unit = 1

Quiz—The Metric System

Fill in the blanks in the following:

1. The metric prefixes used most often are listed below. Express them as decimals:

   Decimal

   a. *milli-*, abbreviated as *m*: a thousand times smaller _____

   b. *centi-*, abbreviated as *c*: a hundred times smaller _____

   c. *kilo-*, abbreviated as *k*: a thousand times larger _____

2. The basic metric unit for measuring length is the _____, which is about _____% larger than the yard. Smaller metric units for measurement of length are the _____ and the _____.

3. There are approximately _____ centimeters in 1 inch.

4. One kilometer is a little longer than _____ of a mile.

5. Multiplication by 10 moves each digit in the other factor _____ _____ to the left; division by 100 moves the decimal point in the dividend _____ _____ to the left.

TEST OF GENERAL KNOWLEDGE: DESCRIPTION, REVIEW, PRACTICE

6. Miss Camp, in discussing athletic contests, asked, "If you had to run a 100-yard dash, how many meters would you be required to run if 1 yard = 0.91 meter? _____.

7. The federal law limits driving speed to 55 miles per hour. Convert this limit to kilometers per hour. (1 mile = 1.61 kilometers.) _____.

8. One inch and 2.54 centimeters are about the same length; therefore, _____ centimeters is about the same length as 4 inches.

9. Bob was told to draw a line 8 centimeters long. How many inches long was the line? _____.

10. If you were changing 25 yards to meters, and the conversion factor is 0.91 for yards to meters and 1.09 for meters to yards, which factor would you use? _____ How many meters would you have? _____

11. Jack's car gets 24 miles to the gallon. How many liters of gasoline must he buy to take a 480-mile trip? (1 gallon = 3.79 liters.) _____.

12. Rosita rented an automobile and traveled in England during the month of June. Her car got 40 miles to the gallon, and she used 606.4 liters of gas. How many miles did Rosita travel? _____.

13. Mr. and Mrs. Sampson bought a house with 7½ acres of land. How many hectares of land do they own? (1 acre = 0.40 hectare.) _____.

14. Betty's brother weighs 140 pounds, and 1 pound = 0.45 kilogram. How many kilograms does Betty's brother weigh? _____.

15. Ruth made scalloped potatoes for a potluck supper. Convert the underlined values in her recipe into their metric equivalents, using the information below the recipe.

Recipe	Metric Equivalent
Heat oven to 350°F.	____ °C
Arrange two layers of peeled, thinly sliced raw potatoes, about 4 cups, in a 1½-quart baking dish.	____ milliliters ____ liters
Sprinkle each layer of potatoes with salt and a little pepper. Dot each layer with 2 to 4 tablespoons butter.	____ milliliters
Pour 1¼ cups hot milk over the potatoes.	____ milliliters
Bake uncovered for about 1¼ hours.	

Conversion to metric equivalents:
Fahrenheit to Celsius: Subtract 32 and multiply by ⅝.
Cups to milliliters: Multiply by 236.
One fluid quart equals 0.95 liter.
Tablespoons to milliliters: Multiply by 15.

MATHEMATICS

16. The local electric plant ordered 1025 short tons of low-sulfur coal. How many metric tonnes did the company order? (1 short ton [2000 lb.] = 0.91 metric tonne.) _____ .

17. Henry's physician told him to mix 2 ounces of medicine with 6 ounces of water. Converting to metric volume, Henry found that he had to take _____ milliliters of fluid. (1 fluid ounce = 30 milliliters.)

18. Jose built a birdhouse 3 inches wide and 5 inches long. The perimeter of the base of the birdhouse was _____ inches or _____ centimeters. The area of the base of the birdhouse was _____ square inches or _____ square centimeters. (Multiply 1 inch by 2.5 to obtain centimeters. Multiply each square inch by 6.5 to obtain square centimeters.)

19. Angela purchased the following items at the supermarket. Using the information below the list, convert each measurement to its metric equivalent.

Item	Metric Equivalent
2 pounds coffee	_____
4 quarts milk	_____
2 pints cream	_____
5 pounds sugar	_____
14 ounces breakfast cereal	_____
3 pounds apples	_____

Conversion to metric equivalents:

1 pound equals 0.45 kilogram
1 gallon equals 3.8 liters
1 pint equals 0.47 liter
1 ounce equals 28.35 grams

20. When Marcia was on vacation in Michigan, the temperature ranged from 10°C to 35°C. What were equivalent temperatures in Fahrenheit degrees? (Multiply the Celsius temperature by $\frac{9}{5}$ and add 32 to obtain the Fahrenheit temperature.)

Celsius	Fahrenheit
10°C	_____
35°C	_____

TEST OF GENERAL KNOWLEDGE: DESCRIPTION, REVIEW, PRACTICE

Answers

1. a. milli-, 0.001; b. centi-, 0.01; c. kilo-, 1000.00

2. meter, 10, centimeter, millimeter

3. 2.5

4. ½ or 0.5 (or even 0.6)

5. one place; two places

6. 91

7. 88.55 or (rounded) 89

8. 10

9. 3.2

10. 0.91, 22.75 or 23

11. 75.8

12. 6400

13. 3

14. 63

15. 350°F = 177°C
    4 cups = 944 milliliters
    1½ quart = 1.425 or 1.43 liters
    2 to 4 tablespoons = 30 to 60 milliliters
    1¼ cups = 295 milliliters

16. 932.75 or (rounded) 933

17. 240

18. 16, 40, 15, 97.5

19. 2 pounds = 0.90 kilogram
    4 quarts = 3.8 liters
    2 pints = .9475 liter
    5 pounds = 2.25 kilograms
    14 ounces = 396.9 grams
    3 pounds = 1.35 kilograms

20. 10°C = 50.0°F
    35°C = 95.0°F

MATHEMATICS

GEOMETRY

Perimeter (distance around)

Finding the perimeter of a square 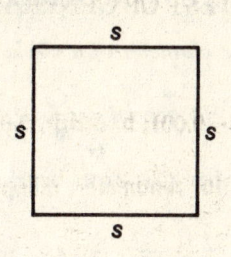
p = 4s
　Find the perimeter when $s = 5\frac{1}{4}$.

　$4 \times 5\frac{1}{4} = 4 \times 5.25 = 21.$

Finding the perimeter of an equilateral triangle 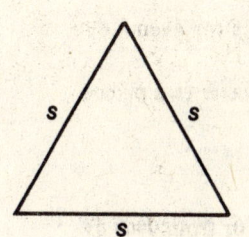
p = 3s
　Find the perimeter when $s = 7.6$.

　$3 \times 7.6 = 22.8.$

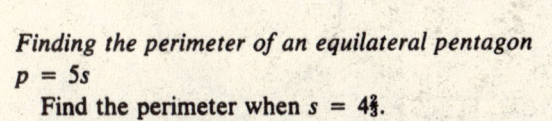

Finding the perimeter of an equilateral pentagon 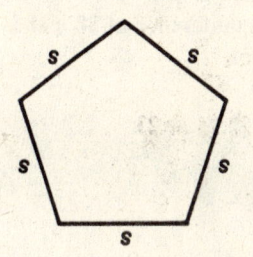
p = 5s
　Find the perimeter when $s = 4\frac{2}{3}$.

　$5 \times 4\frac{2}{3} = 5 \times 4.67 = 23.35.$

Finding the perimeter of a rectangle
p = 2·l + 2·w
A rectangle has length (*l*) and width (*w*).
　Find the perimeter of a room 11.5 feet long and 9 feet wide.

　$2 \times 11.5 = 23$　　$2 \times 9 = 18$
　$23 + 18 = 41$ ft.

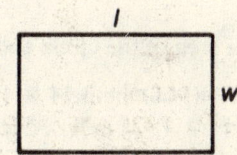

Circumference, Diameter, Radius

Finding the circumference of a circle 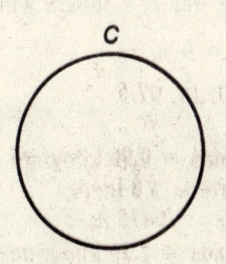
Every circle has a ratio of circumference to a diameter of approximately $3\frac{1}{7}$ or 3.142. The exact ratio is represented by π (pi).

$\dfrac{\text{circumference }(C)}{\text{diameter }(d)} = 3\frac{1}{7} = \dfrac{C}{d} = \pi \text{ (pi)}$　and　$C = \pi d$

　Find c when d is 28 inches.　　$3\frac{1}{7} = \dfrac{22}{7}$

　　　　　　　　　　$C = \dfrac{22}{\cancel{7}} \times \dfrac{\cancel{28}^{4}}{1} = 88$ in.

59

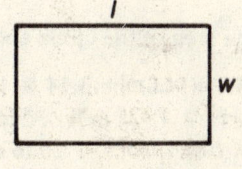

TEST OF GENERAL KNOWLEDGE: DESCRIPTION, REVIEW, PRACTICE

Finding the diameter of a circle

Since $C = \pi d$, then $d = \dfrac{C}{\pi}$.

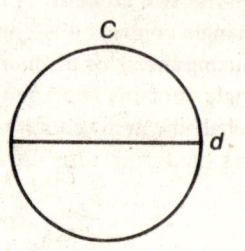

    Find d when C is 88 inches.

$d = \dfrac{88}{1} \div \dfrac{22}{7} = 88 \div 3.14 = 28$ in.

$(3.14 = \pi)$

Finding the radius of a circle
Since the radius of a circle is one-half the diameter, find the diameter and divide by 2. Find the radius of the circle above with a circumference of 88 inches. The diameter of this circle is 28 inches.

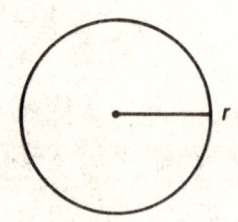

$r = \tfrac{1}{2}d$
$r = \tfrac{1}{2}(28)$
$r = 14$ in.

Area (the size of the interior of a geometric figure)

Finding the area of a circle
$A = \pi r^2$
    Find the area of the circle above whose radius is 14 inches.

$A = (3.14)(14.0)^2 = 3.14 \times 196 = 615.44$ sq. in.

Finding the area of a square 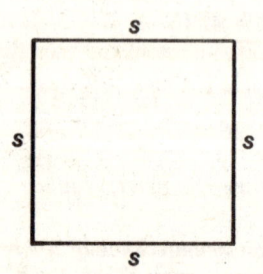
$A = s^2$
    Find the area of a square with sides of 3 inches.

$A = 3^2 = 9$ sq. in.

Finding the area of a rectangle
$A = lw$ **(length times width)** or bh **(base times height)**
    Find the area of the bottom of a box 6 inches long and 4 inches wide.

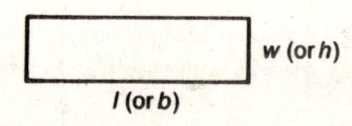

$A = 6 \times 4 = 24$ sq. in.

60

MATHEMATICS

Finding the area of triangles

An equilateral triangle has three equal sides.

A triangle with two equal sides is called an *isosceles* triangle.

A *right* triangle contains a 90° angle (see page 63). A rectangle can be constructed by using the sides of the right angle for its length and width; it can be seen that a rectangle contains two identical right triangles. Therefore, the area of a right triangle is one-half the area of a rectangle that has the same linear measurements.

We express the formula for the area of a right triangle as

$$\text{area} = \frac{\text{base }(b) \times \text{altitude }(h)}{2} \quad \text{or} \quad A = \frac{bh}{2}$$

Example. If a rectangle has a base of 8 inches and an altitude of 4 inches, what is the area of each of the two right triangles?

$$A = \frac{bh}{2} = \frac{8 \times 4}{2} = \frac{32}{2} = 16 \text{ sq. in.}$$

An isosceles triangle can be shown to be composed of two right triangles by drawing a straight line from the vertex of the angle formed by the two equal sides to the midpoint of the base. The area of each of the right triangles is

$$\tfrac{1}{2}\left(\frac{b}{2}h\right) \quad \text{or} \quad \frac{bh}{4}$$

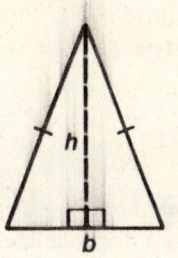

Adding the areas of the two equal right triangles together gives the area of the isosceles triangle

$$A = \frac{bh}{2}$$

A *scalene* triangle, with no equal sides, can also be divided in two by means of a vertical line. Since the sides are unequal, we use DC for the altitude and multiply $DC \times AD \div 2$; then we multiply $DC \times BD \div 2$ and add the two results to obtain the area of the scalene triangle. The area of the scalene triangle is thus

$$A = \tfrac{1}{2}DC \times AB \quad \text{or} \quad \frac{bh}{2}$$

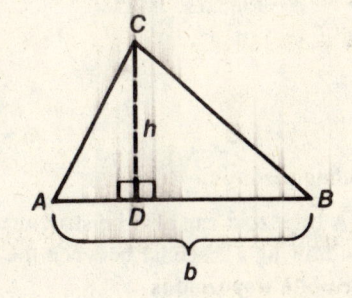

Example. If a scalene triangle has an altitude of 6 inches and a base of 7 inches, what is its area?

$$A = \frac{bh}{2} = \frac{7 \times 6}{2} = \frac{42}{2} = 21 \text{ sq. in.}$$

For any triangle, with base b and altitude h, the area is $\frac{bh}{2}$.

The Pythagorean theorem. In a right triangle the side opposite the right angle is called the *hypotenuse*. Its length is determined by the length of the sides adjacent to the right angle, which are called the *legs* of the right triangle.

The relationship between them, known as the *Phythagorean theorem*, is

$$a^2 + b^2 = c^2$$

where *a* and *b* are the lengths of the legs of the right triangle, and *c* is the length of the hypotenuse.

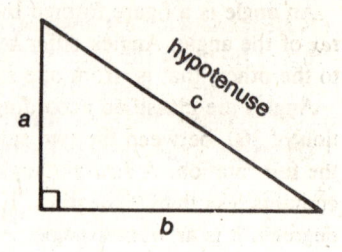

Example. Find the length of the hypotenuse of a right triangle if the length of side *a* is 5 inches and the length of side *b* is 7 inches.

$$a = 5, b = 7$$
$$c^2 = 5^2 + 7^2$$
$$c^2 = 25 + 49$$
$$c^2 = 74$$
$$c = \sqrt{74}$$
$$c = 8.602 \text{ in.}$$

Finding the area of a parallelogram or trapezoid

By drawing a diagonal line between opposite vertices, one can divide a *parallelogram* into two congruent triangles. The area is measured by the product of one side multiplied by the altitude of that side. The area of the parallelogram is equal to the sum of the two triangles within the parallelogram: $A = ab$.

Example. Find the area of a parallelogram whose altitude is 7 inches and whose base is 9 inches.

$$A = 7 \times 9$$
$$A = 63 \text{ in.}$$

A trapezoid can also be structured into triangles, but not congruent ones, by drawing a diagonal between the two parallel sides. The formula for the area of a trapezoid is

$$A = \frac{a}{2}(b_1 + b_2)$$

where b_1 and b_2 are the lengths of the bases and *a* is the altitude.

Example. Find the area of a trapezoid with these dimensions: $a = 4$ feet, $b_1 = 5$ feet, $b_2 = 8$ feet.

$$A = \frac{4}{2}(5 + 8) \qquad A = 2 \times 13$$
$$A = 2(5 + 8) \qquad A = 26 \text{ sq. in.}$$

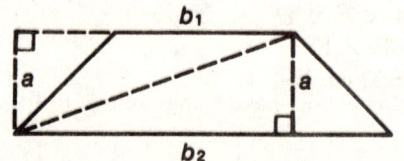

MATHEMATICS

Classification of Angles

An angle is a figure formed by two different rays from a common endpoint, the *vertex* of the angle. Angles differ by the amount of rotation required to move from one ray to the other, that is, from one side of the angle to the other.

Angles are classified according to the number of degrees, out of a possible full rotation of 360, between the two sides. A *right* angle measures 90 degrees or one fourth of the full rotation. A *straight* angle has 180 degrees between its sides. An *acute* angle contains less than 90 degrees. If an angle has more than 90 degrees but less than 180 degrees, it is an *obtuse* angle. A *reflex* angle lies between 180 and 360 degrees.

Volume

The third dimension, in addition to length and width, for quantifying data concerning solids relates to depth. Three-dimensional figures in space have *volume*, which is represented in cubic measurement.

<u>Measures of Volume</u>
1 cubic inch (cu. in.)
1728 cu. in. = 1 cubic foot (cu. ft.)
27 cu. ft. = 1 cubic yard (cu. yd.)

Finding the volume of a rectangular solid
$V = lwh$
  Find the volume of a rectangular box 12 in. long by 6 in. wide by 3 in. high.

  $V = 12 \times 6 \times 3$
  $V = 72 \times 3$
  $V = 216$ cu. in.

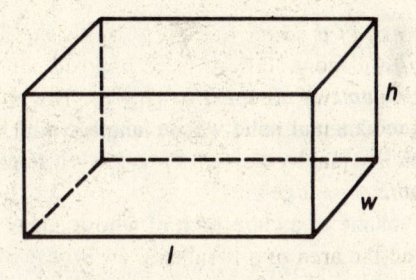

Finding the volume of a prism
$V = bh$ (b = area of base, h = altitude)
  Find the volume of a prism 4 in. high with a base that has an area of 9 sq. in.

  $V = 9 \times 4 = 36$ cu. in.

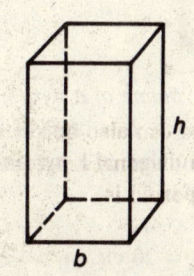

Finding the volume of a cylinder whose base is a circle
$V = \pi r^2 h$, where r = radius of the base and h = altitude of the cylinder
  Find the volume of a cylinder if r = 7 inches and h = 12 inches.

  $V = 3.14 \times 7^2 \times 12$
  $V = 153.86 \times 12$
  $V = 1846.32$ cu. in.

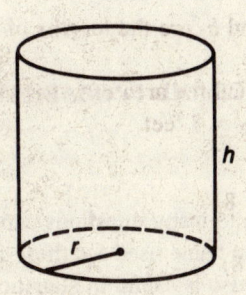

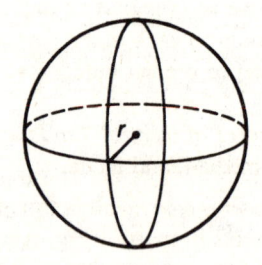

TEST OF GENERAL KNOWLEDGE: DESCRIPTION, REVIEW, PRACTICE

Finding the volume of a cone
$V = \frac{1}{3}\pi r^2 h$, where r = radius of the base and h = altitude of the cone
Find the volume of a cone with r = 6 inches and h = 10 inches.

$V = \frac{1}{3}(3.14 \times 6^2 \times 10)$
$V = \frac{1}{3}(3.14 \times 36 \times 10)$
$V = \frac{1}{3}\left(\frac{1130.4}{1}\right)$
$V = 376.8$ cu. in.

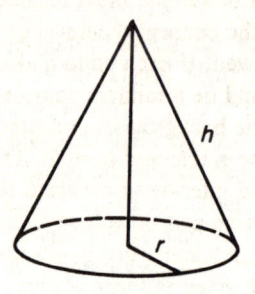

Finding the volume of a sphere
$V = \frac{4}{3}\pi r^3$, where r = radius of the sphere
Find the volume of a sphere with r = 3 inches.

$V = \frac{4}{3}(3.14 \times 3^3)$
$V = \frac{4}{3}(3.14 \times 27)$
$V = \frac{4}{3}(84.78)$

$V = \frac{4}{\cancel{3}} \times \frac{\cancel{84.78}\,^{28.26}}{1} = 113.04$ cu. in.

Finding the volume of a cube
A cube is a rectangular solid whose length, width, and height (i.e., its edges) are all equal.
$V = e^3$, where e = edge
Find the volume of a cube each of whose edges measures 4 inches.

$V = 4^3$
$V = 4 \times 4 \times 4 = 64$ cu. in.

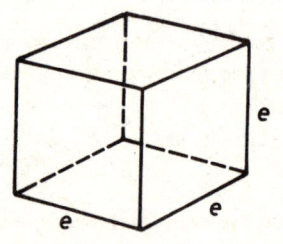

Finding the volume of a pyramid
$V = \frac{1}{3}bh$, where b = area of the base and h = height of the pyramid
Find the volume of a pyramid with a base area of 15 sq. in. and a height of 4 in.
$V = \frac{1}{3}(15 \times 4)$
$V = \frac{1}{3}(60) = 20$ cu. in.

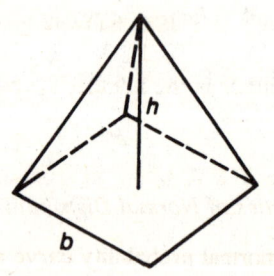

STATISTICS AND PROBABILITY

Statistics

Answers to many questions can be found by collecting facts, *data*, about them. *Statistics* is the name used for these facts and for the interpretation of data. Incomplete information also is useful in statistics for drawing inferences or making predictions. Some answers *probably* are true, and some deductions are derived through *probability* laws.

MATHEMATICS

Since the entire set, or *population*, cannot be observed or studied by collecting data, a subset or *sample* must be selected. Instead of studying the entire fifth-grade population in the county to determine its television-viewing habits, a *random sample* may be interviewed. If each child had an equal opportunity to be selected for the interview, this would be a random sample. If pupils were selected on the basis of age, sex, socioeconomic background, and other factors that teachers considered relevant, the result would be a *selected sample*. This is an example of *inductive statistics* because observations and interviews are used to collect data. Political pollsters use the inductive approach also and draw inferences from such data.

When a teacher gives an examination, collects test scores for all pupils, finds an average or mean of these scores, and then records this information in a record book without drawing inferences, the process can be called *descriptive statistics*, and then deduction is the research method used. The graphs in this section are examples of the use of descriptive or quantitative data; the individual items may or may not have any direct relationship to each other. Descriptive statistics can be used inductively to draw inferences and to predict outcomes.

Measures of Central Tendency. The three measures are called the average (arithmetic mean), median, and mode.

The *average* or *mean* is found by dividing the sum of a set of numbers by the number of items in the set. For example, if José received the following scores in physics on the first five tests: 80, 90, 55, 60, and 75, his average score was

$$\frac{80 + 90 + 55 + 60 + 75}{5} = 72$$

The *median* is the middle number of a set of numbers, arranged in order of size.

When the set of numbers contains an odd number of values, the median is the middle number:

2, 4, 6, $\underline{8}$, 10, 12, 14 (8 is the median)

When the set of numbers contains an even number of values, the median is the value halfway between the two middle numbers:

1, 3, 5, 7, _ 9, 11, 13, 15
(8 is halfway between 7 and 9 and hence is the median)

The *mode* is the number appearing most frequently in a set of numbers:

2, $\underline{3}$, $\underline{3}$, 5, 7 (3 is the mode)

Properties of Normal Distribution Curves

The normal probability curve and the normal frequency curve are symmetric in relation to the *y*-axis. The frequency of the distribution is the area between a normal frequency curve and the *x*-axis, so that one half of the total area lies on either side of the *y*-axis, representing the middle of the distribution:

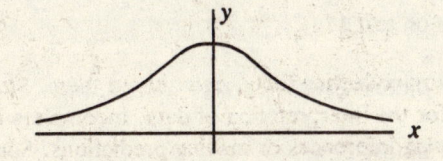

TEST OF GENERAL KNOWLEDGE: DESCRIPTION, REVIEW, PRACTICE

The equation of the y-axis is $x = 0$. Since the curve has a maximum value at $x = 0$, this value will be the mode, as well as the median and the mean. A normal distribution has symmetry. Any score that is above or below the mean on the x-axis is measured in terms of "sigmas" (σ) above or below the mean; σ represents a measure called the *standard deviation* or the *distribution*. The ratio x/σ can be used to show the deviation of any score from the mean as it is turned into a *standard score*.

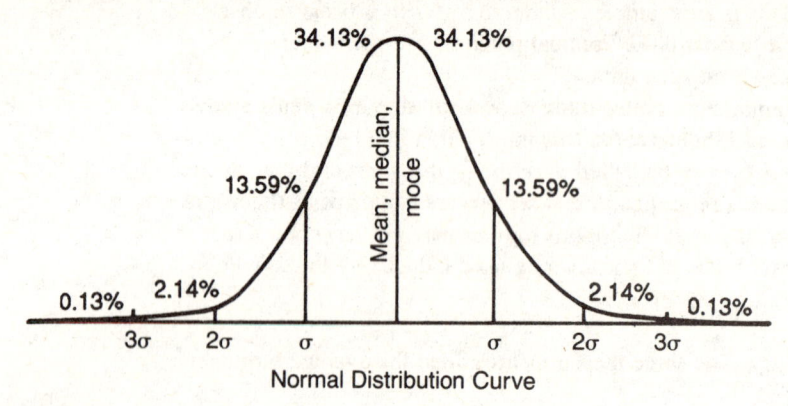

Normal Distribution Curve

Test Scores

A set of test scores may be treated in a variety of ways. Teachers often compare pupils' scores on two tests to determine progress.

Quiz — Statistics

Miss Bianchi obtained the following distribution of scores on two tests, which she has placed in rank order for interpretation. This geometry class had a week of additional review before taking the second test.

	Score	
Student	Test 1	Test 2
1	88	92
2	87	92
3	87	91
4	86	91
5	85	90
6	84	89
7	83	83
8	83	82
9	83	82
10	82	82
11	81	82
12	81	81
13	80	81
14	80	81
15	79	80

Answer the following questions about Miss Bianchi's geometry class:

1. What was the median score of the class on test 1?

2. What was the median score of the class on test 2?

3. What percent of the students improved on test 2?

MATHEMATICS

4. What was the ratio of students receiving the higher score to those receiving a lower score or showing no gain on the second test?

5. What was the net gain in test scores?

6. What was the average gain in test scores?

7. What was the mode on the first test? The second test?

8. On a normal distribution curve how many students should score between 1 standard deviation (σ) above and 1 σ below the mean?

9. If the mode, mean, and the median are at the same point, is this a normal distribution curve?

10. Which test had the wider range of scores?

11. What is the purpose of finding an average of a distribution of scores?

12. What was the mean score on the combined test scores?

13. Which measure of central tendency (mean, median, or mode) can be affected the most by extreme scores at each end of the range?

14. What is one situation when the mean would be the best score to report?

15. What is one situation when the median would be the best score to report?

Answers

1. 83; this is the middle score of the set of 15 numbers.

2. 82.

3. Ten students earned a higher score; this is $\frac{10}{15}$ of the class; $\frac{10}{15} = \frac{2}{3} = 67$ percent.

4. Since 10 students out of 15 got higher scores, 5 students got lower scores or remained at the same level. We compare these numbers: $\frac{10}{5} = \frac{2}{1}$. The ratio is 2 to 1; for every two students who got higher scores, one student got a lower score or remained at the same level.

5. To find the net gain, we add the deviation in scores between the first and second tests by inspection. That leaves a gain of $32 - 2 = 30$ (two students lost 1 point each). The gross gain was 32; the net gain, 30.

6. The mean or average gain is obtained by dividing the net gain (30 points) by the number of students (15); the average gain was 2 points.

7. The mode is the score achieved the most times by the students. On test 1, 83 was the mode; on test 2, 82.

8. On a normal distribution curve 34 percent of the students will achieve 1 sigma (s.d.) above the mean; the same percent will obtain scores 1 σ below the mean: 34 + 34 = 68 percent or 68 out of 100. By multiplying 15 by 68 percent we obtain 10

students out of the 15 who took the two tests; these will achieve scores between 1 σ above the mean and 1 σ below the mean.

9. Yes, on a *skewed* distribution the mean, median, and mode are at different points. To determine skewness we use this formula:

$$\text{skewness} = \frac{\text{mean} - \text{mode}}{\sigma}$$

10. Test 2.

11. For comparison. The mean average is most often used in weather reports for comparing average rainfall or snowfall in different months or seasons and in sport scores, educational testing, and advertising.

12. The mean for the two tests can be found by adding the total scores and dividing by the number of scores (1249 + 1279) ÷ 30 = 84.26. Also, we find that the mean on the first test was 83.26; the mean on the second, 85.26. Then (83.26 + 85.26) ÷ 2 = 84.26. One number checks the other; the two are the same, obtained by different methods.

13. The mean is most susceptible to change because all scores, including extremely high or low ones, are added together. For example, if donations to a school photography club were as follows: $5.00, $4.50, $10.00, $5.00, $5.25, $4.75, and $5.00, what was the average donation?
Answer: $5.64. If we remove the one $10.00 donation, what is the average? Answer: $4.92.
Although four people gave $5.00 or more, and only two people donated less than $5.00, the average, with the $10.00 removed, was less than $5.00.

14. The mean is best when comparisons will be made among or between grades or schools, or when deviation scores are needed for progress reports.

15. The median is more valid for reporting salaries, for example, because one half of the group will be receiving salaries below the median. This gives a better picture of the actual situation.

Probability

In economics, business, politics, education, insurance, the government, and the military the statistics of chance or *probability* is often used. In such cases it is assumed that experiments or events have more than one possible outcome. The probability of the occurrence of a particular happening, $P(h)$, is determined by dividing the number of ways that event can happen by the total number of possible outcomes.

Example. If you flip one coin once, what is the probability of its landing heads up? A coin has two sides, heads and tails, giving two possible outcomes. With only one toss of only one coin there is only one way that can lead to heads, that is, the one coin, tossed once, will land heads up. Therefore

$$P(h) = \frac{1 \text{ (way the event can happen)}}{2 \text{ (possible outcomes)}} = \frac{1}{2}$$

or 1 out of 2 chances heads will be up. The same probability applies to tails, with 1 out of 2 chances that tails will come up in the toss.

MATHEMATICS

Example. If we use the same basic formula, what is the probability of drawing a red ball from a bag containing 3 red balls and 5 black balls?

$$P(r) = \frac{3 \text{ (ways the event can happen—there are 3 red balls)}}{3 + 5 \text{ (possible outcomes—there are 3 red and 5 black balls)}} = \frac{3}{8}$$

Example. What is the probability of drawing a black ball from the same bag?

$$P(b) = \frac{5}{3 + 5} = \frac{5}{8}$$

GRAPHING

The Coordinate System

The coordinate system is based on using two real number lines that intersect at the origin (O), forming four right angles.

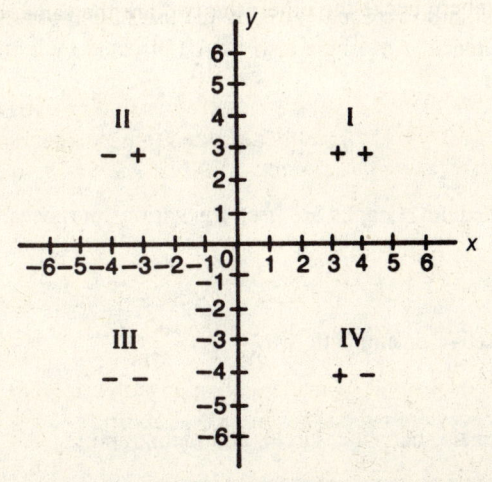

The horizontal number line is called the *x-axis* or *axis of abscissas*; the vertical line is the *y-axis* or *axis of ordinates*. The positive numbers are placed on the right of O and the negative numbers to the left on the *x*-axis line. The perpendicular vertical line has the positive numbers above the *x*-axis and the negative numbers below it. Thus the plane is divided into four sections or quadrants; the coordinates are measured from the origin O.

In quadrant I both the x abscissa and the y ordinate are positive. In quadrant II the abscissa is negative, the ordinate positive. Both the abscissa and the ordinate are negative in quadrant III. In quadrant IV the abscissa is positive and the ordinate is negative.

Plotting Points

To make a graph a point is plotted on the plane. Any point has two coordinates, x and y; x is always plotted and written first.

Graphing a Point

To graph $(3, -2)$, first locate the *x*-coordinate (3) on the *x*-axis. Count three spaces to the right, and then, because -2 is a negative number, count vertically to -2 in quadrant IV.

69

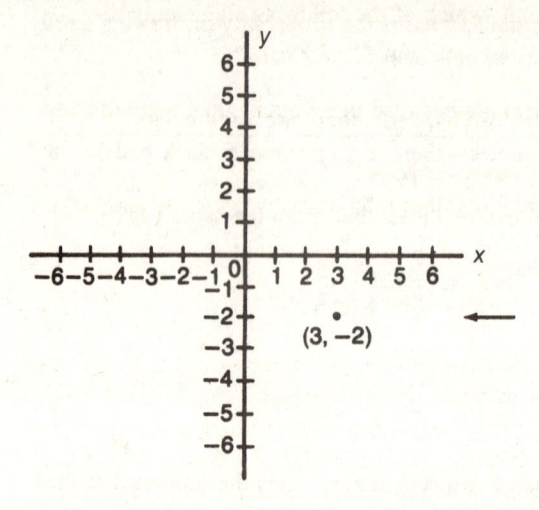

TEST OF GENERAL KNOWLEDGE: DESCRIPTION, REVIEW, PRACTICE

Bisecting a Line

Any line can be bisected or divided into two equal parts by the use of compasses. The length of the line makes no difference. Any angle also can be bisected by a line called a bisector.

GRAPHS AND FLOWCHARTS

A graph presents data in a visual medium. Graphs are used for various purposes, including:

- to show comparisons clearly
- to present information in an attractive or emphatic way
- to make data easy to interpret

There are several types of graphs, namely, bar, line, circle, and pictograph.

Pictograph

This pictograph shows the number of library books read by different types of students in 1 year.

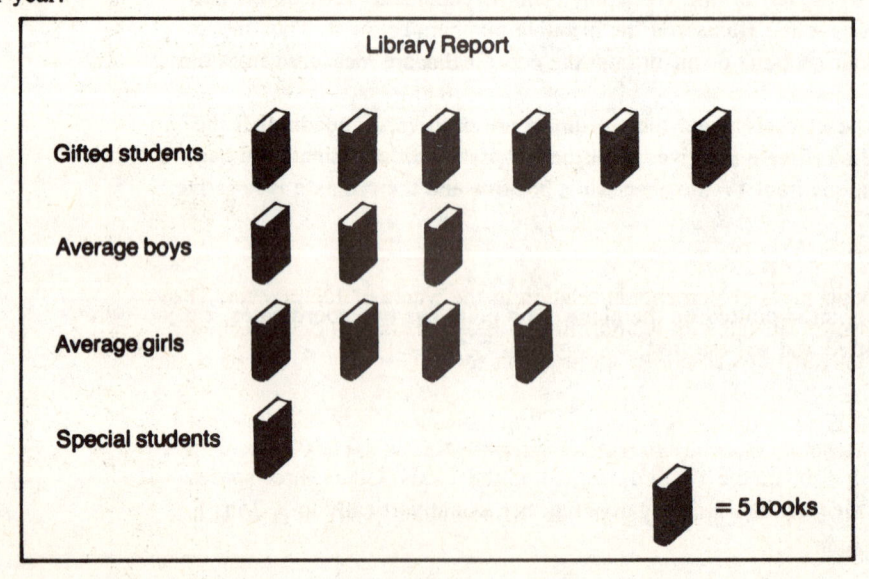

70

MATHEMATICS

From the information in the pictograph, which of the following statements is FALSE?

(A) An average boy and an average girl together read more books than a gifted and a special student together.
(B) Average girls read more books than average boys.
(C) An average boy and a special student together read as many books as an average girl.
(D) Special students read 5 books a year.
(E) Average boys read more books than special students.

The pictograph is very useful when data can be reduced to even-sized units for representation; in this pictograph each book symbol represents 5 books that students read in 1 year. Fractions of symbols are sometimes used to represent, in this case, fewer than five books. However, it is often difficult to interpret the value of a fractional symbol. This is a weakness of the pictograph. One should use separate units, instead of doubling the size of the units to represent 10 books, 20 books, and so on.

In the example (A) is the false statement; an average boy and an average girl together read the same number of books (35) as a gifted student and a special student together.

Circle Graph

This circle graph shows how a student allocated his time on a typical school day.

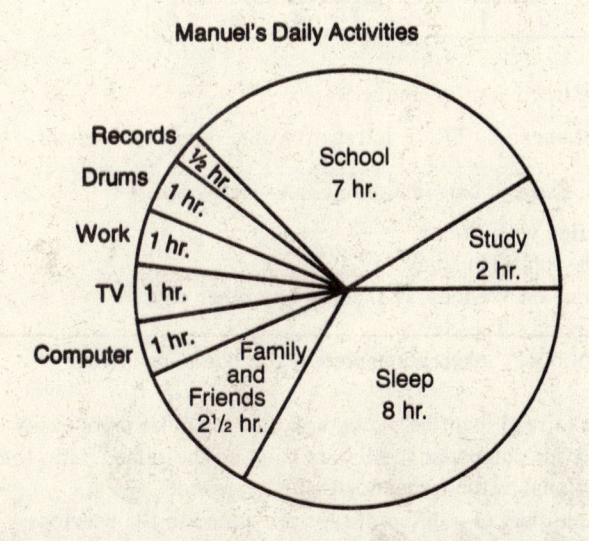

Manuel's Daily Activities

- Records ½ hr.
- Drums 1 hr.
- Work 1 hr.
- TV 1 hr.
- Computer 1 hr.
- Family and Friends 2½ hr.
- Sleep 8 hr.
- Study 2 hr.
- School 7 hr.

The circle graph shows parts or percents in relation to the whole of 100 percent. The relative size of each sector indicates its relationship to the whole and to other sectors.

Answer the following questions about the circle graph shown:

1. Is the computer Manuel's favorite afterschool activity? No; he spends 2½ hr. with friends and family.
   What percent of his total day does he spend on the computer? 1 hr. = $\frac{1}{24}$ of 24 hr.; $\frac{1}{24}$ = 0.04 or 4 percent.

TEST OF GENERAL KNOWLEDGE: DESCRIPTION, REVIEW, PRACTICE

2. What is the ratio of time spent on interpersonal activities to time spent on solitary hobbies? Manuel spends 2½ hr. with family and friends and 3½ hr. on presumably solitary hobbies: television, computer, drums, and records. The ratio is 2½:3½ or $\frac{5}{2}:\frac{7}{2}$ or 5:7.

3. What percent of Manuel's waking time does he spend studying? He spends 8 hr. on sleep, leaving 16 hr. of waking time. He spends 2 hr. studying; $\frac{2}{16} = \frac{1}{8} = 0.125$ or 12.5 percent.

Bar Graph

This bar graph shows the average number of schoolbooks taken home by a student each school day in 1 week.

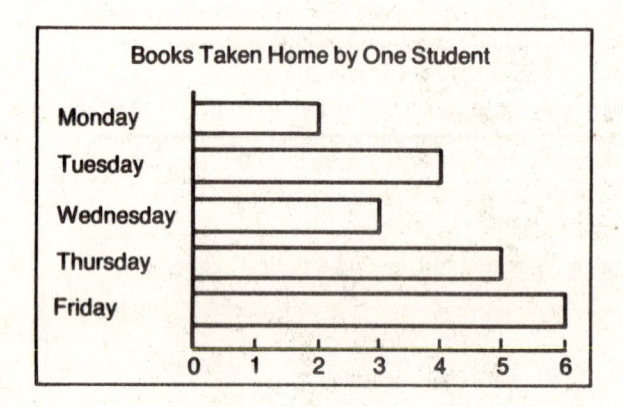

Books Taken Home by One Student

Day	Books
Monday	2
Tuesday	4
Wednesday	3
Thursday	5
Friday	6

Which one of the following statements is TRUE in regard to the number of school books taken home?

(A) Monday plus Wednesday is tied with Friday.
(B) Friday is tied with Wednesday plus Thursday.
(C) More books were carried home on Wednesday than on any other day.
(D) Thursday is tied with Monday plus Tuesday.
(E) This week, 30% of the school books taken home were taken home on Friday.

The bar graph is more difficult to read than the pictograph, but it can be more easily made to represent data accurately for comparison. All bars must be the same width; the length of each bar is then proportional to the frequency that it represents.

In a more complicated bar graph, bars of a different type are added to the previous bars to represent additional data. Comparisons can then be made at a glance. Care must be taken, however, to note what the additional bars represent.

In the example, it can be ascertained by visual inspection of the bar graph that Friday was the day when most school books were taken home by students. To determine whether (A), (B), (C), or (D) is true, inspection plus addition must be used; all are found to be false. That (E) is true can be verified by adding all books taken home on the five school days (20), and finding what percent Friday's books (6) is of the weekly total:

$$\frac{6}{20} = \frac{3}{10} = 30 \text{ percent, or } 10\overline{)3.00} = 30\%.$$

72

MATHEMATICS

Line Graph

This line graph shows temperature changes for 1 day between 8 A.M. and 4 P.M.

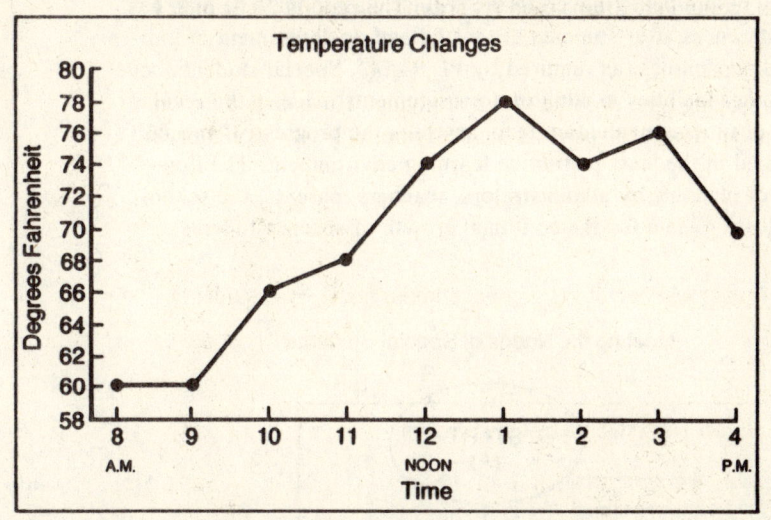

Temperature Changes

[Line graph showing Degrees Fahrenheit (y-axis, 58–80) vs. Time (x-axis, 8 A.M. to 4 P.M.). Values: 8 A.M.=60°, 9 A.M.=60°, 10 A.M.=66°, 11 A.M.=68°, 12 NOON=74°, 1 P.M.=78°, 2 P.M.=74°, 3 P.M.=76°, 4 P.M.=70°.]

The line graph is read by using the points on the line. Care must be taken to watch the degrees on the vertical axis and the hours on the horizontal axis.

Tell whether each of the following is TRUE OR FALSE:

1. The range of temperature during the day was 18°. **True**; the highest temperature for the day (78°) minus the lowest temperature (60°) = 18°.

2. The greatest temperature variation occurred between 9 A.M. and 10 A.M. **False**; the variation of 6° between 11 A.M. and 12 A.M. equaled the variation between 9 A.M. and 10 A.M.

3. The temperature at noon was lower than the temperature at 11 A.M. **False**; the temperature was rising at this time toward its maximum. At 11 A.M. it was 68°, and at noon it was 74°.

4. The hottest time of the day was between 10 A.M. and 12 A.M. **False**; the temperature rose another 4° to 78° at 1 P.M.

5. The coolest time of the day was in the afternoon. **False**; it was cooler in the morning, reaching a peak of only 74° and a low of 60°.

The Flowchart

The flowchart, widely used with computers, is a valuable tool for showing the procedures to be employed in problem-solving because it indicates time and sequence. It is useful in education for planning the curriculum and in administration for providing a visual picture of procedures to be used for long-range goals.

Certain symbols are used in flowcharting:

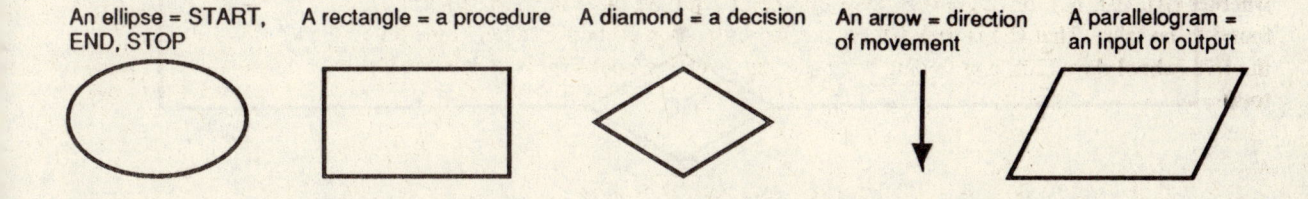

An ellipse = START, END, STOP

A rectangle = a procedure

A diamond = a decision

An arrow = direction of movement

A parallelogram = an input or output

TEST OF GENERAL KNOWLEDGE: DESCRIPTION, REVIEW, PRACTICE

This flowchart shows that all special students are eventually mainstreamed into the regular classroom (B), but that some of them may spend some time in the resource room or reading laboratory before being moved to the regular classroom. The plan has a provision for parent conferences after students are tested and an assessment of individual student's needs and capabilities, as required by PL 94-142. Special students have access to the library and other facilities in addition to assignments made in the regular classroom. After a period of time an evaluation team assesses the progress of special students, and they are placed in the least restrictive learning environment. The flowchart shows the direction of planning by administrators, teachers, parents, the school psychologist, and the evaluation team for the continual growth of special students.

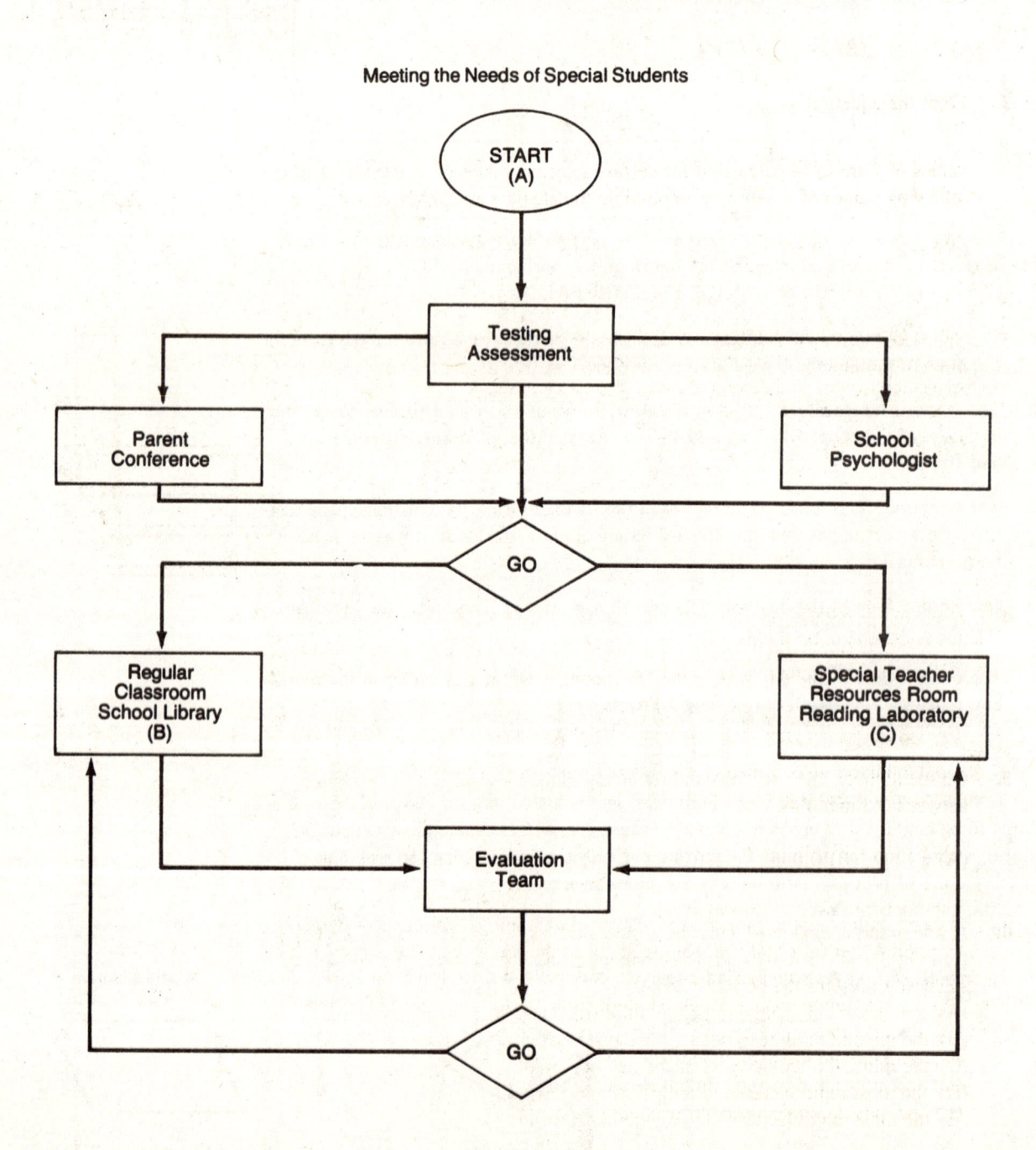

Meeting the Needs of Special Students

MATHEMATICS

Diagnostic Practice Test—Mathematics
Time—30 minutes

Directions: For each question or incomplete statement below there are five suggested answers or completions. Select the one that *best* answers the question or completes the statement. Allow 30 minutes for this test.

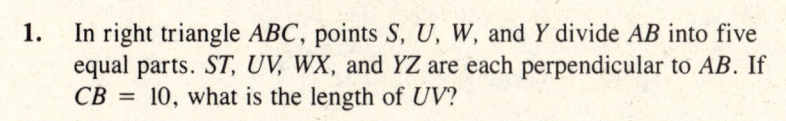

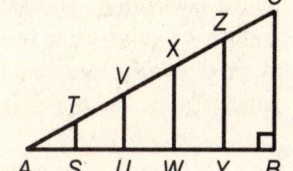

1. In right triangle ABC, points S, U, W, and Y divide AB into five equal parts. ST, UV, WX, and YZ are each perpendicular to AB. If $CB = 10$, what is the length of UV?

    (A) 2 (B) $2\frac{1}{2}$ (C) 4 (D) 5 (E) 6

2. From the equation
$$y = \frac{x^3 - 28x^2 + 5}{x - 5}$$
values of y are to be calculated for certain selected values of x. For which of the following values of x will it be impossible to calculate a value of y?

    (A) -2 (B) 0 (C) $\frac{2}{3}$ (D) 5 (E) 125

3. The figure at the right consists of four rectangles and two squares having the dimensions shown. If the figure is cut out of cardboard and folded to form a closed box, what is the volume of the box in cubic inches?

    (A) 10 (B) 12 (C) 24 (D) 36 (E) 72

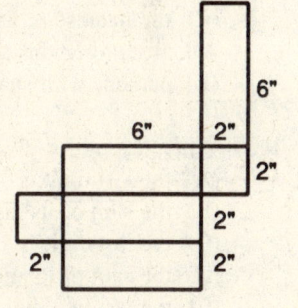

4. A student has marks of 70% and 60% on two mathematics tests. What mark must she obtain on the next test so that her average on all three mathematics tests can be raised to 75%?

    (A) 80% (B) $83\frac{1}{3}$% (C) 90% (D) 95% (E) 100%

5. On the number line, which of the following numbers would NOT be located between 0.3 and 0.4?

    (A) $\frac{3}{8}$ (B) 0.035 (C) $\frac{1}{3}$ (D) 31% (E) $\frac{\pi}{10}$

6. A line graph is drawn showing the temperature readings each hour of the day from 6:00 A.M. to 10:00 P.M. The segment of the line in which the slope is the steepest represents the period when
    (A) the maximum change in temperature from 1 hour to the next occurred.
    (B) the maximum temperature of the day occurred.
    (C) the minimum temperature of the day occurred.
    (D) the most rapid increase in temperature occurred.
    (E) the most rapid decrease in temperature occurred.

TEST OF GENERAL KNOWLEDGE: DESCRIPTION, REVIEW, PRACTICE

7. The numbers of pupils of each sex seated in each of the four rows of seats in a classroom is shown in the accompanying table. One student handed in an assignment paper without putting his or her name on it. The probability that the paper came from a girl in the second row is

	Girls	Boys
Row 1	3	4
Row 2	2	5
Row 3	6	1
Row 4	4	3
Total	15	13

   (A) $\frac{15}{28}$ (B) $\frac{2}{28}$ (C) $\frac{2}{5}$ (D) $\frac{2}{7}$ (E) $\frac{2}{15}$

8. If x, y, and z are natural numbers, then $x(y + z)$ equals
   (A) xyz
   (B) $xy + z$
   (C) $xy + xz$
   (D) $xy + 2x$
   (E) $x(yz)$

9. The concept of one-to-one correspondence can be used in determining the size of a set of objects. If we count the names of all persons in the history class, our answer will be correct if
   (A) all persons are present
   (B) each name is listed only once
   (C) the names are listed by sex
   (D) absent persons are not counted
   (E) persons with similar names are counted once

10. When testing for divisibility, an integer is divisible by 3 if and only if
    (A) the last digit is 3
    (B) the sum of its digits is a number divisible by 3
    (C) the last digit is 1
    (D) the sum of its digits is 9
    (E) the last two digits form a number divisible by 3

11. Which of the following is incorrectly represented as a decimal?
    (A) $\frac{7}{100} = 0.07$
    (B) $2\frac{1}{2}\% = 0.25$
    (C) $\frac{35}{100} = 0.35$
    (D) $150\% = 1.50$
    (E) $\frac{1}{3} = 0.333\ldots$

12. If $\frac{1}{x} < 0$, then x MUST be
    (A) a number greater than 1.
    (B) a negative number.
    (C) a number between 0 and 1.
    (D) a number less than 1.
    (E) a number less than -1.

13. A rectangle is composed of two right triangles. The base of the rectangle is 10 inches, and the width is 6 inches. What is the area of each right triangle?
    (A) 10 sq. in.   (D) 15 sq. in.
    (B) 30 sq. in.   (E) 35 sq. in.
    (C) 20 sq. in.

MATHEMATICS

14. In mathematical logic, if we assume that $A \to B$ is true, and we are then informed that A is true, we can conclude that
    (A) B is false
    (B) the statement is in error
    (C) this is impossible
    (D) B is true also
    (E) the answer is invalid

15. The answer to this problem: Subtract 6 gal. 3 qt. 2 pt. from 9 gal. 1 pt. is
    (A) 2 gal. 1 qt. 1 pt.   (D) 1 gal. 1 qt. 1 pt.
    (B) 1 gal. 2 qt. 1 pt.   (E) 3 gal.
    (C) 2 gal. 1 pt.

16. Fifteen is 20% of what number?
    (A) 100   (D) 65
    (B) 75   (E) $66\frac{1}{2}$
    (C) 70

17. A school budget this year provides for a cut of 20% in the number of pupils receiving subsidized lunches. What percent of increase in next year's budget is necessary to restore lunch subsidies back to their level before the cut?
    (A) 20   (B) $22\frac{1}{2}$ (C) 25   (D) 30   (E) 40

18. Which is the smallest of the following?
    (A) $\frac{1}{0.2}$ (B) $\frac{3}{8}$ (C) $(0.2)^2$ (D) $\frac{3}{100}$ (E) $\sqrt{1.21}$

19. A good estimate of the value of $\frac{24.98 \times 4.001}{9.89}$ is
    (A) 10   (B) 12   (C) 25   (D) 50   (E) 100

20. Mr. Lenardo's science classroom is 20 feet wide and 30 feet long. Mr. Mario's classroom is 15 feet wide and 35 feet long. Which classroom is larger by how many square feet?
    (A) Mr. Mario's, by 25 sq. ft.
    (B) Mr. Mario's, by 10 sq. ft.
    (C) Mr. Lenardo's, by 75 sq. ft.
    (D) Mr. Lenardo's by 25 sq. ft.
    (E) Both are the same size.

21. An airplane is traveling due south. The pilot observes another plane coming toward him at his 9 o'clock position. In which direction is the second airplane traveling?
    (A) East by southeast
    (B) Due north
    (C) West by southwest
    (D) Due west
    (E) Due east

22. An auditorium is a rectangle 60 feet long and 45 feet wide. How long and how wide is a scale drawing of this auditorium if a scale of 1 inch to 9 feet is used?
    (A) 1 × 9 inches   (D) 9 × 5 inches
    (B) 8 × 5¼ inches   (E) 7 × 5 inches
    (C) 6⅔ × 5 inches

TEST OF GENERAL KNOWLEDGE: DESCRIPTION, REVIEW, PRACTICE

23. *ABCD* is a square with a side of 8. The arcs shown in the diagram are portions of circles whose centers are at *A, B, C,* and *D,* respectively. What is the area of the shaded portion?

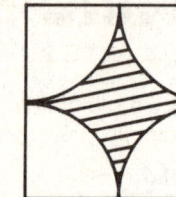

(A) $64 - 4\pi$
(B) $64 - 8\pi$
(C) $64 - 16\pi$
(D) 48π
(E) $64 - 64\pi$

24. It is estimated that two-thirds of all wheat produced in the United States is milled into flour. A farmer sold 30,000 pounds of wheat; each bushel weighs 60 pounds. According to the estimate and the facts given, which of the following statements is true?
(A) The farmer sold 5,000 bushels of wheat.
(B) His crop can be milled into 900 25-pound sacks of flour.
(C) 20,000 pounds of his wheat will be milled into flour.
(D) 500 bushels of his wheat will be used for other purposes.
(E) Only 167 bushels of his wheat will become flour.

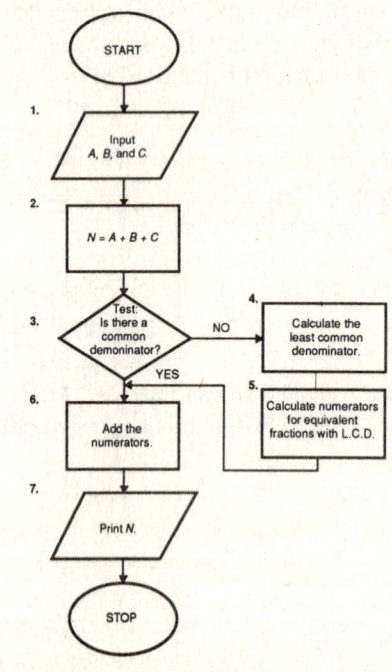

25. In the flowchart above, each of inputs *A, B,* and *C* is a positive rational number. Which of the following values, when input for *A, B,* and *C,* will permit the program to skip steps 4 and 5?
(A) $\frac{1}{2}, \frac{1}{2}, 3$ (B) 4, 8, 7 (C) $\frac{1}{2}, \frac{2}{3}, \frac{1}{4}$ (D) $\frac{1}{2}, 8, -2$ (E) $0, 0, \frac{2}{3}$

Answer Key

1.	C	6.	A	11.	B	16.	B	21.	D
2.	D	7.	B	12.	B	17.	C	22.	C
3.	C	8.	C	13.	B	18.	D	23.	C
4.	D	9.	B	14.	D	19.	A	24.	C
5.	B	10.	B	15.	C	20.	C	25.	B

Literature and Fine Arts

Most of the 35 questions in the Literature and Fine Arts section of the Test of General Knowledge are based on examples taken from the following kinds of materials:

- Passages from literature (short story, novel, essay, poem, play)
- Photographic reproductions of art works and film stills (painting, sculpture, photograph, architecture)
- Photographs of theater or dance productions

About two-thirds of the questions involve analysis and interpretation of literary works or works of art. The remaining third is divided into questions on the ability to recognize basic elements and components of works of literature and fine art and the ability to relate works of literature and fine art to one another and to their social/historical contexts.

Although it is possible that the test you take will have a few questions that require factual knowledge, it is more likely that none of the questions will be based on direct fact-recall. You will not be asked who wrote *War and Peace*, who painted the Mona Lisa, or who created La Pieta. Instead, the questions will be based on a literary passage or a photographic representation of a work of art or a theater or dance production, and the questions will involve understanding and analyzing the works of literature or art.

Note that although music questions were not included in this section in recent years, according to ETS, current tests have between four and six questions based on knowledge of music. Music questions may be on music terminology, or you might be given a line of text and then have to pick the staff that represents the text's rhythm, or you might be given a stanza of notes and be asked to match the lyrics in the answer choices to the stanza.

Preparing for the Literature and Fine Arts Section

Use the review on the following pages to help you recall literary and art-related terms and concepts. Take the Diagnostic Practice Test later in this section to familiarize yourself with the type of questions you will find in this section of the test and to give you an idea of how much study and practice you need. The Model Tests in Part IV of this book will provide further practice.

The review that follows reflects the Literature and Fine Arts test's emphasis on analysis and interpretation and the de-emphasis on factual knowledge. It contains definitions of terms used to describe the structural components and compositional elements of both literary and art works. It does not contain lists of authors, artists, composers and their works, since questions based on factual knowledge of this type are rarely asked.

Literature Glossary

Accent Vocal prominence or emphasis given to a syllable, word, or phrase. In poetry, accented syllables form metrical patterns by contrasting with unstressed syllables. Accented syllables are indicated by the symbol .

Act A major division in a drama; minor divisions within an act are called scenes.

Adage A short, quotable, wise saying that is well known from wide use over a long period of time; usually of anonymous authorship.

TEST OF GENERAL KNOWLEDGE: DESCRIPTION, REVIEW, PRACTICE

Allegory A literary work in which some or all of the characters represent abstract ideas; e.g., *Pilgrim's Progress*.

Alliteration Repetition of the same initial consonant sound in neighboring words, as in "No sound of waters shaken/Nor any sound or sight" (Swinburne).

Allusion An indirect or casual reference to a famous person or event in history, the Bible, a literary work, mythology, or another known source. The allusion may be obvious or esoteric.

Anachronism The representing in literature of a person, scene, object, etc., in a time period that would have been impossible historically (Macbeth wearing a Bulova watch).

Analogy A comparison between two different things in order to clarify or intensify the image or thought.

Apostrophe The addressing of a person or personified thing as if present, as in "O death, where is thy sting?" (*Bible*)

Assonance The close repetition of similar vowel sounds, as in "How now brown cow" or "Like a diamond in the sky."

Ballad A simple narrative, dealing with a single dramatic episode, told as a poem, song, or both.

Baroque A style in art, architecture, literature, and music characterized by flamboyance, elaborate ornamentation, and a symmetrical arrangement. The baroque is a blend of the wild and fantastic with an ordered, formal style, as in the poetry of John Donne and the music of Bach.

Blank verse A type of poetry in which rhyme is not used. Instead, each line has ten syllables with an iambic rhythm (an unstressed syllable followed by a stressed syllable in each poetic foot, as in "abóut thĕ tówn"). Shakespeare's *Othello* was written in blank verse, as in this excerpt:

> If I quench thee, thou flaming minister,
> I can again thy former light restore.

Bombast Inflated, extravagant, pompous, and grandiloquent speech, found in most Elizabethan poems and plays and in many political speeches.

Couplet A stanza consisting of two rhyming lines that often form an independent thought: "Great things are done when men and mountains meet;/These are not done by jostling in the street" (Blake).

Didactic The term used to describe a piece of literature that attempts to serve a cause that is moral, political, social, and so on. A quiet war has been raging since the time of Plato over whether literature should presume to teach, or exist only as aesthetics.

Elegy A lyric poem with death as its theme; a lament.

Elision Omission of an unstressed vowel or syllable to improve the meter, as in *o'er* for *over*, *'tis* for *it is*.

Epic A long, narrative poem recounting the deeds of a person important to the history of his or her race or nation. *The Iliad* and *The Odyssey* are epics.

LITERATURE AND FINE ARTS

Foot A unit of rhythm in poetry. Usually a foot has one stressed syllable and one or more unstressed syllables. The most commonly used feet are as follows:

    iamb (tă tuḿ)   trochee (tuḿ tă)
    anapest (tă tă tuḿ)   dactyl (tuḿ tă tă)

Lines of verse are named according to the number of feet they contain: one foot, monometer; two feet, dimeter; three feet, trimeter; four feet, tetrameter; five feet, pentameter; six feet, hexameter; seven feet, heptameter. The most popular are tetrameter and pentameter.

Free verse Unrhymed verse that does not follow a regular pattern of meter. Amy Lowell, Walt Whitman, and Carl Sandberg often wrote free verse.

Genre A type or classification of literary work. Literary genres are numerous; some examples are the epic, the lyric, tragedy, comedy, and the novel. Until recently writers were expected to adhere to the established rules of the genre in which they were working, but modern eclecticism has broken down this tradition.

Hyperbole Gross exaggeration for effect, as in "tears shall drown the wind" (Shakespeare).

Imagery Descriptive language used to create pictures in the mind of the reader or to evoke various emotions.

Irony A figure of speech used as a literary device in which the meaning stated is contrary to the one intended. In drama, irony is perceived by an audience when a character makes statements not fully understood by himself.

Lyric A short, emotional, imaginative poem characterized by regular rhyme and meter.

Metaphor A direct comparison, without the use of *like* or *as,* of two unlike objects, as in "The moon was a ghostly galleon tossed upon cloudy seas" (Noyes).

Meter The pattern of stressed and unstressed syllables in a line of verse; rhythm.

Mixed metaphor A figure of speech that combines two or more inconsistent or incongruous metaphors, as in Shakespeare's "to take arms against a sea of troubles."

Motif The recurrence of a theme, word pattern, or character in a literary work. This term may also be applied to a major theme which runs through a number of different works. For instance, the isolation of modern man is a frequent motif in contemporary literature.

Ode A lyric poem that deals seriously with a lofty or dignified theme; for example, Keats' "Ode on a Grecian Urn."

Onomatopoeia A combination of sense and sound; the use of words whose sounds convey their meaning, as in *buzz, crackle, howl, murmur, roar.*

Parable A short, simple story conveying a moral lesson. The Bible has the best-known parables; for example, the prodigal son, the Good Samaritan.

Parody A humorous literary work that ridicules a serious work by imitating and exaggerating its style. In media, a parody is a "take-off" on a particular person, event, etc.

Personification The attribution of human qualities to lifeless objects. In the following lines from Donne's *Holy Sonnet 10*, death is personified:

    Death be not proud, though some have called thee
    Mighty and dreadful, for thou art not so;

TEST OF GENERAL KNOWLEDGE: DESCRIPTION, REVIEW, PRACTICE

> For those whom thou think'st thou dost overthrow
> Die not, poor Death, nor yet canst thou kill me.

Point of view A phrase used to denote the vantage point from which an author presents the action in a work of fiction. In the *first person* point of view, the author uses the pronoun *I*, and is part of the story. In the *third* person point of view, the author anonymously chronicles the actions and dialogue of his characters. In the *omniscient* point of view, the author enters the minds of his characters, while taking a third person point of view.

Prose The ordinary language of men in speaking or writing (distinguished from poetry by its greater irregularity and variety of rhythm).

Rhyme Repetition of similar sounds at regular intervals, particularly at the ends of lines. Rhyme depends on pronunciation, not on spelling. Sometimes pronunciations change over the years, so that words that rhymed when a poem was written no longer do.

Rhythm See **meter**.

Simile A comparison using *like* or *as*. "My love is like a red, red rose" is an example of a simile.

Sonnet A verse form consisting of 14 iambic pentameter lines. There are two basic types: (1) the English, or Shakespearean, sonnet consists of three quatrains (4-line stanzas) and a concluding couplet; (2) the Italian, or Petrarchan, sonnet is divided into an octave (8 lines) and a sestet (6 lines).

Stanza A combination of two or more lines that form a unit in a poem, analogous to a paragraph in prose.

Symbol Something that is a meaningful entity in itself and yet stands for, or means, something else. In literature there are so-called universal symbols and others that suggest special meanings because of the way they are used in a novel or other literary work.

Tragedy A serious drama, in prose or poetry, about a person, often of a high station in life, who experiences sudden personal reversals. Tragedies always end with a catastrophic event.

Stage direction Information not part of the dialogue of a play given to the actor, director, or reader. This information may be a description of an action or a setting. Further, the author may describe a character or analyze his personality.

Verse A general name given to all metrical (or poetic) compositions. Used specifically, the word means a line of poetry or the stanza of a song; used generally, it suggests a lower order of poetry, for example, the limerick.

Art Glossary

Abstract Having little or no reference to the appearance of natural objects; pertaining to the nonrepresentational art styles of the 20th century.

Collage A picture built up wholly or partly from pieces of paper, cloth, or any other material stuck onto canvas or some other surface.

Composition The art of combining the elements of a picture or other work of art into a satisfactory visual whole. In art, the whole is very much more than the sum of its

LITERATURE AND FINE ARTS

parts. A picture is well composed if its constituents—whether figures, objects, or shapes—form a harmony that pleases the eye. This is the sole aim of most abstract painting; however, in more traditional art, the task is made much more difficult by the need to piece forms in an ordered sequence without losing their effectiveness as a pattern.

Drawing A work made with the delineated line. This concept is basic to architecture, calligraphy, painting, and sculpture. Works done in chalk, charcoal, crayon, pen, or pencil are drawings. This type of expression emphasizes the belief that form is more important than color.

Engraving A process in which lines are cut with a graver or burin in metal, wood, or other materials. Then the lines are filled with ink; under high pressure the ink is transferred to the surface of the printing press. The earliest engravings printed on paper date to the 15th century.

Etching A method of print making in which lines are cut with acid into metal plates usually made of copper or zinc.

Facade The front of a building, especially an imposing or decorative one.

Fresco A wall painting done on plaster that is still damp, using colors ground up in water or a limewater mixture. Practiced in Italy from the 14th century and perfected in the 16th century, it is one of the most permanent forms of wall decoration known.

Frieze The middle section of a building or structure where relief sculpture was frequently executed. The term also refers to decorative, broad bands between the wall paneling and the ceiling on interior walls.

Gable The triangular end of a wall or building, formed by a sloping roof.

Gothic A term used to describe the medieval architectural style of northern Europe from the early 12th century until the 16th. It is also used to describe the other arts of the same period. The cathedral was Gothic art's greatest contribution, with its elaborate architecture and grand stained-glass panels.

Lithography A form of printing from a prepared stone or metal plate, dating from the late 18th century; plastic plates are now sometimes used in lithography. A drawing is made on the plate with a greasy crayon and then washed with water. When ink is applied, it sticks to the greasy drawing but runs off the rest of the surface.

Mosaic One of the oldest and most durable forms of mural decoration in which the design is formed by embedding small pieces of colored stone or glass in cement.

Perspective A quasimathematical system for the representation of three-dimensional objects in a two-dimensional surface. The basic assumption of all perspective systems is that parallel lines never meet, but that they appear to do so; and that, further, all parallel lines going in any one direction meet at a single point on the horizon known as a vanishing point.

Relief Sculpture that is not free-standing, and, in having a background, approximates painting. The design in this type of sculpture comes from its background, which is either deep (high relief) or shallow (low relief).

Silhouette An outline or profile drawing cut out and pasted to a lighter background. This process was popular in Europe during the 18th century.

Sketch A rough draft of a composition or part of a composition, made in order to satisfy the artist on certain points of scale, composition, lighting, etc. It is the trial run—or one of many—for the full-scale work.

TEST OF GENERAL KNOWLEDGE: DESCRIPTION, REVIEW, PRACTICE

Values The gradations of tone from light to dark in a color. In a painting, value refers to the relation of light and shade.

Woodcut A print made from a design or drawing cut in relief on wood.

Major Art Movements

Abstract Expressionism (1940s–1950s) American art movement stressing spontaneous, nonrepresentational creation. First truly American school of art.

Art Deco (1920s–1930s) Highly decorative art, utilizing streamlined geometric forms inspired by industrial design. Interior designs in glass, plastic, and chrome. Architecturally, New York City's Chrysler Building is an example of this style.

Art Nouveau (1895–1905) Characterized by motifs of highly stylized flowing plants, curving lines, and fluent forms. Found in dress design, illustration, architecture, and interior design.

Ash Can School (c.1908) American Realist painters who abandoned idealized subject matter for representations of the more sordid aspects of urban life.

Barbizon School (1830s–1860s) Landscape artists who rejected the classical and romantic to portray nature directly as they perceived it. Rousseau was the principal artist. The movement was a forerunner of Impressionism.

Baroque (1580–1720) Developed in Italy, a movement of grand theatrical effects and elaborate ornamentation. Palace of Versailles is an excellent example. Baroque's greatest achievement was the fusion of architecture, sculpture, and painting.

Beaux Arts (1890–1920) Primarily an architectural style using formal and classical techniques, derived from the inspiration of the great European academies.

Black (Afro-American) Art The various styles of black American artists, inspired by protest, the search for individual identity, and the desire to trace historical roots.

Classicism Art that emphasizes qualities characteristically Greek or Roman in both spirit and style. Noted for harmony, objectivity, and discipline.

Cubism (1907–1915) A modern art reaction to Impressionism, led by Picasso and Braque, that portrayed geometric forms in nature as a departure from representational art.

Dada (1915–1923) International anti-art movement reflecting the cynicism of the post-World War I era by producing such bizarre works as the *Mona Lisa* with a mustache. Dada represented the absurd and the nonsensical.

Expressionism Twentieth-century art in which the expression of the artist took precedence over rational and faithful rendering of subject matter. Stress on emotion and inner visions.

Fauvism The work of early 20th-century post-Impressionists, characterized by strident color, distortions, and bold brushwork. Matisse and Rouault were leaders of the movement.

LITERATURE AND FINE ARTS

Impressionism Late 19th-century French school that stressed the depiction of light and color in nature at a given moment. Emphasis on visual impressions. Some chief Impressionists: Monet, Renoir, Degas, Pissarro.

Mannerism (1520–1590) School of art and architecture characterized by the exotic and confusing, also the distortion of the elongated human figure. El Greco was a major Mannerist.

Neoclassicism (1790–1830) A rejection of rococo and a return to classical style and motifs. An art form characterized by clarity, restraint and balance.

Op Art (1960s) Nonobjective art based on optical illusions created by geometric forms whose colors the eye must blend at a distance.

Pop Art (1960s) Primarily an American movement derived from both popular culture and commercial art. Representational works culled from everyday life—soup cans, comics, etc. The art of Warhol, Lichtenstein, and Oldenberg, for example.

Rococo (1730–1780) European art of glorified asymmetrical ornamentation on paneling, porcelain, and jewelry to display a love of elegance and gaiety.

Surrealism (1924 ff.) An art form which sought to reveal the psychological reality behind appearances. Subject matter stressed dreams, fantasy, and the subconscious. The art of Magritte, Dali, and Miró.

Music Glossary

Allegro A musical pace described as lively and quick.

Andante A musical pace of medium tempo.

Arpeggio A chord which is performed "spread out," that is, the notes are not sounded simultaneously but in succession.

Ballad A song that tells a story.

Canon A musical composition in which the melody is repeated at different pitch levels and at different times, for example, "Row, Row, Row Your Boat" when sung as a round.

Chord A blending of two or more notes.

Concerto A composition for one or more instruments and orchestra, usually in symphonic form.

Crescendo Music that becomes louder gradually.

Fortissimo Music that is played very loudly.

Key signature The written notation indicating the number of sharps or flats in the prevailing key. The key signature is usually placed at the beginning of each line of

TEST OF GENERAL KNOWLEDGE: DESCRIPTION, REVIEW, PRACTICE

music, and is noted by placing flat or sharp signs on the appropriate lines or spaces in the staff.

Lento Music played slowly.

Libretto The text of an opera.

Melody A succession of notes varying in pitch and having a recognizable musical shape.

Octave The interval that is considered as having eight steps, counting both the bottom and top notes. According to our notation, notes an octave apart from each other have the same letter names.

Orchestra A numerous mixed body of instrumentalists.

Overture A one-movement composition in sonata form for orchestra. The organization lost its sonata form in the late Romantic period and now can use any form to become a type of program.

Overture A piece of orchestral music preceding an opera, an oratorio, or a play and usually musically allusive to what follows.

Phrase A small group of notes forming what is recognized as a unit of melody.

Pitch The highness or lowness of a tone.

Presto A musical direction that means to play fast or quickly.

Rhythm That aspect of music concerned not with pitch but with the distribution of notes in time and their accentuation.

Scale A progression of single notes upward or downward in "steps."

Sonata A musical work in three or four movements, usually performed by a violin or a cello, with piano accompaniment.

Symphony A grand orchestral work in four movements.

Time signature The fractional sign found at the beginning of a composition or movement that tells the kind of beats in the bar and the number of such beats. The denominator indicates the kind of note and the numerator indicates the number of these to the measure.

Musical Instruments

Percussion	Brass	Woodwind	Strings
Snare drum	French horn	Oboe	Cello
Tympani	Trombone	Flute	Violin
Bass drum	Trumpet	Piccolo	Double bass
Cymbals	Tuba	Clarinet	Viola
		Bassoon	
		Saxophone	

LITERATURE AND FINE ARTS

Diagnostic Practice Test—Literature and Fine Arts

Time — 30 minutes

Directions: For each question or incomplete statement below, there are five suggested answers or completions. Select the one that *best* answers the question or completes the statement.

Questions 1–2 refer to the following.

1. The dancers' rigid posture and stiff bearing serve to express
    (A) stability and solidity
    (B) release from stress and conflict
    (C) emotional tension
    (D) rebirth and freedom
    (E) guilt and suffering

TEST OF GENERAL KNOWLEDGE: DESCRIPTION, REVIEW, PRACTICE

2. The costumes and set design indicate this ballet is concerned with
   - (A) twentieth century psychological realism
   - (B) nineteenth century romanticism
   - (C) eighteenth century emphasis on technical proficiency
   - (D) seventeenth century series of dances linked by a common theme
   - (E) ancient folklore

Questions 3–4 refer to the following.

> I am glad of it; for now I shall have reason
> To show the love and duty that I bear you
> With franker spirit; therefore, as I am bound,
> Receive it from me. I speak not yet of proof.
> Look to your wife: observe her well with Cassio;
> Wear your eye thus, not jealous nor secure:
> I would not have your free and noble nature
> Out of self-bounty be abused; look to 't:
> I know our country disposition well;
> In Venice they do let heaven see the pranks
> They dare not show their husbands; their best conscience
> Is not to leave 't undone, but keep 't unknown.

3. In this passage from Shakespeare's *Othello,* Iago is trying to convince Othello
   - (A) that he has no reason to be jealous of Cassio
   - (B) that his wife is going to Venice with Cassio
   - (C) that he should keep watch on his wife
   - (D) that he [Iago] loves him as a true friend
   - (E) that he [Iago] has proof that Othello's wife and Cassio are lovers

4. There is an example of elision in
   - (A) line 2
   - (B) line 4
   - (C) line 6
   - (D) line 8
   - (E) line 10

5. The most unusual feature of this alabaster head of a Sumerian ruler is the
   - (A) overall composition
   - (B) bold facial features
   - (C) large eyes
   - (D) use of light and shadow
   - (E) crown of ringlets

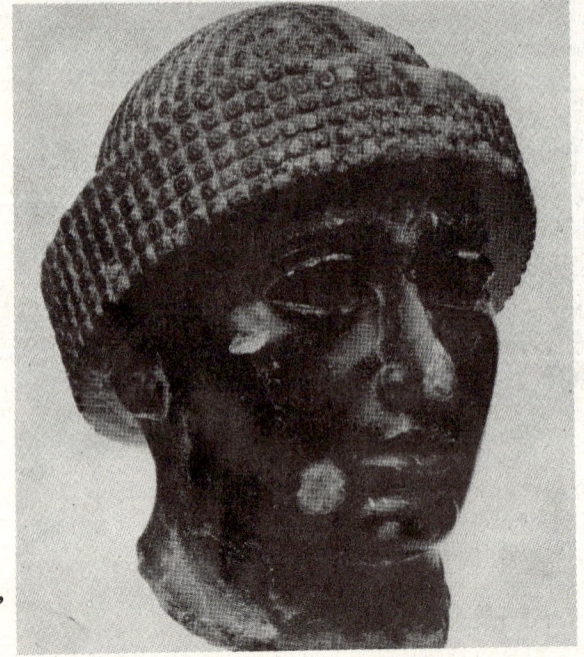

The Metropolitan Museum of Art, Rogers Fund, 1947

LITERATURE AND FINE ARTS

6. ...he took the boy, that cried aloud
   And struggled hard. The wreath of flowers fell
   At Dora's feet. She bow'd upon her hands,
   And the boy's cry came to her from the field.
   More and more distant. She bow'd down her head,
   Remembering the day when first she came,
   And all the things that had been. She bow'd down
   And wept in secret; and the reapers reap'd
   And the sun fell, and all the land was dark.

   Which of the following expresses the main theme of these lines from Tennyson's poem *Dora*?
   (A) By looking backward one can help future situations.
   (B) Life has many bitter moments.
   (C) In spite of tragedy and loss, life goes on.
   (D) Mothers and children are saddened by separation.
   (E) The future will be happier than the past has been.

7. The text for an opera is called a
   (A) madrigal
   (B) masque
   (C) libretto
   (D) prima donna
   (E) barre

Courtesy of
Prado, Madrid

8. The realism of the painting above is enhanced by all of the following EXCEPT
   (A) the bold line of executioners at the right
   (B) the elaborate, extravagant style
   (C) the dark sky
   (D) the facial expressions of the figures
   (E) the upflung arms of one victim

89

9. Some say the world will end in fire,
Some say in ice.
From what I've tasted of desire
I hold with those who favor fire.
But if I had to perish twice,
I think I know enough of hate
To say that for destruction ice
Is also great
And would suffice.

Which of the following best characterizes the speaker's description of "fire"?
(A) passion and desire
(B) murderous hatred
(C) emotional uninvolvement
(D) intellectual intensity
(E) heated revenge

Questions 10–11 refer to the following.

Georges Seurat, SUNDAY AFTERNOON ON THE ISLAND OF A LA GRANDE JATTE, 1884–86, oil on canvas, 207.6 x 308.0 cm, Helen Birch Bartlett Memorial Collection, 1926.224.
© 1988 The Art Institute of Chicago. All rights reserved.

10. The word that best characterizes the mood of this painting is
    (A) realistic   (D) abstract
    (B) emotional   (E) cheerful
    (C) depersonalized

11. The arrangement of the figures and use of light and dark shows the painter's primary concern is
    (A) composition and design
    (B) depicting the character's joyous mood
    (C) portraying life among the upper classes
    (D) describing the typical vacation theme
    (E) creating an "accidental" quality

LITERATURE AND FINE ARTS

12. 'Tis all a Chequer-board of Nights and Days
    Where Destiny with Men for pieces plays:
    Hither and thither moves, and mates, and slays,
    And one and by one back in the Closet lays.

    What do the lines above describe?
    (A) A game
    (B) Life
    (C) A military maneuver
    (D) A housewife straightening a room
    (E) A painting

The Metropolitan Museum of Art,
Gift of Edward S. Harkness,
1926 [26.7, 1412]

13. This statue shows the characteristics of sculptures in the eighth century B.C. This 7-inch gold figure

    (A) shows movement vividly
    (B) looks rigid because it was carved parallel to the four sides of the original block of stone
    (C) is too small
    (D) lacks detail
    (E) is generally crude and primitive

14. Very few of Charles Dickens's novels are based on historical events. One exception to this statement is *A Tale of Two Cities*, the core of which is
    (A) the War of the Roses
    (B) the Irish Rebellion
    (C) the French Revolution
    (D) the Crusades
    (E) the Boer War

91

TEST OF GENERAL KNOWLEDGE: DESCRIPTION, REVIEW, PRACTICE

Ryksmuseum, Amsterdam

15. The focal point of this print is the
    (A) three trees
    (B) light sky
    (C) dark clouds at the top and left
    (D) slight hill at the extreme right
    (E) lighter terrain at the left

Harbinger Dance Company
Detroit, Michigan
Photo by Gary Tafoya

16. The dancers in the scene above are NOT
    (A) expressing anxiety and unhappiness
    (B) expressing youthful lightheartedness
    (C) dancing in a public transportation facility
    (D) dancing in a modern work
    (E) showing harmony of movement

92

LITERATURE AND FINE ARTS

Questions 17–18 refer to the following lines from *The Odyssey*.

(1) Even as he spake,
(2) the great wave smote down upon him,
(3) driving on in terrible wise,
(4) so that the raft reeled again.
(5) And far therefrom he fell,
(6) and lost the helm from his hand.

17. In the course of time, verb forms, like other elements of language, change. In which line above is there a verb form that would not be used in contemporary speech or writing?
    (A) line 1
    (B) line 2
    (C) line 3
    (D) line 4
    (E) line 5

18. In line 3 what does *wise* mean?
    (A) precision
    (B) playfulness
    (C) manner
    (D) madness
    (E) power

19. Which of the following is NOT true of this example of fifteenth-century architecture?
    (A) It has long, low lines.
    (B) Its elements are balanced and harmonious.
    (C) The arches are gently rounded.
    (D) The columns are slender.
    (E) It has a monumental, theatrical quality.

20. Which one of these lines does NOT contain a poetic beat?
    (A) Pine cones and acorns lay on the ground.
    (B) All are needed by each one.
    (C) Teach me your mood, O patient stars!
    (D) Whoever fights, whoever falls, leaves this life too soon.
    (E) Paul thought about it and then laughed.

TEST OF GENERAL KNOWLEDGE: DESCRIPTION, REVIEW, PRACTICE

I.B.M. Institutional Collections

21. This funerary urn is typical of the art of
    (A) pre-Columbian Mexico
    (B) ancient Egypt
    (C) classical Greece
    (D) medieval Italy
    (E) contemporary Nigeria

UNKNOWN.
Emma Van Name. (c. 1795)

Oil on canvas, 29 × 33 inches.
Collection of Whitney Museum of American Art.
Gift of Edgar William and Bernice Chrysler
Garbisch Acq. # 69.142.

22. The portrait above is an example of "Naive" art. All of the following are true of the Naive painters of nineteenth-century America EXCEPT
    (A) they had little or no formal training

LITERATURE AND FINE ARTS

   (B) their knowledge of human anatomy was often faulty
   (C) objects in their paintings are often out of proportion to each other
   (D) their paintings are unappealing because they lack detail
   (E) their pictures appear flat, with little third-dimensional effect

23. "The said Eliza, John, and Georgiana were now clustered around their mama in the drawing-room: she lay reclined on a sofa by the fireside, and with her darlings about her (for the time neither quarrelling nor crying) looked perfectly happy." These lines, which occur on the opening page of a famous novel, suggest that the scene of the novel is
    (A) ancient Greece
    (B) medieval France
    (C) colonial America
    (D) nineteenth-century England
    (E) twentieth-century New York

24. They were always complaining in their magazine that the natives who visited them in physical suffering could not be given the help they desired. To become one day the doctor whom these poor creatures needed, it was worthwhile, so I judged, to become a medical student. Whenever I was inclined to feel that the years I should have to sacrifice were too long, I reminded myself that Hamilcar and Hannibal had prepared for their march on Rome by their slow and tedious conquest of Spain...
    — Albert Schweitzer, "I Resolve to Become a Jungle Doctor"

    Which of the following best describes the meaning of the passage above?
    (A) This goal is worth the required sacrifices.
    (B) Some things are worth fighting for.
    (C) Time means less when one is young.
    (D) Maturity is of value to a physician.
    (E) Attending medical school requires too much time.

25. The violin is usually used in a quartet to
    (A) double the melody an octave lower than the viola
    (B) duplicate the melody of the cello
    (C) play the main melody
    (D) emphasize the beat
    (E) provide a foundation for the harmony

26. The basic element of cubism, as exemplified by, for example, many works of Picasso, is
    (A) analysis of the subject into its component parts and portrayal of these parts in abstract geometrical form
    (B) portrayal of the subject exactly as the human eye perceives it
    (C) infusion of every subject with beauty
    (D) heightening of artistic effect by the use of garish colors
    (E) inclusion of unusual and disturbing effects in regard to composition and perspective

Questions 27–29 refer to the following passage.

Human nature is so well disposed towards those who are in interesting situations, that a young person, who either marries or dies, is sure of being kindly spoken of.

A week had not passed since Miss Hawkins's name was first mentioned in Highbury, before she was, by some means or other, discovered to have every recommendation of person and mind; to be handsome, elegant, highly accomplished, and perfectly amiable: and when Mr. Elton himself arrived to triumph in his happy prospects, and circulate the fame of her merits, there was very little more for him to do, than to tell her Christian name, and say whose music she principally played.

27. The tone of the passage is best described as
    (A) gently humorous
    (B) strident
    (C) sardonic
    (D) matter of fact
    (E) gloomy

28. The passage tells us all of the following about Mr. Elton's fiance EXCEPT
    (A) she was good looking
    (B) she had an agreeable disposition
    (C) she had an unusual first name
    (D) she was an accomplished musician
    (E) she was elegant in appearance and manners

29. The content and style of the passage indicate that it was written by
    (A) Gloria Steinem
    (B) Edna Ferber
    (C) Willa Cather
    (D) Toni Morrison
    (E) Jane Austen

Collection of Hans Neumann, Caracas, Venezuela

30. A startling feature of Chagall's *The Drunkard*, shown above, is the disembodied head at the top of the painting, which
    (A) is a device to secure good composition
    (B) is an attention-getting feature without meaning
    (C) is meant to distract the viewer's attention from the hands and fingers
    (D) detracts from the painting because the top of the head is cut off
    (E) reflects the drinker's desire to be closer to the bottle than the position of his body permits

LITERATURE AND FINE ARTS

31. The church of San Esteban Rey at Acoma Indian Pueblo, New Mexico, shown above, was built by Indians of the area for Spanish settlers around 1642. All of the following features of the building are characteristic of southwest Indian architecture EXCEPT
    (A) the long, low lines
    (B) the lack of ornamentation
    (C) the use of adobe as a building material
    (D) the towers on either side of the main building
    (E) the harmonious blending of the building with the desert

The Metropolitan Museum of Art

32. The most noteworthy feature of the Japanese print shown above is
    (A) the heavy, bold lines of the landscape
    (B) the richness of detail

97

TEST OF GENERAL KNOWLEDGE: DESCRIPTION, REVIEW, PRACTICE

(C) the puzzling small object in the left foreground
(D) the inclusion of an eagle in a Japanese landscape
(E) the use of the eagle as a medium for viewing the scene

Questions 33–35 refer to the following.

They didn't hear the two people coming down the gully path, Dad and the pretty girl with the hard, bright face like a china doll's. But they heard her laugh, and the tune stopped on a wrong, high, startled note. Dad didn't say anything, but the girl came forward and spoke to Granddad prettily: "I'll not be seeing you leave in the morning, so I came over to say good-by."

"It's kind of you," said Granddad, with his eyes cast down; and then, seeing the blanket at his feet, he stopped to pick it up. "And will you look at this," he said in embarrassment, "the fine blanket my son has given me to go away with!"

"Yes," she said, "It's a fine blanket." She turned to Dad, and said to him coldly, "It cost something, that."

33. The music mentioned in the first paragraph suggests
(A) the girl has shattered the family's unity
(B) Granddad has disturbed the family's harmony
(C) the girl has a discordant laugh
(D) it is time for Granddad to leave
(E) Granddad has done something he regrets

34. The phrase "face like a china doll's" is used to
(A) suggest the girl's natural beauty
(B) reveal the girl's character
(C) contrast the girl's appearance to Granddad's
(D) convey the girl's regret at how she treated Granddad
(E) underscore the age difference between Granddad and the girl

35. The last sentence of the passage indicates that the girl
(A) begrudges the expense of Granddad's blanket
(B) suffers from great poverty
(C) had previously been very fond of Granddad
(D) knew about the blanket all along
(E) had planned to surprise Granddad with another gift

Answer Key

1.	C	8.	B	15.	A	22.	D	29.	E
2.	A	9.	A	16.	A	23.	D	30.	E
3.	C	10.	C	17.	A	24.	A	31.	A
4.	D	11.	A	18.	C	25.	C	32.	E
5.	E	12.	B	19.	E	26.	A	33.	A
6.	C	13.	B	20.	E	27.	A	34.	B
7.	C	14.	C	21.	A	28.	C	35.	A

Science

The Science examination contains 30 questions based on topics of current concern in the physical, biological, and earth sciences fields. These topics are considered essential for demonstrating literacy and for teaching elementary or intermediate school science. Test questions are drawn from these current topics:

I. Sources of energy
  The role of the sun
  Stored or potential energy
  Kinetic energy or energy in motion
  Energy used in work: human, solar, water, wind, electrical, chemical
  Changes in the forms of energy
  The food chain
  The transfer, conservation, and conversion of energy
  Kinds of energy—renewable, and nonrenewable

II. The Earth and the universe
  Characteristics of the Planet Earth
  Changes in the structure and composition of the Earth Forces internal (earthquakes, volcanoes) and external (erosion, mining, chemical pollution of land and waters, solid waste disposal) that affect the earth
  Changes occurring in the Earth's atmosphere caused by chemicals, and debris from space exploration
  Storage of heat
  Mineral resources
  Oceans and rivers

III. Living organisms
  Interdependence of plants and animals
  Sunlight and life
  The structure of cells—the nucleus
  Cells as building blocks
  Eight functions of living organisms
  Adaptation to the environment
  Endangered species
  Characteristics of nonliving things
  Changing forms of nonliving things

IV. Matter—definition
  Source of matter
  States of matter
  Gases, liquids, solids
  Composition of matter
  Atoms, molecular composition
  Combination of atoms into diverse substances
  Properties of organic and inorganic substances
  Use of substances
  Mixtures and compounds
  Elements of all matter

TEST OF GENERAL KNOWLEDGE: DESCRIPTION, REVIEW, PRACTICE

Chemical changes
Natural or man-made forces acting upon matter (gravity, nuclear, electromagnetic, mechanical)

V. The environment
Ecological systems and the environment
The use of renewable and nonrenewable resources
How organisms (including humans) affect environmental changes

VI. Science, technology, and human behavior
How pure science, scientific principles and laws, inventions, and research affect human values, safety, prevention of illness and disease, nutrition, medical technology, life extension, management of aging, and the general quality of life

VII. Applying knowledge of scientific methods in the classroom
Reasoning
Experimenting
Analyzing information
Interpreting facts
Inferring from data
Predicting from observation or primary information

Review

†CELLS

The first discoveries of cells were made by such early microscopists as Anthony van Leeuwenhoek (1632–1723), who made his own simple lens microscopes, and saw bacteria and protozoa; and Robert Hooke (1635–1703), who had several lenses in his *compound* microscope, and who first named cells, after studying the tiny boxlike structures in cork. Since then, it has been shown by other biologists such as Dutrochet, Schleiden, and Schwann, that all living things are made of cells, whether they be whale, mouse, oak tree, or human being.

Size of Cells

Cells are so tiny that they are measured in terms of microns (μ). There are 1000 microns in a millimeter (1 μ = 0.001 mm). Bacteria are the smallest cells that can be seen

†The review material on biology is used by permission from *How to Prepare for College Board Achievement Tests–Biology*, by Maurice Bleifeld, Barron's Educational Series, Inc., Hauppauge, N.Y. 1987.

with the light microscope. They average 1–3 microns in size (0.001–0.003 mm). Most other cells are about 10 microns in size. However, a nerve cell, which is microscopic, may extend more than a yard in length. And the yolk of a bird's egg, which is a single cell, may measure several inches across.

Until quite recently, the structure of plant and animal cells was considered to be relatively simple, as shown in the following diagrams:

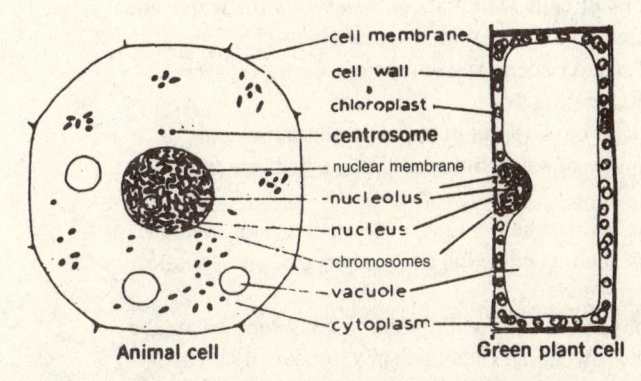

With the aid of the electron microscope, many details of the structure of the cell are being revealed, as shown in the modern version of a generalized cell:

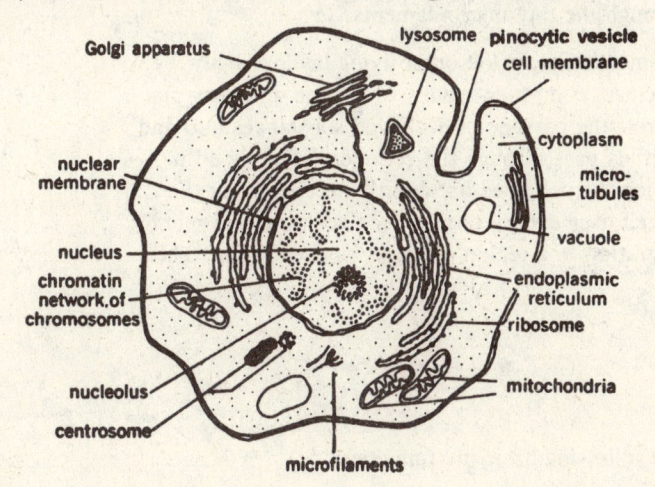

Protoplasm

A cell is a tiny unit of living material called protoplasm. It contains specialized areas called *organelles,* that perform certain functions:

1. Nucleus. A body within the cell, enclosed in a *nuclear membrane*. It contains a distinct number of *chromosomes* on which the *genes* are arrayed. The genes are made of DNA (deoxyribonucleic acid), which controls the production of cell proteins. The proteins control all the chemical activity of the cell. The nucleus also contains *nucleoli,* which are released into the cytoplasm to become ribosomes.

2. Cytoplasm. The rest of the cell, outside the nucleus. It is a complex structure, containing:

   a. Endoplasmic reticulum—a network of channels, or tubes, that extends throughout the cytoplasm. Its membranes connect with the nuclear membrane and the cell membrane. It is thought to function in the transport of materials throughout the cell.

   b. Ribosomes—tiny granules that are distributed along the endoplasmic reticulum. They contain RNA, and function as sites for the synthesis of protein.

c. **Mitochondria**—rodlike structures with inner, folded surfaces called *cristae*. They contain enzymes associated with cellular respiration, leading to the release of energy from food. Most of the ATP molecules are formed here, serving as centers of energy storage. Mitochondria are called the "powerhouses" of the cell.

d. **Lysosomes**—contain digestive enzymes that break down large organic molecules, and worn-out organelles within the cell.

e. **Vacuoles**—are especially large in plant cells. They act as reservoirs for water and dissolved materials.

f. **Golgi apparatus**—produces lysosomes; concentrates enzyme secretions; secretes carbohydrates for plant cell wall formation.

g. **Centrosome**—present in animal cells, outside the nucleus. It contains a pair of *centrioles*, which are composed of a bundle of small filaments, and which are active during nuclear division.

h. **Microtubules**—thin tubular organelles that help support the structure of the cell. They also make up other cell structures such as cilia, flagella, centrioles, and spindle fibers.

i. **Microfilaments**—are involved in movement by pseudopodia in cells such as ameba and white blood cells, and in the tips of growing nerve cells. They appear to consist of very thin strands of the proteins *actin* and *myosin*, which have also been found to be involved in the contraction of skeletal muscle. It was recently determined that food and wastes are transported within a cell through the tiny microfilaments.

3. **Cell Membrane.** The cell, or plasma membrane, is the outer living layer of cytoplasm. It has a complex porous structure, composed mainly of protein and fatty material. It is semipermeable, and controls the passage of dissolved substances into and out of the cell. Some dissolved materials pass through the cell membrane by diffusion; this is *passive transport*, in which the cell does not contribute energy for the movement. In *active transport*, the cell uses energy to move molecules across membranes, from a region of low concentration to a region of higher concentration. This is against the concentration gradient.

Life Activities

Living things are able to carry on the following basic life functions:

Ingestion: The taking in of food.
Digestion: The breaking down of food to simpler soluble form, with the aid of enzymes.
Secretion: The formation of useful substances, such as enzymes.
Absorption: The passage of dissolved materials through the cell membrane, into and out of the cell.
Respiration: Release of energy from food.
Excretion: The waste products are passed out of the cell through the cell membrane.
Transport: Circulation of materials throughout the organism.
Regulation: Maintaining the stability of the organism's chemical makeup under a constantly changing internal and external environment (homeostasis).
Synthesis: The chemical formation of complex molecules from simple compounds.
Assimilation: The nonliving materials in food are changed into more protoplasm, resulting in growth and repair.
Reproduction: More living things are produced.
Irritability: The ability to respond to stimuli.

SCIENCE

Bioluminescence: The production of light by a limited number of organisms (firefly; some bacteria, protozoa, and fungi; deep-sea fish).

PHOTOSYNTHESIS

Photosynthesis is the manufacture of food (carbohydrates) from carbon dioxide and water in the presence of light. It takes place in the cells of green plants containing chlorophyll. During this process, the raw materials, carbon dioxide and water, are combined by the chlorophyll to form simple sugar, glucose. Oxygen is given off as a by-product. The following simplified equation summarizes the process:

$$\text{water} + \text{carbon dioxide} \xrightarrow[\substack{\text{chlorophyll}\\\text{enzymes}}]{\text{energy}} \text{glucose} + \text{water} + \text{oxygen}$$

This equation can be restated with greater chemical detail as:

$$12H_2O + 6CO_2 \xrightarrow[\text{chlorophyll}]{\text{energy}} \underset{\text{glucose}}{C_6H_{12}O_6} + 6H_2O + 6O_2$$

Much information about the various steps in photosynthesis has been obtained recently through the use of isotopes of oxygen and carbon, and the application of refined techniques of chromatography. With the aid of heavy oxygen, oxygen-18, it has been shown that the oxygen that is given off comes from the water. Radioactive carbon, carbon-14, has been traced as a "tagged" molecule through the complex stages of carbon fixation with the aid of instruments such as the Geiger counter. In chromatography, various compounds are separated out at different levels as they are absorbed on a length of filter paper.

Photosynthesis is now known to take place in two sets of reactions: (a) a light reaction, in which oxygen is liberated, and light energy is converted into chemical energy, and (b) a dark reaction, in which the chemical energy is used to convert carbon dioxide into organic compounds, without the necessity of light.

RESPIRATION

Aerobic Respiration

Green plants, like animals, carry on respiration, that is, they take in oxygen, and combine it with food to release energy for their various activities, such as food-making and growth. In the process, carbon dioxide and water are excreted as wastes. Thus, respiration is the reverse process of photosynthesis. As a matter of fact, during the day, both processes go on side by side, in different parts of the green cell. In photosynthesis, an excess amount of oxygen is produced by the chloroplasts. Some of it is used directly by the protoplasm of the cell for oxidizing food, while the rest of it diffuses out and is given off through the stomates. At the same time, while respiration is being carried on by the protoplasm, carbon dioxide and water are given off. These waste products are used up almost at once by the chloroplasts, which are carrying on photosynthesis. Thus two different parts of the cell carry on contrasting activities—the protoplasm takes in oxygen and gives off carbon dioxide and water, to release energy, during respiration; while the chloroplasts in the same cell take in carbon dioxide and water, and give off oxygen, storing energy, during photosynthesis.

At *night*, however, when photosynthesis does not go on, only respiration is carried on; oxygen is taken in from the air through the stomates, and carbon dioxide and water are given off.

TEST OF GENERAL KNOWLEDGE: DESCRIPTION, REVIEW, PRACTICE

COMPARISON OF PHOTOSYNTHESIS AND RESPIRATION

	Photosynthesis	Respiration
When it occurs	Day only	Day and night
What is taken in	CO_2 and H_2O	O_2
What is given off	O_2	CO_2 and H_2O
Where it takes place	In green cells only	In all cells
What happens to glucose	Built up	Broken down
What happens to energy	Used and stored up	Liberated

Anaerobic Respiration

Some of the simpler plants, such as yeast and certain bacteria, carry on anaerobic respiration, in which oxygen is not needed. They produce as wastes carbon dioxide and ethyl alcohol. The process is known as *alcoholic fermentation*. It has commercial values in the brewing, baking and wine-making industries. Other types of bacteria and certain molds carry on *lactic acid fermentation*, in which carbon dioxide and lactic acid are produced. The amount of energy released during anaerobic respiration is relatively small compared to aerobic respiration, since most of the C-C and C-H bonds in the alcohol or the lactic acid have not been broken, and still retain their chemical energy.

FOOD AND ENERGY

Carbohydrates and fats are chiefly used for energy, although proteins may also be used for this purpose. One of the results of oxidation of food in warm-blooded animals is a constant body temperature—in human beings it is 98.6°F; in some birds it may vary from 100°F to 112°F. Oxidation in animals is basically similar to that in plants. Certain respiratory enzymes in each cell are used to break the food down, with the release of energy, and formation of the waste products, carbon dioxide and water.

All cells must be supplied with glucose as a source of energy. In animals, glucose comes from the digestion and other chemical treatment of food materials; in plants, it comes from photosynthesis. Within each cell, a complex series of chemical processes, mostly mediated by enzymes in the mitochondria, oxidizes the glucose to yield energy and the waste products carbon dioxide and water.

In the oxidation of glucose, the chemical energy of the glucose is used to attach an additional phosphate group onto a substance called *adenosine diphosphate* (ADP). The resultant *adenosine triphosphate* (ATP) is a temporary storehouse of energy. All physical and chemical processes in the cell obtain their energy by capturing a phosphate group from ATP, converting the ATP back into ADP.

Food Chain

A food chain represents the pathways along which energy is transferred from one organism to another. The original source of the food energy is almost always sunlight, used by *producers* (green plants, algae, and green and purple bacteria) for photosynthesis. (The only other producer is the sulfur bacteria that grow around volcanic vents in the ocean floor; they get their energy from the chemical products of the volcano.) Energy passes from the producers into animals that eat them, and then into other animals through a chain of carnivores. When animals or plants die, their energy supports the bacteria and fungi that decompose them.

SCIENCE

Classification in a Food Chain

The various links in a food chain may be classified as follows:
(a) Producers—green plants, algae, green and purple bacteria, and sulfur bacteria, are the producers, since they synthesize food from inorganic matter.
(b) Consumers—organisms that feed directly on green plants are called *primary*, or *first-order*, consumers. Animals of this type are known as herbivores. *Secondary*, or *second-order*, consumers are carnivores with sharp tearing teeth, which prey on the primary consumers. There may be *third-order consumers*, which are predators on the secondary consumers, and frequently on the primary consumers.
(c) Decomposers—organisms that break down the wastes and dead bodies of producers and consumers into simpler compounds. These compounds are cycled, or returned to the environment, where they are used over again by other living things.

The sequence in the terrestrial food chain mentioned previously can thus be rewritten in this way: green plants (producers)—mice (first-order consumers)—snakes (second-order consumers)—hawks (third-order consumers on snakes; second-order consumers on mice)—decomposers.

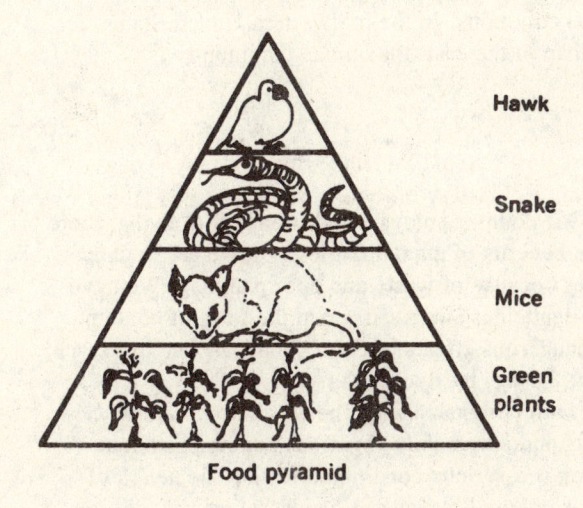

Food pyramid

Food Web

Food chains overlap into food webs, because there are many kinds of producers that may be eaten by different kinds of primary consumers (i.e., insects, rabbits, etc.); these herbivore consumers may shift from one plant to another. Carnivores, which live on herbivores, may likewise shift from one source of prey to another, and may be of different types (e.g., frogs, foxes, owls). An ecological balance is achieved when the numbers of the various populations are kept at relatively stable levels in relation to each other.

Niche

The whole complex of interactions between a species and its environment, including other organisms, is called the *ecological niche* of the species. The niche includes such things as habitat, climate, food supply, nesting sites, predators, parasites, etc. In general, only one species can occupy any particular niche. If two species compete for a niche, the one that makes the most efficient use of the niche, leaving the most offspring, will eventually eliminate the other.

Ecological Succession

As the plants in a pond die, their remains build up and add to the silt that accumulates at the bottom of the pond. At the edge of the pond, where the water is shallow, reeds and cattails grow. A new ecological community has replaced the community within the pond. A whole sequence of communities will follow as the soil continues to build up. Such a sequence is called an *ecological succession*.

At low altitude in the northeastern United States ecological succession that starts in a pond follows a definite pattern. The reeds and cattails eventually produce enough soil to support water-loving shrubs like alder and buttonbush. Swamp-loving herbs, such as marsh marigold, flourish under the shrubs. A community dominated by small trees, red maples and white ashes, then take over. This is followed by a forest of large hardwoods, chiefly sugar maples and beeches. This community can reproduce itself indefinitely; it is a *climax community*.

The details of an ecological succession depend on the starting conditions, the climate, and the geology of the region. In general, each sequence tends toward some stable climax community, depending on local condtions. In the midwestern United States, for example, where there is less rainfall than in the east, the climax community is grassland.

Conservation

America is called a land of plenty. Our country enjoys a high standard of living, there is an excess of food, and we enjoy the benefits of many luxuries. Yet we are in danger of losing our valuable natural resources because of waste and poor planning. We have found that our use of pesticides and insecticides has backfired in the form of contaminated crops and water supplies. The dangerous effects of these chemicals has been well depicted in the best-selling book *Silent Spring*, by Rachel Carson.

In addition, the threat of pollution is affecting our use of the air and the natural waters. Combustion in industrial plants and automobile engines is adding poisonous wastes to the air that we breathe. Smog is a serious condition affecting the health of large city dwellers. The water supply is polluted by sewage, industrial wastes, silt, fertilizers, and salt water. The Great Lakes, which once had pure, fresh water, are in danger of becoming mere sewage basins in which few living things can survive.

We are warned that we must practice *conservation*, the planned use and preservation of our natural resources, especially (1) forests, (2) soil, and (3) wildlife.

MATTER

Phases of Matter

Matter occurs in three phases: solid, liquid, and gas. A solid has a definite shape and size. A liquid has a definite volume, but takes the shape of its container, filling the container up to the level of a definite upper surface. A gas does not have a definite shape or volume; it will spread out to fill its container completely. Change from one phase to another involves heat. Heat must be added to change a solid to a liquid or a liquid to a gas. Change in the other direction releases heat.

SCIENCE

*Composition of Matter

Matter can be subdivided into two general categories: distinct substances and mixtures. The distinct substances are either elements or compounds. If a substance is made up of only one kind of atom, it is called an *element*. If, however, it is composed of two or more kinds of atoms joined together in a definite grouping, it is classified as a *compound*. That a compound always occurs in a definite composition is called the *Law of Definite Composition* or *Proportion*. An example of this is water: it always occurs in a relationship of two hydrogen atoms to one oxygen atom to form the compound water. *Mixtures*, however, can vary in their composition.

† Changes in Matter

Matter may undergo changes in three ways—physical, chemical, and nuclear.

In a *physical change*, atoms and molecules remain unaltered, but their relationships to each other are changed. Examples: water freezes into ice; sugar dissolves in water; a rock is pulverized; a spring is stretched.

In a *chemical change*, atoms are recombined to form new kinds of substances, but the atomic nuclei are not altered and no new elements are formed. Examples: hydrogen and oxygen unite to form water; wood burns; dynamite explodes. If a chemical change releases energy, it is said to be *exothermic;* if it absorbs energy, it is *endothermic*.

In a *nuclear change*, the nucleus of the atom is altered and new elements are formed. Example: the radioactive breakdown of a radium nucleus to form nuclei of helium and radon. Nuclear changes involve very large amounts of energy.

Energy

Energy is a physical quantity, measured in the same units as work, that changes when work is done or heat is added or removed. It takes many forms. *Kinetic energy* is the energy that something has because of its motion. For example, a bowling ball can knock pins down because it has kinetic energy.

Potential energy is the energy a system has because of the forces between its parts. For example, a rock high on a hill has *gravitational energy* because of its separation from the Earth; if it rolls downhill, the gravitational energy becomes kinetic energy. Other forms of potential energy: a stretched spring has *elastic energy;* a battery has *electric energy;* gunpowder has *chemical energy;* a radium nucleus has *nuclear energy*.

† LAW OF CONSERVATION OF ENERGY AND MATTER

Energy may be converted from one form to another but is never destroyed in the change. An example is the battery, which converts chemical energy into electrical energy. The *Law of Conservation of Energy and Matter* states that matter and energy are interchangeable and the total amount in the universe is constant.

Einstein stated the relationship of energy and matter in his famous equation

$$E = mc^2$$

---

*Used by permission from *How to Prepare for College Board Achievement Tests — Chemistry,* by Joseph A. Mascetta, Barron's Educational Series, Inc., Hauppauge, N.Y., 1986.

†Used by permission from *Essentials of Modern Chemistry,* by Philip Perlman, Barron's Educational Series, Inc., Hauppauge, N.Y. 1979.

where E = the amount of energy derived from a quantity of matter,
m = the amount of matter (mass),
c = a constant equal to the velocity of light (3.00×10^{10} cm/sec).

It can be seen from this equation that a small quantity of mass can be converted into a tremendous amount of energy.

SCIENCE GLOSSARY

This is a list of some important concepts that you should be familiar with.

Air mass analysis A theory of weather based on the concept that large masses of air move within the atmosphere. Air masses originating over the continents are dry; those originating over the ocean are moist. Warm masses come from the tropics; cold ones from polar regions. Boundaries between air masses—where weather is stormy—are *fronts*.

Ampere The unit of electric current, equal to one coulomb per second.

Animals One of the five kingdoms of organisms, consisting of those multicellular creatures lacking cell walls and with heterotrophic nutrition.

Atom The smallest part of an element. It consists of a positively charged nucleus surrounded by negatively charged electrons. The charge on the nucleus (the number of protons in the nucleus) specifies the element to which the atom belongs.

Bacteria The most primitive of the five kingdoms of organisms, characterized by very small, single cells lacking nuclei, mitochondria, and other internal structures. Most are parasitic or saphrophytic, but some (blue-green algae, sulfur bacteria, etc.) are autotrophic.

Big bang theory Theory of the origin of the universe that holds that about 15 billion years ago, the entire universe began as a tiny volume of extremely dense material that began to expand explosively. The expansion, according to this theory, continues.

Boyle's law Law stating that at constant temperature, the volume of a gas varies inversely as the temperature.

Carbohydrates Organic chemicals composed of carbon, hydrogen, and oxygen. They include sugars, starches, and cellulose, and are the energy source of cells.

Chlorophyll The green chemical in the cells of plants and algae that contains the chemical mechanism that allows sunlight to be used in photosynthesis.

Chromosome A thread-like structure, composed of protein and DNA, found in the nucleus of all cells. The number and form of chromosomes is uniform in all cells of a given species.

Copernican theory The theory that the sun is the center of the universe and the planets revolve around it.

Coulomb's law Law stating that the electrostatic and magnetic forces of attraction or

SCIENCE

repulsion vary directly as the product of the electric charges or magnetic pole strengths, and inversely as the square of the distance between charges or poles.

Dominance   The situation in which an organism has two different allelic genes, only one of which has an effect on the developing organism. The gene that has no effect is called the *recessive* gene.

Doppler effect   The increase in frequency of a wave as a result of the source moving toward the observer or the observer moving toward the source; the decrease in frequency if the source and observer are moving apart. Astronomers use the Doppler shift of light to measure the motion of stars.

Efficiency   The ratio of the useful energy gotten out of a system to the energy put into it.

Electron   A tiny particle, part of the outer structure of every atom, bearing a single negative electric charge.

Electron microscope   A microscope that uses a beam of electrons (instead of light), controlled by magnetic fields, to produce much higher resolution than is possible with light. The electron beam produces higher resolution because it has a much smaller wavelength than a light beam.

Element   A pure substance, consisting of one kind of atom only. In nature, there are 92 elements; an additional 14 have been created in nuclear reactions. Each element has a unique atomic number, specified by the charge on the nucleus of its atoms.

Energy   A physical quantity, measured in work units, that remains unchanged through many transformations of form. Heat is energy that transfers from one system to another because of a temperature difference. Kinetic energy is the energy that an object has because of its motion. Potential energy is the energy due to forces between parts of a system; it can be gravitational, chemical, electrical, elastic, etc.

Enzyme   A protein that serves as a catalyst in chemical reactions in living things. Some enzymes, such as digestive enzymes, are secreted and function outside the cell that makes them; others, such as the respiratory enzymes, act within the cell.

Evolution   The process by which living organisms change over long periods of time.

First law of thermodynamics   Law stating that total energy is conserved; that is, in any closed system, the form of energy may change, but the total amount of energy cannot increase or decrease.

Fungi   One of the five kingdoms of organisms. They are mostly multicellular and either parasitic or saphrophytic, and the cells have nuclei. The kingdom includes mushrooms, molds, mildews, and yeasts.

Gene   That part of DNA, located on a chromosome, that controls the production of proteins by the cell. The gene is the basic unit of heredity, transmitting specific traits from one generation to the next.

Half-life   The time it takes for half of any given sample of a radioactive material to decay.

TEST OF GENERAL KNOWLEDGE: DESCRIPTION, REVIEW, PRACTICE

Heat Energy transferred from a point of high temperature to a colder place. *Conduction* is transfer through some material, especially a metal. *Convection* is transfer by circulation of a fluid. *Radiation* is transfer by electromagnetic waves, particularly infrared.

Igneous rock Rock formed by the solidification of liquid magma. Magma solidifying inside the crust forms *intrusive* igneous rock, such as granite and basalt. Magma coming to the surface is called *lava*, and hardens into *extrusive* igneous rock.

Ion An atom or group of atoms bearing an electric charge. An *anion* has one or more excess electrons and thus has a negative charge. A *cation* has a positive charge because it is lacking one or more electrons.

Isostasy The theory that blocks of the earth's crust rise and sink into the underlying mantle according to their sizes and densities.

Kelvin scale The temperature scale in which zero is the lowest possible temperature—absolute zero, equal to $-273.16°C$. Temperature in kelvins is equal to the Celsius temperature plus 273.

Linnaeus' system of classification The ordering of organisms into a hierarchy of categories, according to closeness of relationship. The categories, beginning with the largest, are kingdom—phylum—class—order—family—genus—species. Each species is given a two-part name. The first word is the name of the genus and the second is special for the species within the genus. Example: *Canis familiaris* is the scientific name of the dog, in the genus *Canis*.

Machine A device for making it easier to do work. Ideally, the work (force times distance) put into a machine is equal to the work output. Generally, the machine can exert a larger force than the force applied to it, but over a smaller distance. Examples are inclined plane, lever, gears, hydraulic press, screw, etc.

Mass The property of an object that is measured by a platform balance, expressed in grams or kilograms. It must be carefully distinguished from weight. An object's mass does not depend on its location in space; its weight does.

Meiosis The process by which a cell divides twice, in such a way as to insert duplicate copies of one half of its chromosomes into each of four daughter cells. Meiosis occurs in the formation of gametes (eggs and sperm), so that each gamete has the *monoploid* number of chromosomes. (When the gametes unite in fertilization, the resulting *zygote* has the *diploid* number of chromosomes characteristic of the species.) All body cells have the diploid number.

Metamorphic rock Rock that has recrystallized without melting, as the result of great heat and pressure. Examples are marble, slate, gneiss, and quartzite.

Microscope The usual compound optical microscope consists, as a minimum, of two lenses at opposite ends of a tube. The *objective* lens, nearest the object, magnifies up to about 120 diameters, with corresponding increase in the visible detail. The *ocular* lens, nearest the eye, increases the size of the image without producing any additional detail. The ocular can enlarge the image to any desired extent, but more than about 15 diameters enlargement makes the image unacceptably fuzzy.

SCIENCE

Mineral A component of the earth's crust with a definite chemical composition, such as quartz, calcite, bauxite, and biotite.

Mitosis The process by which a cell, in dividing, inserts duplicate copies of all its chromosomes into each daughter cell.

Molds Many kinds of fungi whose cells are connected into long, thin fibers. Some molds produce chemicals that kill bacteria, and these have been used to produce antibiotics, such as penicillin and streptomycin.

Momentum The product of mass and velocity. In any closed system total momentum of all parts is conserved.

Natural selection The theory, stated by Charles Darwin, that individual differences, or variations, within a species result in differences in the ability of individuals to survive and reproduce in a particular environment. Those individuals better adapted to the environment survive and leave the most offspring. Over a period of time this natural selection process leads to changes in the species and eventually to the formation of new species.

Neutralization The reaction of an acid with a base to produce water and a neutral salt.

Neutron The massive, uncharged particles found, along with protons, in the nucleus of an atom.

Newton's law of universal gravitation Law stating that all bodies in the universe are attracted to each other by a force that is directly proportional to the product of their masses and inversely proportional to the square of the distance between them.

Newton's laws of motion Law stating that the acceleration of an object is directly proportional to the force applied and inversely proportional to its mass (second law). Corollaries state that a body remains at rest or in a state of uniform motion unless an external force is applied (first law); and that for every force, there is an equal and opposite force acting on another object (third law).

Nutrition 1. The mechanism by which an organism obtains its energy. In *autotrophic* nutrition, the organism makes its own food from inorganic materials, using the energy of sunlight (photosynthesis) or of available chemicals (chemosynthesis). In *heterotrophic* nutrition, food is taken in in the form of organic substances made by autotrophs. This is the nutrition of animals, saprophytic fungi, parasites, etc.
   2. The foods people eat in relation to their need to maintain health. The U.S. Department of Agriculture has defined 5 food groups: Group 1: fruits and vegetables; Group 2: breads and cereals; Group 3: milk and milk products; Group 4: poultry, fish, meat, eggs, seeds; Group 5: fats, sweets, alcohol. The first 4 groups are needed in proper quantity to supply necessary energy-bearing chemicals: proteins, carbohydrates, and fats. They also supply needed non-energy nutrients: vitamins, minerals, and fiber.

Ohm's law Law stating that in a metallic conductor at constant temperature, potential difference divided by current is a constant, called *resistance*.

Osmosis The diffusion of water (a solvent) through a membrane into a region of higher concentration of solute to equalize the concentration of solute on both sides of the membrane.

Periodic law Rule, first stated by Mendeleyer, that the properties of the elements are periodic functions of their atomic numbers. If the elements are arranged in order of increasing atomic number, their physical and chemical properties are seen to repeat at certain intervals.

pH The concentration of hydrogen ions in a solution. A perfectly neutral material, like pure water, has pH 7; acids are below 7, and bases are over 7, up to 14.

Photosynthesis The process by which green plants, algae, and certain bacteria use the energy of sunlight in the presence of chlorophyll to combine carbon dioxide and water and produce glucose and oxygen.

Plants One of the five kingdoms of organisms, those with complex multicellular structure, cellulose cell walls, and photosynthetic nutrition (usually). Includes the mosses, liverworts, ferns, conifers, and flowering plants.

Plate tectonics The theory that the earth's crust is divided into a set of plates that move over the underlying mantle. Continents move, and the boundaries between plates are zones of active vulcanism and mountain-building.

Power The rate of doing work or performing any other energy transformation. It is measured in joules per second, called watts.

Pressure Force per unit area, measured in pounds per square inch, millibars, millimeters of mercury, or kilopascals.

Protein Giant molecules, composed of long strings of amino acids, that make up the enzymes and many of the structural elements of cells and animal bodies.

Protista One of the five kingdoms of organisms, those that are single-celled, colonial or simply organized. Cells have nuclei and mitochondria. Includes, protozoa, algae, slime molds. Some are heterotrophic; others are photosynthetic.

Proton A positively charged, highly massive constituent of all atomic nuclei. The number of protons in the nucleus is the atomic number of the element.

Second law of thermodynamics Law stating that heat passes by itself only to regions of lower temperature, so that temperatures tend to even out. In every energy transformation, some energy becomes unavailable in the form of low-temperature heat.

Sedimentary rock Rock formed by the consolidation of sediments (sandstone, shale, conglomerate, limestone) or deposited by evaporation of mineral-bearing water (salt, gypsum, travertine).

Segregation The process by which allelic genes separate into different gametes at the time of meoisis.

SCIENCE

Speciation The process by which two populations of a species, usually geographically separated, evolve separately to form two different species.

Species A group of interbreeding populations in nature, unable to interbreed with other populations and occupying a distinct ecological niche.

Stratigraphy The science of deducing the past history of the earth and the life in it by study of the layers of sedimentary rock and the fossils they contain.

Symbiosis A system in which two species live in a permanent, mutually advantageous, and close relationship.

Viruses Submicroscopic particles that cause many kinds of disease by attacking living cells. The particles consist of a core of either DNA or RNA surrounded by a protein coat. The core is injected into a living cell, and uses the cell's own genetic mechanism to reproduce itself.

Volt The unit of electric potential difference, equal to one joule per coulomb.

Water table The upper surface of the ground water, where the earth is saturated. A swamp is a place where the water table is at the surface.

Weight The gravitational pull exerted on an object. It depends on the object's mass and its location in space. An object that weighs 100 newtons on earth will weigh only 16 newtons on the moon, although its mass is no different.

Work The product of force by the distance the force moves in the direction of application of the force. it is measured in foot-pounds or in joules (newton-meters).

Yeast Any of a number of single-celled fungi, reproducing by budding. The common baker's or brewer's yeast obtains its energy saprophytically, by converting sugar into alcohol and carbon dioxide. It is the carbon dioxide that causes the rising of bread and the fizz in beer.

Diagnostic Practice Test — Science

Time—30 minutes

Directions: For each question or incomplete statement below there are five suggested answers or completions. Select the one that *best* answers the question or completes the statement. Allow 30 minutes for this test.

1. The heat from burning fuel vaporizes water to steam; the steam is used to turn a turbine, which powers a generator to produce electricity. How many kinds of energy are represented in this statement?
   (A) One
   (B) Two
   (C) Three
   (D) Four
   (E) Five

TEST OF GENERAL KNOWLEDGE: DESCRIPTION, REVIEW, PRACTICE

2. A person pours boiling water into a cold jar, and the jar breaks. The best explanation is that
   (A) glass is a good conductor of heat
   (B) the jar was made of thin glass
   (C) the inner part of the glass expanded faster than the outer part
   (D) the jar was defective
   (E) air was trapped inside the jar

3. People living in the Andes Mountains have a much higher red blood count than the average person living at sea level; this increased count enables them to absorb more oxygen from the thin air. This is an example of
   (A) adaptation   (D) dominance
   (B) isolation   (E) balance of nature
   (C) commensalism

4. With the growth of industry and population, the following proposals have been made to increase the necessary supplies of water:

   I. Decrease industrial pollution of available water
   II. Recycle waste water
   III. Obtain water from polar ice
   IV. Produce new water from hydrogen and oxygen
   V. Desalinate sea water

   Which of these methods might be useful under conditions of severe water shortage?
   (A) I, II, III, IV, and V
   (B) I and II only
   (C) I, III and IV only
   (D) III and V only
   (E) I, II, III, and V only

5. The moon rotates in the same time that it revolves around the Earth. This fact, plus the Earth's gravitational attraction of the moon, results in
   (A) frequent lunar eclipses
   (B) infrequent solar eclipses
   (C) high tides on Earth
   (D) the same side of the moon always facing the Earth
   (E) the erratic orbit of the moon

6. How many atoms are there in a molecule of ethylene chloride, which has the formula C_2H_5Cl?
   (A) 4   (B) 5   (C) 6   (D) 7   (E) 8

7. A 1-pound rock and a 5-pound rock are dropped together from the roof of a building 12 m high. Then
   (A) both rocks will strike the ground at nearly the same instant and going nearly the same speed
   (B) the 5-pound rock will strike the ground much sooner than the 1-pound rock
   (C) the 1-pound rock will strike the ground much sooner than the 5-pound rock
   (D) the 5-pound rock will be going much faster when it hits the ground
   (E) the 1-pound rock will be going much faster when it hits the ground

SCIENCE

8. Mendel discovered the principle of dominance when he crossed plants that were
   (A) pure tall and pure short
   (B) hybrid tall and hybrid short
   (C) pure tall and hybrid short
   (D) hybrid tall and pure short
   (E) hybrid tall and hybrid tall

9. A teacher who met with eight other committee members in a small room with no ventilation noticed after a time that her rate of breathing had increased. The best explanation is
   (A) nothing was being accomplished
   (B) the lights in the room were too bright
   (C) the temperature of the room had risen
   (D) the oxygen level in the room had increased
   (E) the carbon dioxide concentration in her blood had increased

10. A sedimentary rock formed as a result of the decay, accumulation, and compaction of plant matter is
    (A) limestone
    (B) gypsum
    (C) sandstone
    (D) shale
    (E) coal

11. Which of the following statements about alcohol is NOT true?
    (A) Even one or two drinks can affect judgment, alertness, and coordination.
    (B) In large quantities alcohol causes loss of memory and unconsciousness.
    (C) Alcohol is a stimulant, and the more a person drinks the happier and wittier he or she becomes.
    (D) Regular, heavy drinking lowers resistance to disease.
    (E) In more than one third of automobile accidents the driver has been drinking.

12. All of the following waves can travel through a vacuum EXCEPT
    (A) sound waves
    (B) radio waves
    (C) light waves
    (D) infrared waves
    (E) ultraviolet waves

13. Why do stars appear to move from east to west in the nighttime sky?
    (A) The sun revolves around the Earth.
    (B) The earth revolves around the sun.
    (C) The stars revolve around the Earth.
    (D) The Earth rotates from west to east.
    (E) The Earth rotates from east to west.

14. Cells release energy, but differ from the combustion of a fuel such as coal. Which of the following statements are correct?
    I. The energy released by the combustion of coal is heat and light.
    II. Food molecules combine with oxygen through a series of intermediate steps.
    III. Through metabolism energy is transformed in the cell.
    IV. Food molecules ultimately produce carbon dioxide, water, and energy.

(A) II only
(B) III only
(C) I, II, III, and IV
(D) II and III only
(E) II, III, and IV only

15. Forests are among our most valuable natural resources. They are useful in all of the following ways EXCEPT
    (A) they provide a haven for wildlife
    (B) they help to prevent erosion and flooding
    (C) they provide opportunity for healthful recreation
    (D) useful products are obtained from the wood of trees
    (E) the forest soil is rich in precious minerals

16. A climax community is characterized by
    (A) continual crisis and change
    (B) periodic sharp upheavals, followed by peaceful interludes
    (C) equilibrium and stability
    (D) a continual influx of new species
    (E) a preponderance of species that are in the process of dying out

17. In some ways viruses have puzzled biologists. Which of the following statements is NOT true of viruses?
    (A) They reproduce readily when placed in nutrient broth or jelly.
    (B) They are ultramicroscopic in size.
    (C) They cause many diseases in plants, animals, and human beings.
    (D) When purified from infected tissue, they may resemble dry crystals.
    (E) They do not contain organelles, or specialized areas, like those found in the cells of living things.

18. Every living system incorporates homeostatic systems, which are forms of negative feedback mechanisms. The function of these systems is to make it possible for the organism to
    (A) use food for the production of energy
    (B) adjust its functioning to a changing environment
    (C) pass on its characteristics to its offspring
    (D) obtain a mate and reproduce
    (E) assimilate its food in order to grow

19. In any natural community, energy is transfered from organism to organism. In the simple food chain shown in the diagram, in which level is the total available energy of all the organisms at that level the greatest?
    (A) Green plants
    (B) Rodents
    (C) Snakes
    (D) Hawks
    (E) None; it is the same at all levels

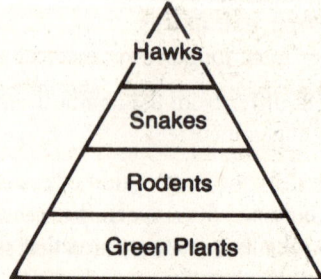

SCIENCE

20. Two individual organisms have been identified as both being members of a single taxonomic group. They might be LEAST closely related if the group is a
    (A) class
    (B) species
    (C) family
    (D) order
    (E) phylum

21. Of the following lunches which one includes all of the four basic food groups recommended by nutritionists?
    (A) A sliced chicken sandwich with lettuce on whole wheat bread, an apple, and a glass of milk
    (B) An egg sandwich on white bread, a piece of cake, and a glass of milk
    (C) A shrimp salad, a dish of ice cream, and a cup of coffee with milk
    (D) Two slices of bran-bread toast with jelly, a banana, and a cup of black coffee
    (E) A ham sandwich on whole wheat bread, a tomato and lettuce salad, and a cola drink

22. If a gas is at a constant temperature, the relation between the volume of the gas and the pressure exerted by the gas
    (A) depends on the particular gases involved
    (B) is inverse
    (C) is direct
    (D) cannot be determined
    (E) is unpredictable

23. For sexual reproduction, every species of flowering plant must have flowers with anthers to produce
    (A) pollen
    (B) nectar
    (C) water
    (D) an odor
    (E) seeds

24. Which of the following is NOT a chemical change?
    (A) Burning of gasoline
    (B) Magnetizing a piece of metal
    (C) Decomposing water by electricity
    (D) Producing hydrogen from iron and hydrochloric acid
    (E) Rusting of iron

25. Science and technology have found many medical applications. For example, the laser, which amplifies visible, ultraviolet, and infrared light, is useful in surgery (e.g., of the eye) because
    (A) it shows in what direction an object is moving
    (B) objects beyond the range of sight can be located
    (C) it produces an echo when it contacts an object
    (D) it can be focused with extreme precision and power on a small area
    (E) it produces a discontinuous beam

TEST OF GENERAL KNOWLEDGE: DESCRIPTION, REVIEW, PRACTICE

26. When a rocket is launched, the amount of energy needed to escape the gravitational pull of the Earth depends largely on
    (A) the orbit of the Earth at the time of launch
    (B) the position of the sun in the solar system
    (C) the length of the spacecraft
    (D) the weight of the spacecraft
    (E) the solar cells on board the spacecraft

27. If large amounts of electrical energy are available, aluminum can be freed from its ore through an economical industrial system called
    (A) electrolysis   (D) diffusion
    (B) photosynthesis   (E) oxidation
    (C) radiation

28. All of the following statements about the handling of toxic waste materials are correct EXCEPT
    (A) The newest technique involves placing invisible microbes in the soil to clean up pollutants.
    (B) The government permits trucking toxic waste to designated sites.
    (C) The safest method of disposal is to place waste in metal drums close to the site of origination and keep it above ground.
    (D) In some states polluted soil is bulldozed and placed in plastic-lined landfills.
    (E) Vegetation and soil contaminated with selenium can kill water birds.

29. The use of defoliants is a matter of grave concern for all of the following reasons EXCEPT
    (A) animals depend upon plants for food
    (B) the existing food chain is disturbed
    (C) water supplies may become contaminated
    (D) the chemical content of the soil may change
    (E) more fertilizer will be needed on croplands

30. A light-year is a measure of
    (A) speed   (D) time
    (B) illumination   (E) distance
    (C) motion

Answer Key

1. D	7. A	13. D	19. A	25. D
2. C	8. A	14. C	20. E	26. D
3. A	9. E	15. E	21. A	27. A
4. E	10. E	16. C	22. B	28. C
5. D	11. C	17. A	23. A	29. E
6. E	12. A	18. B	24. B	30. E

Part II Test of Communication Skills: Description, Review, Practice

The Test of Communication Skills consists of four separately timed 30-minute sections that together test your knowledge and skills in the areas of listening, reading, and writing.

The *Listening* section, which is based on tape-recorded material, assesses your ability to retain and interpret spoken messages. There are 40 questions in this section. Some are based on brief statements or questions, some are based on short dialogs, and some are based on short talks.

The *Reading* section assesses your ability to understand, analyze, and evaluate what you read. The 30 questions in this section are based on long passages, short passages, or brief statements of one or two sentences.

The *Multiple-Choice Writing* section has 45 questions that test your ability to recognize and use standard written English correctly. The test contains three different types of questions; each type is grouped together in a separate part.

The *Essay Writing* section allows you 30 minutes in which to write an essay on an assigned topic. Scored holistically, the essays should give evidence of your ability to write with insight, consistency of point of view, and supporting information, while using appropriate diction, usage, grammar, and punctuation.

TEST OF COMMUNICATION SKILLS: DESCRIPTION, REVIEW, PRACTICE

Listening

The Listening section of the Test of Communication Skills consists of 40 multiple-choice questions that test the ability to listen effectively, a very important skill in teaching. This section is divided into three parts, each having a different question format. Part A contains short statements or questions, Part B short dialogs between two speakers, and Part C several short talks.

Test questions in this section assess the following:

- Ability to comprehend oral messages quickly and accurately, including noting details, paraphrasing and summarizing, and recognizing clues
- Ability to recall information
- Ability to analyze and evaluate messages, including recognizing assumptions and implications, drawing inferences, assessing supporting material, and identifying the speaker's tone and its effect on the listener
- Ability to identify appropriate responses to questions, statements, or dialog

When you take the Listening section of the actual NTE, as when you use this book, you will *hear* the questions and the material on which they are based. You will *see* only the directions and the answer choices. The questions and statements will be spoken just once. After each question, you will have approximately 12 seconds to read the answer choices in the test booklet, choose your answer, and mark your answer sheet. Note that, unlike the other sections of the Core Battery, questions on the Listening test have four instead of five answer choices.

Use the Diagnostic Practice Test, which you will find later in this section, to familiarize yourself with the different types of questions you can expect in each part of the Listening test and to give you an idea of how much further practice you need for this part of the Core Battery.

Strategies for the Listening Section

1. Obviously, the most important strategy for this section is to pay very close attention to what the speakers are saying. Do not let anything distract you.
2. You might find it helpful to look over the answer choices quickly before the speakers begin to talk. If you have the time to do this, it will often give you a good idea of which aspects of the talk are important. For example, if the answers are all different days of the week, you know you have to listen for and remember which day of the week is mentioned in the talk and what it is mentioned in reference to.
3. As with all multiple-choice questions, be sure to read all the choices before choosing your answer. You have about 12 seconds in which to read the choices and choose an answer, which gives you ample time to read all the choices.
4. While listening to the short talks in Part C, try to get a good sense of what is going on, including what the speakers are not saying but might be implying either in words or through intonation. Questions in Part C will often require that you analyze and evaluate what you have heard.

Developing Listening Skills

Listening skills can be developed through frequent practice. Perhaps you know people who have an extreme dependency on reading, one of the slower techniques for ob-

LISTENING

taining new information. Current technology requires the development and daily use of listening skills.

If you think of the speaker as the sender of a message and of the listener as the receiver of that message, you will understand the need to become a skilled listener. A speaker uses guides or clues similar to those used by an author, another sender of information about the world in which we live.

First, the speaker uses an *introductory statement* that sets the tone of the speech. The main statement answers one or more of these questions: What is the problem? Who was involved? What happened or may happen? Where did the action take place? When did this happen? How were the facts gathered? Why does the speaker consider them important? Why should the listener be concerned or get involved?

Supportive statements, two or three, are used to back up the main statement.

A *restatement* may be given for clarification or emphasis.

Details may be provided, or events described in *logical* or *chronological* order to support the speaker's main point or to show a cause and effect relationship.

Examples may be given to clarify meaning or to show how the information can be applied by the listener.

The speaker may inject his or her own *opinion* to influence the listener.

A *personal experience* relating to the topic may be used to stimulate interest, demonstrate feasibility, or prove importance.

A *clincher question* or a *summary statement* may serve to close the speech.

An effective listener thinks while listening. The usual rate of delivery of a speech is about 100 words per minute. The thought processes can function about five times as fast. What relevance does this have for the listener? How do the listener's thought processes and the speaker's message interact from known to unknown ideas?

As you listen, relate the introductory clues given by the speaker to something you already know or to a question you would like answered. Notice the way pitch and rate of speech are used. These elocution changes create attention to emphasize the importance of an idea.

After the speaker is finished, paraphrase the talk in your own words. What was the main topic? Which two or three ideas were used to back up the introductory statement? Were these ideas based on fact or opinion? Did you get the most important information from the introduction, the supportive statements, or the summary conclusion? Are you sure what the speaker's objective was?

If your mind wanders while you listen, you need practice in learning to stay "on course." Here are some helpful tips for more effective listening:

1. Know the title of the talk and anticipate further information.
2. Mentally raise a question about the topic, and listen for an answer to your question.
3. Pay special attention to the introductory statement.
4. Listen for new information.
5. Mentally visualize the outline the speaker is using.
6. Connect each idea to the introductory statement.
7. Mentally raise a question about what is being said, and listen for an answer or for a time when you can ask the question.
8. Begin to agree or disagree with the speaker's reasoning, facts, or personal opinion.
9. Anticipate the next point.
10. Search for assumptions and implied meanings that are not stated in the talk.
11. Anticipate the summary statement.
12. Mentally raise a final question, even if you cannot ask it.

TEST OF COMMUNICATION SKILLS: DESCRIPTION, REVIEW, PRACTICE

Practice Exercise

Have someone read to you a newspaper or magazine article, about 150–200 words long, on a topic of general interest. Ask the person to read clearly, at a normal rate of speed. Then answer as many of the following questions as you can (not all questions will be applicable to every article):

I. Basic Comprehension
   A. *Summarizing.* What is the main idea presented in the article?
   B. *Noting details.* How many persons are or will be affected by this situation? Who was involved? Where did the event take place? How much does the item cost? When did the problem begin? Why do we have the problem? What is the solution? What can you do about it? What will happen if nothing is done?
   C. *Recognizing cognitive clues.* What factual information does the author give to clarify his or her position?
   D. *Understanding the connotation of words.* What words does the author use that suggest associations or feelings? (Some words—*loyalty, liberty, home, warmth*—have pleasant connotations. Others—*thief, mob, cheapskate, dictator*—have acquired unpleasant associations.)
   E. *Interpreting the metaphorical.* Does the author use any figures of speech to compare or to suggest likenesses? (For example, ''The Senator howled and roared his indignation'' suggests a likeness between the Senator and a wild animal and indicates that the speaker is not objective.)

II. Analysis
   A. *Identifying the author's purpose.* What is the author trying to do? (Some common aims are to inform, to incite, to pacify, to amuse, to persuade, and to rebut.)
   B. *Identifying an assumption.* What premise, theory, or supposition is presented by the author?
   C. *Drawing an inference.* What conclusion can be reasonably drawn from evidence given or implied?
   D. *Recognizing the implications.* Is there any suggested or indirect meaning in the author's statements? Can you make any connection between the facts given and a life situation?

III. Evaluation
   A. Was the material logically and effectively arranged?
   B. Was the supporting information appropriate and effective in relation to the main statement?
   C. As far as you are concerned, does the author achieve his or her purpose?

Diagnostic Practice Test—Listening

The questions for this test and the materials on which they are based are recorded. The Diagnostic Practice Test is on the audiocassette. The directions and the answer choices are printed in this book.

There are three parts, A, B, and C, to the Listening test. Allow 30 minutes for the three parts. *Before listening to the recording, familiarize yourself with the directions for all three parts.*

LISTENING

PART A

Directions: You will find two kinds of questions in Part A. One kind presents a short question for you to answer; the other requires you to demonstrate understanding of a short statement. Listen to each question or statement *only once*, and listen very carefully. Then find the answer choices that correspond to the number of the question. Choose the one that best answers the question or is closest in meaning to or best supported by the statement.

Now begin Part A.

1. (A) The percentage will probably be the same as last year—about 10 percent.
   (B) Not all students who are excused exercise this privilege.
   (C) Five years ago no one had this option.
   (D) Taking the test may raise an excused student's grade.

2. (A) There are five genera of marine turtles.
   (B) Sea turtles were among the first groups of animals to receive international attention from conservationists.
   (C) Sea turtle eggs are leathery and golf-ball-sized.
   (D) There is a world demand for high-priced sea turtle products.

3. (A) We eat in a restaurant about twice a week.
   (B) My favorite "eat-out" foods are pizza and enchiladas.
   (C) the waiter was surly, slow, and sloppy.
   (D) The restaurant had been recommended by a friend.

4. (A) Sweden, Japan, and Finland have the best infant survival rates.
   (B) There has been a steady decline in the number of women receiving early prenatal care.
   (C) The United States ranks above Singapore and Ireland in the number of infant deaths per 1000 live births.
   (D) In 1981 there were 12 infant deaths per 1000 live births in the United States.

5. (A) Manuel communicated better in his native language.
   (B) Teachers should speak only English in the classroom.
   (C) Manuel's parents spoke Spanish at home.
   (D) English is not a difficult language for children to learn.

6. (A) Man-made pollution is the chief suspect.
   (B) Some species of softwood trees are losing their foliage and failing to reproduce.
   (C) The damage extends along the eastern coast from Maine to Georgia.
   (D) Forests are among our most valuable natural resources.

7. (A) Women should ignore current and future employment trends.
   (B) Women will be well advised to prepare for jobs in fields related to technology.
   (C) Mathematics and science, required in most technological fields, have always been regarded as difficult subjects for girls.
   (D) When the educational backgrounds of boys and girls are similar, the boys outscore the girls 2 to 1 on mathematics tests.

TEST OF COMMUNICATION SKILLS: DESCRIPTION, REVIEW, PRACTICE

8. (A) If teachers make lessons interesting, pupils will attend school.
   (B) Pupils have the right to choose their assignments.
   (C) "Back to the basics" could be defeated if pupils won't buy it.
   (D) Parental attitudes reinforce and encourage higher standards of school work and attendance.

9. (A) People don't do much local calling anyway.
   (B) The change will benefit those who make many long-distance calls.
   (C) A two-phone household will save more money.
   (D) Digital telephones are cheaper to operate than rotary dialing systems.

10. (A) The sex of the fetus is revealed by amniocentesis.
    (B) Some women don't want to know the sex of their unborn babies.
    (C) Amniocentesis reveals whether the fetus has a chromosomal abnormality, such as that causing Down's syndrome.
    (D) The procedure is relatively simple.

11. (A) Four-year-olds do not have the coordination to do something like that.
    (B) Patience has traditionally been emphasized in China, but not since Chairman Mao.
    (C) American children could do this easily.
    (D) Different cultures teach children in ways suited to their individual goals.

12. (A) A few votes don't make any difference.
    (B) Previous voter registration drives have not brought out the voters.
    (C) It's the candidate that brings out the voters, not drives.
    (D) Women's votes can make a difference in legislation affecting them, their families, and their futures.

13. (A) Consumer awareness, strict laws, and protective packaging are the best preventive measures.
    (B) A number of people died in the Tylenol episode a few years ago.
    (C) People who put injurious substances in food or drug packages are psychotic.
    (D) The best precaution is to take only drugs that are doctor-prescribed.

14. (A) There are not enough licensed, supervised child-care facilities.
    (B) Some women don't care where they leave their children.
    (C) Some large corporations provide child-care centers for their employees.
    (D) Women who have children should stay home and take care of them.

15. (A) Actually, I'd rather watch TV than read.
    (B) I prefer nonfiction, especially biography, to fiction.
    (C) A few years ago I went on an Orwell "kick" and read everything he wrote.
    (D) *Kristin Lavransdatter* is the only novel I've read three times.

PART B

Directions: In Part B you will hear several short dialogs. At the end of each dialog a third person will ask questions about the conversation. Each question will be spoken *only once*. After you hear a dialog and a question about it, read the four answer choices. Decide which is the best answer to the question.

LISTENING

Now begin Part B.

16. (A) They identified with the characters.
    (B) They used it to escape the problems of daily life.
    (C) They liked the commercials shown with it.
    (D) They watched it just because their children liked it.

17. (A) He is an office worker.
    (B) He is a teacher.
    (C) He is an athletic coach.
    (D) It is impossible to tell what he does for a living.

18. (A) Students who cut classes will be suspended.
    (B) Teachers will no longer have to fill out absence reports.
    (C) Requirements for passing a course will include class attendance.
    (D) Parents will be held responsible for preventing truancy.

19. (A) She supports it.
    (B) She is opposed to it.
    (C) She is indifferent.
    (D) She thinks another solution would be better.

20. (A) Its legs are too short for its body.
    (B) It has uncertain, erratic flight.
    (C) It likes to eat pears.
    (D) It has very dull coloring.

21. (A) He doesn't have much sense of humor.
    (B) He doesn't like birds.
    (C) He doesn't like the woman.
    (D) He doesn't think it's right to make fun of people.

22. (A) His daughter sneaked out without telling her parents.
    (B) His daughter spoke disrespectfully to him.
    (C) His daughter is half an hour late.
    (D) His daughter has failed two courses.

23. (A) The man dominates his wife.
    (B) The man is afraid his wife will leave him.
    (C) The woman nags her husband.
    (D) The man and the woman are equal partners in a happy marriage.

24. (A) By intercom
    (B) By radio
    (C) Face to face
    (D) By telephone

25. (A) Conciliatory
    (B) Unfriendly
    (C) Concerned
    (D) Embarassed

26. (A) Mr. Steinfeld will lose his temper and hang up.
    (B) Mrs. Schmidt will burst into tears and apologize for being rude.
    (C) Mrs. Schmidt will agree to come for a conference.
    (D) Mrs. Schmidt will continue to refuse to come for a conference.

27. (A) Help to build his house
    (B) Take up jogging
    (C) Become a carpenter
    (D) Read two books on carpentry

28. (A) She would never work on a house again.
    (B) She and her husband lost money by working on their house.
    (C) She and her husband could have benefitted from more knowledge about house building.
    (D) She and her husband had the help of two carpenters.

29. (A) Her surly coworkers
    (B) The smell of onions
    (C) The perpetual rush
    (D) The customers who sneaked out without paying

30. (A) He would not like to work in a restaurant.
    (B) He disagrees with the woman about the value of work.
    (C) He does not like to eat in fast-food restaurants.
    (D) He shows special consideration to working students who have problems with homework.

PART C

Directions: In Part C you will hear several short talks. Each talk will be followed by three or four questions. You must listen carefully because the talks and the questions will be given *only once*. After hearing each question, select the best answer.

31. (A) Careers in sports medicine
    (B) The value of exercise
    (C) Physical education careers
    (D) The disadvantages of being a trainer

32. (A) 10 percent   (C) 25 percent
    (B) 15 percent   (D) 50 percent

33. (A) Sports medicine is a crowded field with limited opportunities.
    (B) Physicians no longer dominate sports medicine.
    (C) Trainers don't earn their salaries.
    (D) Health spas are dominating the exercise field.

34. (A) Bubble domes are quite inexpensive.
    (B) Bubble-dome enclosures may extend the playing season for several sports.
    (C) Bubble domes are better suited to European weather.
    (D) Air-supported bubbles are the most widely used domes.

LISTENING

35. (A) Dome-enclosed areas will prove economically feasible.
    (B) The air-supported bubble will continue to be the most expensive type.
    (C) The tension bubble is the safest for sport arenas.
    (D) Baseball will be the next game to come under dome enclosure.

36. (A) That the bubble-dome idea be abandoned
    (B) That the use of domes be expanded to include tennis and softball
    (C) That U.S. driving-range owners go to London and Stockholm to see golfing bubbles in operation
    (D) That schools enclose their playing fields and courts

37. (A) The work of the Suncoast Seabird Sanctuary
    (B) The need for fishermen to be careful with hooks and lines
    (C) The dangers of environmental pollution
    (D) The right way to handle an injured bird

38. (A) To keep cats indoors so they won't injure birds
    (B) To rescue any injured birds they see
    (C) To visit the sanctuary
    (D) To support the work of the sanctuary

39. (A) Maine
    (B) Louisiana
    (C) California
    (D) Florida

40. (A) An amazing number of birds are injured every day.
    (B) Birds that have recovered should be released to the wild.
    (C) Permanently injured birds should be put to death to save the cost of feeding them.
    (D) The Suncoast Seabird Sanctuary performs a humane function and is worthy of support.

Answer Key

PART A	PART B	PART C
1. A	16. B	31. A
2. D	17. C	32. D
3. C	18. C	33. B
4. B	19. A	34. B
5. A	20. B	35. A
6. A	21. A	36. B
7. B	22. C	37. A
8. D	23. A	38. D
9. B	24. D	39. D
10. C	25. B	40. C
11. D	26. D	
12. D	27. A	
13. A	28. C	
14. A	29. C	
15. D	30. D	

TEST OF COMMUNICATION SKILLS: DESCRIPTION, REVIEW, PRACTICE

Reading

The Reading section of the Test of Communication Skills contains 30 multiple-choice questions that assess the following skills in relation to written material:

- Ability to understand

  The approximately 15 questions covering this ability area, the ability to understand the explicit content of a passage, will ask about the following:
  1. Main idea
  2. Supporting ideas or details
  3. Relationships among ideas
  4. Recognition of a summary or paraphrase of what was stated in the passage

- Ability to analyze

  The approximately 10 questions covering this ability area will ask about the following:
  1. The author's purpose
  2. The author's assumptions
  3. The author's tone or attitude toward the subject discussed
  4. Inferences from, or implications of, the passage
  5. Fact vs. author's opinion in the passage
  6. Organization of the passage or statement
  7. Application of elements in the passage (ways in which elements can be applied to other situations)

- Ability to evaluate

  The approximately 5 questions on this ability area will ask about the following:
  1. Emotional or manipulative aspects of the passage or statement
  2. Strengths and/or weaknesses of the author's argument
  3. Relevance and/or appropriateness of supporting evidence used by the author to bolster his or her arguments
  4. Relation of the passage or statement to the intended audience

The questions in this section are based on three types of passages: brief statements of one or more sentences; short passages of about 100 words; and long passages of about 200 words. Generally, about 8–10 questions are based on the brief statements, with one question per statement; about 8–10 are on the short passages, with 2 or 3 questions based on a passage; about 11–13 are on the long passages, with 4 to 6 questions on a passage. The passages reflect a variety of writing styles, levels of difficulty, and subject matter. At least one passage is on a technical or scientific topic. About 60 percent of the passages are on education-related topics. All questions can be answered on the basis of the information in the passage. This is a test to measure your reading skills, not factual knowledge.

The Diagnostic Practice Test later in this section and the two Model Tests in Part IV will help you become familiar with the format, style, and content of these questions.

Preparing for the Reading Section

The best way to obtain proficiency in reading is by reading newspapers, magazines, journals, and books of all kinds. As you read, you will develop speed, stamina, and the ability to comprehend the printed page. You have probably read many articles in magazines and journals, as well as many books and textbooks, in the course of your studies. However, in the time you have before the test date, it would be wise to read as much as

READING

you can and to read as many different types of works written on a level appropriate for this exam. As you read, practice reading for comprehension and speed.

Use the many reading questions in this book to give you practice answering this type of question.

Strategies for Answering Reading Questions

1. Answer all the questions on one passage before going on to the next passage. If you do not know the answer to one of the questions, guess, but circle the question so that you can come back to it later if there is time.
2. Use the practice questions in this book to determine whether you do better when you scan the questions before reading the passage. Take one of the model tests in this book using this method. Answer the reading questions in the other model test by reading the passage before looking at the questions. Some people do better on reading comprehension questions when they use the question scanning method and some do better when they just read the passage. Determining which method is better for you now, before you take the test, will improve your chances of achieving a high score.
3. Answer the question based on what is stated or implied in the passage; do not use outside knowledge. This is important to remember since some of the choices may be accurate statements of fact, but not the correct answer to the question.
4. When asked to choose the main idea, watch out for choices that are too specific or too broad. The correct choice should be neither too broad nor too narrow in its scope; it should be specific and yet comprehensive enough to include all the essential ideas presented in the passage.
5. When asked about specific details in the passage, spot key words in the question (the answer choices as well as the stem) and scan the passage to find them (or their synonyms). Then, reread that part of the passage carefully to try to determine the correct answer. Note, however, that the test-writers sometimes use the original wording of the passage in an answer choice to mislead you into thinking that that answer choice is correct.

Reading Exercise

Read each of the following articles, and then answer as many of the questions below as you can (not all questions apply to both articles):

I. Comprehension
   A. What is the *main idea*?
   B. What *details* does the writer use? *Examples*? *Special* or *key words* or *phrases*? *Supporting ideas*?
   C. Are any *relationships* shown by means of sequence of ideas, or cause-and-effect facts and explanations?
   D. How would you *paraphrase* or *summarize* the key elements in the passage?
II. Analysis
   A. What was the writer's *purpose*?
   B. What *assumptions* does the author make?
   C. What is the author's tone or attitude toward the subject discussed?
   D. What are the *implications* of the passage?
   E. What *inferences* can be drawn from the passage?
   F. Do you find any *opinion*, not based on fact, in the passage?
   G. How is the passage *organized*?

H. How correct and effective is the *language*?
I. Can anyone *apply* the information given in the passage?
III. Evaluation
A. Does the author appeal to your *emotions*? Do you feel manipulated by the writer?
B. What are the strengths and/or weaknesses of the writer's *arguments*?
C. How relevant is the *supporting evidence* to the main premise?
D. Is the message intended for a particular or a general *audience*?

HOW SAFE ARE ROBOTS?

Just as people are becoming used to the idea of robots working in industry, the home, the hospital, or the school, safety engineers are raising questions about the possible results of malfunction.

Robots are programmed to do certain tasks and will respond correctly as long as machine parts do not malfunction. Robots can move up or down and go in any direction. Unfortunately, the machine cannot distinguish a human being from an object, and it will deal the way it was programmed to do with anything that is in a certain spot. Therefore most of the 7000 robots now in use in industry are operated behind barriers. Programmers and maintenance people, however, have to work some of the time in these areas.

Most robots are stationary machines with a 9- or 10-foot reach. They do such jobs as spot welding, painting, tool changing, and inspecting. Smaller robots have been tested for use in the home. Robots can mow the lawn, guard the house, or baby sit, by responding to movement across a beam of light. As yet, they cannot serve a meal, do the dishes, or wash windows, but engineers are working on developing more flexible "hands and fingers," improved "vision," and greater speed of movement.

By 1990 it is estimated that there will be 50,000 to 100,000 robots in use, according to the Upjohn Institute for Employment Research in Kalamazoo. It is predicted that additional hazards will arise because of linkages, exposed motors, uncovered nuts, or loose nuts, hoses, or cables.

Research by Hadi Akeel, chief engineer with GMF Robotics, a robot manufacturer, indicates that robots can injure people and damage property unless additional safety devices are built in. Akeel recommends certification by the Underwriters Laboratories and Factory Mutual Engineering Corporation for product safety.

In January 1983 a 16-member safety committee was formed to develop a set of guidelines and to study the potential safety hazards. Kenneth Lauck, a safety administrator for General Motors Corporation, is the committee chairman.

Some of the suggested safety requirements will be costly, but as the use of robots increases, safety will become a matter of significant concern. Therefore it is time that safety guidelines for the manufacture and use of robots be developed.

HIGHER GAS MILEAGE—WHY NOT?

There are about 130 million registered private motor vehicles in the United States; this is nearly one for every adult. In 1980 these vehicles consumed about one half of the U. S. oil imports daily—almost 5.5 million gallons of gasoline.

Automotive engineers frequently report that fuel-efficient cars, capable of up to 100 miles per gallon, can be built. Then why has the industry held back production of such fuel-saving automobiles?

A well-known private-contract research firm, Battelle Memorial Institute of Columbus, Ohio, reported that fuel economy can be achieved by using transmissions with wide-range gear ratios, flywheels that store and redeliver energy lost through braking, and very lightweight structural materials. The Institute actually drew plans for a 100-mpg personal transportation ("Pertran") car. Thus far the Institute can't find anyone to manufacture it!

General Motors has designed its own 95-mpg prototype, the TPC. However, this "two-passenger commuter" car is not likely to be produced in the near future, if ever. To cut down on aerodynamic drag, the TPC has windows that won't roll down. How many consumers would buy a car with that kind of inconvenience?

The fact is that American buyers, no longer concerned about gasoline shortages or high prices, are purchasing more luxury automobiles. If the small, fuel-efficient cars described above were built, they could not be marketed widely at the present time.

If economy is the main consideration, one needs to compare the cost of the fuel-efficient models with other ones. The cost of driving a car for a lifetime of 100,000 miles at 25 mpg is $6000 at present gasoline costs. However, the sticker price of a car might be raised by as much as $1500 if it were made smaller and more fuel efficient. Moreover, many people sell their cars before the full lifetime is reached, so a relatively small saving per gallon of gasoline purchased does not mean that much real economy. Therefore millions of drivers find little incentive to buy small, fuel-efficient models as long as there is plenty of gasoline at an affordable price, and sporty cars with powerful engines are available.

Although buying foreign oil threatens the nation's economy by upsetting the balance of payments, links the United States to somewhat unpredictable governments, and stimulates inflation, millions of car buyers are not yet convinced of the need to purchase smaller automobiles.

Unless the government adds taxes on big cars, or raises the mileage standards, which politicians do not want to do, there is little urgency to change the purchasing habits of American automobile owners. Thus manufacturers must continue to build cars for the fickle marketplace rather than according to advanced technology.

Diagnostic Practice Test—Reading

Directions: Read carefully each statement or passage, and the question(s) and/or incomplete statement(s) that follow it. Then choose from the five choices the best answer or completion for each question or incomplete statement, and fill in the corresponding space completely. Base your answers on what is *stated* or *implied* in the statement or passage, not on any outside knowledge you may possess.

Questions 1–2

Since dogs were domesticated some 8000 years ago, they have undergone most of the cultural and environmental changes that have affected their owners. Since they have shorter lives, however, dogs have gone through some 4000 generations, whereas human beings have gone through about 400. By studying the dog, we can get some idea of the future of mankind. The dog can serve as a genetic pilot for understanding the adaptability of the human race to changing social and environmental conditions.

1. What main point is the author making in this passage?
   (A) Dogs and people have similar life spans.
   (B) Dogs suffer from physical neglect.
   (C) Dogs find it difficult to adapt to environmental changes.
   (D) Dogs and people undergo similar cultural and environmental changes in a particular society.
   (E) Children and dogs have more in common than adults and dogs.

TEST OF COMMUNICATION SKILLS: DESCRIPTION, REVIEW, PRACTICE

2. What assumption does the author make about dogs and human beings?
   (A) Neither species can be studied adequately in isolation of the other.
   (B) The stresses of a particular environment and civilization affect dogs and people in similar ways.
   (C) Comparison studies would not be relevant because owners affect the personalities of their pets.
   (D) Different results would be obtained from the dogs if they lived with different people.
   (E) Dogs have a shorter life span; several dogs live with the same family at different times.

3. If you buy a used car "as is" off the lot, without a written warranty, the dealer will have no further responsibility. If anything goes wrong with the car, even if this happens only a few days later, you will have to pay for the repairs.

   What advice is inherent in this statement?
   (A) Always buy a new car.
   (B) If you buy a used car, be sure to get a written warranty.
   (C) Before you buy a used car, take an auto repair course.
   (D) Buy a used car only from someone you know.
   (E) Before you buy a used car, have a friend or relative check it out.

4. From 1970 to 1980 the number of retired people migrating from Florida to New York was more than double the number for the previous decade. These people, relocating in New York, New Jersey, Pennsylvania, and Ohio, tend to be older, poorer, and more likely to be widowed than those moving in the opposite direction.

   From this statement it can be inferred that
   (A) these people did not like life in Florida
   (B) these people think their chances of remarrying are better in the North than in Florida
   (C) Florida encourages people to move back north when they get older
   (D) the number of people moving north will continue to be double the number moving south
   (E) the northern cities to which these people are moving must prepare to provide support services for them

5. The first half of the nineteenth century was the period of great historical finds. Historians interpreted old documents and published many medieval chronicles and charters. Many of these influential writings were based on false interpretations of events, but in political circles the only truth is what people believe.

   According to the passage, which of the following statements is true?
   (A) People do not believe what they read.
   (B) People resist political manipulation.
   (C) The general public pays little attention to the interpretations of history.
   (D) All historians do extensive research before writing.
   (E) Historians sometimes make faulty interpretations that affect future societal development.

Questions 6–7

After a 20-year decline, in 1982 there was an increase in the scores of college-bound seniors on the Scholastic Aptitude Test (SAT). This change was due primarily to im-

READING

provements in minority-group scores. This gain from 1981 to 1982 in minority scores was greater than the overall national gain. The largest gain was made by black students, whose verbal scores rose 9 points and mathematical scores 4 points, as compared to a 2-point gain in verbal scores and no gain in mathematical scores for the white majority. Increased access to quality education, with an emphasis on achievement, contributed to these results.

6. According to the author of this passage, which of the following is true?
   (A) There has been a constant and continuing decline in SAT scores.
   (B) White students continue to improve their scores more than black students.
   (C) From 1981 to 1982 the largest gains in scores were made by black students.
   (D) The scores of minority groups reduced the national average.
   (E) By 1982 the scores of white students had increased 9 points on the verbal test and 0 on the mathematics test.

7. In this passage, the author is assuming that
   (A) the attitudes of teachers and students toward learning influence achievement on the SAT
   (B) the quality of education has little effect on the performance of students
   (C) SAT scores are not important for success in college
   (D) SAT questions are geared toward the interests of minority-group students
   (E) there is a decline in the number of minority-group students planning to attend college

8. When you move from certain high-risk states, you can become a carrier of gypsy moths. The eggs of the moth can be carried on such articles as toys, camping gear, yard furniture, roofing, and lumber. New federal regulations require inspection of such articles in interstate moves.

   The primary purpose of this passage is to
   (A) urge people to be on the lookout for gypsy moths
   (B) identify insects that carry disease
   (C) make people aware of the federal regulation about gypsy moths
   (D) persuade people not to move to gypsy-moth-infested states
   (E) get people to keep toys, lawn furniture, and similar items inside

9. In England, Germany, and some other European countries fewer than 20% of students are selected, on the basis of academic talent, to go on to high school. In the United States, on the contrary, all students are encouraged to continue their education.

   If this statement is assumed to be true, then which of the following must also be true?
   (A) On average, European young people are smarter than American young people.
   (B) High school seniors in the United States are not likely to score as high on achievement tests as their carefully screened counterparts in England and Germany.
   (C) The United States should also adopt a screening policy for high school entrance.
   (D) In England and Germany fewer than 20% of young people are literate.
   (E) Our top 10% of high school seniors do better on achievement tests than their English and German counterparts.

133

TEST OF COMMUNICATION SKILLS: DESCRIPTION, REVIEW, PRACTICE

Questions 10–11

If the supervisors pass the proposed budget, taxes will rise by about $75 for every family in the county. The local paper has campaigned for the reduction or, hopefully, elimination of "no-show" jobs from the county payroll, but it's not hard to guess what will happen to that idea. Light work for the faithful, or no work at all—that's what makes the political machine run. And all those extra bodies are what makes our taxes go up—and up and up. So start planning how you can supply that extra $75 a year to enable some party hack to sit in the sun.

10. Which of the following adjectives best describes the general tone of the passage?
    (A) Sardonic
    (B) Pleased
    (C) Jocular
    (D) Objective
    (E) Fearful

11. Which of the following inferences regarding the author can be drawn from the passage?
    (A) He has little faith in democracy.
    (B) He will find it hard to pay the extra $75 in taxes.
    (C) He is a member of the political party in power.
    (D) He is jealous of the people who hold "no-show" jobs.
    (E) He sees little hope of reforming the county government.

Questions 12–13

According to the critic Sorokin, Greek architecture was mainly ideational until the fifth century B.C. An example of the ideational style was the Doric form with its simple details, modest size, and sparse exterior sculptural ornamentation. The Parthenon at Athens is an example of another style, the Ionic. The Parthenon demonstrates the use of harmony and architectural proportion to achieve a balance between other worldliness and visual beauty. The sensate period from the fourth century B.C. to the fourth century A.D. was characterized by "visual" emphasis on large size, ornamentation, costly magnificence, the use of illusion techniques, and a mixture of architectural styles. The Greek Corinthian form and the Roman style in the Arch of Titus are good illustrations of the visual emphasis of the period.

12. According to the passage, the most ornate style of architecture developed in
    (A) the fifth century A.D.
    (B) the Renaissance
    (C) the Middle Ages
    (D) the sensate period
    (E) the ideational period

13. The author of the passage would agree with which of the following statements?
    (A) The emphasis in architecture is different in different periods.
    (B) In general, art changes little over the centuries.
    (C) Particular architectural styles are exclusive to different periods in all cultures.
    (D) Every period has had a dominant ideational style.
    (E) Religion has had little impact on art.

Questions 14–16

The Special Olympic games were started in 1968 by the Joseph P. Kennedy, Jr., Foundation. This is an international program of sports and competition for mentally

READING

handicapped children from age 8 up and adults. At the 1983 Special Olympics, more than 4300 athletes from 50 nations and each state participated in 13 individual and team sports. The purpose of the program is to build a more positive self-image. The program aids parents through workshops and enlists volunteers who assist the participants as they test themselves with courage and sportsmanship to gain partial victory over their handicaps. In these Olympics everyone is a winner; each athlete receives a ribbon or a medal and everyone attends the victory banquet.

14. Which of the following would be the best title for this passage?
    (A) The Work of the Kennedy Foundation
    (B) A Very Special Memorial to J.F.K.
    (C) Olympic Games for Special People
    (D) Volunteers for Athletics
    (E) Self-Help for the Physically Handicapped

15. How many political units were represented at the 1983 Special Olympics?
    (A) 50
    (B) 100
    (C) 1000
    (D) 2000
    (E) 4300

16. The author of this passage would be most likely to DISAGREE with which of the following statements?
    (A) Athletes of all ages can get along under supervision.
    (B) Parents play an important role in child development.
    (C) Competition tends to damage the self-image of the handicapped child or adult.
    (D) Self-testing is beneficial in the right environment.
    (E) Athletics furnish a good program for year-round development.

Questions 17–19

One teacher of reading improved the interest level of her pupils by leading discussions on movies that they had seen. As might have been expected, *E.T.* was their favorite. To discuss the movie critically, questions were asked about the main characters, the main events, the problems that had to be solved, and the visual images that the movie-makers had utilized. Children had to stay on track by retelling the story in correct sequence. After *E.T.*, they enthusiastically discussed *The Return of the Jedi*. The unbelievable had happened—reading class was fun!

17. The main purpose of the author of this passage is
    (A) to show how reading can be related to everyday experiences such as movie-going
    (B) to criticize conventional methods of teaching reading
    (C) to point up the inadequacies of reading materials
    (D) to show that movie attendance detracts from reading
    (E) to persuade parents to send children to movies more often

18. The author wrote this passage primarily for
    (A) children
    (B) parents
    (C) elementary-school teachers
    (D) film producers
    (E) remedial-reading teachers in open-admission colleges

135

19. The passage implies that discussion of movies can contribute to reading improvement because
    (A) most children like science fiction
    (B) most children don't like to read
    (C) many children get discouraged in reading class
    (D) children can apply the same techniques to reading materials
    (E) many children find classroom reading materials too easy

Questions 20–24

Dr. Pinin Brambilla Barcilon is doing the seventh restoration of Leonardo da Vinci's *Last Supper*. The restoration is being done very slowly and carefully in a small monastery where the Renaissance artist lived for three years. Da Vinci was a deliberate and meticulous artist who worked from sunrise to sundown, then took a few days off to criticize his work. In 1494 he painted the *Last Supper* on a brick wall that was subject to temperature changes. The calcium carbonate primer failed to anchor his paint securely to the brick wall. The restoration has always been a difficult task. Former restorers repainted the work in dark tones and covered it with glue and wax to anchor the pigment. Some of the harsh solvents destroyed da Vinci's paint. Although his detailed work is almost entirely lost, the present restoration shows some of the luminosity, the design coherence, and the expressiveness of the characters, as verified by sketches he made. Dr. Barcilon uses a 40-power magnifying X-ray machine, a paintbrush, and a scalpel; it takes her a week to clean an area the size of a postage stamp as she seeks the artist's brushstrokes.

20. This account of the restoration of a painting can be characterized as
    (A) subjective   (D) discursive
    (B) argumentative   (E) explanatory
    (C) narrative

21. According to the passage, Dr. Barcilon's restoration of da Vinci's *Last Supper*
    (A) is the first to be done
    (B) is assisted by a powerful magnifying agent
    (C) is facilitated by the skill of previous restorers
    (D) is proceeding more quickly than originally expected
    (E) will be an extremely costly undertaking

22. All of the following factors have contributed to the difficulty of Dr. Barcilon's task EXCEPT
    (A) repainting in dark tones by previous restorers
    (B) earlier applications of glue and wax
    (C) use of harsh solvents
    (D) loss of details in the painting
    (E) lack of information as to how the original painting looked

23. From the passage it can be inferred that
    (A) the *Last Supper* is considered valuable enough to justify any expenditure of time and money to restore it
    (B) Da Vinci joined a religious order in his last years
    (C) the art of restoration reached its peak in the nineteenth century and has declined ever since

READING

    (D) Dr. Barcilon has to do a great deal of skilled guessing as to where brushstrokes should go
    (E) this restoration of the *Last Supper* must be a good one because it will be the last one

24. From the passage we can conclude that the author
    (A) is skilled in art restoration
    (B) has done research on art and art restoration
    (C) has assisted Dr. Barcilon
    (D) lives near the monastery where Dr. Barcilon works
    (E) is an expert on the chemistry of paints and solvents

Questions 25–30

In 1933, when the Museum of Science and Industry opened its doors to celebrate human progress, Chicago and the rest of the nation were in the fourth year of the Great Depression. Only 1000 people visited the museum daily, even with free admission. By comparison, a half century later, the museum has 4 million visitors annually. This attendance is exceeded only by that for the National Air and Space Museum in Washington, America's most frequently visited museum. The Chicago museum covers 14 acres and has exhibits representing 75 major fields and industries. Visitors can descend into a coal mine and ride a hoist and rickety electric cars around the shaft, which has real coal from southern Illinois. They can also view spacecraft or a dollhouse, attend a puppet opera, or walk through "The World of Hardwoods." A model railroad occupying 3000 feet of floor space has 1000 feet of track and 40 switches to operate. One of the most appealing features of the museum is the opportunity for "hands-on" experiences. There are buttons to push, and cranks and levers to manipulate. Computers are used to help people learn about money, diets, and—computers. Everyone will find something appealing and educational at the museum.

25. The primary purpose of the passage is to
    (A) compare the museum to other museums
    (B) encourage school field trips
    (C) interest the general public in visiting the museum
    (D) show still another application of computers
    (E) discuss the need for museums in general

26. The passage is developed chiefly by the use of
    (a) anecdotes
    (B) details
    (C) comparisons and contrasts
    (D) cause and effect
    (E) definitions of terms used

27. In 50 years annual attendance at the museum increased by
    (A) less than 3 million visitors
    (B) less than 3.5 million visitors
    (C) exactly 3.5 million visitors
    (D) more than 3.6 million visitors
    (E) more than 3.75 million visitors

28. Visitors to the museum can do all of the following EXCEPT
    (A) descend into a coal mine
    (B) view a dollhouse
    (C) ride in a spacecraft
    (D) attend a puppet opera
    (E) see a model railroad with 1000 feet of track

29. Which of the following is an unstated assumption by the author of the passage?
    (A) All families enjoy going to museums.
    (B) No other museums have equally appealing exhibits.
    (C) Most people enjoy "hands-on" experiences.
    (D) Teachers helped to plan the educational exhibits.
    (E) The exhibits are changed frequently.

30. Superconductors are now being used by high-school students. In one experiment, students watch as a magnet floats away from a superconductor and hovers in the air above it.

    One inference that can be drawn from this statement is that
    (A) superconductors are a new discovery
    (B) high-school students invented superconductors
    (C) superconductors defy gravity
    (D) superconductors repel magnets
    (E) there are no practical uses for superconductors

Answer Key

1. D	7. A	13. A	19. D	25. C
2. B	8. C	14. C	20. E	26. B
3. B	9. B	15. B	21. B	27. D
4. E	10. A	16. C	22. E	28. C
5. E	11. E	17. A	23. A	29. C
6. C	12. D	18. C	24. B	30. D

Writing: Multiple-Choice

The 45 multiple-choice questions in the Writing section of the Test of Communication Skills assess examinees' knowledge of standard written English and their ability to use it correctly and effectively. A knowledge of formal grammatical terminology is not needed.

The Writing section has three parts.

- Part A consists of approximately 27 *usage questions* in which you have to find the error in the underlined sections of a sentence. You do not have to correct the sentence or explain what is wrong. The errors involve punctuation, capitalization, subject-verb agreement, verb form and tense, pronoun-antecedent agreement, parallel structure, diction, idiom, coordination, subordinations, correlation, comparison, adjective-adverb usage, and other conventions of standard written English. Some sentences contain no errors.
- Part B consists of approximately 9 *sentence correction questions* in which you will be given five different versions of the same sentence and you must choose the best one. These questions involve problems of coherence, word order, economy of statement, appropriateness of diction and choice of idiom, subordination of sentence elements, logical comparison, structure, and clarity of modification and pronoun reference. Many sentence correction questions present faults in the logic or the structure of a sentence.
- Part C, which is a fairly recent addition to the Writing test, consists of approximately 9 *questions involving appropriate composition strategies*. The questions relate to organization, appropriateness, and evaluation of evidence. You are given a passage and asked questions related to the organization of the sentences or paragraphs; the appropriateness of the language; and the evaluation of evidence, such as whether there are gaps in logic or a lack of discrimination between fact and opinion.

Preparing for the Multiple-Choice Writing Section

Use the review and many practice exercises that you will find later in this section to go over points of grammar, usage, diction, sentence structure, and other elements of standard written English.

Then, take the Diagnostic Practice Test at the end of this section to familiarize yourself with the different types of questions and to determine how much further study and practice you need. Use the Model Tests in Part IV for further practice.

Strategies for Answering the Multiple-Choice Writing Questions

1. Remember that, in usage questions, if the sentence contains an error, it involves the underlined words. Don't waste time looking for something wrong in the parts that are not underlined.
2. Look first for the common errors listed in the review that follows.
3. Use your ear for the language. Remember, you don't have to name the error, or be able to explain why it is wrong. All you have to do is recognize that something is wrong. If a word sounds wrong to you, it probably is, even if you don't know why.

TEST OF COMMUNICATION SKILLS: DESCRIPTION, REVIEW, PRACTICE

4. If you spot an error in the underlined section of a sentence correction question, eliminate any answer that repeats it.

5. In sentence corrections questions, if you don't see the error in the underlined section, look at the answer choices to see what is changed. The changes will tell you what kind of problem is being tested in this question.

Review

GRAMMAR AND SENTENCE STRUCTURE

Lack of agreement between subject and verb

A verb agrees in number with its subject. First, identify the subject word. Do not be misled by prepositional phrases or other groups of words between the subject and the verb.

Each of the teachers has been cited for superior performance.
The author of the two biographies and the three novels is my cousin.
There are in New York City approximately 1.5 million persons of Hispanic origin.
No one, including his parents or teachers, is able to control Kevin.
The two girls, not their mother, are responsible for their conduct.
The president, as well as three other board members, has threatened to resign.

If two subjects are connected by *and*, a plural verb is needed.
The boy and the girl are siblings.

Exception. If the compound subject names one person, thing, or idea, a singular verb is used.

The captain and star of the baseball team [one person] has an athletic scholarship.

If two singular subjects are connected by *or*, or *nor*, a singular verb is needed.
Neither Shelley nor her sister is to blame.
If *or* or *nor* connects a singular and a plural subject, the verb agrees with the nearer subject.
Either the dogs or the cat has destroyed this cushion.

A collective noun takes a singular verb when the group is thought of and a plural verb when the individuals are thought of.
The school board is working harmoniously this year.
The school board are unable to agree on which elementary school should be closed.

The plurals of *datum*, *criterion*, and *phenomenon* are *data*, *criteria*, and *phenomena*, respectively. When used as subjects, these plurals require plural verbs.
The data were collected by volunteers.
Two criteria were used for selection.
These phenomena are puzzling to astronomers.

WRITING: MULTIPLE-CHOICE

When *who* or *that* is the subject of an adjective clause, it agrees in number with its antecedent, and accordingly takes either a singular or a plural verb.

She is a person who is easily misled [*person*, the antecedent of *who*, is singular].

This is one of the difficulties that have beset every pioneer [*difficulties*, the antecedent of *that*, is plural].

Wrong tense

The past tense is used for past time.
The satellite, which was launched at 10 o'clock, went into orbit shortly thereafter.

The present perfect tense is used if a particular action is completed in the present time or if its consequences extend to the present time.
Has the speaker arrived yet?
For two centuries Americans have been inspired by the words "All men are created equal."

The past perfect tense is used if a particular action occurred before some other past action.
The teacher said that she had warned Robert three times about his disruptive behavior [the "warning" occurred before the "saying"].

The present tense is used to express something that is always true.
Copernicus said that the sun is the center of the universe.

Wrong mood

The subjunctive mood is preferred for (1) a wish and (2) a condition (an *if* clause) that is untrue.
The principal wished she were anywhere but in her office.
If I were you, I'd take a leave of absence.

Other wrong verb forms

Memorize the following, and study the examples of the correct use of these troublesome verbs:

present tense	*past tense*
sit ("have a seat"); never takes an object	sat
set ("place")	set
lie ("recline" or "rest"); never takes an object	lay
lay ("put down" or "place")	laid
rise ("go up" or "get up"); never takes an object	rose
raise ("elevate")	raised

When I am tired, I sit down to rest.
Since I was tired, I sat down to rest.

TEST OF COMMUNICATION SKILLS: DESCRIPTION, REVIEW, PRACTICE

When I come down in the morning, I <u>set</u> the kettle on the stove.
When I came home yesterday, I <u>set</u> the cake on the table.

Don't disturb me when I <u>lie</u> down on my bed.
After I had finished the dusting, I <u>lay</u> down for a nap.

<u>Lay</u> the book on the shelf.
Yesterday I <u>laid</u> the book on the shelf.

The tradition is that Americans <u>rise</u> when "The Star-Spangled Banner" is played.
When Crenshaw reached the eighteenth green, the spectators <u>rose</u> to applaud him.

<u>Raise</u> your right hand and swear allegiance.
The king <u>raised</u> the old woman to her feet.

Note these other correct verb forms:
She <u>ought not</u> to take the examination [*not* "hadn't ought"].
Luke <u>must have gone</u> with the other group [*not* "must of gone"].

Lack of agreement between pronoun and antecedent

A pronoun agrees in number with its antecedent.
Each of the women agreed to contribute a percentage of <u>her</u> salary.
Not one of the boys returned <u>his</u> uniform.

Wrong case of pronouns

A pronoun used as (1) a subject or (2) a predicate nominative is in the nominative case.
(1) Did <u>you</u> and <u>she</u> understand the speech?
   <u>Who</u> was chosen to head the committee?
   Chris is the one <u>who</u> wrote to me.
   I will speak to <u>whoever</u> answers the telephone.
(2) The committee members are <u>he</u>, <u>she</u>, and <u>I</u>.

A pronoun used as (1) a direct object of a verb, (2) an indirect object, or (3) the object of a preposition is in the objective case.
(1) The chairman praised <u>them</u> and <u>me</u>.
   <u>Whom</u> did you nominate?
   Sarah is the person <u>whom</u> I saw at the game.
(2) Give <u>her</u> and <u>him</u> the help they need.
(3) The will divided the money between my brother and <u>me</u>.
   From <u>whom</u> did you bring this message?
   A hero is a person to <u>whom</u> one looks for inspiration.

Misuse of compound (reflexive) personal pronouns

The simple personal pronoun (e.g., *I, you*) is preferred to the compound personal pronoun (e.g., *myself, yourself*) as subject of a sentence.
My father, my sister, and <u>I</u> are going to the game.
Your family and <u>you</u> will be most welcome.

The incorrect forms *hisself* and *theirselves* should never be used.
The horse hurt <u>himself</u> when he fell.
The men saved <u>themselves</u> by jumping into the sea.

WRITING: MULTIPLE-CHOICE

Misuse of adjectives and adverbs

An adjective agrees in number with the noun it modifies.
Remember that *this* and *that* are singular and *these* and *those* (never use "them" as an adjective!) are plural.
Don't buy those cookies.
This kind of flowers is my favorite.

Faulty comparisons

When two persons or things are compared, the comparative ("-er") form is preferred.
Beth is the better of the two teachers.

When a comparison is made, the object under comparison should be excluded from the group.
The Sahara has higher sand dunes than any other desert.
Louis is more talented musically than any other freshman.

Double comparisons are incorrect.
This book seems funnier (*not* "more funnier") every time I read it.

All the words needed to make a comparison must be included.
Mr. Larkin is as tall as my father, or taller (*not* "as tall or taller than my father").
The birds in Busch Gardens in Tampa are more spectacular than those in our local zoo.

Misuse of correlative expressions

Correlative expressions (*both . . . and, either . . . or, neither . . . nor, not only . . . but also*) are used in pairs. Each conjunction should be placed just before the word(s) it connects.
Both Anne and I have accepted the invitation.
Either the dog or the cat is the culprit.
Tricia showed interest in neither music nor art.
This argument appeals not only to the parents but also to the community at large.

Incomplete sentence

A sentence has a subject and a predicate and makes complete sense when standing alone. In the following sentences the italicized portions cannot stand alone as sentences because they (1) have no verb, (2) have only *-ing* words by themselves, instead of complete predicate verbs, or (3) are subordinate, rather than principal, clauses.
(1) In my senior year I made several good friends, *especially the other three girls in my dormitory suite.*
(2) I will never forget what I saw when I looked in the window—*the old man dozing in his chair and the murderer creeping toward him with a knife.*
(3) Amy showed courage when she defended Billy from his abusive father, *and when she finally left her husband and made a home for herself and her son.*

Run-on sentences

Every sentence should begin with a capital and end with a period. Sentences should not be strung together with commas, but two fairly short, closely related clauses may be joined by a semicolon.

TEST OF COMMUNICATION SKILLS: DESCRIPTION, REVIEW, PRACTICE

At age 14 Donald began to use drugs. This was the beginning of a downward spiral that lasted for 6 years.

To err is human; to forgive is divine.

Failure to use subordination

The coordinate conjunctions *and* and *but* properly connect clauses that are related in thought and equal in importance. In other cases the use of subordinate clauses introduced by appropriate conjunctions (e.g., *after, although, because, before, since, unless, until, when, whenever, where*) **helps to clarify meaning and indicate the relative importance of ideas.** Try changing each of the following complex sentences into a compound sentence with the clauses joined by *and* or *but*, and note how the relationship of ideas becomes obscured and the sentence less effective.

My nephew, who is the shortest boy in his class, is trying out for the cross-country team.

After I went to bed for the night, I heard a loud crash in the kitchen.

Although Mark had won first prize in the essay contest, his parents seemed indifferent to his achievement.

When Lee had finished grading the papers, he entered the marks in his record book and went to bed.

Double negative

Double negatives change the intended meaning and must be avoided. Do not use negative forms with such words as *hardly, scarcely, only*, and *but* when it means "only."

The principal *didn't say anything* about the incident.

I *received no* pay for my day's work.

Yvonne *could scarcely hear* the teacher.

There *is but* one answer to that question.

Do not water the lawn too much *or* [*not* "nor"] cut the grass too short.

Lack of parallel structure

The conjunction *and* properly connects like grammatical elements, such as (1) two nouns, (2) two verbs, (3) two participles, gerunds, or infinitives, or (4) two clauses.

(1) Jane greeted her little pupils with *kindness* and *courtesy*.
(2) The audience *stamped* and *roared* in approval.
(3) Dr. Forman likes *to hunt* and *to fish* [two infinitives].
(4) Juan decided *that he would accept the invitation* and *that he would make a great effort to mingle and to make some new acquaintances.*

Dangling participle

A participle should be clearly attached to the word it modifies. There are three ways to correct a dangling participle: (1) get rid of the participle, (2) put into the sentence some word for it to modify, and (3) place it near the word it modifies. The following sentence can be corrected in either of the first two ways: "Walking on the beach, an unusual shell caught my eye."

(1) As I was walking [predicate verb, *not* participle] on the beach, an unusual shell caught my eye.
(2) Walking on the beach, I saw an unusual shell.

The following sentence can be corrected in the third way mentioned above: "The old

WRITING: MULTIPLE-CHOICE

man sat on the curb in the busy city street with his few possessions lying on the pavement beside him mumbling an incoherent plea for help."

(3) The old man, mumbling an incoherent plea for help, sat on the curb in the busy city street with his few possessions lying on the pavement beside him.

Practice Exercise

Five of the following sentences are correct. First identify these five, and write C next to the number of each one on a piece of paper. Then rewrite the other sentences correctly.

1. This is one of the incidents that has aroused suspicion and fear in our neighborhood.

2. Each girl leaving the classroom placed their examination paper on the teacher's desk.

3. If I was President of this country, things would be different.

4. In 200 years the Constitution has been amended 26 times.

5. Clark decided not only to major in mathematics but also Spanish.

6. The birds building their nests, the flowers coming up, and Joe beginning to think of Vera.

7. Steaming into the harbor, a large crowd waited on the pier to greet the ship.

8. Everyone, including my parents, grandparents, aunts, and uncles, were opposed to my plan.

9. The teacher's tense, anxious face was evidence of the problems that had beset her during the past six months.

10. Just between you and I, I don't understand this lesson.

11. My little sister seems to have more problems than any person I know.

12. Rosa was advised to file a complaint with the rent stabilization board and that she should put her rent money in an escrow fund.

13. Sometimes it seems as though life in New York is fraught with more hazards than any other city.

14. In the town of Wakulla Springs there isn't but one place for tourists to stay.

15. Neither the principal nor the teachers have agreed to the board's offer.

16. My family and myself are leaving for England on May 24.

17. Give the message to whoever comes to the door.

18. The phenomena reported in the last issue of the *Journal of Physics* was of particular interest to my uncle.

TEST OF COMMUNICATION SKILLS: DESCRIPTION, REVIEW, PRACTICE

19. I can't resist these kind of books, even though I know they're a waste of time.

20. Virginia couldn't decide what to do, she could discipline the unruly girls or she could ignore them and hope that they would stop of their own accord.

21. Just as I laid down to rest, the telephone rang and the neighbor's dog began to bark.

22. He is the man who I met under traumatic circumstances in the emergency room of our local hospital.

23. Mr. Lowry is a talented amateur artist, and last year he ran unsuccessfully for the school board.

24. Did every boy fill out his application correctly and hand it to the receptionist on the way out?

25. Dr. Dunne told me not to remove the bandage nor to use the hand for several days.

Answers

1. C

2. Each girl leaving the classroom placed her examination paper on the teacher's desk.

3. If I were President of this country, things would be different.

4. C

5. Clark decided to major not only in mathematics but also in Spanish. *Or* . . . to major in not only mathematics but also Spanish.

6. The birds were building their nests, the flowers were coming up, and Joe was beginning to think of Vera. *Or* Now that the birds were building their nests and the flowers were coming up, Joe was beginning to think of Vera.

7. Steaming into the harbor, the ship was greeted by a large crowd waiting on the pier. *Or* . . . As the ship steamed into the harbor, it was greeted by a large crowd waiting on the pier.

8. Everyone, including my parents, grandparents, aunts, and uncles, was opposed to my plan.

9. C

10. Just between you and me, I don't understand this lesson.

11. My little sister seems to have more problems than any other person I know.

12. Rosa was advised to file a complaint with the rent stabilization board and to put her rent money in an escrow fund.

WRITING: MULTIPLE-CHOICE

13. Sometimes it seems as though life in New York is fraught with more hazards than life in any other city.

14. In the town of Wakulla Springs there is but one place for tourists to stay.

15. C

16. My family and I are leaving for England on May 24.

17. C

18. The phenomena reported in the last issue of the *Journal of Physics* were of particular interest to my uncle. *Or* The phenomenon . . . was . . . .

19. I can't resist this kind of books, even though I know they're a waste of time.

20. Virginia couldn't decide what to do. She could discipline the unruly girls or she could ignore them and hope that they would stop of their own accord. *Or* . . . do; she . . . .

21. Just as I lay down to rest, the telephone rang and the neighbor's dog began to bark.

22. He is the man whom I met under traumatic circumstances in the emergency room of our local hospital.

23. Mr. Lowry, who is a talented amateur artist, ran unsuccessfully for the school board last year. *Or* Mr. Lowry, a talented amateur artist, ...

24. C

25. Dr. Dunne told me not to remove the bandage or to use the hand for several days.

DICTION, IDIOMS, AND MECHANICS

Redundancy

To be redundant is to use more words than are grammatically necessary to do the job, that is, to use words that serve no purpose in the sentence. In searching for redundancy, look with particular suspicion at pronouns, prepositions, and conjunctions.

The runner who wins the Boston Marathon he receives a great deal of publicity.
That noisy boy has just fallen off of the diving board.
Sabrina's day to receive visitors in the big, gloomy living room was on Wednesday.
Inside of the basket were six brightly colored Easter eggs.
The last speaker stated that, since the United States had dropped the first atom bomb, that this nation has a particular obligation to stop the nuclear arms race.

Idioms

Every language has picturesque or unusual forms of expression, called *idioms*, that add life and color to the language, but do not mean exactly what the meanings of the separate words would indicate.

TEST OF COMMUNICATION SKILLS: DESCRIPTION, REVIEW, PRACTICE

Here are some common idioms in the English language. What does the speaker mean in each instance?

The clock ran down.	(The clock stopped.)
Put out the light.	(Extinguish the light.)
He didn't have a red cent.	(He was very poor.)
in the long run	(over a period of time)
in hot water	(in difficulty)
in apple-pie order	(in good order)
in the black, paying its own way	(yielding a profit, lucrative)
by the same token	(similarly)
to strike a bargain	(to get something at a low price)
to come to grief	(to get into trouble)
to leave stranded	(to abandon)
to take by storm	(to surprise)
to be up in arms	(to be very angry)
to win one's spurs	(to achieve a goal)
to stand up for	(to champion)
to make a face	(to show disapproval)
to turn one's back on	(to abandon)
to be rotten to the core	(to be evil)
to eat humble pie	(to apologize or retract, usually under pressure)
to run its course	(to come to an end)
to put up with	(to endure, to tolerate)
to have what it takes	(to have the ability to succeed)
to eat one's words	(to renounce, to recant)
to hold in abomination	(to detest, to loathe, to abominate)
to do the disappearing act	(to abscond, to flee, to escape)
to take French leave, to skip out	(to escape, to flee)
to do dirt to	(to abuse, to betray)
to put up with	(to endure, to accept)
to go hand in hand	(to accompany)
to squirrel away	(to store up, to accumulate)
to laugh in one's sleeve	(to be slyly or cynically amused)
to run for office	(to be a candidate)
to hit it off with	(to agree with, to get on well with)
to reach for the stars	(to aim high)
to be all eyes and ears	(to be alert, wide-awake, vigilant)
to hold a brief for	(to encourage, to advocate)
ace in the hole, inside track	(advantage)
cup of tea	(something one likes or excels in)
slap in the face	(affront, insult)
enough and to spare	(abundance)
bed and board	(lodging and meals)
flash in the pan	(something that appears promising but turns out to be disappointing)
red-letter day	(very significant or important day)
month of Sundays	(long time)
once in a blue moon	(very infrequently)
frightened out of one's wits, in a blue funk	(apprehensive, afraid)

WRITING: MULTIPLE-CHOICE

Word Choice

accept, except. *Accept* is a verb meaning "to receive with consent." As a verb, *except* means "to leave out"; as a preposition, it means "excluding."

We *accept* the donation with thanks.

If you *except* the cost of heating and lighting, your budget will not reflect all your expenses.

Everyone *except* the parents approved of the field trip.

affect, effect. Except in a specialized sense in psychiatry, *affect* is always a verb, meaning "to influence." *Effect* may be either a verb meaning "to bring about" or a noun meaning "the result of an action or situation."

Arnold's defection *affected* the agency in a strange way.

The teacher *effected* a change in the attitude of the class toward handicapped people.

What was the *effect* of the salary increase on the teachers' morale?

amount, number. *Amount* refers to quantity and, as a rule, should not be used as a synonym for *number*.

A small *number* of children can consume a large *amount* of lemonade.

compare, contrast. To *compare* is to indicate similarities *and* differences; to *contrast* is to point out differences alone.

Compare the populations of New York City and Chicago [point out likenesses and differences].

Contrast the populations of New York City and Omaha [point out differences only].

credible, credulous, creditable. All are adjectives. *Credible* means "believable"; *credulous* means "believing" or "inclined to believe"; *creditable* means "worthy of belief or of praise."

Tom's account of the events on the camping trip is highly *credible*.

Miguel is very *credulous* where his girlfriend is concerned.

To the teacher's surprise Elise gave a *creditable* performance at the recital.

discover, invent. To *discover* is to find, for the first time, something that already exists; to *invent* is to produce something entirely new.

Columbus *discovered* several islands in the Caribbean Sea.

Benjamin Franklin *invented* bifocal spectacles.

due to, because of. The use of *due to* as a prepositional phrase meaning "because of" is recognized by Webster and is gaining widespread acceptance. In formal written English, however, *because of* is still preferred by some authorities.

Because of the unusually cold weather in January much of the orange crop was ruined.

fewer, less. *Fewer* is used for number; *less*, for quantity.

There are *fewer* pupils this year in the elementary schools than last year.

There is *less* soil pollution with this grade of fertilizer than with that one.

good, well. *Good* is an adjective and cannot be used to modify a verb. *Well* can be used either as (1) an adverb or (2) an adjective.

TEST OF COMMUNICATION SKILLS: DESCRIPTION, REVIEW, PRACTICE

It was a *good* day for swimming.
(1) Barbara reads very well for a six-year-old.
(2) Is your sister *well* ["healthy"]?
All is *well* ["satisfactory"] with her marriage.

hanged, hung. *Hanged* is used with reference to capital punishment; otherwise, *hung* is correct.

The murderer *was hanged* in the courtyard of the prison.
With great care the painting was *hung* above the fireplace.

imply, infer. An author or speaker *implies*, that is, "hints" or "insinuates." The reader or listener *infers*, that is, "draws a conclusion" from what is read or heard.

The coach implied that he did not want girls on the track team.
From the ending of the story, we infer that the couple remarried.

learn, teach. A student *learns*, that is, "acquires knowledge or skills." A teacher *teaches*, that is, "gives instruction."

Angelo *learned* to read before he entered kindergarten.
I asked her to *teach* me skydiving.

leave, let. To *leave* is "to go away from" or "to allow to remain." To *let* is "to allow" or "to permit."

I plan to *leave* on the early flight tomorrow.
Leave your test paper on the desk.
Let me do this for you.

like, as, as if, as though. *Like* is correctly used as a preposition. Its use as a conjunction is widespread, for example, in advertising, but to many authorities is not acceptable in written English. To avoid criticism use *as, as if,* or *as though* to introduce a clause.

Betsy looks *like* her mother.
Betsy does *as* her mother says.
The casserole tastes *as if* a master chef had concocted it.

majority, plurality. Let's assume that 300 votes are cast for president of the freshman class. Al, Bob, and Chris are candidates. If Al receives at least 151 votes, he has a *majority*, that is, more than half the votes cast. If, however, Al receives 125 votes, Bob receives 100 votes, and Chris receives 75 votes, Al has a *plurality*, that is, more votes than any other candidate, but *not* a majority.

oral, verbal. *Oral* means "in spoken words"; *verbal*, "in words (either spoken or written)."

In the absence of pen and paper let's make an *oral* agreement.
Rather than taking military action, the government sent a *verbal* protest.

principal, principle. As a noun, *principal* means "the head of a school"; as an adjective, it means "chief" or "main." A *principle* (noun) is "a law, doctrine, or rule of conduct."

The *principal* of Berry Lane School will retire next spring.
Miss Florio's *principal* worry is failure to be granted tenure.
As a knight, Sir Gawain upheld the *principles* to which he had sworn allegiance.

WRITING: MULTIPLE-CHOICE

respectfully, respectively. *Respectfully* means "with respect"; *respectively*, "in the order given."

Behave *respectfully* in a place of worship.
Al, Bob, and Chris received 125, 100, and 75 votes, *respectively*.

Practice Exercise

Complete each of the following sentences by selecting, from the choices given, the correct word to fill the blank:

1. Elsie received 150 of the 200 votes cast and therefore enjoyed a comfortable _____. (majority, plurality)

2. How will this ruling _____ your status? (affect, effect)

3. When my grandchild tells me anything, I am a very _____ listener. (credible, credulous)

4. Act _____ you know the answer. (as if, like)

5. The new judge swore to uphold the _____ of truth and justice. (principals, principles)

6. Trenton and Albany are the capitals of New Jersey and New York, _____. (respectfully, respectively)

7. The next speaker _____ that he favored the ERA. (implied, inferred)

8. Vinny did _____ on the algebra test. (good, well)

9. Alexander Graham Bell _____ the telephone. (discovered, invented)

10. _____ me the right way to swing a golf club. (Learn, Teach)

11. The _____ contract was upheld in court because two witnesses testified that they had heard it made. (oral, verbal)

12. The _____ denied indignantly that a drug problem existed in his school. (principal, principle)

13. The young man _____ petitioned the court for permission to visit his child. (respectfully, respectively)

14. A large _____ of visitors sign the guest book every year. (amount, number)

15. Fran and I have _____ his invitation to go skiing. (accepted, excepted)

16. Dr. Riley's casual attitude had a calming _____ on the frightened students. (affect, effect)

17. Mounting a stepladder, Claire _____ the living room drapes. (hanged, hung)

18. Annie Sullivan _____ Helen to communicate with her hands. (learned, taught)

TEST OF COMMUNICATION SKILLS: DESCRIPTION, REVIEW, PRACTICE

19. The _____ reason for going today is that I won't have the car tomorrow. (principal, principle)

20. Writing on parchment with a quill pen, the governor drew up the first _____ contract with the Indians. (oral, verbal)

21. In listing my assets, I _____ some stocks that had declined greatly in value and seemed destined to go even lower. (accepted, excepted)

22. I _____ from the introduction that this biography by the poet's wife is not strictly objective. (imply, infer)

23. _____ me take care of your plants while you're on vacation. (Leave, Let)

24. Over the years several scientists _____ various facts about electricity. (discovered, invented)

25. Did _____ pupils register for the course this semester? (fewer, less)

Answers

1. majority	6. respectively	11. oral	16. effect	21. excepted
2. affect	7. implied	12. principal	17. hung	22. infer
3. credulous	8. well	13. respectfully	18. taught	23. Let
4. as if	9. invented	14. number	19. principal	24. discovered
5. principles	10. Teach	15. accepted	20. verbal	25. fewer

Other Words Often Confused

1. already = previously

2. all ready = all are ready

3. altogether = entirely

4. all together = everyone or everything is in the same place

5. capital = a city; working assets

6. capitol = a building

7. coarse = rough

8. course = path; plan of action

9. desert (noun) = a dry area

10. desert (verb) = to leave

11. dessert = the last course of a meal, usually fruit or a sweet

WRITING: MULTIPLE-CHOICE

12. here = this place

13. hear = to perceive or learn through the ear

14. its = belonging to it

15. it's = it is

16. lead = to go first (present tense)

17. led = went first (past tense)

18. loss = the act or result of losing possession

19. loose = free, apart

20. piece = a part of something

21. peace = the opposite of war, tranquility

22. plain = a flat area of land; not fancy

23. plane = a tool or airplane; a flat surface

24. stationery = writing paper

25. stationary = not moving

26. there = that place

27. their = belonging to them

28. they're = they are

29. to = in the direction of, toward

30. too = also, in addition

31. two = 2, sum of two units, a pair

32. weather = local atmospheric conditions

33. whether = if, in the event of, in case

34. whose = belonging to whom

35. who's = who is

36. your = belonging to you

37. you're = you are

TEST OF COMMUNICATION SKILLS: DESCRIPTION, REVIEW, PRACTICE

Punctuation

Apostrophe

   Use an apostrophe to

   • take the place of an omitted letter or omitted letters in a contraction

Examples. wasn't, you're, I'll, I'm, who's, there's, o'clock

   • denote possession

Rules:

   a. Form the possessive of a singular noun by adding an apostrophe and an *s*.

Examples. the boy's sled, the child's desk, the monkey's tail, Burns's poems, Mr. Jones's house

Exceptions. conscience' admonition, righteousness' sake, Jesus' name, Moses' life, Demosthenes' speeches

   b. To form the possessive plural of a noun, first write the plural. (1) If the plural ends in *s*, as most plurals do, add only an apostrophe. (2) If the plural does not end in *s*, add an apostrophe and an *s*.

Examples. (1) the girls' lockers, the teachers' lounge, the Joneses' house; (2) the women's coats, the children's toys, the mice's tails

   c. For joint possession use only one apostrophe: Procter and Gamble's new product. If the possession is individual, however, each name must be in the possessive form: Annette's and Mike's tastes in music are very different.

   • express duration

Examples. one week's notice, three days' sick leave

   • indicate monetary worth

Example. a dime's worth of candy, five dollars' worth of gasoline

Brackets

Use brackets to enclose corrections, explanations, or comments that are inserted in a quoted sentence.

Example. "For his last record [*Songs to a Lost Love*] John won an award."

Colon

   Use a colon

   • after the salutation in a business letter

WRITING: MULTIPLE-CHOICE

Examples. Dear Sir: Gentlemen: Dear Mrs. Patrick:

- after *as follows* or *the following* to indicate a list of items

Example. Ranked in order, the most popular foods are as follows: hamburgers, ice cream, pizza, apple pie, and chocolate cake.

- before a formal statement

Example. This is the situation: The district is 1 million dollars in the red, and we cannot afford to hire more teachers or coaches at this time.

- in expressions of time, to separate the numbers

Examples. 12:30 P.M., 8:30 A.M.

- after the speaker's name in a dialog

Example. MR. BATES: Use the car as long as you like on Saturday.

Comma

Use a comma to

- set off responses like *yes* and *no* at the beginning of a sentence

Example. Yes, I agree that it is too cold to hold a class in that room.

- separate the items in a date or an address

Examples. Jason Robert was born on January 17, 1983, in Hartford.
I live at 25 Rock Street, Chicago, Illinois 60636.

- separate items in a series

Example. He started the car, shut the garage door, and then turned on the air conditioning.
You forgot the cereal, the bread, and the apples.

- set off a direct quotation

Example. She smiled warmly and said, "Welcome to our family, Maria. I'm glad you are going to marry our son."

- indicate thousands in a large number

Example. He won a prize of $100,000.

- set off words in direct address

Example. Welcome, dear friends, to our new home.

- separate the clauses in a compound sentence when the clauses are joined by a conjunction, unless the clauses are very short and closely related

TEST OF COMMUNICATION SKILLS: DESCRIPTION, REVIEW, PRACTICE

Example. Angry parents marched and demonstrated outside the high school, and a campaign of vilification began in the local newspaper.

- emphasize the contrast between two expressions connected by *not*

Example. He should have been given a medal, not a reprimand.

- set off an introductory adverbial clause or participial phrase

Example. Whenever Isabel could manage to sneak out on Thursday night, she went to choir practice.
Having tasted the cake, the boy ran out of the room.

- set off appositives

Example. Felicio, the class president, was given a scholarship.

- set off parenthetical expressions, that is, expressions that interrupt the main thought of a sentence

Example. This is, I think, the best class I have ever taught.

- set off nonrestrictive modifiers, that is, modifiers that give more information but are not essential to the original meaning

Examples. He takes the time, whenever he comes, to visit the kindergarten room.
I offered the parakeet a small piece of lettuce, which he eyed at first with great suspicion.

- prevent misreading

Example. Above, the helicopter hovered as it dropped lower and lower to pick up the frantic swimmer.

- follow the closing phrase of a letter

Examples. Sincerely yours,   Yours truly,

- separate a title or degree from a person's name

Examples. Andrew Clark, Esq.   Frederick J. Bradford, Ph.D.

Do *not* use a comma

- between a *subject* and its *verb*

Incorrect: The day after, was hot and dry.
                              x

- between an *adjective* and the *noun* it modifies

Incorrect: This was a long, confusing, difficult, test.
                                              x

- between a *verb* and its *complement*

Incorrect: She soon received, the reward she deserved.
⠀⠀⠀⠀⠀⠀⠀⠀⠀⠀⠀⠀⠀⠀⠀⠀⠀x

- before an *indirect quotation*

Incorrect: The man yelled, that the ladder was falling.
⠀⠀⠀⠀⠀⠀⠀⠀⠀⠀⠀⠀⠀⠀⠀x

- for commonly used or closely related *appositives*

Incorrect: He, himself, did the work.
⠀⠀⠀⠀⠀⠀⠀x⠀⠀⠀⠀⠀x

Incorrect: The poet, Frost, was a good speaker.
⠀⠀⠀⠀⠀⠀⠀⠀⠀⠀⠀⠀x⠀⠀⠀⠀x

Dash

Use a dash to

- indicate a significant break in the main thought

Example. Louise quickly made up her mind—a decision that surprised everyone—to become an astronaut.

- introduce a clause that summarizes preceding particulars

Example. Dirt, noise, heat, poverty, and crime—those were my impressions after three days in the city that July.

Exclamation point

Use an exclamation point to show strong or sudden emotion.

Examples. "Ouch!" he screamed in agony. "Your dog bit my ankle!"
⠀⠀⠀⠀⠀⠀⠀⠀Out, out! Get out and stay out!
⠀⠀⠀⠀⠀⠀⠀⠀Oh, what a horrible movie!
⠀⠀⠀⠀⠀⠀⠀⠀Hurray! The Islanders won again!

Caution. Avoid overuse of the exclamation point. In particular, never use more than one exclamation point at the end of a sentence, thereby suggesting hysteria. If exclamation points are used sparingly throughout, one will do the job when it is really needed.

Hyphen

Use the hyphen to

- divide, between two syllables, a word that will not otherwise fit at the end of a line

Example. It is a growing problem, a diffi-
⠀⠀⠀⠀⠀⠀⠀cult situation that could bring ruin to many people.

Exception. Do not divide the word before or after a single-letter syllable.

- separate the parts of compound numbers

TEST OF COMMUNICATION SKILLS: DESCRIPTION, REVIEW, PRACTICE

Example. My mother is forty-five years old.

- link the two or more words in some compound adjectives when the adjective precedes the noun modified

Examples. He made a station-to-station call.
She came from a well-to-do family in the South.

Caution. Hyphenation of compound adjectives is not always logical. Unless you are sure, consult a dictionary.

Parentheses

Use parentheses to indicate a comment that is not part of the sentence and does not affect its structure.

Example. Theresa's father (he travels widely) is an artist.

Period

Use a period

- at the end of a declarative or imperative sentence

Examples. His name is, rather incredibly, John Jones.
Tell me why you are late.

- after an abbreviation

Example: Mrs. Brown spoke to Col. James Colvert, Jr., at the meeting.

Key Point. There is a strong trend now away from periods after abbreviations. Note particularly that abbreviations for government agencies, broadcasting companies, unions, and other groups do not take periods: NASA, CBS, AFL-CIO, UNESCO.

Question Mark

Use a question mark

- after a direct question, but not after an indirect question or a request worded in interrogative form

Examples. Who is that new student?
Mark asked who the new student was.
Will you please return the book as soon as possible.

- after each of a series of interrogative words, phrases, or clauses within a sentence.

Examples. How much of your allowance did you spend for clothes? for tennis balls? for pizzas and hamburgers?
What have I been doing? And for how long? he wondered.

- to indicate editorial doubt

158

WRITING: MULTIPLE-CHOICE

Example. Stuart left college in 1981(?) and was readmitted in 1984.

Quotation Marks

   Use double quotation marks to

- enclose a direct quotation, but *not* an indirect quotation

Examples. Janet said, "I am going to pass this course with a high grade."
Janet said that she was going to pass the course with a high grade.

- enclose the titles of chapters in books, articles in magazines, and short poems

Example. That night I read an article entitled "Economic Predictions for the Coming Year" and Keats's poem "Ode on a Grecian Urn."

Use single quotation marks around a quotation within a quotation.

Example. Julie remarked, "Those were her words as she left: 'See you in Chicago.'"

Key Points. The *comma* and the *period* are placed inside the quotation marks.
The *semicolon* and the *colon* are placed outside the quotation marks.
The *question mark* and the *exclamation point* are placed inside the quotation marks if they are a part of the quotation; otherwise they are placed outside.

Examples. "It is as much the parent's fault," the principal said, "as the teacher's."
I hastened to say, "I'm sorry"; Bob, however, refused to accept my apology.
"Well, I won't take that grade!" the student shouted angrily.
Did you hear the child say, "I'm not going"?

Semicolon

   Use a semicolon

- to separate the clauses of a compound sentence if they are not joined by one of the coordinate conjunctions *and, but, or, nor, for, yet*. The clauses should deal with the same topic and should express related or contrasting ideas.

Examples. The board of education voted in favor of a competency examination for teachers; a committee has been appointed to select the best examination.
The military leaders are seeking nuclear arms superiority; the citizens' groups, a nuclear freeze. [The comma takes the place of the omitted verb *are seeking*.]
I thought the train ride was too long; however, if the opportunity arises, I will take it again.
The purse cost too much; therefore I did not buy it.
In some ways Tim was very attractive to Olivia; nevertheless she declined to marry him.

- to separate main clauses or other coordinate parts of a sentence that have commas within themselves

Examples. Ellen Hancock, top runner on the girls' track team, has the best opportunity to win an award; and if she does, she will be the youngest girl to receive this

159

honor, which is highly prized by our students.

I flew into Kennedy Airport with more baggage than I had when I left: five cashmere sweaters, purchased in Scotland for my daughters, sons-in-law, and grandchild; several pieces of Waterford crystal for various friends, relatives, and myself; and a bone china bell to add to my neighbor's collection.

Italics

Use italics for
- words to be emphasized, unfamiliar foreign words or phrases, and words or letters referred to as such

Examples. Let's discuss his *covert*, as opposed to his *overt*, activities.
Can you conjugate both *kommen* and *können*?
The word *antediluvian*, the letters *x* and *y*

- the titles of books, motion pictures, magazines, and newspapers

Examples. Have you read *Return of the Native* and *Jude the Obscure*?
That year *Terms of Endearment* won the Oscar for best motion picture.
I cancelled my subscription to the *New Yorker* and the *Wall Street Journal*.

- the titles of long musical compositions and of works of art

Examples. Her favorite opera is *Carmen*.
That critic has commented on both Wyeth's *Christina's World* and Rodin's *The Thinker*.

- the names of ships

Example. The new, beautiful *Atlantic* has replaced the *Doric* on the Bermuda run.

- the names of genera and species

Example. It's hard to believe that Snowball, our little kitten, is known scientifically as *Felis domestica*.

Practice Exercise

For each of the following questions, there are five possible answers. Select the one *best* answer.

1. Which sentence is NOT punctuated correctly?
   (A) People who have money are lucky.
   (B) My uncle, a good mechanic, fixed my car.
   (C) Her new dress which was pink was lost on the train.
   (D) New York, which I haven't visited for two years, has many attractions.
   (E) No, the girls are not ready.

2. In which of these sentences should the italicized part be set off by commas?
   (A) A ticket was obtained by everyone *who waited in line*.
   (B) Boys *who are good dancers* are usually popular.
   (C) Girls *who work in the summer* will have spending money.
   (D) Mary *the girl we hired today* is the receptionist.
   (E) The people *who arrive late* will not be seated.

WRITING: MULTIPLE-CHOICE

3. Which of these statements about the use of the comma is INCORRECT?
   (A) Restrictive statements are set off by commas.
   (B) Restrictive statements are not set off by commas.
   (C) Words in a series are set off by commas.
   (D) Nonrestrictive expressions are set off by commas.
   (E) If a nonrestrictive expression is left out, the meaning of the sentence is the same.

4. Which one of the following sentences is correctly punctuated?
   (A) The bills were mailed on Friday December 30 1961.
   (B) Wednesday, February 12 1961 was the date of his birth.
   (C) We visited relatives in Detroit, Michigan during Christmas vacation.
   (D) He was born in Kansas City, Missouri, on Wednesday, September 15, 1954.
   (E) Address the letter to 15 Elm Street Atlanta, Georgia.

5. Which sentence has a nonrestrictive expression?
   (A) Children who eat candy have many cavities.
   (B) Our house, which is rather old, is on Oak Street.
   (C) The bowl that Linda broke lies on the floor.
   (D) Few pupils like to go through the door that leads to the principal's office.
   (E) The necklace that was on the dresser has disappeared.

6. Which sentence is correctly punctuated?
   (A) I cooked the meal while you were away.
   (B) I cooked the meal, while you were away.
   (C) Carla will leave her husband, unless he stops abusing her.
   (D) When the noise began again and became even more unbearable the children screamed loudly.
   (E) Running after his mother David screamed for her to come back.

7. In which sentence is the semicolon used correctly?
   (A) One sister is talented, the other is not.
   (B) I want the first question; and you can have the second.
   (C) Olivia went to college; but she stayed only one term.
   (D) My sister sings; my brother plays the guitar.
   (E) The girls like to swim; but the boys prefer tennis.

8. Which one of the following sentences is punctuated correctly?
   (A) Hurrah, we won the football game.
   (B) The floors are brown: the walls are white.
   (C) John likes school; but Joe does not.
   (D) My brother has pneumonia; he is in the hospital.
   (E) I wanted to go to Europe but, I did not have the money.

9. Select the one sentence that is punctuated INCORRECTLY.
   (A) My Mother, is coming for a visit.
   (B) Yes, I solved that problem.
   (C) We are going to the mountains, not the seashore.
   (D) Come in, Marcy, and stay for a while.
   (E) We were served clam chowder, fishcakes, and fresh fruit.

10. In which sentence would you make a correction?
    (A) Almost everyone is familiar with Grant Wood's *American Gothic*.
    (B) We are late, nevertheless, we should go.

TEST OF COMMUNICATION SKILLS: DESCRIPTION, REVIEW, PRACTICE

    (C) The nurse said, "The doctor is out."
    (D) Harry said that Lorraine had called.
    (E) "She will be late," Ann replied.

11. Which sentence is punctuated INCORRECTLY?
    (A) The rule is as follows: Anyone who is five minutes late is not admitted.
    (B) "Will you, he asked, hurry with the medicine?"
    (C) "I love you," she said softly.
    (D) Betty said—and I believed her—that she had seen him.
    (E) "Am I too late?" Mary asked.

12. Which sentence would you correct?
    (A) "Who is there?" she asked in a frightened voice.
    (B) Did you say, "Mary is late"?
    (C) Mike said, "I heard your father say, 'One o'clock.'"
    (D) As soon as I finish *My Antonia*, I'm going to start *Death Comes for the Archbishop*.
    (E) The old woman said that she was lost.

13. Which sentence is correct?
    (A) The teacher asked, "Why don't you look where you are going!"
    (B) Did you hear the speaker say, "It is late"?
    (C) Did she say, "Where is Sammy?"
    (D) "This" Father said "is too much for me!"
    (E) Tom said that "he was feeling sick."

14. Which sentence is punctuated INCORRECTLY?
    (A) "We are moving to Chicago," Alice told us.
    (B) "Come quickly," she urged.
    (C) He yelled, "Eureka, we struck oil!"
    (D) When a package is marked "Special Delivery", it moves quickly.
    (E) "Tell me a story," said the child. " I am not sleepy."

15. Which sentence is INCORRECT?
    (A) The following people attended the symposium; Mary, Tom, Annette, and Kent.
    (B) When I left the house for the last time that winter night, it was snowing.
    (C) Don't tell me you never heard of the word *simile*!
    (D) She said, "I went; however, no one else was there."
    (E) "I will be away," Lynn said, "until Sunday."

Answer Key

1. C	4. D	7. D	10. B	13. B
2. D	5. B	8. D	11. B	14. D
3. A	6. A	9. A	12. C	15. A

Capitalization

Capitalize

• the first word of (1) a complete sentence, (2) a quoted sentence, or (3) a sentence that is part of another sentence

Examples. (1) She was the owner of a bakery shop.
          (2) "Good morning," she said. "We are going to have another great day on our tour."
          (3) I rise to inquire, Who is behind this proposal?

WRITING: MULTIPLE-CHOICE

- the first word and all other words except articles, short prepositions, and short conjunctions in the title of a book, motion picture, or article

Example. Have you read *Death Comes for the Archbishop* or *To the Lighthouse*?

- the names of languages but not of other school subjects except in course designations

Examples. English, Spanish, Italian; art, botany, history, mathematics; Biology II, Accounting 12

- kinship names when used before a proper name or alone without a modifier

Examples. Uncle Robert, Cousin Lupe
Tell me a story, Grandma.
I heard Father come quietly into the house.

But: My mother was a single parent at a time when this status was still uncommon.
His brother lives in a houseboat on Long Island Sound.

- the names of specific persons and places (parts of the world, political divisions, topographical names, buildings, streets, etc.)

Examples. Jimmy Carter, Sandra Day O'Connor; the South, the Orient, the North Pole, Tropic of Cancer; New Mexico, New York City, the Union of South Africa, La Porte County, Second Congressional District; Lake Louise, Rocky Mountains, Dead Sea, Pacific Ocean; the Capitol, the Statue of Liberty, the Sphinx, the Empire State Building, Grand Central Station, Kennedy Airport, Park Avenue, Picadilly Circus, U.S. Route 80

But: To reach Connecticut from Texas he drove first east and then north; the state of New Mexico, the city of New York, the county, the lake, the ocean, the sea, the statue, the building, the station

- a title preceding a name or used with no name in direct address

Examples. President Reagan, Pope John Paul II, Queen Elizabeth II, Professor O'Ryan
I presume, Governor, that you are serious.

But: Among those present were three professors, two doctors, and a senator.

- the names of organizations and institutions

Examples. State Department, United Nations, New York Court of Appeals, University of Michigan, John F. Kennedy High School, Exxon Corporation, Boy Scouts of America, National Institutes of Health, American Airlines

But: the department, the court, the university, the high school, the corporation, the institute, the airline

- the names of days of the week, months of the year, and holidays but not of seasons

Examples. Monday; April; Easter, Passover, Fourth of July, Martin Luther King's Birthday; summer, fall, midwinter, autumnal equinox

- the names of political parties, nations, and races, tribes, and other groups of people

TEST OF COMMUNICATION SKILLS: DESCRIPTION, REVIEW, PRACTICE

Examples. Democrats, Republicans, Liberals; Canadian, Polish, Brazilian; Hispanic(s), Chicano(s), Mongol(s), Oriental(s)

- cultural or historical epochs, events, and documents

Examples. Stone Age, Middle Ages, Renaissance; Vietnam War, Reformation, Boston Tea Party; Magna Charta, Declaration of Independence

- religious names and terms

Examples. Christianity, Judaism, Muslim, Islam; Catholic, Protestant, Jewish, Gentile, Southern Baptist; God, the Lord, the Almighty, Jesus Christ, the Saviour, Buddha, Great Spirit

Words Often Misspelled

1. absence
2. accidentally
3. accommodate
4. acknowledgment
5. advice (noun)
6. advise (verb)
7. aisle
8. all right
9. appearance
10. argument
11. assistant
12. athletics
13. attacked
14. awful
15. bachelor
16. bargain
17. believe
18. bicycle
19. biscuit
20. bookkeeper
21. brake
22. breathe
23. bulletin
24. bureau
25. calendar
26. changeable
27. column
28. coming
29. committee
30. comparatively
31. conscience
32. convenience
33. courageous
34. criticism
35. description
36. despair
37. develop
38. dictionary
39. dilapidated
40. disappear
41. discipline
42. dissatisfied
43. efficient
44. eighth
45. embarrass
46. exaggerate
47. exercise
48. exhausted
49. existence
50. fascinate
51. February
52. finally
53. forty
54. fourth
55. grammar
56. grievous
57. gymnasium
58. handkerchief
59. height
60. hoping
61. incidentally
62. indispensable
63. intercede
64. irresistible
65. laboratory
66. license
67. losing
68. maneuver
69. medieval
70. microphone
71. mischievous
72. misspelled
73. monotonous
74. movable
75. necessarily
76. necessary
77. ninety
78. nuisance
79. occasionally
80. occurred
81. o'clock
82. optimistic
83. orchestra
84. original
85. outrageous
86. parallel
87. particularly
88. permissible
89. perseverance
90. picnicking
91. pneumonia
92. practice
93. preceding
94. prejudice
95. privilege
96. probably
97. procedure
98. proceed
99. pronunciation
100. psychology
101. purpose
102. pursue
103. questionnaire
104. quiet
105. quite
106. realize
107. receive
108. recognize
109. recommend
110. referred
111. rehearse
112. relief
113. repetition
114. representative
115. restaurant
116. rhythm
117. sandwich
118. satisfactorily
119. schedule
120. scissors
121. semester
122. separate
123. seize
124. siege
125. similar
126. sophomore
127. souvenir
128. specimen
129. strategy
130. subtle
131. sufficient
132. syllable
133. sympathy
134. symphony
135. synonym
136. tariff
137. temperament
138. thoroughly
139. tournament
140. tragedy
141. transferred
142. truly
143. unanimous
144. unnecessary
145. until
146. using
147. vacuum
148. vengeance
149. waste (verb)
150. waist (noun)
151. Wednesday

WRITING: MULTIPLE-CHOICE

Practice Exercise

For each of the following questions, there are five possible answers. Select the one *best* answer.

1. Which sentence is correctly capitalized?
   (A) He shouted, "Where is the fire?"
   (B) My question is, who has seen Mary?
   (C) Gary, have you memorized "the Birches"?
   (D) He was raised by his aunt Phoebe.
   (E) Have you ever been in Detroit, mother?

2. Which of these statements is correct? (Consult the dictionary if you need help.)
   (A) A word that does not fit at the end of a line can be divided between any two letters.
   (B) A hyphen is used to divide a word into syllables.
   (C) *Bough* can be divided at the end of the line.
   (D) The *y* in *murky* can be carried over to the next line.
   (E) Any three letters form a syllable.

3. Which sentence is correct?
   (A) The capitol of Florida is Tallahassee.
   (B) I'm afraid I will loose my purse.
   (C) Whose boat is moored to the dock?
   (D) The rabbit had lost most of it's fur.
   (E) We were already to start on the hike.

4. Which sentence is INCORRECTLY capitalized?
   (A) Did you see *Chariots Of Fire*?
   (B) The last two speakers were Senator Moynihan and Governor Cuomo.
   (C) I'm taking Algebra 2 and French 3 next semester at Westfield High School.
   (D) My grandmother was born in Scotland and my Uncle Patrick in County Cork, Ireland.
   (E) The Young Men's Hebrew Association will dedicate its new building on Parkway Drive this Thursday night.

5. Which line contains a misspelled word?
   (A) preceding, siege, occurred, truly
   (B) parallel, incidentally, license, tragedy
   (C) irresistable, vengeance, hoping, permissible
   (D) perseverance, changeable, coming, aisle
   (E) indispensable, exhausted, fascinate, intercede

6. Which word contains an extra letter?
   (A) dilapidated   (D) outrageous
   (B) accommodate   (E) mischievious
   (C) rhythm

7. Which word should be capitalized?
   (A) algebra   (D) orient
   (B) county   (E) summer
   (C) governor

TEST OF COMMUNICATION SKILLS: DESCRIPTION, REVIEW, PRACTICE

8. Which line contains a misspelled word?
   (A) fourth, pursue, quiet, synonym
   (B) comparative, despair, committee, discipline
   (C) tragedy, unanimous, predjudice, height
   (D) psychology, questionnaire, receive, outrageous
   (E) privilege, proceed, grievous, develop

9. Which sentence is INCORRECTLY capitalized?
   (A) In July the Democrats held their convention in San Francisco.
   (B) I have attended Christian Science, Episcopalian, and Lutheran churches with my mother and father.
   (C) In the British Museum I saw the Magna Charta and the original manuscript of *Beowulf*.
   (D) The prisoner told the Judge that he had lived in the city of Phoenix for the past 5 years.
   (E) At Ohio State University he majored in art history under Professor Weinstein.

10. In which word is a letter missing?
    (A) argument   (D) occasionally
    (B) forty   (E) preceding
    (C) embarass

Answer Key

1. A   3. C   5. C   7. D   9. D
2. B   4. A   6. E   8. C   10. C

Diagnostic Practice Test—Writing: Multiple Choice

Time—30 minutes

Part A

Directions: Four portions of each of the sentences below are underlined and lettered. After reading the sentence, decide whether any one of the underlined parts contains an incorrect grammatical construction, faulty sentence structure, incorrect word usage, or incorrect or omitted punctuation or capitalization. If this is the case, note the letter underneath the underlined portion. If there is no error in any underlined portion of the sentence, choose (E). No sentence contains more than one error.

Example. Neither my father or my brother would take me to the basketball game with-
                    A   B   C
out my mother or sister. No error
              D   E
                                              Ⓐ ● Ⓒ Ⓓ Ⓔ

WRITING: MULTIPLE-CHOICE

1. I know that <u>either</u> Mary or Vicky <u>were</u> here, <u>because</u> <u>she</u> left a note for us.
                 A   B   C   D
   <u>No error</u>
   E

2. She spoke <u>clearly</u> and <u>forcefully</u> to <u>we</u> students about the problems <u>encountered</u>
                A   B   C   D
   by blacks and Hispanics in this university. <u>No error</u>
                                                E

3. The <u>issue of equal pay</u> for the same work <u>may be</u> more important than <u>any issue</u>
            A   B   C
   in <u>women's</u> struggle for equal rights. <u>No error</u>
        D   E

4. Tony was <u>one of those</u> arrested, although Jane told the police that he <u>didn't</u>
                   A   B   C
   <u>participate</u> in the crime. <u>No error</u>
       D   E

5. The <u>principal</u>, <u>feeling</u> <u>like</u> he does, could not talk to the students <u>without scolding</u>
        A   B C   D
   them. <u>No error</u>
          E

6. After we <u>had closed</u> the door, the house was <u>warmer</u> and the <u>wind</u> did not sound
               A   B   C
   so <u>loudly</u>. <u>No error</u>
       D   E

7. The new committee <u>agreed</u> that <u>everyone</u> should <u>stand</u> on <u>their</u> own feet.
                             A   B   C   D
   <u>No error</u>
   E

8. <u>Angelo's</u> boss said, "I <u>expect</u> my secretary to be not only efficient <u>but friendly</u>."
       A   B C   D
   <u>No error</u>
   E

9. The <u>principal</u>, as well as the <u>supervisors</u>, <u>were</u> present at the banquet
         A   B C
   on <u>Thursday</u>. <u>No error</u>
       D   E

10. <u>Dr. Langley</u> is <u>expected</u> to <u>accept</u> the invitation for <u>ten o'clock</u> on Friday.
        A   B   C   D
    <u>No error</u>
    E

11. The common deity of the <u>English</u> people was Woden, the war god, <u>whom</u> every
                               A   B   C
    tribe <u>thought to be</u> the first ancestor of its kings. <u>No error</u>
          D   E

TEST OF COMMUNICATION SKILLS: DESCRIPTION, REVIEW, PRACTICE

12. Looking very stern, Father advised my brother neither to be a borrower or to be
       A   B   C   D
    a lender. No error
                E

13. I like walking over the fields and to swim in the pond. No error
         A   B   C   D   E

14. Overseas trade upon which the colonies depended for their livelihood,
                   A   B   C
    was now cut off. No error
        D   E

15. The printing press was perhaps the greatest invention of the latter part of the
                          A   B   C
    Middle Ages. No error
        D   E

16. The girls showed particular interest in Joe being that he was the son of a senator.
              A   B   C   D
    No error
       E

17. What affect did the new licensing law have upon you and your family? No error
            A   B   C   D   E

18. My Aunt Clara, whom I greatly admire, is a tall woman of about fifty years old.
           A   B   C   D
    No error
       E

19. "What we should do," Steve said, "is to keep this a secret between you and I."
                   A   B   C   D
    No error
       E

20. California has more persons of Mexican descent than any state in the union.
             A   B   C   D
    No error
       E

21. As the play opens, Wendy, along with her two brothers, are playing in the nursery.
     A   B   C   D
    No error
       E

22. Before I knew it, she had talked me into buying an album and start to collect
             A   B   C   D
    stamps. No error
             E

23. There wasn't no way to combat the blind prejudice and mistreatment Randy
                   A   B   C
    encountered in Smithville. No error
        D   E

WRITING: MULTIPLE-CHOICE

24. If the board of directors controls the company, they may vote themselves bonuses.
         A   B   C   D
    No error
    E

25. You'll have to give me a real good reason for giving up this seat. No error
     A   B   C D   E

26. Fortunately she was one of those teachers who has good rapport with students.
         A   B   C D
    No error
    E

27. Last year Mr. Romano introduced a new innovation into his teaching of math.
                                      A   B   C   D
    No error
    E

Part B

Directions: In each of the following sentences there is an underlined portion that may be correct or may contain an error in grammar, diction (word use), sentence construction, or punctuation. Sometimes the entire sentence is underlined. Beneath each sentence are five ways of writing the underlined part. Choice (A) repeats the original, whereas the other four choices are different. If you think that the original sentence is correct, choose (A); otherwise choose the best answer from the other four choices given. *Do not choose an answer that changes the meaning of the original sentence.*

Example. The students are learning how to get along with others, to depend on themselves, and managing their own money.
      (A) to depend on themselves, and managing their own money.
      (B) to depend on themselves, and manage their own money.
      (C) to depend on themselves, and to manage their own money.
      (D) depend on themselves, and to manage their own money.
      (E) depending on themselves, and managing their own money.
                                         Ⓐ Ⓑ ● Ⓓ Ⓔ

28. What we need is a list of students broken down alphabetically.
    (A) is a list of students broken down alphabetically.
    (B) is a list of broken down students alphabetically.
    (C) is a broken down list of students.
    (D) is an alphabetical list of students.
    (E) is an alphabetical students' list.

29. You should see that the tank is full, the sparkplugs cleaned, the points adjusted; then your car will be ready to go.
    (A) the sparkplugs cleaned, the points adjusted;
    (B) the sparkplugs cleaned, the points are adjusted;
    (C) the sparkplugs cleaned and the points adjusted;
    (D) the sparkplugs are cleaned, and the points are adjusted;
    (E) the sparkplugs are cleaned, and the points adjusted;

30. While flying low, the windmills were seen.
 (A) While flying low, the windmills were seen.
 (B) When flying low, the windmills were seen.
 (C) We saw the windmills flying low.
 (D) While flying low, we saw the windmills.
 (E) While we are flying low, we saw the windmills.

31. Juan can run faster than any boy in Lakeville High and is captain of the cross-country team.
 (A) can run faster than any boy in Lakeville High and is
 (B) , running faster than any boy in Lakeville High, is
 (C) can run faster than any other boy in Lakeville High and is
 (D) can run as fast as any boy in Lakeville High and is
 (D) can run as fast as any other boy in Lakeville High and is

32. Not having seen Mrs. Larkin for five years, I didn't hardly recognize her.
 (A) didn't hardly recognize her
 (B) didn't recognize her hardly
 (C) hardly didn't recognize her
 (D) didn't recognize her
 (E) hardly recognized her

33. The reason Mr. Hirsch did not speak at the meeting was that his secretary forgot to remind him of the appointment.
 (A) that his secretary forgot
 (B) because his secretary forgot
 (C) why his secretary forgot
 (D) due to the fact that his secretary forgot
 (E) that his secretary has forgotten

34. The Coast Guard reported that it could reach the survivors neither by boat or by plane.
 (A) reach the survivors neither by boat or by plane
 (B) reach the survivors by neither boat or by plane
 (C) reach the survivors neither by boat nor by plane
 (D) neither reach the survivors by boat or by plane
 (E) neither reach the survivors by boat nor by plane

35. The child was unusually small for his age, and he lived with his Spanish-speaking grandmother.
 (A) The child was unusually small for his age, and he lived
 (B) The child, who was unusually small for his age, lived
 (C) The child was unusually small for his age, but he lived
 (D) Although the child was unusually small for his age, he lived
 (E) Being that the child was unusually small for his age, he lived

36. The symptoms of these young people include cough, fever, and that exertion makes them short of breath.
 (A) cough, fever, and that exertion makes them short of breath
 (B) cough, fever, and shortness of breath upon exertion
 (C) cough, fever, and exertion that makes them short of breath
 (D) that they cough, fever, and exertion makes them short of breath
 (E) cough, fever, and shortness of breath

WRITING: MULTIPLE-CHOICE

Part C

Directions: Select the best answer for each of the questions or incomplete statements that follow.

Questions 37–39 refer to the following passage.

(1) Cheating was, in a sense, almost *de rigueur* in the 1960's, a decade characterized by rebellion and anti-establishment attitudes. (2) And no one was much surprised by it in the 1970's, the "me-generation" years when selfishness was supposedly the cornerstone of youthful behavior. (3) In fact, reports of cheating were so prevalent in the 1970's that the Carnegie Council on Policy Studies in Higher Education undertook a full-scale study of the phenomenon. (4) Its findings, published in 1979, showed a "significant and apparently increasing amount of cheating by students in academic assignments." (5) Similar findings at specific colleges, including the Johns Hopkins University and Barnard College, prompted deans there to scrap longstanding honor systems in favor of proctored tests. (6) If anything, it has become worse.

37. Which of the following would be the best sentence to insert between (5) and (6) above?
    (A) When word of this got out, parents of college-age children got very angry; they felt it was all the fault of the colleges.
    (B) The bigshots who run colleges and universities tried to keep the report quiet.
    (C) Informal polls at numerous colleges show that the problem has by no means abated.
    (D) College students throughout the country, very annoyed by what the report said about them, promised never to cheat again as long as they lived.
    (E) Findings like these only make everyone worry for no reason.

38. Which of the following would the writer be most likely to use in the paragraph following the one above to begin a discussion of the possible causes of widespread cheating on today's college campuses?
    (A) The constant threat of nuclear war makes students feel so hopeless; therefore, they figure why not cheat.
    (B) On the surface, the reasons are painfully apparent: Television newscasts and newspaper headlines blare revelations of breach-of-ethics scandals on an almost daily basis.
    (C) Who knows why young people today are carrying on like this; they sure didn't do it in my day.
    (D) Certainly to be found are reasons for students to act in this manner.
    (E) As you all know, causes can always be found for any actions under discussion.

Questions 39–41 refer to the following passage.

(1) All the books reviewed exhibit the group consciousness that has so affected our sense of the past during the last generation. (2) Christopher Columbus has not left the scene, but women and blacks are two new groups prominent in the American history textbook. (3) The new groups can be incorporated into the larger parade of American

TEST OF COMMUNICATION SKILLS: DESCRIPTION, REVIEW, PRACTICE

history with integrity and even passion. (4) In some cases the textbooks reviewed do so admirably. (5) The stories of Clara Barton, Booker T. Washington, and Custer's Last Stand endure. (6) Items like *Plessy* v. *Ferguson* and the Seneca Falls resolutions have gained deserved prominence. (7) But in some cases the textbooks' effort to focus on women, blacks, Indians, and other groups is superficial, forced, and occasionally ridiculous. (8) Color photographs help students understand the textual information on the science of histology.

39. Which sentence does NOT belong in the passage?
    (A) Sentence (1)
    (B) Sentence (3)
    (C) Sentence (4)
    (D) Sentence (7)
    (E) Sentence (8)

40. Which of the following sentences would be a likely continuation of the statement made in Sentence (7) above?
    (A) The running text is the skeletal and muscular system of a textbook.
    (B) The quality of writing in textbooks reviewed varied considerably by individual text.
    (C) But do they convey to the reader a sense of excitement about the past, about human achievements and frailties?
    (D) American history is a linchpin in the school curriculum and it is a potentially exciting subject.
    (E) Trivial examples and strained statements crowd out significant and exciting political, economic, or cultural events in order to engage in a kind of textual affirmative action.

41. Which two sentences belong in the passage, but nevertheless could be omitted without disturbing the coherence of the paragraph?
    (A) Sentences (1) and (2)
    (B) Sentences (2) and (3)
    (C) Sentences (3) and (4)
    (D) Sentences (5) and (6)
    (E) Sentences (6) and (7)

42. Today's high school students are not being educated, they are being trained. Their teachers demand little of them other than that they memorize facts and follow directions. The current emphasis on training in basic math and verbal skills, while a useful first step, rarely leads to the essential second step: development of independent critical thinking.

    Which of the following, if added to the passage above, would support the writer's claim that teaching basic math and verbal skills is only the beginning of a teacher's job?

    (A) A recent study involving 25,000 students in grades 7 through 11 showed that 87 percent of the students did better than their counterparts of twenty years ago on standardized reading and vocabulary tests, while they did worse than their counterparts on standardized math tests.
    (B) A recent study involving 25,000 students in grades 7 through 11 showed that there is very little correlation between students' mathematical and verbal abilities.

(C) A recent study involving 25,000 students in grades 7 through 11 proved for the third time in the past ten years that getting back to the basics is the way to go in education today.
(D) A recent study involving 25,000 students in grades 7 through 11 trained junior high school students to do well in math and verbal skills.
(E) A recent study involving 25,000 students in grades 7 through 11 found that only 10 percent of the students were capable of analyzing what they read.

43. A church found that their facilities were too small to accommodate the crowd for a special two-day religious service. They received a license to use the public park, and a public address system was promptly installed. Citizens who were not members of that church protested the action of the Park Department for having issued this license.

Which of the following would be the best argument the writer could give to urge that the church be allowed to keep its license?

(A) Since there has been wide publicity announcing the location of the special service, the church should be permitted to keep its license.
(B) The public address system was installed at great expense to the church, therefore, they should be permitted to keep their license.
(C) The church, after all, is a local taxpayer, so why shouldn't they be allowed to use the public park?
(D) The park has been used before by religious organizations for rallies, concerts, and meetings, so why should there be a problem with using it for this particular meeting?
(E) The license to use the park does not mean that other community members would be excluded from entering the park during the service, so what could possibly be causing all the objection?

Questions 44–45 refer to the following passage.

(1) Justice Byron White wrote the majority opinion: "School officials may impose reasonable restrictions on the speech of students, teachers, and other members of the school community." (2) A recent 5–3 ruling by the Supreme Court placed limits on articles in student newspapers. (3) As this is now interpreted, articles on abortion, divorce, suicide, runaways, and drugs, considered by school boards and administrators not to contain information which serves educational purposes, can be excluded from school newspapers. (4) Several hundred student editors reported prior censorship and adverse administrative rulings before the Court ruled. (5) In other actions the Court has supported the search of student lockers by school officials without search warrants, and the disciplining of students who use lewd language.

44. Which one of the following would be the best sentence to use as a concluding statement for the paragraph above?

(A) These Court rulings suggest that high school students do not have the same constitutional rights as adults.
(B) Student complaints about loss of rights are unfounded.
(C) Parents also object to censorship of student newspapers.
(D) School newspapers in private schools and colleges will be affected by these rulings.
(E) Teachers disagree with these Supreme Court rulings.

45. Which two sentences are out of sequence and should be transposed?

(A) (1) and (2)
(B) (2) and (3)
(C) (3) and (4)
(D) (2) and (5)
(E) (4) and (5)

Answer Key

PART A		PART B	PART C
1. B	14. A	28. D	37. C
2. C	15. A	29. D	38. B
3. C	16. A	30. D	39. E
4. C	17. A	31. C	40. E
5. C	18. D	32. E	41. D
6. D	19. D	33. A	42. E
7. D	20. D	34. C	43. D
8. D	21. D	35. B	44. A
9. C	22. D	36. B	45. A
10. E	23. A		
11. E	24. B		
12. D	25. D		
13. D	26. D		
	27. B		

Writing: Essay

This section of the Test of Communication Skills requires the examinee to write on an assigned topic that does not require any specialized knowledge but relates to situations or problems familiar to members of both the educational and the general community.

For the actual test, experienced teachers will evaluate each essay and assign a single score for overall quality. Essays will be evaluated on the following:

- quality of insight or central idea
- evidence of knowledge of purpose in writing
- choice of vocabulary and style appropriate for intended audience
- consistency of point of view (impersonal, *you*, *we*)
- adequate and well-chosen supplementary information or arguments
- use of specific examples to support generalizations
- appropriateness of organization (chronological order, order of relative importance, etc.)
- cohesiveness of ideas and overall coherence
- correctness of grammar, diction, and mechanics
- general rhetorical and/or literary quality

The topic on which you will be asked to write will not require specialized knowledge; rather, it will deal with some general aspect of teaching, learning, or education in general.

WRITING: ESSAY

Review

Good modern writing, whether in an essay, a report, a novel, a letter, or any other literary form, has certain qualities: it is grammatically correct, cohesive, reasonably concise, clear, and natural.

Recently the third annual competition for the worst opening sentence for a novel produced this prize-winning entry:

"The lovely woman-child Kaa was mercilessly chained to the cruel post of the warrior-chief Beast, with his barbarian tribe now stacking wood at her nubile feet, when the strong clear voice of the poetic and heroic Handsomas roared, 'Flick your Bic, crisp that chick, and you'll feel my steel through your last meal.'"

According to the judges, the entry had all of the following aspects of bad writing: anticlimax, wordiness, misplaced modifiers, overblown language, triteness, and parody. The prize, incidentally, was a word processor.

Although the example above involves the novel, the same principles of good writing style apply to the essay. Here are some hints to help you do well on the essay question of the National Teacher Examination.

ESSAY WRITING HINTS

1. Read the question *very carefully*. Notice (a) the limitations of the topic (e.g., "Choose one side of this question"); (b) the reader(s) for whom the essay is intended (e.g., an administrator to whom you are applying for a teaching position); and (c) any other instructions (e.g., "Give specific details regarding your qualifications and experience").
2. Allow a brief time (perhaps 5 minutes) to think about what you will say, and to decide how you will organize your ideas. Will chronological order be best? Or is a cause-and-effect relationship evident between certain points you want to make? Or would an enumerative order, arranging ideas from the least to the most important, work well?
3. Jot down on the bottom of the instruction sheet important points that you want to include.
4. Begin to write slowly, carefully, and *legibly* on the special answer sheet provided. Bear in mind that there is no requirement as to length. A good essay of reasonable length will be rated higher than a poor one that is twice as long.
5. When you express a generalization, be sure to back it up with examples or other supporting evidence.
6. Before writing a sentence, ask yourself, "Is this idea expressed correctly, concisely, and clearly?"
7. Allow time to read your essay critically. Look for misspellings, grammatical errors, ambiguities, and wordiness. Make necessary corrections and other changes as neatly as you can.

Practice Exercise

Rewrite each of the following sentences. Find the main idea, eliminate unnecessary words, use correct grammar and sentence structure, and, if possible, use the active rather than the passive voice.

1. My philosophy is that if more consideration was given in school on learning to write, the graduating seniors would be better prepared for life and to face a job interview.

2. In high school not much need for economics is thought to be the case by most students until they get married and have a family.

3. Why Larry chose this career in professional football where he doesn't know anyone bothers his father, an engineer.

4. The fact that students have to make up days lost during a strike until July is not sensible according to community leaders who travel.

5. When some question which he didn't know was asked him by the teacher he just laughed and nudged the student sitting ahead of him.

6. The causes of mediocrity in education are not the fault of teachers but the parents blame you for everything.

Now compare your rewritten sentences with the following ones:

1. I believe that schools should stress writing in order to prepare students for careers and for life in general.

2. Until they marry and have a family, few students see a need to study economics.

3. Larry's father, an engineer, does not understand his son's choice of a career in professional football.

4. Community leaders who travel object to extending the school year into the summer to make up "strike" days.

5. When the teacher asked him a question that he didn't understand, he just laughed and nudged the student who sat in front of him.

6. Parents blame teachers unjustly for the current mediocrity in education.

CONNECTING CLAUSES

If a clause can stand alone, it is a main clause. Other (subordinate) clauses must be joined to main clauses because they cannot stand alone as sentences. The connections used to join clauses must be chosen appropriately to show the relationship of ideas.

Effective double-clause sentences give balance and interest to the essay, but they must meet two criteria: (1) The ideas expressed in the clauses must be related; and (2) the connecting word or words must show this relationship.

Here is a list of frequently used connectives:

and (greatly overused)   joins ideas that go together

but, yet, although, though   introduce a different idea

or, nor   introduce an alternative

when, while, after, as, since, before, until   express time relationships

because, as, for, since   introduce a reason

if, even if, unless   introduce conditions

as, than   introduce a comparison

WRITING: ESSAY

Practice Exercise 1

Complete each of the following sentences by adding an appropriate clause. Be guided by the clause given and by the connective used.

1. Either the teachers will sign the contract, or
2. Frank and Joe did not know biology, but
3. The Puerto Rican children were placed in a bilingual program, and
4. Since women make only 57 cents in salary for every $1.00 made by men,
5. The child could not read, although
6. Behavior modification will be tried until
7. A child leaped from the swing after
8. Although the playground equipment was new,
9. Even if she had wanted to go,
10. Choose a career carefully because
11. He won't talk to a counselor unless
12. Mrs. Lopez is a mother whom I admire, for
13. I will not go, though
14. Please don't talk while
15. Laura walked farther in the March of Dimes than

Practice Exercise 2

Write two sentences to illustrate the correct use of each kind of connective described in the text on page 66.

WRITING EFFECTIVE ESSAYS

Here are four important steps to follow in writing an effective paragraph or essay:

1. State the main idea.
2. Supply supporting evidence, such as examples.
3. Organize for logical sequence and for clarity.
4. Draw conclusions and summarize to convince the reader.

Read the following badly organized, confusing, short essay.

IMPROVING SCHOOL DISCIPLINE

Wars are used to settle international differences, so why should children talk, not fight, to settle their differences? Most teachers are somewhat frightened the first time a fight breaks out in the classroom, and the first impulse is to stop it as quickly as possible. Some respect must be shown for the fighters. Who began the fight? Why did they think it necessary to resort to physical violence? Sometimes the teacher threatens to get physical, if the fighters do not stop immediately. What does that teach the child? Should the teacher demonstrate that "might makes right"? Should the stronger person win?

Many children from the inner city fight with their fingernails and fists as well as with foulmouthed words. Violence is glorified in television and in video games. The teacher is working against the powerful influence of violence in our culture. Telling the children to shake hands and be friends does not deal adequately with feelings. As the teacher tells children that they should talk about their differences, children see examples. Some students have been involved in rapes, murders, thefts, and assaults on the streets. Therefore subtle plans to "get even" may lie dormant for months. A sudden outburst of anger may not be so sudden after all. One of the most difficult ideas that teachers must help children put into action is that interpersonal differences can be solved by reason instead of force. That is why the teacher must find a way to deal with angry words and flailing fists the first time a fight erupts. Because the teacher is a role model, all eyes are upon him or her in a conflict situation.

When a sudden burst of anger erupts, it may not be so detrimental if the teacher deals with the pupils' feelings. Role playing and group discussion and counseling techniques can help the teacher with discipline problems. Teachers need more information about cultural, emotional, and personal aspects of discipline. They can bring about changes in pupil behavior.

Now study the rewritten version below, and note how the improvements were made.

IMPROVING SCHOOL DISCIPLINE

Main topic: One of the most difficult ideas that teachers must help children put into action is that interpersonal quarrels can be solved successfully by reason instead of force.

Statement of problem: For this reason the teacher must find a way to deal with angry words and flailing fists the first time a fight erupts.

Supporting evidence, logically arranged: Many children from the inner city fight with their fingernails and fists as well as with foulmouthed words. When such an outburst occurs, many teachers are frightened. The first time a fight breaks out in the classroom, the immediate impulse is to stop it as quickly as possible by any means. But should the teacher use threats of physical violence? Should the teacher demonstrate that "might makes right"? Should the stronger person win? What does this action teach the children? Since the teacher is a role model, all eyes are upon him or her in a conflict situation.

A teacher who does not permit the use of physical action in conflict situations is working against the powerful influences in the culture that glorify violence.

Examples: Countries use war to settle international disputes; video games and television programs present violence as acceptable behavior. Some children living in the inner city either have been involved in rapes, thefts, murders, and assaults on the streets or have witnessed such crimes of violence.

Teachers are not prepared to cope with such situations.

Solutions to problem: For this reason, teachers need to have experience with discussion techniques, the use of role playing, and counseling in groups. In this way pupils will learn that teachers have respect for them, even for those who fight in the classroom. Questions about why the fight occurred, why the pupil took physical action, and how each one felt before and during the struggle must be openly discussed. Then, when a sudden burst of anger erupts, it may not so detrimental, for the child will have some understanding of the source of anger and the ways in which it can be expressed safely.

WRITING: ESSAY

Concluding statement: School discipline covers a wide spectrum of cultural, emotional, and personal aspects. Teachers need to have wide experience with conflict resolution so that they can be influential in bringing about changes in the habitual behavior of pupils.

Practice Exercise 1

After reading the paragraph below, write a short essay (300 words or fewer) *describing* some of the possible effects of poverty on infants and children, and incorporating additional information.

THE ECONOMY CAN HANDICAP CHILDREN FOR LIFE

In 1983, a group of scholars and social workers met at the University of Michigan to discuss poverty and its impact on families. Since 1981, when the recession deepened, the number of children living in poverty-stricken families has increased considerably. To add to the difficulty, since that year the federal government has tightened eligibility for most welfare programs.

Recent statistics show that chances are higher today than in previous years that a baby will die before birth, or if it is born alive, that it will die in infancy. There has been an increase in the number of infants suffering from water intoxication. This is caused when mothers dilute infant formula with water to save money on food.

Practice Exercise 2

Since the best way to learn to write is by writing, write each of the following. When you have finished, read the letter or essay critically and try to improve it.

1. You are a teacher applying for a position as a school principal. Write a letter selling yourself and your qualifications to the board of education.

2. Your school association has just called a strike. Write a letter explaining the association's viewpoint to the school newspaper.

3. Write an essay explaining your philosophy of education.

4. Write an essay describing the benefits of merit pay for teachers.

5. Write an essay explaining why you believe that teachers should *not* have tenure in your district.

Diagnostic Practice Test—Writing: Essay

Directions: Take 30 minutes to plan and write an essay on the topic in the box below. Take time to organize your thoughts and perhaps make a rough outline before beginning to write.

> Congress should (should not) pass a constitutional amendment authorizing prayer in public schools.
>
> Choose one side of this question, and in a letter to the editor of your local newspaper (general circulation) state your point of view and give arguments to support it.

TEST OF COMMUNICATION SKILLS: DESCRIPTION, REVIEW, PRACTICE

When you have finished your essay, ask two or three honest critics—teachers or other persons whose knowledge of written English you respect—to evaluate your essay in terms of the items listed on page 64 and to point out any aspects of your writing that need improvement. Request them to indicate specific types of errors in grammar, sentence construction, diction, and mechanics (capitalization and punctuation) to which you are prone and which you must be careful to avoid.

Part III
Test of Professional Knowledge: Description, Review, Practice

The purpose of the Test of Professional Knowledge is to examine the basic knowledge and intellectual elements that the beginning teacher, with up to 2 years of experience, will use as a learning facilitator in two areas of teaching, (1) the structure of teaching and (2) the methodology of teaching.

I. The Structure of Teaching
   The legal rights of students in the classroom.
   The content of laws regarding handicapped children (Public Law 94-142), sex discrimination, racial rights, and school attendance.
   The out-of-school influences on the teacher, pupils, and school—parents, board of education, community at large, district policy, and state interpretation of laws and regulations.
   The forces that support education in a particular community, such as business and the media. The changing social milieu in which schools exist.
   Basic child and adolescent development theory in regard to home and parent influences, and the meaning of peer pressure at certain ages.
   Professional organizations, current literature on education, and research relevant to the field.
   Teacher's professional rights and responsibilities.
   Meaningful goals and expectations for personal growth.

TEST OF PROFESSIONAL KNOWLEDGE: DESCRIPTION, REVIEW, PRACTICE

II. The Methodology of Teaching

Diagnosing pupil problems and needs, arranging for individual and group instruction, and appraising pupil progress.

Determining common and particular individual and group goals.

Designing pupil participation with classroom and community resources.

Developing standards with pupils and school administrators.

Facilitating learning through manipulation of the physical environment, pupil-teacher interaction, pupil-pupil relationships, and home-parent involvement.

Orienting students to learning through special introductory procedures, pupil involvement in planning, and evaluation.

Managing the classroom through positive reinforcement and rewards.

Showing flexibility in meeting classroom crises and changing pupil needs.

Providing different experiences and various activities according to pupil capacity to understand and relate new information to previously learned facts and hypotheses.

Measuring pupil progress with adequate instruments, both commercial and self-designed.

Participating periodically in self-evaluation and teaching success.

Developing professional attitudes with colleagues, parents, and community leaders as a public relations person for the school system.

Knowing personal strengths and weaknesses and taking appropriate measures to improve and up-date teaching skills and the application of theories and research in the field of specialty.

Teaching Principles and Practices—Topics for Review

THE TEACHER IN THE CLASSROOM

Nondirected Learning
Directed Learning
Dominated Learning
Learning Objectives
Laboratory Approaches and Learning
Classical Conditioning
Instrumental Learning
Selective Learning
Rote Learning
Discrimination Learning
Problem Solving
Maturation and Readiness
Transfer of Training
Current Research on Learning

REINFORCEMENT AND LEARNING

Emitted Behavior
Respondent Behavior
Primary and Secondary Reinforcers
Negative Reinforcement

TRANSFER OF TRAINING

Level of Learning and Amount of Transfer
Utility and Transfer
Difficulty of Task and Transfer
Interference with Learning
Principles and Learning Sets
Transfer Mechanisms
Overlearning and Transfer
Retention Curves
Theories of Forgetting

TEACHER AND PUPIL ATTITUDES

Imitative Behavior
Habitual Responses
Prejudice
Measurement Devices for Attitudes
Group Pressures and Peer Relations
Resistance to Attitudinal Changes
Learning Problems and Resistance to Change

TEST OF PROFESSIONAL KNOWLEDGE: DESCRIPTION, REVIEW, PRACTICE

Reward and Punishment
Delay in Reinforcement
Anticipatory Goal Responses
Extinction of Behavior
Motivation and Reinforcement

MOTIVATION

Need Systems
Conceptual Systems
Hierarchy of Needs
Anxiety as Motivation
Interest and Motives
Level of Aspiration and Goal-seeking Behavior

INDIVIDUAL DIFFERENCES

Exceptional Children
Range of Individual Differences
Problems of Grouping
Mainstreaming
The Gifted Child
The Slow Learner
Bilingual Education

PUPIL ADJUSTMENT

Defense Mechanisms
Nonadjustive Reactions
Social Adjustment
Peer Relations
School Adjustment
Discipline and Motivation

THE SCHOOLS AND THE LAW *

Teachers' Rights
Pupils' Rights

* See NOTES ON SCHOOLS AND THE LAW.

MEASUREMENT OF INTELLIGENCE AND APTITUDES

Current Research on Measurement and Evaluation
Relationship Between Intelligence and Academic Achievement
Constancy of the IQ
School Achievement As a Predictor of Future Success

EDUCATION AND TECHNOLOGY

Audiovisual Aids to Learning
Use of Teaching Machines for Subject Areas
Programmed Learning and Creativity
Research on Educational Television
The Computer and Individualized Instruction *

* See NOTES ON COMPUTERS.

THE SCHOOL CURRICULUM

Objectives of Language Arts Programs
Objectives of Teaching the Sciences
Problems of Modern Language Instruction
Teaching the New Mathematics
New Trends in Social Studies
Junior High School Curriculum
Articulating the School Curriculum
Censorship

COCURRICULAR ACTIVITIES

Place in the School Program
Objectives
Special Problems

NOTES ON COMPUTERS

Computer terminology is so unique that it could be considered another world language. However, there is no standardized computer language. Three widely used versions are BASIC, FORTRAN, and ALGOL. As schools increasingly adopt computer-related courses, it is important for the teacher to know basic computer terms and concepts.

Keyboard. The simplest version of a personal computer may be a typewriter-like keyboard with a small built-in display. Words, numbers, and symbols typed on the keyboard appear on the display, as do the results of computer computations. What appears on the display is easily erased and replaced, thus making the computer a more flexible medium than the typewritten or handwritten page.

Video screen. Usually, instead of the built-in display, a personal computer is connected to a separate screen, or *monitor*; in many cases, the screen of an ordinary TV set is used.

Terminal. In schools and businesses where several keyboard-plus-screen units are connected to the same central computer, each working unit is called a terminal.

CPU. The heart of any computer is its central processing unit (CPU). This processor has two main components: (a) the arithmetic-logic unit (ALU), which combines and compares numbers; and (b) the control unit, which regulates the flow of signals coming into and going out of the computer.

Memory. The computer has a permanent memory of certain instructions installed by the manufacturer. This is called *read-only memory* (ROM). It also has the capacity to "remember" instructions entered during the time it is in use, but such *random-access memory* (RAM) disappears as soon as the computer is turned off.

Kilobyte (K). Computer memory is measured in kilobytes—literally, a thousand *bytes*. (A byte is the equivalent of a letter, number, or symbol.) It takes 2000 bytes, or 2K, to enter the contents of a double-spaced, typewritten, $8\frac{1}{2}''$ times $11''$ page into a computer.

Peripherals. Other computer units that a user may add include a printer, a disk drive or cassette recorder, and a modem for sending computer data over the phone. Both the disk drive and the cassette recorder are used for putting information into the computer's RAM, and for saving data for future use. Of these two, the cassette recorder is less expensive, but also less efficient.

Disk drive. This unit records, or "writes," data on computer disks and transfers, or "reads" data from the disks back to the computer on request.

Disks. Also called diskettes and floppies, computer disks are permanently encased in a square envelope. They are usually $5\frac{1}{4}''$ or $8''$ in diameter, and are coated with a magnetic substance. The Winchester, or hard disk, is a circular platter of solid aluminum also covered with a magnetic medium. This disk spins at a very rapid speed and can hold a large number of data.

File. Each separate document or set of data a user "saves," or writes to a disk, is called a file. Depending on the number of tracks on a disk and the length of documents a disk for a personal computer may hold one or several dozen files.

Program. A program tells the computer what to do and how to do it. Some programs—for example, the Disk Operating System (DOS)—tell the computer how to work. Programs, or *software*, for educational purposes are steadily increasing in number and quality. Some are even useful for meeting the needs of individual students.

Word wrap. As data are entered at the keyboard, the computer recognizes when it reaches the end of a line and automatically "wraps" the text around to the next line.

Graphic displays. Many computers can display charts, graphs, and individualized art. Programs incorporating this ability are useful for teaching various educational subjects.

Hundreds of new programs, applicable to nearly every subject, are being developed in several computer languages to meet the needs of children of different ages and skills.

TEST OF PROFESSIONAL KNOWLEDGE: DESCRIPTION, REVIEW, PRACTICE

Before purchasing any of these, a committee should investigate the skills required to operate and understand the program. Teachers should try the program with children, to see if learning actually does take place. Excellent programs make it worth the additional cost of getting a computer, and taking the time to learn its operation.

NOTES ON SCHOOLS AND THE LAW

A knowledge of tort law is important for teachers, who have legal responsibilities toward those in their care.

A **tort** is a civil cause of action, based on noncontractual legal responsibilities that individuals have, to avoid harming or injuring another's person, property, or reputation. *Negligence* is the most common tort case. There are four elements to consider in negligence cases.

1. *Duty of Due Care*. The individual in charge of care must "act as an ordinary, prudent, reasonable person" in the protection of others from unreasonable risks. This care may be specified by statute or by common law. The school and teachers have a duty to protect the health and safety of their pupils while in the custody of the school.
2. *Breach of Duty*. Such a breach is defined as the failure to fulfill in a just and proper manner the duties of an office or fiduciary (trusted) employment. During supervision, a teacher can be charged either with violation of duty or with failure to take proper action.
3. *Causation*. There must be a close causal connection between an alleged action and a consequent injury.
4. *Actual Damages*. A plaintiff must show an actual loss or real injuries to win a suit.

Other terms that arise in connection with tort law and the schools include the following:

School setting. During school hours such incidents as playground scuffles, falls caused by floor wax in the hallway, injuries from falling plaster or an explosion in the science room raise the question of liability. The same is true for the use of the building after school hours by community groups.

Buildings and grounds. These include playground equipment and school buses—both en route to and from school, loading and unloading and so on.

Assumption of risk. A student, for example, assumes some risk when choosing to play football at school.

Contributory negligence. A high school student who runs in front of a school bus may contribute to an accident.

Immunity. A statute can limit the liability of a school district. In some instances, the district is protected from tort suits while engaged in its exercise of government functions.

Statute of limitations. The law may indicate the time during which a certain type of suit can be filed—for example, 4 years after the cause of the legal action.

Liability standards. Standards vary from state to state according to the descriptions of acts and injuries.

Assault and battery. Suits under these headings usually involve the use of corporal punishment by school personnel. *Battery* is the intentional and unpermitted touching of another person. *Assault* is the act of putting another person in fear of such touching.

Teachers' Rights

Free speech. Suits have been brought involving a teacher's loss of employment because of his or her political involvement or expression of personal opinion.

Due process rights. Teachers have sued over noncontractual changes in, for example, assignments.

Bargaining. During bargaining, teachers may claim the right to continue under provisions in their current contract, even if it has expired.

Strike. Whether or not a strike exists may determine the eligibility of teachers for unemployment compensation.

Injunction. A school district can get a court order against a strike brought by a teachers' union.

Pupils' Rights

The Education for All Handicapped Children Act of 1975 (PL 94-142). Most recent suits under this law have arisen from parental claims of improper pupil placement in a classroom or school, in contradiction to the law's "least restrictive" environment clause.

Elementary and Secondary Education Act of 1965 (PL 89-313). Some districts claim that they operate programs for the handicapped under a previous law such as PL 89-313. This has been challenged in the courts.

Religion in the schools. Federal circuit courts of appeal have struck down prayer during school hours in classrooms and assemblies; voluntary prayer group meetings for students before school hours; Bible Club meetings during the noon hour; and a Bible literature course which, it was ruled, advanced religion.

The Supreme Court defined several points during a trial on religion in the schools in 1971.

1. School law has a *secular purpose*.
2. Religion is *promoted* through a religious ritual.
3. Religious rituals in the classroom require *excessive* government *entanglement* with a religion.

Students won a case against a Texas school that restricted the number of excused absences for religious holidays.

Other cases have raised the propriety of having students in public and sectarian schools share the same buildings or special transportation, and of allowing tuition support for handicapped children who attend private schools that offer programs for the handicapped.

Discipline and expulsion. The courts have upheld the right of a school to expel students for fighting, for smoking marijuana, and for certain other violations of rules.

Compulsory attendance. Amish children and parents have been brought to court for nonattendance and truancy. The Amish are leaving certain states because of the conflict between state laws regarding compulsory education and Amish beliefs regarding what their children need to learn.

Bilingual and bicultural programs. The Supreme Court ruled that the state of Texas must study Mexican American children in its system for 6 years to learn when these children become ready for the use of English as the language of instruction.

School sports. Students transferring from a private school to a public school have challenged rules requiring a wait of 1 year before they became eligible to participate in sports. Girls are still receiving unequal funding for athletics in many school sports.

Search and seizure. Practices involving the use of dogs to sniff-search school lockers and student cars were declared to be unconstitutional on grounds that school personnel did not know whether drugs were in specific lockers at the time the search commenced. The court reversed this decision in January, 1985; teachers and principals may conduct searches to improve discipline.

First Amendment, freedom of expression. District courts ruled that

1. a school can regulate which plays it will sponsor and the nights they will be presented;
2. schools can decide whether a band has permission for specific trips;
3. a student can be suspended for wearing a button with a vulgar slogan;
4. a student can be suspended for starting a fire or for fighting;
5. a student or parent can be dismissed or fined for striking a teacher or administrator.

Education accountability tests. Students won a Florida case testing the state's Education Accountability Act of 1976. The court ruled that, since the state did not prove that the test was a measure of what was taught in the schools of Florida, mandated accountability tests must be checked for "curricular validity." It was found that black students were being penalized by such tests because of earlier lapses in their curriculum requirements.

In a Georgia case, the court ruled that the state could continue to use the California Achievement Test only if its student tracking system was changed.

Desegration. According to the courts, a pupil cannot be forced to attend a school other than the one geographically nearest or next nearest to his or her home.

Continue to Check School Laws with Your College Education Department or Your School Administrators. You Need to Know State Statutes and Rulings of Both District Courts and the Supreme Court As Important New Cases Are Decided.

Bibliography

All persons taking the National Teacher Examinations should review current publications in their fields. Journals, reports, and publications, as well as tapes from meetings, seminars, and national symposia on education are available from many university and local libraries. Curriculum libraries in teacher training institutions contain teacher's manuals plus samples of current textbooks in reading and the language arts, mathematics, science, music, business, home economics, physical education, and the social studies.

Interpretations of federal laws relating to education are contained in articles in state school journals and *Today's Education*, published by the National Education Association. Other helpful publications are *Learning, The Arithmetic Teacher, Journal of Educational Psychology, Teaching Exceptional Children, The Reading Teacher*, and *The Instructor*. For those working with handicapped students, the *Journal of Learning Disabilities* is available.

TEST OF PROFESSIONAL KNOWLEDGE: DESCRIPTION, REVIEW, PRACTICE

Worksheets for Applying Principles

WORKSHEET 1

Teaching Exceptional Children

Complete the following statements:

1. The Education for All Handicapped Children Act is also known as Public Law (number) __94-142__

2. "__mainstreaming__" is the popular term for providing education for exceptional children in the least restrictive environment.

3. The decision to place an exceptional child in a regular classroom on a part-time or full-time basis depends on two attributes of the individual child, __personal characteristic__ and __special needs educational__

4. The least restrictive environment for the severely handicapped child who has been removed from an institution may be, not the regular classroom, but a public school program characterized as __special__ education.

5. Generally speaking, when may a handicapped child be removed from a regular classroom setting? __When supplemental aid in that class does not meet the child's need__

6. Under the act dealing with handicapped children, an appropriate public education program for such children must meet several criteria.
   (a) The program must be provided at public expense, with no cost to the parents or guardians of the child.
   (b) It must meet state department of education standards.
   (c) It must meet instructional criteria for the appropriate school level, __preschool__, __elementary__, or __secondary__.
   (d) It must include provision for __individualized__ instruction.

7. Three other purposes of this law are
   (a) __help states & local school districts provide for the education of all handicapped children__
   (b) __to protect the rights of all handicapped children & their parents or guardian__
   (c) __to evaluate the effectiveness of educational programs for handicapped children in all 50 states__

8. A handicapped child may be one who is __visually impaired, EMH, TMH, deaf orthopedically impaired__

9. The term *special education* includes various types of programs, such as __institutional classroom, home instruction, physical education, other especially designed programs.__

10. Supportive educational services include __counseling services, psychological services, diagnostic & evaluative medical service, occupational, speech pathology and audiology__

11. Before the passage of the law dealing with handicapped children, there were approximately __1 million__ such children who were not receiving a free public education.

12. With respect to children, what does "due process" mean? __Children are entitled to fair legal procedures before a state can deny any of their rights & priviledges.__

TEST OF PROFESSIONAL KNOWLEDGE: DESCRIPTION, REVIEW, PRACTICE

13. List three situations related to mainstreaming that might cause parents to seek due process owed to them or their children.
    (a) _without appropriate notification of parents — places a child in a special class_
    (b) _" removes a child from a special class_
    (c) _" changes a child educational program_

14. Teachers are required to give parents written notice whenever the school proposes to initiate or change the evaluation or _placement_ of a child.

15. A coach who wants to place a student in a special physical education program must provide the student's guardian with _written notice_ before making such a change in instruction.

16. The mother of a visually handicapped child claims the right to question any and all aspects of the educational program developed for her child. Comment on the mother's rights in this situation.
    The mother has a right to refuse any change or approve in her child's educational program

17. A physically handicapped student has been denied the right to take a course in Introductory Shop. His parents and school officials have not been able to resolve this problem. What are the next two steps that the student's parents can take?
    (a) _request a due process hearing_
    (b) _appeal to the state department of education for a review of the findings_

18. Under what circumstances, if any, could the case described in question 17 be brought to court?
    either parents or school officials may bring the civil action to the US district court if the party objects to results of the appeal made to the department of instruction education

19. While a legal action is pending, what is the status of the handicapped student involved in the action?
    the child remains in the classroom which he or she was assigned before the action commenced

20. The law stipulates that a child who has been classified as mentally retarded must be evaluated in a multi-faceted testing procedure. List five factors that should be covered in such an assessment.
    (a) _language & communication skills_
    (b) _school achievement so far_
    (c) _growth & physical health_
    (d) _social skills & activities_
    (e) _psychological well being_

21. Educational assessment of each child should include two types of tests, _criterion_ tests and _standardized / norm-referenced_ tests. _referenced_

22. Tests for communication skills may cover both oral and _written_ skills.

23. What are two general purposes of a physical examination for students?
    to detect health problems and _identify physical defects_.

24. Emotional behaviors and problems can be measured by _direct observations_, _psycological tests_ _checklists_, and _scales_.

25. Social skills can be measured by _direct observations_, _adaptive behavior_, and _parent & teacher conferences_.

26. Two reasons why a child might score poorly on a test are that
    (a) _does not understand the directions_,
    (b) _sensory problems related to hearing & vision_

189

TEST OF PROFESSIONAL KNOWLEDGE: DESCRIPTION, REVIEW, PRACTICE

27. If a child is not familiar with the English language, tests must be administered in _child's native language_.

28. An intelligence test could be considered to be _discriminatory_ if a child's physical handicap prevents him or her from being able to do well on it.

29. Three tests often used with children who have language difficulties are
    (a) _draw a man test_,
    (b) _Leiter International Performance scale_,
    (c) _Raven's Progressive matrices_.

30. Under law, what are a parent's rights with regard to his or her child's school records? _Parents have a right to see their child's school records and to receive an interpretation of data thereon_

WORKSHEET 2

Individualizing Instruction

Complete the following statements:

1. One of the current thrusts in education is called humanism. What is the difference between the way humanism views the individual child and the way children were viewed in earlier decades? _new humanism in education stresses the welfare & growth of the individual pupil. The old concept of individual differences included the premise that the individual was subordinate to that group_

2. The following aspects of individual growth are emphasized by humanistic teachers. According to the humanist, how should each of these aspects of growth influence the teacher's approach to the individual student?
    (a) Dignity. _every child has worth & considered competent by the teacher_
    (b) Values. _new humanism does not impose new values but emphasizes the clarification of values that the pupil already holds_
    (c) Emotions. _a child's feelings are worthy of attention as the child's level of critical thinking_
    (d) Morality. _help makes pupils sensitive to justice & injustice & behave in ways that are consistent with moral judgements_
    (e) Freedom. _teacher will help the child to choose, totry, and even to fail_
    (f) Concern and responsibility. _develop concern for the feelings & needs of others and to give others the same freedom he or she expects to receive_

3. Combs says that teachers should eliminate practices that tend to dehumanize pupils. Name six such practices related to classroom procedures.
    (a) _expressing distrust toward a pupil_
    (b) _always requiring the right answer_
    (c) _using the single-textbook approach to all instruction_
    (d) _requiring all students to complete work at the same pace_
    (e) _overcrowding classes & offering all pupils the same instructional program_
    (f) _fostering undesirable competition for grades & increasing pressure to achieve high test scores_

4. Carl Rogers has urged teachers to stop "teaching" and to start "_facilitating learning_."

5. Identify five steps a teacher might take to implement Rogers's suggestion.
    (a) _Draw out & clarify what a pupil wants to do_
    (b) _Provide a wide range of learning experiences & multi media_
    (c) _Establish a comfortable working climate in the classroom_
    (d) _Serve as a flexible resource to be used by members of the class_
    (e) _Act as a participate learner_

TEST OF PROFESSIONAL KNOWLEDGE: DESCRIPTION, REVIEW, PRACTICE

6. Behaviorists believe strongly in the value of setting _behavioral_ objectives and using _behavior_ modification.

7. Define *self-concept*. — the image we have of ourselves

8. List two ways by which a teacher can learn about the self-concepts of students.
   (a) use pictures or verbal descriptions of people to elicit students' reactions or interpretations (projective technique)
   (b) administer self-reporting scales on which students respond orally or in writing to checklist of items designed to reveal their self images

9. Self-concept has been described by several writers in the field of human development. How have the following four writers defined positive self-concept?
   (a) Combs. a person who perceives himself well liked & possessing worth & integrity has good self concept
   (b) Maslow. a good self concept allows a person's "inner nature" to receive love, respect and acceptance from one's peers
   (c) Kelley. has good human values, is secure, thinks well of him or herself as well as others
   (d) Rogers. one who has a sense of openness to new experiences and does not use defense mechanisms

10. Teachers, although not therapists, should be able to recognize the following symptoms of high anxiety in a student: _nervousness_, _low self esteem_, _projection_, and _rationalization_ misbehavior

11. Ned Flanders, in reporting his research, shows that in a typical classroom the teacher and students talk for __2/3__ of the time, and the teacher talks for __2/3__ of that time.

12. Through interaction analysis, Flanders learned that teachers use three different types of talk with students. These types are
   (a) _eliciting talk_,
   (b) _informing talk_,
   (c) _reacting talk_.

13. Thomas Harris writes of four kinds of interaction postures taken by people as they communicate. One of these may be characterized as "I'm OK, you're OK." List the other three kinds of interaction postures.
   (a) _I'm not OK, you're OK_
   (b) _I'm not OK, you're not OK_
   (c) _I'm OK, you're not OK_

14. A teacher is developing experience-referenced individualized instruction for his eighth-grade English class. Three types of experiences he might plan are _manageable selections of_, _differing levels of difficulty_, and _self correcting_ learning centers, open ended projects, informal discussion

15. Individualized instructional programs prepared by publishers usually have the following characteristics:
   (a) _manageable selections of subject matter_,
   (b) _differing levels of difficulty_,
   (c) _self correcting devices_.

16. In an exploratory learning center, the emphasis is on _quality of experience_ rather than on specific outcomes.

17. A classroom is being arranged to facilitate individual work. List three matters that require special attention.
   (a) _____
   (b) _____
   (c) _____

191

TEST OF PROFESSIONAL KNOWLEDGE: DESCRIPTION, REVIEW, PRACTICE

18. When teacher and student meet to decide on activities that the student will complete during the week, this schedule is often called a *negotiated* schedule.

19. Prescription after diagnostic testing is related directly to *needs identification*.

20. What are task cards? *individual assignments, directions for completing them and sources that maybe helpful*

21. Modularized instruction bears a strong resemblance to its predecessor, *unit teaching*.

22. A good set of modules suggests activity topics that appeal to students with *differing* interests.

23. Alternative enabling activities will assist students in reaching *behavioral objectives specified by the teacher*.

24. List four educators who have given form to the open education movement. *Kohl*, *Bruner*, *Silberman*, *Kozol*.

25. What is the difference between open education and "open experience" in education?
_____

26. Under open education, what is the chief characteristic of each of the following?
    (a) Time structuring. _____
    (b) Role of inquiry. _____
    (c) Teacher-student relations. _____
    (d) Evaluation. _____
    (e) Teacher behavior. _____

27. List five ways to check up on student progress.
    (a) _____
    (b) _____
    (c) _____
    (d) _____
    (e) _____

28. When a teacher notes that children are having difficulty with individualized instruction, he or she can play the role of providing _____, and can do _____ teaching.

TEST OF PROFESSIONAL KNOWLEDGE: DESCRIPTION, REVIEW, PRACTICE

29. What types of problems or behaviors does Berkowitz cluster under each of the following categories?
    (a) Learning problems. _____
    (b) Social adjustment problems. _____
    (c) Behavior problems. _____

30. According to Piaget, what type of intellectual development should you expect from pupils in each of the following stages?
    (a) Intuitive thought stage. _____
    (b) Concrete operations stage. _____
    (c) Formal operations stage. _____

31. A seventh-grade teacher plans to teach her class through "success structuring." What does this approach involve?
    (a) Activities are broken down into small steps; each step leads easily to the next, more difficult step. Another name for this process is _____.
    (b) A wealth of multimedia materials would be provided to meet each pupil's needs. These would include such things as _____, _____, and _____.
    (c) Activities are planned to meet the pupil's individual learning style. Most pupils fall into one of three cognitive styles, which are defined as follows:
        (1) The adventurer. _____
        (2) The ponderer. _____
        (3) The drifter. _____

32. A fifth-grade teacher, following behavior modification principles developed by Skinner in his research on operant conditioning, uses five forms of approval to change pupil behavior. Define each one and give an example.
    (a) Personal reactions. _____
    (b) Activity reinforcers. _____
    (c) Token systems. _____
    (d) Prize systems. _____
    (e) Graphic symbols. _____

33. Ogden Lindsley devised a system for changing behavior, called "precision teaching." State five ways in which Lindsley's approach differs from behavior modification.
    (a) _____
    (b) _____
    (c) _____
    (d) _____
    (e) _____

TEST OF PROFESSIONAL KNOWLEDGE: DESCRIPTION, REVIEW, PRACTICE

WORKSHEET 3

Providing Education for All Children

Complete the following statements:

1–8. You have been assigned to check the school building and grounds for accessibility to handicapped children, in compliance with suggestions provided by the American Institute of Architects. What are the standards you will use?

1. (a) Public walks should be at least ___48___ inches wide.
   (b) The platform extends at least 1 foot beyond each side of the ___doorway___.
   (c) Walks should blend to a ___common___ level as they cross other walks, driveways, and parking lots.
   (d) The gradual rise of any walk is not more than ___5___ percent.
   (e) Whenever a door swings out onto the platform, the platform is at least 5 feet by ___5___ feet or, if no door swings out onto a platform, is at least 3 feet by ___5___ feet.

2. (a) There is a ___handrail___ on at least one side of each ramp.
   (b) The slope creates no more than a 1-foot rise for every _____ feet on each ramp.
   (c) All ramps have a _____ surface.
   (d) The height of handrails is _____ inches from the surface of the ramp.
   (e) There are at least _____ feet of open clearance at the bottom of each ramp.
   (f) There are level platforms at 30-foot intervals for _____.

3. (a) When doors are ajar, they leave an access opening of no fewer than _____ inches.
   (b) When doors are opened, there are no sharp changes in incline at the _____.
   (c) The floor is level for _____ feet in the direction of the door swing.

4. (a) Risers on stairways are no more than _____ inches in height.
   (b) Do stairs have handrails which extend at least _____ inches beyond the top and bottom step?
   (c) Steps are _____ and evenly textured.

5. (a) There is a turning space _____ inches by 60 inches in toilet cubicles for people in wheelchairs.
   (b) In both men's and women's (boys' and girls') lavatories, there are safety provisions for a _____.
   (c) Drain pipes and hot water pipes are _____ for safety.
   (d) The lavatory door should be _____ inches wide and should swing _____.
   (e) Mirrors and shelves are no higher than _____ inches above the floor.

6. (a) Spouts and other controls on water founts are at the front and are operated by _____.
   (b) When mounted on a wall, basins of water founts are _____ inches or less above the floor.
   (c) Spouts are no higher than _____ inches on floor-mounted fountains.

7. (a) There are telephones accessible to people in wheelchairs, with the height of the dial no more than _____ inches from the floor.
   (b) The coin slot on such phones is not more than _____ inches from the floor.
   (c) Telephone facilities for persons with hearing difficulties are clearly _____.

8. (a) Controls and switches for elevators, heat, light, fire alarms, and ventilation are _____ inches or less from the floor.

TEST OF PROFESSIONAL KNOWLEDGE: DESCRIPTION, REVIEW, PRACTICE

    (b) Controls are labeled with raised or _____ letters.
    (c) Controls and switches are easy to push or are touch-_____.
    (d) The elevator cab is at least _____ feet by _____ feet.
    (e) Doorhandles and knobs are made identifiable for a blind person by their _____.
    (f) For persons with visual or hearing disabilities, there are warning signals that are _____ and _____.
    (g) Signs, ceiling lights, and other fixtures protruding into regular corridors are not less than _____ feet from the floor.
    (h) Exits and entrances are identified by _____.

9. What is a disability? _____

10. What is a handicap? _____

11. In order to work effectively with handicapped students, teachers should know the characteristics of various disabilities. What is the identifying description of each of the following?
    (a) Amputation. _____
    (b) Arthritis. _____
    (c) Cerebral palsy. _____
    (d) Kyphosis and scoliosis. _____
    (e) Multiple sclerosis. _____
    (f) Muscular dystrophy. _____
    (g) Poliomyelitis. _____
    (h) Spina bifida. _____
    (i) Spinal cord injury. _____

12. Define diabetes mellitus and epilepsy.
    (a) Diabetes mellitus. _____
    (b) Epilepsy. _____

13. What signs should alert a teacher to the fact that a child is having an epileptic seizure in the classroom?
    (a) Grand mal seizure. _____
    (b) Petit mal seizure. _____
    (c) Psychomotor seizure. _____

14. Pupils who have recently become handicapped usually go through a grieving process that has five stages. Name and characterize each stage.
    (a) _____
    (b) _____
    (c) _____
    (d) _____
    (e) _____

15. State three ways a teacher can help students set productive goals and develop positive attitudes, in spite of handicaps.
    (a) _____
    (b) _____
    (c) _____

16. Name and describe four observable behaviors of a hyperactive child.
    (a) _____
    (b) _____

TEST OF PROFESSIONAL KNOWLEDGE: DESCRIPTION, REVIEW, PRACTICE

    (c) _____
    (d) _____

17. List five strategies a teacher can use when working with a child who demonstrates hyperactivity.
    (a) _____
    (b) _____
    (c) _____
    (d) _____
    (e) _____

18. What does the acronym DLD stand for? _____

19. State the definition for mental retardation developed by Grossman in 1973.
    _____

20. For children with learning disabilities, three levels of testing are usually pursued, with a variety of tests available at each level. Complete the following outline with appropriate examples of tests for each level.
    (a) *Level I: Classroom Screening*
        (1) _____
        (2) _____
        (3) _____
    (b) *Level II: Differential Diagnosis*
        (1) _____
        (2) _____
        (3) _____
        (4) _____
    (c) *Level III: Personal History*
        (1) _____
        (2) _____
        (3) _____
        (4) _____
        (5) _____

21. Describe each of the following impairments of a child with speech disorders.
    (a) Omissions. _____
    (b) Substitutions. _____
    (c) Distortions. _____
    (d) Organic or functional problems. _____
    (e) Generally poor speech. _____

22. Sometimes, a child's difficulty in speaking arises from environmental circumstances, for example
    (a) _____ ;
    (b) _____ ;
    (c) _____ .

23. The dyslexic child is often confused about words relating to *time* and *direction*. In 1971 Boder suggested the following three categories of dyslexic children. Define each.
    (a) Dysphonetic dyslexic child. _____
    (b) Dyseidetic dyslexic child. _____
    (c) Mixed dysphonetic-dyseidetic dyslexic child. _____

TEST OF PROFESSIONAL KNOWLEDGE: DESCRIPTION, REVIEW, PRACTICE

24. Primary reading retardation is presumed to be neurologically based, related to parietal lobe dysfunction. What are some of the symptoms of this retardation?
    (a) _____
    (b) _____
    (c) _____

25. Brain injury, accompanied by some reading retardation, demonstrates _____.

26. Children with secondary reading retardation demonstrate _____.

27. Children with visual agnosia demonstrate _____.

28. *Dyscalculia* is a term used to describe _____.

29. From birth, the autistic child is _____.

30. (a) Receptive aphasia is _____.
    (b) Expressive aphasia is _____.

WORKSHEET 4

Teaching Mathematics

Complete the following statements:

1. The increase in mathematical knowledge within the society requires the school to _____.

2. Experimental mathematics programs have had a profound influence on the content, _____, and _____ used in the schools since the mid-1950s.

3. From 1955 to 1965, primary emphasis was placed on introducing new content into mathematics courses. Since that time, the emphasis has shifted to improving _____, _____, and _____.

4. Several experimental projects in the field of elementary school mathematics contributed to new materials. Among these projects were the School Mathematics Study Group (SMSG), and
    (a) _____,
    (b) _____,
    (c) _____,
    (d) _____.

5. Since the first new programs were implemented in the mid-1950s, both new experimentation and reappraisal of mathematical programs have continued. Many unanswered questions remain. Among them are
    (a) _____
    (b) _____
    (c) _____
    (d) _____
    (e) _____

TEST OF PROFESSIONAL KNOWLEDGE: DESCRIPTION, REVIEW, PRACTICE

6. Much emphasis is now placed on scope and sequence planning in mathematics education. Show how this affects the teaching of math in grades K through 3, by commenting on each of the following:
   (a) Sets. _____
   (b) Addition. _____
   (c) Subtraction. _____
   (d) Multiplication and division. _____
   (e) Symbols. _____
   (f) Measurements. _____
   (g) Geometric shapes. _____
   (h) Problem solving. _____

7. Explain each of the following new trends in the mathematics program.
   (a) The laboratory approach. _____
   (b) The systems approach. _____
   (c) The relevant-experiences approach. _____

8. One of the changes taking place in the teaching of mathematics is an increasing emphasis on having pupils explore a process and discover the rules themselves. The three major steps involved in this approach are _____, _____, and _____.

9. Learning mathematics is achieved most effectively when the emphasis is on structure, _____, and _____.

10. The study of multiplication and division becomes meaningful for students when they grasp _____ and _____.

11. If a teacher wants to begin a math lesson with interesting materials, he or she should begin with things which interest pupils and which they have _____.

12. A pupil's interest in a new mathematics activity is usually based upon the belief that he or she can _____.

13. What is likely to happen if a teacher ignores the rule "one difficulty at a time" when introducing new math material?
    _____

14. A teacher need not always "follow the interests of the children" but should guide pupils from _____ to _____

15. For transfer of learning, the teacher should emphasize _____, _____, and _____.

16. In order to transfer a learned principle successfully, a pupil must recognize both the principle and the _____.

17. The mathematical formula $A = lw$ expresses a _____ that the pupil can apply to many situations.

18. Mere repetition does not lead to learning. _____ should precede drill and practice.

19. A small number of well-selected exercises, spaced in short, intensive practice periods, is better than _____.

TEST OF PROFESSIONAL KNOWLEDGE: DESCRIPTION, REVIEW, PRACTICE

20. It is essential that pupils practice correct routines under careful supervision. Without guidance, it is possible for a pupil to develop _____ that later require considerable unlearning.

21. Practice in the use of an algorithm must be rational and exploratory to keep pupils aware of _____.

22. The development of mathematical concepts begins with the manipulation of _____ and proceeds gradually toward the use of _____.

23. When the instructional purpose is to "fix" skills, a certain amount of overlearning assures _____.

24. With an eye to the flowchart of upcoming skills lessons, a teacher can be alert to the value of everyday occurrences for _____, _____, and _____.

25. The abacus is useful for teaching the concept of _____ as a placeholder.

26. A "hundreds board" can be used for counting by 5's and _____.

27. Flannel board cutouts can be used to show the meaning of _____ numbers, such as first or second.

28. When a pupil tends to group addends out of order because they are easiest to combine, there is an increased probability of _____.

29. One way to add 47 and 28 mentally is to think of the problem as (47 + 20) + 8. The steps for this would be 47 + 20 = 67, and 67 + 8 = 75. What other technique can be used for adding 47 to 28?

30. Which is the better form for stating the problem to a child?
    (a) Change the fraction $\frac{1}{2}$ to $\frac{4}{8}$.
    (b) Express the fraction $\frac{1}{2}$ as $\frac{4}{8}$.

31. One way of helping pupils learn addition and subtraction of fractional numbers is to start with examples in which all fractions have the same _____.

ANSWERS FOR WORKSHEETS

Worksheet 1

1. 94-142

2. "Mainstreaming"

3. personal characteristics, educational needs

4. special

5. When it becomes evident that supplemental aid in that class does not meet the child's needs

6. (c) preschool, elementary, secondary
   (d) individualized

199

7. (a) to help states and local school districts provide for the education of all handicapped children
   (b) to protect the rights of all handicapped children and their parents or guardians
   (c) to evaluate the effectiveness of educational programs for handicapped children in all 50 states

8. visually handicapped, hard of hearing, deaf, speech-impaired, mentally retarded, orthopedically impaired, or otherwise health-impaired; seriously emotionally disturbed; or significantly learner-disabled

9. institutional, classroom, or home instruction; physical education; other specially designed programs

10. counseling services, psychological services, diagnostic and evaluative medical services, occupational therapy, speech pathology, and audiology

11. 1 million

12. Children are entitled to fair legal procedures before the state can deny any of their rights and privileges.

13. (a) Without appropriate notification of parents, a teacher removes a child from a special class.
    (b) Without appropriate notification of parents, a teacher places a child in a special class.
    (c) Without appropriate notification of parents, a teacher changes the educational program for a child.

14. placement

15. written notice

16. The child's mother has the right to approve or refuse any change that is to be made in her daughter's educational program.

17. (a) Parents in such a situation can ask for a due process hearing, which is informal and impartial. The parents may be accompanied by counsel and someone knowledgeable in the special problems of the handicapped. They can cross-examine witnesses and ask for both a written report of the informal hearing and the findings and decisions of the agency that conducted the hearing.
    (b) If they are not satisfied with the findings of the informal hearing, such parents may appeal to the state department of education for a review of the findings.

18. Either the parents or school officials may bring civil action in a state or U.S. District Court if the party objects to the results of the appeal made to the state department of education.

19. The student remains in the class to which he or she was assigned before the action commenced.

20. (a) The child's language and communication skills
    (b) The child's school achievement thus far
    (c) The child's growth and physical health
    (d) The child's social skills and activities
    (e) The child's psychological well-being

21. criterion-referenced tests; standardized, norm-referenced tests

22. written—or other nonvocal

23. To detect health problems, to identify physical defects

24. direct observations, psychological tests, checklists, scales

TEST OF PROFESSIONAL KNOWLEDGE: DESCRIPTION, REVIEW, PRACTICE

25. direct observations, adaptive behavior scales, parent and teacher conferences

26. (a) he or she does not understand the directions
    (b) he or she has sensory problems related to vision or hearing

27. the child's native language.

28. discriminatory

29. (a) the Draw-a-Man Test
    (b) the Leiter International Performance Scale
    (c) Raven's Progressive Matrices

30. Parents have the right to see their child's school records and to receive an interpretation of data thereon.

Worksheet 2

1. The new humanism in education stresses the welfare and growth of the individual pupil. The old concept of individual differences included the premise that the individual was subordinate to the group.

2. (a) Every individual has worth and should be considered potentially competent by the teacher.
   (b) The new humanism does not impose new values, but emphasizes the clarification of values that the pupil already holds.
   (c) The humanistic teacher believes that a child's feelings and emotions are as worthy of attention in the classroom as the child's level of critical thinking.
   (d) Education should help to make pupils sensitive to justice and injustice, and help them behave in ways that are consistent with their moral judgments.
   (e) The noncoercive teacher will protect the child's freedom to choose, to try, and even to fail.
   (f) Humanist teachers will help the child to develop concern for the feelings and needs of others, and to give others the same freedom he or she expects to receive.

3. (a) Expressing distrust toward a pupil
   (b) Always requiring the "right answer"
   (c) Using the single-textbook approach to all instruction
   (d) Requiring all students to complete work at the same pace
   (e) Overcrowding classes and offering all pupils the same instructional program
   (f) Fostering undesirable competition for grades and increasing pressure to achieve high test scores

4. facilitating learning

5. (a) Draw out and clarify what a pupil wants to do.
   (b) Provide a wide range of learning experiences and multimedia.
   (c) Establish a comfortable working climate in the classroom.
   (d) Serve as a flexible resource to be used by members of the class.
   (e) Act as a participant learner.

6. behavioral, behavior

7. Self-concept is the "image" we have of ourselves. If a child has a positive, or good, self-concept, he or she will be motivated to pursue fulfilling expectations in life.

201

TEST OF PROFESSIONAL KNOWLEDGE: DESCRIPTION, REVIEW, PRACTICE

8. (a) Use pictures or verbal descriptions of people to elicit students' reactions and interpretations. This is the projective technique.
   (b) Administer self-reporting scales, on which students respond either orally or in writing to a checklist of items designed to reveal their self-images.

9. (a) According to Combs, a person who sees him- or herself as generally well liked and possessing worth and integrity has a good self-concept.
   (b) For Maslow, a good self-concept allows a person's "inner nature" to receive love, respect, and acceptance from one's peers.
   (c) According to Kelley, a fully functioning person (that is, one with a good self-image) has good human values, is secure, and thinks well of him- or herself and others.
   (d) For Rogers, a good self-concept is the mark of a person in the process of becoming, of one who has a sensitive openness to new experiences and does not use defense mechanisms.

10. nervousness, low self-esteem, use of projection and rationalization, misbehavior

11. two thirds, two thirds

12. (a) eliciting talk (teachers ask questions and give commands that require either verbal or behavioral response)
    (b) informing talk (teachers provide factual information and/or give directions, explanations, and assignments to students)
    (c) reacting talk (teachers respond to student talk, giving approval or disapproval)

13. (a) "I'm not OK, you're OK"
    (b) "I'm not OK, you're not OK"
    (c) "I'm OK, you're not OK"

14. use of learning centers, open-ended projects, informal discussions, others

15. (a) manageable selections of subject matter
    (b) differing levels of difficulty
    (c) self-correcting devices

16. the quality of experiences

17. (a) The room should be set up to allow maximum student involvement and easy management of activities by the teacher.
    (b) Collection, storage, and retrieval of materials should be made easy.
    (c) Placement of pupils for group activities and for self-scheduled tasks should both be possible without delay.

18. negotiated

19. needs identification

20. Task cards contain individual assignments, directions for completing them, and sources that may be helpful. They may also include self evaluation activities. They are usually used in learning centers.

21. unit teaching

22. differing

TEST OF PROFESSIONAL KNOWLEDGE: DESCRIPTION, REVIEW, PRACTICE

23. behavioral objectives specified by the teacher

24. Kohl, Bruner, Silberman, Kozol, Piaget, Rousseau, Froebel, Pestalozzi, Dewey, Neill

25. An "open experience" in education provides the student with freedom within a defined time or activity. "Open education" implies a total, all-day involvement in learning experiences.

26. (a) There is no set amount of time or fixed sequence for learning activities.
    (b) Students are encouraged to show independence, responsible self-direction, and decision making as they pursue their projects.
    (c) Teacher and students maintain a cooperative and collaborative approach in developing lessons.
    (d) Successes, not failures, are emphasized. The teacher uses reinforcement of student responses to encourage mastery learning.
    (e) The teacher's attention is student-centered. His or her attitude is facilitative for learning.

27. (a) By reviewing completed activities
    (b) By conferencing with students
    (c) By listening to oral reports
    (d) By testing students on content materials
    (e) By observing student behavior in the learning center

28. ideas and information, facilitative

29. (a) The major difficulty here lies with slow learning or failure to learn in certain subject areas.
    (b) The student demonstrates isolation, fears, withdrawal, feelings of rejection, depression, or dependency.
    (c) Behaviors include aggression, hyperactivity, destructiveness, inattention, and other disruptive actions that interfere with learning.

30. (a) From ages 4 to 7, normal children reason and act on the basis of hunches or intuition. They cannot follow lists of rules, use logic, or conserve or reverse operations.
    (b) From ages 7 to 11, normal children can conserve quantities and mentally reverse operations, or "undo" many thought processes. This enables them to perform experiments and comprehend mathematical problems, provided they can work with concrete or manipulable materials. They can do logical thinking, remember regulations, and work in steps or sequences.
    (c) From ages 11 to 15, normal children can use a variety of abstractions, think about thought, and form hypotheses and theories. At the completion of this stage the normal child thinks like an adult.

    Different students enter and leave these three stages at different chronological ages, but they all go through the same sequence of intellectual development. Pupils need activities appropriate to their level of understanding. They cannot be pushed into a higher level by threats of academic failure.

31. (a) programmed instruction
    (b) books, records, tapes, filmstrips, films, computer-assisted instruction
    (c) (1) tends to be active, eager to learn, and spontaneous in response, but may not stay with a task long enough to complete it
        (2) starts tasks slowly, but may continue them to completion, pays attention to details, works well with sequenced activities
        (3) has difficulty beginning a new lesson and finishing it on time, needs success experiences and close supervision

TEST OF PROFESSIONAL KNOWLEDGE: DESCRIPTION, REVIEW, PRACTICE

32. (a) Teacher reactions such as nods, smiles, pats on the back, or comments like "You are improving" work well with some students.
    (b) For students who prefer to do free reading, play learning games, or listen to tapes, such "work" activities can be used to reward the completion of less pleasing assignments.
    (c) Small cards, play money, plastic chips, or disks can be accumulated by students who complete assignments. These "tokens" are later cashed in for privileges, or for objects such as candy, buttons, or pencils.
    (d) The prize system is often used in addition to a token system. Some pupils will work for such prizes as theater tickets, ribbons, certificates, and other rewards.
    (e) Desirable symbols include points, grades, drawings, "smiling faces," and gold stars given for acceptable behavior and school work.

33. (a) Tokens or extrinsic reinforcers are not used in precision teaching.
    (b) The teacher defines the behavior(s) to be changed in specific terms—for example, "talking when other pupils recite" or "walking around the room after the bell rings."
    (c) The frequency of record keeping depends on the specified behavior. Often the student assists in record keeping and plots his or her own progress.
    (d) Interesting materials, instead of rewards, are employed to interest the pupil and to improve behavior.
    (e) Each pupil works to improve his or her own record and is not competing with others.

Worksheet 3

1. (a) 48   (b) doorway   (c) common   (d) 5   (e) 5, 5
2. (a) handrail   (b) 12   (c) nonslip   (d) 32   (e) 6   (f) rest
3. (a) 32   (b) doorsill   (c) 5
4. (a) 15   (b) 18   (c) level
5. (a) 60   (b) handrail   (c) insulated   (d) 32, outward   (e) 40
6. (a) hand   (b) 36   (c) 30
7. (a) 48   (b) 48   (c) identified
8. (a) 48   (b) indented   (c) sensitive   (d) 5, 5   (e) knurled surface   (f) audible, visual   (g) 7   (h) large signs, flashing lights, audible signals
9. A disability is an actual physical or psychological impairment.
10. A handicap is a disadvantage imposed upon a person by a disability.
11. (a) The removal of a limb or other part of the body
    (b) A disease that often involves painful movement of the joints, the adjacent structures, or both
    (c) An impairment of voluntary movement by a central nervous system disease, often with some degree of spastic movement
    (d) Curvature of the spine
    (e) The hardening of brain or spinal tissue, usually associated with some paralysis and muscular tremor
    (f) A central nervous system disorder that causes slowly progressive wasting of the skeletal or cardiac muscle fibers, with respiratory complications. Legs and arms may be weak and spastic.

TEST OF PROFESSIONAL KNOWLEDGE: DESCRIPTION, REVIEW, PRACTICE

    (g) An acute viral infection that may lead to motor paralysis and atrophy of skeletal muscles
    (h) A disorder of the spinal column
    (i) Concussion or compression of the spinal cord, leading to loss of neurologic function, muscular weakness, and poor tendon reflexes

12. (a) A metabolic disease related to an insufficiency of insulin, leading to elevated blood glucose and—over time—to some injury of sensory and motor nerves
    (b) A recurrent disorder of cerebral function, resulting in sudden, brief convulsive attacks, an altered state of consciousness, and a loss of some sensory and motor control

13. (a) In a grand mal seizure, the child becomes tense, falls on the floor, shows muscle jerking, breathing difficulties, and loss of bladder control, and may be unconscious for several minutes. The teacher should be calm, place the child on the floor, turn his or her head to one side, and remove any objects that may be in the child's mouth. It's a good idea to loosen any tight clothing the child may be wearing, and to let him or her rest after the seizure.
    (b) A petit mal seizure is only a brief interruption of consciousness; the eyelids may twitch or the face make slight movements. The child appears to be daydreaming and is not aware of the seizure.
    (c) A psychomotor seizure is a temporal lobe seizure that brings out the most complex behavior. The child may engage in purposeless chewing, lip smacking, repetitive walking, or hand-and arm-movement. Such a seizure can last for only a minute or for several hours, during which the child may be dizzy or confused.

14. (a) Denial: "If I behave the way I always did, the problem won't bother me."
    (b) Anger: "Why did God, my parents, or my teacher let this happen to me?"
    (c) Bargaining: "If I do this or you help me do this, the problem will go away."
    (d) Depression: "I feel so bad that I don't want to eat or sleep or play or do anything."
    (e) Acceptance: "I can't run as well as the other children, but I can still play ball."

15. (a) The teacher should listen to individual pupils, and work one-on-one or with small groups to provide a success experience for each handicapped pupil.
    (b) Goals should be discussed and worked out realistically with each pupil.
    (c) Reinforcement strategies may have to be adapted and increased to help a handicapped child develop a good self-concept.

16. (a) Impulsiveness, mainly involuntary behavior, not aggressive behavior with an emotional content
    (b) Excitability, demonstrated by a low frustration level, irritability, occasional temper tantrums, or destructiveness
    (c) Excessive activity, manifested by inability to sit still, by continual running around the room, by incessant talking, and the like
    (d) Distractibility, evidenced by a very short attention span, inability to stay on task, forgetfulness, and overstimulation by aural and visible distractions

17. (a) Listen to the child's interests and plan realistic small goals that he or she can probably achieve.
    (b) Use study carrels to minimize distractions.
    (c) Develop a routine procedure that the child will learn to expect.
    (d) Begin with positive reinforcement and provide for success experiences.
    (e) Be consistent in following through when enforcing class rules.

18. Developmental and Learning Disabilities

19. Grossman defined mental retardation as "significantly subaverage general intellectual functioning, existing concurrently with deficits in adaptive behavior, and manifested during the developmental period."

TEST OF PROFESSIONAL KNOWLEDGE: DESCRIPTION, REVIEW, PRACTICE

20. (a) (1) A teacher-made design-copying test
    (2) The Classroom Screening Instrument (CSI), with 50 observable behavioral indices
    (3) The Draw-a-Man Test
   (b) (1) The Wide-Range Achievement Test (WRAT)
    (2) Subtests from the Durrell Reading Achievement Analysis Test
    (3) Spache Reading Test
    (4) Wechsler Intelligence Scale for Children (WISC), the Frostig Developmental Test of Visual Perception (DTVP), the Illinois Test of Psycholinguistic Abilities (ITPA—experimental edition), the Templin-Darley Articulation Test, an audiometric screening, the Beery Visual Motor Integration Test (VMI)
   (c) (1) Social-behavioral histories, including family background
    (2) Neurological examination, medical history, laboratory tests, vision and hearing tests
    (3) Occupational therapy evaluation, the Southern California Tests, the Purdue Perceptual-Motor Survey
    (4) Electroencephalogram (EEG)
    (5) Other tests, including the Peabody Picture Vocabulary Test, Picture Story Language Test, Abstract-Concrete Rating, Concept Utilization

21. (a) The child may omit the same sounds in all words.
    (b) The child produces substitute sounds for the correct one such as "p" for "f," or "f" for "ch."
    (c) The child approximates the correct sound, such as "fp" for "t," or "t" for "th."
    (d) The child may have a cleft lip or palate, cerebral palsy, or dental abnormalities such as overbite or the loss of front teeth.
    (e) The child may pronounce the words, but shows the influence of poor speech models in the home or the continuance of infantile speech habits.

22. (a) anxiety over giving an answer, speaking before large groups, etc.
    (b) interruptions by listeners or by the teacher
    (c) lack of skills in telephone conversations

23. (a) A dysphonetic dyslexic child has a limited sight vocabulary, and has no phonic or word analysis skills. Reading from context is easier than reading single words.
    (b) A dyseidetic dyslexic child can read phonetically, but has difficulty remembering specific letters of words and so analyzes their components. He or she makes errors in reading and spelling because of this tendency to rely on such analysis.
    (c) The dysphonetic-dyseidetic dyslexic child has "hard core" dyslexia, according to Boder. Because this child cannot work out the visual or auditory clues to written words, he or she may remain a nonreader.

24. (a) Inability to translate sounds into letter symbols
    (b) Left-right directional confusion
    (c) Inadequate visual and auditory information processing

25. aphasia, with some history of birth trauma, head injury, or encephalitis

26. the normal capacity to read, but are nonreaders because of emotional problems or lack of motivation

27. a loss of spatial organization and visual discrimination, plus some loss of understanding of numbers

28. difficulty in understanding mathematics, including mathematical symbols, ideas, and relationships

29. withdrawn and uncommunicative, developing no speech, gestures, or tonal quality until later years, when communication tends to be echolalic

30. (a) the inability to understand the speech of others
    (b) a loss of speech—a loss in the motor ability to produce word sounds

Worksheet 4

1. teach essential skills more effectively in less time, add some (not all) information previously reserved for secondary programs to the elementary school curriculum

2. methods, materials

3. methods, materials, the evaluation of learning

4. (a) University of Illinois Arithmetic Project
   (b) Madison Project
   (c) Nuffield Project
   (d) Syracuse University Project

5. (a) What minimum level of achievement in fundamental skills should be required for every pupil?
   (b) At what age level should each particular skill be introduced?
   (c) How can the math education needs of handicapped and disadvantaged learners be met?
   (d) Should more emphasis be placed on the application of mathematics to pupils' daily lives?
   (e) Should the accelerated pupil have the equivalent of 3 years of college mathematics by the end of grade 12, as recommended in the Cambridge Conference Report?

6. (a) The concept of set is taught: some sets are equal and others are not equal. Students form subsets of a set, join them, and separate them. They count members of sets and identify a number with a set. They study sets of numbers and geometric figures.
   (b) The addition of whole numbers is studied after joining sets is objectified. Addition facts, column addition, and algorithms are studied by the end of grade 2.
   (c) Subtraction of whole numbers is related to addition, and related skills are learned concurrently.
   (d) At about grade 2, the multiplication and division of whole numbers are taught.
   (e) The pupil uses a symbol instead of a number, and is introduced to base 10 and to place value through concrete experiences.
   (f) Measurement is introduced through familiar objects.
   (g) Different geometric shapes are learned through hands-on experiences.
   (h) Problem solving is introduced early.

7. (a) Learning by experimenting in real and immediate situations, the pupil discovers mathematical ideas, reports observations, and draws conclusions.
   (b) Concepts are taught (and learned) with the aid of coordinated materials such as texts, laboratory projects, TV tapes, models, filmstrips, films, overlays, manipulable materials, computer-assisted programs, and resource persons.
   (c) Mathematics is correlated with other subjects such as art, music, science, social science, geography, reading, and health. Problems are drawn from activities such as scouting, sports, students' jobs, and other daily experiences in and out of the classroom.

8. exploration, discovery, generalization

9. organization, relationships

10. the principle underlying each process, the relationship between the two processes

11. selected for study

12. successfully solve the problem involved

13. Students may be overwhelmed by too many new problems and give up trying to achieve.

14. interests they already have; new, related topics

15. rules, principles, understandings that can be applied to other situations

16. type of situation to which it applies

17. relationship

18. Understanding

19. one long practice session

20. incorrect habits

21. reasons for the steps involved in the algorithm

22. concrete objects, abstract symbolism

23. retention

24. developing prerequisite skills, reviewing concepts, developing new vocabulary

25. zero

26. 10's

27. ordinal

28. error

29. Think of the problem as 45 + 30: (47 − 2) = 45, and (28 + 2) = 30.

30. Choice (b) is better, since the term *change* has other connotations for a child. *Rename* would be an appropriate term, also.

31. denominator

TEST OF PROFESSIONAL KNOWLEDGE: DESCRIPTION, REVIEW, PRACTICE

Diagnostic Practice Test—Test of Professional Knowledge

SECTION 1

Time—30 minutes

Directions: For each question or incomplete statement below, there are five suggested answers or completions. Select the one that *best* answers the question or completes the statement.

1. A poor attention span, lack of persistence in completing an assignment, and requiring more time than their peers to complete a task are behaviors most indicative of which of the following conditions?
   (A) Poor oral communication skills
   (B) A high level of intellectual ability resulting in boredom with everyday class activities
   (C) A motor impairment
   (D) Overindulgence resulting in a child's resistance to the teacher's authority
   (E) A task-related behavior deficit

2. Some psychologists find that the development of cognitive ability occurs in stages. Which of the following stages of cognitive development is usually thought to begin at adolescence?
   (A) The sensorimotor stage
   (B) The formal operational stage
   (C) The intuitive stage
   (D) The preoperational stage
   (E) The symbolic stage

3. A teacher can best foster the growth of inductive thinking, by which students increase their understanding of concepts or principles, through the use of
   (A) recitation of memorized data
   (B) films
   (C) computer-assisted instruction
   (D) personal-discovery activities
   (E) deductive problem solving

4. If you wanted to evaluate a program in the social studies to revise it for greater correspondence to the program objectives, you would use
   (A) accountability tests
   (B) assessment surveys
   (C) a behavior sample
   (D) standardized aptitude tests
   (E) essay tests

5. What is the difference between norm-referenced and criterion-referenced tests?
   (A) Test reliability is lower for criterion-referenced tests.
   (B) Norm-referenced tests in a particular subject or skill are better for determining the performance of any two students, relative to a national or large-group norm.
   (C) It is easier to structure a criterion-referenced test.
   (D) Criterion-referenced tests are standardized.
   (E) There is no significant difference between these two types of test.

6. A teacher prepared a unit test in arithmetic, but based questions only on the final week's work. The test
   (A) will have content validity, but not reliability
   (B) will have high construct validity
   (C) will not measure what the teacher wants to know about pupil performance
   (D) will be a broad sample of pupil learnings
   (E) will have criterion-referenced validity, but not reliability

7. Results of noncognitive tests are useful for counseling because these tests
   (A) provide stanine scores on mental abilities
   (B) measure opinions, attitudes, or interests
   (C) measure achievement
   (D) measure aptitude
   (E) provide a constant baseline

8. Reliability is lost in true-false tests because the testees tend to
   (A) guess
   (B) use an acquiescent response set
   (C) respond differently when retested
   (D) find questions are either too easy or too difficult
   (E) do all of the above

9. A teacher wants to obtain an index of item difficulty on a geometry test. Which of the following formulas should he use?
   (A) Add the proportion of students who scored high on the test and got a particular item correct to the proportion of students who scored low but got that item correct, then divide by 2.
   (B) Add the scores obtained by all students, then divide by 2.
   (C) Count the number of pupils who missed a particular item, then divide by 3.
   (D) Count the number of pupils who scored low and missed a particular item.
   (E) Count the number of students who scored high but missed a particular item.

10. A teacher wants to use brainstorming as a technique in problem solving. This teaching approach requires that
    (A) each participant give a logical suggestion for solving the problem
    (B) each participant express any ideas that come to mind, even though they may seem ridiculous
    (C) all participants vote on the best idea
    (D) the only students who speak be those who have researched the topic
    (E) the teacher call on the participants likely to have the best ideas

11. If a teacher wants to improve divergent thinking in an English literature class, he or she should
    (A) always require the correct answer
    (B) use creative approaches to a story or poem
    (C) be critical of all comments that do not lead to a set interpretation
    (D) discourage intensive questioning by pupils
    (E) provide daily practice quizzes in punctuation

TEST OF PROFESSIONAL KNOWLEDGE: DESCRIPTION, REVIEW, PRACTICE

12. Habitual set is a deterrent to creative thinking for which of the following reasons?

    I. It is genetic in origin.
    II. It is based on convergent thinking.
    III. It is critical of ad hoc solutions.
    IV. It is inflexible in patterns of decision-making.

    (A) I only
    (B) II only
    (C) III only
    (D) I, II, and III only
    (E) II, III, and IV only

13. Children with visual perception disorders may have greatest difficulty with which of the following skills?
    (A) Understanding what is read to them
    (B) Paying attention to what the teacher is saying
    (C) Repeating aloud a sequence of words
    (D) Participating in a group game
    (E) Recognizing letters and numerals

14. Kohler's study of apes led to the understanding of insight learning. What kind of teaching does insight learning encourage?

    I. Discovery teaching
    II. Encouragement of experimentation
    III. Engineering situations with potential for learning
    IV. Freeing students to learn

    (A) I only
    (B) II only
    (C) I and III only
    (D) II and III only
    (E) I, II, III, and IV

15. In discovery teaching the teacher
    (A) sets up a contract
    (B) teaches the solution
    (C) makes students memorize a procedure
    (D) helps students learn the principles underlying a procedure
    (E) closely monitors science projects

16. Certain learnings are more likely to take place in one or the other hemisphere of the brain. Which of the following statements about the brain is true?
    (A) Schools tend to emphasize development of the right hemisphere of the brain.
    (B) The left hemisphere of the brain is dominant in human beings.
    (C) The left hemisphere of the brain processes conceptual information.
    (D) Both hemispheres of the brain have an equal role in processing perceptual information.
    (E) The right hemisphere of the brain diminishes in size after adolescence.

17. A teacher is planning an exercise in multiple discrimination. Which of these learning activities should he or she use?
    (A) Pupils plant sunflower seeds in milk cartons.
    (B) Pupils classify birds from drawings on picture cards.
    (C) Pupils feed a rabbit in its cage.
    (D) Pupils change clothes for gym class.
    (E) Pupils march to the sound of appropriate music.

18. By following Bloom's taxonomy of the cognitive domain when writing objectives, a teacher chooses an approach in which
    (A) attitudinal experiences are emphasized
    (B) movement practices will be increased
    (C) levels of thinking can be expanded or increased
    (D) verbal-association practices can be emphasized
    (E) many signal concepts can be used

19. A teacher is developing lessons for providing children with experiences from the simple to the complex. Which of the following series is arranged from the simplest to the most complex?
    (A) Principle, signal, multiple discrimination
    (B) Problem solving, signal, multiple discrimination
    (C) Principle, problem solving, verbal association
    (D) Problem solving, verbal association, signal
    (E) Multiple discrimination, concept, principle

20. Many teachers do not use behavioral objectives because they
    (A) do not like the limitations of teaching for certain outcomes
    (B) prefer taking the time to write specific objectives
    (C) do not like describing behaviors that would require pupil individuality
    (D) prefer structuring groups toward common goals
    (E) believe in encouraging students to take responsibility on their own

21. School enrollment indicates that which of the following classifications is most prevalent today?
    (A) Learning disabled
    (B) Multihandicapped
    (C) Orthopedically impaired
    (D) Emotionally disturbed
    (E) Mentally retarded

22. Which of the following behaviors is an example of psychological *contiguity*?
    (A) Clarissa does not speak loudly in class because the teacher will not recognize her when she does.
    (B) Jane smiles at the coach when she enters the basketball court. The coach praises Jane for her skill in making baskets.
    (C) Bob doesn't talk much on a date because Mary likes to listen to the music on the stereo system.
    (D) Whenever Karen passes a florist shop, she thinks of her former boyfriend because he frequently gave her a red rose.
    (E) Sam hurries to clean up his table in the laboratory because the teacher lets him get in line first if he finishes quickly.

TEST OF PROFESSIONAL KNOWLEDGE: DESCRIPTION, REVIEW, PRACTICE

23. For teachers working with a mentally retarded boy, the behavior-shaping technique that usually works best involves
    (A) rewards for successive approximations of a desired behavior
    (B) a negative stimulus following an undesirable behavior
    (C) punishment, when needed, by social isolation from the class
    (D) nonreinforcement of an undesirable response
    (E) an emotional stimulus

24. Which of the following personal characteristics influences the learning of individual students at the eighth-grade level?

    I. Incentives
    II. Attitudes
    III. Interests and needs
    IV. Values and expectation level

    (A) I only
    (B) II only
    (C) I and II only
    (D) III only
    (E) I, II, III, and IV

25. P.L. 94-142, the Education for All Handicapped Children Act of 1975, guarantees
    (A) that all handicapped children be mainstreamed
    (B) that all handicapped children receive educational services from birth to age 21
    (C) that all handicapped children be provided with personal teacher aides
    (D) that all handicapped children be educated in the least restrictive environment
    (E) that all handicapped children be exempted from taking standardized tests

26. Jake received a percentile rank of 75 on the SAT test. The counselor told him that
    (A) his score is too low for success in college
    (B) one fourth of the students ranked higher on the test than he did
    (C) three fourths of the students ranked higher than he did
    (D) Jake got 75% of the questions correct
    (E) Jake got less than one fourth of the questions correct

27. A teacher desires to evaluate his third-grade reading class for comprehension skills. He should select a standardized test that will provide
    (A) an analysis of factors in reading comprehension
    (B) a standard deviation score
    (C) the median score
    (D) percentile ranks
    (E) prediction scales

213

TEST OF PROFESSIONAL KNOWLEDGE: DESCRIPTION, REVIEW, PRACTICE

28. A teacher indicates that she has several students in the seventh grade who are products of an education poverty circle. What does she mean?
    (A) Parents with low scholastic ability tend to create poor learning environments for their children.
    (B) Test bias creates a cycle of poor scholarship.
    (C) Teachers who give students failing marks develop circles of unemployment poverty.
    (D) The students in question are the children of immigrants.
    (E) Teachers have to use culture-fair tests to avoid penalizing students of low-income families.

29. A principal wants to improve home-school relationships so that pupil potential and achievement are developed to the optimum. Research shows that the home-school interaction can be significantly improved by which of the following?
    I. early intervention to aid infant and preschool learners
    II. a linguistic-deficiency program
    III. the "giant-word" approach developed by Bereiter and Engelmann
    IV. a preschool child-centered curriculum
    (A) I only
    (B) II only
    (C) I and II only
    (D) III and IV only
    (E) I, II, III, and IV

READ THE FOLLOWING DIRECTIONS BEFORE PROCEEDING.
Directions: The following questions contain the word NOT or EXCEPT. Read each question very carefully, then find the answer that applies.

30. A teacher has selected the Personalized System of Instruction (PSI) for his seventh-grade English class. Which one of these will NOT be a part of his planning?
    (A) Student-paced assignments
    (B) Mastery requirements
    (C) Individualized instruction
    (D) Tutoring
    (E) Relative standards

31. The following factors influence the effectiveness of classroom teaching. Which factor is NOT correctly defined?
    (A) *Preinteractive phase*, the planning phase before teaching begins
    (B) *With-it-ness*, the teacher's awareness of pupils' activities throughout the classroom
    (C) *Momentum*, the teacher's interaction with some students more than others
    (D) *Group alerting*, the teacher's use of suspense techniques to keep students on task
    (E) *Overlappingness*, the teacher's ability to deal with several problem pupils at the same time

TEST OF PROFESSIONAL KNOWLEDGE: DESCRIPTION, REVIEW, PRACTICE

32. Learning is enhanced for each pupil when a teacher uses any of the following approaches EXCEPT
    (A) probing for the desired answer among several students
    (B) asking higher-order questions that require analysis, synthesis, application, or evaluation
    (C) giving signals for transition from one part of the lesson to another
    (D) directly structuring the classroom learning process
    (E) promptly giving postperformance feedback to pupils

33. Which of the following is NOT an environmental factor in operant conditioning?
    (A) A token economy
    (B) Teacher praise
    (C) Teacher use of incentives
    (D) Motivation contracts
    (E) Reflex actions

34. A fifth-grade teacher manipulates several environmental factors to motivate her students toward more effective learning. Which of the following is NOT one of these factors?
    (A) A lenient grading policy
    (B) Self-grading by the students
    (C) Students epistemic curiosity to know
    (D) The student's functional autonomy to work alone
    (E) The student's use of referent power as leader

35. Which of the following devices would NOT be used by a teacher in a fifth-grade geography class?
    (A) *Manding stimuli*, verbal statements that carry no consequence
    (B) *Mediation*, the creation of links between unrelated materials
    (C) *Cue dependence*, use of cues for information retrieval
    (D) An *advance organizer*, short overview of new material
    (E) *Overlearning*, review of material already learned

S T O P

IF YOU FINISH BEFORE TIME IS CALLED, YOU MAY CHECK YOUR WORK ON THIS SECTION ONLY.
DO NOT WORK ON ANY OTHER SECTION IN THE TEST.

TEST OF PROFESSIONAL KNOWLEDGE: DESCRIPTION, REVIEW, PRACTICE

SECTION 2

Time — 30 minutes

Directions: For each question or incomplete statement below, there are five suggested answers or completions. Select the one that *best* answers the question or completes the statement.

1. Which of the following abilities embodies the current concept of intelligence?

    I. The ability to deal with abstractions
    II. The ability to learn
    III. The ability to solve problems
    IV. The ability to deal with new situations

    (A) I only
    (B) II only
    (C) I and II only
    (D) I, II, and III only
    (E) I, II, III, and IV

2. A teacher uses the aptitude-treatment-interaction (ATI) approach. You would expect him to write learning objectives that
    (A) fit the student's characteristics
    (B) require setting up special classroom experiences
    (C) indicate special treatment after aptitude testing
    (D) allow for sex-related differences
    (E) are based on current development norms

3. When Jean was tested she was asked to repeat several digits forwards and backwards and to take a vocabulary subtest. The kind of test she was given was
    (A) an achievement test
    (B) a reading test
    (C) an arithmetic placement test
    (D) an intelligence test
    (E) a grade-placement test

4. A teacher's lesson plan includes both emotional and intellectual objectives. Her philosophy of learning is based primarily on
    (A) behaviorism
    (B) activism
    (C) rationalism
    (D) humanism
    (E) classicism

5. Ted's score of 600 on the SAT is 1 standard deviation above the mean. What percent of high school students scored lower than Ted?
    (A) 16 percent
    (B) 75 percent
    (C) 84 percent
    (D) 10 percent
    (E) 68 percent

TEST OF PROFESSIONAL KNOWLEDGE: DESCRIPTION, REVIEW, PRACTICE

6. Which of the following statements represents the relationship between intelligence and age?
   (A) Intelligence is usually stabilized by age 25.
   (B) Usually, intelligence is highly stable by age 10.
   (C) Intelligence increases at a set rate until age 21.
   (D) Intelligence remains constant from birth.
   (E) Intelligence declines rapidly after age 35.

7. To avoid vagueness in objectives for a fifth-grade social studies class, a teacher should do which of the following?
   I. State the objectives in terms of learner behavior that can be observed easily.
   II. Specify clearly the objectives for each topic.
   III. State criteria by which achievement of the objectives can readily be evaluated.

   (A) I only
   (B) II only
   (C) III only
   (D) I and III only
   (E) I, II, and III

8. A teacher wants to improve students' reading comprehension. The best initial approach would be to
   (A) experiment with a variety of methods with individual pupils
   (B) give textbook reading assignments to everyone in the class
   (C) plan computer-aided instruction for all students
   (D) use filmstrips with the first unit of lessons
   (E) begin with the look-say method

9. Mary performed well on an examination including card-sorting, a vocabulary comprehension test, and an arithmetic reasoning test. A teacher summarizing the results of Mary's exam would say she scored high in
   (A) abstract reasoning
   (B) numerical reasoning
   (C) affective learning
   (D) general mental abilities
   (E) verbal abilities

10. Although Betty seems anxious and questions directions given by the teacher's aide and the parent-helper, she follows the teacher's directions well. Which of the following theories does she exemplify?
    (A) Erikson's theory of trust and mistrust
    (B) Kohlberg's theory of moral development
    (C) Maslow's theory of the hierarchy of needs
    (D) Rogers' theory of phenomenal field
    (E) Bandura's theory of modeling

TEST OF PROFESSIONAL KNOWLEDGE: DESCRIPTION, REVIEW, PRACTICE

11. As Mitchell and Martin watched television many hours each week, their aggressive behavior increased. Which of the following opportunities should their teachers provide for them?

    I. To model or imitate more desirable behavior
    II. To obtain reinforcement for desirable behavior
    III. To see and discuss role-playing that involves different behaviors

    (A) I only
    (B) II only
    (C) I and II only
    (D) I and III only
    (E) I, II, and III

12. Educational research has shown that written objectives work best when
    (A) students do not see them.
    (B) they specify intentional learnings.
    (C) students prefer incidental activities.
    (D) teachers think they make the most difference for above-average students.
    (E) the learning tasks are too difficult.

13. A teacher plans to provide significant individual learning for her biology classes by using the greenhouse for plant study. For such a project, she should institute
    (A) autocratic class control
    (B) hands-on experiences for each student
    (C) self-initiated projects
    (D) a temporary halt on all evaluation measures
    (E) the recommendations in (B) and (C) above

14. Under the Tenth Amendment of the United States Constitution,
    (A) education is recognized as being under the authority of the national government
    (B) education is one of the powers reserved to the states
    (C) a free public education for all citizens is guaranteed
    (D) the Supreme Court is given responsibility for the direction of education throughout the nation
    (E) education is made compulsory for all children

15. A teaching certificate is an assurance that its possessor is qualified to teach. Teaching certificates are issued by which of the following?
    (A) The college or university from which the teacher graduated
    (B) The school district employing the teacher
    (C) The federal department of Health and Human Services
    (D) The school employing the teacher
    (E) Each state's department of education

16. Which of the following terms is incorrectly defined?
    (A) *Dyslexia*—a disturbance in reading
    (B) *Autism*—extreme withdrawal from reality
    (C) *Hyperkinesis*—abnormal, purposeless muscular movement
    (D) *Educable mentally retarded*—those with an IQ below 50
    (E) *Gifted children*—those having an IQ of 130 or above

TEST OF PROFESSIONAL KNOWLEDGE: DESCRIPTION, REVIEW, PRACTICE

17. Studies in the United States and England indicate that direct instruction is associated with
    (A) group gains in reading and creative writing at all levels
    (B) gains in mathematics at the primary-grade level
    (C) gain in mathematics at the secondary level
    (D) higher than average achievement in reading and mathematics for elementary pupils from poor socioeconomic backgrounds
    (E) higher average pupil achievement in all subjects

18. Research indicates that the home can make a positive difference in children's intellectual development through the influences of which of the following?

    I. Parents' conversations with children
    II. Parents' reading habits, and books available to their children
    III. Parental values
    IV. Behavior models within the family group

    (A) I only
    (B) II only
    (C) II and III only
    (D) I, II, and III only
    (E) I, II, III, and IV

19. Nursery schools and other preschool programs can do the most to improve a child's intellectual responses through the use of
    (A) adequate custodial care
    (B) direct instruction
    (C) various open activities
    (D) child-centered planning
    (E) attractive, learning-oriented toys and other equipment

20. In one school district, parent conferences are held twice each school year. Mrs. Carris is planning the format by which she will meet with each parent and conduct each conference. To present her information and obtain the parent's understanding and cooperation, Mrs. Carris should do which of the following?
    (A) Start by listing the child's areas of deficit, so that the parent will have no problem in understanding the teacher's educational goals and will be able to help with the most difficult homework assignments.
    (B) Start by listing the child's areas of strength, so that the parent will understand why the teacher is no longer stressing these areas in class or when giving homework assignments.
    (C) Start by showing samples of the child's poor schoolwork, so that the parent can take the papers home and tutor the child on work which was done incorrectly at school.
    (D) Start by explaining that the child has social difficulties, poor attention span, and little interest in the curriculum, so that the parent understands why the child is doing poorly and can help correct these problems at home.
    (E) Start by praising the child's areas of strength, then proceed to areas of need, so that the parent understands that the teacher is viewing the child from an unbiased perspective.

TEST OF PROFESSIONAL KNOWLEDGE: DESCRIPTION, REVIEW, PRACTICE

21. Research on language usage indicates that the teacher must provide a variety of experiences for children who come from low-socioeconomic homes and have reading difficulties because
    (A) they use a fused-word language structure
    (B) their language usage is limited by their environment
    (C) their language makes it difficult to transfer from speech to reading
    (D) they have many stereotyped expressions
    (E) in the formulation of concepts, poor language habits affect learning

22. Bob had written a poem for his English class. At a club meeting, he was asked to recite the poem, and he did so. This is an example of
    (A) slight positive transfer
    (B) mediated transfer
    (C) marked positive transfer
    (D) slight negative transfer
    (E) marked negative transfer

23. Jim passed a driver education course. When he took the driver's test at the courthouse, however, he failed. All factors being equal, his failure was the result of
    (A) extinction of a learned behavior
    (B) a transfer of training
    (C) poor motivation
    (D) poor encoding
    (E) a combination of factors other than (A), (B), (C), and (D)

24. In physical education classes, the teacher can help students avoid developing feelings of inferiority by
    (A) providing success experiences for each pupil
    (B) blocking individual pupil initiative
    (C) posting the list of pupils failing to pass a physical-activities test
    (D) grading physical activities such as the number of push-ups a student can do
    (E) ridiculing pupils who are awkward

25. Which of the following is the best definition of learning?
    (A) A tentative bonding between stimulus and response
    (B) A short-term acquisition of knowledge
    (C) A permanent change in behavior, based on experience
    (D) The ability to decode a telegram
    (E) The habit of responding to the teacher's signals

26. For the nutrition class in home economics, Betty and Howard prepared a meal including a fish casserole that several students did not eat. The next time the two prepared a menu for the class, they excluded fish. This is an example of
    (A) extinction of behavior through lack of reward
    (B) fear of punishment
    (C) forgetting
    (D) imitation learning
    (E) inquiry learning

TEST OF PROFESSIONAL KNOWLEDGE: DESCRIPTION, REVIEW, PRACTICE

27. Which of the following associated ideas is correctly matched?
(A) behaviorism—teacher-initiated learning activities
(B) humanism—goal-centered philosophy of education
(C) cognitive goal—personal competence
(D) behaviorist goal—intellectual development
(E) affective domain—discrimination, precision

Questions 28–29 are based on the following standardized test results for a student over a four-year period.

Grade — 4.1
Date of Testing — 10/85

Subtests	NUMBER RIGHT	GRADE EQUIV	STANINE	NATL PCT
READING				
Word Study Skills	31	4.1	5	54
Comprehension	26	5.8	7	79
TOTAL READING	57	4.9	6	61
MATHEMATICS				
Applications	19	2.9	3	21
Computation	27	4.2	5	56
TOTAL MATHEMATICS	46	3.5	4	38
LANGUAGE				
Mechanics	41	2.2	2	9
Usage	39	2.5	3	20
TOTAL LANGUAGE	80	2.4	3	18
SPELLING	33	2.7	4	30
TOTAL BATTERY	216	3.5	4	37

Grade — 5.1
Date of Testing — 10/86

Subtests	NUMBER RIGHT	GRADE EQUIV	STANINE	NATL PCT
READING				
Word Study Skills	37	6.1	7	78
Comprehension	39	6.3	7	82
TOTAL READING	76	6.2	7	80
MATHEMATICS				
Applications	21	3.2	3	15
Computation	34	4.8	5	48
TOTAL MATHEMATICS	55	4.0	4	33
LANGUAGE				
Mechanics	27	2.8	1	3
Usage	30	3.4	3	10
TOTAL LANGUAGE	57	3.1	2	7
SPELLING	39	3.9	4	30
TOTAL BATTERY	227	4.5	5	40

Grade — 6.1
Date of Testing — 10/87

Subtests	NUMBER RIGHT	GRADE EQUIV	STANINE	NATL PCT
READING				
Word Study Skills	41	5.2	4	37
Comprehension	36	4.7	4	30
TOTAL READING	77	4.8	4	31
MATHEMATICS				
Applications	31	4.8	4	23
Computation	39	5.7	5	42
TOTAL MATHEMATICS	70	5.2	4	32
LANGUAGE				
Mechanics	32	3.0	3	10
Usage	40	3.3	3	17
TOTAL LANGUAGE	72	3.2	3	12
SPELLING	22	4.4	3	18
TOTAL BATTERY	241	4.2	3	21

Grade — 7.1
Date of Testing — 10/88

Subtests	NUMBER RIGHT	GRADE EQUIV	STANINE	NATL PCT
READING				
Word Study Skills	31	7.7	6	66
Comprehension	38	8.5	7	80
TOTAL READING	69	8.1	7	79
MATHEMATICS				
Applications	38	7.2	5	57
Computation	41	6.8	5	46
TOTAL MATHEMATICS	79	7.0	5	49
LANGUAGE				
Mechanics	26	5.3	4	24
Usage	44	6.2	5	41
TOTAL LANGUAGE	70	5.7	4	31
SPELLING	34	4.9	3	21
TOTAL BATTERY	252	6.5	5	44

TEST OF PROFESSIONAL KNOWLEDGE: DESCRIPTION, REVIEW, PRACTICE

28. In which skills area does this student regularly score within the average range as compared to students on whom this test was normed?
    (A) Word study skills
    (B) Comprehension
    (C) Computation
    (D) Applications
    (E) Spelling

29. At which grade is this student generally having the greatest academic difficulty?
    (A) 4
    (B) 5
    (C) 6
    (D) 7
    (E) It cannot be determined from the information given.

READ THE FOLLOWING DIRECTIONS BEFORE PROCEEDING.
Directions: The following questions contain the word LEAST, NOT, or EXCEPT. Read each question very carefully, then find the answer that applies.

30. A teacher sets out to plan learning experiences that will aid elementary children in linguistic comprehension and performance. Believing that students' difficulties in reading arise from environmental factors, he will incorporate all of the following guidelines in his plans EXCEPT the one holding that
    (A) linguistic functioning is modifiable
    (B) linguistic functioning is based on innate competence
    (C) the teacher should reduce severe-anxiety-producing situations
    (D) the teacher should use dialog often
    (E) the teacher should not reward impulsivity in speech

31. Jimmy's teacher notices his shyness and fear of new experiences. When conferring with the school psychologist, she learns all of the following about Jimmy EXCEPT that he
    (A) has experienced overcontrol by his parents
    (B) lacks a sense of trust
    (C) lacks a sense of autonomy
    (D) can develop a sense of initiative if the appropriate behavior is reinforced
    (E) should be reprimanded frequently by his teacher

TEST OF PROFESSIONAL KNOWLEDGE: DESCRIPTION, REVIEW, PRACTICE

32. A social-studies teacher wants to write statements specifying conditions and levels of performance that will demonstrate student success in a unit on Georgia. Which of the following statements should she NOT use?
    (A) *Condition*—using an outline map of Georgia, pupils will locate the state capital and three cities with populations of 35,000 or more.
    (B) *Condition*—to obtain A as a grade, the pupil must correctly answer 9 out of 10 multiple-choice questions.
    (C) *Level*—the pupil will spell correctly 9 out of 10 words on each geography word list.
    (D) *Condition*—given an outline map of the state, pupils will locate where 90 percent of the agricultural products are grown in Georgia.
    (E) *Level*—given any topic of the pupil's choice, the pupil will write a report.

33. A teacher makes a summary of various theories of mental development. Which of the following summaries is NOT an accurate statement?
    (A) According to Bruner, pupils at every grade level use all three modes of representation.
    (B) According to Bruner, during the iconic-representation stage, pupils think pictorially.
    (C) According to Bruner, the symbolic stage compares to the stage of formal operations.
    (D) In humanism, the key element is the self-concept theory.
    (E) According to Skinner, children develop through mental stages.

34. A teacher desires to improve transfer of learning in the language arts, especially in spelling. Which of the following concepts would NOT apply to this goal?
    (A) Stimulus predifferentiation
    (B) Identity of substance
    (C) Identity of procedure
    (D) Negative transfer-of-learning
    (E) Aptitude-treatment interaction

35. When planning programs for learning-disabled children, teachers should be guided by all of the following assumptions, EXCEPT that
    (A) the learning-disabled have normal overall intelligence
    (B) the learning-disabled have behavioral and emotional problems
    (C) the learning-disabled have no major physical handicaps
    (D) the learning-disabled are "normal" children with learning problems
    (E) problems for the learning-disabled arise from a specific cause rather than a defect in global functioning

STOP

IF YOU FINISH BEFORE TIME IS CALLED, YOU MAY CHECK YOUR WORK ON THIS SECTION ONLY. DO NOT WORK ON ANY OTHER SECTION IN THE TEST.

TEST OF PROFESSIONAL KNOWLEDGE: DESCRIPTION, REVIEW, PRACTICE

SECTION 3

Time—30 minutes

Directions: For each question or incomplete statement below, there are five suggested answers or completions. Select the one that *best* answers the question or completes the statement.

1. Bruce was drawing funny faces of the teacher and passing the drawings around in the arithmetic class. The teacher ignored this behavior and concentrated on praising those who did their work. Last week, instead of drawing, Bruce spent his time doing arithmetic problems. According to Skinner's theory of operant conditioning, Bruce began to exhibit the effects of
   (A) classical conditioning
   (B) classification of activities
   (C) extinction of a learned behavior
   (D) distributed practice
   (E) chaining

2. The major characteristic of operant conditioning is the use of
   (A) reinforcement procedures
   (B) massed practice
   (C) patterned practice
   (D) the Premack principle
   (E) a configuration of experiences

3. An instructor is planning lessons for a new tennis class. After initial learning, the best way for her pupils to maintain new skills will be through
   (A) a variety of sports activities
   (B) solo practice
   (C) distributed practice
   (D) applying the Gestalt principle
   (E) mass practice

4. Teachers who frequently experience role-conflict are those who
   (A) set pupil standards too low
   (B) are inconsistent in discipline
   (C) have inadequate training
   (D) have to meet several different kinds of responsibilities
   (E) use innovative methods

5. Pupils and teachers work in a psychological climate fundamentally created by
   (A) the board of education
   (B) the community
   (C) the school administrators
   (D) the students themselves
   (E) the teachers themselves

TEST OF PROFESSIONAL KNOWLEDGE: DESCRIPTION, REVIEW, PRACTICE

6. In the broadest sense, a teacher is a facilitator of learning in that
   (A) pupils are in charge of planning their work
   (B) parents become involved in learning situations
   (C) the teacher plans for individual differences
   (D) guidance is a part of education
   (E) the teacher assists pupils in planning and evaluation

7. In addition to academic competency, one of the most significant benefits a high school student can gain from education is
   (A) self-understanding
   (B) college counseling
   (C) test confidence
   (D) preparation for marriage
   (E) career counseling

8. High schools that have reduced truancy and dropout rates did so by developing policies to
   (A) punish truancy
   (B) involve students in planning activities
   (C) increase guidance and counseling time
   (D) reinforce school attendance
   (E) expel disinterested students

9. Emotional problems of students may be of interest to teachers when
   I. parents criticize teachers
   II. pupils create discipline problems
   III. lack of pupil adjustment interferes with learning

   (A) I only
   (B) II only
   (C) III only
   (D) II and III only
   (E) I, II, and III

10. Exceptional children sometimes have needs that the school cannot meet without support services. Forming a liaison among the school, mental health clinics, welfare agencies, the juvenile court, and the home is usually the responsibility of the
    (A) guidance counselor
    (B) principal
    (C) school psychologist
    (D) vice principal
    (E) social worker

11. Studies show that when older students with reading difficulties tutor younger pupils, the tutors
    (A) show more gain in reading than the tutees
    (B) decrease in reading ability
    (C) show about the same gain as the tutees
    (D) show no gain in reading comprehension
    (E) cause younger readers to lose interest in reading

TEST OF PROFESSIONAL KNOWLEDGE: DESCRIPTION, REVIEW, PRACTICE

12. When using a preschool program for disadvantaged learners, the program's effectiveness can be increased through home visits made by
    (A) administrators of the program
    (B) community social workers
    (C) mothers employed by the program
    (D) school nurses
    (E) school psychologists

13. For those who teach disadvantaged learners the overriding goal should be to help these children to
    (A) develop excitement about achieving
    (B) handle possible failures
    (C) express their opinions
    (D) learn to spell
    (E) learn academic English

14. One of the major problems in counseling disadvantaged students, by comparison with middle-class students, is to get them to
    (A) take directive counseling
    (B) come to the counselor's office
    (C) make long-range plans
    (D) attend class regularly
    (E) reduce their anxiety about tests

15. A teacher likes to use small candies as a reward for students who complete assignments in arithmetic. Such immediate rewards are useful for working with
    (A) high achievers in arithmetic
    (B) retarded learners
    (C) boys of any age
    (D) girls of any age
    (E) students who are goal-oriented

16. A teacher reprimands his algebra class with the following comment: "I have never had a class that does as poorly as you do on tests. What is the matter with you? I give you plenty of review materials and a lot of time in class to get help. I am not at fault. The fault lies with you! Now get busy and do all the problems that you missed on this test!" Such a statement would give the most cause for anxiety to students who
    (A) are highly competent in mathematics
    (B) are generally insecure about their schoolwork and dislike algebra
    (C) are generally high achievers
    (D) are emotionally mature
    (E) are not reading on grade level

17. In lower income families, the anxiety most often expressed by parents about their children is that
    (A) they are likely to get into trouble
    (B) they will not succeed in school
    (C) they will not get into a good college
    (D) they will drop out of school
    (E) teachers will not like them

TEST OF PROFESSIONAL KNOWLEDGE: DESCRIPTION, REVIEW, PRACTICE

18. The number of children living at or below the poverty level increases
    (A) as the number of one-parent households increases
    (B) as an increase is noted in one-parent households headed by a woman
    (C) as the population increases
    (D) as the average income of families declines
    (E) for none of the reasons given above

19. One of the beliefs that disadvantaged learners need help to overcome is that
    (A) social progress is a matter of luck
    (B) people are responsible for their own actions
    (C) personal development is a matter of hard work
    (D) education counts in the job market
    (E) setting long-term goals is important

20. Studies show that teachers who work well with delinquent or emotionally disturbed students
    (A) are more self-confident than other teachers
    (B) use punitive measures daily
    (C) seldom punish misbehavior
    (D) are very successful also with children not so diagnosed
    (E) are better educated than most teachers

21. Which of the following is the most probable reason why gifted children may have adjustment problems?
    (A) They expect very little of themselves.
    (B) Other students in the class resent them.
    (C) They constantly feel the pressure of parents' and teachers' expectations.
    (D) School seems boring to them.
    (E) They tend to be very shy.

22. A teacher of mentally retarded children should
    (A) deal with just one aspect of the retardation
    (B) realize that the developmental potential of such children is negligible
    (C) limit the children's opportunities for social contact to avoid ridicule
    (D) provide a variety of communication opportunities
    (E) avoid the use of reward and punishment

23. A pupil above the third grade who repeats a grade is likely to
    (A) show marked improvement in reading
    (B) develop new skills in arithmetic
    (C) gain in self-confidence
    (D) show little gain from the experience
    (E) show a gain in IQ

24. What percentage of children classified as mentally retarded are found to be socially deprived?
    (A) Approximately 75 percent
    (B) Approximately 35 percent
    (C) Approximately 25 percent
    (D) Approximately 10 percent
    (E) Approximately 50 percent

25. Which of the following would be required by a student contract for a unit of work in a social studies class?
    (A) That the teacher set a terminal goal
    (B) That the student determine how to reach a goal
    (C) That the student get the materials necessary to reach a goal
    (D) That the student develop a way to evaluate his or her goal achievement
    (E) Any of the above

26. One of the myths that humanistic philosophy debunks is the notion of
    (A) learning as an isolated intellectual activity
    (B) accommodation
    (C) Gestalt psychology
    (D) relevant education for today's living
    (E) affective learnings

27. The process by which a student converts information to permanent learnings involves
    (A) interference   (D) classification
    (B) encoding   (E) discrimination
    (C) correlation

28. Which of the following is associated with the arousal of curiosity?
    I. Novelty of an object
    II. Incongruity of a situation
    III. Incompleteness of an explanation

    (A) I only
    (B) II only
    (C) III only
    (D) I and III only
    (E) I, II, and III

29. A teacher wants to write a series of lesson plans to help students develop good problem-solving skills. Which of the following skill sequences is in the correct order for this series of lesson plans?
    (A) Perception, generation of solutions, evaluation
    (B) Deduction, generation of solutions, reporting
    (C) Memory, deduction, perception
    (D) Reporting, evaluation, memory
    (E) Evaluation, generation of solutions, perception

TEST OF PROFESSIONAL KNOWLEDGE: DESCRIPTION, REVIEW, PRACTICE

READ THE FOLLOWING DIRECTIONS BEFORE PROCEEDING.

Directions: The following questions contain the word LEAST, NOT, or EXCEPT. Read each question very carefully, then seek the answer that applies.

30. Which of the following is NOT an example of encoding?
    (A) Craig lists the telephone numbers of the companies he calls most often in clusters of three digits.
    (B) Mark draws an illustration of the gas meter so that he will remember how to read it.
    (C) Ann underlines key ideas and makes notes in the margin of the history textbook.
    (D) Manley will remember that he wore a blue shirt the day he lost the lead part in the school play.
    (E) Marta uses the memory device ROY G BIV to remember the order of the colors in the spectrum.

31. Children with physical handicaps include all of the following EXCEPT
    (A) those who are partially paralyzed
    (B) those who have sensory defects such as problems with hearing or vision
    (C) those who have individual learning needs
    (D) those who have spastic problems
    (E) those who have minimal brain dysfunction

32. A teacher's questions should focus on the kind of knowledge that is relevant to the lesson plan and objectives. Which of the following questions does NOT relate to the knowledge category preceding it?
    (A) *Symbols:* "How many quarter notes are in this melody line?"
    (B) *Composition:* "Which of these is an example of haiku?"
    (C) *Object recognition:* "What stain is being used to darken this shelf?"
    (D) *Relationship of behaviors:* "How does aerobic exercise affect the large muscles in the arm?"
    (E) *Analysis of meaning:* "What is the current GNP of the United States?"

33. Classroom discipline is essential for learning. Students will accept rules LEAST readily if
    (A) they help formulate the regulations
    (B) there are very few rules to break
    (C) rules apply to the students' needs and welfare
    (D) clear-cut rules are always enforced, and punishment always follows
    (E) rules are not consistently enforced

34. Penny constantly breaks the rules, leaves her seat, and interrupts the teacher during orientation procedures. All of the following methods will help the teacher get Penny to cooperate EXCEPT
(A) ignore her completely
(B) reinforce any acceptable behavior she demonstrates
(C) determine whether she is seeking attention through misbehavior
(D) give her a responsibility in the classroom to build her self-concept
(E) talk to Penny about the situation

35. A teacher plans to use programmed learning on a daily basis with his ninth-grade science class. Since he does not have a computer or standardized material, he should plan to do all of the following EXCEPT
(A) analyze the content of the unit to be taught
(B) divide the content into small steps
(C) elicit each student's response every day
(D) conduct frequent evaluations
(E) provide occasional feedback to each student

S T O P

IF YOU FINISH BEFORE TIME IS CALLED, YOU MAY CHECK YOUR WORK ON THIS SECTION ONLY. DO NOT WORK ON ANY OTHER SECTION IN THE TEST.

TEST OF PROFESSIONAL KNOWLEDGE: DESCRIPTION, REVIEW, PRACTICE
SECTION 4

Time—30 minutes

Directions: For each question or incomplete statement below, there are five suggested answers or completions. Select the one that *best* answers the question or completes the statement.

1. Your fourth-grade students have taken an intelligence test. What part of the report for that test would be of most value to you?
    (A) Raw scores
    (B) Rank of each student within the class group
    (C) Reported correlation between this and other intelligence tests
    (D) Subtest data for each pupil
    (E) Item analysis for a question on analogies

2. Most teachers of children who are physically or emotionally handicapped or who are learning-disabled like to have their students take at least one IQ test that is individually administered. Why?
    (A) Such a test can be used for assessing group strengths.
    (B) Its subtest results can be used to shape the development of new curricula.
    (C) A handicapped or learning-disabled child may achieve a higher score on such a test.
    (D) Any faulty perceptual processing by such a child can be located with an individual test.
    (E) The results of individually administered IQ tests are more predictable.

3. A teacher's mathematics class achieved the following scores on a weekly examination: 45, 47, 52, 52, 54, 57, 59, 62, 64, 68, 71, 75, 75, 80, 87, 88, 89, 90, 93, 93, 93, 95, 96. What was the median on this test?
    (A) 75
    (B) 71
    (C) 73
    (D) 64
    (E) 93

4. A teacher wants to test the computational ability of his fourth-grade pupils. Which of the following types of question would contribute most to the validity of the test he prepares?
    (A) Story problems
    (B) Multiple-choice items
    (C) Problems demanding very little reading
    (D) True-false items
    (E) Problems invented by the pupils

TEST OF PROFESSIONAL KNOWLEDGE: DESCRIPTION, REVIEW, PRACTICE

5. The *Stanford-Binet Intelligence Test* is based on the ratio of the testee's mental age to his or her
   (A) environment
   (B) achievement
   (C) heredity
   (D) chronological age
   (E) interests

6. A curriculum committee has asked a teacher to serve as evaluator of its foreign-language program. The teacher should base her evaluation on
   (A) students' ability to translate a given passage
   (B) different standards that she sets for each grade level
   (C) student attitudes toward the language they are studying
   (D) results of standardized vocabulary tests
   (E) specific criteria or goals set by each teacher prior to instruction

7. Frank usually gets a high score on science tests. Despite the fact that he studied for it, he did very poorly on the last test. All other things being equal, which of the following factors most probably accounted for his poor score?
   (A) He took the test on a very hot day.
   (B) His teacher changed his seating location.
   (C) Most of the test questions were in essay form instead of the usual multiple-choice items.
   (D) Too many days had been spent discussing key concepts in the lesson tested.
   (E) More time had been spent in group work than on individual assignments.

8. A teacher wants to use behavior modification techniques with his third-grade reading class. First he must establish a baseline of performance for each pupil by
   (A) giving pretests to the class
   (B) checking last year's reading scores for the class
   (C) having everyone read aloud
   (D) having a few pupils take a comprehension test
   (E) giving creative writing assignments

9. Every teacher should be concerned about the validity of tests given for the purpose of grading. Assuming that appropriate lessons on each subject had been taught, which of the following is the best example of a valid test question?
   (A) List the important characteristics of a baseball player.
   (B) Define civilization.
   (C) Identify the elements of a successful presidential campaign.
   (D) State three reasons why the Battle of Gettysburg was a turning point in the Civil War.
   (E) Explain why you like or dislike movies about teenagers.

10. When you want to assess each student's achievement by comparison with the achievement of others in the same grade, you have to use a
    (A) criterion-referenced test   (D) norm-referenced test
    (B) developmental test   (E) personal inventory test
    (C) psychomotor test

TEST OF PROFESSIONAL KNOWLEDGE: DESCRIPTION, REVIEW, PRACTICE

11. A culturally disadvantaged pupil with poor penmanship received a low grade on an essay test, even though he knew the basic information. The probable explanation for this is that the teacher graded the test
    (A) objectively
    (B) subjectively
    (C) with prejudice
    (D) on a curve
    (E) from the standpoint of validity

12. Criterion-referenced evaluation is based on fixed standards. Which one of the following represents grading practices usually associated with this form of evaluation?
    (A) Students compete against one another for grades.
    (B) Pupils receive grades of A, B, C, etc.
    (C) A student receives only one mark, "Credit," whenever he or she has completed a behavior designated in the objectives.
    (D) Students are expected to achieve a "Passing" grade every week.
    (E) The total number of correct student responses is computed at the end of 6 weeks.

13. When a test has been standardized and a norm has been determined, it means that
    (A) a particular score has been derived as "abnormal" for a particular population
    (B) the test has not been validated
    (C) test results can establish whether a testee has achieved an "average" score for his or her grade level
    (D) in the case of intelligence tests, norms are not referenced to age level
    (E) the class can be ranked on the basis of achievement alone

14. On the seventh-grade mathematics test, Sam received a score of 80, which converted to the 92nd percentile. This means that
    (A) Sam did as well or better than 80% of the students taking the test
    (B) 8% of the students taking the test did not do as well as Sam did
    (C) Sam did better than most students at his grade level
    (D) Sam is an average student
    (E) 20% of the students taking the test did better than Sam did

15. Aptitude tests are valuable for counseling a student because they give information that is appropriate for which of the following?
    I. Making an occupational prognosis
    II. Determining language and readiness development
    III. Determining skills and strengths

    (A) I only
    (B) II only
    (C) I and II only
    (D) I and III only
    (E) I, II, and III

16. Morton received a score on a Spanish test that placed him in the ninth stanine. In conference, what should his parents be told about stanine scores?

   I. From lowest to highest, converted scores are divided into nine stanines.
   II. All those who failed the test will be in the first stanine.
   III. The fifth stanine includes the average score.
   IV. The ninth stanine includes the highest achievers on the test.

   (A) I only
   (B) II only
   (C) III only
   (D) III and IV only
   (E) I, III, and IV only

17. Under what circumstance would the averaging of converted scores distort the relative standing of students?
   (A) When more than 25 scores are averaged
   (B) When there is a large difference in the range of variability from test to test
   (C) When each test has the same range of variability
   (D) When criterion-referenced tests are used
   (E) In none of the above circumstances

18. By definition, a person with an IQ score of 130
   (A) has twice as much aptitude for reading as someone with an IQ of 65
   (B) achieved a very high score on an intelligence test
   (C) should be able to achieve grades twice as high as a student with an IQ of 100
   (D) achieved a relatively high performance on a norm-referenced aptitude test
   (E) has a grade equivalent of 10.2

19. A teacher serves as a day-to-day counselor for many pupils. The basis for such counseling is the teacher's
   (A) acceptance of the worth of each student
   (B) criticism of the student's shortcomings
   (C) conferences with parents
   (D) skill in presenting lesson plans
   (E) interpretation of the student's standardized intelligence scores

20. An example of a teacher-constructed evaluation of students' ability to analyze and synthesize would be an assignment to
   (A) obtain information through a survey
   (B) conduct a political poll, interpret the data, and write a one-page report on its import
   (C) write a paper on home computers
   (D) memorize the names of 30 insects
   (E) explain the relationship between dieting and weight loss

21. One of the key obstacles to testing in the affective domain arises from
   (A) pupil resistance to such tests
   (B) poor values-clarification techniques
   (C) lack of parental involvement
   (D) the disputed ethics of testing students' beliefs, attitudes, and values
   (E) the nonemotional content of standardized tests

TEST OF PROFESSIONAL KNOWLEDGE: DESCRIPTION, REVIEW, PRACTICE

22. If you were evaluating results of the Socratic method of teaching, you would focus your assessment on students'
    (A) use of inquiry questions in pursuing a research assignment
    (B) deductive reasoning abilities in answering written questions
    (C) use of the scientific method in a class project
    (D) free associations in a creative-writing assignment
    (E) mastery of the set of criterion-referenced objectives established by the teacher at the start of the unit

23. At the beginning of the new semester, Maria and Bob transferred to a new school. On their first reading test, Bob got a score of 80 and Maria, a score of 68. Their new teacher concluded that
    (A) Bob is smarter than Maria
    (B) Maria has reading difficulties that need further assessment
    (C) the test should be discounted because girls are better readers than boys
    (D) though the test was reliable, the children were probably distracted by being in a new school
    (E) Bob's score is the equivalent of one grade higher than Maria's

24. Compared with a teacher-made test, the one weakness of a standardized test is that
    (A) it has less construct validity
    (B) it has less content validity
    (C) it does not save the teacher time
    (D) it takes too long to obtain the scores
    (E) it is more difficult to score

25. Determine the mode and median of the following arithmetic scores for one test: 45, 72, 74, 47, 48, 49, 53, 53, 83, 80, 75, 65, 65, 65, 84.
    (A) Mode, 65; median, 53
    (B) Mode, 53; median, 65
    (C) Mode, 65; median, 65
    (D) Mode, 53; median, 53
    (E) Mode, 53; median, 75

26. T-scores are useful standard scores because the deviation is 10 and the range is
    (A) −1 to +1
    (B) −3 to +3
    (C) 1% to 99%
    (D) 20 to 80
    (E) 200 to 800

27. Which of the following tests is matched correctly with the purpose for which it is used?
    (A) *Bender Visual Motor Gestalt Test*—diagnosing cerebral dysfunction
    (B) *California Achievement Test*—assessing mastery of developmental tasks
    (C) *Cattell's Culture-Fair Test*—measuring mental ability in a nonverbal manner
    (D) *Draw-a-Man Test*—measuring intelligence as objectively as possible
    (E) *Kuder Preference Record*—measuring attitudes and values

28. What is the relationship between measurement and evaluation?
   (A) Evaluation is a part of measurement.
   (B) Measurement is a part of evaluation.
   (C) Measurement has more validity than evaluation.
   (D) Measurement is better for determining the reliability of test items.
   (E) The terms are synonymous.

29. The essay test is the best type of measurement to use when you want to know whether pupils can
   (A) organize their ideas about a current issue and write under pressure of time
   (B) express aesthetic values
   (C) compare two chemical reactions
   (D) demonstrate a mastery of objective facts in a geography lesson
   (E) defend their points of view in a debate

30. In education, the main purpose of multiple evaluation procedures is to
   (A) obtain class ranks for students
   (B) obtain the mean of all test scores
   (C) test individual pupil achievement
   (D) establish the basis for curriculum revision
   (E) develop a profile of teacher competency

READ THE FOLLOWING DIRECTIONS BEFORE PROCEEDING.
Directions: The following questions contain the word LEAST, NOT, or EXCEPT. Read each question very carefully, then find the answer that applies.

31. A major reason why some teachers favor an essay test rather than an objective one is that an objective test does NOT
   (A) indicate students' affective skills
   (B) cover course content as thoroughly
   (C) require as close supervision
   (D) have constant validity
   (E) have consistent reliability

32. When Mr. K gives a true-false test, he should adjust for the factor of guessing by using all of the following EXCEPT
   (A) test-retest measurements
   (B) correction formulas
   (C) oral testing
   (D) standard deviations
   (E) item analysis

33. Teachers who try to help pupils improve individual performance obtain the LEAST gains in pupil performance when they
   (A) reinforce individual pupils
   (B) reinforce the entire class
   (C) postpone reinforcement to the end of the period
   (D) let the children reinforce each other
   (E) reinforce only high performance on two-week tests

34. Multiple-choice test items should be all of the following EXCEPT
    (A) plausible
    (B) expressed in parallel form
    (C) short and clear
    (D) short and complex
    (E) content-related

35. A criterion-referenced system of grading may show the following EXCEPT
    (A) every student may get an A.
    (B) grades may have to be defended to parents.
    (C) every student may get a C.
    (D) no student may get an F.
    (E) every student's grade is compared to other students' performance.

S T O P

IF YOU FINISH BEFORE TIME IS CALLED, YOU MAY CHECK YOUR WORK ON THIS SECTION ONLY. DO NOT WORK ON ANY OTHER SECTION IN THE TEST.

TEST OF PROFESSIONAL KNOWLEDGE: DESCRIPTION, REVIEW, PRACTICE

ANSWER KEYS

Section 1

1.	E	8.	E	15.	D	22.	D	29.	E
2.	B	9.	A	16.	C	23.	A	30.	E
3.	D	10.	B	17.	B	24.	E	31.	C
4.	B	11.	B	18.	C	25.	D	32.	A
5.	B	12.	E	19.	E	26.	B	33.	E
6.	C	13.	E	20.	A	27.	A	34.	A
7.	B	14.	E	21.	A	28.	A	35.	A

Section 2

1.	E	8.	A	15.	E	22.	B	29.	C
2.	A	9.	D	16.	D	23.	E	30.	B
3.	D	10.	A	17.	D	24.	A	31.	E
4.	D	11.	E	18.	E	25.	C	32.	E
5.	C	12.	E	19.	D	26.	A	33.	E
6.	B	13.	E	20.	E	27.	A	34.	D
7.	E	14.	B	21.	B	28.	C	35.	B

Section 3

1.	C	8.	D	15.	B	22.	D	29.	A
2.	A	9.	E	16.	B	23.	D	30.	D
3.	C	10.	E	17.	A	24.	A	31.	C
4.	D	11.	A	18.	B	25.	C	32.	E
5.	C	12.	C	19.	A	26.	A	33.	E
6.	E	13.	A	20.	D	27.	B	34.	A
7.	A	14.	C	21.	C	28.	E	35.	E

Section 4

1.	D	8.	A	15.	E	22.	A	29.	A
2.	E	9.	D	16.	E	23.	B	30.	C
3.	A	10.	D	17.	B	24.	B	31.	A
4.	C	11.	B	18.	D	25.	C	32.	D
5.	D	12.	A	19.	A	26.	D	33.	E
6.	E	13.	C	20.	B	27.	A	34.	D
7.	C	14.	C	21.	D	28.	B	35.	C

Part IV Model Tests: Core Battery

The following Model Tests are similar in format, number, type, and level of difficulty to the actual Core Battery. Their purpose is to help you measure your improvement and readiness to take the actual test. There is no penalty for guessing; your score is the number of correct answers.

Adhere to the 30-minute time limits for the various sections. If possible, follow the timetable used for the actual test:

8:00 A.M.	Begin General Knowledge Test
10:30 A.M.	End test
10:45 A.M.	Get set for Communication Skills Test
11:00 A.M.	Begin Communication Skills Test
1:30 P.M.	End test
2:15 P.M.	Get set for Professional Knowledge Test
2:30 P.M.	Begin Professional Knowledge Test
5:00 P.M.	End test

ANSWER SHEET FOR MODEL TEST 1

Test of General Knowledge

BE SURE EACH MARK IS DARK AND COMPLETELY FILLS THE INTENDED SPACE. DO NOT MAKE ANY STRAY MARKS. MAKE ALL ERASURES COMPLETE.

Test of Communication Skills

BE SURE EACH MARK IS DARK AND COMPLETELY FILLS THE INTENDED SPACE. DO NOT MAKE ANY STRAY MARKS. MAKE ALL ERASURES COMPLETE.

MODEL TEST 1

Test of Professional Knowledge

BE SURE EACH MARK IS DARK AND COMPLETELY FILLS THE INTENDED SPACE. DO NOT MAKE ANY STRAY MARKS. MAKE ALL ERASURES COMPLETE.

Model Test 1
Test of General Knowledge

SECTION 1

SOCIAL STUDIES

Time—30 minutes

Directions: For each question or incomplete statement below, there are five suggested answers or completions. Select the one that *best* answers the question or completes the statement.

POPULATION MOVEMENTS, CENTRAL COUNTY, U.S.A.

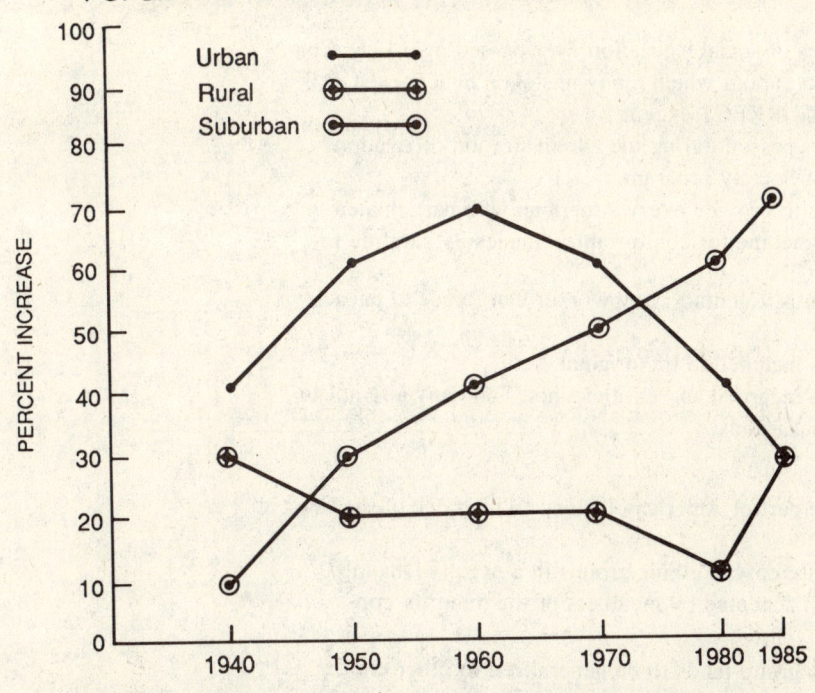

1. The line graph above indicates that all of the following population movements took place in Central County between 1940 and 1985 EXCEPT:
   (A) The suburban population grew consistently.
   (B) The rural population growth rate declined consistently.
   (C) By 1985, suburban and urban growth rates stood in juxtaposition.
   (D) From 1970–1985, the rate of urban growth declined 30 percent.
   (E) The urban and rural growth rates were the same between 1940 and 1950.

243

2. Economic growth declined in the United States during 1982 under stringent government policies. As a result, which of the following occurred?
   (A) Demand for OPEC oil increased
   (B) Industrial employment decreased.
   (C) The federal budget was balanced.
   (D) Industrial production remained steady.
   (E) Inflation increased.

3. The illiteracy rate is declining, but the actual number of illiterate persons in the world continues to rise. A probable reason is that
   (A) illiteracy has increased in advanced countries
   (B) less money is being spent on education
   (C) there has been a worldwide increase in population
   (D) fewer teachers are being trained
   (E) Third World countries oppose education

4. One of the most important pieces of social legislation ever passed by a U.S. Congress was the Social Security Act, about which many mistaken beliefs exist. All the following statements are INCORRECT except
   (A) The Social Security Act was passed during the administration of Lyndon Johnson as part of his Great Society program.
   (B) The purpose of the Act was to provide every American who participated in the program with an ample income for comfortable, financially carefree retirement.
   (C) Participation in the program is voluntary; any worker can refuse to participate.
   (D) The Medicare program was included in the original Act.
   (E) Social Security benefits are regarded as "entitlements," and any attempt to reduce them is politically hazardous.

5. Prejudice and discrimination are part of American history. Which one of the following statements is NOT true?
   (A) American society tends to stereotype ethnic groups in a negative manner.
   (B) Ethnic stereotypes are often accepted by members of the minority concerned.
   (C) Prejudice toward one ethnic group tends to be generalized to other ethnic groups.
   (D) Prejudice and discrimination are acquired and are not innate.
   (E) Stereotyped minority members are identified less readily by prejudiced people.

6. Here are the names of four Republican Presidents:
   I. Nixon
   II. Hoover
   III. Eisenhower
   IV. Ford

TEST OF GENERAL KNOWLEDGE

In which of the following are these Presidents listed in correct chronological order?

(A) I, III, II, IV
(B) II, III, I, IV
(C) III, I, II, IV
(D) IV, III, II, I
(E) I, IV, III, II

Questions 7 and 8 refer to the map of Central America below, on which the letters A–E designate five countries:

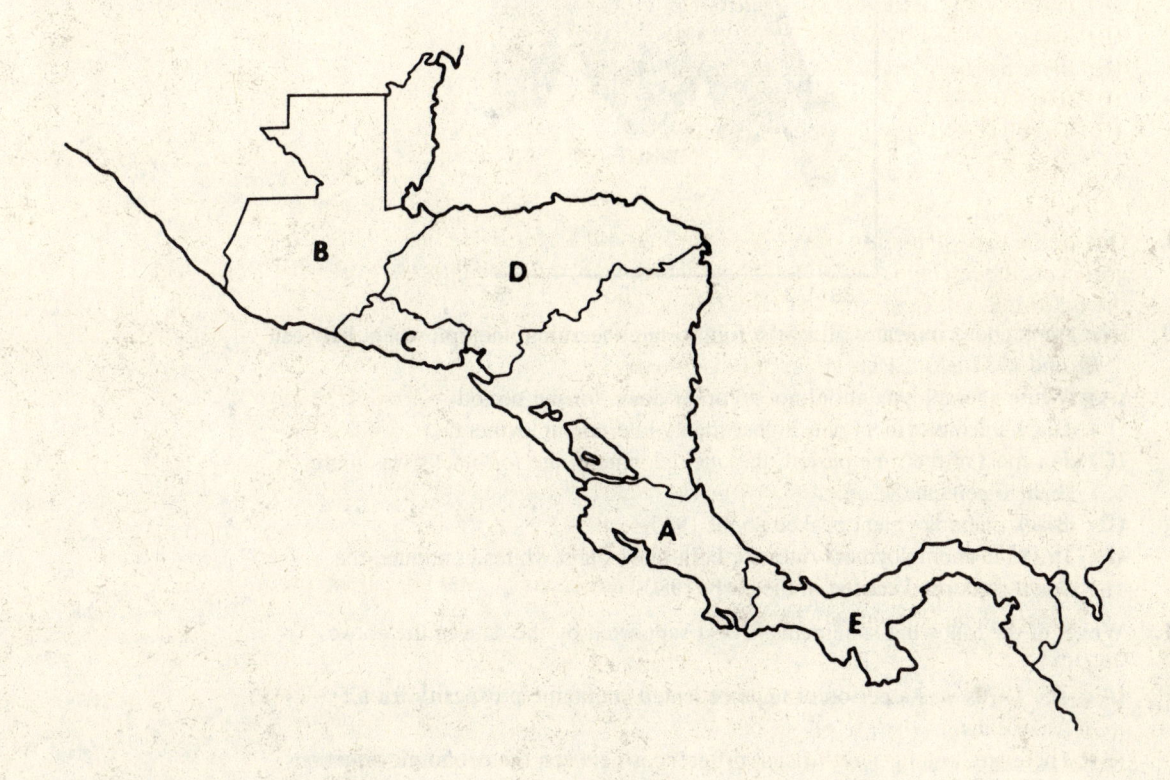

7. Which country has been ravaged by civil war for several years and accused of gross violation of human rights?

8. With which country did the United States sign two important and hotly debated treaties during the Carter administration?

9. Which one of the following is NOT compatible with the philosophy of free enterprise?
   (A) Private property
   (B) Profit motivation
   (C) Competition
   (D) Economic freedom
   (E) National production quotas

Questions 10–11 are based on the following graph.

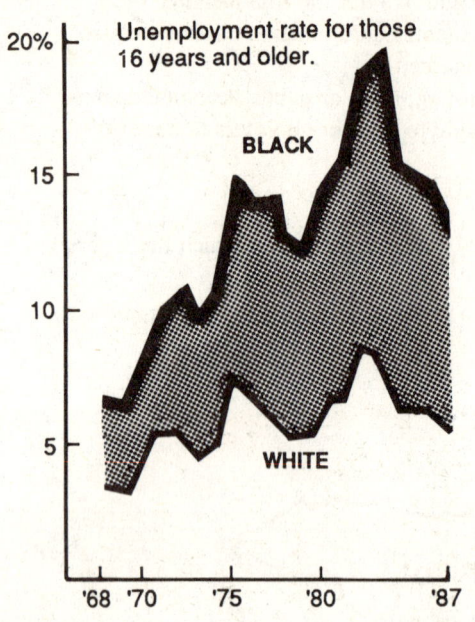

[Graph: Unemployment rate for those 16 years and older, showing BLACK and WHITE unemployment rates from '68 to '87, with y-axis from 0 to 20%]

10. The graph above indicates all of the following concerning unemployment between 1968 and 1987 EXCEPT:
    (A) White unemployment did not go up or down for the period.
    (B) Black unemployment was higher than white unemployment.
    (C) For most of the time period, the unemployment rate for blacks was more than 10 percent.
    (D) Black unemployment peaked about 1985.
    (E) In 1987, unemployment rates for both blacks and whites continued the downward trend started in the early 1980s.

11. Which of the following statements is best supported by the data in the above graph?
    (A) The 1970s was a period of unprecedented economic prosperity for all Americans.
    (B) There are no longer significant differences between the economic situations of black and white Americans.
    (C) Most Americans have learned to live with double-digit unemployment.
    (D) A black American is more likely to be unemployed than his white neighbor.
    (E) There was a sharp decrease in unemployment from 1980 to 1982.

12. In the United States the Federal Reserve Board controls the money supply. When the Board curtails the amount of money available, we may expect that
    (A) interest rates will rise
    (B) mortgage rates will be low
    (C) the construction industry will boom
    (D) large corporations and small businesses will expand
    (E) inflation will sharply decline

13. Economic goods differ from services in their
    (A) materiality   (D) transferability
    (B) scarcity   (E) productivity
    (C) utility

TEST OF GENERAL KNOWLEDGE

14. In 1963 Dr. Martin Luther King made the famous speech in which he said, "I have a dream that this nation will rise up and live out the true meaning of its creed: 'We hold these truths to be self-evident: that all men are created equal.'" The next year Congress passed a bill providing that
    (A) there could be no discrimination in voting, jobs, or public accommodations
    (B) a federally funded effort would be made to register all voters in minority neighborhoods
    (C) equality of rights would not be denied on the basis of sex
    (D) immediate measures would be taken to remedy school desegregation
    (E) universities and businesses were to give preference to minority applicants

15. The development of the town form of local government in the New England colonies was fostered by
    (A) the Indian raids
    (B) the unsuitability of the land for agricultural use
    (C) the unfavorable climate
    (D) the English background and traditions of the colonists
    (E) the strict religious beliefs of the settlers

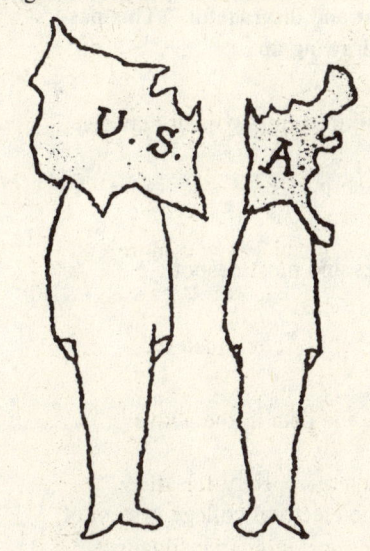

Balanced Ticket

16. In a U.S. presidential election, the vice-presidential candidate is selected by the chosen presidential candidate to balance the political party ticket. The cartoon above suggests that the vice-presidential candidate should provide a balance in which of the following areas?
    (A) Ethnic support
    (B) Urban support
    (C) Financial support
    (D) Philosophical support
    (E) Demographic support

17. The greatest economic value of capital is that it
    (A) belongs to everybody
    (B) is government-controlled
    (C) is nonmaterialistic
    (D) can be used to produce other goods
    (E) can always be readily obtained

18. One proposal for stopping the escalation of medical costs in the United States is to limit by law the charges that physicians and hospitals can make. Which of the following groups would benefit most from such legislation and would therefore be most likely to lobby for its passage?
    (A) The American Medical Association
    (B) The National Association of Manufacturers
    (C) The American Federation of Teachers
    (D) The American Association of Retired Persons
    (E) The American Nurses Association

19. "Every body wishes, every body expects something from the convention; but what will be the final result of its deliberation, the book of fate must disclose. Persuaded I am, that the primary cause of all our disorders lies in the different State governments, and in the tenacity of that power, which pervades the whole of their systems. Whilst independent sovereignty is so ardently contended for, whilst the local views of each State, and separate interests, by which they are too much governed, will not yield to a more enlarged scale of politics, incompatibility in the laws of the different States, and disrespect to those of the general government, must render this great country weak, inefficient and disgraceful." This passage is descriptive of the difficulties encountered in drawing up
    (A) The Declaration of Independence
    (B) The Articles of Confederation
    (C) The Constitution
    (D) The Bill of Rights
    (E) The Monroe Doctrine

20. One main difference between modern totalitarian states and most despotic monarchies is the
    (A) interest of present states in education
    (B) neglect of the masses in totalitarian states
    (C) autocratic leadership
    (D) delegation of authority
    (E) restrictions on citizens

21. Which of the following is a correct statement about the electoral college system of electing United States presidents?
    (A) The electoral college consists of delegates chosen by the 50 states and the District of Columbia.
    (B) Some U.S. presidents have had a majority of votes in the electoral college, but only a minority in the national election.
    (C) The states send their congressional representatives to vote in the electoral college.
    (D) A presidential candidate must have three-quarters of the votes in the electoral college to be elected.
    (E) If the electoral college is unable to choose a candidate, the U.S. Senate selects the president by a majority vote.

22. The significance of the Ordinance of 1787 lies in its
    (A) plan for constitutional union
    (B) plan for territorial government
    (C) plan for colonial expansion
    (D) provision for the building of roads in western lands
    (E) provision for homesteading western lands

TEST OF GENERAL KNOWLEDGE

23. Edmund Burke contributed greatly toward the shaping of
    (A) a conservative British political and social philosophy
    (B) British antagonism against the American colonies
    (C) the American Revolution
    (D) French prerevolutionary philosophy
    (E) the social-contract philosophy of government

24. "If the past to a man is nothing but a dead hand, then in common honesty he must be an advocate of revolution. But if it is regarded as the matrix of present and future, whose potency takes many forms but is not diminished, then he will cherish it scrupulously and labour to read its lessons, and shun the heady shortcuts which end only in blank walls."

    Which of the following can be inferred about history based on the quotation above?
    (A) The past has little meaning for present generations.
    (B) He who reads the lessons of the past well will save time and effort.
    (C) Each cultural period slightly diminishes the human strength of each succeeding generation.
    (D) Change only comes about through revolution.
    (E) The future has little to learn from the past because of the influence of technology.

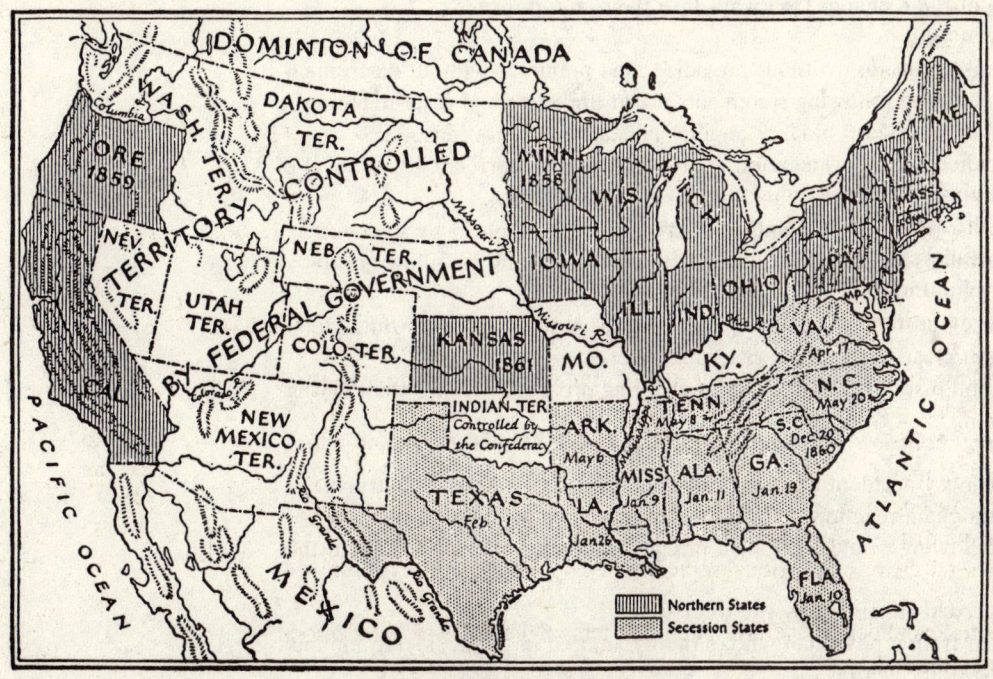

THE DIVIDED UNION IN 1861
with dates of secessions from the Union

25. Based on the map above, which of the following statements is true?
    (A) The first state to secede from the Union was Mississippi.
    (B) The first and last states to secede from the Union, in order, were Alabama and Tennessee.
    (C) A majority of the states seceded from the Union.
    (D) By February 2, 1861, six states had seceded from the Union.
    (E) A minority of the states seceded from the Union.

MODEL TEST 1

26. Four American presidents were assassinated. Select the answer that lists them in correct chronological order.
    (A) Lincoln, Garfield, McKinley, Kennedy
    (B) Kennedy, McKinley, Garfield, Lincoln
    (C) McKinley, Garfield, Lincoln, Kennedy
    (D) Lincoln, McKinley, Kennedy, Garfield
    (E) Garfield, Lincoln, McKinley, Kennedy

27. "Prices Rise a Steep 0.6 Percent in January." Which one of the following factors would NOT have contributed to the price increase described in the headline?
    (A) A December freeze in Florida
    (B) An abundant supply of home heating oil
    (C) A summer drought in the Plains States
    (D) A sharp rise in pleasure driving
    (E) An upward adjustment of telephone rates

28. Cultural lag exists in most societies because
    (A) there is little transfer of training
    (B) there is fierce opposition to new ideas
    (C) human behavior is unpredictable
    (D) the nonmaterial aspects of culture lag behind the material ones in growth rate
    (E) in periods of rapid change, folkways lose their importance

29. There can be discrimination without prejudice, and prejudice without discrimination. Which one of the following statements about prejudice and discrimination is also true?
    (A) Both prejudice and discrimination are always directly correlated with level of education.
    (B) Charges of "reverse discrimination" have never been upheld by the courts.
    (C) Societal attitudes and behavior toward ethnic groups tend to follow group norms.
    (D) In most desegregated schools the pattern has been for black and white children to form close friendships with each other.
    (E) Prejudice and discrimination are greater during prosperous times than during a depression.

30. In a serious highway accident a tractor trailer jumped a guard rail and struck a car, setting off a chain reaction that resulted in three deaths and five injuries. Which of the following would NOT be a primary source of information about this disaster?
    (A) A tape-recorded statement by the truck driver
    (B) A statement from a physician who, although injured in the accident, administered to the other victims
    (C) A newspaper account by a reporter who interviewed witnesses
    (D) A description of the accident from one of the injured persons
    (E) A report by the police officer at the scene

S T O P

IF YOU FINISH BEFORE TIME IS CALLED, YOU MAY CHECK YOUR WORK ON THIS SECTION ONLY. DO NOT WORK ON ANY OTHER SECTION IN THE TEST.

TEST OF GENERAL KNOWLEDGE
SECTION 2

MATHEMATICS

Time—30 minutes

Directions: For each question or incomplete statement below, there are five suggested answers or completions. Select the one that *best* answers the question or completes the statement.

1. $\sqrt{40}$ is between
   (A) 6 and 7
   (B) 5 and 6
   (C) 36 and 49
   (D) 5.5 and 5.96
   (E) 4.9 and 5.95

2. Ms. Burke's class has 21 pupils on register, and Mr. Korngraff's class has 28. The pupils in each class are to be assigned to groups in such a way that every student is in exactly one group and all groups in both classes contain the same number of pupils. How many groups will there be in all?
   (A) 3 (B) 4 (C) 6 (D) 7 (E) 14

3. The fraction $\frac{2}{5}$ lies between each of the following pairs EXCEPT
   (A) $\frac{1}{10}$ and $\frac{9}{10}$
   (B) 0.3 and 0.5
   (C) $\frac{1}{2}$ and $\frac{3}{4}$
   (D) 0.2 and 0.6
   (E) 0 and 1

4. In each of the following pairs the first number is less than the second number EXCEPT in
   (A) $-2, -1$
   (B) 2, 1
   (C) $-4, -3$
   (D) 3, 4
   (E) 0.1, 1

5. The high temperature during the day was 93°F, and the low temperature was 70°F. If we change these readings to Celsius, what were the highest and lowest temperatures during this day? [The formula for converting Fahrenheit to Celsius temperatures is $C = \frac{5}{9}(F - 32)$.]
   (A) 61°C and 21°C
   (B) 34°C and 17°C
   (C) 26°C and 13°C
   (D) 55°C and 40°C
   (E) 34°C and 21°C

6. Fernando bought $4\frac{1}{2}$ bushels of apples and $2\frac{1}{4}$ bushels of pears. The difference between the two quantities is
   (A) $2\frac{1}{4}$ bushels
   (B) $1\frac{3}{4}$ bushels
   (C) $1\frac{1}{2}$ bushels
   (D) $1\frac{3}{8}$ bushels
   (E) $2\frac{1}{4}$ bushels

251

MODEL TEST 1

7. The price of gasoline dropped from $1.33 a gallon to $1.21 a gallon. How much money did Jack get back from a $20.00 bill when he refilled a 15-gallon tank?
   - (A) $18.79
   - (B) $2.54
   - (C) $1.85
   - (D) $1.80
   - (E) $18.67

8. A jar contains three dozen cookies. How many total trips will be necessary for three children to empty the jar, if each child takes two cookies each trip?
   - (A) 6
   - (B) 18
   - (C) 12
   - (D) 9
   - (E) 15

9. John earns $4.00 an hour during the day as a lifeguard, but after 6:00 P.M. he earns $5.00 an hour. The ratio of his day pay to his evening pay is
   - (A) 2:3
   - (B) 4:5
   - (C) 1:2
   - (D) 5:4
   - (E) 3:4

10. The fraction $\frac{1}{100}$ can also be written as
    - (A) 0.100
    - (B) 10.00
    - (C) $\frac{1}{10^2}$
    - (D) 0.001
    - (E) $\frac{1}{10^3}$

11. The school recreational area has three outdoor playgrounds arranged as shown. What is the perimeter of the total area?
    - (A) 282'
    - (B) 186'
    - (C) 202'
    - (D) 242'
    - (E) 196'

12. In the formula $x = 12y$, if the value of y is reduced to $\frac{1}{4}$ of its original value, the value of x
    - (A) is reduced to 25% of its original value
    - (B) is reduced to 75% of its original value
    - (C) remains the same
    - (D) is increased 50%
    - (E) is tripled

13. If $A = BC$, which of these equations is incorrect?
    - (A) $BC = A$
    - (B) $C = A \div B$ or A/B
    - (C) $B = A \div C$ or A/C
    - (D) $A - B = C$
    - (E) $A - BC = 0$

TEST OF GENERAL KNOWLEDGE

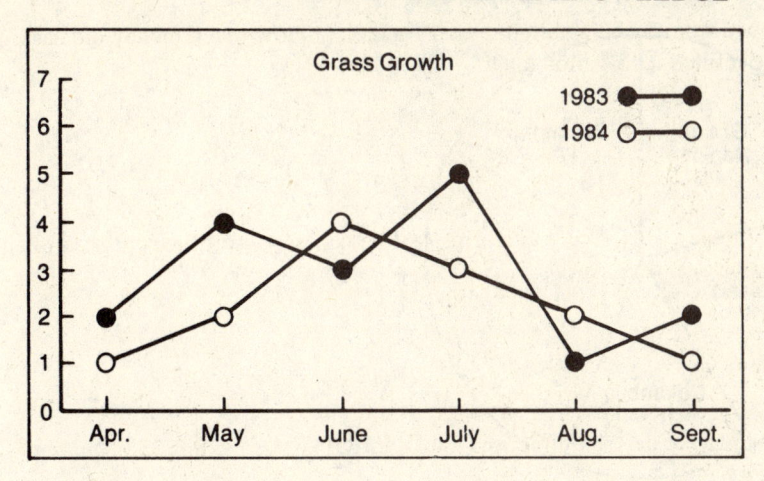

Grass Growth

14. The line graph above reveals that grass grew the most in which pair of months in 1983?

    (A) April and September
    (B) July and August
    (C) May and August
    (D) June and July
    (E) May and July

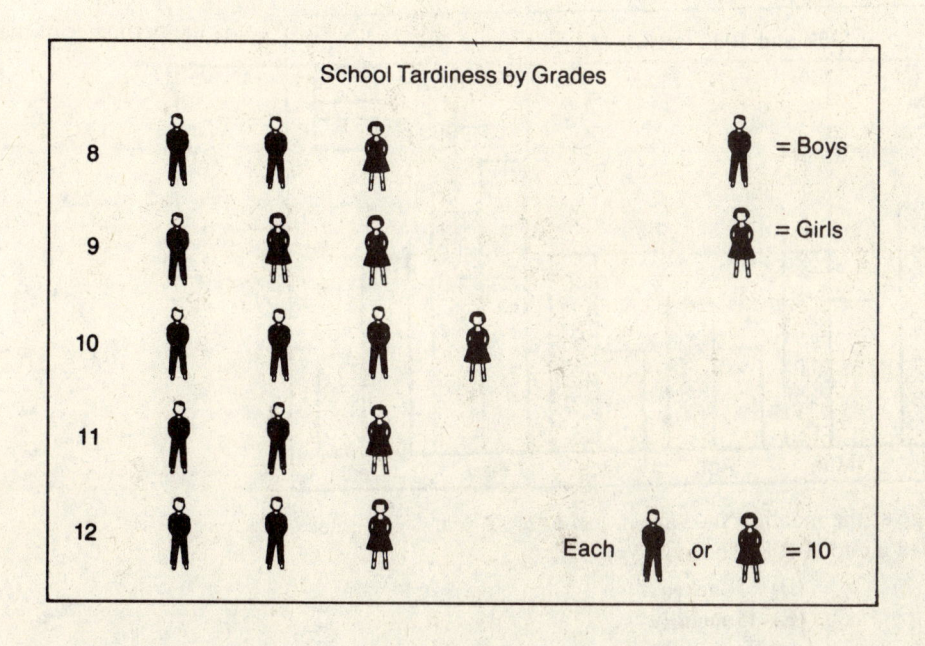

School Tardiness by Grades

15. In the pictograph above for a school year, the ratio of tardiness for girls to boys was

    (A) 1:4
    (B) 3:5
    (C) 4:3
    (D) 3:1
    (E) 3:2

253

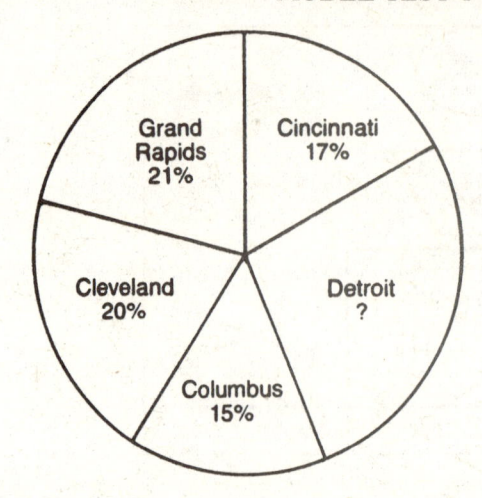

16. The circle graph above shows the percentage of new cars sold with special paint trim in selected Michigan and Ohio cities. What was the percentage in Detroit?
    (A) 24%
    (B) 36%
    (C) 40%
    (D) 27%
    (E) 20%

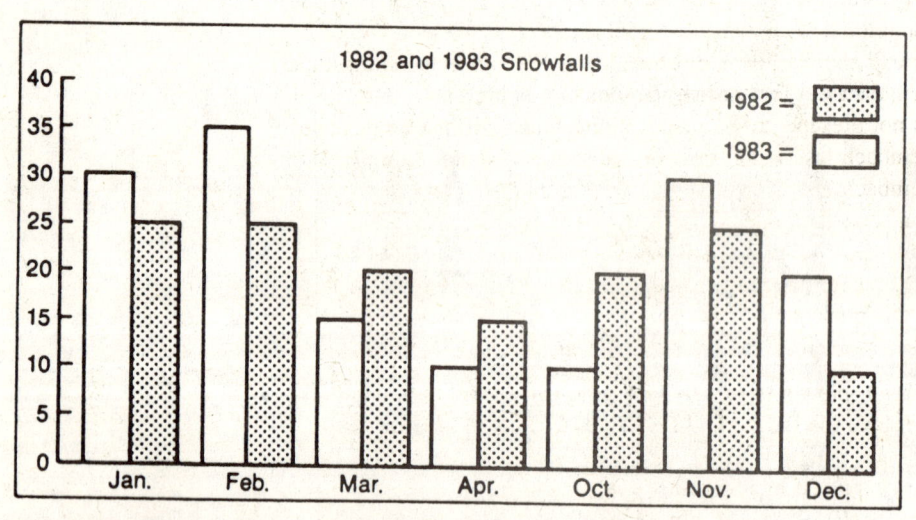

17. The bar graph above gives the monthly snowfall in inches for 2 years. The total 1983 snowfall exceeded the total 1982 snowfall by
    (A) 20 inches
    (B) 10 inches
    (C) 25 inches
    (D) 5 inches
    (E) 15 inches

18. In a book, the printing of a three-place number is blurred so that the middle digit is illegible. The first digit is 3, and the last digit is 4. What must the middle digit be if it is known from the context that the number is divisible by 7?
    (A) 2   (B) 3   (C) 4   (D) 5   (E) 6

TEST OF GENERAL KNOWLEDGE

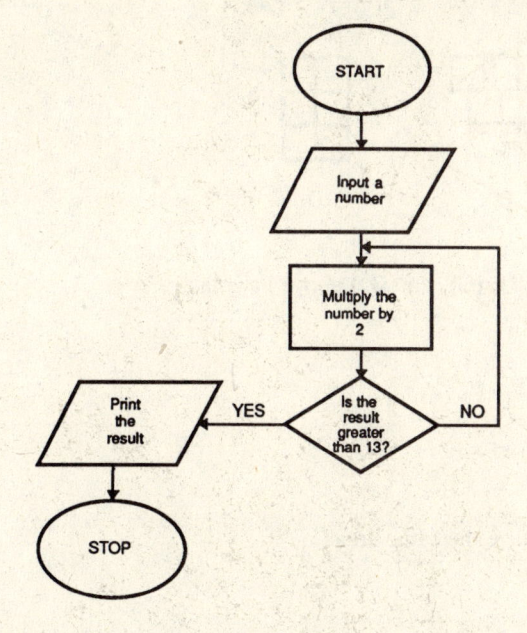

19. If the number 5 is input in the computer program represented by the flowchart above, what number will be printed?
    (A) 5 (B) 10 (C) 13 (D) 20 (E) none

20. A medical laboratory uses the Muller-Kleinbach test to detect the presence of substance X in a blood sample. It is known that, if substance X is present, the Muller-Kleinbach test will show a positive result. It may be validly concluded that
    (A) if the Muller-Kleinbach test is positive, substance X is present
    (B) if substance X is not present, the Muller-Kleinbach test will not be positive
    (C) if the Muller-Kleinbach test is not positive, substance X is not present
    (D) if the Muller-Kleinbach test is positive but a different test shows that substance X is not present, then one of the tests was improperly performed
    (E) if a properly performed Muller-Kleinbach test reveals no presence of substance X, a second performance of the test may nevertheless reveal that some substance X is present

21. It takes a farmer 4 hours to plow a field. His farmhand can do the same job in 6 hours. How long will it take the farmer and his helper to plow the field if they both work together?
    (A) 10 hr.   (D) 3 hr., 36 min.
    (B) 5 hr.   (E) 2 hr., 24 min.
    (C) 3 hr.

22. In the formula $\frac{y}{4} = 3x$, if y and x are positive and the value of y is tripled, what will be the effect on the value of x?
    (A) It will be divided by 4.
    (B) It will be multiplied by $\frac{3}{4}$.
    (C) It will be divided by 12.
    (D) It will remain unchanged.
    (E) It will be tripled.

MODEL TEST 1

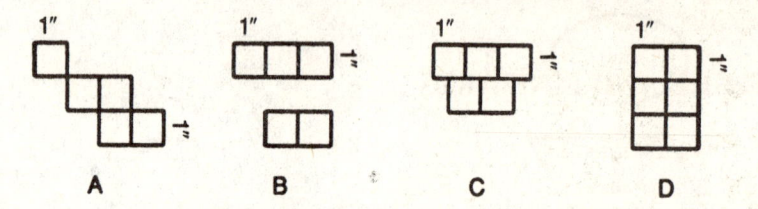

23. Which of the separate figures shown in (A), (B), (C), and (D) above have the same perimeter?
    (A) A, B, and C
    (B) B and C
    (C) A and C
    (D) C and D
    (E) B and D

24. Which of the separate figures in Problem 23 have the same area?
    (A) A, B, and C
    (B) A and C
    (C) A and D
    (D) B and C
    (E) C and D

25. The sixth grade had 60 magazine subscriptions to sell. If the students sold 51, what percentage of their assignment did they sell?
    (A) 85%
    (B) 80%
    (C) 78%
    (D) 90%
    (E) 89%

STOP

IF YOU FINISH BEFORE TIME IS CALLED, YOU MAY CHECK YOUR WORK ON THIS SECTION ONLY. DO NOT WORK ON ANY OTHER SECTION IN THE TEST.

TEST OF GENERAL KNOWLEDGE
SECTION 3
LITERATURE AND FINE ARTS

Time—30 minutes

Directions: For each question or incomplete statement below, there are five suggested answers or completions. Select the one that *best* answers the question or completes the statement.

1. The pose of the dancers and the design of their costumes in the photograph above combine to suggest
   (A) the poise of their classic style
   (B) great passion and despair
   (C) a light, ebullient mood
   (D) the indecision of experimental ballet
   (E) the excitement of tension and strain

Questions 2–4 refer to the following.

   The world is too much with us; late and soon,
   Getting and spending, we lay waste our powers;
   Little we see in Nature that is ours;
   We have given our hearts away, a sordid boon!
(5) This Sea that bares her bosom to the moon,
   The winds that will be howling at all hours,

257

And are up-gathered now like sleeping flowers,
For this, for everything, we are out of tune;
It moves us not. Great God! I'd rather be
(10) A Pagan suckled in a creed outworn;
So might I, standing on this pleasant lea,
Have glimpses that would make me less forlorn;
Have sight of Proteus rising from the sea;
Or hear old Triton blow his wreathed horn.

2. The general tone of the poem is one of
   (A) joy
   (B) disillusionment
   (C) fear
   (D) rage
   (E) hope

3. In lines 13 and 14, the speaker refers to figures from
   (A) Greek mythology
   (B) Egyptian mythology
   (C) the Old Testament
   (D) Arthurian legends
   (E) Old English ballads

4. All of the following statements about the poem are true EXCEPT
   (A) The word *boon* (line 4) means "benefit" or "favor."
   (B) There is a simile in line 7.
   (C) The speaker states that human beings and nature are "out of tune."
   (D) The speaker would rather be a pagan than lose contact with nature.
   (E) The speaker recommends that modern religions be replaced with paganism.

5. The recessed facade of this building is created in part by
   (A) the two projecting wings
   (B) its elegant Corinthian columns
   (C) the length of the hall
   (D) the richly carved moldings
   (E) the tri-part roof treatment

TEST OF GENERAL KNOWLEDGE

6. This rug made centuries ago by Navajo Indians in what is now Arizona shows all of the following characteristics EXCEPT
    (A) balance
    (B) good composition
    (C) fantasy
    (D) sophistication
    (E) geometric harmony

    IBM Institutional Collections

7. The artistic impact of this gold drinking cup is derived basically from the
    (A) incongruity of the lion's head and bird's wings
    (B) snarling mouth
    (C) color of the object
    (D) precious metal from which it is made
    (E) bold form and well-defined patterns

    The Metropolitan Museum of Art

8. *The Woman* All flying is not toward, much is from.
    Danger's four-cornered in the compass-rose,
    and flying south is dreaming, nothing more.
    What do you know of a bird's loneliness?
    I tell you freedom is a lonely word.

    Which of the following best describes the central theme of the passage above?
    (A) A bird's life is as lonely as that of the rose.
    (B) Danger comes from every direction and lies all around us.
    (C) Flying south will cure the caged bird's loneliness.
    (D) Freedom is appreciated most by those who have lost it.
    (E) It is possible to have freedom, but also to feel a deep lack in one's life.

MODEL TEST 1

9. The hero of *David Copperfield*, considered to be the most autobiographical of Dickens's novels, experiences an abuse common in Victorian society of which Dickens himself had first-hand knowledge. This was
   (A) debtor's prison
   (B) banishment to Australia on conviction of a minor crime
   (C) child labor
   (D) racial discrimination
   (E) sexual mistreatment of children

10. The term "Renaissance man," designating a person having many interests and skilled in many areas, is often applied to
    (A) Leonardo da Vinci
    (B) Jan van Eyck
    (C) Hieronymus Bosch
    (D) Claude Monet
    (E) Paul Cezanne

Questions 11–13 refer to the following.

The young man was sincerely but placidly in love. He delighted in the radiant good looks of his betrothed, in her health, her horsemanship, her grace and quickness at games, and the shy interest in books and ideas that she was beginning to develop under his guidance. (She had advanced far enough to join him in ridiculing the Idyls of the King, but not to feel the beauty of Ulysses and the Lotus Eaters.) She was straightforward, loyal, and brave; she had a sense of humour (chiefly proved by her laughing at *his* jokes); and, he suspected, in the depths of her innocently gazing soul, a glow of feeling that it would be a joy to waken. But when he had gone the brief round of her he returned discouraged by the thought that all this frankness and innocence were only an artificial product. Untrained human nature was not frank and innocent; it was full of the twists and defences of an instinctive guile. And he felt himself oppressed by this creation of factitious purity, so cunningly manufactured by a conspiracy of mothers and aunts and grandmothers and long-dead ancestresses, because it was supposed to be what he wanted, what he had a right to, in order that he might exercise his lordly pleasure in smashing it like an image made of snow.*

11. According to the passage, a wealthy young girl living in New York at the turn of the twentieth century could be expected to be all of the following EXCEPT
    (A) skilled in horsemanship
    (B) literate but not well educated
    (C) adept at games
    (D) able to converse knowledgeably about politics and economics
    (E) ready to subordinate herself to her husband's wishes

12. What is disturbing to the young man about his fiancée is that
    (A) she cannot appreciate the Greek literature he loves
    (B) she never tells *him* jokes
    (C) she appears incapable of deep emotion
    (D) she seems at times to be concealing some aspect of her past
    (E) her nature is not natural but is artificial, created for his supposed pleasure

*Edith Wharton, excerpted from *The Age of Innocence*. Copyright © 1920, D. Appleton and Company; copyright renewed 1948 William R. Tyler. Reprinted with permission of Charles Scribner's Sons.

TEST OF GENERAL KNOWLEDGE

13. The word "factitious" in the last sentence means
    (A) produced by human rather than natural forces
    (B) intended to reveal
    (C) designed to appeal to the emotions
    (D) conveyed by actions rather than words
    (E) expressed in subtle ways

Questions 14–16 refer to the following.

(A)

(B)

(C)

(D)

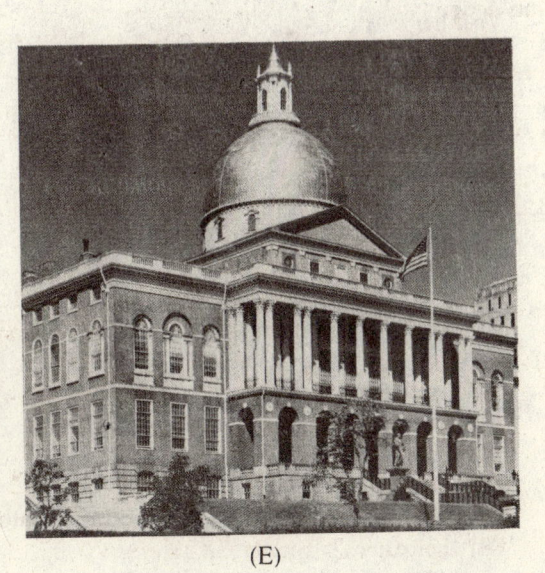

(E)

MODEL TEST 1

14. An element common to each building is
    (A) bold, arched entrances
    (B) steeply arched roofs
    (C) adaptations of classical columns
    (D) recessed arcades
    (E) an extensive use of glass

15. When considered as a group, these buildings can best be described as
    (A) stately
    (B) functional
    (C) ornate
    (D) experimental
    (E) flamboyant

16. Which building incorporates a design element not found in the other buildings?

Questions 17–19 refer to the following.

    O, that this too too solid flesh would melt,
    Thaw and resolve itself into a dew!
    Or that the Everlasting had not fix'd
    His canon 'gainst self-slaughter! O God! God!
(5) How weary, stale, flat and unprofitable
    Seem to me all the uses of this world!
    Fie on 't! ah fie! 'tis an unweeded garden
    That grows to seed; things rank and gross in nature
    Possess it merely. That it should come to this!
(10) But two months dead! Nay, not so much, not two;
    So excellent a king; that was, to this,
    Hyperion to a satyr; so loving to my mother,
    That he might not beteem the wind of heaven
    Visit her face too roughly.

17. The general tone of this passage is best described as
    (A) scornful
    (B) resigned
    (C) sorrowful
    (D) joyful
    (E) fearful

18. The speaker expresses a desire to
    (A) reduce his weight
    (B) die
    (C) kill someone
    (D) avenge his father's death
    (E) take as good care of his mother as his father did

TEST OF GENERAL KNOWLEDGE

19. All of the following statements are true in regard to the passage EXCEPT
    (A) *the Everlasting* refers to God
    (B) *canon* is a church regulation or dogma
    (C) *beteem* means "forbid"
    (D) the world is compared to a neglected garden
    (E) lines 3, 4, and 7 contain examples of elision

The Metropolitan Museum of Art

20. The composition of this Egyptian painting gives a sense of unity through
    (A) the horizontal dividing line of pool and canal
    (B) having all figures engaged in agricultural activities
    (C) the large tree at the left balancing the cow at the right
    (D) the use of human and animal figures
    (E) the trees scattered throughout the painting

LuPone in *Anything Goes*
TIME, November 2, 1987

21. The position and stance of the singer in the above scene from Cole Porter's *Anything Goes* suggest
    (A) trouble and disharmony
    (B) strength and heart
    (C) love and hate
    (D) distress and sadness
    (E) good and evil

263

22. Which one of the following is a well-known American composer and orchestra conductor?
    (A) Strauss
    (B) Bernstein
    (C) Stravinsky
    (D) Kreisler
    (E) Franck

Questions 23–24 refer to the following.

No man is an island, entire of itself; every man is a piece of the continent, a part of the main. If a clod is washed away by the sea, Europe is the less, as well as if a promontory were, as well as if a manor of thy friend's or of thine own were: any man's death diminishes me, because I am involved in mankind, and therefore never send to know for whom the bell tolls; it tolls for thee.

23. The main thought expressed by this passage is that
    (A) Europe is not an island
    (B) man is part of the universe
    (C) there is a bond uniting all humankind
    (D) a bell should be tolled whenever anyone dies
    (E) one person's death does not concern another

24. A phrase from this passage became the title of a famous modern novel by
    (A) Theodore Dreiser
    (B) James Baldwin
    (C) Willa Cather
    (D) Virginia Woolf
    (E) Ernest Hemingway

Hessisches Landesmuseum, Darmstadt

25. Art nouveau, produced chiefly in the late nineteenth century, has been interpreted as a reaction against the commercialism and mass production of the Machine Age. As shown by the brooch above, all of the following are common elements in specimens of art nouveau EXCEPT
    (A) complexity of design
    (B) use of semiprecious stones
    (C) delicate floral patterns
    (D) dreamlike women's faces
    (E) simplicity of detail

TEST OF GENERAL KNOWLEDGE

Collection of Rijksmuseum, Amsterdam

26. This drawing of an old man is notable chiefly for
    (A) its imaginative quality
    (B) its faulty composition
    (C) its lack of perspective
    (D) its lack of facial expression
    (E) its realism

27. This well-known song is
    (A) "Greensleeves"
    (B) "My Old Kentucky Home"
    (C) "On Wisconsin!"
    (D) "The Star-Spangled Banner"
    (E) "He's Got the Whole World in His Hands"

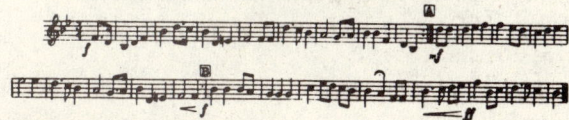

28. Which of the following styles of architecture influenced the design of Frank Lloyd Wright's Unity Temple, shown above?
    (A) Greek
    (B) Roman
    (C) Japanese
    (D) Gothic
    (E) Baroque

265

Questions 29–31 are based on the passages below.

(A) Safe in their Alabaster Chambers —
Untouched by Morning —
And untouched by Noon —
Lie the meek members of the Resurrection —
Rafters of satin — and Roof of Stone!

(B) And even like the precurse of feared events,
As harbingers preceding still the fates
And prologue to the omen coming on,
Have heaven and earth together demonstrated
Unto our climatures and countrymen.

(C) Let us go then, you and I,
When the evening is spread out against the sky
Like a patient etherized upon a table;
Let us go, through certain half-deserted streets,
The muttering retreats

(D) Why is it no one ever sent me yet
  One perfect limousine, do you suppose?
Ah no, it's always just my luck to get
  One perfect rose.

(E) How like the winter hath my absence been
From thee, the pleasure of the fleeing year!
What freezings have I felt, what dark eyes seen!
What old December's bareness everywhere!

29. Which describes an object by substituting a part for the whole?

30. Which exaggerates to create a specific effect?

31. Which treats an inanimate object as if it were animate?

Questions 32–34 refer to the following.

In Southwerk at the Tabard as I lay
Redy to wenden on my pilgrymage
To Caunterbury with ful devout corage,
At nyght was come into that hostelrye
Wel nyne and twenty in a compaignye,
Of sondry folk, by aventure yfalle
In felaweshipe, and pilgrimes were they alle,
That toward Caunterbury wolden ryde.

32. The Tabard (line 1) is
(A) a hospital
(B) an inn
(C) a youth hostel
(D) a private home
(E) a duke's palace

TEST OF GENERAL KNOWLEDGE

33. What did all these people intend to do?
    (A) Hold a meeting
    (B) Join the Crusades
    (C) Go on a pilgrimage
    (D) Go hunting
    (E) Search for the Holy Grail

34. Which of the following statements is NOT true?
    (A) The narrator felt courageous.
    (B) The narrator was joined by 29 other travelers.
    (C) The other travelers were a sundry, that is, a mixed, group.
    (D) The other travelers arrived at night.
    (E) The other travelers had all met by prearrangement.

35. Like poetry, music has a beat to express the ideas and emotions of the composer. The following excerpt has the beat of a

    (A) march
    (B) gigue
    (C) boogie
    (D) waltz
    (E) polka

STOP

IF YOU FINISH BEFORE TIME IS CALLED, YOU MAY CHECK YOUR WORK ON THIS SECTION ONLY. DO NOT WORK ON ANY OTHER SECTION IN THIS TEST.

MODEL TEST 1

SECTION 4

SCIENCE

Time — 30 minutes

Directions: For each question or incomplete statement below, there are five suggested answers or completions. Select the one that *best* answers the question or completes the statement.

1. A majority of the Earth's volcanoes are found near the edges of continents. The reason for this is that
   (A) tectonic plates collide at continental edges
   (B) tectonic plates are separating at continental edges
   (C) hot spots in the underlying magma are located mostly at continental edges
   (D) the impact of waves on the shore creates instabilities in the crust
   (E) accumulated offshore sediments create unusual pressures on the crust

2. A lunar eclipse occurs
   (A) whenever the Earth is between the sun and the moon
   (B) whenever the moon is between the Earth and the sun
   (C) sometimes when the moon is new
   (D) every time the moon is new
   (E) every time the moon is full

3. The possible interconnected feeding relationships among organisms in an ecosystem are termed a
   (A) food pyramid   (D) food group
   (B) food web   (E) food vacuole
   (C) food chain

4. Why can't a magnet be used to pick up a dime inside a glass of water?
   (A) The glass acts as an insulator.
   (B) The water destroys the magnetism.
   (C) The dime does not contain a magnetic substance.
   (D) A wet magnet will not work.
   (E) The dime will be repelled by the magnet.

5. A group of organisms in which the cells are most different from all others is the
   (A) ferns
   (B) protozoa
   (C) vertebrates
   (D) bacteria
   (E) algae

TEST OF GENERAL KNOWLEDGE

6. There are three modes by which heat can be transferred from place to place:

   I. conduction
   II. convection
   III. radiation

   The energy of the sun comes to the earth by
   (A) III only
   (B) II and III only
   (C) II only
   (D) I and II only
   (E) I, II, and III

7. The function of a motor is to convert
   (A) power to mechanical energy
   (B) electrical energy to magnetism
   (C) electrical energy to mechanical energy
   (D) mechanical energy to electrical energy
   (E) electrical energy to power

8. Which of the following factors affect regional climate?

   I. Global wind patterns
   II. Latitude
   III. Altitude
   IV. Bodies of water
   V. Phases of the moon

   (A) I only
   (B) II and III only
   (C) I, II, and III only
   (D) IV and V only
   (E) I, II, III, and IV only

9. Which of the following terms denotes the most closely related group of organisms?
   (A) Phylum
   (B) Order
   (C) Species
   (D) Genus
   (E) Class

10. If you weigh 100 pounds on Earth and step on a bathroom scale on the moon,
    (A) the scale would read much less because weight is a measure of the pull of gravity
    (B) the scale would read the same because weight is the same throughout the universe
    (C) the scale would read much less because mass is a measure of the pull of gravity
    (D) the scale would read the same because mass is the same throughout the universe
    (E) you would find that the bathroom scale would not work on the moon

11. An unqualified nutritionist suggests that the following situations could be contributing to the development of rickets in a boy:

    I. He eats meat.
    II. He gets little exposure to sunshine.
    III. He drinks too much milk.
    IV. His diet contains too little vitamin D.
    V. He does not eat enough fish.

    Which of these could actually be contributing causes?
    (A) II and IV only
    (B) I and V only
    (C) III and V only
    (D) IV only
    (E) II and III only

12. RESIDENTIAL WATER CONSUMPTION IN THE UNITED STATES

Average annual residential consumption	107,000 gallons
Each person daily average	168 gallons
To take a shower	25 to 50 gallons
To flush a toilet	5 to 7 gallons
To shave (water running)	10 to 15 gallons
To brush teeth (water running)	2 gallons
To wash dishes by hand	20 gallons
To wash dishes by dishwasher	10 gallons

    (*Source*: American Water Works Association)

    Which of the following statements is evident from the data?

    I. A family of five persons that used only two quarts each for brushing teeth could save more than 50 gallons of water a week.
    II. The largest amount of water was saved after the family began to use the dishwasher.
    III. A new showerhead, reducing water usage by 35 percent, resulted in a greater saving of water than the dishwasher.
    IV. Using only one-half the amount of water for shaving resulted in each man saving 35 to 50 gallons a week.

    (A) I and III only
    (B) I only
    (C) I and II only
    (D) I, II, and III only
    (E) IV only

13. Which one of the following is a correct statement about the beneficial service performed by earthworms?
    (A) They act as seed dispersers.
    (B) They destroy harmful insects.
    (C) They destroy weeds.
    (D) They loosen the soil.
    (E) They add nitrogen to the soil.

TEST OF GENERAL KNOWLEDGE

14. H_2O is the formula for a(n)
    (A) element
    (B) ionic compound
    (C) organic compound
    (D) molecular compound
    (E) solution

15. Which one of the following is an example of a simple machine?
    (A) Pulley
    (B) Bicycle
    (C) Engine
    (D) Automobile
    (E) Flashlight battery

16. A boulder at the top of a cliff, compared with one at the bottom of the cliff, has more
    (A) kinetic energy
    (B) gravitational potential energy
    (C) radiant energy
    (D) chemical potential energy
    (E) electromagnetic energy

17. Electrical errors in a household circuit may cause a number of different problems:

    I. A fuse may blow.
    II. Wires in the walls may overheat and melt.
    III. A circuit breaker may open.
    IV. An appliance may catch fire.

    In a vacuum cleaner, the insulation of the wires wears out and the two leads touch each other. If the household circuit is in normal condition, which of the above events may happen?
    (A) I or III only
    (B) I or IV only
    (C) II or IV only
    (D) IV only
    (E) I, II, III, or IV

18. A compound is a chemical union of two or more
    (A) electrons
    (B) neutrons
    (C) protons
    (D) isotopes
    (E) elements

19. In a scientific experiment, the investigator uses a control that differs from the part of the experiment being tested by
    (A) one theory
    (B) several theories
    (C) one factor
    (D) several factors
    (E) no factor

MODEL TEST 1

20. In the United States, the amount of water used every day is the equivalent of several thousand gallons per person. Which activity utilizes the greatest amount of water?
    (A) Drinking
    (B) Cooking
    (C) Washing and laundry
    (D) Flushing toilets
    (E) Industry

21. Which of these nutrients are sources of energy?
    (A) Fats and minerals
    (B) Vitamins and fats
    (C) Vitamins and minerals
    (D) Sugars and starches
    (E) Starches and minerals

22. DNA, the molecule which contains the hereditary information of the cell, is located in the
    (A) cell nucleus
    (B) cell walls
    (C) cytoplasm
    (D) blood
    (E) enzymes

23. In a cell, the information that controls functioning passes from the
    (A) cytoplasm to the mitochondria
    (B) nucleus to the cytoplasm
    (C) cytoplasm to the nucleus
    (D) mitochondria to the nucleus
    (E) vacuoles to the cytoplasm

24. Which of the following is a good way of preventing soil from eroding on a hill?
    (A) Plant the hill with grass or trees.
    (B) Plow the hill regularly.
    (C) Plant only in alternate years.
    (D) Add earthworms to the soil.
    (E) Irrigate the area.

25. A geologic fault is
    (A) a rock formation produced by the cooling of magma
    (B) a break in rock layers caused by pressure
    (C) cementation of sediments to form rock
    (D) a layer of lava between sedimentary layers
    (E) a layer of sediments on top of an unrelated layer

26. The scientific name of the American Robin, in the thrush family, is *Turdus migratorius*. Some other members of the thrush family are

    I. *Sialia sialis*, in North America
    II. *Turdus pilaris*, in Europe
    III. *Cantharus fuscescens*, in North America
    IV. *Turdus fuscator*, in South America
    V. *Catharus ustulatus*, in the entire western hemisphere

272

TEST OF GENERAL KNOWLEDGE

The species that has the most recent common ancestor with the American Robin is probably

(A) I or III only
(B) V only
(C) II or IV only
(D) I or V only
(E) IV only

27. The object in the sky that is nearest the Earth is
    (A) the sun
    (B) the moon
    (C) Halley's comet
    (D) Venus
    (E) the North Star

28. If thousands of observations uphold a theory and one (verified several times) comes along that contradicts it, then
    (A) the contradictory observation should be ignored
    (B) nothing should be done
    (C) the theory should be discarded because it is wrong
    (D) the theory should be modified because it is probably basically right
    (E) a new theory should be sought

29. A foreign material in the blood may lead to any of the following outcomes:

    I. the number of white blood cells may increase
    II. the antibodies in the blood may increase
    III. the number of red blood cells may increase
    IV. the temperature may rise

    If a flu vaccine is injected to produce active immunity to a current strain, which of the above may happen?
    (A) I only
    (B) I and III only
    (C) I, II, and IV only
    (D) III and IV only
    (E) IV only

30. All of the following are examples of arthropods EXCEPT the
    (A) fly
    (B) spider
    (C) crayfish
    (D) starfish
    (E) shrimp

S T O P

IF YOU FINISH BEFORE TIME IS CALLED, YOU MAY CHECK YOUR WORK ON THIS SECTION ONLY.
DO NOT WORK ON ANY OTHER SECTION IN THIS TEST.

MODEL TEST 1

Answer Keys and Explanations — Test of General Knowledge

SOCIAL STUDIES

Answer Key

1.	B	7.	C	13.	A	19.	C	25.	E
2.	B	8.	E	14.	A	20.	A	26.	A
3.	C	9.	E	15.	D	21.	B	27.	B
4.	E	10.	A	16.	E	22.	B	28.	D
5.	E	11.	D	17.	D	23.	A	29.	C
6.	B	12.	A	18.	D	24.	B	30.	C

Explanations

1. **(B)** The rural population rate declined 20 percent from 1940 to 1980, but then rose 20 percent from 1980 to 1985.

2. **(B)** The economic recession, the worst since World War II, caused a significant decrease in industrial employment.

3. **(C)** The number of illiterate persons in the world continues to rise because of the worldwide population explosion.

4. **(E)** Although further changes in the Social Security system are manifestly necessary if it is not to become bankrupt, because of the growing number of elderly persons and the emotional aspects involved the issue is a politically sensitive one (E). The Social Security Act was passed in 1935 in Franklin Roosevelt's, not Johnson's, administration (A). Its purpose was to *supplement*, not to constitute the only, retirement income (B). Participation is mandatory for most workers (C). Legislation establishing the Medicare program was passed more than 30 years later, in 1966 (D).

5. **(E)** Prejudiced people seem to identify stereotyped minorities more readily, through prejudgment based on partial information regarding the facts involved.

6. **(B)** Hoover was president from 1929 to 1933; Eisenhower, from 1953 to 1961; Nixon, from 1969 to 1974; Ford, from 1974 to 1977.

7. **(C)** In 1979 a military coup overthrew the Romero government of El Salvador, and the country has been torn by violence and unrest ever since. The question of U.S. economic and military aid to El Salvador has been volatile and politically divisive.

8. **(E)** In 1978 the Senate ratified two treaties that provide for the gradual transfer of the Panama Canal to Panama and the withdrawal of U.S. troops.

9. **(E)** National production quotas (E) are characteristic of command (e.g., Communist), not capitalistic, economic systems.

TEST OF GENERAL KNOWLEDGE

10. **(A)** In 1968 white unemployment was approximately 4 percent, while in the early 1980s it was close to 8 percent, so it did go up and down for the period shown.

11. **(D)** For the entire period shown the line indicating black unemployment is above the line indicating white unemployment.

12. **(A)** When the money supply tightens, interest rates rise, reflecting the decreased supply of money. Mortgage rates are high because money is not available to lend (B); the construction industry and businesses lack funds to function and expand (C, D), and inflation rises (E).

13. **(A)** Economic goods represent tangible materials; services include intangible things like professional treatment by physicians.

14. **(A)** The civil rights bill of 1964 banned discrimination. The Equal Rights Amendment (C) was never ratified by the required number of states. School desegregation (D) was ordered in 1956. Choice (E) refers to Affirmative Action.

15. **(D)** The town form of local government was fostered in New England by the fact that the settlers came from England.

16. **(E)** Although all five of the choices represent areas in which the vice-presidential candidate would hopefully complement the presidential candidate, the cartoon, with its map of the United States, is clearly referring to demographic support. A balanced ticket, according to the cartoon, is one in which together the presidential and vice-presidential candidates can account for the support of the whole country.

17. **(D)** Capital is the third factor, besides raw material and labor, in the economic production of goods for consumption.

18. **(D)** Choice (D), which consists of persons in the age group that has the most illnesses, would benefit most from such legislation and would most strongly support it. Choices (B) and (C) would probably favor it also, but to a lesser degree. The American Medical Association (A) and, to a lesser extent, the American Nurses Association (E) could be expected to oppose legislation of the type described because of the adverse effect on the earnings of members.

19. **(C)** This quotation from a letter by George Washington describes the difficulties encountered in persuading the individual states to compromise and to surrender their self-interests in favor of a strong central government. Note that the references to states rule out (A).

20. **(A)** Although some absolute monarchs of the past were benevolent despots, most of them did not believe in educating their people. Modern totalitarian states, on the other hand, use mass education to indoctrinate and thus maintain their authority.

21. **(B)** Ten presidents have been elected by the electoral college who received only a minority vote in the national election. They were: James Buchanan (1856), Abraham Lincoln (1860), Rutherford B. Hayes (1876), James A. Garfield

275

MODEL TEST 1

(1880), Grover Cleveland (1884), Benjamin Harrison (1888), Woodrow Wilson (1912 and 1916), Harry S. Truman (1948), John F. Kennedy (1960), and Richard M. Nixon (1968).

22. **(B)** The Ordinance of 1787 dealt with the procedures for creating new states north of the Ohio River, with the same privileges and rights as the original thirteen.

23. **(A)** The writings of Edmund Burke (1729–1797) influenced conservative political thought in England, France, and the United States.

24. **(B)** The quotation mentions the need to read the lessons of the past to avoid quick decisions which "end only in blank walls."

25. **(E)** A total of eleven states seceded from the Union to establish the Confederacy.

26. **(A)** Lincoln (1865), Garfield (1881), McKinley (1901), and Kennedy (1963).

27. **(B)** As a rule, the greater the supply of a commodity, the lower the price; therefore an ample supply of home heating oil would reduce the cost to consumers. A December freeze in Florida (A), causing damage to fruits, and a summer drought in the Plains States (C), reducing the grasslands available for grazing cattle, would result in higher food prices. A rise in pleasure driving (D) would reduce the supply of gasoline and hence raise the price.

28. **(D)** Cultural adaptation lags behind technical changes or new ideas; for example, social legislation lags behind economic needs. Material progress makes more rapid gains than changes in traditions, attitudes, and laws.

29. **(C)** Social organizations tend to foster prejudice and poor intergroup relations, through loyalty of the individual to the norms of his or her group. Moreover, it is difficult for other persons to enter such a group; therefore group members are limited in their personal contacts.

30. **(C)** The reporter (C) was neither an eyewitness nor a participant in the accident. All the other choices represent primary sources, which might have been used by the reporter in writing his account.

MATHEMATICS

Answer Key

1. A	6. E	11. C	16. D	21. E
2. D	7. C	12. A	17. B	22. E
3. C	8. A	13. D	18. E	23. D
4. B	9. B	14. E	19. D	24. B
5. E	10. C	15. B	20. C	25. A

TEST OF GENERAL KNOWLEDGE

Explanations

1. **(A)** What number multiplied by itself equals 40?
$$6 \times 6 = 36; \qquad 7 \times 7 = 49$$
   Therefore the square root of 40 lies between 6 and 7.

2. **(D)** The registers, 21 and 28, must be evenly divisible by the same number in order to form groups with the same number of members in both classes. The only number divisible into both 21 and 28 is 7. Therefore, each group must have 7 pupils in it. Ms. Burke's class will have $21 \div 7$ or 3 groups, and Mr. Korngraff's class will have $28 \div 7$ or 4 groups. This makes a total of 7 groups.

3. **(C)** Change $\frac{2}{5}$ to tenths: $\frac{2}{5} = \frac{4}{10}$ or 0.4. It is easy by visual inspection of the numbers to see that $\frac{4}{10}$ lies between $\frac{1}{10}$ and $\frac{9}{10}$ (A) and between 0.3 and 0.5 (B). However, $\frac{1}{2}$ is 0.5 and $\frac{3}{4} = 0.75$; therefore 0.4 does not lie between these decimal numbers, and (C) is incorrect. It does lie between 0.2 and 0.6 (D) and between 0 and 1, that is, $\frac{10}{10}$ (E).

4. **(B)** A number line

$$\overline{-6\ -5\ -4\ -3\ -2\ -1\ \ 0\ \ +1\ +2\ +3\ +4\ +5\ +6}$$

   makes the relationships of the numbers clear. Only in (B) is the first number (2) larger than the second (1).

5. **(E)** To obtain Celsius readings for the Fahrenheit temperatures, follow the formula given in the problem: $C = \frac{5}{9} \times (F - 32)$.
   Step 1. Subtract 32 from 93: $93 - 32 = 61$.
   Step 2. Multiply: $\frac{61}{1} \times \frac{5}{9} = \frac{305}{9}$.
   Step 3. Divide: $305 \div 9 = 33.88$, which, rounded to the next highest number $= 34°C$.
   To obtain the Celsius temperature for 70°F, use the same formula.
   Step 1. Subtract 32 from 70: $70 - 32 = 38$.
   Step 2. Multiply: $\frac{38}{1} \times \frac{5}{9} = \frac{190}{9}$.
   Step 3. Divide: $190 \div 9 = 21.11$, which, rounded to the next lowest number is 21°F.

6. **(E)** When subtracting fractions, we change to a common denominator. In this case $4\frac{1}{2}$ becomes $4\frac{2}{4}$, from which we subtract $2\frac{1}{4}$, leaving $2\frac{1}{4}$.

7. **(C)** The previous price of $1.33 has nothing to do with the problem.
   Step 1. Multiply the current cost of $1.21 per gallon by 15 gallons. The answer is $18.15.
   Step 2. Subtract: $20.00 - $18.15 = $1.85.

8. **(A)** Step 1. Multiply: 12 cookies per dozen $\times$ 3 dozen = 36.
   Step 2. Multiply: 3 children $\times$ 2 cookies per trip = 6 cookies per trip.
   Step 3. Divide 6 into 36; the answer is 6 trips.

MODEL TEST 1

9. **(B)** A comparison is made between the two hourly wages; the ratio of $4.00 John earns in the daytime to $5.00 he earns in the evening is 4 to 5, or 4:5. For every $4.00 John earns in the daytime, he earns $5.00 in the evening.

10. **(C)** Step 1. Write $\frac{1}{100}$ as a decimal; 0.01 is equal to none of the numbers given in (A), (B), or (D).
    Step 2. Multiply: $\frac{1}{10} \times \frac{1}{10} = \frac{1}{100}$. Choice (C) is correct.

11. **(C)** Step 1. To find the perimeter we add the total distance around an area. In this problem, we are fencing the entire outside area, not just the distance around each playground.
    Add: 18 + 4 + 25 + 4 + 30 + 20 (width on one end) = 101.
    Step 2. Multiply this distance by 2; there are two equal sides and two equal lengths to the total area: 2 × 101 = 202.

12. **(A)** If $x = 12y$ and y is reduced by $\frac{1}{4}$, what is the value of x?
    Select an "old" value for y, for example, $y = 8$.
    Since $x = 12y$, $x = 12 \times 8$, or $x = 96$, when $y = 8$.
    If y is reduced to $\frac{1}{4}$ of its old value, its new value is $\frac{1}{4}(8) = 2$.
    Since $x = 12y$, $x = 12 \times 2$, or $x = 24$, when $y = 2$.
    Thus x has changed from 96 to 24. Since 24 = 25% of 96, x is reduced to 25% or $\frac{1}{4}$ of its old value.

13. **(D)** By the reflexive property of equality, if $A = BC$, then $BC = A$, so (A) is true.
    In the equation $BC = A$, divide both sides by B:
    $$\frac{BC}{B} = \frac{A}{B} \quad \text{or} \quad C = \frac{A}{B},$$
    so (B) is true.
    In the equation $BC = A$, divide both sides by C:
    $$\frac{BC}{C} = \frac{A}{C} \quad \text{or} \quad B = \frac{A}{C},$$
    so (C) is true. If BC is subtracted from both sides of the equation $A = BC$, the result is $A - BC = 0$, so (E) is true. The only incorrect equation is (D).

14. **(E)** Step 1. Total the grass growth for the 2 months in each pair.
    (A) April (2) and September (2) = 4 inches
    (B) July (5) and August (1) = 6 inches
    (C) May (4) and August (1) = 5 inches
    (D) June (3) and July (5) = 8 inches
    (E) May (4) and July (5) = 9 inches
    Step 2. Compare your findings.
    Step 3. Select the highest total: (E) May and July.

15. **(B)** Step 1. Count the number of girls: 60.
    Step 2. Count the number of boys: 100.
    Step 3. Reduce to the smallest denominator or fraction. The ratio of girls to boys is 60 to 100, which can be written as the fraction $\frac{60}{100}$. Reducing the fraction, we have:
    $$\frac{60}{100} = \frac{3}{5}$$

TEST OF GENERAL KNOWLEDGE

Step 4. Read as a ratio: 3 girls are absent for every 5 boys.

16. **(D)** Inspect the circle graph. There is a question mark in the Detroit sector. We know that the percentages for all the sectors must total 100 percent.
    Step 1. Add the percentages given on the graph:

    $$21 + 20 + 15 + 17 = 73.$$

    Step 2. Subtract: $100 - 73 = 27\%$.

17. **(B)** Step 1. Begin with January and add the number of inches of snowfall in 1983 that exceeded the snowfall of 1982; do the same for 1982 as compared to 1983.

1983 over 1982		1982 over 1983	
January	5 in.	March	5 in.
February	10 in.	April	5 in.
November	5 in.	October	10 in.
December	10 in.		20 in.
	30 in.		

    Step 2. Subtract 30 in. − 20 in. = 10 in.
    Step 3. Select the correct answer: (B).

18. **(E)** Let 3–4 represent the number. The first digit, 3, is not divisible by 7, but 35 is. However, the middle digit cannot be 5 because the last digit, 4, is not divisible by 7. If, however, 1 was carried over from the middle digit division, it would provide 14 for the final division, and 14 is divisible by 7. Therefore, the middle digit must be $5 + 1$ or 6.

19. **(D)** 5 multiplied by 2 gives 10. However, 10 is not greater than 13, so 10 is multiplied by 2, giving a result of 20. Since 20 is greater than 13, 20 is printed.

20. **(C)** We are given the true proposition "If substance X is present, the Muller-Kleinbach test will show a positive result." Choice (A) is the converse of this proposition, and choice (B) is the inverse of it. The converse and the inverse of a true proposition may or may not be true. In the case under consideration in this question, some substance other than substance X may also produce a positive Muller-Kleinbach result. This explains why an alternative test showing no presence of substance X does not mean that a positive Muller-Kleinbach test was improperly performed — choice (D). Since the presence of substance X always results in a positive Muller-Kleinbach result, choice (C) is always true, and it will be unnecessary to conduct a second test when a negative result occurs — choice (E).

21. **(E)** If the farmer takes 4 hours to plow the field, he does $\frac{1}{4}$ of it in 1 hour. The farmhand takes 6 hours to do the whole job, so he does $\frac{1}{6}$ of it in 1 hour. Together, the two men do $\frac{1}{4} + \frac{1}{6}$ in 1 hour, or $\frac{3}{12} + \frac{2}{12}$ or $\frac{5}{12}$. To do a complete job, they must do $\frac{12}{12}$. The number of hours required can be represented as $\frac{12}{12} \div \frac{5}{12}$.

    $$1 \div \frac{5}{12} = 1 \times \frac{12}{5} = 2\frac{2}{5} \text{ or 2 hr, 24 min.} - \text{choice (E)}.$$

MODEL TEST 1

Note that the question can be solved very simply by ruling out choices (A), (B), (C), and (D) since each of these is more than $\frac{1}{2}$ the time the slower worker takes. When helped by a faster worker (the farmer), the job should be finished in less than half of the 6 hours the farmhand takes alone.

22. **(E)** Choose a convenient "original" value for y, say 12. Then $\frac{12}{4} = 3x$, or $3 = 3x$, or $x = 1$ (this is the "original" value of x).

If y is now tripled, its "new" value is 3×12 or 36. Then, $\frac{36}{4} = 3x$, or $9 = 3x$, or $x = 3$ (this is the "new" value of x). Since x changes from 1 to 3, x is tripled.

23. **(D)** Perimeter is the distance around an object or figure. Figures C and D have the same number of 1-inch sides — C has two $\frac{1}{2}$-inch sides, which make 1; 1 + nine 1-inch sides = 10 inches.

Note that A and the combination of the two figures in B have the same perimeter — 14 inches — but this is not one of the choices.

24. **(B)** The same area, 5 square inches, is covered by A and C. The separate figures in B have areas of 3 square inches and 2 square inches; D has 6 square inches.

25. **(A)** To find the percentage, use 60 as the base and 51 as the rate. In this case, we have $p = \frac{r}{b}$. Therefore, we divide 60 into 51 to determine the percentage of the total sold; the result is 85 percent.

LITERATURE AND FINE ARTS

Answer Key

1.	A	8.	E	15.	A	22.	B	29.	A
2.	B	9.	C	16.	E	23.	C	30.	E
3.	A	10.	A	17.	C	24.	E	31.	C
4.	E	11.	D	18.	B	25.	E	32.	B
5.	A	12.	E	19.	C	26.	E	33.	C
6.	C	13.	A	20.	B	27.	D	34.	E
7.	E	14.	C	21.	B	28.	C	35.	D

Explanations

1. **(A)** The dancers' formal attire and traditional pose combine to suggest their mastery of classical ballet. There is nothing in their pose to suggest (B), great despair. Further, their pose is too stiff for (C), ebullience. The classic costumes and pose clearly mark this as traditional rather than experimental ballet, eliminating choice (D). The ballerina's seeming ease argues against (E), tension and strain.

TEST OF GENERAL KNOWLEDGE

2. **(B)** Disillusionment prevails. Human beings have become so preoccupied with worldly concerns that they have lost the ability to respond to nature and appreciate its beauty; in this regard the pagans were more fortunate.

3. **(A)** The speaker refers to figures from Greek mythology: Proteus, a sea-god who, according to the *Odyssey,* can take on any shape he wills; and Triton, another sea-god, whose lower body is that of a fish and who is usually represented as blowing on a conch shell.

4. **(E)** The speaker praises one aspect of paganism: appreciation and love of nature, but refers to paganism as "a creed outworn."

5. **(A)** The recessed center hall is partly created by the two projecting wings. The columns are not Corinthian (B); the hall's length has nothing to do with its depth (C). In the same way, the moldings (D) do not affect the recessed facade. (E) confuses cause and effect; the tri-part roof is a result of the projecting wings.

6. **(C)** Early American Indians were talented artists, producing articles of sophistication and beauty. They were particularly adept at intricate geometrical designs, with which they ornamented such utilitarian objects as baskets and blankets. The one characteristic the rug does *not* show is fantasy, or imagination.

7. **(E)** The winged lion, used originally by the Assyrians, was adopted for decoration by the Persians when they conquered the Near East. The bold outlines and strong patterns make this drinking cup stand out visually.

8. **(E)** The Woman speaks about danger, about dreaming, and about freedom, and loneliness. She makes the point that one may fly toward or away from something which is lacking or dangerous in one's life. One can be free and still be lonely.

9. **(C)** At 10 years of age David went to work in the wine warehouse of Murdstone and Grinby; as a child in a debt-ridden family Dickens worked in a blacking factory.

10. **(A)** Leonardo was interested in everything—weapons, fortifications, waves, currents, storms, floods, trees, grass: he was a painter and sculptor, a designer of machinery and buildings, a musician, a scientist, and an inventor.

11. **(D)** Note "the shy interest in books and ideas that she was *beginning* to develop."

12. **(E)** Note the last three sentences. He is not really disturbed by (A) and (B); he suspects that (C) is not true; and (D) is eliminated by "She was straightforward."

13. **(A)** *Factitious* is the opposite of *natural*; a clue is *cunningly manufactured*.

14. **(C)** Each building uses columns in some fashion.

MODEL TEST 1

15. **(A)** The word that best describes these buildings is (A), stately. Their dignified facades, elegant columns, and classical, balanced lines combine to create an impressive tone. Although they may indeed be functional (B), that does not best describe their appearance as a group. Buildings (B) and (D) are not ornate (choice C); neither are any of them experimental (D) or flamboyant (E), excessively showy.

16. **(E)** Building (E) is the only one of the five edifices that has a dome.

17. **(C)** Note the first six lines in particular.

18. **(B)** If his religion did not forbid it, the speaker (Hamlet) would commit suicide (lines 3 and 4).

19. **(C)** The word *beteem* means "allow" or "permit." A loving husband *would* forbid the wind to blow too roughly on his wife's face.

20. **(B)** The pool and canal line divides the painting horizontally, but unity is gained by having all the workers engaged in hoeing, plowing, or breaking up clods of earth—essential tasks before the seeds could be planted.

21. **(B)** The outstretched arms, thrown back head, facial expression, etc., all suggest strength and heart.

22. **(B)** Leonard Bernstein, composer of *West Side Story*, is the only native American among the choices.

23. **(C)** Note "every man is...a part of the main" and "I am involved in mankind."

24. **(E)** Ernest Hemingway's *For Whom the Bell Tolls*, a novel about the Spanish Civil War, was later made into a motion picture.

25. **(E)** Objects produced during this period tended to be rich in detail, like the brooch shown, which represents Sarah Bernhardt in the role of Melisande and was created by Alphonse Mucha.

26. **(E)** The drawing of an old man was done by Van Gogh in his early years. Van Gogh has shown the old man realistically in his grief. Note such details as the clenched hands, the bunched arm muscles, the wisps of hair on the otherwise bald head, and the sturdy workman's shoes. The drawing is not imaginative (A), nor does it lack good composition (B) or perspective (C). The lack of facial expression (D) is not a valid criticism.

27. **(D)** This is the national anthem, "The Star-Spangled Banner." At (A) we have a repetition of the first eight measures, which makes the song complete.

28. **(C)** The simplicity of the concrete building, with its flat lines and essential lack of ornamentation, reflects the Japanese influence.

29. **(A)** The poem describes a coffin by substituting its inner lining for the entire coffin.

TEST OF GENERAL KNOWLEDGE

30. **(E)** We realize that the speaker did not literally freeze when he was apart from his loved one, nor did the days turn dark. Rather, the speaker is exaggerating to illustrate the depth of his despair at his separation from his beloved.

31. **(C)** The poet treats the evening, an inanimate thing, as though alive by comparing it to a patient anesthetized on a table.

32. **(B)** Note the reference to "that hostelrye," that is, an inn. Hostels (C) are a relatively modern form of accommodation. The passage quoted is from Chaucer's *Canterbury Tales*, as you probably have realized.

33. **(C)** Note "ready to wenden on my pilgrymage" and "pilgrimes were they all."

34. **(E)** The travelers had "aventure yfal in felaweshipe" — in other words, had fallen into fellowship by adventure (chance).

35. **(D)** The beat here has the accent on the first syllable; the second and third syllables are played with a staccato touch. The waltz is written in three-beats-to-the-measure time.

SCIENCE

Answer Key

1. A	7. C	13. D	19. C	25. B
2. A	8. E	14. D	20. E	26. C
3. B	9. C	15. A	21. D	27. B
4. C	10. A	16. B	22. A	28. D
5. D	11. A	17. A	23. B	29. C
6. A	12. D	18. E	24. A	30. D

Explanations

1. **(A)** As one tectonic plate moves against another, one will force its way below the edge of the other, in a *subduction zone*. This is happening at the western edge of both the North and South American continents. The resultant instability creates regions of violent tectonic and volcanic activity in zones parallel to the coast.

2. **(A)** In a lunar eclipse, the shadow of the Earth is cast onto the moon, so that the illumination of the moon is shut off. This can happen only during the full moon, when the sun and the moon are on opposite sides of the Earth. It does not happen every full moon because the Earth is usually not aligned with the moon and the sun, or, in other words, the Earth is usually above or below an imaginary line stretching between the moon and the sun.

3. **(B)** The term *ecosystem* refers to the interactions of a community with its environment. A food web (B) describes how the populations in an ecosystem feed on each other. A food pyramid (A) shows the relationship among consumers (at the top of the pyramid), producers (in the middle), and decomposers (at the bottom) in an ecosystem. A food chain (C) is one part of a food web; it shows the links along which food is passed from one type of organism to another. Food groups and food vacuoles are not related to the first three choices. The term *food groups* refers to the basic four types of foods recommended for a balanced daily diet. Food vacuoles are spaces in the protoplasm of organisms, such as amoebae, that serve to digest food.

4. **(C)** Only certain materials are attracted to a magnet. Iron and steel are highly attracted, and, to a lesser extent, cobalt and nickel. (However, there is not enough nickel in a U.S. coin to be attracted.) The old silver dimes, as well as the present copper-filled coins, do not contain any materials that are attracted to magnets.

5. **(D)** Bacterial cells are hardly cells at all. They are prokaryotic. They lack an organized nucleus and do not have the complex internal structure of eukaryotic cells—those of ferns, algae, protozoa, vertebrates, and virtually all other organisms. Prokaryotes lack mitochondria, endoplasmic reticulum, and other membrane-bound organelles. The bacterial genetic material is a single strand of DNA.

6. **(A)** Conduction is the transfer of heat through a material, particularly through a metal. Convection is the transfer of heat by the circulation of a fluid, either a liquid or a gas. Since there is no substance between the Earth and the sun, neither of these two methods is possible. Electromagnetic radiation, however, can pass through a perfect vacuum. The Earth is heated by radiation, especially infrared.

7. **(C)** Energy and power are dimensionally different, and it is not possible to convert one into the other. Different forms of energy can be interconverted. In a motor, electricity is fed in; the outcome is movement. In other words, electrical energy is converted into mechanical energy.

8. **(E)** Prevailing winds affect climate in several ways—for example, by carrying moisture. Latitude also affects climate: it is colder at higher latitudes because the sun's rays strike the Earth more obliquely. The higher the altitude also the cooler. A large body of water stores heat, and tends to make summers cooler and winters warmer. The phases of the moon have no effect on climate.

9. **(C)** The correct order of the answer choices, in terms of increasingly close relationship, is as follows: (A) → (E) → (B) → (D) → (C). The family (not given as a choice) comes between the order and the genus.

10. **(A)** Mass, defined as the amount of matter an object contains, remains the same throughout the universe. However, the question is concerned with weight, not mass, thereby eliminating (C) and (D). Weight is defined as a measurement of the pull of gravity, and this differs according to where a person or object is in the universe, eliminating (B). On the moon, a 100-pound person would weigh about 16 pounds (A) because the moon exerts one-sixth the pull of gravity that the Earth does.

TEST OF GENERAL KNOWLEDGE

11. **(A)** Rickets is a growth abnormality of the skeletal system, caused primarily by a deficiency of vitamin D. This vitamin can be obtained in certain foods, and it is produced in the skin by the action of sunlight.

12. **(D)** Based on the information in the table, four statements about birth and death rates and about literacy are incorrect. Only one statement (D) is correct. The country with the highest birth rate—41 per 1,000— is Central Africa, which also has the lowest life expectancy—33 years for men, 36 for women.

13. **(D)** Earthworms eat their way through the soil as they burrow, taking in nutrients as well as soil. The soil passes through their digestive canal and into the ground again. In the process, the earthworms loosen the soil (D), thus areating it and allowing water to enter.

14. **(D)** Any chemical formula represents a compound, a combination of elements. In water, the three atoms (2 of hydrogen and 1 of oxygen) are firmly bound into a molecule. Water is not an ionic compound, easily broken apart into charged ions; nor is it an organic compound because it does not contain carbon.

15. **(A)** According to classical physics, there are 6 simple machines: pulley, wheel-and-axle, lever, screw, wedge, and inclined plane. A number of others have been invented since this list was made: hydraulic press, gears, belt drive, etc. All of these machines, except the hydraulic press, are based on only two really basic principles: the lever and the inclined plane.

16. **(B)** Since it takes work to move a boulder up to a higher position, it has more potential energy at the higher location. The energy is gravitational because the work has to be done against the pull of gravity.

17. **(A)** The two leads of a cord touching each other constitute a short circuit, allowing an enormous surge of current. In the absence of protection, the vacuum cleaner might burn up, or the wires in the wall might melt. However, a normally operating household circuit is protected by a fuse or by a circuit breaker, which opens to shut off the current.

18. **(E)** All matter is made up of about 100 basic substances called elements. The smallest particle of an element, containing all of its properties, is an atom. When two or more elements combine chemically (E), a compound is formed. The smallest particle of a compound is a molecule.

19. **(C)** When doing an experiment, several factors may be suspected of being responsible for a certain result. It is important, therefore, to perform a series of controlled experiments where all conditions are alike except for one variable factor at a time (C). When a difference in the result is noted for one experiment, it is then evident which factor was responsible.

20. **(E)** By far, industrial uses (E) for water surpass all other uses combined. It is estimated that over 150,000 gallons per person per year is needed by industry. Personal uses of water (A, B, C, D), including watering lawns and operating air conditioning and heating, require less than one-tenth the amount consumed by industry.

21. **(D)** The human body requires six nutrients to maintain good health: carbohydrates, fats and oils, proteins, vitamins, minerals, and water. Carbohydrates, which include sugars and starches (D), provide energy. Fats (A, B) are an energy source and also serve as insulation and protection. The proteins (B) are the building blocks of the cell. A lack of proper vitamins (C) may result in

deficiency diseases. Minerals (C, E) serve the body in several ways, including bone formation. Water is necessary in the digestion of food and the production of certain body fluids. Choice (D) is the only one in which both nutrients provide energy.

22. **(A)** Deoxyribonucleic acid (DNA) is the organic molecule found in the nuclei of cells (A). More specifically, DNA is located within the chromosomes (structures in the nuclei). The DNA molecules determine the hereditary traits of the individual.

23. **(B)** In a eukaryotic cell, the DNA in the chromosomes controls the production of RNA, which carries the code for the manufacture of proteins. The RNA passes out of the nucleus to the ribosomes in the cytoplasm, where it controls the production of proteins.

24. **(A)** The action of running water is the principal agent of erosion. Water loosens the soil, and gravity takes the soil from one level to a lower one. Several methods are helpful in reducing this loss. Among them is the use of ground cover, that is, planting grass and trees to hold the water and thus the soil.

25. **(B)** Pressures on the rocks in the Earth's crust from overlying rock, or from the molten magma below, may cause them to bend and, if great enough, to break (B). These breaks in the Earth's crust are called faults. Crustal pressure can cause shifting of the rocks up or down relative to each other. When strong enough, this may lead to earthquakes.

26. **(C)** Species are placed in the same genus when the evidence indicates that they have the most recent common ancestor. Since II and IV belong to the same genus as the American Robin (*Turdus*), one of them is most likely the closest relative of the robin.

27. **(B)** The moon (B) is our nearest neighbor in space. Its average distance from the Earth is about 240,000 miles. The sun (A) is 93 million miles away. Even at its closest approach, Halley's comet (C) will be much farther away than the moon. At times Venus (D) comes closer to the Earth than any other planet, about 30 million miles. The distance to the North Star (E) is over 1000 light-years.

28. **(D)** Even if, as stated, the contradictory observation has been checked several times, the theory should not be abandoned (C, E). It is probably basically correct and, with some modification, will be even better (D). On the other hand, the contradictory observation should not be ignored (A, B).

29. **(C)** The flu vaccine is a weakened flu virus, which elicits the same kind of immune reaction in the body as the live virus would. It provides increased protection against the live virus by causing the body to increase the production of white cells and antibodies. This may be accompanied by an increase in temperature. The red blood cells have nothing to do with the immune system.

30. **(D)** Arthropods belong to the phylum of invertebrate animals with jointed legs and segmented bodies. The major classes of arthropods are the crustaceans (crayfish, lobsters, shrimps, crabs, barnacles); the centipedes; the millipedes; the arachnids (spiders, scorpions, ticks, mites); and the insects (the largest class of all). Starfish (D) belong to the echinoderm (spiny-skinned) phylum.

Model Test 1
Test of Communication Skills

SECTION 1
LISTENING

Approximate time—30 minutes

PART A

Directions: You will find two kinds of questions in Part A. One kind presents a short question for you to answer; the other requires you to demonstrate understanding of a short statement. Listen to each question or statement (on the audiocassette) *only once*, and listen very carefully. Then find the answer choices that correspond to the number of the question. Choose the one that best answers the question or is closest in meaning to or best supported by the statement, and fill in the appropriate space completely.

1. (A) The banks closed in Michigan that year, and teachers were paid in scrip.
   (B) Our local school board was disappointed with the teachers' qualifications.
   (C) The school attendance was average in spite of the very hot weather that prevailed all year.
   (D) I did not like the textbooks for my physics course.

2. (A) It was not in the textbook.
   (B) John did not know the answer.
   (C) Bob and I had a discussion during lunch.
   (D) It was in my notes from Tuesday's lecture.

3. (A) Bob had the best qualifications.
   (B) Fred was the president last year.
   (C) George received the most votes.
   (D) Andy was very popular, but he did not want the job.

4. (A) He had a 14–12 record.
   (B) Voters eliminated varsity basketball for economic reasons.
   (C) He did not like to bring problems to the school board meetings.
   (D) His wife taught school in the next county.

5. (A) Teachers feel the need to assemble and share experiences.
   (B) School districts are being increased in physical size.
   (C) The National Commission on Excellence in Education issued a critical report entitled "A Nation at Risk."
   (D) Class size seldom relates to quality in education.

6. (A) The Russians graduated more new physics teachers last year than the total number in the United States.
   (B) U.S. industry is outbidding educational institutions for science and mathematics personnel.
   (C) In 1980 there was no shortage of secondary science teachers.
   (D) More than half of the mathematics teachers in the United States have been hired on an emergency basis.

7. (A) When she makes a committee report to the board of education
   (B) When she attends a summer workshop session at the school
   (C) When she attends an athletic event at the school
   (D) When she converses with the parents and other adults in the community

8. (A) There are fewer children per family.
   (B) The single-parent family has less income.
   (C) There is a shortage of child-care facilities.
   (D) Opportunities for conversation with adults are reduced.

9. (A) Residents of Centralia feel no worse than any one else.
   (B) For 20 years a fire has been burning in the coal mines beneath the town.
   (C) A nuclear bomb might hit a neighboring state.
   (D) The winter seasons are longer than they used to be.

10. (A) The pay is excellent.
    (B) There is high risk of injury or even death.
    (C) Jane's brother is a police officer.
    (D) Jane concluded that the advantages of the firefighter's job outweighed the disadvantages.

11. (A) It's amusing that stores can't read some customers' orders.
    (B) The low level of penmanship is cause for concern.
    (C) Penmanship is relatively unimportant, in and out of school.
    (D) Illegible penmanship should not be held against a job seeker.

12. (A) All need for funds to start a business is met by the Small Business Administration.
    (B) Minority groups should try to meet their needs through special banking facilities, as well as through conventional sources.
    (C) Business ownership is too risky for minority groups.
    (D) The owners of small businesses have poor credit ratings.

13. (A) In 1983 the "doomsday clock" was set ahead for the first time.
    (B) Atomic scientists delight in alarming the public.
    (C) Setting the clock ahead expresses the concern of scientists for human survival when international relations are deteriorating.
    (D) Few people pay attention to atomic scientists and what they think.

14. (A) Public shelters accommodate many during severe weather conditions.
    (B) Only the aged and the poor are affected by bad weather.
    (C) Unusually severe weather prevailed all over the world in 1983.
    (D) The Midwest was affected most by severe weather conditions in 1983.

15. (A) Many people believe that "raped women ask for it" and that "only bad girls get raped."
    (B) A victim of rape needs physical and psychological assistance.
    (C) People should not pass moral judgments on others.
    (D) Every police department should set up a rape prevention program.

TEST OF COMMUNICATION SKILLS
PART B

Directions: In Part B you will hear several short dialogs. At the end of each dialog a third person will ask questions about the conversation. Each question will be spoken *only once*. After you hear a dialog and a question about it, read the four answer choices. Decide which is the best answer to the question, and fill in the corresponding space completely.

16. (A) In person
    (B) By telephone
    (C) By telegram
    (D) By letter

17. (A) He is happy.
    (B) He is angry.
    (C) He is indifferent.
    (D) He is jealous.

18. (A) The district cannot afford new books.
    (B) He doesn't know anything about the reading program.
    (C) He does not believe the evaluator.
    (D) He does not teach reading.

19. (A) Students are better motivated if they are allowed to choose their reading matter.
    (B) The evaluator is unqualified to judge the textbooks.
    (C) Students learn better with new materials.
    (D) The district can afford new books.

20. (A) She uses computers to teach math herself.
    (B) She thinks the man has too many computers.
    (C) She is not a math teacher.
    (D) She thinks the man will rely too much on the new computer.

21. (A) She thinks a computer is an essential teaching tool.
    (B) She wishes computers had never been invented.
    (C) She never uses computers.
    (D) She thinks the teacher is the most important teaching tool, with the computer playing a secondary role.

22. (A) His books have not sold well.
    (B) His writing, and people's attitude toward it, are very important to him.
    (C) Reviewers have criticized his books harshly.
    (D) His publishers want to cancel the contract for a forthcoming book.

23. (A) The public often identifies an author with his or her work.
    (B) People are unkind and like to insult others.
    (C) Children are unimportant in our culture.
    (D) People don't appreciate writers.

24. (A) The woman was abroad alone when it happened.
    (B) She lost her credit cards and couldn't pay her hotel bill.
    (C) It was her first time abroad.
    (D) She lost her passport and travel checks.

MODEL TEST 1

25. (A) Her passport (C) Her camera
 (B) Her jewelry (D) Her credit cards

26. (A) She will never go abroad again.
 (B) She will travel only with a large group.
 (C) She will leave cameras and other valuables at home.
 (D) She will continue to travel.

27. (A) To convey statistical information in a factual manner
 (B) To tease an unhappy listener
 (C) To sympathize with the man's dismay
 (D) To be very tactful in breaking unwelcome news

28. (A) He favors it.
 (B) He is opposed to it.
 (C) He is indifferent to it.
 (D) He is amused by it.

29. (A) He does not think there are any qualified black candidates.
 (B) He does not want to work with blacks.
 (C) The school board is negative toward blacks in administration.
 (D) No blacks have applied for administrative posts.

30. (A) He has had past experience with poor administrators.
 (B) He is prejudiced against blacks.
 (C) His concern is genuine; he wants the best administrators regardless of color.
 (D) He really doesn't care one way or another as long as he avoids controversy.

PART C

Directions: In Part C you will hear several short talks. Each talk will be followed by three or four questions. You must listen carefully because the talks and the questions will be given *only once*. After hearing each question, select the best answer and fill in the appropriate space completely.

31. (A) Obstacles to creating a learning environment
 (B) Lack of awareness of students' wants
 (C) Students' prejudices against authority
 (D) The need for stricter discipline in the classroom

32. (A) Encourage students to listen carefully.
 (B) Ignore the attitudinal factors that students bring to the classroom.
 (C) Use awareness exercises to reveal attitudinal factors in the classroom.
 (D) Expel inattentive students.

33. (A) Their lack of awareness results in automatic reactions that interfere with learning.
 (B) Students trust new teachers.
 (C) Students' outside experiences interfere with learning.
 (D) Students and teachers have had different experiences.

TEST OF COMMUNICATION SKILLS

34. (A) Long-range educational goals for handicapped students
    (B) Short-term goals for handicapped students
    (C) Needs of exceptional students
    (D) Assessment of progress by handicapped students

35. (A) Develop handicapped pupils' reading comprehension skills.
    (B) Limit handicapped students to short-range goals to meet current needs.
    (C) Make similar plans for all handicapped students through limited assessment techniques.
    (D) Assess current instruction of handicapped students in relation to long-term goals.

36. (A) Achievement of short-term goals is unimportant for these students.
    (B) Few of them will finish 12 years of schooling.
    (C) While in school they need to prepare for life in the working world.
    (D) Handicapped students don't need to develop social skills.

37. (A) How conventional computer programs limit creativity
    (B) The value of computers in learning
    (C) The computer as a toy
    (D) Mechanical problems with computers

38. (A) Computers are essential for learning.
    (B) Computers are only one learning tool.
    (C) Computers limit creative thinking.
    (D) New programs that encourage choices and decision-making are needed.

39. (A) Highly admiring
    (B) Unreservedly opposed
    (C) Indifferent
    (D) Judiciously critical

40. (A) Students in computer classes
    (B) Manufacturers and programmers
    (C) Parents
    (D) Teachers

S T O P

IF YOU FINISH BEFORE TIME IS CALLED, YOU MAY CHECK YOUR WORK ON THIS SECTION ONLY. DO NOT WORK ON ANY OTHER SECTION IN THE TEST.

MODEL TEST 1

SECTION 2

READING

Time—30 minutes

Directions: Read carefully each statement or passage, and the question(s) and/or incomplete statement(s) that follow it. Then choose from the five choices the best answer or completion for each question or incomplete statement, and fill in the corresponding space completely. Base your answers on what is *stated* or *implied* in the statement or passage, not on any outside knowledge you may possess.

1. Anne, Beth, and Claire are friends. Anne and Beth attend Bicounty High School; Claire attends Tricounty High. Anne plays varsity golf and tennis; Beth plays varsity tennis, basketball, and field hockey; Claire plays varsity golf and basketball and is on the cross-country team.

   If the information above is true, then which of the following statements must also be true?

   I. Bicounty High School has a cross-country team.
   II. Tricounty High School has a varsity tennis team.
   III. Both Bicounty High School and Tricounty High School offer varsity golf.

   (A) I only
   (B) II only
   (C) III only
   (D) I and II only
   (E) II and III only

2. Since approximately 70 percent of the Earth's plants and animals exist in the tropics, the leaders of developing or Third World countries must develop land-use policies that strike a balance between the needs of wildlife (giraffes, rhinos, etc.) and the needs of expanding human populations.

   With which of the following would the author of this statement most probably agree?
   (A) Most wild animals now in the tropics should be rounded up and shipped to zoos in established nations.
   (B) Unlimited hunting of all wild animals should be actively encouraged.
   (C) Since animals were there before people, they should be allowed to roam at will over as much land as they wish.
   (D) Available land should be apportioned so that there is enough to sustain wildlife and also enough for people to grow crops.
   (E) Leaders of the Third World should be made aware of the ethical and esthetic values of wildlife and of the need to preserve it regardless of the cost to the human population.

TEST OF COMMUNICATION SKILLS

Questions 3–8

"Teaching students to write clearly and effectively should be a central objective of the school," states Dr. Ernest L. Boyer, principal author of a recent report on secondary education issued by the Carnegie Foundation for the Advancement of Teaching. This opinion is supported by mounting evidence that students at all levels have been doing very little writing, and that students who have not learned to write clearly are not likely to reason clearly and critically. This decline in writing ability, therefore, has grave portent in regard to these individuals' future role in society and to the leadership of the community, the state, and the nation in years to come.

Apparently the decline in writing skills developed during the 1960s, when liberalization on college campuses resulted in the abolishment of the more rigorous basic requirements for admission, such as skill in expository writing. Fortunately, however, the situation in regard to writing skills is beginning to change. Now even mathematics- and science-oriented institutions like Massachusetts Institute of Technology are setting composition requirements. New York State has added a writing test to its requirements for a high school diploma, as have several other states. In Florida extra state aid is given to districts that reduce the size of high school English classes and that require students to write at least one composition each week.

3. According to the passage, the decline in students' writing ability is caused by
   (A) relaxation of college requirements in regard to basics
   (B) too much emphasis on science
   (C) failure of school boards to allocate special funds to teach writing
   (D) lack of student interest in writing
   (E) ineffective teaching of writing skills

4. According to the passage, one consequence of inability to write clearly is
   (A) failure to pass college courses in expository writing
   (B) failure to reason clearly and critically
   (C) difficulty in gaining admission to college
   (D) inability to hold a job that requires writing skills
   (E) failure to graduate from high school

5. In this passage the word *portent* means
   (A) political risk
   (B) unknown peril
   (C) potential hazard
   (D) prophetic significance
   (E) educational implication

6. The author of this passage uses examples to illustrate the statement that
   (A) liberalization of college requirements resulted in the decline of students' writing skills
   (B) teaching students to write clearly and effectively should be a central objective of the school
   (C) students at all levels are doing very little writing
   (D) students who are unable to write clearly are not likely to think clearly
   (E) the situation in regard to writing skills is beginning to change

MODEL TEST 1

7. If the quotation at the beginning of the passage is assumed to be true, then which of the following statements must also be true?
    (A) Every high school should set up a course in logic.
    (B) Schools should pay more attention to developing qualities of leadership in their students.
    (C) Specially trained teachers should be hired to teach writing.
    (D) The size of English classes should be increased, so that students will have more opportunity to criticize each other's writing.
    (E) Every elementary and high school should establish and/or maintain an effective program to teach writing.

8. The author's personal concern with the decline in writing standards is indicated by the
    (A) use of a quotation from an authority
    (B) inclusion of background information
    (C) use of examples
    (D) choice of language
    (E) introduction of opposing viewpoints.

Questions 9-10

A recent report prepared by the Cabinet Council on Human Resources indicated that vandalism costs schools more than textbooks and that lack of discipline is the greatest concern about American schools. Nearly three million secondary school pupils are victims of school crime every month, and minority students, especially blacks, are the most likely victims. The report recommended that the federal government become involved. It was suggested that the U.S. Justice Department provide training and technical assistance, where needed, to fight crime in the schools. Teachers alone cannot solve this problem, which is a national disgrace, and the federal government should indeed come to the rescue.

9. The author quotes the relative costs of school vandalism and textbooks in order to show that
    (A) vandalism is a school crime
    (B) schools do not purchase enough textbooks
    (C) many textbooks are overpriced
    (D) school vandalism results in damaged textbooks
    (E) school crime is serious

10. The author assumes that
    (A) local school boards would welcome and utilize federal assistance in dealing with crime
    (B) the public would reject federal assistance with local crime control
    (C) more students will be arrested for school crime in the future
    (D) minority students are largely responsible for school crime
    (E) federal assistance is not available

11. The teachers' association reported to the board of education at a special meeting that the median salary for beginning teachers in a neighboring district was $14,000, as compared to the median salary in the local district—$12,800. In a gesture of extraordinary generosity the board then gave the teachers a 2 percent increase!

    The author's tone is
    (A) factual   (D) indifferent
    (B) sarcastic   (E) happy
    (C) angry

TEST OF COMMUNICATION SKILLS

12. Although the total school budget was reduced by 18 percent, funding for the reading program will be increased by 2 percent. One reduction will involve transportation; busing will no longer be provided for high school students who live less than two miles from school.

    One inference that can be drawn from this statement is that
    (A) the school board members disagreed about the budget
    (B) little consideration has been given to the needs of high school students
    (C) many secondary students will transfer to other schools
    (D) increased parental cooperation and involvement will be required
    (E) basic-skill subjects received little consideration

Questions 13-14

For several years the bicounty Affirmative Action Program, responsible for placing blacks, Hispanics, and women in construction jobs, has been funded by Sharon and Lake counties. Next year, however, it faces the loss of half or even all of its $250,000 funding, because Sharon County has decided that its own county Affirmative Action office can provide the same services. Now Lake County is also assessing the situation in light of Sharon County's decision to withdraw support. Henry Blackwell, executive director of Affirmative Action Programs, attributes Sharon's decision to pressure to keep women and minorities out of construction jobs.

13. According to the passage, which of the following statements is true?
    (A) Because of pressure from minority groups more blacks and Hispanics have been placed in construction jobs in Sharon County.
    (B) Both Sharon and Lake counties have withdrawn funding for the Affirmative Action Programs for the next year.
    (C) The number of construction jobs in Sharon and Lake counties has dwindled sharply in recent years.
    (D) Sharon County will not pay its $125,000 share of funding for the Affirmative Action Programs next year.
    (E) The Affirmative Action Programs have placed substantial numbers of women and minorities in construction jobs.

14. On the basis of its content, in which of the following would the passage be LEAST likely to appear?
    (A) A local newspaper
    (B) A doctoral thesis on Affirmative Action Programs
    (C) A guide on how to fund social welfare programs
    (D) A newsletter for construction workers
    (D) A bulletin put out by Sharon County

15. After a study by the state legislature, one state added one-half hour to the school day and increased the school year from 180 to 190 days. Parents and pupils objected to these changes because vacation time would be shortened. Teachers, however, agreed that the changes were necessary.

    In this statement the author
    (A) shows a bias in favor of the legislation
    (B) reports the facts objectively
    (C) agrees with the parents and pupils
    (D) praises the teachers for supporting the changes
    (E) questions the cost of lengthening the school day and the school year

295

MODEL TEST 1

Questions 16–21

A person with ten years' experience as a programmer or analyst may find a new career in computer networking. The challenge posed by the explosion of microcomputers is to provide access to more than one system and to integrate single computers into a local area network (LAN) or a regional or national network so that computers can talk to each other and share data.

One terminal can be made to do many things. Each one can talk to the main computer and distribute the information obtained to many individuals or businesses. To do this, computer language must become more standardized. International computer language committees are studying the possibility of developing a language more like English, which will be more useful and easier to learn than the symbolic and technical languages now in use. Telephones and cable will be used to mix voice and data. Television sets will perform the functions of transmitting, receiving, printing, copying, and talking. Small microcomputers will be linked in a national network that will create a demand for writing, demonstrating, and servicing the new software. A person with an analytical mind will find a creative challenge in developing new hardware and software. Today's computer industry is seeking greater accessibility, availability, and compatability through wider interconnecting systems. This will provide many jobs for the right people.

16. The author's purpose in writing the passage is to
    (A) amuse
    (B) correct an injustice
    (C) inform
    (D) incite to action
    (E) arouse emotion

17. The main idea of the passage is best expressed by which of the following titles?
    (A) Coming Opportunities in the Computer Field
    (B) The Shortcomings of Computer Languages
    (C) How the Local Area Network (LAN) Will Work
    (D) New Types of Hardware and Software
    (E) The Functions of Computer Terminals

18. According to the passage, one reason for trying to develop a computer language like English is that
    (A) computers are used only in English-speaking countries
    (B) English is grammatically simple and easy to learn
    (C) English is the native language of more people than any other language
    (D) such a language would be easier to use than symbolic and technical languages
    (E) all of the persons developing the new language are English-speaking

19. According to the passage, the computer industry will need new workers because
    (A) there are many people with ten years' experience as programmers
    (B) LAN will integrate personal home computers to other home computers only
    (C) each terminal can have only a single function
    (D) television sets will replace computer analysts
    (E) networking will require new software and hardware

TEST OF COMMUNICATION SKILLS

20. Which of the following is an unstated assumption made by the author of this passage?
    (A) Competing computer designers will accept a new, standard language.
    (B) Prices will come down so more people can buy computers.
    (C) There is sufficient software for networking.
    (D) New computer firms will be formed.
    (E) Data processing will be done by word processors.

21. The content of the passage indicates that the passage would be LEAST likely to appear in which of the following?
    (A) A popular science journal
    (B) A computer magazine
    (C) A magazine for retired people
    (D) A magazine for working women
    (E) A magazine for men

---

22. It has been said that habit is not a kitten to be thrown out the window, but rather a tiger to be led down the stairs and carefully out of the house.

    A cigarette smoker who wishes to apply this statement to break the tobacco habit should
    (A) buy a kitten to keep his or her mind off smoking
    (B) quit "cold turkey"
    (C) cut down on the number of cigarettes very gradually over a long period
    (D) punish him- or herself every time he or she lights a cigarette
    (E) switch to cigars or a pipe

Questions 23–25

The results of a recent Foundations of Literacy study must surely cause grave misgivings among those involved with American education. According to the study, which was conducted in 1985, fully two-thirds of the high-school students tested by the foundation did not know the dates of the Civil War, while one-third did not know the date of the Declaration of Independence or the year that Columbus landed in the New World. Half the students failed to identify Joseph Stalin or Winston Churchill, and three-quarters of them were unfamiliar with Thoreau and Walt Whitman.

23. The primary purpose of the passage is to
    (A) point out several facts with which American high school students are unfamiliar
    (B) discuss the functions of the Foundations of Literacy
    (C) suggest that there is reason for concern about American education
    (D) identify a statistical basis for curriculum analysis
    (E) argue that today's high school students are not as knowledgeable as students of the past

24. Which of the following is an unstated assumption made by the author of the passage?
    (A) It is important for high school students to know certain dates and facts.
    (B) Education is everybody's business.
    (C) Society as we know it is possible only because of education.
    (D) Television is responsible for a decline in educational standards.
    (E) Modern students should not be burdened with irrelevant information.

MODEL TEST 1

25. If the findings of the study mentioned in the passage are true, then which of the following statements must also be true?

    I. American high school students are more familiar with English literature than with American literature.
    II. Most high school students know the date of the Declaration of Independence.
    III. Students forget much of what they learn in high school.

    (A) I only
    (B) II only
    (C) III only
    (D) II and III only
    (E) I, II, and III

26. A survey by a women's group found that 70% of the school districts that responded included on job applications improper questions concerning age, previous jobs, height, weight, number of children, and family situations.

    The author of the statement assumes which of the following?
    (A) Persons looking for work should not apply to school districts that ask improper questions.
    (B) Factors such as age may adversely affect a candidate's chance of employment.
    (C) A school district has the right to refuse employment to overweight persons.
    (D) The 30% of school districts that did not ask improper questions have lower standards.
    (E) The group that conducted the survey was delighted to find evidence of discrimination against women.

Questions 27–28

Educators and lawmakers are currently debating increased federal testing of students in United States schools. Under a new plan, a sample of elementary and high school students would be tested in reading, mathematics, writing, science, geography, history, and civics. Those in favor of such a national system of testing believe that it would lead to improved education. Those against it are worried that it would result in regimentation, destroying the diversity of the traditional school systems controlled by states and local districts. However, some educators are of the opinion that educational curricula are already pretty much the same throughout the nation.

27. The main idea of the passage is that
    (A) something should be done to improve United States schools at the national level
    (B) traditional school systems are based on diversity
    (C) standardization of school subjects has already begun
    (D) a democracy has no right to impose tests
    (E) a program for testing students at the national level has been proposed

TEST OF COMMUNICATION SKILLS

28. According to the passage, as compared to federal authority, traditional school systems are
    (A) more responsive to individual needs
    (B) under more regional jurisdiction
    (C) less concerned with core subjects
    (D) less likely to test students
    (E) laxer in administration

---

29. True learning involves doing. Athletes learn by practicing their sport. Actors rehearse, and student musicians play their instruments.

    Which of the following is the most accurate inference from the statement above?
    (A) Practice is important in the performing arts.
    (B) Students should be given opportunities to practice academic subjects.
    (C) Every field of endeavor has its specialized mode of training.
    (D) Students are better able to learn extracurricular activities.
    (E) Teachers should motivate students by comparing school activities to those in which they have practical experience.

30. Children in some 10,000 elementary schools nationwide are participating in an innovative program that will increase motivation and greatly sharpen their problem-solving skills. The program is called Invent America, and under its auspices, children are actively taught how to invent things.

    The author's tone in this passage can best be described as
    (A) unrealistically hopeful
    (B) somewhat critical
    (C) highly enthusiastic
    (D) cautiously optimistic
    (E) mildly negative

S T O P

THIS IS THE END OF THIS SECTION.
IF YOU FINISH BEFORE TIME IS CALLED, YOU MAY CHECK YOUR WORK ON THIS SECTION ONLY.
DO NOT WORK ON ANY OTHER SECTION IN THE TEST.

MODEL TEST 1

SECTION 3

WRITING: MULTIPLE-CHOICE

Time—30 minutes

Part A

(Suggested time—10 minutes)

Directions: Four portions of each of the sentences below are underlined and lettered. After reading the sentence, decide whether any one of the underlined parts contains an incorrect grammatical construction, incorrect word usage, or incorrect or omitted punctuation or capitalization. If this is the case, note the letter underneath the underlined portion and fill in completely the corresponding letter on the answer sheet. If there is no error in any underlined portion of the sentence, fill in space (E). No sentence contains more than one error.

Example Ila served a <u>real</u> good dinner <u>during</u> the <u>Easter</u> <u>holidays</u>. <u>No error</u>
　　　　　　　　　　A　　　　　　　　　　B　　　　　　　C　　　　D　　　　　　E

● Ⓑ Ⓒ Ⓓ Ⓔ

Explanation. An adverb is needed to modify the adjective *good*. The adjective *real* cannot be substituted for the adverb *really, very,* or *unusually*. Therefore (A) is the incorrect part of the sentence.

1. <u>Us</u> teachers had <u>better</u> speak out <u>promptly</u> and <u>decisively</u> on this issue. <u>No error</u>
　　A　　　　　　　　　B　　　　　　　　C　　　　　　　D　　　　　　　　　　E

2. <u>My Aunt Marge</u> is the town mayor, <u>and she</u> <u>has always been</u> the best pie-maker
　　A　　　　　　　　　　　　　　　　　B　　　　　　C
　for miles around. <u>No error</u>
　　　　　　D　　　　　E

3. <u>Among</u> the great jazz bands of the 1920s, none <u>were</u> <u>more popular than</u>
　　A　　　　　　　　　　　　　　　　　　　　　　　B　　　　C
　that of Duke Ellington. <u>No error</u>
　　　　　　D　　　　　　　　E

4. I <u>read in the paper</u> where a strike <u>had been called</u> by the <u>airline pilots' union</u>.
　　　　A　　　　　　B　　　　　　　C　　　　　　　　　　　D
　<u>No error</u>
　　E

5. My father, George Buckley, is <u>as tall</u>, if not taller <u>than</u>, I am. <u>No error</u>
　　　　　　　A　　　　　　　B　C　　　　　　　　D　　　　　　E

6. In response to <u>my inquiry</u> Rita said that her wristwatch <u>has been stolen</u> last
　　　　　　　　A　　　　　　　　　　B　　　　　　　　　　　　C
　spring. <u>No error</u>
　D　　　　E

7. Give <u>these</u> <u>leftovers</u> to <u>whomever</u> wants <u>to take</u> them home. <u>No error</u>
　　　　A　　　B　　　　　　C　　　　　　　D　　　　　　　　　　E

8. If the student <u>would take</u> me into his confidence, I <u>might</u> be <u>able</u> to help him.
　A　　　　　　　　B　　　　　　　　　　　　　　　　　　　C　　　D
　<u>No error</u>
　E

300

TEST OF COMMUNICATION SKILLS

9. He, as well as his sisters, were happy to be taking the final examinations in
      A   B   C
   English literature. No error
        D   E

10. Neither she or he works at the Rapid Plastics Manufacturing Company plant in
               A   B   C D
    Belsan City. No error
              E

11. Some of the coats were damaged by the fire that occurred last week. No error
         A   B   C   D   E

12. Sarah, whom I have known since high school, is the youngest of the two sisters.
          A   B   C   D
    No error
      E

13. Your question about how the accident occurred would require a long explanation,
                       A   B   C
    what I do not have time to give. No error
      D   E

14. Is it true, senator, that you disagree with the Secretary of Defense on the size of
      A B   C   D
    this missile? No error
                  E

15. I remember studying about the treaty of Ghent in my course in United States
                               A   B   C
    history. No error
      D   E

16. I'll buy these kind of flowers and those fish for the teachers' banquet at the
       A   B   C
    Crillion Hotel on Wednesday. No error
        D   E

17. He ran passed me, only to return a moment later with the book I had been asking
          A   B   C
    about tucked under his arm. No error
                  D   E

18. Joe's attitude is somewhat better than it used to be; he searched diligently to find
       A   B   C   D
    a suitable topic for his thesis. No error
                               E

19. He, not his brothers, is the one who I called to inquire about the position at the
                                A   B   C
    oil company. No error
      D   E

20. The panel's report criticized the history textbook severely; among the alleged defects
          A
    were inaccuracies, bias, and that many important facts were omitted. No error
       B   C   D   E

21. The vase that was stolen from the Metropolitan Museum of Art,
          A   B
    had been appraised at half a million dollars. No error
          C   D   E

MODEL TEST 1

22. In an eloquent speech James Lee, the lawyer, claimed that the courts never
                                    A   B   C
    showed no justice to homeless persons like his client. No error
           D   E

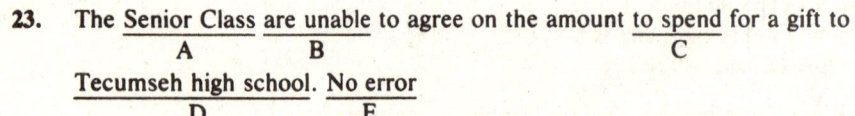

23. The Senior Class are unable to agree on the amount to spend for a gift to
                    A   B   C
    Tecumseh high school. No error
         D   E

24. For several months irate parents have been arguing with the school board about
                                    A
    the affects, good and bad, of closing the elementary school on Split Rock Road.
        B   C   D
    No error
      E

25. The editorial in the *Evening News* urged everyone to be understanding;
                                                     A
    neither the women nor William are to blame for the tragic accident that took the
             B   C   D
    lives of two children. No error
                            E

26. Coming home exhausted, I set down with a sigh of relief in my favorite chair.
                            A   B   C   D
    No error
      E

27. Some Assembly members advocate a plan under which schools designated as
                                              A   B
    merit schools because of improved student achievement would receive a bonus.
         C   D
    No error
      E

PART B

(Suggested time — 10 minutes)

Directions: In each of the following sentences there is an underlined portion that may be correct or may contain an error in grammar, diction (word use), sentence construction, or punctuation. Sometimes the entire sentence is underlined. Beneath each sentence are five ways of writing the underlined part. Choice (A) repeats the original, whereas the other four choices are different. If you think that the original sentence is correct, fill in space (A); otherwise choose the best answer from the other four choices given. *Do not choose an answer that changes the meaning of the original sentence.*

Example. All I have done to improve my vocabulary is to look up words I don't know and learning their meanings.
- (A) know and learning their meanings
- (B) know and learn their meanings
- (C) know and learning what their meanings are
- (D) know, learning their meanings
- (E) know and then I learn their meanings   Ⓐ ● Ⓒ Ⓓ Ⓔ

Explanation. The conjunction *and* connects like elements: nouns, verbs, clauses, and so on. Choice (B) is correct because *and* then connects two infinitives: *to know* and *(to) learn.*

302

TEST OF COMMUNICATION SKILLS

28. Steve <u>is smarter than any boy in his class and is</u> the best musician in the band.
    (A) is smarter than any boy in his class and is
    (B) is as smart as any other boy in his class and is
    (C) is as smart as any boy in his class and is
    (D) is smarter than any other boy in his class and is
    (E) , being smarter than any boy in his class, is

29. The year 1884 was an epochal one for American culture, <u>yielding an extraordinary work by a writer who called himself Mark Twain</u>.
    (A) yielding an extraordinary work by a writer who called himself Mark Twain
    (B) that yielded an extraordinary work by a writer who called himself Mark Twain
    (C) it yielded an extraordinary work by a writer who called himself Mark Twain
    (D) yielding an extraordinary work by a writer who called hisself Mark Twain
    (E) yielding an extraordinary work by a writer that called himself Mark Twain

30. <u>He had worked hard all his life, and when</u> he died he left nothing but a run-down shack and a mongrel dog.
    (A) He had worked hard all his life, and when
    (B) Although he had worked hard all his life, when
    (C) Working hard all his life, when
    (D) He had worked hard all his life; when
    (E) He had worked hard all his life, when

31. <u>Walking to school today</u>, a car passed me with a bumper sticker that said, "If you think education is expensive, try ignorance."
    (A) Walking to school today,
    (B) When I had walked to school today,
    (C) As I was walking to school today,
    (D) While walking to school today,
    (E) When walking to school today,

32. Alice Walker is a talented writer whose essays have been highly praised and <u>awarded the Pulitzer Prize in literature for her novel *The Color Purple*</u>.
    (A) awarded the Pulitzer Prize in literature for her novel *The Color Purple*
    (B) whose novel *The Color Purple* has been awarded the Pulitzer Prize in literature
    (C) she will be awarded the Pulitzer Prize in literature for her novel *The Color Purple*
    (D) her novel *The Color Purple* has been awarded the Pulitzer Prize in literature
    (E) and have been awarded the Pulitzer Prize in literature

33. Letty Cottin Pogrebin is the <u>mother of three teenagers, a wife of 20 years' standing, and the author of books that</u> espouse the ideals of feminism.
    (A) mother of three teenagers, a wife of 20 years' standing, and the author of books that
    (B) mother of three teenagers, is a wife of 20 years' standing, and the author of books that
    (C) mother of three teenagers, a wife of 20 years' standing, and she has written books that
    (D) mother of three teenagers, a wife of 20 years' standing, and the author of books which
    (E) mother of three teenagers, a wife of 20 years' standing, and the author of books, that

MODEL TEST 1

34. The name of the sculpture is "Eagle Warrior" and was dug up in downtown Mexico City last year.
    (A) The name of the sculpture is "Eagle Warrior" and was dug up in downtown Mexico City last year.
    (B) The name of the sculpture is "Eagle Warrior," it was dug up in downtown Mexico City last year.
    (C) The name of the sculpture, "Eagle Warrior," was dug up in downtown Mexico City last year.
    (D) The name of the sculpture is "Eagle Warrior," dug up in downtown Mexico City last year.
    (E) The sculpture, named "Eagle Warrior," was dug up in downtown Mexico City last year.

35. A teacher must not know only subject matter but also the process of teaching.
    (A) must not know only subject matter but also the process
    (B) must know subject matter but also the process
    (C) not only must know subject matter but also the process
    (D) must know not only subject matter but also the process
    (E) must know not only subject matter but the process

36. Major reasons for the recent rise in compulsive gambling among women are the increasing number of gambling facilities and that credit has become more available to women.
    (A) that credit has become more available to women
    (B) that credit will become more available to women
    (C) the greater availability of credit to women
    (D) that more credit has become more available to women
    (E) the greater number of women who use credit to gamble

Part C

(Suggested time — 10 minutes)

Directions: Each of the questions or incomplete statements below is followed by five suggested answers or completions. Select the one that is best in each case.

Questions 37–39 refer to the following passage.

(1) The teachers and pupils of Elmwood Elementary School invite all parents to attend the Annual Open House on Friday evening at 6:30 P.M. (2) Two one-half hour periods, beginning at 7 P.M., will provide an opportunity for parents to attend classes with their children. (3) The school orchestra will present a short program at 8 P.M. (4) After this program, refreshments will be served in the school cafeteria. (5) Awards night is next Wednesday.

37. Which of the following would be the best sentence to place between (1) and (2) above?
    (A) Parents must make arrangements for teacher conferences next week.
    (B) Teachers have to talk with parents about their children's schoolwork next week.
    (C) Fathers also should attend parent-teacher conferences.
    (D) Teacher conference appointments for next week can be made at this time or by calling the school on Monday.
    (E) Teachers expect parents to take an interest in their children's schoolwork.

TEST OF COMMUNICATION SKILLS

38. Which of the following statements, if added to the passage above, would indicate parental concern for education?
    (A) Last year only ten parents attended the Open House.
    (B) Disinterested parents seldom find time to attend the annual Open House.
    (C) Between 85 percent and 90 percent of the parents of elementary pupils visit school during the Open House.
    (D) Attending the Open House will give children an opportunity to explain their projects.
    (E) Children like to have their parents attend a class with them.

39. Which sentence is NOT necessary in the passage above?
    (A) Sentence (1)
    (B) Sentence (2)
    (C) Sentence (3)
    (D) Sentence (4)
    (E) Sentence (5)

Questions 40–41 refer to the following passage.

(1) Yesterday thirty families vacated their waterlogged homes along the Green River. (2) The present ice jam, caused by the early January thaw, is now twenty feet wide and three feet deep; this has caused a backup of water, which is three feet above flood level at the Blacking damsite. (3) A public hearing was called by the county commission to obtain comments on proposed changes in township drainage policy. (4) As a tentative measure, large culverts are being placed along 100th Avenue near the airport. (5) The state has appropriated $100,000 for airport expansion in 1990.

40. Which sentence should NOT be in the passage above?
    (A) Sentence (1)
    (B) Sentence (2)
    (C) Sentence (3)
    (D) Sentence (4)
    (E) Sentence (5)

41. Which of the following sentences, if added to the passage above, would most likely question the motivation of the township officials?
    (A) The township chairman insisted that the ice jam was an unusual situation.
    (B) Two previous meetings have produced no action.
    (C) The airport manager urged the installation of additional culverts.
    (D) The sheriff's department is assisting in the evacuation.
    (E) Dynamite may have to be used to break up the ice jam.

Questions 42–43 refer to the following passage.

(1) There are several basic methods of teaching from which an instructor can make a selection. (2) Every teacher must decide which method or methods will be the most effective in each different learning situation. (3) Two of the criteria that must be considered are, first, the pupils to be taught, and second, the special skills and capabilities of the teacher. (4) It must be determined whether the subject matter is knowledge-oriented, skill-oriented, or value-oriented. (5) Pupil participation should include information-gathering, discussion, and decision-making; thus, allowing pupils to become involved in democracy in action.

MODEL TEST 1

42. Which one of the following would be the best sentence to place between (4) and (5) in the above passage?
(A) Role playing should be used more often.
(B) Lecture is the best method for teaching history.
(C) Slow pupils do not like to gather information.
(D) Students need to be confronted with questions, facts, and contrary viewpoints.
(E) Discussions often lead to arguing.

43. From the information in the passage above, one can infer that it was written by
(A) a high school student
(B) an experienced teacher
(C) a disgruntled supervisor
(D) a first-year teacher
(E) a curriculum coordinator

Questions 44–45 refer to the following passage.

In November 1987 scientists met with the International Joint Commission on Great Lakes Water Quality. The Commission decided that citizens must be concerned and informed if water quality was to be improved in the Great Lakes Basin. The major concern was about the ecosystem concept for the integration of economic, social, and environmental effects, which emphasizes stewardship of natural resources. The Commission has identified forty-two areas of concern in this basin. Toxic substance pollution is currently regulated for big industrial plants and municipal sewage plants.

44. Which of the following, if added to the above passage, would most likely lead to further legal action?
(A) Another meeting is scheduled for 1989.
(B) Drinking water is unaffected thus far.
(C) Unrestricted run-off from farms and city lawns continue to occur.
(D) Canada and the U.S. have been cooperating on Water Quality Agreements since 1978.
(E) Continued monitoring of fish in the Lake Erie region is a first priority.

45. Which one of the following, if added as the last sentence to the passage above, would best sum up and restate the point of the passage?
(A) Water quality is an international problem.
(B) The Great Lakes Commission was organized in 1978.
(C) Industrial waste is the greatest source of pollution.
(D) Water clean-up is a federal problem.
(E) The ecosystem concept of stewardship must be understood and implemented by everyone if we are to protect the quality of our water.

S T O P

THIS IS THE END OF THIS SECTION.
IF YOU FINISH BEFORE TIME IS CALLED, YOU MAY CHECK YOUR WORK ON THIS SECTION ONLY.
DO NOT WORK ON ANY OTHER SECTION IN THE TEST.

TEST OF COMMUNICATION SKILLS

SECTION 4

WRITING: ESSAY

Time—30 minutes

Directions: Take 30 minutes to plan and write an essay on the topic in the box below. Take time to organize your thoughts and perhaps make a rough outline before beginning to write.

Teachers should (should not) be allowed to serve as members of local school boards.

Choose one side of this question, and in a letter to the editor of your local newspaper (general circulation) state your point of view and give arguments to support it.

Answer Keys and Explanations—Test of Communication Skills

LISTENING SKILLS

Answer Key

PART A	PART B	PART C
1. A	16. B	31. A
2. D	17. A	32. C
3. C	18. C	33. A
4. B	19. C	34. A
5. C	20. D	35. D
6. B	21. D	36. C
7. D	22. B	37. A
8. D	23. A	38. A
9. B	24. D	39. D
10. D	25. D	40. B
11. B	26. D	
12. B	27. B	
13. C	28. B	
14. C	29. A	
15. A	30. C	

307

MODEL TEST 1

Explanations

Part A

1. **(A)** This is the only answer that relates to teaching "in Michigan 50 years ago."

2. **(D)** This is the only statement that directly answers the question. The other answers give negative statements (A, B) or ignore the question (C).

3. **(C)** We can eliminate (A), (B), and (D) because we know that officers are usually chosen by a vote of the group. Hence (C), "George received the most votes," is correct.

4. **(B)** The coach's record was satisfactory (A), so (B) gives the only plausible reason for eliminating his position. Choices (C) and (D) are unrelated to the question.

5. **(C)** Although (A), (B), and (D) are related to education, (C) is the only choice that explains the reason for nationwide concern.

6. **(B)** Choices (A) and (C) make general statements, and (D) is concerned with math, not science, teachers. Choice (B) directly supports the original statement about a "brain drain."

7. **(D)** Choices (A) and (B) do not call for interaction with the general public; in (C) Mrs. Rosselini's role is that of a spectator (passive), rather than a participant (active), as in (D).

8. **(D)** Choices (A), (B), and (C) concern the family, but only (D) relates specifically to the learning of language.

9. **(B)** Choice (B) is the only one that relates directly to the present problem in Centralia, as opposed to any other city. Choice (D) would not justify "a sense of doom."

10. **(D)** Choices (A) and (B) give arguments pro and con, respectively, and (C) is irrelevant. Choice (D) is closest in meaning to the original statement.

11. **(B)** Choices (A) and (C) are untrue, in light of the statement, and no opinion is expressed about (D).

12. **(B)** This is the only answer supported by the statement. Choice (A) is untrue, and (C) and (D) are based on opinions.

13. **(C)** This is the only true answer; the other choices are false.

14. **(C)** This choice is the only one related directly to the information given. The other statements may or may not be true.

15. **(A)** This directly supports the statement that rape victims suffer from moral judgments and myths about rape. Choices (B), (C), and (D), although true, are not supported by the statement.

TEST OF COMMUNICATION SKILLS

Part B

16. **(B)** The only logical choice is (B), "By telephone." The reference to "your happy voice" rules out (C) and (D), and the words "I can tell" indicate that the man can't see the woman's face (A).

17. **(A)** The clue is "That's great!"

18. **(C)** The man mentions that the evaluator is biased; therefore it can be assumed that he doubts the accuracy of her assessment of the need for new readers. The other choices may or may not be true.

19. **(C)** From the conversation we know that the woman is concerned about the evaluator's specific criticism of the reading series as too old. The other choices may or may not be true.

20. **(D)** This answer relates best to the woman's statement that "I don't think we should rely on computers to do our teaching for us."

21. **(D)** The conversation indicates that she values the teacher more highly than the computer as a teaching tool.

22. **(B)** The man is irritated because he has not received adult recognition for his work. He takes his work very seriously, although he writes for children.

23. **(A)** Authors are often identified with their books; thus a humorist, for example, is not expected to have opinions on serious matters.

24. **(D)** This is the only choice justified by the conversation.

25. **(D)** The other choices are untrue.

26. **(D)** There is no justification for the other choices. The clue to (D) is the words "Next time."

27. **(B)** The references to "ruffle your feathers" and "Someday we'll get that [The ERA] passed" justify this choice. The woman is not speaking in a factual, sympathetic, or tactful manner.

28. **(B)** "I should have lived a hundred years ago" indicates opposition.

29. **(A)** The only negative statement the man makes about black administrators relates to their qualifications, so the other choices are not justified by the conversation.

30. **(C)** The man does not seem to be prejudiced against blacks ("I regret," "Unfortunately"). He seems to want to fill the administrative positions with qualified people.

MODEL TEST 1

Part C

31. **(A)** The topic sentence "It is difficult to create an optimum learning environment" sets the scene for the discussion of major obstacles to the achievement of this environment. Therefore (A) is the best answer.

32. **(C)** The lack of pupil awareness is discussed in relation to the effects of the "hidden agendas" and students' automatic responses. Since "awareness exercises are necessary to release students' learning potential," (C) is the correct answer, based on the contents of the talk.

33. **(A)** The speaker talks about how the students' lack of awareness of "hidden agendas" leads to automatic responses and negative attitudes. Since (A) refers to automatic reactions that interfere with learning, it is the best choice. The talk contains nothing to justify (B), (C), or (D).

34. **(A)** Long-range goals for handicapped students are emphasized, although short-term goals are mentioned in relation to success experiences. The other answers are supportive of the main topic.

35. **(D)** In the talk long-range goals are emphasized, so that after graduation handicapped students will fit into the world as it is. There is no justification in the talk for (A), (B), or (C).

36. **(C)** The assumption that school should be a preparation for life in the future relates most closely to the speaker's concerns for handicapped students.

37. **(A)** Although there is no clear-cut topic sentence, the main idea is the need for programs that "allow for choices, decision making, and creative input" and that help the "human spirit find the ultimate challenge." Choices (B) and (C) are details, not main ideas, and (D) is not mentioned in the talk.

38. **(A)** The speaker would agree with (B), (C), and (D). He considers the computer only one "toy or tool for learning," not an essential component.

39. **(D)** The speaker is not "highly admiring" (A), "unreservedly opposed" (B), or "indifferent" (C). He recognizes the "excitement and adventure in learning to work with computers," but also calls attention to what he perceives as the danger.

40. **(B)** The clue is "unlike you, I'm neither a manufacturer nor a programmer."

READING

Answer Key

1. C	7. E	13. D	19. E	25. B
2. D	8. D	14. C	20. A	26. B
3. A	9. E	15. B	21. C	27. E
4. B	10. A	16. C	22. C	28. B
5. D	11. B	17. A	23. C	29. B
6. E	12. D	18. D	24. A	30. C

TEST OF COMMUNICATION SKILLS

Explanations

1. **(C)** Anne and Beth attend Bicounty High School; neither is on the cross-country team; therefore we cannot say that I *must* be true. Claire attends Tricounty High School; she is not on the tennis team; therefore we cannot say that II *must* be true. Both Anne (Bicounty) and Claire (Tricounty) play varsity golf; therefore both high schools *must* offer this sport (III).

2. **(D)** This choice is supported by "the leaders...must develop land-use policies that strike a balance between the needs of wildlife...and the needs of expanding human populations." There is no justification in the statement for the other choices.

3. **(A)** The first sentence of the second paragraph directly supports this choice.

4. **(B)** The passage states that "students who have not learned to write clearly are not likely to reason clearly and critically." The other consequences may or may not follow.

5. **(D)** "Prophetic" is implied by "future" and "in years to come."

6. **(E)** Three examples support this statement: actions taken by (1) mathematics- and science-oriented institutions, (2) New York State, and (3) Florida.

7. **(E)** this is the only choice that follows directly from the quotation. There is no support for (A) or (B), (C) may or may not be desirable, and (D) is certainly undesirable.

8. **(D)** The author's choice of words such as *fortunately* reflects his or her relief that the situation in regard to writing skills is beginning to change. Choices (A), (B), and (C) do not indicate the author's feelings, and choice (E) is not included in the passage.

9. **(E)** A strong statement is made by comparing the cost of vandalism to the cost of textbooks. Nothing in the passage justifies the other choices.

10. **(A)** The author makes the assumption that, since local school boards cannot control school crime, they would accept and utilize assistance from the federal government.

11. **(B)** The last sentence ("In a gesture of extraordinary generosity the board then gave the teachers a 2 percent increase!") indicates sarcasm (2 percent is very small in relation to the discrepancy of $1,200 between the districts).

12. **(D)** If high school students who live less than 2 miles from school have to find their own transportation, many parents will be involved in furnishing cars, driving, or obtaining insurance for teenage drivers.

13. **(D)** This choice is supported by the second sentence of the passage. Choices (A), (C), and (E) may or may not be true; (B) is untrue (Lake County has not decided whether to withdraw funds).

MODEL TEST 1

14. **(C)** A guide on how to fund social welfare programs would be least likely to report this matter, which is not about how to raise funds.

15. **(B)** The author makes no interpretation of the report and offers no clue as to how he or she feels about the new regulations or attitudes toward them.

16. **(C)** The author's purpose is to inform. There is nothing to support the other choices.

17. **(A)** The main idea is expressed in the opening sentence of the passage.

18. **(D)** This choice is justified by the description of the language that may be developed: "which will be more useful and easier to learn than the symbolic and technical languages now in use." All of the other choices, in addition to finding no support in the passage, are untrue.

19. **(E)** The best choice is "networking will require new software and hardware." The other choices are either irrelevant (A) or untrue (B, C, D).

20. **(A)** The author discusses the networking system in light of a new, standard computer language. He assumes that this will be acceptable to the manufacturers and designers of computers (A), who presently compete for sales by offering various languages. The passage affords no justification for assumption (B), (C), (D), or (E).

21. **(C)** An article about computers could be written for the readers of any of these publications. However, a passage dealing with future job opportunities would not be likely to appear in a magazine for retired people (C).

22. **(C)** A habit (cigarette smoking) is compared to a tiger, which cannot be thrown out the window, as implied in (B), but must be dealt with gradually and carefully (C). There is no justification for (A), (D), or (E).

23. **(C)** The main idea is expressed in the first sentence of the passage. Choice (A) is a supporting detail, (E) is an unjustified assumption, and there is little justification in the passage for (B) and none for (D).

24. **(A)** The assumption that high school students must know certain dates and facts relates most closely to the author's concern about education.

25. **(B)** If, as stated in the passage, one-third of the students do not know the date of the Declaration of Independence, then the other two-thirds must know it. There is no support in the passage for I or III.

26. **(B)** This is the only choice justified by the contents of the statement. The term "improper questions" implies that the author assumes such questions to have an adverse effect on chance of employment.

27. **(E)** The main idea is expressed in the first sentence of the passage. The other choices are unjustified by the content of the passage.

28. **(B)** The passage mentions "traditional school systems controlled by states and local districts." The other choices are not mentioned.

TEST OF COMMUNICATION SKILLS

29. **(B)** The first sentence mentions the importance of "doing" for learning. Then three examples are given. By analogy, academic subjects should also be practiced.

30. **(C)** The author's word choice ("innovative," "increase motivation," "greatly sharpen," "actively taught") shows enthusiasm. The other choices are not supported by the content.

WRITING: MULTIPLE-CHOICE

Answer Key

PART A		PART B	PART C
1. A	14. B	28. D	37. D
2. B	15. A	29. A	38. C
3. B	16. B	30. B	39. E
4. B	17. A	31. C	40. E
5. C	18. E	32. B	41. B
6. C	19. B	33. A	42. D
7. C	20. D	34. E	43. B
8. E	21. B	35. D	44. C
9. B	22. D	36. C	45. E
10. A	23. D		
11. E	24. B		
12. D	25. C		
13. D	26. B		
	27. C		

Explanations

Part A

1. **(A)** The subject of a sentence must be in the nominative case. Therefore the nominative pronoun *we*, not the objective *us* (A), must be used.

2. **(B)** "My Aunt Marge is the town mayor" and "she has always been the best pie-maker for miles around" are two unrelated ideas that should not be joined by *and* (C) to form a compound sentence.

3. **(B)** The subject *none*, when it means "no one" or "not one" as it does here, needs the singular verb *was*, not the plural verb *were* (B).

4. **(B)** The adverb *where* (B) should not be used in place of the subordinate conjunction *that*.

5. **(C)** Part (C) should read *as tall as*, rather than *as tall*, to make an accurate comparison.

6. **(C)** The present tense *has* (C) should be *had*; the stealing occurred in the past, even before Rita *said* (past) that it had.

313

MODEL TEST 1

7. **(C)** Since the pronoun *whoever* is the subject of the clause "whoever wants to take them home," it should be in the nominative case (*whoever*), not in the objective case (*whomever*).

8. **(E)** No error.

9. **(B)** The subject of the sentence is *he*, not *his sisters*, so the singular verb *was*, not the plural verb *were* (B), is needed.

10. **(A)** *Nor* is used with *neither*, so *or* (A) is incorrect.

11. **(E)** No error.

12. **(D)** When two persons or things are compared, the comparative form (*-er*) is used, not the superlative (*-est*), as in (D).

13. **(D)** *Which* or *that* refers to things; one of these words should be used here in place of *what* (D), which is equivalent to "that which" and hence sounds awkward.

14. **(B)** The word *senator* (B), used in place of a proper name, should be capitalized.

15. **(A)** The word *treaty* (A) is part of a formal title (Treaty of Ghent) and should be capitalized.

16. **(B)** An adjective must agree in number with the word it modifies. In this case *these* (B) is plural, whereas *kind* is singular.

17. **(A)** The adverb *past* should not be used in place of the verb *passed*.

18. **(E)** No error.

19. **(B)** The case of a relative pronoun is determined by its use in the sentence. The word *whom*, not *who* (B), must be used because the pronoun is the object of the verb *called*. The verb *is* (A) agrees with the subject *he* and is therefore correct.

20. **(D)** The sentence lacks parallel structure because (D) is a clause whereas (B) and (C) are nouns. The sentence should read: ". . . among the alleged defects were inaccuracies, bias, and the omission of many important facts."

21. **(B)** There is no reason for a comma (B) after *Art*.

22. **(D)** Since the word *never* is negative, it should not be followed by another negative; *no* (D) should be deleted, or replaced by *any*.

23. **(D)** The term *high school* (D) is part of a formal name and should be capitalized. The plural verb *are* (B) is correct because *unable to agree* indicates that the members of the class are referred to as individuals, rather than as a unit.

TEST OF COMMUNICATION SKILLS

24. **(B)** Except in a highly specialized sense in psychiatry, the word *affect* is a verb, not a noun. In this sentence *affects* (B) should be *effects*.

25. **(C)** When *or* or *nor* joins two subjects, the verb agrees with the nearer one. In this sentence *are* (C) is incorrect, since the verb must agree with the singular subject William.

26. **(B)** To *set* (B) means to place. Here *sat*, the past tense of *sit* is the correct word for the sense of the sentence.

27. **(E)** No error.

28. **(D)** This is the only choice that avoids (1) saying that Steve is smarter than himself (A, E) or (2) changing the meaning (B, C).

29. **(A)** The original sentence is correct. The other choices introduce various types of errors.

30. **(B)** The two clauses are not of equal importance and hence should not be joined by *and* or *but*. In (B) the first clause is properly subordinate and, unlike in (C), the tense is correct.

31. **(C)** In the original sentence *Walking* is a dangling participle that appears to refer to "a car" rather than "me." In (C) the participle has been replaced by the predicate verb *was walking*, there is a subject (I), and the tense is correct, unlike (B).

32. **(B)** This is the only choice that results in two parallel clauses introduced by *whose* and connected by *and*.

33. **(A)** The original sentence is correct. The other choices are less preferable in regard to construction (B, C), choice of relative pronoun (D), and punctuation (E).

34. **(E)** The original sentence and (C) state that the name of the sculpture was dug up in Mexico City—an absurdity. Choice (D) is ambiguous (What was dug up?), and (B) is a run-on sentence. In (E) the less important information about the name is properly subordinated, and the meaning is clear.

35. **(D)** The two parts of the correlative expression "not only . . . but also" must be placed properly, following the verb *must know* and preceding the nouns *subject matter* and *process*. Choice (D) is the only answer that meets this criterion.

36. **(C)** *And* cannot properly be used to connect a noun (*number*) and a clause (*that credit has become more available to women*). Choices (B) and (D) repeat this error, and (E) changes the meaning.

37. **(D)** By inserting (D) at this point it accounts for the one-half hour between the opening of the building at 6:30 P.M. and the first classes at 7 P.M.

38. **(C)** This sentence indicates that between 85 and 90 percent of the parents show their concern for education by participating in a school-related activity such as Open House.

MODEL TEST 1

39. **(E)** Sentence (5) is irrelevant because nowhere is Awards Night mentioned.

40. **(E)** Sentence (5) refers to another topic: airport improvement. It does not refer to local flooding. The other sentences add to the unity of the paragraph by giving information related to the local flooding.

41. **(B)** This sentence raises the question as to whether meetings and discussions about the problem produce any results.

42. **(D)** This sentence best continues the idea of the types of subject-matter to be taught, and it leads into the ideas of the need for pupil-involvement. Sentence (5) gives a concluding statement about pupil participation and preparation for life in a democracy.

43. **(B)** The passage was most likely written by an experienced teacher who knows teaching techniques and pupils well.

44. **(C)** If industrial plants and sewage treatment facilities are controlled by law, then the next big source of pollution must be the herbicides and pesticides used on farms and city lawns.

45. **(E)** The main idea of the passage has been the concept of stewardship, the individual's responsibility to manage his or her life and property with proper regard to the rights of others.

WRITING: ESSAY

When you have finished your essay, ask two or three honest critics—teachers or other persons whose knowledge of written English you respect—to evaluate your essay in terms of items listed on page 64 and to point out any aspects of your writing that need improvement. Request them to indicate specific types of errors in grammar, sentence construction, diction, and mechanics (capitalization and punctuation) to which you are prone and which you must be careful to avoid.

Model Test 1
Test of Professional Knowledge

SECTION 1

Time — 30 minutes

Directions: For each question or incomplete statement below, there are five suggested answers or completions. Select the one that *best* answers the question or completes the statement.

1. You have been assigned to a curriculum improvement committee. What steps must your committee take before altering the curriculum?

    I. Conduct a needs-assessment activity.
    II. Collect data on student performance.
    III. Interpret data collected and relate it to school objectives.
    IV. Obtain information from other teachers, parents, and students.

    (A) I only
    (B) I and II only
    (C) III only
    (D) I and IV only
    (E) I, II, III, and IV

2. If teaching mirrors learning, then learning and teaching have some similar components. In which of the following is the learning theory matched incorrectly with the teaching technique(s)?

    (A) Bruner: cognitive development—readiness, structure, intuition, motivation.
    (B) Skinner: operant conditioning—reinforcement.
    (C) Nagel and Richman: competency-based instruction—classical conditioning with rewards and punishment.
    (D) Carroll: mastery learning—time, aptitude, quality of instruction.
    (E) Popham and Baker: instructional sequencing—specifying behavioral objectives and giving opportunities for practice.

3. A teacher who grades a student lower than she deserves because she does not always agree with the teacher is most probably contributing to the student's
    (A) creativity
    (B) greater interest in the subject
    (C) control of her undesirable behavior
    (D) feelings of insecurity in this classroom
    (E) respect for the teacher

4. A teacher who wants to identify test questions that are too difficult or too easy will use
    (A) validity studies
    (B) the test-retest technique
    (C) item analysis
    (D) correlation
    (E) a frequency polygon

MODEL TEST 1

5. If, as a teacher, you encounter a persistent teaching-learning problem in the classroom, the best way to work out a solution is to
   (A) help your students improve their goals
   (B) make adjustments in your own goals and/or strategies
   (C) improve the learning environment by removing distractors
   (D) incorporate all of the above in a plan of action
   (E) change the course of study

6. The most stable measure of central tendency is the
   (A) mean   (D) standard error
   (B) mode   (E) standard deviation
   (C) median

7. The major categories within the cognitive domain, as classified by Bloom, are
   (A) knowledge, comprehension, application
   (B) analysis, synthesis, evaluation
   (C) knowledge, accommodation, conservation
   (D) (A) and (B) above
   (E) (B) and (C) above

8. It is generally agreed that a teacher's way of teaching depends most on his or her
   (A) basic reasons for teaching
   (B) professional training
   (C) constructive supervision
   (D) social interest
   (E) past experiences of success in the classroom

9. A teacher should be cautious about giving parents their child's exact IQ score because
   (A) there are marked differences among students within the same range on the normal curve
   (B) a genius is difficult to define
   (C) a student's score may vary as he or she grows older
   (D) performance varies at different IQ levels
   (E) the IQ is a constant, and parents may categorize the child on this basis

10. Following child-development principles, a teacher can safely make the assumption that
    (A) normal children can differ in both rate of growth and awareness of themselves as individuals
    (B) a child who tries hard enough can learn anything
    (C) it is fair to demand that every child reach the average or norm for his or her group
    (D) since children grow at different rates, there can be no goals for individual children
    (E) normal children can differ in both rate of growth and social maturity

318

TEST OF PROFESSIONAL KNOWLEDGE

11. A student questions adult values and standards. It would be best for the teacher to
    (A) reprimand the student
    (B) argue in support of adult values and standards
    (C) side with the student
    (D) ridicule him or her
    (E) encourage open discussion

12. At a recent faculty meeting, a teacher suggested the use of modular scheduling at the junior high school level to meet pupil needs. He was referring to
    (A) 40-minute periods
    (B) 50-minute periods
    (C) standard block scheduling
    (D) area teaching variations
    (E) scheduling small blocks of time that can be clustered variously

13. The average boy reaches the age of puberty at
    (A) 10 years   (D) 14 years
    (B) 11 years   (E) 15 years
    (C) 13 years

14. The junior high school teacher who attempts to draw every student into the discussion understands the adolescent's need
    (A) to be active   (D) to excel
    (B) to be creative   (E) to compete
    (C) to belong

15. Students become more proficient in using the problem-solving approach when
    (A) they are left to solve problems without help
    (B) the teacher guides and assists them, as needed
    (C) they select their own problems for study
    (D) the use of textbooks is kept to a minimum
    (E) the emotional and social climate of the classroom is established by them

16. Generally, a most frustrating aspect of public criticism of the schools is the fact that
    (A) no clear mandate has been given by the public to educators
    (B) the public changes its demands from year to year
    (C) the public is not really interested in the schools
    (D) teachers are blamed for taking progressive action
    (E) many parents do not attend school meetings

17. Three situations related to the mainstreaming of children are listed below. Which of them might cause parents to seek due-process procedures, if not given prior notification?
    I. A teacher removes a child from a special class.
    II. A teacher places a child in a special class.
    III. Teachers change their evaluation procedures.

    (A) I only   (D) I and II only
    (B) II only   (E) I, II, and III
    (C) III only

18. A teacher's initial attempt to teach diagramming in a tenth-grade English class fails. In seeking to explain this failure, the teacher could examine whether
    (A) there is a lack of pupil interest
    (B) the students have already acquired this skill
    (C) they dislike having a new teacher
    (D) they see no purpose in learning
    (E) there is a combination of factors (A), (B), (C), and/or (D)

19. A physical education teacher should consider that the emotional climate in his or her class is
    (A) not important to student learning
    (B) under the control of the students
    (C) one that should always foster competitiveness
    (D) dependent on what happens in other classes
    (E) set by the teacher as part of the course orientation.

20. In a group situation, such as the classroom, the factor having the greatest effect on the efficiency of learning has to do with
    (A) the characteristics of the teacher
    (B) the material to be learned
    (C) the composition of the group
    (D) the characteristics of the learners
    (E) the classroom environment

21. Teachers are required to give the parents of a handicapped child written notice whenever the school proposes to initiate or change the child's

    I. identification of needs
    II. evaluation of progress
    III. placement

    (A) I only
    (B) II only
    (C) III only
    (D) I, II, and III
    (E) II and III only

22. The teacher who uses a classroom newspaper should
    (A) rewrite all the children's stories for publication
    (B) encourage children to revise their own work, and permit them to use their "finished" product
    (C) demand perfect writing
    (D) use as few pupils' names as possible
    (E) worry about public relations if some stories seem imperfect

23. Currently the most widely recognized theory of the influence of heredity and environment holds that there is
    (A) an interaction between the two factors in an individual's development
    (B) an isolated operation of one factor or another on an individual
    (C) an independent contribution of each factor to growth
    (D) an equal significance to both factors in every person's life
    (E) little significance of either factor in a person's life

TEST OF PROFESSIONAL KNOWLEDGE

24. A coach wants to place a pupil in a special physical education program. Before making this change in instruction, the coach must provide the child's guardian with
    (A) an evaluation report
    (B) a set of test results
    (C) a verbal message, sent through a third party
    (D) a written notice
    (E) a telephone call

25. A researcher uses an "optimum environment" to measure the influence of heredity. What erroneous conclusion would this probably produce?
    (A) Belief that the operation of heredity has been merely obscured by poor environmental factors
    (B) Belief that an "optimum environment" is difficult to achieve
    (C) Belief that the "true" contribution of heredity may not be revealed under optimum environmental conditions
    (D) Belief that an "optimum environment" is not necessary for the influence of heredity
    (E) Belief that there is no continuum of effectiveness on which the environment can be rated

26. By comparison with other boys his age, a boy whose physical maturity is late has an increased probability of
    (A) feeling socially inferior
    (B) being physically smaller
    (C) being poorly adjusted to school
    (D) being either aggressive or introverted
    (E) all of the above

27. Under "due process," the punishment must fit the offense. With regard to this principle, which of the following statements is true?
    (A) A student under suspension does not have the right to a hearing.
    (B) Parents have no right to object to the punishment given to a child by a teacher.
    (C) Joe can be suspended, although Sam was given a lesser punishment for the same infringement of a school regulation.
    (D) If a student has a hearing, this proves his or her innocence.
    (E) Suspensions are usually imposed by a school administrator.

28. A student objects on religious grounds to the requirement that he participate in ROTC training as a prerequisite for a diploma. Is he within his rights?
    (A) No, he must take ROTC training.
    (B) No, he loses his diploma if he chooses not to take ROTC training.
    (C) Yes, because of his religious beliefs regarding war.
    (D) No, not if other students take the course.
    (E) Yes, but he must do community service while others are taking the ROTC classes.

321

29. Which of the following characteristics of a test would lead you to believe that you have chosen a good assessment instrument?
    (A) High performance levels of those taking the test
    (B) A reliability coefficient of 0.00
    (C) Its national norms
    (D) National standing of its publisher
    (E) Its high content validity

30. A teacher was asked to provide the "least restrictive environment" for Jane, a fourth-grade handicapped student. Where should the teacher place Jane?
    (A) In a resource room
    (B) With the remedial reading teacher
    (C) In a special education classroom
    (D) In a modular library assistance program
    (E) In a "regular" classroom if Jane's needs can be met there

READ THE FOLLOWING DIRECTIONS BEFORE PROCEEDING.

Directions: The following questions contain the word LEAST, NOT, or EXCEPT. Read each question very carefully, then find the answer that applies.

31. An exchange teacher asks about the American educational system. Which one of these statements would NOT be true?
    (A) The American system is government-controlled because of federal aid.
    (B) Local districts generally elect their school board members.
    (C) Each state seeks solutions for its own educational problems.
    (D) The state board of education is usually led by a professional educator.
    (E) No federal law requires a state to maintain a system of public education.

32. One of the functions of guidance is to deal with real problems of pupils. A real problem is characterized by all of the following EXCEPT
    (A) its uniqueness for the individual pupil
    (B) its emotional content
    (C) the student's essential role in its outcome
    (D) the simplicity, rather than the complexity, of its causation
    (E) the availability of alternatives for its resolution

33. The teacher who understands classroom management techniques can remove problems that pupils cannot master. All of the following are positive situational assistance techniques EXCEPT
    (A) provide timely assistance and give clear directions
    (B) consistently rebuke a pupil who is not settling down to the learning task
    (C) change the pace and vary the daily routine
    (D) prevent distractions
    (E) tell pupils what they may expect and what behavior is acceptable

TEST OF PROFESSIONAL KNOWLEDGE

34. Which of the following is LEAST consistent with the guidelines of adaptive teaching?
    (A) Contingency contracting
    (B) Behavioral objectives
    (C) Norm-referenced grading
    (D) Competition for grades
    (E) Drill instruction

35. Criterion-referenced grading is LEAST likely to be done with
    (A) grading on the curve
    (B) reinforcement techniques
    (C) group instruction
    (D) selective instruction
    (E) the regular classroom

STOP

IF YOU FINISH BEFORE TIME IS CALLED, YOU MAY CHECK YOUR WORK ON THIS SECTION ONLY.
DO NOT WORK ON ANY OTHER SECTION IN THIS TEST.

MODEL TEST 1
SECTION 2

Time — 30 minutes

Directions: For each question or incomplete statement below, there are five suggested answers or completions. Select the one that *best* answers the question or completes the statement.

1. Which of the following is a *value* assumption?
    (A) Girls tend to mature faster than boys.
    (B) Reality, for the individual, is the way he or she perceives the world.
    (C) Students should participate in self-government to prepare for life in a democracy.
    (D) Some first-graders are not ready to learn to read.
    (E) Some first-graders are farsighted.

2. Value assumptions influence teachers as they
    (A) measure intelligence
    (B) grade pupil achievement
    (C) set outcomes for a course of learning
    (D) interpret pupil behavior
    (E) punish delinquent acts

3. Knowledge of the psychological principles of education helps the teacher to
    (A) understand the motivations of each learner
    (B) use audiovisual materials more effectively
    (C) incorporate a variety of teaching strategies in a lesson plan
    (D) be more creative in the classroom
    (E) solve his or her own personal problems

4. Which of the following is an empirical statement about education?
    (A) Competency in civic matters is a worthwhile educational goal.
    (B) Fatigue reduces the effectiveness of the learner.
    (C) Popular teachers are the best teachers.
    (D) There is a place for vocational education in the high school.
    (E) The main purpose of education is to prepare students for life.

5. Adolescence is a time of rapid growth. How many adolescents manifest definite anxiety about their physical development?
    (A) About 1 out of 6
    (B) About 1 out of 8
    (C) About 1 out of 3
    (D) About 1 out of 10
    (E) About 1 out of 50

6. Persons who advocate teaching reading to babies believe that
    (A) readiness depends on the method used in teaching.
    (B) children can learn anything at anytime.
    (C) parents are the only teachers a child needs
    (D) age six is too late to learn disciplined habits of study
    (E) boys, especially, need a headstart in learning to read

TEST OF PROFESSIONAL KNOWLEDGE

7. The rate at which a boy grows and develops muscular coordination often affects his
   (A) social experience
   (B) height and weight
   (C) competence in vocal music
   (D) interest in art
   (E) capacity to do arithmetic

8. A boy's concern about his physical size depends most on
   (A) his age and grade level
   (B) acceptance by his peers
   (C) acceptance by his teacher
   (D) his relations with siblings
   (E) family stability

9. Girls mature more rapidly than boys. A typical girl of 11 to 13 years is as mature as a boy who is
   (A) 1 year younger
   (B) 2 years younger
   (C) 1 year older
   (D) 2 years older
   (E) 3 years older

10. The effects of parental rejection are generally
    (A) demonstrated by the child's aggressiveness
    (B) demonstrated by the child's apathy
    (C) shown by the child's shyness
    (D) different for individual children
    (E) demonstrated by the child's lack of trust

11. An adolescent boy who makes a good adjustment to high school usually has a father who
    (A) is competent and adequate as a father
    (B) is indifferent and easy-going
    (C) is very indulgent to his son
    (D) demands high achievement by his son
    (E) leaves all decisions to the boy's mother

12. Stressing a curriculum that emphasizes relating new concepts to the experiences of the learner would probably find the greatest support from teachers of
    (A) the languages
    (B) English
    (C) natural and social sciences
    (D) speech
    (E) the fine arts

13. For six-year-olds, what is the optimum size of a classroom working group?
    (A) Three or four children
    (B) Five or six children
    (C) Seven or eight children
    (D) Appropriate size for maturity level and kind of activity
    (E) Appropriate for hearing and seeing the teacher

14. Rousseau believed that education should be
    (A) strict and rigid
    (B) paced to the unfolding growth patterns of the child
    (C) for mental discipline only
    (D) for practical application only
    (E) for the development of aesthetic senses only

15. Terman's study of gifted children found that they—by comparison with others their age—are usually
    (A) smaller in height
    (B) socially maladjusted
    (C) lighter in weight
    (D) less critical of their peers
    (E) above average in moral attitudes

16. When teaching coeducational social activities to preadolescent pupils one finds that the attitude of boys toward girls is typically that of
    (A) contemptuous rejection   (D) exploitation
    (B) tolerance   (E) affection
    (C) hostility

17. Scientific inquiry, coupled to the philosophy of determinism, made its most serious impact on education by using mathematics to
    (A) teach mental discipline
    (B) make inferences and predictions about student performance
    (C) develop a positive mind-set toward science
    (D) teach research techniques in all curriculum areas
    (E) prepare students to take other science courses

18. The teaching of biology underwent considerable changes when textbook writers began to include Darwin's theory of
    (A) natural selection
    (B) population and food ratio
    (C) determinism
    (D) the immutability of the species
    (E) the origin of fossils

19. Mr. G gave a diagnostic test in mathematics. Four students failed all of the problems involving fractions. Which of the following will serve as positive reinforcement and thus increase the learning of these students?
    I. Pairing immediate feedback with problems solved correctly
    II. Scolding students for failing to complete work correctly
    III. Making students rework all incorrect problems before taking a recess break

TEST OF PROFESSIONAL KNOWLEDGE

    IV. Praising students for work completed correctly
    V. Giving gold stars for correct papers

    (A) I, IV, and V only
    (B) I and V only
    (C) I and II only
    (D) I and III only
    (E) III and IV only

20. In social-climate classroom studies it was demonstrated that frustration, anger, and poor morale were observed the most in classrooms in which teachers
    (A) exerted autocratic control
    (B) used little or no control
    (C) let pupils share in the planning
    (D) had frequent conferences with parents
    (E) functioned frequently as sources of knowledge

21. The knowledge of good, according to Rousseau, comes to the child
    (A) through education
    (B) through life in the family
    (C) from the example of his peers
    (D) through great literature
    (E) from the child's soul

22. Which is uncharacteristic of the activity curriculum?
    (A) a unitary group of activities
    (B) flexible organization
    (C) a fusion of subject-matter fields
    (D) the addition of activities to each content-based curriculum
    (E) learning through activities

23. A teacher may find it necessary to have professional assistance in diagnosing the learning disabilities of a particular pupil. Which of the following would be useful for such a diagnosis?
    (A) A social-behavior history including data about the family background
    (B) A neurological examination
    (C) A medical history, including results of vision and hearing tests
    (D) A perceptual-motor survey or an electroencephalogram (EEG)
    (E) All of the above

24. Among instructional materials that can be selected for use with young children, flat (two-dimensional) pictures are appropriate when
    (A) students are involved in large-group instruction
    (B) motion is significant for understanding the idea or concept
    (C) the lesson-plan calls for interpreting perspective cues
    (D) motion is not significant for understanding the idea or concept
    (E) there is no time to get around to individual students

25. Community resources are still not used as widely as they could be. Given the following options for using his or her community resources, what order of priority should a teacher assign to them?
    1. A student's report to the class about his or her independent visit to a local historical site
    2. Class use of booklets supplied by the local 4-H club
    3. Demonstration of a community craft during a visit to the class by a local leatherworker
    4. A class trip to the archives of the local newspaper
    5. Class use of reading materials supplied by the local chamber of commerce
    (A) 4, 5, 1, 2, 3
    (B) 5, 1, 4, 3, 2
    (C) 3, 2, 1, 5, 4
    (D) 4, 2, 5, 1, 3
    (E) 5, 4, 3, 2, 1

26. The "inquiry process" refers to an educational approach that
    (A) encourages the learner to evaluate experiences
    (B) makes the learner an observer
    (C) places the learner in the context of real-life situations or simulations of them
    (D) does all of the above
    (E) does none of the above

27. Children who watch much television during the preschool years often develop a problem that teachers must provide the means to correct. This is a difficulty with
    (A) visual discrimination
    (B) auditory discrimination
    (C) assimilation of ideas
    (D) visual sequencing
    (E) verbal responses

28. Which of the following steps is (are) essential to providing pupils with practice in visual literacy?
    (A) Giving them experience in identifying objects as visually different or similar
    (B) Providing exercises for finding common characteristics among pictures
    (C) Having them "read" different types of expressions in sequence
    (D) Having them arrange different pictures in sequence to tell a story
    (E) All of the above

29. Planned learning experiences for disadvantaged children should include
    (A) a variety of entry levels
    (B) a variety of exit levels
    (C) a variety of recycling experiences
    (D) none of the above
    (E) all of the above

TEST OF PROFESSIONAL KNOWLEDGE

READ THE FOLLOWING DIRECTIONS BEFORE PROCEEDING.

Directions: The following questions contain the word LEAST, NOT, or EXCEPT. Read each question very carefully, then find the answer that applies.

30. According to research on the use of computers in the classroom, which statement is NOT true?
    (A) CAI is as effective as teachers for some classroom purposes.
    (B) Computer programs use branching and dialog effectively.
    (C) Time can be saved by using the computer for drill and review.
    (D) Educational planning must be done more thoroughly to use computers effectively.
    (E) Computer software for classroom use lacks quality control.

31. A teacher compiled the following report on Keith after giving him a battery of tests: C.A. 9-8; M.A. 10-4; IQ 103. The diagnostic reading tests showed a grade equivalent of 1.0, and in oral reading a grade equivalent of 1.7, with special performance at the Pre-Primer II level. He made 14 errors at the Pre-Primer II level. He is 2.4 years below the 4.1 expected grade equivalent level. Which of these recommendations will his teacher be LEAST likely to use for improving Keith's reading skills?
    (A) Watch for reversals while making him read from left to right.
    (B) Emphasize both consonant and vowel sounds (medial work).
    (C) Develop word recognition skills with word list scanning.
    (D) Utilize the Kinesthetic approach.
    (E) Initially use 2.5 grade level reading materials to challenge him.

32. Parents ask a teacher for the cause of their child's poor progress in his school subjects. Which of the following explanations may NOT be the basic cause?
    (A) He dislikes school.
    (B) He is smaller than most of the boys in his class.
    (C) He has multiple problems, including hyperactivity.
    (D) He has an IQ of 90 with some coordination problems.
    (E) His attention span is short.

33. Research indicates that children with the learning disability syndrome need corrective-remedial learning tasks based on symptomology rather than etiology. Which one of the following characteristics would usually NOT be true of such children?
    (A) Inconsistent performance in more than one subject
    (B) Hetereogeneity within a grade
    (C) Underachievement
    (D) Predictable similarity of behavior
    (E) Short attention span or impulsivity

329

MODEL TEST 1

34. When planning lessons to meet the needs of any class, the teacher's knowledge of instruction tasks and individual differences should focus on receptors and effectors by using all of the following EXCEPT
    (A) Effectiveness of encoding skills
    (B) Physical impairments
    (C) Sex of child
    (D) Memory components
    (E) Visual-motor coordination

35. Research on test construction indicates that teachers can improve the effectiveness of self-constructed tests LEAST by
    (A) Using different measuring techniques
    (B) Writing questions from a wide sampling of material studied
    (C) Avoiding clues to correct answers
    (D) Relating difficulty level to student capability
    (E) Giving optional choices for several questions

STOP

IF YOU FINISH BEFORE TIME IS CALLED, YOU MAY CHECK YOUR WORK ON THIS SECTION ONLY.
DO NOT WORK ON ANY OTHER SECTION IN THE TEST.

TEST OF PROFESSIONAL KNOWLEDGE
SECTION 3

Time — 30 minutes

Directions: For each question or incomplete statement below, there are five suggested answers or completions. Select the one that *best* answers the question or completes the statement.

1. Students who adopt the philosophy of the affiliation ethic will probably have some
   (A) conflicts in relation to learning achievement
   (B) difficult times making friends
   (C) shallow values
   (D) difficulty getting along with their parents
   (E) conflict over group values

2. Transfer of learning is increased when
   (A) much time is spent in drill of essentials
   (B) pupil interest is the basis of course selection
   (C) understanding underlies learning
   (D) pupils choose their own topics for study
   (E) frequent examinations are given

3. Students who find themselves in a situation calling for guidance should be helped to realize that
   (a) they have no choices for action
   (B) they have alternative choices of behavior
   (C) they need conditioned responses
   (D) they need more insight into why they have problems
   (E) there are no precedents to follow

4. For most learners, personal goals are
   (A) easily surrendered
   (B) set with great reluctance
   (C) rejected in favor of parents' and teachers' goals
   (D) used as the basis for self-direction
   (E) ignored until attainment seems easy

5. In learning a skill, if a pupil does not get the desired results on the first attempt, he or she will be most likely to
   (A) give up in disgust
   (B) try to think the effort through
   (C) change the goal
   (D) go through a trial-and-error procedure
   (E) continue to repeat the unsuccessful step

6. Children who are overprotected at home generally have a tendency, at school, to be
   (A) overaggressive
   (B) selfish
   (C) unable to work for sustained periods of time
   (D) lacking in independence
   (E) unable to imagine outcomes of proposed activities

331

MODEL TEST 1

7. The right to due process of law requires that all people get fair treatment from the government. Since the school is a government agency, which of the following is true?
   (A) A student may be punished for misconduct without first determining his or her guilt or innocence.
   (B) Schools are not courtrooms; students have the responsibility to prove their innocence when accused of misconduct.
   (C) Expulsion from school is permitted in all misconduct cases.
   (D) The denial of a diploma is not excessive punishment.
   (E) A student must be given the opportunity to tell his or her story when accused of misconduct.

8. Psychologists who favor operant conditioning criticize teaching techniques that are characterized by
   (A) permissiveness
   (B) specific-goal orientation
   (C) immediate reinforcement
   (D) infrequent reinforcement
   (E) an experiential approach

9. The "activities-program" approach to meeting pupil needs in the classroom is best characterized by the use of
   (A) multiple projects
   (B) teacher-pupil planning
   (C) flexibility in pupil assignments
   (D) self-evaluation techniques
   (E) group evaluation techniques

10. All teachers work with pupils who have both positive and negative attitudes towards their studies. A pupil moves most effectively towards educational goals when he or she
    (A) is receiving praise from the teacher
    (B) is punished for poor work
    (C) is allowed to abandon these goals for periods of time
    (D) is told that failure is probable, without doubled efforts
    (E) is actively involved in group work

11. Team teaching by pupils allows those involved to learn not only specific subject matter but also
    (A) group dynamics
    (B) parliamentary procedure
    (C) classroom organization
    (D) theories of social development
    (E) new attitudes, values, understanding of others

TEST OF PROFESSIONAL KNOWLEDGE

12. Every local school should have an organization for curriculum improvement. An effective curriculum-planning organization will
    (A) control the expression of individual ideas
    (B) utilize the experience of individual teachers
    (C) be dominated by the principal
    (D) be directed by district supervisors
    (E) show little concern for staff morale

13. The basic functional unit for all curriculum planning is the
    (A) community
    (B) child
    (C) individual classroom
    (D) school district
    (E) individual school

14. The chief priority of a system-wide curriculum council should be to
    (A) enforce a unified but flexible program of instruction in each school
    (B) leave the curriculum problems of individual schools to their own (local) solutions
    (C) furnish supervision for program implementation
    (D) utilize preschool work conferences for in-service education
    (E) encourage individual school planning, within broad guidelines

15. The main function of the effective guidance program should be to
    (A) furnish information about students to the teachers
    (B) coordinate home, school, and community efforts to place graduates in jobs
    (C) help pupils understand and use their abilities to achieve realistic goals
    (D) help pupils fit into existing school programs
    (E) counsel potential college students

16. Mr. Braun caught Paula cheating on a mathematics test. "If I catch you cheating again, you will be expelled from school," Mr. Braun remarked in front of the class. In response to his threats, which of the following are likely to occur?

    I. Some students will not cheat because they believe it is wrong.
    II. Some students will avoid getting caught cheating.
    III. Some students will think Mr. Braun doesn't really mean it.
    IV. A few students will cheat if they think the test is unfair.
    V. None of the students will cheat in his class again.

    (A) I only
    (B) I and II only
    (C) III and IV only
    (D) II, III, and IV only
    (E) I, II, III, and IV only

MODEL TEST 1

17. Educators who punish undesirable behavior and reward desirable behavior are probably influenced by the studies on stimulus and response learning by
    (A) Wundt
    (B) Darwin
    (C) Bain
    (D) Thorndike
    (E) Cattell

18. Films and audiovisual aids are generally most effective when used with
    (A) follow-up writing assignments
    (B) supplementary text materials
    (C) discussion of information before and after viewing
    (D) no discussion of information
    (E) a follow-up test

19. Teachers cannot be sure that the words they use to describe an idea, object, or process convey appropriate meanings to all pupils. A teacher describing a planned visit to a farm was surprised to hear one child tell another, "We'll see the cow that has one faucet for milk and another one for cream." The child's comment provides an example of
    (A) sensorimotor learning
    (B) referent confusion
    (C) conservation
    (D) assimilation
    (E) accommodation

20. Teachers who use flexible lesson plans are not using the system of presentation devised by
    (A) Dewey
    (B) Guilford
    (C) Herbart
    (D) Skinner
    (E) Bruner

21. Much of the success of a unit of work depends on the pupils' orientation to it. Which of the following is inappropriate in orientation to new material?
    (A) Evaluating the unit
    (B) Helping students to see the significance of the unit topic
    (C) Relating the unit to past learning experiences
    (D) Identifying appropriate community resources
    (E) Providing a stimulating classroom environment

TEST OF PROFESSIONAL KNOWLEDGE

22. In what order do children develop the ability to use past, present, and future verb tenses in their early speech patterns?
    (A) First past, then future, then present tenses
    (B) First past, then present, then future tenses
    (C) First present, then future, then past tenses
    (D) First present, then past, then future tenses
    (E) First future, then present, then past tenses

23. Media-related teaching must recognize individual differences among learners. During an auditory learning activity, at what point can individual differences in sound discrimination first be measured?
    (A) When sound waves reach the eardrum
    (B) When sound vibrations reach the cochlea
    (C) When nerve impulses are transmitted over the auditory nerve
    (D) When auditory impulses are "recognized" in the cerebrum
    (E) When the individual pupil responds to an auditory stimulus

24. Our sense receptors send impressions to the brain, where important learning activities take place. The most important for the activities-oriented school program is
    (A) information-processing
    (B) listening
    (C) forgetting
    (D) memorizing
    (E) coding

25. After showing a science film, a teacher provided the opportunity for a creative experience in using the scientific method. Which of the following steps is a cognitive exercise rather than part of the scientific method?
    (A) Pupils classified a group of insects.
    (B) Pupils formulated their own hypothesis.
    (C) Pupils assembled their own scientific instruments.
    (D) Pupils conducted their own experiment.
    (E) Pupils selected their own observations and conclusions.

26. A computer does not "play" games. However, it can
    I. store information that can be retrieved for gaming
    II. facilitate playing games and using simulations
    III. process information that has been programmed into it
    IV. limit the playing of games of skill to the programmer's level

    (A) I only
    (B) II only
    (C) I and III only
    (D) III and IV only
    (E) I, II, III, and IV

27. A pupil whose performance with conceptual material is low will be aided most by
    (A) an increasing exposure to abstract ideas
    (B) a series of individual, "hands-on" experiences
    (C) a program tailored to his or her current limits
    (D) recurrent testing
    (E) a variety of experiences calculated to fill gaps in his or her understanding

MODEL TEST 1

28. Sometimes a child needs help to change an attitude that interferes with his or her success as a learner. Which of the following steps can the teacher take to facilitate this change?

    I. Develop a stimulating bulletin board relating to the lessons in which the student is having difficulty.
    II. Show a motion picture that portrays the attitude(s) involved in the sought-for change.
    III. Expose the student to models, role-playing, and experiences with various social interactions.

    (A) I only
    (B) II only
    (C) III only
    (D) I and III only
    (E) I, II, and III

29. A classroom teacher keeps a record of her observations for a week. Which of the following should she allow to influence her as she plans next week's media activities?

    I. Students exhibited apathy while watching filmstrips.
    II. Students participated more frequently in activities that they helped to plan.
    III. Students created opportunities to learn when they set their own goals.

    (A) I only
    (B) II only
    (C) I and II only
    (D) I, II, and III
    (E) III only

30. In planning ways to help students develop an orderly process of thinking, the teacher should emphasize
    (A) skills in selecting information that applies to a problem
    (B) skills in discarding information that does not apply to a problem
    (C) the acquisition of a broad background of perceptual experiences
    (D) skills of concentration
    (E) skills in the use of symbols

READ THE FOLLOWING DIRECTIONS BEFORE PROCEEDING.

Directions: The following questions contain the word LEAST, NOT, or EXCEPT. Read each question very carefully, then seek the answer that applies.

31. All of the following audio-cued learning materials are effective for skills development EXCEPT
    (A) a cassette recording of introductory directions for using shop equipment
    (B) a card reader
    (C) a cartridge recording of a story, to accompany an illustrated book
    (D) a tape-recorded tutorial in science
    (E) a cassette recording of foreign-language conversations

TEST OF PROFESSIONAL KNOWLEDGE

32. Which of the following ways of beginning a parent–teacher conference would be LEAST objectionable to the parents?
    (A) Begin with the student's deportment and point out the relation of bad to good behavior during the term
    (B) Begin with examples of pupil's work and emphasize improvement
    (C) Begin with a chart showing the rank of the student among his classmates; he is near the bottom of the class
    (D) Ask why he never does his homework on time
    (E) Begin with a list of rules and explain how you try to enforce them

33. All of the following statements about teachers as mental health workers relate to pupil learning progress EXCEPT:
    (A) Teachers are catalytic agents.
    (B) Teachers serve as models for students.
    (C) Pupils change just because teachers are in the classroom.
    (D) Some teachers lack self-understanding.
    (E) Teachers accept and respect each student as an individual.

34. Research on students from impoverished environments indicates that all of the following statements are unacceptable EXCEPT:
    (A) Teachers do make important contributions to students from impoverished environments.
    (B) Parental influence is so strong that teachers make little difference at any stage of development.
    (C) A school can do little for students from impoverished homes.
    (D) Teachers have more influence on boys from low-income backgrounds than on girls from the same economic backgrounds.
    (E) The positive influence of teachers is seen with adolescents only.

35. High school students who lack skills in standard English can succeed. Which of the following strategies would NOT be helpful?
    (A) The first steps toward better study habits must be taken by the students to foster self-direction.
    (B) The lessons must be simple enough to understand, but difficult enough to challenge the students.
    (C) The first steps must be taken by the teacher.
    (D) The classroom environment should be partially structured.
    (E) Immediate positive reinforcement should be given daily.

S T O P

IF YOU FINISH BEFORE TIME IS CALLED, YOU MAY CHECK YOUR WORK ON THIS SECTION ONLY. DO NOT WORK ON ANY OTHER SECTION IN THE TEST.

MODEL TEST 1
SECTION 4

Time — 30 minutes

Directions: For each question or incomplete statement below, there are five suggested answers or completions. Select the one that *best* answers the question or completes the statement.

1. Essay tests tend to
   (A) be objective
   (B) cover a narrow range of content area
   (C) be good discriminators of student performance
   (D) be more reliable than objective test items
   (E) favor the student who can write and organize thoughts

2. Which is the best kind of evaluation for encouraging pupil participation?
   (A) Daily quizzes
   (B) Weekly tests
   (C) Gold stars for achievement
   (D) Teacher's praise
   (E) Pupil's self-evaluation

3. For studying the interpersonal behavior of pupils in the fourth grade a useful device is the
   (A) sociogram
   (B) Wetzel grid
   (C) Wechsler test
   (D) California Personality test
   (E) Stanford-Binet test

4. Children can learn to cope with failure. With guidance, they can learn to
   (A) avoid tasks at which they may fail
   (B) accept failure as their level of performance
   (C) rationalize failure
   (D) abandon goals that are not easy to achieve
   (E) try to solve problems through self-direction

5. Current research on the effect of group ratings (standards) on individual students shows that
   (A) pupils will not change their opinions to meet group standards
   (B) group ratings affect pupil attitudes to a high degree
   (C) group ratings have little effect on individual pupils
   (D) teacher ratings have more effect than group ratings
   (E) group ratings occur infrequently

6. The school program should be evaluated
   (A) on objective evidence of the goals and outcomes
   (B) on the basis of teachers' comments about the school
   (C) according to objectives formulated by the board of education
   (D) according to criteria established by the supervisors
   (E) on the basis of parental satisfaction

TEST OF PROFESSIONAL KNOWLEDGE

7. The earliest use of testing instruments was coupled with the philosophy that
    (A) nature was more important than nurture in accounting for individual differences
    (B) guidance could develop student interests
    (C) good teaching would change student aptitudes
    (D) the level of aspiration could modify the influence of heredity
    (E) student failure would be reduced by aptitude testing

8. A teacher gave an objective test to a ninth-grade algebra class. An implication of this fact is that
    (A) different individuals could score this test and find the same set of results
    (B) the test is valid
    (C) this test can be used with other students
    (D) the test is norm-referenced
    (E) the test is probably unreliable

9. Which of the following is an example of an objective question?
    (A) "How does the eardrum help a person to hear?"
    (B) "What was Rosa Parks's role in the civil-rights movement?"
    (C) "What are two causes of air pollution?"
    (D) "Which of these is a prime number: (a) 3; (b) 6; (c) 9; (d) 12?"
    (E) "What economic factors contributed to the Great Depression?"

10. The investigator who uses the cross-sectional approach in child study will
    (A) study different children at different ages
    (B) study one segment of personality at a time
    (C) study only one age group at a time
    (D) compare boys with girls of different ages
    (E) compare the results of three different tests administered to the same student

11. Using the experimental method of child study, a researcher would
    (A) work with children one group at a time
    (B) ignore children's emotions in evaluating maturity
    (C) ignore maturation levels of children working in the experiment
    (D) be concerned only with intellectual development
    (E) use a control group and an experimental group

12. Marks, or grades, for student work should
    (A) be used as incentives
    (B) not be used as ends in themselves
    (C) be used to reward good students
    (D) be used to punish poor students
    (E) reflect the normal curve

13. A teacher attempts to make her tests reliable. In other words, she is trying to
    (A) get her tests to measure what has been taught
    (B) make her tests consistent
    (C) make all questions equally difficult
    (D) have some questions more difficult than others
    (E) conform to a percentage distribution

MODEL TEST 1

14. When a committee of teachers discuss the possibility of promotion or nonpromotion for a pupil, a very important consideration is the
    (A) IQ
    (B) home conditions
    (C) educational age and performance level
    (D) mental ability
    (E) physiological maturity

15. The search for knowledge through research is based on the philosophy of
    (A) realism
    (B) rationalism
    (C) nihilism
    (D) essentialism
    (E) eclecticism

16. The culminating activity of a unit should be
    (A) a comprehensive evaluation of students' work
    (B) a test to determine students' mastery of skills
    (C) a test to determine students' mastery of information
    (D) a summary of each pupil's achievements
    (E) an assembly program

17. For the teacher who uses the scientific approach, the first basic step in planning a program probably will be
    (A) determining the learners' goals
    (B) determining the teacher's own goals
    (C) formulating class objectives
    (D) diagnosing individual differences
    (E) making a unit plan

18. *Measurement*, *evaluation*, and *testing* are not synonymous terms. Although *evaluation* is more inclusive than *measurement*, good measurement
    (A) is a basis for good evaluation
    (B) is required for good testing
    (C) is more important than evaluation
    (D) is based on the teacher's judgment
    (E) has little relationship to testing

19. To determine the habits, skills, and information most useful to successful adults, educational researchers use a technique called
    (A) correlation
    (B) measuring the central tendency
    (C) interpreting a frequency distribution
    (D) applying the mean
    (E) factor analysis

20. The testing instrument constructed by Binet and revised for American use by Terman is
    (A) a group test
    (B) an individual intelligence test
    (C) a preference test
    (D) an achievement test
    (E) a personality test

TEST OF PROFESSIONAL KNOWLEDGE

21. The use of individual psychological testing in education is best left to
    (A) the school psychologist and his or her staff
    (B) guidance counselors
    (C) school supervisors
    (D) the classroom teacher
    (E) clinical psychologists

22. The use of defense mechanisms for coping with stress is an attempt to
    (A) protect the ego
    (B) reject id domination
    (C) gain control of the supergo
    (D) overcome the will
    (E) utilize the superego

23. Why do many teachers and students dislike essay tests?

    I. They are time-consuming in regard to scoring.
    II. Methods of scoring can affect the reliability of the test.
    III. Their content validity can be affected by subjective questions.
    IV. Such tests favor students who can work under pressure.

    (A) I and II only
    (B) I and III only
    (C) III and IV only
    (D) I, II, and III only
    (E) I, II, III, and IV

24. Which of the following represent common errors in evaluating a pupil's academic growth?

    I. Failing to reward a pupil who received a low grade, but who was making consistent progress
    II. Grading students against teacher expectations that may be too low or too high
    III. Setting inappropriate standards for underprivileged pupils
    IV. Adjusting standards as growth continues

    (A) I only
    (B) I and II only
    (C) I, II, and III only
    (D) II and III only
    (E) I, II, III, and IV

25. One disadvantage of grading on a curve is that
    (A) it provides little objective evidence of what students can do
    (B) it is norm-referenced
    (C) the system is misunderstood by parents and pupils
    (D) the teacher does not have to set standards
    (E) it is criterion-referenced

26. A sociometric device can be useful if the teacher
    (A) wants to have a highly structured classroom
    (B) uses a learning center
    (C) wants to seat students according to ability
    (D) wants to determine which pupils will work together in a small group
    (E) wants to send certain pupils to the counselor for aptitude testing

341

27. Which of these conditions would affect the reliability of a student's test score?
    I. A busy highway just outside of the school, visible from the testing room
    II. A cold testing room
    III. An administrative error in giving test directions
    IV. The pupil's ability to guess correctly

    (A) I only
    (B) I and III only
    (C) III and IV only
    (D) I, II, and III only
    (E) I, II, III, and IV

28. Test reliability is determined by which one of the following?
    (A) Validity
    (B) Consistency
    (C) Length
    (D) Ease of scoring
    (E) Intelligence of the pupils

29. When planning to evaluate any pupil performance, it is most essential to
    (A) relate the test to the objectives of the course
    (B) have a balance between factual and conceptual items
    (C) use the inquiry method
    (D) ask factual questions most often
    (E) emphasize the concepts taught

30. What is the median of the following scores?
    9 10 12 13 13 14 15 16 18
    (A) 15
    (B) 14
    (C) undeterminable because of skewness
    (D) the same as the mode
    (E) none of the above

READ THE FOLLOWING DIRECTIONS BEFORE PROCEEDING.

Directions: The following questions contain the word LEAST, NOT, or EXCEPT. Read each question very carefully, then find the answer that applies.

31. Which statement about correlation studies is NOT true?
    (A) A correlation study can be used to compare the performance of two groups in regard to one variable.
    (B) A correlation study can be used to determine whether variable *A* causes variable *B*.
    (C) A correlation study shows the degree of relationship between variables.
    (D) A correlation study cannot show whether *A* causes *B* or whether *B* causes *A*.
    (E) A study that shows a low negative correlation between two variables may be important.

TEST OF PROFESSIONAL KNOWLEDGE

32. Multiple-choice tests are difficult to compose. Which statement about multiple-choice-test preparation is NOT true?
    (A) Each question must test logical thought processes.
    (B) In writing each question, it is important to reduce the number of plausible answers.
    (C) The test as a whole must cover a wide range of content area.
    (D) In writing the questions, it is important to use as few words as possible in each item.
    (E) It is not possible to write valid questions for such a test.

33. When preparing a multiple-choice test, it is necessary to do all of the following EXCEPT
    (A) check the objectives of the course
    (B) keep the reading level at the pupils' level
    (C) watch for items that could be confusing
    (D) make sure there is only one correct answer per question
    (E) prepare a standardized curve for grading

34. A teacher has several handicapped pupils in her sixth-grade class. Which of the following would be LEAST likely to help them develop productive goals and positive attitudes?
    (A) Listen to these pupils read, talk, and explain their work.
    (B) Set their goals for them.
    (C) Use reinforcement techniques—praise, privileges, and so on—to develop good self-concepts.
    (D) Let them work in small groups.
    (E) Arrange some activities in small steps so that each handicapped child can be successful frequently.

35. A teacher tried the following strategies with pupils who demonstrated distractibility or hyperactivity. Which strategy would NOT help these pupils?
    (A) Setting long-range goals for their work
    (B) Assigning study carrels for individual work
    (C) Using routine procedures and clearly written directions
    (D) Making the consequences of different choices clear, and enforcing them
    (E) Providing success experiences and using positive reinforcement

S T O P

IF YOU FINISH BEFORE TIME IS CALLED, YOU MAY CHECK YOUR WORK ON THIS SECTION ONLY. DO NOT WORK ON ANY OTHER SECTION IN THE TEST.

MODEL TEST 1

Answer Keys and Explanation — Test of Professional Knowledge

SECTION 1

Answer Key

1. E	8. E	15. B	22. B	29. E
2. C	9. C	16. A	23. A	30. E
3. D	10. E	17. E	24. D	31. A
4. C	11. E	18. E	25. A	32. D
5. D	12. E	19. E	26. E	33. B
6. A	13. D	20. D	27. E	34. D
7. D	14. C	21. D	28. C	35. A

Explanations

1. **(E)** A needs assessment must be done, including the obtainment of input from other teachers, parents, and students. After the data have been collected, they must be interpreted, and school objectives must be analyzed in relation to student and community needs.

2. **(C)** Competency-based instruction requires the student to perform at a level that has been previously established by teacher and student. The teacher sets out to make instruction effective so that the student can achieve these goals.

3. **(D)** A student's security and motivation depend in large degree on a teacher's fairness and support.

4. **(C)** An item analysis will yield a record of the number of students who answered each question correctly and the number who did not. Items answered correctly by everyone are probably too easy; while items answered correctly by only one or two students, or by none, are probably too difficult.

5. **(D)** If a teaching-learning problem is persistent, changes probably need to be made in the environment (by eliminating distractors, etc.); the teacher-pupil relationship can be changed by the teacher's use of positive reinforcement; realistic goal-setting by both pupils and teacher should be an ongoing process.

6. **(A)** The mean (the average) is more stable than the mode (which is the score that occurs most frequently) and the median (which is the midpoint on any test). Standard deviation and standard error are calculated on the basis of the mean.

7. **(D)** Choice (C) is part of Piaget's theory of the stages of development.

8. **(E)** A teacher develops his or her own style from past success in the classroom, that is, by learning what works with students and what does not.

TEST OF PROFESSIONAL KNOWLEDGE

9. **(C)** The IQ score can change with time and environmental stimulation, so parents and teachers must be flexible about assisting pupils to set realistic goals at different steps of growth. Parents may expect too much from a student who has a high IQ.

10. **(E)** So-called normal children can differ in rate of growth, depending on heredity and environmental factors. They can also differ in social maturity. But "normal" children are aware of themselves as individuals.

11. **(E)** Open discussion gives students an opportunity to express their ideas, to find out what others think, and to anticipate clarifying values through further experiences.

12. **(E)** Modular scheduling is flexible. It is based on small blocks of time (less than an average class period) that can be arranged in various ways to meet teacher and pupil goals. Periodically larger blocks can also be used.

13. **(D)** The maturation ages of both boys and girls are changing; children are maturing at younger ages because of better nutrition.

14. **(C)** The affiliation need is high among adolescents; the classroom teacher can provide opportunities for all to share ideas and experiences.

15. **(B)** Less time is wasted and more success experiences are possible for students when the teacher is available and serves as a facilitator.

16. **(A)** Public demands on the schools differ from community to state to national levels. Yet no generally supported set of educational goals exists. Teachers often are blamed for not preparing students to meet widely varying expectations.

17. **(E)** If parents are not notified of such changes, they can initiate due-process procedures.

18. **(E)** A teacher always has to seek more than one cause for a particular situation. The orientation and past experiences of the students, their goals, and their need for this approach to learning syntax would have to be considered, in addition to a possible lack of pupil interest.

19. **(E)** Emotional, social, intellectual, and physical factors are all significant to the development of psychomotor activities. The physical education teacher sets goals dealing with all these factors.

20. **(D)** Characteristics of learners will affect their motivation, goal-setting, need for feedback, and the types of evaluation the teacher can consider using.

21. **(D)** Whenever identification of pupil needs, evaluation of progress, and/or a change in placement (including initial placement) is decided, parents must be given written notice, according to the federal law governing the education of all handicapped pupils.

22. **(B)** A school newspaper is a good way to teach the language arts. However, if the teacher rewrites all articles before publication, pupils will lose interest and motivation because of the (implied) negative feedback: "Your work is not good enough now, and may never be."

23. **(A)** Current research favors the theory that there is an interaction between heredity and environment, with both having significance in a person's development.

24. **(D)** A telephone call is not sufficient; the coach must give the guardian written notification of the proposed change.

25. **(A)** It is very difficult to separate the influence of heredity from the influence of environment. The notion that an "optimum environment" would isolate the phenomenon of heredity for study is a false premise.

26. **(E)** The late-maturing boy may have many problems, including those related to the items listed.

27. **(E)** A school administrator is usually the one who suspends a pupil. The practice is determined by the legal responsibilities of the school within a particular system or district.

28. **(C)** A diploma cannot be withheld from a student when his or her religious beliefs conflict with school requirements of this nature.

29. **(E)** High content validity in a test is essential for testing what have been identified as important knowledge and skills.

30. **(E)** She should be placed in a regular classroom, provided that the classroom teacher understands her needs, and the classroom has the facilities to meet them.

31. **(A)** The American school system is not controlled by the federal government, although guidelines are given and laws are enforced regarding the use of federal funds.

32. **(D)** Problems of students usually have more than one cause. Care must be taken during counseling to assist the counselee to find the causes of the difficulty, to resolve the need to project blame, and to accept personal responsibility for the outcome.

33. **(B)** Nagging or scolding does not lead to motivation or enthusiasm for staying on a learning task to its completion. Many students encountering consistent rebukes give up, become frustrated, or engage in misconduct.

34. **(D)** Adaptive teaching is concerned with meeting the needs of individual pupils who compete against themselves for growth and progress. Competing for grades leads to comparing the performance of one student with that of others.

TEST OF PROFESSIONAL KNOWLEDGE

35. **(A)** Criterion-referenced testing (and grading) is concerned with specific objectives.

SECTION 2

Answer Key

1. C	8. B	15. E	22. D	29. E
2. C	9. D	16. B	23. E	30. E
3. A	10. D	17. B	24. D	31. E
4. B	11. A	18. A	25. C	32. A
5. C	12. C	19. A	26. D	33. D
6. A	13. D	20. B	27. D	34. C
7. A	14. B	21. E	28. E	35. E

Explanations

1. **(C)** Choices (A), (B), (D), and (E) are based on observations or data taken from research. Value assumptions in education are based on cultural considerations of what is important in preparing children for life in a particular society.

2. **(C)** In planning a course and its goals, a teacher incorporates what he or she assumes to be most worthwhile for students to experience.

3. **(A)** Knowledge of educational psychology helps the teacher understand the needs, interests, drives, and motivations of each learner. Teachers can plan to meet pupils' needs if they have knowledge of the pupils' individual differences.

4. **(B)** Empirical information is based on observation or research. In this case, research shows that fatigue reduces learner effectiveness and that performance declines as a result.

5. **(C)** About one third of adolescents are concerned about their physical development. Boys among this group want to be strong and muscular; girls do not want to be too tall, or weigh too much. Many girls at this age seem to be constantly dieting.

6. **(A)** Such advocates believe that readiness is affected by the environment, and that parents play a key role in the education of children.

7. **(A)** Research shows that social skills are related to physical competence. Often, a boy will not be chosen to play in sports games if his coordination is inadequate. Thus, by comparison with his peers, his range of social experience may be limited.

8. **(B)** All children have a basic need for acceptance by their peers. No one wants to be different to the extent that it makes for neglect or ridicule by others.

9. **(D)** Girls tend to mature more rapidly. For that reason they tend to seek the company of boys who are older. During late adolescence these differences in maturity decrease.

10. **(D)** Some children are able to compensate for parental rejection by having many friends or by doing very well in scholastic work. Other children withdraw from social contact or become hostile toward siblings and/or other children.

11. **(A)** Although the roles of men and women in childrearing are becoming more similar, boys who identify with a competent and caring father tend to be effective learners—meeting both parental expectations and their own goals.

12. **(C)** The natural and social sciences are concerned with many problems having a certain immediacy: the environment, our sources of energy, and global economic conditions. Educators in these subject areas relate the past to the present by applying what is known to contemporary problems.

13. **(D)** Children vary greatly in their readiness for school. Under different teaching–learning experiences class size would vary so each child could participate and get help from the teacher. Attention spans are short so young children need to become involved visually and perceptually.

14. **(B)** Rousseau believed that education could not be rushed but should be matched to the child's inner growth patterns. Educators today find much value in his approach to individual learning differences among children.

15. **(E)** Terman's studies of gifted children showed they had an above-average ability to cope with life situations, and commensurate moral attitudes. Results of such studies today might be different, owing to intensive peer pressure on all children, including the gifted.

16. **(B)** Preadolescent boys tend merely to tolerate girls and even, in some cases, to avoid them. Boys of this age are likely to have their own friends and to stay together for activities, games, and so on.

17. **(B)** Mathematics can be used to make inferences, predict outcomes, and indicate the probability of a student's passing or failing a course under certain circumstances. Educators who were affected by a determinist philosophy made fewer efforts to assist students who were predicted to have marginal chances for success in the system.

18. **(A)** Darwin's theory of natural selection emphasizes the survival of the species that are strongest and most adaptable to environmental changes.

19. **(A)** Positive reinforcement is given to encourage the pupil to work harder, continue a task, complete work on time, and have a feeling of success. Immediate feedback gives children an idea of how their performance rates and whether they are doing the problems correctly. If a child is having difficulty, questions can be answered before additional errors are made. Scolding students for making errors and using problems as punishment (deprivation of recess) can have an aversive effect; the pupil begins to dislike arithmetic. Praising for correct work and giving a tangible reward, such as gold stars, gives the pupil a sense of achievement and of being accepted by the teacher. Students with low self-esteem do better with encouragement and rewards than they do with scolding and deprivation of privileges.

TEST OF PROFESSIONAL KNOWLEDGE

20. **(B)** Pupil morale is higher in all classrooms with a social-climate that fosters learning through teacher assistance, specific guidelines (sometimes set by pupils with the teacher's help), and parental cooperation. The poorest place to learn is in a classroom frequently disrupted by students and in a climate of inconsistency and uncertainty.

21. **(E)** Rousseau believed that children are born good, but that they may be adversely affected by the people with whom they come in contact. They become bad, he felt, through environmental influences—thus, the need to limit children's social contacts.

22. **(D)** In an activity curriculum, the entire curriculum is experience-based. According to Dewey, its two main objectives are to increase effective learning and to prepare the child to live competently in a democratic society. Today's schools reflect "learning by doing" through the incorporation of learning centers and laboratories, workshops, activity-centered units of instruction, and a wide range of community resources.

23. **(E)** Learning disabilities can have multiple causes. In addition to getting a medical history, a psychologist will sometimes have to use assessment devices to determine the individual's extent of perceptual-motor impairment or other neurological damage.

24. **(D)** Flat (two-dimensional) pictures can be used if there is time for individual students to examine the pictures, and if the concept of motion is not relevant to the learning situation.

25. **(C)** Time is a factor in the use of field trips. Many classes do not work effectively unless there is additional supervision, which may or may not always be available. Therefore other community resources—including speakers to the class—should be considered ahead of field trips.

26. **(D)** Inquiry learning is planned to provide opportunities for learners to be selectors, observers, experimenters, and evaluators in their learning experiences.

27. **(D)** Children who view television are exposed to sequencing that often does not reflect the normal order of occurrence. Flashbacks and frequent change of pace hold the child's interest but do not require him or her to develop a sense of order and sequence to understand the story. The child who is learning to read or to develop skills in arithmetic must use sequencing for extracting information and for problem-solving. These skills can be improved through practice that the teacher must provide.

28. **(E)** Multiple experiences in developing visual literacy can be provided. The choices listed are just a few that are available for daily use.

29. **(E)** Children who are disadvantaged should be offered flexible learning experiences with a variety of entry and exit levels. Their earliest learning experiences can be used in the language arts for building self-concepts.

MODEL TEST 1

30. **(E)** Quality control of publishers software programs is provided continuously through teacher reviews and other forms of input.

31. **(E)** A child with reading difficulties is frustrated and discouraged. He needs to begin at a level from which he can derive success experiences and still make progress. In this case at the Pre-Primer I level.

32. **(A)** His dislike for school may not be the cause of his low grades but one of the symptoms that his learning needs are not being met by the school.

33. **(D)** The behavior will vary from child to child and from hour to hour.

34. **(C)** There is no indication that girls and boys have different receptors and effectors for learning, so they should generally be given the same information to process. Individual differences will be demonstrated but not in learning capability based on sex differences only.

35. **(E)** Optional choices create difficulty in grading and giving equal weight to each choice.

SECTION 3

Answer Key

1. A		8. D		15. C		22. C		29. D
2. C		9. C		16. E		23. A		30. C
3. B		10. A		17. D		24. A		31. A
4. D		11. E		18. C		25. A		32. B
5. D		12. B		19. B		26. E		33. D
6. D		13. E		20. C		27. E		34. A
7. E		14. E		21. A		28. E		35. A

Explanations

1. **(A)** The affiliation ethic emphasizes belonging to groups; thus these students will probably be under peer pressure to engage in many social activities. Emphasis on such activities can affect the amount of time spent in studying and doing homework.

2. **(C)** Rote learning involves memorization of facts and information. Learning with understanding increases the student's awareness, helps to relate past and present learnings, and builds a foundation for problem-solving in new situations. Learning is thus transferred from one experience to another.

3. **(B)** When a teacher or counselor works with a student in a problem situation, alternatives are pointed out to the student so that responsible choices can be made.

TEST OF PROFESSIONAL KNOWLEDGE

4. **(D)** An individual's actions spring from choices that are based on personal goals. Students are usually in conflict situations until their personal goals are established and sustained.

5. **(D)** In learning a skill, students tend to use the trial-and-error approach whenever the desired results cannot be obtained by following the teacher's directions.

6. **(D)** Children who are overprotected at home have often had little experience in making decisions or in problem-solving. A teacher should provide opportunities for such children to achieve success after they initiate a learning action.

7. **(E)** A student's rights must be protected so that punishment is not given on the basis of circumstantial evidence, preconceived labeling, or a teacher's or administrator's opinions.

8. **(D)** Behaviorists favor consistent reinforcement. They consider it essential for helping pupils who are not functioning effectively in the classroom to learn specified appropriate responses. B. F. Skinner is the best known psychologist of this school of thought.

9. **(C)** With this approach, modifications are frequently made in the choice of pupil activities and in the amount of time spent on each one.

10. **(A)** Praise from the teacher is the most important stimulus. Each such experience motivates the student to try again.

11. **(E)** Students can work in teams to plan lessons and teach them to younger or less experienced pupils. These pupil-teachers work harder to prepare lessons so that they can teach them to others. Persistence, patience, courtesy, and the need for communication skills are some of the behaviors learned by pupil teaching teams. Many classroom teachers use older students who have computer skills to write programs to assist pupils with special learning problems or interests.

12. **(B)** The curriculum committee should utilize the skills of teachers who have planned, implemented, and evaluated learning programs at the various grade levels. Participation in curriculum planning improves the morale of teachers and thus increases their support for innovation and continuous evaluation.

13. **(E)** Each school within a district has unique requirements based on the individual differences of its pupils and the materials and facilities that are available. To ensure that these factors are taken into consideration by a district, each of its schools should be allowed maximum input to curriculum planning.

14. **(E)** System-wide planning must permit schools to develop individual curriculum programs within overall guidelines.

15. **(C)** The school guidance program involves more than working with pupils who have problems. It should be a program that assists all pupils in planning and achieving realistic personal goals.

16. **(E)** Students under threat of punishment will respond in unpredictable ways. Some students will do (I), (II), and (III). Other students will accept his threat as a dare; they will cheat and try to outwit him without being caught. A number of students may think he will not really expel them from school because he has made other threats and has not followed through. A few students will continue to cheat when he includes test questions on material never covered in class discussions or assignments. It is unlikely that no students will attempt to cheat again, especially after some time has passed.

17. **(D)** Thorndike did research on the relationship between stimulus and response learning, with results that indicated the behavior of children could be changed by strengthening or weakening specific stimulus-response connections or associations.

18. **(C)** Audiovisual materials are most effective when their use is preceded by general discussion of the topic they cover. Pupils often do not extract information from viewing such materials unless they are first made aware of questions for which they can seek answers while viewing and listening. Follow-up discussion allows students to confirm and/or correct their impressions.

19. **(B)** Context information available to the teacher from his or her experience and reading is often not known to pupils. Referent confusion arises from a student's limited information or from a lack of the maturity needed to understand and use information obtained previously.

20. **(C)** Herbart set up five steps to be followed in teaching a lesson. He would not permit teacher flexibility in the presentation.

21. **(A)** The evaluation procedure follows the conclusion of a unit of work, so it would not be appropriate at the orientation stage. However, it is appropriate to involve pupils in evaluation while planning other aspects of the unit.

22. **(C)** In their development of speech, children tend to be oriented first toward the present (now), with some ability to anticipate the very near future. The past is the last concept to make sense to them.

23. **(A)** From the moment sound waves reach the eardrum, they are uniquely transmitted to the brain and "processed" in each individual. Every person has a different set of sound-discrimination "cues."

24. **(A)** Sensory information is processed, "selected," and placed in short- or long-term memory. Particular stimuli will elicit these responses later, as needed by the learner.

25. **(A)** Besides not being a step in the scientific method, classifying insects would not be a "creative response." It would be a cognitive exercise involving materials provided by the teacher.

26. **(E)** A computer stores information that is programmed into it. This information can be retrieved and changed by anyone knowing the program language.

TEST OF PROFESSIONAL KNOWLEDGE

27. **(E)** A planned variety of experiences will help such a pupil to build new concepts. In the process, he or she would need help to connect new ideas to ideas or concepts previously formed.

28. **(E)** Because attitudes develop from experiences within the individual's social environment, many kinds of new experiences are required to change an attitude. Learning activities that involve the use of personal contact and all the senses—visual, tactile, and auditory—can be used to help a pupil bring about such change.

29. **(D)** If students exhibit lack of interest during a media activity, allowing them to select topics and materials and to operate the equipment will raise their interest.

30. **(C)** A broad background of perceptual experiences helps children understand and relate better to the social and physical world; they begin to recognize the order in the environment and the sequence of events, ideas, and so on, as they occur.

31. **(A)** Shop equipment is so dangerous that the teacher has to demonstrate the safety rules to individuals and small groups.

32. **(B)** Parents are apprehensive about a conference with a child's teacher, particularly if the teacher has called the meeting. The best way to relax the tension that exists in both the teacher and the parents is to begin with positive comments about the student's strong points and, if possible, by showing examples of successful classwork the child has done. Criticism may anger the parents, who may react by criticizing the teacher.

33. **(D)** Teachers are models in the classroom who stimulate responses. If they accept and respect students as individuals, the students try harder and change because the teacher has created a warm, interactive environment. However, some teachers have difficulty counseling students because they don't understand their own motivation and lack of adjustment to stress and personal problems.

34. **(A)** Teachers make considerable difference and can contribute much to student motivation. The desire of the teacher for student success, as shown through interest, reinforcement of acceptable performance, and steady encouragement, leads to pupil progress.

35. **(A)** Students cannot face the responsibility alone for helping themselves to learn standard English. The first steps need to be taken by the teacher, who evaluates performance, sets practice time with oral reading and speaking, using other students, tapes, or small groups for reading and conversation.

MODEL TEST 1

SECTION 4

Answer Key

1.	E	8.	A	15.	B	22.	A	29.	A
2.	E	9.	D	16.	D	23.	E	30.	D
3.	A	10.	A	17.	C	24.	E	31.	B
4.	E	11.	E	18.	A	25.	A	32.	E
5.	B	12.	B	19.	E	26.	D	33.	E
6.	A	13.	B	20.	B	27.	E	34.	B
7.	A	14.	C	21.	A	28.	B	35.	A

Explanations

1. **(E)** Essay tests are useful, but they are limited. Because of time, only a few questions can be asked. The student who writes rapidly and can organize his or her thoughts well has an advantage over the student who needs more time to think and then writes more slowly than others.

2. **(E)** Self-evaluation lets the student know what kinds of errors he or she made and how a particular score compares to other pupils' achievements. Self-evaluation may also be just an ongoing comparison that the student makes between his or her work and personal goals. In either case, because the pupil makes the assessment of his or her work, there is more potential for motivation.

3. **(A)** A sociogram is useful for finding which pupils are friends, and which pupils prefer to work together. Children who are not chosen by anyone (isolates) need the special attention of the teacher so that group cohesion can be obtained.

4. **(E)** Children who learn how to cope with failure set realistic goals for themselves and work independently toward those goals.

5. **(B)** Young people have a deep desire to belong and to be accepted by their peers. Thus, group standards exert pressure on individual students to conform.

6. **(A)** Objective evidence of the goals and outcomes of a school program have value for curriculum committees, teachers, and ultimately pupils. If parents have been involved in the planning of the program, they should receive information on its outcomes.

7. **(A)** Early testing was accompanied by the idea that intelligence scores were constant throughout life. One was born with a certain mentality and little could be done in the classroom to change it.

TEST OF PROFESSIONAL KNOWLEDGE

8. **(A)** An objective question has only one correct answer. Therefore several teachers could score an objective test, using its answer key, and find the same results for the class.

9. **(D)** For an objective question, there is only one right answer—in this case, the teacher's judgment does not enter into scoring students' responses.

10. **(A)** An investigator using the cross-sectional approach would take children from various groups and study them according to certain criteria or characteristics.

11. **(E)** The experimental method calls for two groups of children for each study. This allows the researcher to compare selected variables and to measure the cause(s) of change in behavior. For instance, an experimental group might be taught reading with the use of a filmstrip based on the reading material. The control group would be taught reading by the usual textbook method. At the end of the study, the two groups of children would be compared for growth in reading skills. The sampling for the experimental and control groups would have to be similar in all other variables except for the use of the audiovisual reading material.

12. **(B)** Grades or marks should not be ends in themselves. Pupils should use them—and any other form of evaluation—as cues for setting goals that they can achieve.

13. **(B)** Consistency of test results, established on a test-retest basis, is the fundamental factor in test reliability.

14. **(C)** Educational age is important. It is related to the child's performance consistency, potential, and motivation.

15. **(B)** Rationalism bases knowledge on one's ability to reason. Knowledge is derived from experience and reason rather than from the senses or emotions.

16. **(D)** Different types of culminating activities can be used to determine each pupil's achievement in relation to the goals that were set when the unit was initiated. The teacher usually confers with each pupil to determine his or her strengths and weaknesses, and to decide how these can be improved. New goals may be set for the pupil, materials selected, and lessons assigned.

17. **(C)** With the scientific approach, a teacher's first consideration in planning for a particular unit or topic of study would be to set objectives for the program.

18. **(A)** Measurement includes several forms of assessment that can be used in the evaluation of pupil progress. The teacher's observation of a pupil's attitude toward school, reading ability, and other skills can also be added to test information to provide a fuller picture of his or her learning abilities.

19. **(E)** By using factor analysis, researchers have discovered more than 100 specialized abilities that "cluster" in successful adults. This information has influenced the development of aptitude tests used by many schools.

20. **(B)** The Stanford-Binet Scale is an individual intelligence test that is usually given by psychologists. It is useful with children who do not take group tests well.

21. **(A)** Educational testing, such as standardized achievement tests and certain diagnostic tools, can be used by teachers but psychological testing often requires more highly trained personnel. This is true both for testing children with emotional or behavioral problems and for interpreting the test results. Using results from all such tests, teachers and school psychologists can work together to plan a program for meeting each child's needs and interests.

22. **(A)** Such mechanisms as projection, rationalization, and suppression are useful in protecting a person from undue anxiety. Each is a way of gaining time to resolve some conflict at a later date.

23. **(E)** Essay tests are scored subjectively by each grader; therefore the reliability of such tests can be questioned. The phrasing of essay questions can reduce their content validity. The fact that some students organize ideas and write well under pressure of time raises the issue of fairness, too.

24. **(E)** Evaluation techniques need to be used that will not penalize a student because of mental, physical, or emotional handicaps, rate of maturation, or learning disabilities. Even very small gains, if used effectively, can build a pupil's self-confidence and motivation to learn.

25. **(A)** Grading on the curve is based on the performance of individuals in one class. This is a disadvantage because a student's relative success from one class to the next may be constantly changing, making it difficult to assess a pupil's growth.

26. **(D)** Sociometric devices are useful in the elementary grades as a quick source of information for the teacher who wants to establish temporary working groups. Young children change friendships often and choose different companions to meet different needs.

27. **(E)** Many things influence a pupil's test score. Room temperature, noise, instructional errors, and guessing will all affect a pupil's achievement on the test.

28. **(B)** The reliability of a testing instrument is determined by the consistency with which it measures performance. On a test-retest basis, with the same pupils taking the same test a second time, both sets of scores can be compared for consistency.

29. **(A)** Pupil performance needs to be evaluated against the material taught and the objectives set for the course. If a measuring instrument does not serve this purpose, pupils' scores will not provide valid evidence of their learning.

30. **(D)** The midpoint score (the median) is determined by counting the scores listed in rank order. In this case, it is 13, the same as the mode. The mode is the score most often achieved on a test.

31. **(B)** Correlation studies can be used for (A), (C), (D), and (E). They can be used to show the relationship between two variables, but not that one variable causes the other.

32. **(E)** It is possible to write valid statements for a multiple-choice test. Each question must pertain to the course objectives and to the material taught.

33. **(E)** Chocies (A), (B), (C), and (D) apply to the teacher who prepares multiple-choice test items. Since the test is objective, each question must be clear and relevant to the content studied by the pupils. A standardized curve is not needed to grade a classroom test.

34. **(B)** The teacher must find where such pupils are, in terms of interests and motivation. Handicapped pupils need to learn how to set realistic personal goals so that they can look forward to a success experience at the conclusion of an educational challenge.

35. **(A)** Hyperactive children need consistent guidelines, short-range goals, firm limits, and a teacher sensitive to their particular needs.

ANSWER SHEET FOR MODEL TEST 2

Test of General Knowledge

BE SURE EACH MARK IS DARK AND COMPLETELY FILLS THE INTENDED SPACE. DO NOT MAKE ANY STRAY MARKS. MAKE ALL ERASURES COMPLETE.

SECTION 1		SECTION 2		SECTION 3		SECTION 4	
1 Ⓐ Ⓑ Ⓒ Ⓓ Ⓔ	26 Ⓐ Ⓑ Ⓒ Ⓓ Ⓔ	1 Ⓐ Ⓑ Ⓒ Ⓓ Ⓔ	26 Ⓐ Ⓑ Ⓒ Ⓓ Ⓔ	1 Ⓐ Ⓑ Ⓒ Ⓓ Ⓔ	26 Ⓐ Ⓑ Ⓒ Ⓓ Ⓔ	1 Ⓐ Ⓑ Ⓒ Ⓓ Ⓔ	26 Ⓐ Ⓑ Ⓒ Ⓓ Ⓔ
2 Ⓐ Ⓑ Ⓒ Ⓓ Ⓔ	27 Ⓐ Ⓑ Ⓒ Ⓓ Ⓔ	2 Ⓐ Ⓑ Ⓒ Ⓓ Ⓔ	27 Ⓐ Ⓑ Ⓒ Ⓓ Ⓔ	2 Ⓐ Ⓑ Ⓒ Ⓓ Ⓔ	27 Ⓐ Ⓑ Ⓒ Ⓓ Ⓔ	2 Ⓐ Ⓑ Ⓒ Ⓓ Ⓔ	27 Ⓐ Ⓑ Ⓒ Ⓓ Ⓔ
3 Ⓐ Ⓑ Ⓒ Ⓓ Ⓔ	28 Ⓐ Ⓑ Ⓒ Ⓓ Ⓔ	3 Ⓐ Ⓑ Ⓒ Ⓓ Ⓔ	28 Ⓐ Ⓑ Ⓒ Ⓓ Ⓔ	3 Ⓐ Ⓑ Ⓒ Ⓓ Ⓔ	28 Ⓐ Ⓑ Ⓒ Ⓓ Ⓔ	3 Ⓐ Ⓑ Ⓒ Ⓓ Ⓔ	28 Ⓐ Ⓑ Ⓒ Ⓓ Ⓔ
4 Ⓐ Ⓑ Ⓒ Ⓓ Ⓔ	29 Ⓐ Ⓑ Ⓒ Ⓓ Ⓔ	4 Ⓐ Ⓑ Ⓒ Ⓓ Ⓔ	29 Ⓐ Ⓑ Ⓒ Ⓓ Ⓔ	4 Ⓐ Ⓑ Ⓒ Ⓓ Ⓔ	29 Ⓐ Ⓑ Ⓒ Ⓓ Ⓔ	4 Ⓐ Ⓑ Ⓒ Ⓓ Ⓔ	29 Ⓐ Ⓑ Ⓒ Ⓓ Ⓔ
5 Ⓐ Ⓑ Ⓒ Ⓓ Ⓔ	30 Ⓐ Ⓑ Ⓒ Ⓓ Ⓔ	5 Ⓐ Ⓑ Ⓒ Ⓓ Ⓔ	30 Ⓐ Ⓑ Ⓒ Ⓓ Ⓔ	5 Ⓐ Ⓑ Ⓒ Ⓓ Ⓔ	30 Ⓐ Ⓑ Ⓒ Ⓓ Ⓔ	5 Ⓐ Ⓑ Ⓒ Ⓓ Ⓔ	30 Ⓐ Ⓑ Ⓒ Ⓓ Ⓔ
6 Ⓐ Ⓑ Ⓒ Ⓓ Ⓔ	31 Ⓐ Ⓑ Ⓒ Ⓓ Ⓔ	6 Ⓐ Ⓑ Ⓒ Ⓓ Ⓔ	31 Ⓐ Ⓑ Ⓒ Ⓓ Ⓔ	6 Ⓐ Ⓑ Ⓒ Ⓓ Ⓔ	31 Ⓐ Ⓑ Ⓒ Ⓓ Ⓔ	6 Ⓐ Ⓑ Ⓒ Ⓓ Ⓔ	31 Ⓐ Ⓑ Ⓒ Ⓓ Ⓔ
7 Ⓐ Ⓑ Ⓒ Ⓓ Ⓔ	32 Ⓐ Ⓑ Ⓒ Ⓓ Ⓔ	7 Ⓐ Ⓑ Ⓒ Ⓓ Ⓔ	32 Ⓐ Ⓑ Ⓒ Ⓓ Ⓔ	7 Ⓐ Ⓑ Ⓒ Ⓓ Ⓔ	32 Ⓐ Ⓑ Ⓒ Ⓓ Ⓔ	7 Ⓐ Ⓑ Ⓒ Ⓓ Ⓔ	32 Ⓐ Ⓑ Ⓒ Ⓓ Ⓔ
8 Ⓐ Ⓑ Ⓒ Ⓓ Ⓔ	33 Ⓐ Ⓑ Ⓒ Ⓓ Ⓔ	8 Ⓐ Ⓑ Ⓒ Ⓓ Ⓔ	33 Ⓐ Ⓑ Ⓒ Ⓓ Ⓔ	8 Ⓐ Ⓑ Ⓒ Ⓓ Ⓔ	33 Ⓐ Ⓑ Ⓒ Ⓓ Ⓔ	8 Ⓐ Ⓑ Ⓒ Ⓓ Ⓔ	33 Ⓐ Ⓑ Ⓒ Ⓓ Ⓔ
9 Ⓐ Ⓑ Ⓒ Ⓓ Ⓔ	34 Ⓐ Ⓑ Ⓒ Ⓓ Ⓔ	9 Ⓐ Ⓑ Ⓒ Ⓓ Ⓔ	34 Ⓐ Ⓑ Ⓒ Ⓓ Ⓔ	9 Ⓐ Ⓑ Ⓒ Ⓓ Ⓔ	34 Ⓐ Ⓑ Ⓒ Ⓓ Ⓔ	9 Ⓐ Ⓑ Ⓒ Ⓓ Ⓔ	34 Ⓐ Ⓑ Ⓒ Ⓓ Ⓔ
10 Ⓐ Ⓑ Ⓒ Ⓓ Ⓔ	35 Ⓐ Ⓑ Ⓒ Ⓓ Ⓔ	10 Ⓐ Ⓑ Ⓒ Ⓓ Ⓔ	35 Ⓐ Ⓑ Ⓒ Ⓓ Ⓔ	10 Ⓐ Ⓑ Ⓒ Ⓓ Ⓔ	35 Ⓐ Ⓑ Ⓒ Ⓓ Ⓔ	10 Ⓐ Ⓑ Ⓒ Ⓓ Ⓔ	35 Ⓐ Ⓑ Ⓒ Ⓓ Ⓔ
11 Ⓐ Ⓑ Ⓒ Ⓓ Ⓔ	36 Ⓐ Ⓑ Ⓒ Ⓓ Ⓔ	11 Ⓐ Ⓑ Ⓒ Ⓓ Ⓔ	36 Ⓐ Ⓑ Ⓒ Ⓓ Ⓔ	11 Ⓐ Ⓑ Ⓒ Ⓓ Ⓔ	36 Ⓐ Ⓑ Ⓒ Ⓓ Ⓔ	11 Ⓐ Ⓑ Ⓒ Ⓓ Ⓔ	36 Ⓐ Ⓑ Ⓒ Ⓓ Ⓔ
12 Ⓐ Ⓑ Ⓒ Ⓓ Ⓔ	37 Ⓐ Ⓑ Ⓒ Ⓓ Ⓔ	12 Ⓐ Ⓑ Ⓒ Ⓓ Ⓔ	37 Ⓐ Ⓑ Ⓒ Ⓓ Ⓔ	12 Ⓐ Ⓑ Ⓒ Ⓓ Ⓔ	37 Ⓐ Ⓑ Ⓒ Ⓓ Ⓔ	12 Ⓐ Ⓑ Ⓒ Ⓓ Ⓔ	37 Ⓐ Ⓑ Ⓒ Ⓓ Ⓔ
13 Ⓐ Ⓑ Ⓒ Ⓓ Ⓔ	38 Ⓐ Ⓑ Ⓒ Ⓓ Ⓔ	13 Ⓐ Ⓑ Ⓒ Ⓓ Ⓔ	38 Ⓐ Ⓑ Ⓒ Ⓓ Ⓔ	13 Ⓐ Ⓑ Ⓒ Ⓓ Ⓔ	38 Ⓐ Ⓑ Ⓒ Ⓓ Ⓔ	13 Ⓐ Ⓑ Ⓒ Ⓓ Ⓔ	38 Ⓐ Ⓑ Ⓒ Ⓓ Ⓔ
14 Ⓐ Ⓑ Ⓒ Ⓓ Ⓔ	39 Ⓐ Ⓑ Ⓒ Ⓓ Ⓔ	14 Ⓐ Ⓑ Ⓒ Ⓓ Ⓔ	39 Ⓐ Ⓑ Ⓒ Ⓓ Ⓔ	14 Ⓐ Ⓑ Ⓒ Ⓓ Ⓔ	39 Ⓐ Ⓑ Ⓒ Ⓓ Ⓔ	14 Ⓐ Ⓑ Ⓒ Ⓓ Ⓔ	39 Ⓐ Ⓑ Ⓒ Ⓓ Ⓔ
15 Ⓐ Ⓑ Ⓒ Ⓓ Ⓔ	40 Ⓐ Ⓑ Ⓒ Ⓓ Ⓔ	15 Ⓐ Ⓑ Ⓒ Ⓓ Ⓔ	40 Ⓐ Ⓑ Ⓒ Ⓓ Ⓔ	15 Ⓐ Ⓑ Ⓒ Ⓓ Ⓔ	40 Ⓐ Ⓑ Ⓒ Ⓓ Ⓔ	15 Ⓐ Ⓑ Ⓒ Ⓓ Ⓔ	40 Ⓐ Ⓑ Ⓒ Ⓓ Ⓔ
16 Ⓐ Ⓑ Ⓒ Ⓓ Ⓔ	41 Ⓐ Ⓑ Ⓒ Ⓓ Ⓔ	16 Ⓐ Ⓑ Ⓒ Ⓓ Ⓔ	41 Ⓐ Ⓑ Ⓒ Ⓓ Ⓔ	16 Ⓐ Ⓑ Ⓒ Ⓓ Ⓔ	41 Ⓐ Ⓑ Ⓒ Ⓓ Ⓔ	16 Ⓐ Ⓑ Ⓒ Ⓓ Ⓔ	41 Ⓐ Ⓑ Ⓒ Ⓓ Ⓔ
17 Ⓐ Ⓑ Ⓒ Ⓓ Ⓔ	42 Ⓐ Ⓑ Ⓒ Ⓓ Ⓔ	17 Ⓐ Ⓑ Ⓒ Ⓓ Ⓔ	42 Ⓐ Ⓑ Ⓒ Ⓓ Ⓔ	17 Ⓐ Ⓑ Ⓒ Ⓓ Ⓔ	42 Ⓐ Ⓑ Ⓒ Ⓓ Ⓔ	17 Ⓐ Ⓑ Ⓒ Ⓓ Ⓔ	42 Ⓐ Ⓑ Ⓒ Ⓓ Ⓔ
18 Ⓐ Ⓑ Ⓒ Ⓓ Ⓔ	43 Ⓐ Ⓑ Ⓒ Ⓓ Ⓔ	18 Ⓐ Ⓑ Ⓒ Ⓓ Ⓔ	43 Ⓐ Ⓑ Ⓒ Ⓓ Ⓔ	18 Ⓐ Ⓑ Ⓒ Ⓓ Ⓔ	43 Ⓐ Ⓑ Ⓒ Ⓓ Ⓔ	18 Ⓐ Ⓑ Ⓒ Ⓓ Ⓔ	43 Ⓐ Ⓑ Ⓒ Ⓓ Ⓔ
19 Ⓐ Ⓑ Ⓒ Ⓓ Ⓔ	44 Ⓐ Ⓑ Ⓒ Ⓓ Ⓔ	19 Ⓐ Ⓑ Ⓒ Ⓓ Ⓔ	44 Ⓐ Ⓑ Ⓒ Ⓓ Ⓔ	19 Ⓐ Ⓑ Ⓒ Ⓓ Ⓔ	44 Ⓐ Ⓑ Ⓒ Ⓓ Ⓔ	19 Ⓐ Ⓑ Ⓒ Ⓓ Ⓔ	44 Ⓐ Ⓑ Ⓒ Ⓓ Ⓔ
20 Ⓐ Ⓑ Ⓒ Ⓓ Ⓔ	45 Ⓐ Ⓑ Ⓒ Ⓓ Ⓔ	20 Ⓐ Ⓑ Ⓒ Ⓓ Ⓔ	45 Ⓐ Ⓑ Ⓒ Ⓓ Ⓔ	20 Ⓐ Ⓑ Ⓒ Ⓓ Ⓔ	45 Ⓐ Ⓑ Ⓒ Ⓓ Ⓔ	20 Ⓐ Ⓑ Ⓒ Ⓓ Ⓔ	45 Ⓐ Ⓑ Ⓒ Ⓓ Ⓔ
21 Ⓐ Ⓑ Ⓒ Ⓓ Ⓔ	46 Ⓐ Ⓑ Ⓒ Ⓓ Ⓔ	21 Ⓐ Ⓑ Ⓒ Ⓓ Ⓔ	46 Ⓐ Ⓑ Ⓒ Ⓓ Ⓔ	21 Ⓐ Ⓑ Ⓒ Ⓓ Ⓔ	46 Ⓐ Ⓑ Ⓒ Ⓓ Ⓔ	21 Ⓐ Ⓑ Ⓒ Ⓓ Ⓔ	46 Ⓐ Ⓑ Ⓒ Ⓓ Ⓔ
22 Ⓐ Ⓑ Ⓒ Ⓓ Ⓔ	47 Ⓐ Ⓑ Ⓒ Ⓓ Ⓔ	22 Ⓐ Ⓑ Ⓒ Ⓓ Ⓔ	47 Ⓐ Ⓑ Ⓒ Ⓓ Ⓔ	22 Ⓐ Ⓑ Ⓒ Ⓓ Ⓔ	47 Ⓐ Ⓑ Ⓒ Ⓓ Ⓔ	22 Ⓐ Ⓑ Ⓒ Ⓓ Ⓔ	47 Ⓐ Ⓑ Ⓒ Ⓓ Ⓔ
23 Ⓐ Ⓑ Ⓒ Ⓓ Ⓔ	48 Ⓐ Ⓑ Ⓒ Ⓓ Ⓔ	23 Ⓐ Ⓑ Ⓒ Ⓓ Ⓔ	48 Ⓐ Ⓑ Ⓒ Ⓓ Ⓔ	23 Ⓐ Ⓑ Ⓒ Ⓓ Ⓔ	48 Ⓐ Ⓑ Ⓒ Ⓓ Ⓔ	23 Ⓐ Ⓑ Ⓒ Ⓓ Ⓔ	48 Ⓐ Ⓑ Ⓒ Ⓓ Ⓔ
24 Ⓐ Ⓑ Ⓒ Ⓓ Ⓔ	49 Ⓐ Ⓑ Ⓒ Ⓓ Ⓔ	24 Ⓐ Ⓑ Ⓒ Ⓓ Ⓔ	49 Ⓐ Ⓑ Ⓒ Ⓓ Ⓔ	24 Ⓐ Ⓑ Ⓒ Ⓓ Ⓔ	49 Ⓐ Ⓑ Ⓒ Ⓓ Ⓔ	24 Ⓐ Ⓑ Ⓒ Ⓓ Ⓔ	49 Ⓐ Ⓑ Ⓒ Ⓓ Ⓔ
25 Ⓐ Ⓑ Ⓒ Ⓓ Ⓔ	50 Ⓐ Ⓑ Ⓒ Ⓓ Ⓔ	25 Ⓐ Ⓑ Ⓒ Ⓓ Ⓔ	50 Ⓐ Ⓑ Ⓒ Ⓓ Ⓔ	25 Ⓐ Ⓑ Ⓒ Ⓓ Ⓔ	50 Ⓐ Ⓑ Ⓒ Ⓓ Ⓔ	25 Ⓐ Ⓑ Ⓒ Ⓓ Ⓔ	50 Ⓐ Ⓑ Ⓒ Ⓓ Ⓔ

Test of Communication Skills

BE SURE EACH MARK IS DARK AND COMPLETELY FILLS THE INTENDED SPACE. DO NOT MAKE ANY STRAY MARKS. MAKE ALL ERASURES COMPLETE.

SECTION 1 – LISTENING			SECTION 2 – READING		SECTION 3 – WRITING		
1 Ⓐ Ⓑ Ⓒ Ⓓ	16 Ⓐ Ⓑ Ⓒ Ⓓ	31 Ⓐ Ⓑ Ⓒ Ⓓ	1 Ⓐ Ⓑ Ⓒ Ⓓ Ⓔ	16 Ⓐ Ⓑ Ⓒ Ⓓ Ⓔ	1 Ⓐ Ⓑ Ⓒ Ⓓ Ⓔ	16 Ⓐ Ⓑ Ⓒ Ⓓ Ⓔ	31 Ⓐ Ⓑ Ⓒ Ⓓ Ⓔ
2 Ⓐ Ⓑ Ⓒ Ⓓ	17 Ⓐ Ⓑ Ⓒ Ⓓ	32 Ⓐ Ⓑ Ⓒ Ⓓ	2 Ⓐ Ⓑ Ⓒ Ⓓ Ⓔ	17 Ⓐ Ⓑ Ⓒ Ⓓ Ⓔ	2 Ⓐ Ⓑ Ⓒ Ⓓ Ⓔ	17 Ⓐ Ⓑ Ⓒ Ⓓ Ⓔ	32 Ⓐ Ⓑ Ⓒ Ⓓ Ⓔ
3 Ⓐ Ⓑ Ⓒ Ⓓ	18 Ⓐ Ⓑ Ⓒ Ⓓ	33 Ⓐ Ⓑ Ⓒ Ⓓ	3 Ⓐ Ⓑ Ⓒ Ⓓ Ⓔ	18 Ⓐ Ⓑ Ⓒ Ⓓ Ⓔ	3 Ⓐ Ⓑ Ⓒ Ⓓ Ⓔ	18 Ⓐ Ⓑ Ⓒ Ⓓ Ⓔ	33 Ⓐ Ⓑ Ⓒ Ⓓ Ⓔ
4 Ⓐ Ⓑ Ⓒ Ⓓ	19 Ⓐ Ⓑ Ⓒ Ⓓ	34 Ⓐ Ⓑ Ⓒ Ⓓ	4 Ⓐ Ⓑ Ⓒ Ⓓ Ⓔ	19 Ⓐ Ⓑ Ⓒ Ⓓ Ⓔ	4 Ⓐ Ⓑ Ⓒ Ⓓ Ⓔ	19 Ⓐ Ⓑ Ⓒ Ⓓ Ⓔ	34 Ⓐ Ⓑ Ⓒ Ⓓ Ⓔ
5 Ⓐ Ⓑ Ⓒ Ⓓ	20 Ⓐ Ⓑ Ⓒ Ⓓ	35 Ⓐ Ⓑ Ⓒ Ⓓ	5 Ⓐ Ⓑ Ⓒ Ⓓ Ⓔ	20 Ⓐ Ⓑ Ⓒ Ⓓ Ⓔ	5 Ⓐ Ⓑ Ⓒ Ⓓ Ⓔ	20 Ⓐ Ⓑ Ⓒ Ⓓ Ⓔ	35 Ⓐ Ⓑ Ⓒ Ⓓ Ⓔ
6 Ⓐ Ⓑ Ⓒ Ⓓ	21 Ⓐ Ⓑ Ⓒ Ⓓ	36 Ⓐ Ⓑ Ⓒ Ⓓ	6 Ⓐ Ⓑ Ⓒ Ⓓ Ⓔ	21 Ⓐ Ⓑ Ⓒ Ⓓ Ⓔ	6 Ⓐ Ⓑ Ⓒ Ⓓ Ⓔ	21 Ⓐ Ⓑ Ⓒ Ⓓ Ⓔ	36 Ⓐ Ⓑ Ⓒ Ⓓ Ⓔ
7 Ⓐ Ⓑ Ⓒ Ⓓ	22 Ⓐ Ⓑ Ⓒ Ⓓ	37 Ⓐ Ⓑ Ⓒ Ⓓ	7 Ⓐ Ⓑ Ⓒ Ⓓ Ⓔ	22 Ⓐ Ⓑ Ⓒ Ⓓ Ⓔ	7 Ⓐ Ⓑ Ⓒ Ⓓ Ⓔ	22 Ⓐ Ⓑ Ⓒ Ⓓ Ⓔ	37 Ⓐ Ⓑ Ⓒ Ⓓ Ⓔ
8 Ⓐ Ⓑ Ⓒ Ⓓ	23 Ⓐ Ⓑ Ⓒ Ⓓ	38 Ⓐ Ⓑ Ⓒ Ⓓ	8 Ⓐ Ⓑ Ⓒ Ⓓ Ⓔ	23 Ⓐ Ⓑ Ⓒ Ⓓ Ⓔ	8 Ⓐ Ⓑ Ⓒ Ⓓ Ⓔ	23 Ⓐ Ⓑ Ⓒ Ⓓ Ⓔ	38 Ⓐ Ⓑ Ⓒ Ⓓ Ⓔ
9 Ⓐ Ⓑ Ⓒ Ⓓ	24 Ⓐ Ⓑ Ⓒ Ⓓ	39 Ⓐ Ⓑ Ⓒ Ⓓ	9 Ⓐ Ⓑ Ⓒ Ⓓ Ⓔ	24 Ⓐ Ⓑ Ⓒ Ⓓ Ⓔ	9 Ⓐ Ⓑ Ⓒ Ⓓ Ⓔ	24 Ⓐ Ⓑ Ⓒ Ⓓ Ⓔ	39 Ⓐ Ⓑ Ⓒ Ⓓ Ⓔ
10 Ⓐ Ⓑ Ⓒ Ⓓ	25 Ⓐ Ⓑ Ⓒ Ⓓ	40 Ⓐ Ⓑ Ⓒ Ⓓ	10 Ⓐ Ⓑ Ⓒ Ⓓ Ⓔ	25 Ⓐ Ⓑ Ⓒ Ⓓ Ⓔ	10 Ⓐ Ⓑ Ⓒ Ⓓ Ⓔ	25 Ⓐ Ⓑ Ⓒ Ⓓ Ⓔ	40 Ⓐ Ⓑ Ⓒ Ⓓ Ⓔ
11 Ⓐ Ⓑ Ⓒ Ⓓ	26 Ⓐ Ⓑ Ⓒ Ⓓ		11 Ⓐ Ⓑ Ⓒ Ⓓ Ⓔ	26 Ⓐ Ⓑ Ⓒ Ⓓ Ⓔ	11 Ⓐ Ⓑ Ⓒ Ⓓ Ⓔ	26 Ⓐ Ⓑ Ⓒ Ⓓ Ⓔ	41 Ⓐ Ⓑ Ⓒ Ⓓ Ⓔ
12 Ⓐ Ⓑ Ⓒ Ⓓ	27 Ⓐ Ⓑ Ⓒ Ⓓ		12 Ⓐ Ⓑ Ⓒ Ⓓ Ⓔ	27 Ⓐ Ⓑ Ⓒ Ⓓ Ⓔ	12 Ⓐ Ⓑ Ⓒ Ⓓ Ⓔ	27 Ⓐ Ⓑ Ⓒ Ⓓ Ⓔ	42 Ⓐ Ⓑ Ⓒ Ⓓ Ⓔ
13 Ⓐ Ⓑ Ⓒ Ⓓ	28 Ⓐ Ⓑ Ⓒ Ⓓ		13 Ⓐ Ⓑ Ⓒ Ⓓ Ⓔ	28 Ⓐ Ⓑ Ⓒ Ⓓ Ⓔ	13 Ⓐ Ⓑ Ⓒ Ⓓ Ⓔ	28 Ⓐ Ⓑ Ⓒ Ⓓ Ⓔ	43 Ⓐ Ⓑ Ⓒ Ⓓ Ⓔ
14 Ⓐ Ⓑ Ⓒ Ⓓ	29 Ⓐ Ⓑ Ⓒ Ⓓ		14 Ⓐ Ⓑ Ⓒ Ⓓ Ⓔ	29 Ⓐ Ⓑ Ⓒ Ⓓ Ⓔ	14 Ⓐ Ⓑ Ⓒ Ⓓ Ⓔ	29 Ⓐ Ⓑ Ⓒ Ⓓ Ⓔ	44 Ⓐ Ⓑ Ⓒ Ⓓ Ⓔ
15 Ⓐ Ⓑ Ⓒ Ⓓ	30 Ⓐ Ⓑ Ⓒ Ⓓ		15 Ⓐ Ⓑ Ⓒ Ⓓ Ⓔ	30 Ⓐ Ⓑ Ⓒ Ⓓ Ⓔ	15 Ⓐ Ⓑ Ⓒ Ⓓ Ⓔ	30 Ⓐ Ⓑ Ⓒ Ⓓ Ⓔ	45 Ⓐ Ⓑ Ⓒ Ⓓ Ⓔ

MODEL TEST 2

Test of Professional Knowledge

BE SURE EACH MARK IS DARK AND COMPLETELY FILLS THE INTENDED SPACE. DO NOT MAKE ANY STRAY MARKS. MAKE ALL ERASURES COMPLETE

Model Test 2
Test of General Knowledge

SECTION 1

SOCIAL STUDIES

Time — 30 minutes

Directions: For each question or incomplete statement below, there are five suggested answers or completions. Select the one that *best* answers the question or completes the statement.

1. Here are four events important in American history:

    I. Monroe Doctrine
    II. Mexican War
    III. Louisiana Purchase
    IV. Assassination of Abraham Lincoln

    In which of the following are these events listed in correct chronological order?
    (A) I, III, II, IV
    (B) III, I, II, IV
    (C) II, I, IV, III
    (D) IV, III, II, I
    (E) II, I, IV, III

2. The Syrian territory of the Golan Heights was occupied by Israel during the 1967 Arab-Israeli War. The initial Israeli purpose for this control was to
    (A) turn the area over to the United Nations
    (B) exploit the vast oil reserves
    (C) destroy the center of world terrorism
    (D) end terrorist attacks on Israeli settlements in the valley below
    (E) establish a community of Israeli settlers

3. The United States census indicates that, at the present growth rate, by the 1990s the largest ethnic minority in this country will be
    (A) Hispanic   (D) Arab
    (B) black   (E) Indian
    (C) Asian

4. The longest river in the world is the
    (A) Amazon   (D) Mississippi
    (B) Congo   (E) Nile
    (C) Danube

MODEL TEST 2

World Population Growth   10,000 BC to 1982

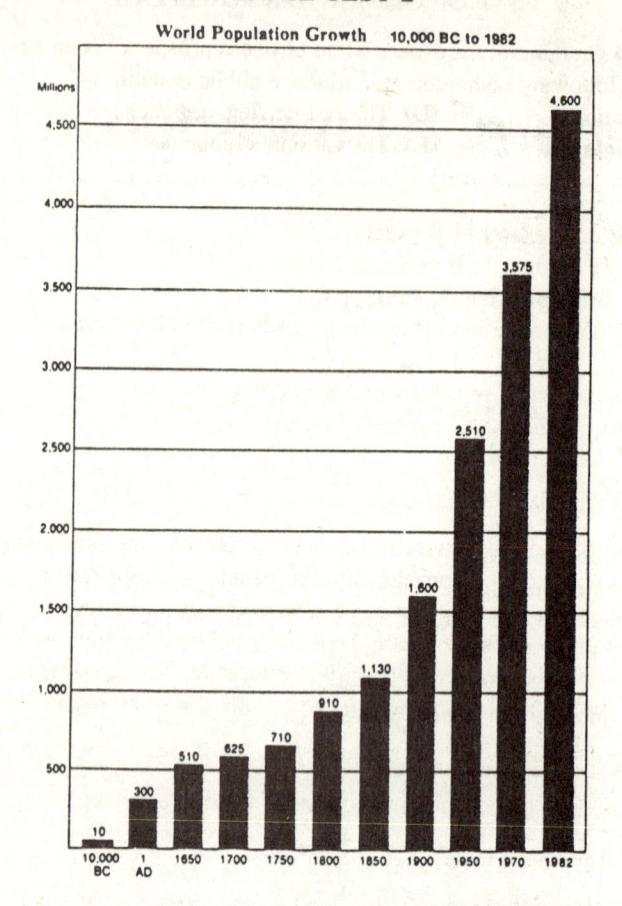

Year	Population (Millions)
10,000 BC	10
1 AD	300
1650	510
1700	625
1750	710
1800	910
1850	1,130
1900	1,600
1950	2,510
1970	3,575
1982	4,600

5. There has always been a steady growth in world population. According to the bar graph above, which of the following statements are NOT correct?

   I. In 1982 the world population was less than 5 billion.
   II. The rate of population growth was slower between 1 A.D. and 1650 than during any period since the beginning of the Christian era.
   III. Between 1850 and 1900 the rate of growth nearly tripled.
   IV. During the two decades 1950–1970 the population growth amounted to nearly half of the entire increase for the twentieth century.

   (A) I only
   (B) II only
   (C) III and IV only
   (D) IV only
   (E) II, III, and IV only

6. The concept of culture is useful for the study of anthropology, other social sciences, and the humanities. Human societies are distinguished by all of the following characteristics EXCEPT

   (A) shared customs, ideas, and structure
   (B) the transmission of traditions and attitudes by biological inheritance
   (C) established systems of rewards and punishments
   (D) social organization, religion, and economic system(s)
   (E) possible adaptation of some cultural traits from other groups by diffusion

TEST OF GENERAL KNOWLEDGE

7. The statement that "the community prospers when business prospers" is an example of which of the following techniques to influence public opinion?
   (A) Appeal to the emotions
   (B) Alleged common interest
   (C) Disguised identity
   (D) The red-herring approach
   (E) The rational argument

8. Which of the following is an example of isolationism?
   (A) World sanctions against apartheid in South Africa
   (B) The 19th century British colonial system
   (C) Theodore Roosevelt's negotiation of the Treaty of Portsmouth between Japan and Russia
   (D) The Soviets not withdrawing forces from Afghanistan
   (E) United States refusal to join the League of Nations

Questions 9–10 are based on the following passage.

Though religion has changed much from ancient times to the present, the fundamental importance of its role has not altered. From the simplest beliefs in animism and ancestor worship to the most sophisticated of the modern monotheisms, one finds religion playing a key role: it gives moral guidance, helps to structure daily life, and provides solace when the mysteries of birth and death must be faced. Though science has greatly added to our understanding of the universe, there will always be mysteries that no amount of laboratory work can solve.

9. Which of the following statements reflects a hypothesis contained in the above passage?
   (A) Religion will continue to be very important.
   (B) Animism is an early and simple form of religion.
   (C) There is more than one religion.
   (D) Modern religions include monotheisms.
   (E) Moral guidance can be found in some religions.

10. Which of the following, if true, would LEAST support the opinion contained in the above passage?
    (A) Church attendance has continued to rise.
    (B) Statistics indicate few Bibles are sold anymore.
    (C) Television ministers have very high ratings.
    (D) Decreasing numbers of people identify themselves as being atheists.
    (E) Many public meetings are opened with the reciting of a prayer.

11. The Common Market, known officially as the European Economic Community, has as one of its basic purposes
    (A) common membership in the World Bank
    (B) manipulation of the world supply of gold
    (C) gradual elimination of tariff barriers and trusts between member nations
    (D) production of its own independent supply of oil
    (E) control of world steel production

12. A person studying the cultural geography of a region would be particularly interested in which one of the following features?
    (A) Topography
    (B) Weather and climate
    (C) Minerals
    (D) Population distribution and settlement
    (E) Surface and ground water

MODEL TEST 2

13. People today have considerable mobility. When people move on the same social level, this is referred to as
    (A) horizontal mobility
    (B) vertical mobility
    (C) group dynamics
    (D) inaction
    (E) social stability

14. In a Fascist state, the will of the majority
    (A) is replaced by the rule of a single person
    (B) is used to raise group standards
    (C) prevails in the government
    (D) governs through organized labor
    (E) is used to increase production

15. In the twentieth century, for the first time, a Vice President succeeded to the presidency of the United States because of the resignation, rather than the death, of his predecessor. Of which of the following is this statement true?
    (A) John F. Kennedy
    (B) Richard Nixon
    (C) Gerald Ford
    (D) Jimmy Carter
    (E) Ronald Reagan

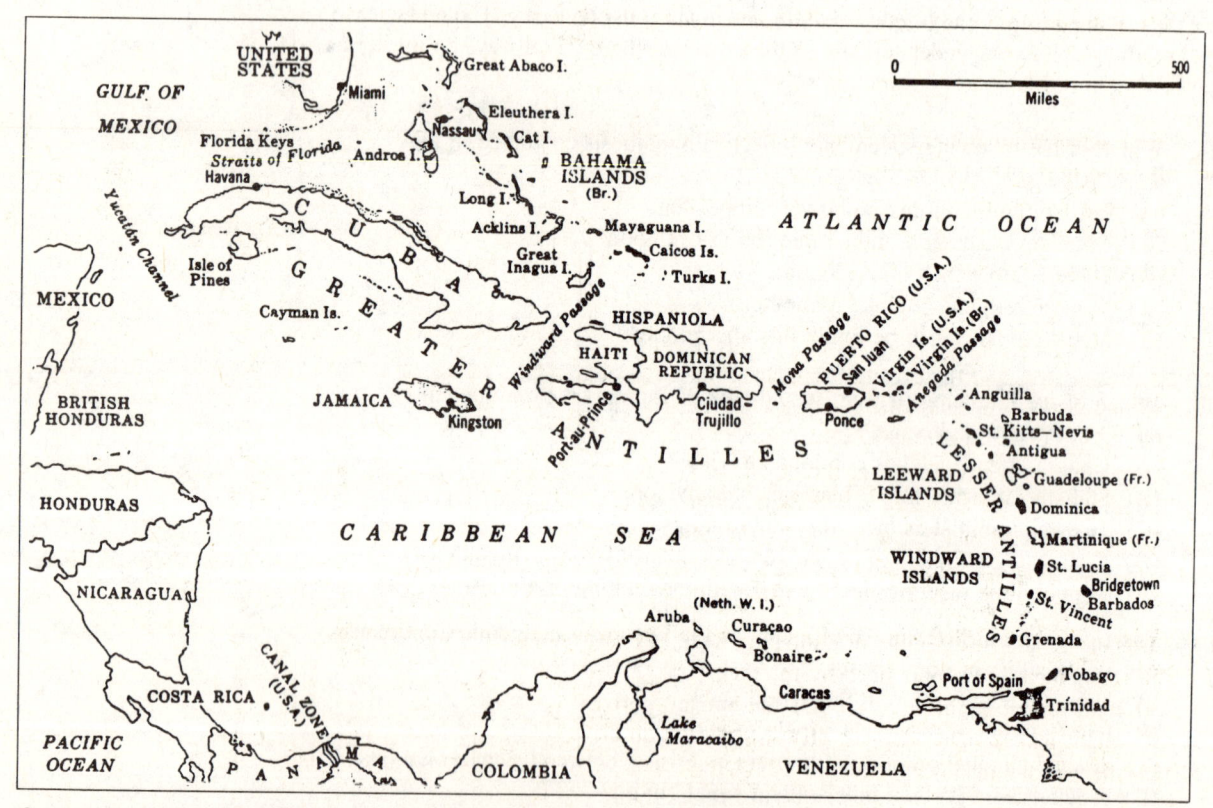

Source: Paul Hamlyn, *Children's Picture Atlas*, Golden Press, 1960.

16. All of the following statements about the region in the above map are false EXCEPT:

    I. The U.S. was concerned during the 1980s about the increasing military and political involvement of the U.S.S.R. in Cuba and Central America.

TEST OF GENERAL KNOWLEDGE

II. The entire region shown on the map is called "The West Indies."
III. The U.S. has little need for concern about the Panama Canal Zone because of its distance from the U.S.
IV. Cuba once belonged to France and was traded for Canada in 1763.
V. Nassau has belonged to the U.S. since World War II.

(A) I and II only
(B) III only
(C) I only
(D) III and IV only
(E) V only

17. The size of the national debt is a matter of grave concern to many Americans. Which one of the following is an economic measure related to our national debt that, if taken, could result in severe damage to the financial system of the United States?
    (A) Curtailing Social Security benefits
    (B) Abolishing Medicare
    (C) Closing half the post offices
    (D) Reducing the Army and Navy to a fraction of their present sizes
    (E) Failing to pay the interest on bonds issued by the federal government

18. The English philosopher who first set down the system of checks and balances as followed in the U.S. Constitution was
    (A) Thomas Malthus   (D) David Hume
    (B) John Locke   (E) Adam Smith
    (C) George Berkeley

19. Karl Marx rejected the capitalistic system on the grounds that
    (A) no system can be a pure democracy
    (B) the class system is inefficient
    (C) a small group profits from the efforts of labor
    (D) profits should be taken only by the government
    (E) industries should be controlled by the government

20. In recent times the attempts of nations to keep any one nation from dominating the scene have been influenced by the theory of
    (A) right makes might   (D) the hunger motive
    (B) might makes right   (E) the population drive
    (C) the balance of power

21. The 1987 nuclear arms agreement signed by Ronald Reagan and Mikhail Gorbachev set the stage for
    (A) immediate implementation of arms reduction by presidential proclamation
    (B) ratification by the Warsaw Pact countries
    (C) further study and ratification by the United States Senate

365

(D) rejection by the NATO countries and formation of their own agreement with the U.S.S.R.
(E) a new treaty between England and the NATO countries

22. A major change took place in the Supreme Court during the 1980s. Which one of the following occurred?
    (A) Minority opinions were eliminated.
    (B) The Court decided to convene only in odd-numbered years.
    (C) Justices were confirmed without Senate approval.
    (D) The number of Court justices was increased to twelve.
    (E) Sandra Day O'Connor became one of the Justices of the Court.

23. To remain competitive, an industry must replace outmoded methods, procedures, and equipment as more efficient ones become available. A U.S. industry that has suffered devastating financial losses in recent years, partly because of failure to apply this principle, is the
    (A) aerospace industry
    (B) garment industry
    (C) pharmaceutical industry
    (D) shipbuilding industry
    (E) steel industry

24. A labor dispute that cannot be resolved by mediation is sometimes settled by arbitration. Under the rules of arbitration,
    (A) the disputing parties agree to accept the arbitrator's decision
    (B) a "gentlemen's agreement" cannot be used
    (C) the negotiations are "out in the open"
    (D) one side can refuse to accept the arbitrator's decision
    (E) sessions must be held continuously until agreement is reached

25. Certain human characteristics can be explained by the climate and geographical features of a particular region. This philosophy is known as
    (A) the Malthus theory
    (B) the process of segregation
    (C) the law of least resistance
    (D) geographical determinism
    (E) humanism

26. The skill of a teacher can fulfill the criteria of being scarce and of being useful and yet *not* be considered
    (A) a service   (D) a material
    (B) a personal ability (E) a utility
    (C) an economic good

27. Which one of the following countries has a command-type economic system?
    (A) Brazil   (D) Republic of China
    (B) England   (E) Union of South Africa
    (C) Mexico

28. Several years ago, when Angelo Bartlett Giamatti was installed as president of Yale University, a newspaper described him as "flip, funny, iconoclastic" and

TEST OF GENERAL KNOWLEDGE

added "one can almost close one's eyes and hear him addressed as 'Don Giamatti.'" This is an example of

(A) a racial slur
(B) ethnic stereotyping
(C) yellow journalism
(D) jingoism
(E) objective reporting

Questions 29 and 30 refer to the partial map of Asia below (the U.S.S.R. is not included), on which the letters A–E designate five countries. To answer each question choose one of the letters. A letter may be used once, twice or not at all.

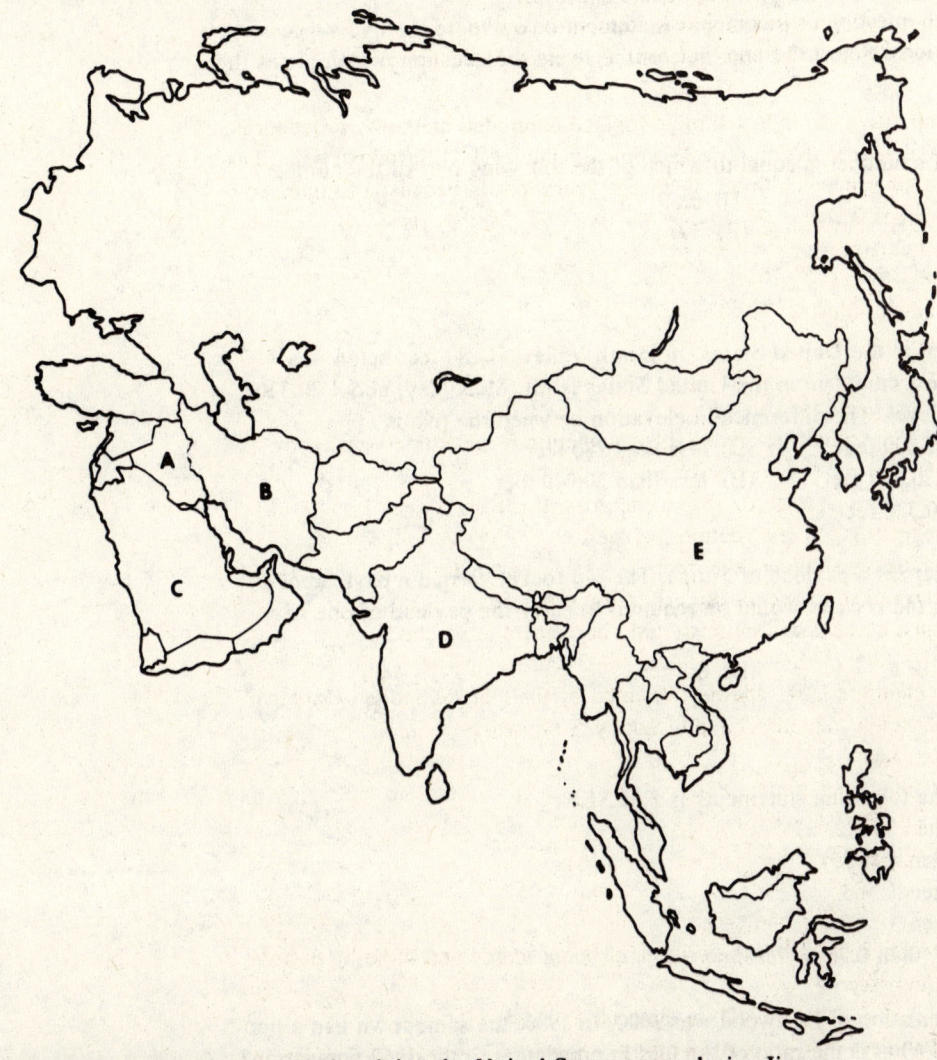

29. In which country did a crisis involving the United States occur during Jimmy Carter's administration?

30. In which country was a woman the prime minister from 1966 to 1977, assuming the same office again in 1980?

S T O P

IF YOU FINISH BEFORE TIME IS CALLED, YOU MAY CHECK YOUR WORK ON THIS SECTION ONLY. DO NOT WORK ON ANY OTHER SECTION IN THIS TEST.

MODEL TEST 2

SECTION 2

MATHEMATICS

Time — 30 minutes

Directions: For each question or incomplete statement below there are five suggested answers or completions. Select the one that *best* answers the question or completes the statement.

1. Five percent of a number is equal to which of the following part of the number?
   (A) $\frac{5}{8}$
   (B) 0.05
   (C) 0.005
   (D) 0.50
   (E) 5.0

2. The lowest point in the United States, in Death Valley, is 280 feet below sea level. The highest mountain in the United States is Mt. McKinley, about 20,320 feet above sea level. The difference in elevation between the two is
   (A) less than 15,000 feet
   (B) more than 20,500 feet
   (C) less than 20,320 feet
   (D) less than 280 feet
   (E) less than 20,040 feet

3. A new rocket carries a payload of 5 tons. The old rocket carried a payload of $\frac{3}{4}$ ton. How many old rockets would be required to carry the payload of one new rocket?
   (A) 5
   (B) 6
   (C) 7
   (D) 8
   (E) 9

4. Which one of the following statements is FALSE?
   (A) If 4 = 4, then 2 = 2.
   (B) If 8 > 4, then 4 > 2.
   (C) If 3 < 7, then 7 > 3.
   (D) If 4 < 6, then 3 > 6.
   (E) If $\frac{3}{4}$ = 0.75, then 0.75 = 75%.

5. In 1960, the population of Eastwood was 3000. In 1980, the same town had a population of 2000. What is the ratio of the loss in population to the 1960 population?
   (A) 2:5
   (B) 1:2
   (C) 3:4
   (D) 3:5
   (E) 1:3

6. You wish to change 2500 miles to scientific notation expressed as a decimal multiplied by 10 raised to the appropriate exponent. Which of the following is correct?
   (A) 2.0×10^3
   (B) 2.3×10^2
   (C) 2.5×10^2
   (D) 2.5×10^3
   (E) 2.0×10^3

TEST OF GENERAL KNOWLEDGE

7. In which of the following pairs are the figures NOT congruent?

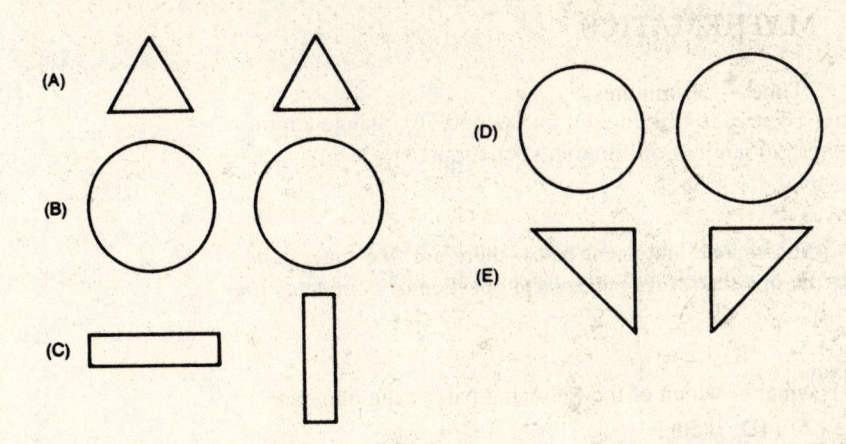

(A) [two triangles]
(B) [two circles]
(C) [two rectangles]
(D) [two circles]
(E) [two right triangles]

8. Which of the figures have the same area?

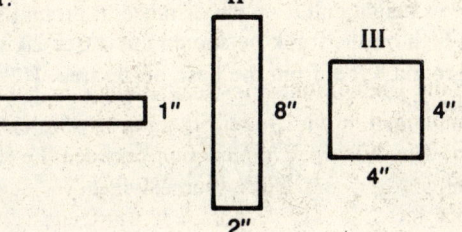

I: 16" × 1"
II: 8" × 2"
III: 4" × 4"

(A) I and II
(B) I and III
(C) I, II, and III
(D) II and III
(E) All have different areas.

9. $\sqrt{100}$ is between
   (A) 5 and 15
   (B) 20 and 25
   (C) 50 and 75
   (D) 100 and 500
   (E) 1000 and 2000

10. If $x = y \div z$ or $y = xz$, then which one of these equations is correct?
    (A) $z = y \div x$
    (B) $x = yz$
    (C) $z = yx$
    (D) $z = x \div y$
    (E) $x = z \div y$

11. A farmer wants to raise catfish. The circumference of his pond is 20 rods and 14 feet. (One rod = 16.5 feet.) He plans to use three strands of fence wire. Can he fence this pond with 950 feet of fence wire?
    (A) No; he needs 2080 feet of wire.
    (B) No; he needs 1032 feet of wire.
    (C) Yes; he needs only about 350 feet of wire.
    (D) Yes; he needs between 700 and 800 feet of wire.
    (E) No; he needs 1174 feet of wire.

12. The point halfway between $\frac{3}{4}$ and $\frac{1}{4}$ is
    (A) $\frac{8}{16}$
    (B) $\frac{7}{16}$
    (C) $\frac{1}{8}$
    (D) $\frac{7}{8}$
    (E) $\frac{1}{8}$

MODEL TEST 2

13. Frannie paid $3.50, or one fourth of her money, for a notebook. How much money did she have before she bought the notebook?
    - (A) $12.50
    - (B) $10.50
    - (C) $13.00
    - (D) $14.00
    - (E) $14.50

14. A kilogram is 1000 grams. There is 0.45 kilogram in 1 pound. To change a number of pounds into an equivalent number of kilograms, one must
    - (A) multiply the number by 0.45
    - (B) divide the number by 0.45
    - (C) multiply the number by 0.45 and then divide the result by 1000
    - (D) divide the number by 0.45 and then multiply the result by 1000
    - (E) multiply the number by 450

15. A forester used this formula

    $$\frac{h^2 - b^2}{2h} = \text{height to cut}$$

    where h = the tree's height and b = the distance to ground-striking point, to determine how high on the trunk he should cut a tree 20 feet high so that it would strike the ground 8 feet from the base of the tree. How high on the trunk should he make the cut?
    - (A) 8.4 feet
    - (B) 11.5 feet
    - (C) 7 feet
    - (D) 15 feet
    - (E) 17 feet

16. If the probability that an event will occur is $\frac{3}{5}$, the probability that it will not occur is
    - (A) $\frac{3}{8}$
    - (B) $\frac{2}{8}$
    - (C) $\frac{2}{5}$
    - (D) $\frac{5}{3}$
    - (E) $\frac{5}{8}$

17. Marge will be 2 years more than twice as old as she is now in 14 years. How old is Marge now?
    - (A) 14 years
    - (B) 7 years
    - (C) 12 years
    - (D) 16 years
    - (E) 13 years

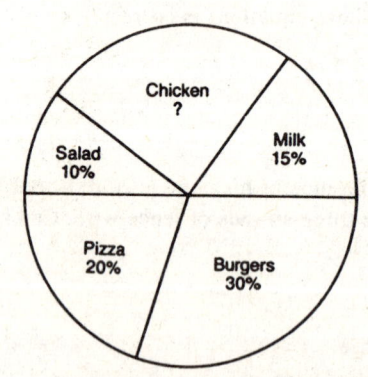

18. The percentages of students selecting various foods for lunch in a high school cafeteria are shown in the circle graph above for all foods but one. What was the percentage of students who chose chicken?
    - (A) 5%
    - (B) 10%
    - (C) 35%
    - (D) 20%
    - (E) 25%

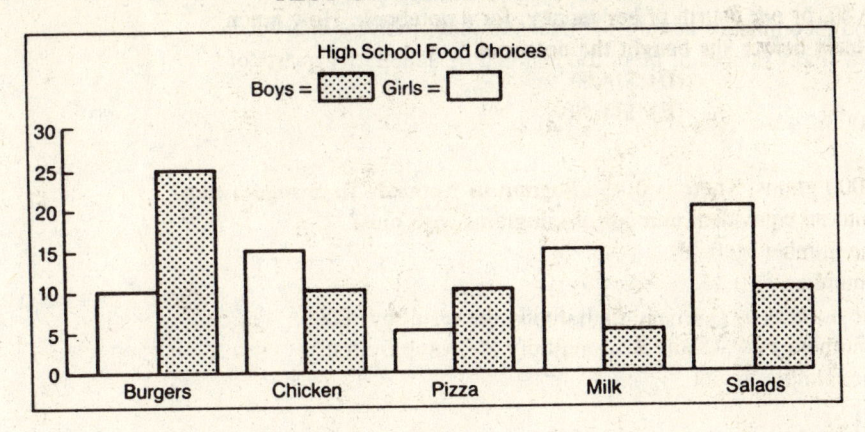

19. From the information in the bar graph, which of the following statements is INCORRECT?
    (A) Burgers were chosen more often by boys.
    (B) Salads were chosen more often by girls.
    (C) More girls than boys chose chicken.
    (D) Fewer girls than boys chose pizza.
    (E) The ratio of girls to boys choosing burgers was 5:2.

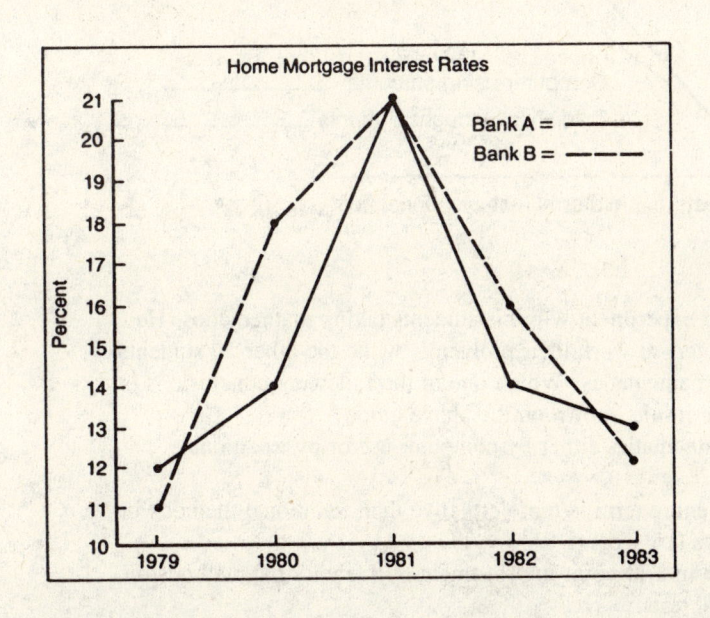

20. The line graph shows the interest rates for home mortgages offered by two banks. On the basis of the information given, which of the following statements is INCORRECT?
    (A) Bank B's interest rates were lowest in 1979.
    (B) Interest rates for both banks were highest in 1981.
    (C) The median interest rates for the two banks are the same.
    (D) For the 5-year period shown, interest rates were higher overall at Bank B.
    (E) The interest rate mode for Bank A was 14%.

21. A box of plant food recommends adding $1\frac{1}{2}$ ounces of plant food for every 3 pints of water. How many ounces of plant food should be added to 4 quarts of water?
   (A) $2\frac{1}{2}$ (B) $3\frac{1}{2}$ (C) 4   (D) 6   (E) 8

Learning Mathematics

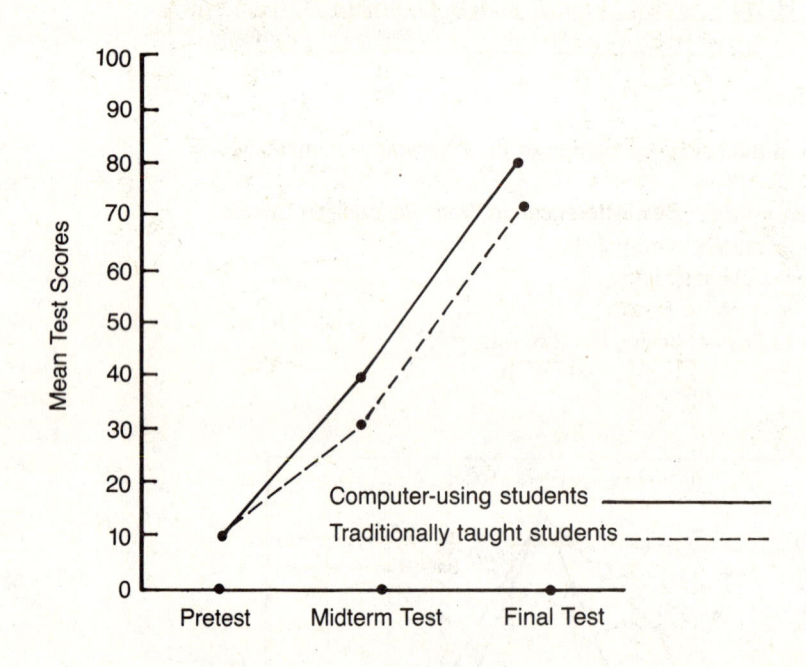

22. Mr. Cassiano conducted an experiment with his students taking mathematics. He had 50 students use computers to work their problems, while the other 50 students continued with traditional mathematics. Which one of the following conclusions is NOT valid according to the results shown on the above graph?
   (A) Students can learn mathematics either by computer use or by traditional teaching methods.
   (B) Computer use for the entire term is more effective than traditional methods in improving mathematics test scores.
   (C) Computer use resulted in a 10-point improvement over traditional methods on both midterm and final tests.
   (D) Computer use is initially more effective than traditional methods, but results in no more rapid improvement after the midterm test.
   (E) The computer group's performance on the midterm test was one-third better than the traditional group's, and improved more rapidly than the traditional group's thereafter, since computer use resulted in these students being able to answer correctly more of the difficult questions than the traditional group.

TEST OF GENERAL KNOWLEDGE

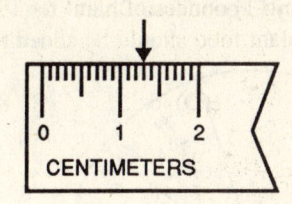

23. A 2-centimeter portion of the scale on a metric ruler is shown above. The arrow points to a reading of
    (A) $1\frac{3}{8}$ cm (B) $1\frac{3}{16}$ cm (C) 13 mm (D) 1.03 mm (E) 13 m

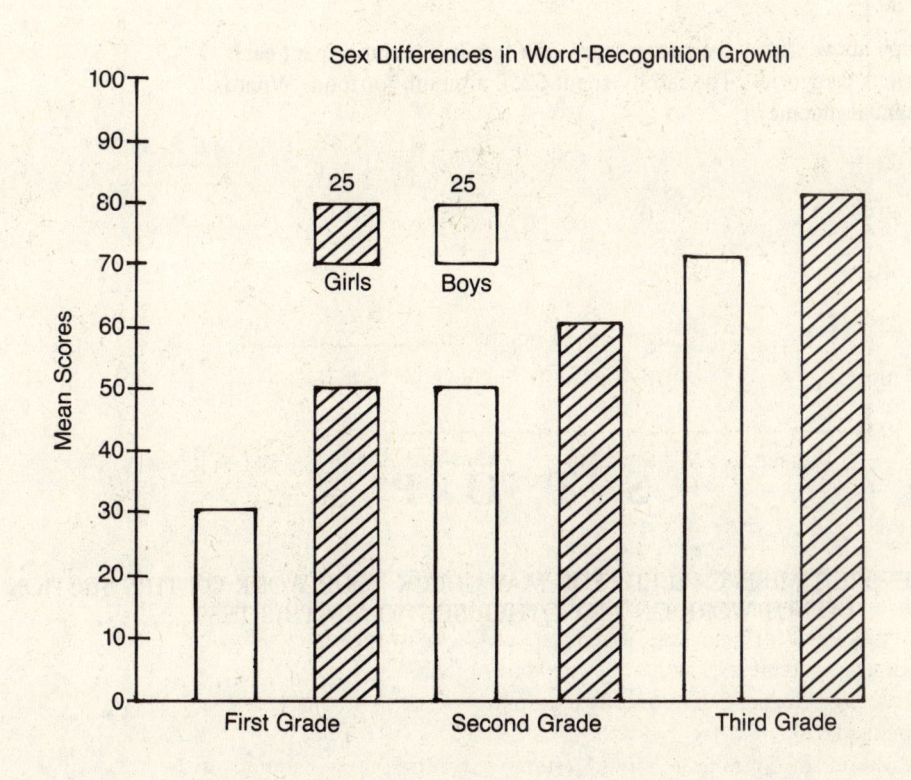

24. In Lawrence Elementary School 25 boys and 25 girls in reading classes were studied for 3 years to determine their growth in word-recognition skills. Which of the following results from the remedial classes is FALSE?
    (A) Girls outperformed boys in each grade.
    (B) Boys made equal gains between the first and second grades and the second and third grades.
    (C) Girls in the second and third grades outperformed the boys by 10 points.
    (D) Girls showed a greater mean score gain than boys for the three grades.
    (E) Boys more than doubled their scores during these three grades.

MODEL TEST 2

Annual Family Expenditure Chart

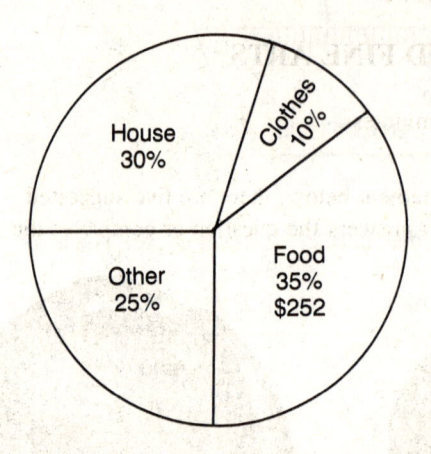

25. The circle graph above shows the percentages of a family's income spent each month for various categories. The family spent $252 a month for food. What is the family's annual income?
    (A) $5616
    (B) $6410
    (C) $7420
    (D) $8640
    (E) $9860

S T O P

IF YOU FINISH BEFORE TIME IS CALLED, YOU MAY CHECK YOUR WORK ON THIS SECTION ONLY.
DO NOT WORK ON ANY OTHER SECTION IN THIS TEST.

TEST OF GENERAL KNOWLEDGE

SECTION 3

LITERATURE AND FINE ARTS

Time — 30 minutes

Directions: For each question or incomplete statement below, there are five suggested answers or completions. Select the one that *best* answers the question or completes the statement.

The Metropolitan Museum of Art, gift of Edmund Kerper, 1952.

1. From the rough shape and the ornamentation of this object, dating from the fifth century B.C., one can assume that it was used in Athens as
   (A) a piece of jewelry
   (B) an amulet for good luck
   (C) a prize in the Olympics
   (D) a coin for exchange purposes
   (E) a utensil for some unknown purpose

Questions 2–3 refer to the following.

"The truth is," I said, "I promised to give them quilts to Maggie, for when she marries John Thomas."

She [Dee] gasped like a bee had stung her. "Maggie can't appreciate these quilts!" she said. "She'd probably be backward enough to put them to everyday use."

"I reckon she would," I said. "God knows I been saving 'em for long enough with nobody using 'em. I hope she will!" I didn't want to bring up how I had offered Dee a quilt when she went away to college. Then she had told me they were old-fashioned, out of style.

"But they're *priceless*!" she was saying now, furiously; for she has a temper. "Maggie would put them on the bed and in five years they'd be in rags. Less than that!"

"She can always make some more," I said. "Maggie knows how to quilt."

Alice Walker, "Everyday Use"*

* Excerpt from "Everyday Use," copyright © 1973 by Alice Walker. Reprinted from *In Love and Trouble* by permission of Harcourt Brace Jovanovich.

375

MODEL TEST 2

2. One function of dialog is to provide information essential to the plot. From the dialog above we learn all of the following EXCEPT
   (A) that Dee wants the quilts
   (B) that Dee speaks more correctly than her mother and is presumably better educated
   (C) that the mother has promised the quilts to Maggie
   (D) how Dee feels about her sister
   (E) why the mother promised to give the quilts to Maggie rather than to Dee

3. Another function of dialog is to reveal character. The dialog above shows the mother to be
   (A) vacillating
   (B) determined
   (C) conciliatory
   (D) short-tempered
   (E) slow-witted

4. The design of this painting on a Greek vase is most reminiscent of which one of the following?
   (A) a modern photograph
   (B) a contemporary advertisement
   (C) an aquarium
   (D) a planetarium
   (E) a terrarium

The Metropolitan Museum of Art

TEST OF GENERAL KNOWLEDGE

5. Which of the following best describes the picture above?
   (A) Breaking up the shapes of the figures and the background creates a dynamic pattern.
   (B) The subject matter suggests the figures may be sad beneath their jolly appearance.
   (C) The artist has conveyed great sympathy and pity.
   (D) The use of vertical lines unifies the scene.
   (E) Its theme is tense and highly dramatic.

Questions 6–8 are based on the following.

> You see me here, you gods, a poor old man,
> As full of grief as age; wretched in both:
> If it be you that stirs these daughters' hearts
> Against their father, fool me not so much
> To bear it tamely; touch me with noble anger,
> And let not women's weapons, water-drops,
> Stain my man's cheeks! No, you unnatural hags,
> I will have such revenges on you both
> That all the world shall—I will do such things—
> What they are, yet I know not, but they shall be
> The terrors of the earth. You think I'll weep;
> No, I'll not weep:
> I have full cause of weeping; but this heart
> Shall break into a hundred thousand flaws,
> Or ere I'll weep. O fool, I shall go mad!
>
>   William Shakespeare

6. This passage indicates that the theme of the play from which it is taken is
   (A) marital infidelity   (D) indecision
   (B) filial ingratitude   (E) jealousy
   (C) overriding ambition

MODEL TEST 2

7. The tone of the passage is best described as
   - (A) fearful
   - (B) angry
   - (C) piteous
   - (D) vacillating
   - (E) confused

8. All of the following statements are true in regard to the passage EXCEPT
   - (A) the subject of *fool* in line 4 and *touch* in line 5 is *you* (understood)
   - (B) "women's weapons" are tears
   - (C) the passage gains power from the repetition of *weep* in the last 5 lines
   - (D) the speaker, although upset, is fully in control of himself
   - (E) the word *flaws* in the next to the last line means "fragments"

Questions 9–10 refer to the following.

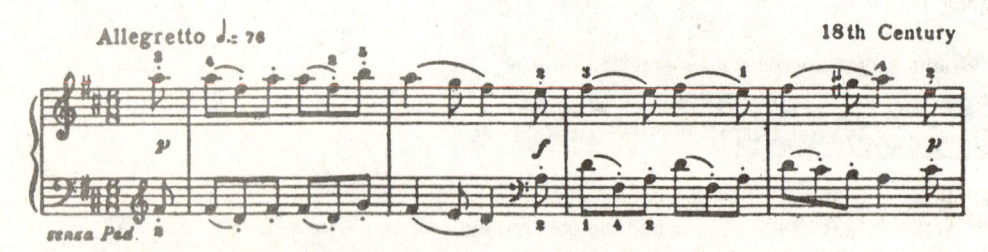

9. A pianist playing this composition will use how many beats to the measure?
   - (A) Eight
   - (B) Six
   - (C) Four
   - (D) Three
   - (E) Two

10. The composition should be played
    - (A) slowly
    - (B) very slowly
    - (C) at moderate tempo
    - (D) fairly fast
    - (E) loudly

The Metropolitan Museum of Art, Rogers Fund, 1907

11. On this vase, dating from about 455 B.C., one apple tree serves to represent a whole orchard. The reason is that
    - (A) there were not many apple trees in ancient Greece
    - (B) Greek artists found it difficult to paint trees

TEST OF GENERAL KNOWLEDGE

(C) the ancient Greeks did not like apples
(D) there was a belief that painting fruit trees on vases would result in a poor harvest the following year
(E) Greek artists preferred to paint people rather than landscapes

12. 'Well, mamma,' said she, when they were all returned to the breakfast room, 'and what do you think of my husband? Is not he a charming man? I am sure my sisters must all envy me. I only hope they may have half my good luck. They must all go to Brighton. That is the place to get husbands. What a pity it is, mamma, we did not all go.'

    The content of this passage suggests that it is taken from a novel by
    (A) Jane Austen
    (B) Alice Walker
    (C) Willa Cather
    (D) Virginia Woolf
    (E) Edna Ferber

13. Frank Lloyd Wright is best known for his contributions to
    (A) sculpture
    (B) literature
    (C) history
    (D) music
    (E) architecture

Questions 14–16 refer to the following.

For having lived in Westminster—how many years now? over twenty,—one feels even in the midst of the traffic, or waking at night, Clarissa was positive, a particular hush, or solemnity; an indescribable pause; a suspense (but that might be her heart, affected, they said, by influenza) before Big Ben strikes. There! Out it boomed. First a warning, musical; then the hour, irrevocable. The leaden circles dissolved in the air. Such fools we are, she thought, crossing Victoria Street. For Heaven only knows why one loves it so, how one sees it so, making it up, building it round one, tumbling it, creating it every moment afresh; but the veriest frumps, the most dejected of miseries sitting on doorsteps (drink their downfall) do the same; can't be dealt with, she felt positive, by Acts of Parliament for that very reason: they love life. In people's eyes, in the swing, tramp, and trudge; in the bellow and the uproar; the carriages, motor cars, omnibuses, vans, sandwich men shuffling and swinging; brass bands; barrel organs; in the triumph and the jingle and the strange high singing of some aeroplane overhead was what she loved; life; London; this moment of June.

Virginia Woolf, *Mrs. Dalloway**

14. This passage appeals primarily to the sense of
    (A) sight
    (B) hearing
    (C) taste
    (D) smell
    (E) touch

15. The chief emotion experienced by Clarissa as she crossed Victoria Street was
    (A) love of life
    (B) fear of the derelicts sitting on doorsteps
    (C) dislike of the "bellow and uproar"
    (D) pleasure at the "particular hush" that hung over London
    (E) unhappiness at being a fool

* Excerpt from Mrs. Dalloway by Virginia Woolf, copyright © 1928 by Harcourt Brace Jovanovich, Inc., renewed 1953 by Leonard Woolf. Reprinted by permission of the publisher.

16. One example of onomatopeia in the passage is the word
    (A) *dissolved*   (D) *boomed*
    (B) *tumbling*   (E) *crossing*
    (C) *dejected*

17. Which of the following descriptions best characterizes the building pictured above?
    (A) It shows an amalgam of architectural styles.
    (B) It possesses a quiet elegance.
    (C) It makes inspired use of a tight, awkward space.
    (D) It makes a bold, utilitarian statement.
    (E) It has a free and informal manner.

18. If they be two, they are two so
        As stiff twin compasses are two;
    Thy soul, the fixed foot, makes no show
        To move, but doth, if th'other do.

    This passage compares the two legs of a draftsman's compass to
    (A) two ice skaters twirling in a fixed pattern
    (B) two people working together smoothly on a project
    (C) the souls of twin sisters
    (D) the souls of two lovers moving in harmony and unison
    (E) a dance routine where one person's foot remains fixed on the floor

TEST OF GENERAL KNOWLEDGE

19. The dancers' big leaps suggest
    (A) lightness and ebullience
    (B) acrobatic daring
    (C) exuberant fantasy
    (D) tradition and heritage
    (E) delicate gracefulness

20. This sixteenth-century German woodcut derives much of its effect from the artist's utilization of
    (A) religious subject matter
    (B) vivid colors
    (C) light and shadow
    (D) imagination and fantasy
    (E) unity of figures and movement

The Metropolitan Museum of Art

381

MODEL TEST 2

21. A thin, acrid pall as of the tomb seemed to lie everywhere upon the room decked and furnished as for a bridal: upon the valance curtains of faded rose color, upon the rose-shaded lights, upon the dressing table, upon the delicate array of crystal and the man's toilet things backed with tarnished silver, silver so tarnished that the monogram was obscured.

    Overall, the setting conveys the impression of
    (A) femininity
    (B) wealth and beauty
    (C) caring and hope
    (D) lightness and delicacy
    (E) disappointment and decay

Adams National Historical Site

22. A characteristic feature of seventeenth-century American portrait art, as shown in this painting known as *Alice Mason*, is that
    (A) the child looks relaxed and at ease
    (B) the child is dressed as an adult
    (C) the hands are particularly well drawn
    (D) the anatomical elements are well proportioned
    (E) there is an excellent use of light and shadow

382

TEST OF GENERAL KNOWLEDGE

WYETH, Andrew. *Christina's World*. (1948) Tempera on gesso panel, 32¼ × 47¾ inches. Collection of the Museum of Modern Art, New York. Purchase.

23. The dominant impression conveyed by Andrew Wyeth's *Christina's World*, shown above, is one of
    - (A) simplicity
    - (B) joy in nature
    - (C) struggle
    - (D) poverty
    - (E) entrapment

24. The background design and the dancer's posture and costume in the example above combine to evoke
    - (A) a thoroughly idealized Romantic portrait
    - (B) great energy and control
    - (C) a return to the ridigity of the Neoclassical style
    - (D) an electrifying stage personality
    - (E) prodigious speed

The Metropolitan Museum of Art

25. All of the following statements are true of this photograph of the Temple of Horus at Edfu (237–257 B.C.) EXCEPT
    (A) the photograph was taken by an observer flying over the temple
    (B) the entrance is through the gateway
    (C) the most striking feature is the two flat towers
    (D) an open court connects the towers and the porch
    (E) the composition has unity

Questions 26–27 refer to the following.

(1) What happens to a dream deferred?
(2) Does it dry up
(3) Like a raisin in the sun?
(4) Or fester like a sore—
(5) And then run?
(6) Does it stink like rotten meat?
(7) Or crust and sugar over—
(8) Like a syrupy sweet?
(9) Maybe it just sags
(10) Like a heavy load.
(11) *Or does it explode?*   Langston Hughes, "Dream Deferred"

26. The message expressed by the poem is developed through the use of
    (A) personification   (D) onomatopoeia
    (B) simile   (E) hyperbole
    (C) alliteration

27. Which one of the following statements about the poem is NOT true?
    (A) It begins and ends with a question.
    (B) The general tone is one of hope and expectation of improvement.
    (C) Each of the images in lines 2–10 produces a different impact.
    (D) The message is timeless in that it can be applied to any oppressed race, culture, or nation.
    (E) The poem ends with a warning.

TEST OF GENERAL KNOWLEDGE

Questions 28–30 refer to the following.

(A)

Courtesy of Prado, Madrid

(B)

The Metropolitan Museum of Art, bequest of Joseph Pulitzer, 1933.

385

(C)

(D)

The Metropolitan Museum of Art, Gift of Junius S. Morgan, 1919.

(E)

The Museum of Modern Art, Gift of Mrs. Simon Guggenheim.

28. In which does the facial expression most clearly evoke the subject's personality?

29. In which does the flat, decorative treatment have a direct, childlike quality?

30. In which is an atmosphere of dream and fantasy created in part by the bright edges of light surrounding each important form?

TEST OF GENERAL KNOWLEDGE

31. One of the functions served by the costumes, the poses of the dancers, and the stage setting pictured above is to
    (A) suggest the joyfulness of pioneers settling in the West
    (B) divide the characters into evenly spaced, parallel groups
    (C) block groups of characters from interacting
    (D) fashion a cheerful backdrop to counterbalance the bleak dress
    (E) suggest a religious ritual practiced in colonial America

Questions 32–34 are based on the passages below.

(A) Robert did not come that day. She was keenly disappointed. He did not come the following day, nor the next. Each morning she awoke with hope, and each night she was prey to despondency. She was tempted to seek him out. But far from yielding to the impulse, she avoided any occasion which might throw her in his way.

(B) "No, it's my dad who's the doctor."
"You should read a book about it."
Wilhelm said, "But this means that the world is full of murderers. So it's not the world."

(C) In English writing we seldom speak of tradition, though we occasionally apply its name in deploring its absence. We cannot refer to "the tradition" or to "a tradition"; at most, we employ the adjective in saying that the poetry of So-and-So is "traditional" or even "too traditional."

(D) "Likely hit ain't fitten for hawgs," one of the sisters said. "Nevertheless, fit it will and you'll hog it and like it," his father said. "Get out of them chairs and help your Ma unload."

(E) The young girl seemed to be the very ideal of that pure good woman to whom every young man dreams of entrusting his future. All who knew her kept saying, "The man who gets her will be lucky. No one could find a nicer girl than that."

32. Which provides the most detailed description of a character's emotional response to disappointment?

33. Which uses dialect to establish setting?

34. Which suggests a gap between appearance and reality?

35. Which of the following design elements suggests the building pictured above was designed as a fort?
    (A) the gabled parapet and blind entrance
    (B) the strategically placed trees and shrubbery
    (C) the dormer built at right angles to the street
    (D) the sharply arched doorway
    (E) the elegant central tower

S T O P

**IF YOU FINISH BEFORE TIME IS CALLED, YOU MAY CHECK YOUR WORK ON THIS SECTION ONLY.
DO NOT WORK ON ANY OTHER SECTION IN THIS TEST.**

TEST OF GENERAL KNOWLEDGE

SECTION 4

SCIENCE

Time — 30 minutes

Directions: For each question or incomplete statement below there are five suggested answers or completions. Select the one that *best* answers the question.

1. Machines are used to
    (A) do a job using less work
    (B) make it easier to do the same amount of work
    (C) increase the amount of power being used
    (D) conserve energy
    (E) reduce the friction in a system

2. Which sequence best illustrates a food chain?
    (A) Fish, frog, larvae, algae
    (B) Trees, deer, rabbit, lion
    (C) Grasses, grasshopper, lizard, hawk
    (D) Grasses, mouse, lion, shrew
    (E) Rabbit, hawk, fox, tree

3. For the most part, plant and animal cells perform the same essential functions. Which of the following is an exception to this statement?
    (A) Absorption
    (B) Photosynthesis
    (C) Excretion
    (D) Respiration
    (E) Reproduction

4. A fossil is the remains of a living thing that existed long ago. All of the following are fossil fuels EXCEPT
    (A) oil
    (B) coal
    (C) uranium
    (D) lignite
    (E) natural gas

5. Which of the following is NOT considered a renewable natural resource?
    (A) soil
    (B) coal
    (C) air
    (D) forests
    (E) water

6. The flash of lightning is seen before the thunder is heard because
    (A) light travels faster than sound
    (B) the lightning and the thunder are not produced at the same time
    (C) eyes are more sensitive than ears
    (D) sound travels better in solids than in air
    (E) sounds do not travel in a vacuum

7. To extinguish a fire in a pan of burning fat, one would place a cover over the pan to
    (A) add oxygen
    (B) cut off oxygen
    (C) raise the kindling temperature
    (D) remove the fuel
    (E) remove carbon dioxide

8. The program that is a combined effort of the United States and some foreign countries to conduct scientific experiments in space is
    (A) Sputnik
    (B) Apollo
    (C) Mercury
    (D) Soyuz
    (E) the Space Shuttle

MODEL TEST 2

9. The list below contains four changes that can take place in materials:
   - I. A dish breaks
   - II. Water boils
   - III. A light bulb is turned on
   - IV. Paper burns

   Which of these is (are) chemical change(s)?
   - (A) II and IV only
   - (B) II and III only
   - (C) I only
   - (D) IV only
   - (E) I, II, III, and IV

10. Which one of the following is the primary reason why nutritionists advise against cooking vegetables too long? Overcooked vegetables
    - (A) look unappetizing
    - (B) lose much of their taste
    - (C) have a mushy texture
    - (D) lose their vitamin C
    - (E) lose their phosphorus and zinc

11. The chemical changes taking place inside cells are most directly controlled by
    - (A) the cell membrane
    - (B) the genes
    - (C) the nucleus
    - (D) enzymes
    - (E) ribosomes

12.

Wind Chill Table

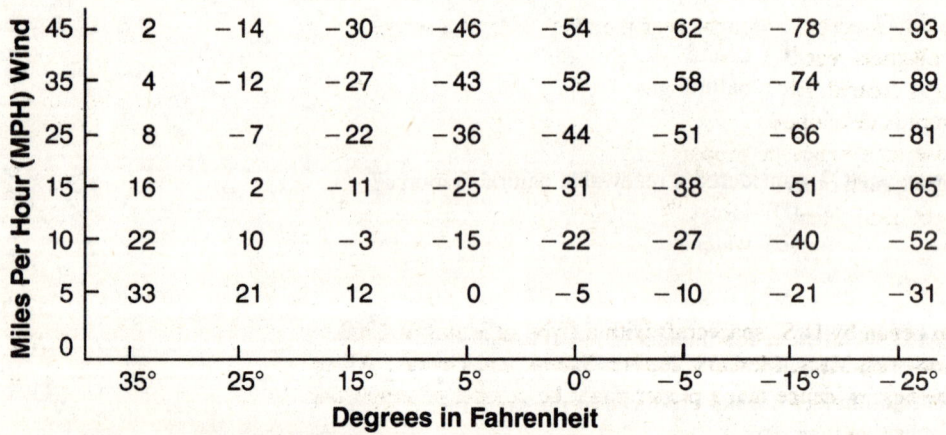

Miles Per Hour (MPH) Wind	35°	25°	15°	5°	0°	−5°	−15°	−25°
45	2	−14	−30	−46	−54	−62	−78	−93
35	4	−12	−27	−43	−52	−58	−74	−89
25	8	−7	−22	−36	−44	−51	−66	−81
15	16	2	−11	−25	−31	−38	−51	−65
10	22	10	−3	−15	−22	−27	−40	−52
5	33	21	12	0	−5	−10	−21	−31

Degrees in Fahrenheit

Source: U.S. Weather Service

The effect of cold weather on the human body due to loss of warmth may lead to increased health risks. In the Wind Chill table, note the difference between the actual temperature and the wind chill temperature with its variable miles per hour (MPH) wind. Which one of the following statements is false?

- (A) At 25°F, a 10 MPH wind lowers the effective temperature by 15°F
- (B) A 5 MPH wind produces a larger drop in effective temperature at lower actual temperatures
- (C) Effective temperature is the same at 25°F and a wind of 15 MPH as at 35°F with a 45 MPH wind
- (D) A 35 MPH wind makes 25°F feel colder than 0°F with no wind
- (E) A 45 MPH wind makes 0°F feel like −62°F

TEST OF GENERAL KNOWLEDGE

13. A steel bridge may sag in the summer because
    - (A) steel becomes brittle in summer
    - (B) metals expand when heated
    - (C) winter temperatures keep steel rigid
    - (D) metals contract when heated
    - (E) there is more traffic in the summer

14. Each of the following consists of the scientific names of two kinds of birds. According to the binomial system of classification, in which pair are the two birds most closely related?
    - (A) *Spizella pusilla* and *Sitta pusilla*
    - (B) *Puffinus puffinus* and *Puffinus gravis*
    - (C) *Parus carolinensis* and *Parula americana*
    - (D) *Icteria virens* and *Icterus spurius*
    - (E) *Canachites canadensis* and *Grus canadensis*

15. If a green plant opens its stomata when the sun is shining, it can photosynthesize. However, it also suffers from loss of
    - (A) water
    - (B) carbon dioxide
    - (C) glucose
    - (D) nitrogen
    - (E) oxygen

16. When the north pole of a magnet is brought near the south pole of a second magnet, how do the magnets react?
    - (A) Static electricity is created.
    - (B) An electric current is developed.
    - (C) Both magnets lose their magnetic properties.
    - (D) The magnets attract each other.
    - (E) The magnets repel each other.

17. Planetary exploration began by U.S. spacecraft with a flyby of Venus in 1962, followed by encounters with Mars, Mercury, Jupiter, Saturn, and Uranus. Which of the following is the best evidence that a planet might be capable of supporting some form of life?
    - (A) Venus has a surface temperature of 869°F which is evenly distributed.
    - (B) A day on Mars is similar in length to that on Earth, 23 hours 56 minutes compared to 24 hours and 37 minutes on Mars.
    - (C) Erosion on Mars shows that there has been liquid water there.
    - (D) Pluto is made of frozen methane and water.
    - (E) The surface temperature of Saturn is about $-288°F$.

18. A possible explanation for an event or a phenomenon is called a(n)
    - (A) hypothesis
    - (B) experiment
    - (C) conclusion
    - (D) control
    - (E) observation

MODEL TEST 2

19. Industrial waste water dumped into rivers and lakes may result in thermal pollution, which includes
    (A) decrease in water temperature, growth of algae, increase in oxygen, loss of aquatic life
    (B) decrease in water temperature, decrease of algae, increase of oxygen, rise of aquatic life
    (C) increase in water temperature, decrease of algae, decrease in oxygen, rise of aquatic life
    (D) increase in water temperature, growth of algae, decrease in oxygen, loss of aquatic life
    (E) increase in water temperature, growth of algae, increase in oxygen, rise of aquatic life

20. In the last 250 million years the land areas of the Earth have been dominated, in turn, by three different classes of vertebrates. In what order did the three classes achieve dominance?
    (A) Reptiles, mammals, amphibians
    (B) Birds, mammals, amphibians
    (C) Amphibians, reptiles, mammals
    (D) Mammals, amphibians, birds
    (E) Amphibians, mammals, reptiles

21. The following effects depend on the relationship of the Earth to the sun:
    I. The change of seasons
    II. Differing length of daylight throughout the year
    III. Differing level of insulation throughout the year

    Which of these effects depends on the fact that the Earth's orbit is tilted at an angle of $23\frac{1}{2}°$ with respect to the plane of its orbit?
    (A) I only
    (B) II only
    (C) I and II only
    (D) I, II and III
    (E) II and III only

22. The smallest particle of an element is its
    (A) nucleus
    (B) ion
    (C) formula
    (D) molecule
    (E) atom

23. A number of morbid conditions may have been associated with cigarette smoking:
    I. coronary disease
    II. cirrhosis of the liver
    III. emphysema
    IV. lung cancer
    V. severe depression

392

TEST OF GENERAL KNOWLEDGE

Which of these are now known to result from smoking?
(A) I and II only
(B) II and IV only
(C) I, III, and IV only
(D) II, IV, and V only
(E) I and V only

24. The water cycle includes all of the following EXCEPT
(A) precipitation
(B) condensation
(C) clouds
(D) air pressure
(E) evaporation

25. Igneous rock is produced by
(A) consolidation of sediments
(B) volcanoes only
(C) pressure from earthquakes
(D) solidification of magma and lava
(E) chemical deposition from water

26. Which of the following statements about energy is NOT correct?
(A) It can be measured by the work done by a system.
(B) It cannot be made.
(C) It can be converted from one form to another.
(D) It is produced from nothing by a generator.
(E) It can be changed into more useful forms.

27. The science class wants to measure wind velocity on a daily basis. Which one of the following instruments should be used?
(A) anemometer
(B) barometer
(C) hygrometer
(D) thermometer
(E) psychrometer

28. The air we breathe consists of several gases. The order, from most to least abundant, of the following three gases is
(A) nitrogen, carbon dioxide, oxygen
(B) oxygen, nitrogen, carbon dioxide
(C) oxygen, carbon dioxide, nitrogen
(D) nitrogen, oxygen, carbon dioxide
(E) carbon dioxide, oxygen, nitrogen

29. In his theory of natural selection, Charles Darwin set out to explain
(A) how we inherit eye color from our parents
(B) the relationship between fossils of extinct organisms and living plants and animals
(C) how our environment has undergone changes
(D) how invertebrates differ from vertebrates
(E) why the forms of life change over long periods of time

30. Some birds will build nests characteristic of their species even if they have never seen one. This kind of behavior is classified as a(n)
    (A) conditioned reflex
    (B) instinct
    (C) taxis
    (D) acquired learning skill
    (E) conditioned response

S T O P

IF YOU FINISH BEFORE TIME IS CALLED, YOU MAY CHECK YOUR WORK ON THIS SECTION ONLY. DO NOT WORK ON ANY OTHER SECTION IN THIS TEST.

TEST OF GENERAL KNOWLEDGE

Answer Keys and Explanations — Test of General Knowledge

SOCIAL STUDIES

Answer Key

1.	B	7.	B	13.	A	19.	C	25.	D
2.	D	8.	E	14.	A	20.	C	26.	C
3.	A	9.	A	15.	C	21.	C	27.	D
4.	E	10.	B	16.	C	22.	E	28.	B
5.	C	11.	C	17.	E	23.	E	29.	B
6.	B	12.	D	18.	B	24.	A	30.	D

Explanations

1. **(B)** Louisiana Purchase: 1803; Monroe Doctrine: 1823; Mexican War: 1846–1848; assassination of Lincoln: 1865.

2. **(D)** The first purpose of the Israeli occupation of the Golan Heights was to protect the people living below in the valley. In September, 1967, Prime Minister Eshkol announced plans to establish settlements in the Golan Heights.

3. **(A)** The 1980 U.S. census revealed a national growth rate of 11.4% during the 1970s; however, the Hispanic growth rate was 61%.

4. **(E)** The Nile (E) is 4145 miles long; the Amazon, 4000; the Congo, 2900; the Mississippi, 2348; the Danube, 1776.

5. **(C)** III is incorrect because the total growth was 470 million; during the previous period (1800–1850), the increase was 220 million. IV is also incorrect. The total population growth during 1950–1970 was 1.06 billion compared to a growth of 3 billion for the period from 1900–1982.

6. **(B)** Human societies have common goals, traditions, and customs (A). Systems of rewards and punishments (C) are used to enforce customs, religious values, and social organization (D). Such attitudes and traditions are passed from one generation to another through learning and experiences, not by inheritance (B).

7. **(B)** The alleged common interest of the people in a community with business is a device to persuade the public at large that prosperity depends on business, as it does to some extent. The same, however, is claimed by labor unions, agriculture, and teacher's organizations, and thus the illusion is created that each group is fighting for the interests of all. In (C), the real identity of a group is disguised by ambiguity to conceal its real purpose. Terms such as *communism, socialism, bureaucracy,* and *collectivism* are used by an opposition that offers its own "integrity," "morality," and "the American way" to gain emotional support (A). The red-herring technique (D) is used as a scare tactic to divert public attention from the real issues involved.

395

8. **(E)** The refusal of the United States to join the League of Nations after World War I marked its temporary withdrawal from active involvement in world affairs.

9. **(A)** The central theme of this passage is that religion has and will have an important role.

10. **(B)** If Bible sales decreased that might indicate a lessening interest in religion, which would contradict the central theme of the passage.

11. **(C)** The purpose of the Common Market is to work cooperatively among the member European nations for agreement on tariffs, the movement of labor and capital, and eventual economic and political union. Associate members have been accepted, including some African nations. (A), (B), (D), and (E) are worldwide involvements.

12. **(D)** Cultural geography is concerned with the phenomena and effects of human occupation of the earth. The other choices (A, B, C, E) are natural features of the region.

13. **(A)** In the game of life, people who move up or down have vertical mobility; people who move across the same plane have horizontal mobility.

14. **(A)** For example, this was true of Benito Mussolini in Italy before World War II.

15. **(C)** In 1974 Gerald Ford became President when Richard Nixon resigned because of the Watergate scandal.

16. **(C)** The U.S. is concerned about the influence of the Soviet Union in the Western Hemisphere. Soviet influence is increasing in Cuba and Nicaragua.

17. **(E)** In a financial crisis all of the other measures (A–D), however undesirable, could be taken. To default on interest payments would destroy the financial creditability of the government.

18. **(B)** Locke, the founder of British empiricism, is best known for his political theory, including the system of checks and balances. He also held that under some circumstances revolution is not only a right but also an obligation.

19. **(C)** In *Das Kapital*, Karl Marx stated that in capitalism the small ruling class exploits the laborer—the working class; Marx's goal was a classless society: from each according to his ability, to each according to his needs.

20. **(C)** The balance of power, through competition in arms, implies that the resources of two or more states for war are equal. When such a balance exists, neither power can hope to win and peace is preserved.

21. **(C)** The president cannot implement a treaty without the approval and ratification of the U.S. Senate.

22. **(E)** President Reagan appointed the first woman to serve as a Justice of the Supreme Court, Sandra Day O'Connor.

TEST OF GENERAL KNOWLEDGE

23. **(E)** For many years the domestic steel industry, unlike its foreign competitors, clung to outmoded, inefficient methods and procedures. Recently the president of the American Institute for Imported Steel (the United Steelworkers of America want a global quota on imported steel) charged that America producers "neglected to restructure their plants, modernize equipment, and contain employment costs." In arguing for the imposition of a 15 percent quota on imported steel, the chairman of Bethlehem Steel said, "With relief, the domestic industry will be fully competitive in five years. Without relief, the industry will be denied the cash flow to finance the modernization recognized by all as needed."

24. **(A)** In arbitration, a third party decides the issue and his or her decision must be accepted; in mediation, the two parties compromise the issue.

25. **(D)** Geographical determinism is based on diffusion of geographical influences and cultural contacts, which produce conditions that mold some human characteristics.

26. **(C)** An economic good is consumable.

27. **(D)** The command economic system is characteristic of communist countries.

28. **(B)** The implication that an Italian is always joking and is not to be taken seriously represents an ethnic stereotype. A racial slur (A) is more clearly derogatory. Choices (C) and (D) denote extreme nationalism and belligerence, and the example given is clearly not objective reporting (E).

29. **(B)** In 1979, 63 Americans were taken hostage at the American embassy in Teheran, Iran.

30. **(D)** Indira Gandhi took office as the prime minister of India for the second time in 1980.

MATHEMATICS

Answer Key

1.	B	6.	D	11.	B	16.	C	21.	C
2.	B	7.	D	12.	B	17.	C	22.	E
3.	C	8.	C	13.	D	18.	E	23.	C
4.	D	9.	A	14.	A	19.	E	24.	D
5.	E	10.	A	15.	A	20.	C	25.	D

Explanations

1. **(B)** Percents are based upon 100 percent. When a percent is changed to a decimal, it represents a relationship to 100. Therefore 5 percent is equal to 0.05.

397

MODEL TEST 2

2. **(B)** Step 1. Think of sea level as 0 on the scale; then Death Valley will be 280 feet below that point. The elevation of Mt. McKinley will be 20,320 feet above point 0.

$$280 - 0 + 20{,}320 \text{ feet}$$

Step 2. Add the two figures: 280 + 20,320 feet = 20,600 feet, which is more than 20,500 feet (B).

3. **(C)** Step 1. Obtain the weight of the payload for the new rocket in pounds: 5 × 2000 = 10,000 pounds. The old rocket moved ¾ × 2000 = 1500 pounds.
Step 2. Divide 1500 (old payload) into 10,000 (new payload) = 6.66.
Step 3. Round to highest number (a partial rocket cannot be used). The answer is 7 (C).

4. **(D)** These equations and inequalities are all correct except (D). If 4 is less than 6, then 3, the number below 4, also is less than 6.

5. **(E)** To find the loss subtract the 1980 population from the 1960 population: 3000 − 2000 = 1000. The ratio is 1000 over 3000:

$$\frac{1000}{3000} = \frac{1}{3}$$

or a ratio of 1 to 3 (E).

6. **(D)** In scientific notation a large number is written as a factor between 0 and 10 multiplied by a power of 10. For example 37,000,000 is $3.7(10)^7$ and 180,000,000 is $1.8(10)^8$.
For 2500 the factor between 0 and 10 is 2.5, which must be multiplied by 1000 (or 10^3) to make it equal 2500. Therefore $2500 = 2.5 \times 10^3$, and (D) is the correct answer.

7. **(D)** To be congruent two figures have to be exactly the same in shape and size, so that one can be superimposed on the other. Choices (A), (B), (C), and (E) show congruent figures. The circles in (D) are of different sizes; therefore they are not congruent.

8. **(C)** To determine the areas of the figures, multiply length by width: for I, 16 × 1 = 16; for II, 2 × 8 = 16; for III, 4 × 4 = 16. All the figures have the same area (C), although they have different dimensions.

9. **(A)** The square root of 100 = 10 (10 times 10 equals 100), and 10 is between 5 and 15 (A).

10. **(A)** We are given that $y = xz$. To get an expression for z alone, divide both sides of this equation by x:

$$\frac{y}{x} = \frac{xz}{x} \quad \text{or} \quad \frac{y}{x} = z.$$

This is equivalent to $y \div x$, which is (A), the correct answer.

398

TEST OF GENERAL KNOWLEDGE

11. **(B)** Step 1. Multiply 20 rods × 16.5 feet to convert all the measurements into feet: 20 × 16.5 = 330. Add the other 14 feet: 330 + 14 = 344 feet.
    Step 2. Multiply 344 feet × 3 for three strands of wire: 344 × 3 = 1032 feet of wire (B).

12. **(B)** Since there are no 8ths between $\frac{3}{8}$ and $\frac{1}{2}$, we need to change these numbers to 16ths.
    Step 1. Multiply $\frac{3}{8}$ and $\frac{1}{2}$ by 2, obtaining $\frac{6}{16}$ and $\frac{8}{16}$.
    Step 2. Choose the only answer that lies between $\frac{6}{16}$ and $\frac{8}{16}$, that is, $\frac{7}{16}$ (B).

13. **(D)** Let x represent the original amount of money. Then
    $$\frac{x}{4} = \$3.50$$
    $$x = 4 \times \$3.50$$
    $$x = \$14.00 \text{ (D)}$$

14. **(A)** 1 lb. = 0.45 kg. Therefore, 2 lb. = 2 (0.45) kg, 3 lb. = 3 (0.45) kg, etc. Hence, we multiply the number of pounds by 0.45 to obtain the number of kilograms (A). The fact that a kilogram = 1000 grams is extraneous information.

15. **(A)** Step 1. Multiply to find h^2: 20 × 20 = 400.
    Step 2. Multiply to find b^2: 8 × 8 = 64.
    Step 3. Subtract: 400 − 64 = 336.
    Step 4. Multiply to find $2h$: 20 × 2 = 40.
    Step 5. Divide 40 into 336: 336 ÷ 40 = 8.4. This equals the unknown side of the triangle. The cut should be made 8.4 feet from the ground (A).

16. **(C)** The probability that an event will occur is the ratio of the number of favorable outcomes to the total possible number of outcomes. If there are 3 favorable outcomes out of a total possible number of 5 outcomes, then there must be 2 unfavorable outcomes out of the total of 5. Thus the probability of the event not occurring is $\frac{2}{5}$ (C).

17. **(C)** Let x = Marge's age now. Then $x + 14$ will represent her age in 14 years. Also, 2 years more than twice her present age can be represented by $2x + 2$. The equation is
    $$2x + 2 = x + 14$$
    $$2x - x = 14 - 2$$
    $$x = 12$$

18. **(E)** Since a circle graph must represent a total of 100 percent, we need to find how much of this total is missing.
    Step 1. Add the percentages that are given: 15 + 30 + 20 + 10 = 75%.
    Step 2. Subtract 75% from 100%: 100 − 75 = 25% (E).

19. **(E)** To solve this problem visually, inspect both the horizontal and vertical bar heights and note carefully which symbol is used for boys and which for girls.

399

MODEL TEST 2

Choices (A), (B), (C), and (D) are correct, as can be determined by inspection. The ratio in (E) is incorrect; for every 2 girls choosing burgers, 5 boys chose them, a ratio of 2:5.

20. **(C)** Choices (A), (B), (D), and (E) are correct, as can be determined by inspection. Choice (C) is incorrect because the median rate is not the same for the two banks.
Bank A had these interest rates: 12%, 13%, <u>14%</u>, 14%, 21%.
Bank B had these interest rates: 11%, 12%, <u>16%</u>, 18%, 21%.
The median is the midvalue; for Bank A it is 14; for Bank B, 16.

21. **(C)** $1\frac{1}{2}$ ounces $= \frac{3}{2}$ ounces. If $\frac{3}{2}$ ounces are used for 3 pints, then $\frac{1}{2}$ ounce is used for 1 pint. There are 2 pints in 1 quart, therefore, there are 4x2 or 8 pints in 4 quarts. For 8 pints, we need $8 \times \frac{1}{2}$ or 4 ounces of plant food (C). We can also solve by letting $x =$ the number of ounces for 8 pints and writing a proportion:

$$\frac{x}{8} = \frac{\frac{3}{2}}{3}$$
$$3x = 8(\tfrac{3}{2})$$
$$3x = 12$$
$$x = 4$$

22. **(E)** Since scores increase under both computer use and traditional methods, both are effective — choice (A). Computer use results in higher final scores, so the use of the computer is more effective for the whole term — choice (B). The graph shows the computer results to be 10 points ahead of the traditional at both the midterm and final tests — choice (C). The steeper slope of the computer line up to the midterm tests indicates its superiority in the first half of the term; it rises at the same slope as the traditional line in the last half of the term, indicating that it is equally effective (but not better) during that period — choice (D). Choice (E) is false since we have no way of knowing whether the larger number of questions correctly answered by the computer group on the final test included the more difficult questions or whether the two groups were able to answer *different types* of questions.

23. **(C)** Since 100 centimeters equal 1 meter and 1000 millimeters equal 1 meter, there are 10 millimeters in a centimeter. Each of the 10 divisions between centimeters on the scale represents 1 millimeter. Therefore, the arrow points to a reading of 13 millimeters, abbreviated as 13 mm (C).

24. **(D)** Boys had a mean score gain of 40; girls, of 30. Therefore choice (D) is false.

25. **(D)** Let $x =$ the family's monthly income.
Then $0.35x = 252$.
Multiply each side of the equation by 100 to clear fractions: $35x = 25{,}200$.
Divide each side by 35:
$$\frac{35x}{35} = \frac{25{,}200}{35}$$
$$x = 720$$

If the monthly income is $720, then the annual income is 12 x $720 or $8640, which is choice (D).

400

TEST OF GENERAL KNOWLEDGE

LITERATURE AND FINE ARTS

Answer Key

1.	D	8.	D	15.	A	22.	B	29.	B
2.	E	9.	B	16.	D	23.	E	30.	E
3.	B	10.	D	17.	B	24.	A	31.	A
4.	C	11.	E	18.	D	25.	A	32.	A
5.	A	12.	A	19.	A	26.	B	33.	D
6.	B	13.	E	20.	E	27.	B	34.	E
7.	B	14.	B	21.	E	28.	C	35.	A

Explanations

1. **(D)** This is an Athenian drachma and typically has the head of Athena on one side, and her sacred owl and the first letters of the name Athens on the other.

2. **(E)** Choices (A) and (C) are obvious. In regard to (B) note "them quilts" and "'em" (the mother) versus "these quilts" and "them" (Dee). As for (D), "Maggie can't appreciate the quilts" and "She'd . . . be backward enough . . . ."

3. **(B)** The mother is not vacillating (A); her mind is clearly made up. In her conversation with Dee she is matter of fact, neither conciliatory (C) nor short-tempered (D). Her final response to Dee rules out the possibility that she is slow-witted (E).

4. **(C)** This painting is most like an aquarium because it is possible to see what is happening under water.

5. **(A)** The division of the background and figures into geometric shapes creates an active and compelling pattern. (B) is incorrect because there is nothing to suggest the figures in the picture are jolly, while (C) errs by attributing emotion not present in the picture. There are no vertical lines that unify the scene, eliminating (D), and the picture is neither tense nor dramatic in theme, only in treatment.

6. **(B)** Note lines 3 and 4 and "you unnatural hags."

7. **(B)** There are some piteous elements—"a poor old man, as full of grief as age; wretched in both"—but the overriding impression is one of anger.

8. **(D)** The last exclamation ("O fool, I shall go mad!") shows that the speaker is so torn by anger and grief that he has nearly lost all self-control. In regard to (E) the modern meaning of *flaws* ("defects") would make no sense here; the word has the archaic meaning given.

9. **(B)** There are six beats to the measure.

10. **(D)** *Allegretto* indicates that the piece is to be played more rapidly than *andante*, but more slowly than *allegro*.

MODEL TEST 2

11. **(E)** In general, Greek painters and sculptors preferred to portray human beings and gods and goddesses. They studied anatomy and proportion, as well as optics and the laws of motion and perspective.

12. **(A)** The passage, from Jane Austen's *Pride and Prejudice*, reflects the relief of the nineteenth-century English woman who had found a suitable husband and thus avoided the emotional, social, and often financial onus of spinsterhood.

13. **(E)** Frank Lloyd Wright, pre-eminent in American architecture, stressed harmony of a structure with its environment. Two of his innovations were the use of concrete as a building material and the fusion of interior and exterior space.

14. **(B)** Notice all the words that appeal to hearing, for example, *hush, boomed, musical, tramp, trudge, bellow, uproar, shuffling, bands, organs, jingle, singing*.

15. **(A)** Note particularly the last sentence: "what she loved; life, London, this moment of June."

16. **(D)** The sound of the word *boomed* conveys its meaning.

17. **(B)** The broad facade, evenly spaced windows, detailed moldings, and classic arches combine to suggest a quiet elegance. The styles are unified, eliminating (A); the structure occupies an enviable expanse of space (C). It is neither functional (D); nor informal (E).

18. **(D)** The final two lines reveal the poem concerns two lovers, their souls united as a compass' legs.

19. **(A)** Note how the dancers' wide arm motions combine with their leaps to suggest exhilaration. Although the leaps are high, they are not acrobatic (B). Do not confuse the dancers' costumes, which do suggest tradition and heritage (D); the question specified "big leaps," not costumes. While (C) is correct in "exuberant," there is nothing in the leap to suggest the second half of the choice, "fantasy." Finally, the leaps are too high and powerful to convey "delicate gracefulness," (E).

20. **(E)** The figures are lifting, placing, sawing, and hammering on various parts of a building that they are constructing. The unity comes from having the carpenters all engaged in their occupation and spaced throughout the woodcut. Color (B) and light and shadow (C) are not elements of a woodcut, and there is no religious subject matter (A) or imagination (D) in this portrayal of the construction of a building.

21. **(E)** The words and phrases "thin," "acrid pall as of the tomb," "faded," and "tarnished" give the impression of great disappointment and decay. There is evidence of wealth, but the beauty is long gone, eliminating choice (B). There is nothing hopeful about the current remains of the scene, although the room was obviously once decorated with a vision for the future. The *overall* impression is neither (D) lightness and delicacy nor (E) femininity.

TEST OF GENERAL KNOWLEDGE

22. **(B)** The fact that the child is dressed as an adult reflects a characteristic of colonial life: children were expected to take care of younger siblings and to help their parents in other ways as well. None of the other choices is true of this portrait or of colonial portraits in general.

23. **(E)** In this painting, one of the most famous of modern times, the viewer shares the crippled girl's feeling of being trapped in a world that ends at the boundaries of the isolated farm.

24. **(A)** The ballerina's apparent weightlessness combines with the shadowy flowers and hazy background to suggest a completely Romantic view of the ballerina. There is nothing in the ballerina's impossible pose to suggest (B) great energy and control, or (D) an electrifying stage personality. In the same way the portrait suggests weightlessness rather than speed, choice (E). Finally, choice (C), a rigid Neoclassic style, does not fit with the dreaminess of the picture.

25. **(A)** The photograph was taken from the ground.

26. **(B)** Lines 3–10 contain a series of similes.

27. **(B)** The general tone is one of disillusionment and bitterness.

28. **(C)** The facial characteristics reveal the nature of a great and powerful man. Note the intelligence, determination, and aggressiveness of a conqueror suggested by the way the sculptor modeled and stressed the various features. Note especially the deep lines around the forehead and around the mouth which show the effects of heavy responsibilities.

29. **(B)** Here we see Jonah who, after emerging from the body of the whale, is reaching for a garment that is being brought to him by a swiftly flying angel. The whale resembles the flat, decorative treatment accorded to Chinese or Japanese paper fish that we can buy in America today. There is a direct, childlike quality to the flatness and relatively simple figures.

30. **(E)** The bright edges of light, along with the two-dimensional objects, the bright surface of the mandolin, and the detailed texture of the lion's mane, create an atmosphere of dream and fantasy.

31. **(A)** The rough, open-framed structure combines with the exuberant dance and clearly nineteenth century costumes to suggest the happiness of establishing a shelter on the frontier.

32. **(A)** Only choice (A) gives a detailed description of a character's emotional response to disappointment, telling of hopes that by nightfall turn to despondency.

33. **(D)** Dialect is a regional variety of language distinguished by vocabulary, grammar, and pronunciation. Here, the author indicates pronunciation by spelling: "hit" for "it," "hawgs" for "hogs." The dialect indicates the story is set in the South.

MODEL TEST 2

34. **(E)** The word "seems" indicates that there is a gap between what the young woman appears to be and what she actually is.

35. **(A)** Both the gabled parapet (the elevated wall) and the blind entrance are designs especially effective in repelling attackers and thus would be suitable for use on a fort. There is nothing in the sparsely planted trees to suggest they would effectively repel an attack (B). There is no dormer (B). The doorway is not *sharply* arched. The central tower is functional, not elegant (E).

SCIENCE

Answer Key

1. B	7. B	13. B	19. D	25. D
2. C	8. E	14. B	20. C	26. D
3. B	9. D	15. A	21. D	27. A
4. C	10. D	16. D	22. E	28. D
5. B	11. D	17. C	23. C	29. E
6. A	12. E	18. A	24. D	30. B

Explanations

1. **(B)** In any machine, less work is gotten out than is put in, because of friction and other losses. The work may be easier to do, however, because the machine can make it possible to do it with a smaller force, exerting the force over a greater distance. The reverse is also possible.

2. **(C)** The producer in a food chain is a green plant. A herbivore, or plant-eater, is the first-order consumer—the grasshopper in (C) answer. A carnivore, or flesh-eater, becomes the second-order consumer (the lizard). Other carnivores (the hawk) will feed on the second-order carnivores.

3. **(B)** Only plants cells, not animal cells, carry on photosynthesis, whereby carbohydrates are manufactured from carbon dioxide in the presence of light.

4. **(C)** Fossil fuels, such as (A), (B), (D), and (E), are formed from the remains of animals and plants that lived many millions of years ago. Plant matter was compressed to coal (B), while both plant and animal remains were changed by pressure to form oil and natural gas (E). Lignite (D) is an intermediate stage between peat and soft coal. Uranium (C) is a radioactive element.

5. **(B)** With proper replanting (by nature or by people) forests (D) can be considered one of our valuable renewable natural resources. Crop rotation and fertilization both help to replace the soil (A) used by plants, so soil too is a renewable resource. Through the water cycle, water (E) is returned to the Earth for renewed use. Although we are continuously adding pollutants to the air (C), the Earth's wind patterns are helpful in the circulation of this renewable resource. On the other hand, fossil fuels (coal, oil, natural gas) (B) and minerals taken from the Earth are considered nonrenewable resources that are not replaced once they are removed.

TEST OF GENERAL KNOWLEDGE

6. **(A)** Although lightning and thunder occur simultaneously, lightning is noticed first because light travels much faster than sound (A). Light travels at 186,000 miles per second, while sound travels at 1087 feet per second; in other words, light travels 900,000 times faster than sound.

7. **(B)** The three requirements of a fire are fuel, kindling temperature, and oxygen. To extinguish a fire, you can shut off the oxygen supply (B), lower the kindling temperature, or remove the fuel (this will not be done by covering the pan).

8. **(E)** The Space Shuttle (E) is an orbiting space station designed to help scientists perform various experiments in space. It is also designed to make repairs on other satellites in space. Sputnik (A) was the first successful artificial satellite, launched by the Soviet Union in 1957. Soyuz spacecraft (D) carry Russian cosmonauts in orbit. The Apollo and Mercury projects (B, C) were part of the American space program that culminated in landing astronauts on the moon.

9. **(D)** In a chemical change, new substances are formed with different properties. When paper is burned (D), the charred remains have properties different from the original ones. Choices (A), (B), and (C) are examples of physical change, where the substances remain the same, even though the form differs.

10. **(D)** Vitamin C is destroyed by heat. Choices (A), (B), and (C) are secondary reasons to avoid overcooking vegetables; (E) is incorrect because vegetables are not a source of phosphorus or zinc.

11. **(D)** While all the listed components have some influence on chemical activity in cells, it is the enzymes that are directly involved in the details of each chemical change. The genes act indirectly, by specifying the production of enzymes. The ribosomes make the enzymes. Cell membranes control the passage of chemicals into and out of the cell. The nucleus is the locus of the genes.

12. **(E)** The chart shows that with a 45 MPH wind, the effective temperature at 0°F is $-54°F$.

13. **(B)** Solids expand when heated (B). For this reason, bridges (and sidewalks, railroad tracks, etc.) are constructed to allow room for this expansion. Since different solids expand at different rates, the characteristics (called the coefficient of linear expansion) of each must be known. Contraction in the winter must also be compensated for by engineers.

14. **(B)** This is the only choice in which the two birds belong to the same genus, indicating a close relationship. Having the same species name (A, E) is not indicative of close relationship unless the generic names are also the same. In (C) and (D) the generic names are similar but not identical.

15. **(A)** The stomates must open to allow the passage of carbon dioxide into the leaf and oxygen out. However, the tissues of the leaf are moist, and water will evaporate from them and pass out through the stomates. Desert plants cannot open their stomates in the heat of the day for this reason.

MODEL TEST 2

16. **(D)** Each magnet has two poles, a north and a south pole. These are named for the direction each pole in a bar magnet would face if freely suspended by a string. Similarly, a compass needle, which is nothing more than a magnetized needle on a pivot, aligns itself in a north-south position. The greatest magnetic attraction is at the poles. With magnets, unlike poles attract (D), and like poles repel.

17. **(C)** Life as we know it can exist only in the presence of liquid water. Venus is too hot and Pluto and Saturn are too cold for liquid water. The length of the Martian day is irrelevant. However, the surface of Mars shows valleys similar to those carved by rivers on Earth, and there is water in the Martian polar ice caps. This indicates that there was once liquid water on Mars, so life may have evolved there.

18. **(A)** The scientist begins by making observations (E) in order to gather data. A pattern may be noted that can give rise to a hypothesis (A), that is, a tentative statememt based on the observations. To test the hypothesis, an experiment (B), with controls (D), is performed. If the hypothesis is borne out (or revised), conclusions (C) may be drawn.

19. **(D)** When the water of streams is used to cool industrial processes, the water warms up, promoting the growth of algae. Masses of algae eventually die, and in their decay they use up oxygen. Fish die.

20. **(C)** The fossil record shows that the first vertebrates to come out of the water and dominate the land, in the middle Paleozoic era, were amphibians. Reptiles appeared in the late Paleozoic and were the dominant creatures of the land throughout the Mesozoic (if the dinosaurs are considered reptiles, which is now disputed). The first mammals appeared early in the Mesozoic, but they were a small, obscure group until the great extinction of the reptiles at the end of the Mesozoic. Then the mammals took over.

21. **(D)** During winter in the Northern Hemisphere, the North Pole is tilted away from the sun, causing that part of the Earth to receive its most indirect sunlight of the year. Six months later, the Northern Hemisphere experiences summer because the North Pole is tilted most toward the sun, and receives its most direct sunlight. During spring and autumn, the sun's direct rays strike the equator.

22. **(E)** Each of the 92 natural and 14 artificial elements is composed of its own unique kind of atoms. A molecule is a combination of atoms and is the smallest part of a compound. The nucleus is a part of an atom; an ion is an atom that has acquired an electric charge.

23. **(C)** Medical evidence leads to the conclusion that cigarette smokers run a higher risk of developing coronary disease, bronchitis, emphysema, and lung cancer than do nonsmokers. Tobacco contains the chemicals nicotine, tars, and carbon monoxide. Lung cancer occurs 20 times more frequently in smokers than in nonsmokers, and smokers have 3 times the death rate of nonsmokers from coronary disease (C).

TEST OF GENERAL KNOWLEDGE

24. **(D)** The water (or hydrologic) cycle is the movement of water from the oceans, rivers, lakes, streams, plants, and so on into the atmosphere and back to the Earth again. Water is constantly evaporating (E) from the liquid state to gaseous water vapor. It then condenses (B), or changes from vapor back to liquid, in the form of clouds (C). Tiny particles of matter in the air, such as salt, act as condensation nuclei, further allowing the process of condensation from water vapor into small droplets to occur. The next step in the water cycle is precipitation (A) in the form of rain, snow, hail, drizzle, or sleet. In this way, the water returns to the Earth and eventually winds up back in the bodies of water, whereupon the cycle begins again.

25. **(D)** Igneous rocks are formed by the solidification of molten rock. Volcanoes produce it in the form of lava, but much igneous rock solidifies from magma inside the crust. Rock formed from sediments or deposition from water are called sedimentary rocks.

26. **(D)** Energy is measured in the same units as work. It cannot be made or destroyed, but it can be transformed. A generator does not produce energy from nothing, but converts the kinetic energy put into it into an electric energy output.

27. **(A)** In all of the choices the suffix -*meter* means to "to measure." The anemometer (A) is the instrument meteorologists use to determine the velocity of the wind. The barometer (B) measures air pressure. Both the hygrometer (C) and the psychrometer (E) are used to determine relative humidity. The thermometer (D) is used to measure temperature.

28. **(D)** The gases in the Earth's atmosphere include many more than the three listed, but these are the best known by most people. By far the most abundant is nitrogen, making up over 78% by volume of the total atmosphere. Oxygen is next with nearly 21%. Together, these two gases account for 99% of the atmosphere. Third (not listed in the choices) is the inert gas argon, with 0.93%, and carbon dioxide is fourth, with 0.03%. The four gases listed comprise 99.96% of air.

29. **(E)** In 1859, Charles Darwin explained the theory of natural selection in his book *On the Origin of Species by Means of Natural Selection*. A summary of his ideas is as follows:
    1. A favorable environment can support only a limited number of organisms.
    2. Organisms vary in the traits that help them adapt to the environment.
    3. The organisms whose variations are most suitable to the environment are more likely to survive than the others.
    4. The survivors pass these favorable genetic traits on to their offspring.

    Of the choices given, only (E) expresses these ideas.

30. **(B)** An instinct (B) is an inborn tendency to behave in a way that is characteristic of a species (e.g., butterfly larva spinning a cocoon, or a bird building a nest). A conditioned reflex (A) is a response to a secondary stimulus, such as a dog salivating when a bell rings after the ringing has been repeatedly associated with the primary stimulus, the sight of food. A taxis (C) is a simple response toward or away from a stimulus (e.g., a worm moving away from light). An example of acquired learning (D) is a trick that a dog has been taught to perform, such as sitting up on his hind legs to beg. A conditioned response (E) is the same as a conditioned reflex.

Model Test 2
Test of Communication Skills

SECTION 1

LISTENING

Approximate time—30 minutes

PART A

Directions: You will find two kinds of questions in Part A. One kind presents a short question for you to answer; the other requires you to demonstrate understanding of a short statement. Listen to each question or statement *only once*, and listen very carefully. Then find the answer choices that correspond to the number of the question. Choose the one that best answers the question or is closest in meaning to or best supported by the statement, and fill in the appropriate space completely.

1. (A) The tickets were all sold a month ago.
    (B) The Syosset Braves are playing their arch rivals, the Hicksville Devils.
    (C) The Syosset coach gave me the tickets.
    (D) My best friend is captain of the Hicksville team.

2. (A) We left on the spur of the moment.
    (B) Our car broke down in Georgia.
    (C) We ran into heavy snow in Delaware.
    (D) We didn't allow enough time in the Everglades.

3. (A) Nobody in education lacks position power.
    (B) Teachers always respond to parent-pupil demands.
    (C) Teachers respond to what they perceive to be true in a situation, although these perceptions are subject to error.
    (D) Authority is always defined by the school district.

4. (A) This approach cannot be very useful.
    (B) Pupils sometimes dislike a teacher's style.
    (C) Parents object to frequent changes in the classroom.
    (D) Teachers translate decisions into behavior in accordance with their task and interpersonal skills.

5. (A) Mrs. Pollard has six grandchildren and bakes wonderful cookies.
    (B) The Boy Scouts maintained that she could not be a scoutmaster because of her sex.
    (C) She had periodically been the unofficial leader of a troop since 1953.
    (D) The state Commission on Human Rights and Opportunities ordered the "clearly erroneous" Boy Scouts to give her both the title of scoutmaster and the volunteer job.

TEST OF COMMUNICATION SKILLS

6. (A) Some pupils are brighter than others.
   (B) Many pupils are negative thinkers.
   (C) Education research shows that "cognitive modifiability" is possible.
   (D) The ability to think clearly is innate and cannot be taught.

7. (A) He lost his compass as he crossed a stream.
   (B) He was caught in a rainstorm.
   (C) He stopped to look at some wild violets.
   (D) He was an experienced woodsman and was familiar with the terrain.

8. (A) There is no American education system.
   (B) There has been a loss of national identity.
   (C) Local school governance is losing effectiveness; closer cooperation is needed between school officials and citizens.
   (D) School busing laws have not always been upheld by the courts.

9. (A) As babies these animals are cute and appealing.
   (B) When the animal reaches sexual maturity, it becomes aggressive and destructive indoors.
   (C) When raised as pets, these animals have no fear of human beings.
   (D) A raccoon or squirrel raised as a pet never learns to fend for itself in the wild.

10. (A) Last year's programs will not be evaluated.
    (B) There will be less funding for testing materials in the future.
    (C) Evaluation may produce hidden truths about the program, if the right formula is used.
    (D) Teachers are held responsible for the outcome of programs, even those used for the first time.

11. (A) Minority recruits were addressed by derogatory epithets and assigned to the most disagreeable tasks.
    (B) The state police had been ordered to increase the number of minority members on the force.
    (C) The training academy was located upstate, far from the homes of most minority members.
    (D) The training academy has been ordered to turn over all its records on these minority recruits.

12. (A) Performance tests are demonstrations of learning in areas such as music.
    (B) Pupils like paper and pencil tests and do well on them.
    (C) Teachers may not know how to give other kinds of tests.
    (D) With written tests, teachers have papers to grade.

13. (A) To become law, an amendment must be ratified by three fourths of the state legislature.
    (B) Two hours after clearing Congress, the ERA was ratified by Hawaii, and one year later it had been ratified by 30 states.
    (C) Some women, as well as some men, opposed the amendment.
    (D) The ERA read simply, "Equality of rights under the law shall not be denied or abridged by the United States or by any state on account of sex."

MODEL TEST 2

14. (A) Few teachers have the skills to lead group interviews.
    (B) Many pupils dislike group interviews and participate reluctantly if at all.
    (C) During individual interviews, the teacher can usually obtain more insight into pupil comments and responses.
    (D) Group interviews take more of the teacher's time.

15. (A) The Voting Rights Act was passed in the administration of President Johnson.
    (B) One section of the Voting Rights Act was extended for another 25 years in 1982.
    (C) By federal law there can be no discrimination in regard to employment or public accommodations.
    (D) In 1964 there were 103 black elected officials in the United States; now there are more than 5500.

PART B

Directions: In Part B you will hear several short dialogs. At the end of each dialog a third person will ask questions about the conversation. Each question will be spoken *only once*. After you hear a dialog and a question about it, read the four answer choices. Decide which is the best answer to the question, and mark the corresponding space.

16. (A) He did not answer the question.
    (B) He told the woman his preference.
    (C) He did not hear the woman's question.
    (D) He is indifferent to heat and cold.

17. (A) He is patient.
    (B) He is rude.
    (C) He is pleased at her interest.
    (D) He is indifferent.

18. (A) She does not like science.
    (B) She does not like any teacher.
    (C) She really never liked Mr. Klein.
    (D) She is hurt that Mr. Klein has not kept in touch.

19. (A) Teachers should be pals to their students.
    (B) Teachers' responsibilities toward their students extend beyond the classroom.
    (C) All teacher-pupil relationships are completely satisfactory.
    (D) No teachers can be trusted.

20. (A) She is a pessimist.
    (B) She is afraid to disagree with anyone.
    (C) She tends to view situations in the best light possible.
    (D) She did not increase her communication skills in the group activity project.

21. (A) The new friendships will be maintained.
    (B) Friendships are fragile and don't last long.
    (C) Group activities are of little permanent value.
    (D) She made a major contribution to the course.

TEST OF COMMUNICATION SKILLS

22. (A) Central Americans exist in a perpetual state of revolution.
    (B) Central Americans and the lives they lead are different from their counterparts in the United States.
    (C) Central Americans willingly embrace foreign ideologies.
    (D) Life in Central America can be readily changed because the people are very receptive to new ideas.

23. (A) She thinks the United States should provide economic help to Central America.
    (B) She thinks conditions in Central America will never change.
    (C) She thinks the United States should keep its hands off Central America.
    (D) She thinks Russia will foment continual revolutions in Central America.

24. (A) The threat posed by computers to the human intellect
    (B) The probability that human executives will be replaced by computers
    (C) The growing capabilities of artificial intelligence machines
    (D) The fact that computers no longer require human programmers

25. (A) Serious   (C) Alarmed
    (B) Deferential   (D) Joking

26. (A) It is impossible to tell.
    (B) Yes, he is a petroleum engineer and expects to be replaced by a computer.
    (C) No, he perceives that computers are not self-sufficient.
    (D) No, he is a programmer.

27. (A) To make the woman angry
    (B) To make the woman feel guilty
    (C) To present facts objectively
    (D) To persuade the woman to give the black children more help

28. (A) She remains unsympathetic to the man's remarks.
    (B) She will give the black children extra help.
    (C) She thinks the children's parents should help them.
    (D) She resents the man's request.

29. (A) As journalist   (C) As teacher
    (B) As student   (D) As mother

30. (A) He is conciliatory toward the woman.
    (B) He is glad the woman came to speak with him.
    (C) He is indifferent about the whole matter.
    (D) He is defensive about what he perceives as criticism.

PART C

Directions: In Part C you will hear several short talks. Each talk will be followed by three or four questions. You must listen carefully because the talks and the questions will be given *only once*. After hearing each question, select the best answer and fill in the appropriate space.

31. (A) The conveniences made possible by batteries
    (B) Cameras and computers
    (C) The safety of battery-operated vehicles
    (D) Our dependence on batteries in everyday life

32. (A) Manufacture larger, more powerful batteries.
    (B) Invent a replacement for batteries.
    (C) Make batteries cheap and uniform in size.
    (D) Make cars that run without batteries.

33. (A) We have become too dependent on a costly, unreliable product.
    (B) We buy too many portable telephones.
    (C) Batteries are safe for children's toys.
    (D) The value of smoke detectors is greatly overrated.

34. (A) A critique of Poe's poetry
    (B) An orgy at Poe's graveside
    (C) Odd ways of celebrating birthdays
    (D) The celebration of Poe's 175th birthday

35. (A) To entertain
    (B) To frighten people with a graveyard story
    (C) To increase people's appreciation of Poe's poetry
    (D) To increase the sales of cognac and roses

36. (A) In January   (C) In July
    (B) In May   (D) In September

37. (A) Teachers' performance
    (B) Coming school reforms
    (C) Student deficiencies
    (D) Parents' demands for computers

38. (A) California   (C) Washington
    (B) New York   (D) New Jersey

39. (A) Teachers will oppose them.
    (B) The changes will be costly.
    (C) Reforms can be achieved within current school budgets.
    (D) Parents are uninterested in reforms.

40. (A) Resist all of the proposed changes
    (B) Hire untrained people as teachers
    (C) Dismiss incompetent teachers
    (D) Find new methods of school financing

STOP

THIS IS THE END OF THE LISTENING SECTION.
IF YOU FINISH BEFORE TIME IS CALLED, YOU MAY CHECK YOUR WORK ON THIS SECTION ONLY.
DO NOT WORK ON ANY OTHER SECTION IN THE TEST.

TEST OF COMMUNICATION SKILLS

SECTION 2

READING

Time—30 minutes

Directions: Read carefully each statement or passage, and the question(s) and/or incomplete statement(s) that follow it. Then choose from the five choices the best answer or completion for each question or incomplete statement, and fill in the corresponding space completely. Base your answers on what is *stated* or *implied* in the statement or passage, not on any outside knowledge you may possess.

1. Thomas Jefferson, in 1786, equated education with democracy. He wrote, "No other sure foundation can be devised for the preservation of freedom and happiness."

   Jefferson would be most likely to agree with which of the following statements?
   (A) Educated citizens tend to participate in government.
   (B) An educated man is a threat to his leader.
   (C) Educated people don't vote in national elections.
   (D) The survival of democracy is based solely on elected leaders.
   (E) Schools have little impact on the society in which they function.

2. Cocaine abusers develop such serious emotional problems as anxiety and depression; only cocaine will keep the depression under control and enable the user to function. As addiction increases, so does the amount spent on the drug, forcing many persons to turn to crime to finance the habit.

   The purpose of this statement is to
   (A) identify the persons most likely to become cocaine abusers
   (B) clarify the effects of cocaine on the nervous system
   (C) explain the dangers of cocaine abuse
   (D) point out the cost to society of cocaine addiction
   (E) suggest a solution to the problem of cocaine addiction

Questions 3–5

This unusual table is several hundred years old, and yet it is as sound and strong as ever, as good as new! It is not made of wood or iron, but it will last forever. Nobody uses it to hold a lamp or a television set or a computer. No one eats a meal on it. This table came all the way from Arabia and is ornamented with many figures. We do not know who made it, but millions of people use it every day in their homes and businesses. What is this most unusual table that you will be using before the end of this year? It is the Multiplication Table!

3. For which audience was this passage written?
   (A) High school students
   (B) Parents of preschool children
   (C) Elementary school children
   (D) Math teachers
   (E) The general public

MODEL TEST 2

4. What unstated assumption does the author make?
   (A) Children love arithmetic.
   (B) Children hate mysteries.
   (C) Children can be aroused to interest in a subject.
   (D) Children would rather snack than eat at a table.
   (E) Children dislike school.

5. To which of the following feelings or drives does the passage appeal?
   (A) Anxiety   (D) Fear
   (B) Curiosity   (E) The competitive instinct
   (C) Anger

Questions 6–7

There are two kinds of stress: (1) good stress and (2) distress. Good stress moves us to get up in the morning, arrive at work on time, finish our tasks, and set long-range goals. Distress, on the other hand, affects the whole body and may cause immobilization or even illness. The damage comes from being geared up for a fight or a flight response. The autonomic ductless glandular system moves more adrenalin into the bloodstream; then, more blood sugar is burned, the heartbeat increases, and digestion slows down. It becomes more and more difficult to relax from an "adrenalin high" at the end of a stressful day. Stress can be a positive force; distress is dangerous to health!

6. The primary purpose of this passage is to
   (A) persuade people to avoid any stress
   (B) encourage people to change jobs
   (C) show the effects of the two kinds of stress
   (D) emphasize the motivational value of stress
   (E) explain the nervous system

7. What is the most important question left unanswered by the author?
   (A) What is the dividing line between good stress and distress?
   (B) What are the beneficial effects of stress?
   (C) How does the autonomic ductless system work?
   (D) What is the autonomic nervous system?
   (E) What is an "adrenalin high"?

---

8. Man seldom applies to the conduct of human affairs the scientific approach, which has been used to control and direct the forces and materials supplied by nature and put to work in the physical sciences. The tragedy is that human relations have floundered between the nonscientific and the pseudoscientific.

   Which of the following is an unstated assumption made by the author of the statement?
   (A) People don't want to solve their problems.
   (B) Social scientists don't know how to use other methods.
   (C) The scientific method is the best way to solve problems of human relations.
   (D) The physical sciences belong to the Age of Science.
   (E) We are living in a postscientific period.

9. About 31,000 of New York City's elementary and junior high school pupils almost never go to school. For many the trials of everyday life are so overwhelming that

school seems relatively unimportant. The parents, often deeply depressed, find it easier to let the children stay home than to get them off to school.

With what school problem is the statement concerned?
(A) Pupil tardiness
(B) Classroom discipline
(C) Parental indifference
(D) Student truancy
(E) Inadequate and outdated teaching aids

10. The defendant in a murder trial referred to herself as "a person in an empty chair."

What did she mean by this statement?
(A) She felt removed from the mainstream of life and condemned to sit home alone.
(B) She felt that she had lost her identity as an individual and had become a non-person.
(C) She felt like a social outcast, that if she sat down in an empty chair, everyone else would leave the room.
(D) She felt sad that there was no one to sit in the empty chairs in her home.
(E) She felt that she was the only person in a room full of empty chairs.

Questions 11–15

Studies indicate that 1,000,000 American children are listed as runaways, but that some 300,000 really are "throwaway kids," children who have been pushed out of their homes by adults. Child Find, an organization that aids in the location of missing children, reports that these young people are heavily exploited by prostitution, pornography, and drugs. Many of these children wind up in John Doe graves because nobody knows who they are—they were never reported missing by their parents! Reform schools and jails hold many teenagers placed there because parents considered them incorrigible. Thousands of children hitchhike to New York, California, or Florida to find a better life, only to wind up sleeping in alleys and eating from garbage cans. A federal study reported that from 20 to 40 percent of the children at shelters for runaways had been beaten and another 8 percent had been sexually assaulted. At this time there are no answers to this horrifying problem, but there is growing public awareness that these wasted lives will affect parenting into the next generation. Parenting is a learned skill; thousands of young people have no role models!

11. The main idea of this passage is best expressed by which of the following titles?
(A) Children in Trouble
(B) Parents and the Courts
(C) The Responsibilities of Society toward the Home
(D) The Failure of the School to Educate Parents
(E) The Role of the Federal Government in Child Care

12. According to the passage, almost one third of a million children have left home because
(A) they are on drugs
(B) their parents were too strict with them
(C) they are afraid of being placed in reform schools
(D) they have been forced out by adults
(E) they are seeking excitement and easy wealth

415

13. Which of the following is always true about the occupant of a John Doe grave?
    (A) He was named John Doe.
    (B) His or her identity is unknown.
    (C) He died in jail and relatives wouldn't claim the body.
    (D) He or she was an incorrigible young person who disgraced the family.
    (E) He or she was never reported to be missing.

14. The author argues that
    (A) parents should be role models
    (B) children don't need role models
    (C) children won't accept role models
    (D) children's friends are the best role models
    (E) teachers are ideal role models

15. What conclusion does the author draw about the long-range effects of homelessness upon children?
    (A) It will affect them little in the long run.
    (B) Children survive most of their problems very well.
    (C) Some of them will die of neglect.
    (D) They will be inadequate parents.
    (E) They will be strengthened by their experiences and will make better parents because of them.

Questions 16–17

Reflecting the frustration endemic on Indian reservations, the leaders of the American Indian Movement (AIM) are preparing for a confrontation with the U.S. government. The AIM is demanding the return of Indian lands, such as the Black Hills of Dakota, sacred to the Lakota-Sioux. The United States has offered to pay the Indians for the land, but they would have to relinquish all further claims. Neither side is disposed to yield. "The U.S. government is fighting a fire here," states one Indian leader. "And if they don't put it out, there'll be a revolution."

16. Which of the following adjectives best describes the tone of the passage?
    (A) Hopeful
    (B) Objective
    (C) Fearful
    (D) Somber
    (E) Sarcastic

17. If the quotation at the end of the passage is assumed to be true, which of the following must also be true?
    (A) The AIM leaders are temperate people and are ready and willing to compromise.
    (B) The mood on Indian reservations is grim, desperate, and determined.
    (C) The AIM is interested chiefly in negotiating to improve conditions on the reservations.
    (D) The AIM is prepared to accept a nominal sum in settlement of its claims.
    (E) Although the Indians want the Black Hills back, they have abandoned their old religious beliefs and no longer consider the area sacred.

TEST OF COMMUNICATION SKILLS

18. Recently it became legal for merchants to impose a fee on customers using credit cards. In arguing for such a fee, the Consumer Federation of America pointed out that the previous ban on surcharges obscured the true cost of credit and forced cash customers to subsidize credit purchasers.

    Which of the following groups would be LEAST likely to publish this statement?
    (A) Merchants
    (B) Travelers
    (C) Consumers in general
    (D) Business executives
    (E) Credit card companies

19. The Parkfield Civic Association has determined that the school board will submit to the voters a $40 million budget, a startling increase over the current one. This year property owners will also be burdened by tax increases resulting from the installation of sewers.

    From this statement it can be inferred that
    (A) the school board is reckless with the taxpayers' money
    (B) the sewer tax will not take effect for some time
    (C) the civic association has a policy of neutrality in regard to school matters
    (D) the civic association will recommend defeat of the school budget
    (E) the civic association will work for the passage of the school budget

Questions 20–22

Many women combine homemaking and a career with outstanding success. One of these women is Dr. Rosalyn Yalow, nuclear physicist; she is the wife of Aaron Yalow, physicist, and the mother of two children. In 1977 she won the Nobel Prize for her work with radioimmunoassay (RIA), a technique for determining diseased or normal states in the body through the use of radioactive isotopes that measure hormones, enzymes, vitamins, drugs, and viruses. Potential blood donors can be screened for hepatitis and other diseases. Dr. Yalow is the first woman to win the prestigious Albert Lasker Medical Research Award and to be elected to the National Academy of Sciences.

20. What is the main point of the passage?
    (A) Women should not take science.
    (B) Homemaking and careers don't mix well.
    (C) Women can marry, have children, and achieve at a high level in a career.
    (D) It is very difficult for women to combine child-rearing and a career.
    (E) Scientific careers are now open to women.

21. This passage is of special interest to women because
    (A) many women are afraid to give blood
    (B) it shows how physics contributes to medicine
    (C) women in particular will benefit from R I A
    (D) Dr. Yalow is a woman who has combined an outstanding career with marriage and motherhood
    (E) women don't like to take science courses

417

22. The author makes the unstated assumption that
    (A) women will accept role models
    (B) women dislike science
    (C) women like mathematics
    (D) teachers do not encourage girls to take science courses
    (E) husbands discourage their wives from having careers

---

23. Students of the '80s are experiencing the growth of self-discipline and the challenges of difficult courses and more homework. In 1950, 57.1 percent of white students and 25.7 percent of black students graduated from high school. In 1983, 85 percent and 77.3 percent, respectively, graduated.

    The main topic of this statement is
    (A) American education during the last decade
    (B) the growing number of black teachers
    (C) the impact of the home on the school
    (D) recent increases in the number of high school graduates
    (E) "the rising tide of mediocrity" in education

24. Jack, Ken, and Luigi are friends. Jack is planning to attend X College; Ken and Luigi, to go to Y College. Jack will major in business administration, physics, or chemistry; Ken will major in math, chemistry, or biology; Luigi will major in English, drama, or business administration.

    Which of the following statements must then be true?

    I. X College offers a major in biology.
    II. Y College offers a major in business administration.
    III. Both X College and Y College offer majors in drama.

    (A) I only   (D) I and II only
    (B) II only   (E) II and III only
    (C) III only

Questions 25–30

Several selective high schools are listed among the top schools in the nation. Entrance requirements usually include competitive examinations and high grade-point averages. Access for superior minority students is provided. At Boston Latin High School the study of Latin is mandated. The New York City Bronx High School of Science, founded in 1938, has produced three Nobel Prize winners in physics. The curriculum offers eight languages, including Hebrew, Chinese, and Japanese. Every year about 7000 students apply but only 950 are accepted. For six straight years Stuyvesant High School, New York City, has had the top number of National Merit Scholarship semifinalists. The school emphasizes engineering and has many advanced placement courses, including 14 in mathematics. At Central High in Philadelphia, students are exposed to the largest public school library in the United States (50,000 volumes). Advanced placement courses in six foreign languages and in chemistry, biology, physics, and mathematics are available. At Lowell High in San Francisco nearly 58 percent of the students are Asian, mostly Chinese; 95 percent of the graduates attend college, many assisted by scholarships. These selective high schools provide quality education through high levels of expectation for students and the challenge of advanced placement courses in several fields.

TEST OF COMMUNICATION SKILLS

25. The primary purpose of this passage is to
    (A) present information about selective high schools in an objective way
    (B) encourage all students to apply to selective high schools in the hope of securing a better education
    (C) persuade more minority students, particularly Asians, to apply to selective high schools
    (D) urge that admission requirements for selective high schools be liberalized so that more students could benefit
    (E) emphasize the value of advanced placement courses for all students

26. Which of the following statements summarizes the contents of the passage most accurately?
    (A) Only private secondary schools offer quality educational programs.
    (B) Selective high schools are the best schools for everyone to attend.
    (C) Selective high schools offer superior curricula and sometimes better facilities than other high schools, and their students generally achieve at high levels.
    (D) All selective high schools receive high ratings and deserve public support.
    (E) Nearly 95 percent of selective high school graduates win scholarships and go on to college.

27. The main idea of the passage is developed primarily through the use of
    (A) cause and effect
    (B) comparison and contrast
    (C) examples
    (D) details
    (E) all of the above

28. At Boston Latin High School the study of Latin is
    (A) recommended   (D) traditional
    (B) required   (E) optional
    (C) offered

29. The ratio of number of acceptances to number of applications at the Bronx School of Science is approximately
    (A) 1 to 3   (D) 1 to 6
    (B) 1 to 4   (E) 1 to 7
    (C) 1 to 5

30. Joy excels in mathematics and science, and wants to become an engineer. If she could attend any selective high school mentioned in the passage, which school would you recommend?
    (A) Lowell High
    (B) Bronx High School of Science
    (C) Central High
    (D) Boston Latin High
    (E) Stuyvesant High

S T O P

IF YOU FINISH BEFORE TIME IS CALLED, YOU MAY CHECK YOUR WORK ON THIS SECTION ONLY. DO NOT WORK ON ANY OTHER SECTION IN THIS TEST.

MODEL TEST 2

SECTION 3

WRITING: MULTIPLE-CHOICE

Time — 30 minutes

Part A

(Suggested time — 10 minutes)

Directions: Four portions of each of the sentences below are underlined and lettered. After reading the sentence, decide whether any one of the underlined parts contains an incorrect grammatical construction, incorrect word usage, or incorrect or omitted punctuation or capitalization. If this is the case, note the letter underneath the underlined portion and fill in completely the corresponding letter on the answer sheet. If there is no error in any underlined portion of the sentence, fill in space (E). No sentence contains more than one error.

Example. The season of the year, the depth of the water, and the types of food avail-
　　　　　　　　　　　　　　　　　　　　　　A　　　　　　　　　　　　B
able influences the number of species of wildlife seen in the pool. No error
　　　C　　　　　　　　　　　　　　　　　　　　　D　　　　　　　　E

Ⓐ Ⓑ ● Ⓓ Ⓔ

Explanation. The sentence has a compound subject (*season*, *depth*, and *types*) so a plural verb (*influence*) is needed. Therefore (C) is the incorrect part of the sentence.

1. Each of the women who performed tonight have contributed something valuable
　　A　　　B　　C　　　　　　　　　　D
to this orchestra. No error
　　　　　　　　　E

2. The analysts refuse to return to work without the company raises their salaries
　　　A　　　　　　　　　　　　　　　B　　　　　　　　C
substantially. No error
　　D　　　　E

3. The teacher who he described is my brother, an excellent athlete and a talented
　　　　　　A　　B　　　　　　　　　C
flutist. No error
　D　　E

4. By early evening the hurricane had turned toward the Pacific Ocean, although it
　　　　　　　　　　　　　　A　　　　　　　　　B　　　　　C
had been expected to hit the coast. No error
　　　D　　　　　　　　　　　　　E

5. Education is overwhelmingly a service industry, teachers perform the bulk of the
　　　　　　　　　A　　　　　　　　　　　B
service, material requirements being relatively small. No error
　　　　　　　　　　　　　C　　　D　　　　　　E

6. Plants growing in both open water and on high sites are greatly affected by soil
　　　A　　　B　　　　　　　　　　　　　　　C　　　　D
type and amount of sunlight. No error
　　　　　　　　　　　　E

7. On Wednesday, the day before we left on our trip, Eric and myself watered the
　　A　　　　　　　　　　　　　　　　　　　B　　　C　　　D
flowers and mowed the lawn. No error
　　　　　　　　　　　　E

420

TEST OF COMMUNICATION SKILLS

8. In the depths of her <u>frustration</u> Sarah felt like <u>throwing</u> the book through the win-
                        A   B
   dow or <u>tear</u> it to <u>pieces</u>. <u>No error</u>
          C   D   E

9. A <u>complete</u> list of Thomas <u>Hardy's</u> poems and novels <u>is given</u> in the <u>appendix</u>.
       A   B   C   D
   <u>No error</u>
     E

10. When <u>pope John Paul II</u> <u>arrived</u> in the <u>Philippines</u>, he found hundreds of men,
               A   B   C
    women, and children <u>waiting</u> in the rain to greet him. <u>No error</u>
                         D   E

11. The <u>wildlife refuge</u> pools are open to the public from <u>March 15</u> through
            A   B
    <u>October 15</u> for fishing, crabbing, and <u>to go canoeing</u>. <u>No error</u>
       C   D   E

12. Two dogs, three horses, two <u>lions</u>, and an elephant <u>was</u> in the small circus <u>that</u>
                                  A   B   C
    <u>visited</u> our town last week. <u>No error</u>
      D   E

13. On Christmas <u>Eve</u> the temperature <u>fell to</u> an <u>unbelievable</u> −18 degrees
                A   B   C
    below zero. <u>No error</u>
       D   E

14. From literature received in the mail Ted and <u>I</u> learned that Maine <u>has</u> more pine
                                            A   B
    trees than <u>any</u> state in the <u>Northeast</u>. <u>No error</u>
                C   D   E

15. The instructions stated, "Do not give assistance <u>nor</u> receive assistance <u>while</u> tak-
                         A   B   C
    ing <u>this test."</u> <u>No error</u>
         D   E

16. The dead marsh plants and other nutrients <u>that</u> <u>are carried</u> into the bay by tidal
                                         A   B
    action <u>form</u> the start of the food chain <u>essential</u> to most marine life. <u>No error</u>
         C   D   E

17. One reason the teacher resigned <u>was</u> <u>because</u> she <u>was offered</u> more money to
                                  A   B   C
    work <u>fewer</u> hours as a consultant. <u>No error</u>
          D   E

18. Stephanie comes from a <u>single-parent</u> home, <u>and</u> in her senior year she
                               A   B
    <u>was elected</u> <u>class</u> president. <u>No error</u>
        C   D   E

19. My new job <u>is</u> neither interesting <u>or</u> profitable, and I am <u>embarrassed</u> that I <u>made</u>
               A   B   C   D
    such a bad decision. <u>No error</u>
                        E

20. <u>Struggling</u> to keep back the tears, Liz admitted that the casserole she
        A
    had prepared so <u>carefully</u> did indeed smell <u>strangely</u>. <u>No error</u>
      B   C   D   E

MODEL TEST 2

21. There are, if I see correctly in this heavy snow, three trucks and a car pulled off
    　　　A　　　　　　B　　　　　　　　C　　　　　　　　　　　　　　D
    at the side of the road. No error
    　　　　　　　　　　　　　E

22. The article points out not only that spending per pupil has increased by 165 per-
    　　　　　　　　　　　A　　　　　　　　　　　　　　B
    cent but that also teachers' salaries per pupil have increased by only 114 percent.
    　　　C　　　　　D
    No error
    　E

23. When I reached Snow Shoe, I discovered to my amazement that there wasn't but
    　　　　A　　　　B　　　　　　　　　　　　　　C　　　　　　　　　　D
    one street in the town. No error
    　　　　　　　　　　　　E

24. The account of the Revolutionary War given in this textbook is the
    　　　　　　　　　　A　　　　　　　　　　　　　B
    most complete one that I have ever read. No error
    　　C　　　　　　　　D　　　　　　　　E

25. John is shorter than Tom, Tom is shorter than Bill, and Bill is shorter than me.
    　　　　　　　A　　　　　　　　　　　　　　B C　　　　　　　　　　　D
    No error
    　E

26. Between longer-lived birds such as geese, swans, and raptors, where there is an
    　　A　　　　　　　　　　　　　　　　　　　　　　　　　　　　　　B
    advantage to faithfulness, pairs are often maintained as long as both partners live.
    　　　　　　　　　　　　　　　　C　　　　　　　　　D
    No error
    　E

27. They had ought to have gone earlier; they were late for the game. No error
    　　　　A　　　　　　　B　　　　　C　　　　　D　　　　　　　　E

Part B

(Suggested time — 10 minutes)

Directions: In each of the following sentences there is an underlined portion that may be correct or may contain an error in grammar, diction (word use), sentence construction, or punctuation. In the example the entire sentence is underlined. Beneath each sentence are five ways of writing the underlined part. Choice (A) repeats the original, whereas the other four choices are different. If you think that the original sentence is correct, fill in space (A); otherwise choose the best answer from the other four choices given. *Do not choose an answer that changes the meaning of the original sentence.*

Example. The pie will be divided among Meg, Jenny, and I.
- (A) The pie will be divided among Meg, Jenny, and I.
- (B) The pie will be divided among Meg, Jenny, and me.
- (C) Let's divide the pie among Meg, Jenny, and me.
- (D) The pie will be divided between Meg, Jenny, and I.
- (E) The pie will be divided between Meg, Jenny, and me.

Ⓐ ● Ⓒ Ⓓ Ⓔ

TEST OF COMMUNICATION SKILLS

Explanation. The objective case is needed after the preposition *among* (B). Choice (C) changes the meaning, and *between*, used in (D) and (E), commonly applies to two, not three, persons or things.

28. Most women queried in the poll preferred job security <u>to high but uncertain income</u>.
    (A) to high but uncertain income
    (B) than high but uncertain income
    (C) rather than to have high but uncertain income
    (D) instead of having high but uncertain income
    (E) more than high but uncertain income

29. <u>Being the fog was so thick</u>, we got lost on the lake.
    (A) Being the fog was so thick
    (B) Due to the fog being so thick
    (C) Due to the thick fog
    (D) Because the fog was so thick
    (E) Being that the fog was so thick

30. The governor often signs minor spending bills in exchange for support for bills he <u>favors, which he considers good strategy</u>.
    (A) favors, which he considers good strategy
    (B) favors, he considers this good strategy
    (C) favors that he considers good strategy
    (D) favors, a practice that he considers good strategy
    (E) favors and considers good strategy

31. On Thursday there is a television program <u>at 8 P.M. in the evening that I don't want to miss</u>.
    (A) at 8 P.M. in the evening that I don't want to miss
    (B) at 8 P.M. in the evening what I don't want to miss
    (C) at 8 P.M. in the evening, and I don't want to miss it
    (D) at 8 P.M. in the evening; I don't want to miss it
    (E) at 8 P.M. that I don't want to miss

32. <u>Bryan didn't study much for the test, and he</u> did surprisingly well.
    (A) Bryan didn't study much for the test, and he
    (B) Not studying much for the test, Bryan
    (C) Not having studied much for the test, Bryan
    (D) Although Bryan didn't study much for the test, he
    (E) Bryan didn't study much for the test; he

33. Miss Wiley's way of teaching reading is <u>different from the other teachers</u>.
    (A) different from the other teachers
    (B) different than the other teachers
    (C) different than the others teachers' way
    (D) different than the ways of the other teachers
    (E) different from the other teachers' way

MODEL TEST 2

34. <u>Roger Baldwin, the founder of the American Civil Liberties Union, frequently said, "No</u> fight for civil liberty ever stays won."
    (A) Roger Baldwin, the founder of the American Civil Liberties Union, frequently said, "No
    (B) Roger Baldwin the founder of the American Civil Liberties Union, frequently said, "No
    (C) Roger Baldwin, the founder of the American Civil Liberties Union frequently said, "No
    (D) Roger Baldwin the founder of the American Civil Liberties Union frequently said, "No
    (E) Roger Baldwin, the founder of the American Civil Liberties Union, frequently said "No

35. The report that Dr. Illmensee had successfully cloned mice <u>was under review because of assertions by his staff that there had been</u> irregularities in record keeping.
    (A) was under review because of assertions by his staff that there had been
    (B) were under review because of assertions by his staff that there had been
    (C) was under review due to assertions by his staff that there had been
    (D) was under review due to assertions by his staff, that there had been
    (E) was under review because of assertions by his staff that there was

36. One of the most frightening problems is contamination of the environment with chemicals that, to most of us, are strange <u>and their effects are hard to understand.</u>
    (A) and their effects are hard to understand
    (B) and with effects that are hard to understand
    (C) and whose effects are hard to understand
    (D) and having effects that are hard to understand
    (E) and we can't understand their effects

Part C

Directions: Select the best one of the five answers relating to the following questions or incomplete statements.

Questions 37–38 refer to the following passage.

(1) The Kara Young Human Relations Awards will be presented this year to those who have, through their actions, demonstrated a sincere concern for others. (2) The awards were established in 1971 to honor the memory of Kara Young, a former teacher, who was devoted to the cause of Human Rights. (3) Kara organized the Human Relations Committee in our school district to make all of us more aware of and sensitive to the needs of others. (4) The Human Relations Committee believes that it may be helpful if school staff and faculty have an opportunity to react to individual nominations before they are submitted to the committee. (5) The awards, special framed certificates, were set up to recognize those students who have shown they possess the qualities which best exemplify the spirit and accomplishments of Kara Young.

TEST OF COMMUNICATION SKILLS

37. Which of the following would be the best sentence to insert after (5) above?
    (A) Nominations for the awards may be made by teachers or fellow students.
    (B) You can nominate a friend for the award, or a teacher can nominate a student he's crazy about.
    (C) Nominating a deserving youngster will make you feel proud.
    (D) Pupils should be profusely rewarded whenever they exhibit tendencies to goodness.
    (E) We're lucky if we have two kids to nominate this year.

38. Which of the following does not belong in the passage above?
    (A) Sentence (1)
    (B) Sentence (2)
    (C) Sentence (3)
    (D) Sentence (4)
    (E) Sentence (5)

Questions 39–40 refer to the following passage.

(1) A special faculty workshop on problems of classroom management will take place on Saturday. (2) Dr. Allan Frantzen will present "A Classroom Control Model." (3) The three subtopics are: "Causes of Misbehavior," "Preventive Control Tactics," and "Corrective Control Tactics." (4) Dr. Frantzen will be leaving Wednesday for his three-week tour of Japanese Schools. (5) Dr. Frantzen's research findings indicate that some of the misbehavior arises from ignorance, poor study habits, mimicry, and displacement. (6) Even special events, such as a fire drill, or winning a varsity game, can affect classroom behavior.

39. Which one of the following should be placed between (5) and (6) above?
    (A) Fatigue, boredom, frustration, and learning tasks can also cause misbehavior.
    (B) Teachers and pupils should review the rules frequently.
    (C) Fantasy is less painful than reality.
    (D) Slow learners cause most of the management problems.
    (E) Pupil involvement makes little difference in attitudes.

40. Which sentence does NOT belong in the passage?
    (A) Sentence (1)
    (B) Sentence (2)
    (C) Sentence (3)
    (D) Sentence (4)
    (E) Sentence (5)

Questions 41–42 refer to the following passage.

(1) We, the teachers of Hillsdale School, appreciate your frequent visits as supervisor of our district. (2) Your availability has made it easier to implement the new science program at all grade levels. (3) We had some difficulty planning the field trips because of the bad weather. (4) Please, thank the principal for the use of the secretary to send permission slips to all the parents. (5) Several teachers from other school districts have visited our classrooms to learn about our new program; they commented about the pupils' avid interest in science. (6) We look forward to the planning sessions you will offer in September.

41. Which sentences do NOT belong in the passage?
    (A) Sentences (1) and (2)
    (B) Sentences (2) and (3)
    (C) Sentences (3) and (4)
    (D) Sentences (4) and (5)
    (E) Sentences (5) and (6)

42. Which of the sentences in the passage indicates an increasing acceptance of the science program at Hillsdale School?
- (A) Sentence (2)
- (B) Sentence (3)
- (C) Sentence (4)
- (D) Sentence (5)
- (E) Sentence (6)

Questions 43–45 refer to the following pasage.

(1) Infants and young children are not just sitting twiddling their thumbs, waiting for their parents to teach them to read and do math. (2) They are expending a vast amount of time and effort in exploring and understanding their immediate world. (3) Healthy education supports and encourages this spontaneous learning. (4) Early instruction miseducates, not because it attempts to teach, but because it attempts to teach the wrong things at the wrong time.

43. Which of the following best describes the function of sentence (4)?
- (A) It provides evidence to support the main idea of the passage.
- (B) It anticipates an objection to the argument advanced later in the passage.
- (C) It suggests a solution to the problem presented in the passage.
- (D) It eliminates the need for a thesis statement
- (E) It expresses the main idea of the passage.

44. Which of the following, if added to the passage above, would provide support for the author's position that "early instruction miseducates...because it attempts to teach the wrong things at the wrong time?"
- (A) In books addressed to parents a number of writers are encouraging parents to teach infants and young children reading, math, and science.
- (B) The weight of solid professional opinion opposes the formal instruction of infants and young children and advocates providing young children with a rich and stimulating environment that is, at the same time, warm, loving, and supportive of the child's own learning priorities and pacing.
- (C) The threat of miseducation is greatest in public education, where the most children will be affected.
- (D) Too little attention is placed upon reading for pleasure; therefore, children do not associate reading with enjoyment.
- (E) If we do not wake up to the potential danger of these harmful practices, we may do serious damage to a large segment of the next generation.

45. Which of the following would be the best sentence to insert after sentence (4)?
- (A) We'd better get on the ball and teach our little tykes what they need to know.
- (B) Too often one attempts to teach the correct subject matter but is unable to carry the attempt to fruition.
- (C) When we ignore what the child has to learn and instead impose what we want to teach, we put infants and young children at risk for no purpose.
- (D) Canning the whole idea about giving instruction in this format seems like the best thing to do at this point.
- (E) If we concentrate on teaching the right things at the right times, we may lick this yet.

S T O P

IF YOU FINISH BEFORE TIME IS CALLED, YOU MAY CHECK YOUR WORK ON THIS SECTION ONLY. DO NOT WORK ON ANY OTHER SECTION IN THE TEST.

TEST OF COMMUNICATION SKILLS
SECTION 4
WRITING: ESSAY

Time — 30 minutes

Directions: Take 30 minutes to plan and write an essay on the topic in the box below. Take time to organize your thoughts and perhaps make a rough outline before beginning to write.

> A system of merit pay for teachers should (should not) be substituted for the uniform wage scales now in use in this district.
>
> Choose one side of this question, and in a letter to the president of the school board state your point of view and give arguments to support it.

MODEL TEST 2

Answer Keys and Explanations — Test of Communication Skills

LISTENING SKILLS

Answer Key

PART A	PART B	PART C
1. C	16. A	31. D
2. D	17. B	32. B
3. C	18. D	33. A
4. D	19. B	34. D
5. D	20. C	35. A
6. C	21. A	36. A
7. A	22. B	37. B
8. C	23. A	38. D
9. B	24. C	39. B
10. D	25. D	40. D
11. A	26. C	
12. A	27. D	
13. D	28. B	
14. C	29. D	
15. D	30. D	

Explanations

Part A

1. **(C)** The other choices give additional information; they do not answer the question.

2. **(D)** Choice (A) is untrue in view of the planning mentioned in the statement. Choices (B) and (C) were fortuitous happenings that basically could not have been prevented by planning. Allotting time in various places (D), however, is a fundamental part of planning a trip.

3. **(C)** Perception is related to a sense of awareness and appropriateness in a given situation. The other statements do not relate to decision-making on a personal basis.

4. **(D)** Self-knowledge includes self-evaluation as an effective teacher. The teacher has to make decisions with the best interests of pupils in mind and a knowledge of his or her ability to implement these requirements. Choice (A) contradicts the premise of the question; (B) and (C) do not answer the question.

5. **(D)** Choice (A) may or may not be true. Choices (B) and (C) explain the situation but do not support the statement that Mrs. Pollard had won a victory.

6. **(C)** Research shows that teachers can make an impact on children's thinking. Practice in thinking helps pupils to keep an open mind and to take in more possibilities for choices. Choices (A) and (B) are true but irrelevant, and (C) contradicts, not supports, the statement.

7. **(A)** Choices (B) and (C) are insufficient reasons to get lost; with a compass (A) John could have found his way in spite of the storm and the distraction of the violets. Choice (D) deepens the mystery, rather than answering the question.

428

TEST OF COMMUNICATION SKILLS

8. **(C)** Since schools are still basically controlled by local boards, communities that are becoming victims of their own systems lack local leadership. For example, many bond issues do not pass because of poor public relations on the local level. Choices (A), (B), and (D) are irrelevant to the statement.

9. **(B)** This is the only choice that answers the question. Choice (A) explains the appeal of these animals, and (C) and (D) deal with the effects on the animals of being raised as pets.

10. **(D)** This statement indicates the current attitude that teachers are responsible for pupil learning, even the first year a program is used. If this were not the case, pupils would be the losers every time materials or textbooks are changed.

11. **(A)** This is the only choice directly related to "systematic harrassment."

12. **(A)** In some courses, such as music, physical education, and foreign languages, performance tests may be more valuable than written ones. Skills need to be observed and evaluated directly by the teacher on an individual basis.

13. **(D)** The other choices provide additional information about the ERA but do not answer the question.

14. **(C)** In interpersonal interviews, the teacher who listens to pupil comments and responses can often gain insight, from just one or two questions, into thinking skills, prejudices, and lack of information. Choices (A), (B), and (D) do not relate to *analysis* of the interview.

15. **(D)** The increase in the number of elected officials (one evidence of political gain) supports the statement given. Choices (A) and (B) provide additional information about the Voting Rights Act, and (C) is irrelevant since it does not deal with political gains.

Part B

16. **(A)** He did not answer the question (B), but his response indicates that he heard the question (C) and that he is not indifferent to heat and cold (D). Choice (A) is the only one left.

17. **(B)** The reference to "dumb questions" rules out patience (A), pleasure (C), and indifference (D). Color him rude (B).

18. **(D)** There is no evidence in the conversation to support any other choice.

19. **(B)** The other generalizations are obviously untrue, and there is no reason to choose them. The woman has given a specific reason why she is disappointed in one teacher.

20. **(C)** The woman has mentioned two benefits from participation in the group project. Therefore she is not a pessimist (A), and she is disagreeing with the man, thereby eliminating (B). Choice (D) contradicts the dialog.

MODEL TEST 2

21. **(A)** This is the only logical choice; she would not mention new "friends" unless she thought they would be kept. There is no support in the dialog for any of the other choices.

22. **(B)** Note "It is difficult to understand Central Americans" and "the quietness of village life."

23. **(A)** "Helping them achieve a more prosperous lifestyle" implies providing economic aid. There is no support for any of the other choices.

24. **(C)** There is no justification in the conversation for any of the other choices. Both of the man's contributions deal with new or forthcoming capabilities of the computer.

25. **(D)** The woman's attitude is irreverent and jocular. The man, on the other hand, is serious.

26. **(C)** Note "When properly programmed." Nowhere is it stated that the man himself is a programmer (D).

27. **(D)** The clue is "Please consider how you can give them this help."

28. **(B)** The woman's final statement is "I'll go to work on it."

29. **(D)** Note "As parents we . . . ."

30. **(D)** "I can't be expected to know everything that's going on" is defensive.

Part C

31. **(D)** The speaker says, "Batteries are taking over my home" and "Why must we depend . . . ."

32. **(B)** "Blessed will be the person who invents something to replace batteries!"

33. **(A)** The entire talk is on this theme. The cost and unpredictability of batteries are specifically mentioned.

34. **(D)** The talk describes specifically the birthday celebration for Poe, thereby eliminating (C). There is nothing in the talk about Poe's poetry (A), and the celebration, although unusual, hardly qualifies as an orgy (B).

35. **(A)** The talk has no other purpose than to entertain. It will not frighten (B), educate (C), or inflate the market for cognac and roses (D).

36. **(A)** The date of the celebration, January 19, is mentioned at the start of the talk.

37. **(B)** The other topics are all subordinate to this one.

38. **(D)** This information is given: "New Jersey may decide to hire people to teach who have taken no education courses."

39. **(B)** "This year could be the costliest one yet for American education."

40. **(D)** The final statement is "A top priority is creative financing."

TEST OF COMMUNICATION SKILLS

READING

Answer Key

1.	A	7.	A	13.	B	19.	D	25.	A
2.	C	8.	C	14.	A	20.	C	26.	C
3.	C	9.	D	15.	D	21.	D	27.	C
4.	C	10.	B	16.	D	22.	A	28.	B
5.	B	11.	A	17.	B	23.	D	29.	E
6.	C	12.	D	18.	E	24.	B	30.	E

Explanations

1. **(A)** Educated persons are more likely to understand the responsibilities of citizenship and to participate in government.

2. **(C)** The dangers of emotional problems and of obtaining the money to finance the habit are mentioned.

3. **(C)** The simple sentences are typical of writing aimed at children. Also note "you will be using before the end of this year"; this rules out the other choices.

4. **(C)** The author assumes that teachers can arouse interest with certain presentation techniques, in this case arousing curiosity and satisfying it at the end of the passage.

5. **(B)** The passage appeals to children's curiosity: What is this strange table being described?

6. **(C)** The main purpose of the author is to show that some stress is good, whereas distress affects the human body in a negative way. The second sentence rules out (A), and (D) is only briefly mentioned. There is no support for (B) or (E).

7. **(A)** Everyone needs to know when stress (the motivator) urges people to do too much or to take on too many responsibilities, thereby incurring distress. The answers to (B) and (C) are given. The autonomic nervous system is not mentioned (D), and the answer to (E) can be inferred.

8. **(C)** The author assumes that the scientific method would work as well for the social as for the physical sciences.

9. **(D)** Note "almost never go to school."

10. **(B)** She is saying that although she was sitting in the chair, the chair was still empty. In other words, no one was sitting in the chair—she was no longer a person.

11. **(A)** The main idea is that a million American children are in trouble, either as voluntary runaways or as "throwaways" through home problems.

12. **(D)** These are the "throwaway kids."

13. **(B)** "Nobody knows who they [John Does] are."

431

MODEL TEST 2

14. **(A)** The author is concerned that poor parenting techniques, due to the lack of effective parent models, will be continued in the families of these troubled children.

15. **(D)** The author assumes that parental models are the most significant factors in determining the kind of homes people establish. The troubled children of today will become the inadequate parents of tomorrow.

16. **(D)** The tone is not hopeful (A), objective (B), or sarcastic (E). There is the fearful (C) element of revolution, but the prevailing tone is somber—"frustration," "confrontation," "Neither side . . . disposed to yield."

17. **(B)** The AIM leaders are preparing for a confrontation; therefore they are not willing to compromise (A) or likely to accept a nominal sum in settlement of their claims (D). According to the passage, they are focusing on the return of their lands, not on improvement of conditions on the reservations (C). The words "sacred to the Lakota-Sioux" rule out (E).

18. **(E)** Credit card companies would oppose a surcharge or any other measure that would discourage use of credit cards. Merchants (A) as a whole might well favor the surcharge. Choices (B), (C), and (D) would probably also oppose a surcharge, but not to the same extent as credit card companies; they would have the option of using cash or checks.

19. **(D)** Note the cues—"startling increase" and "will also be burdened."

20. **(C)** The author is stressing the idea that women can have successful marriages and careers.

21. **(D)** Dr. Yalow is an example of a competent wife, parent, and scientist—living evidence of what women can achieve.

22. **(A)** The author assumes that women who know about successful high achievers will seek to emulate these role models.

23. **(D)** The main topic is the increased number of high school graduates, both black and white, due to improved attitudes and more challenging school work.

24. **(B)** Jack is going to X College and will major in business administration, physics, or chemistry; therefore we cannot say that either I or III *must* be true. Luigi will attend Y College and will major in English, drama, or business administration; therefore II (B) is the only choice that *must* be true.

25. **(A)** Information is presented objectively. Readers are not encouraged (B), persuaded (C), or urged (D), nor are advanced placement courses advocated for all students.

26. **(C)** The other statements are not supported by the passage.

27. **(C)** Several examples of excellent selective high schools are discussed. Some details (D) about these schools are given, but the primary means of development is by the use of example.

TEST OF COMMUNICATION SKILLS

28. **(B)** The meaning of *mandated* can be inferred, if not known, in two ways: (1) from the name of the high school—this, however, would not rule out "traditional" (D), and (2) from the emphasis on more difficult courses and generally high levels of expectation.

29. **(E)** Dividing 950, the number of students accepted, into 7000, the number of applicants, gives a ratio of about 1 to 7.

30. **(E)** Stuyvesant High emphasizes engineering, Joy's career choice.

WRITING: MULTIPLE-CHOICE

Answer Key

PART A		PART B	PART C
1. D	15. B	28. A	37. A
2. B	16. E	29. D	38. D
3. A	17. B	30. D	39. A
4. E	18. B	31. E	40. D
5. B	19. B	32. D	41. C
6. B	20. D	33. E	42. D
7. C	21. E	34. A	43. E
8. C	22. C	35. A	44. B
9. E	23. D	36. C	45. C
10. A	24. C		
11. D	25. D		
12. B	26. A		
13. D	27. A		
14. C			

Explanations

Part A

1. **(D)** *Each*, the subject of the sentence, is singular; therefore a singular verb (*has contributed*) is needed.

2. **(B)** *Without* is correct as a preposition or an adverb; its use as a conjunction, as here, should be avoided. In this case the correct word is *unless*.

3. **(A)** The pronoun is the object of the verb *described*; hence the objective case (*whom*) is needed.

4. **(E)** The sentence, including the verbs, capitalization, and conjunction *although*, is correct.

5. **(B)** When two coordinate clauses are not joined by a conjunction, the semicolon, not the comma, is required between them.

6. **(B)** The words are transposed; the plants are growing *both in* open water and *on* high sites.

7. **(C)** The compound personal pronoun *myself* should be replaced by *I*. *Myself* is correctly used in "I hurt myself" and "I myself must bear the blame."

MODEL TEST 2

8. **(C)** The sentence lacks parallel structure. Since *throwing* is a gerund, the corresponding form *tearing* should be used.

9. **(E)** The sentence has no errors. The possessive is spelled correctly, and the singular verb *is given* agrees with the singular subject *list*.

10. **(A)** A religious title preceding a name should be capitalized.

11. **(D)** The sentence lacks parallel structure. A third gerund (*canoeing*) is required.

12. **(B)** The sentence has a compound subject (*dogs, horses, lions, elephant*) and therefore requires a plural verb (*were*).

13. **(D)** The words *below zero* are redundant; −18 degrees *is* below zero.

14. **(C)** Maine can't have more pine trees than itself; *any other state* is correct.

15. **(B)** The sentence suffers from a double negative: *not* and *nor*; the latter should be *or*.

16. **(E)** The sentence is correct.

17. **(B)** The word *because* should be replaced by *that* to introduce a noun clause used as a predicate nominative; *because* introduces an adverbial clause.

18. **(B)** That Stephanie comes from a single-parent home and that she was elected class president are two unrelated ideas that should not be joined by *and* to form a compound sentence.

19. **(B)** The correct correlatives are *neither . . . nor*; *or* should be replaced by *nor*.

20. **(D)** Verbs like *look, feel, smell,* and *touch* are often followed by predicate adjectives; here *strange* is needed.

21. **(E)** The sentence is correct; a plural verb (*are*) and the two commas are needed.

22. **(C)** The correlative expression is *not only . . . but also*; the second *that* is misplaced. The correct order is *but also that*.

23. **(D)** The words *wasn't but* constitute a double negative; *wasn't* should be replaced by *was*.

24. **(C)** The word *complete*, like *perfect* or *unique*, is an absolute term and cannot be compared. Here *most nearly complete* or *most comprehensive* would be correct.

25. **(D)** The nominative case (*I*) is needed as subject of the verb *am* (understood).

26. **(A)** As a general rule, *among*, not *between*, is used when referring to more than two.

27. **(A)** *Had* should not be used with *ought*.

TEST OF COMMUNICATION SKILLS

Part B

28. **(A)** The original sentence is correct. One thing is preferred *to* another; the other choices are unidiomatic or clumsy.

29. **(D)** In the original sentence (A) and in (E) *being* is a dangling participle that appears to relate to *we*. In (B) and (C) *due to* is not the preferred form; *because of* would be the better phrase.

30. **(D)** In the original sentence (A) *which* has no antecedent; in (D) the noun *practice* has been added, and *that* refers to it. Choice (B) is incorrectly punctuated; a semicolon is needed between the clauses since no conjunction is used. Choices (C) and (E) change the meaning.

31. **(E)** The phrase *in the evening* in all the other choices is redundant; 8 P.M. *is* in the evening.

32. **(D)** The two clauses are not of equal weight and should not be joined by *and*; the compound sentence does not express the relationship between the ideas. Only (D) expresses the idea that Bryan did well *in spite of* his lack of study.

33. **(E)** Miss Wiley's way of teaching is not different from the other teachers; it is different from their way of teaching. *Different from* is preferable to *different than* (B, C, D).

34. The original sentence is correct. The first two commas set off words in apposition, and the third introduces a quotation.

35. **(A)** The original sentence is correct. The singular verb *was* agrees with *report*, ruling out (B); *because of* is preferable to *due to* in (C) and (D); and *had been* is the proper tense. In (E) *was* is wrong also because a plural verb is needed.

36. **(C)** This is the only choice in which there are two parallel adjective clauses joined by *and* and both modifying *chemicals*.

37. **(A)** Only choice (A) continues not only the substance of the passage but the style and tone as well.

38. **(D)** Sentence (4), although it discusses the Human Relations Committee mentioned in sentence (3), is not related to the main idea, which is a description of the Kara Young Human Relations Award.

39. **(A)** This sentence gives additional examples of causes of misbehavior, a logical continuation of sentence (5), which is then further developed in sentence (6).

40. **(D)** Sentence (4) does not belong in the passage. The main idea of this paragraph is stated in the first sentence: a special faculty workshop on problems of classroom management. Dr. Frantzen's tour plans are not related to either the workshop or the subject of the workshop.

MODEL TEST 2

41. **(C)** Sentences (3) and (4) do not belong in the passage. They might be part of a later paragraph in this letter, but they are out of place in this paragraph.

42. **(D)** The interest shown by teachers from other districts indicates an increasing acceptance of the program.

43. **(E)** The function of sentence (4) is to express the main idea of the passage.

44. **(B)** The fact that "the weight of solid professional opinion opposes . . . formal instruction" supports the author's position.

45. **(C)** Only this sentence has a style appropriate for this passage.

WRITING: ESSAY

When you have finished, ask two or three honest critics—teachers or other persons whose knowledge of written English you respect—to evaluate your essay in regard to the items listed on page 64 and to point out any aspects of your writing that need improvement. Request them to indicate specific errors in grammar, sentence structure, diction, and mechanics (capitalization and punctuation) to which you are prone and which you must be careful to avoid on the actual test.

Model Test 2
Test of Professional Knowledge

SECTION 1

Time — 30 minutes

Directions: For each question or incomplete statement below, there are five suggested answers or completions. Select the one that *best* answers the question or completes the statement.

1. The teacher must be aware that both heredity and environment represent complex factors, exerting many specific influences on an individual's growth. Which of the following statements best represents the influence of heredity and environment?
   (A) Heredity counts; environment is less important.
   (B) If the environment is changed, heredity becomes less important.
   (C) The relative influences of heredity and environment can vary widely in an individual's growth.
   (D) In the long run, both tend to cancel each other's influence.
   (E) None of the above

2. The best possible way to measure the influence of heredity is by
   (A) keeping the environment constant
   (B) ignoring the environment
   (C) studying fraternal twins of normal capability
   (D) studying identical twins of normal capability
   (E) doing none of the above

3. The teacher who encourages students to develop their own questions, to set their own goals, to search for answers, and to use new information in creative ways is using
   (A) the "engineering" approach to learning
   (B) the inquiry method
   (C) the classical-school approach
   (D) the field-theory method
   (E) the Herbartian method

4. Excessive verbalism on a teacher's part may create a psychological barrier to learning, particularly for
   (A) hyperactive children
   (B) disadvantaged learners
   (C) gifted children
   (D) physically handicapped students
   (E) artistic children

437

MODEL TEST 2

5. Knowledge that children differ in their capacity to learn has led to the continued development of tools for testing the child's
   (A) special aptitudes
   (B) musical ability
   (C) motor skills
   (D) clerical ability
   (E) artistic interests

6. If a teacher accepts Maslow's theory on the hierarchy of needs, he or she will probably structure objectives to
   (A) meet both the physiological and intellectual needs of students
   (B) eliminate testing
   (C) eliminate extrinsic motivations
   (D) maintain a certain anxiety level for increased competition
   (E) do none of the above

7. A widespread misbelief held by parents and teachers is that adolescents
   (A) will become self-disciplined solely through autocratic control
   (B) do best when no discipline is given
   (C) dislike discipline, therefore, should not have it
   (D) develop self-control by modeling parents and teachers
   (E) get too much discipline in school

8. Those who favor open education support

   I. Rigid time structuring
   II. Responsible student self-direction
   III. An emphasis on success rather than failure

   (A) I only
   (B) II only
   (C) I and II only
   (D) III only
   (E) II and III only

9. Which behavior is atypical of a student with social adjustment problems?
   (A) Isolation and hyperactivity
   (B) Anxiety or dependency
   (C) Withdrawal from others
   (D) Feelings of depression
   (E) Excessive shyness

10. Under which of the following circumstances are teachers mandated to report child sexual abuse?
    (A) When a child regularly comes to school with soiled underwear.
    (B) When a teacher suspects sexual abuse but has no evidence that this is true.
    (C) When a teacher sees a child touching her or his own genitals.
    (D) Only when a teacher personally has observed an adult abusing a child.
    (E) When a child frequently plays doctor or nurse and is seen examining a doll's genitals.

11. Carl Rogers urged teachers to stop "teaching" and to start "facilitating learning." A teacher who follows Rogers' urging would probably
    (A) establish a competitive climate in the classroom
    (B) always require the correct answer
    (C) use multimedia materials to provide a variety of learning experiences
    (D) permit pupils to use classroom computers only for spelling programs
    (E) plan lessons around lengthy lectures

TEST OF PROFESSIONAL KNOWLEDGE

12. A teacher wants to develop experience-referenced individualized instruction for his eighth-grade English class. He will probably use
    (A) learning centers
    (B) diagnostic-prescriptive teaching techniques
    (C) programs developed around student's interests
    (D) state-developed syllabi
    (E) educational software

13. In measuring a child's social skills, the most useful and least costly results can be attained by using
    (A) direct observations and parent-teacher conferences
    (B) psychological tests
    (C) adaptive behavior scales
    (D) records of extracurricular activities
    (E) parent questionnaires

14. Which of the following authorities is legally responsible for teacher certification?
    (A) The federal government
    (B) The National Association of Teachers
    (C) State governments
    (D) Local school boards
    (E) Undergraduate and graduate schools of education

15. Which of the following mental maturity tests can be used with children who have language difficulties?

    I. Draw-A-Man Test
    II. Leiter International Performance Scale
    III. Raven's Progressive Matrices Test

    (A) I only
    (B) II only
    (C) I and II only
    (D) I, II, and III
    (E) II and III only

16. In *Diana v. State Board of Education* (1970), a suit was brought on behalf of nine Mexican-American students who were placed in classes for the educable mentally retarded based on IQ scores obtained from administration of either the Stanford-Binet or Wechsler intelligence tests. This resulted in legislation requiring that children be tested in their primary language based on the argument that
    (A) these IQ tests were based on a dominant white, middle class culture and standardized on groups that were English-speaking
    (B) these IQ tests were standardized before large numbers of Mexican-Americans entered schools in the United States
    (C) the IQs of children from other cultures should be expected to differ from those of middle-class American-born children.
    (D) most of the children in special education classes do not speak English
    (E) children who come from other cultures should always be placed in regular education classes as there is no way to test their abilities

MODEL TEST 2

17. Lee obtained a percentile rank of 30 on a mathematics test. Lee's parents will learn that
    (A) Lee is a top student in the advanced class
    (B) Lee got 30% of the test items correct
    (C) Lee obtained a score higher than 30% of the students in the class
    (D) Lee got 70% of the items correct
    (E) Lee obtained a score higher than 70% of the students who took the test

18. A teacher uses behavior modification techniques in his classes. Which of the following student behaviors would he find most difficult to change?
    (A) Aggressive tendencies toward classmates
    (B) Poor habits in organizing work materials
    (C) Interrupting a speaker
    (D) Abandoning a project before it is finished
    (E) Failure to read the full question before answering

19. To improve their athletic performance, a coach appeals to her students' capacity for self-motivation. Which of the following motivations would be counterproductive to good team performance?
    (A) Curiosity about the plays that other teams develop
    (B) A desire for affiliation with team members
    (C) The use of goal-setting in developing strength and skills
    (D) The desire for athletic competence
    (E) The desire for independence in decision-making

20. Shaping, a form of operant conditioning, is successful with educable mentally retarded children because it
    I. provides frequent feedback
    II. begins with easily achieved goals
    III. provides multiple success experiences

    (A) I only
    (B) II only
    (C) III only
    (D) I and III only
    (E) I, II, and III

21. Learning-disabled children most characteristically have
    (A) low IQs
    (B) poor socioeconomic backgrounds
    (C) an average level of intelligence
    (D) minimal brain damage
    (E) maladaptive social behaviors

22. Hyperactive children and emotionally disturbed children are alike in that both tend to
    (A) have behavior problems
    (B) dislike teachers
    (C) be given drug therapy
    (D) come from broken homes
    (E) fight with other children

TEST OF PROFESSIONAL KNOWLEDGE

23. Which of the following is true about educable mentally retarded children?
    (A) Their IQs range between 75 and 100.
    (B) They have short attention spans and experience difficulty in generalizing.
    (C) Their reading, writing, and arithmetic skills cannot be improved.
    (D) Their reading scores generally go up one grade level every six years.
    (E) They respond well to the use of delayed rewards.

24. Which of the following would most likely be the purpose behind a teacher using role-playing in her civics class?
    (A) To get students in front of the class so they become accustomed to speaking before an audience of their peers
    (B) To present difficult material in a simple way
    (C) To learn to act independently
    (D) To speed up the course content
    (E) To help pupils learn to interact with others in solving common problems

25. Which of the following strategies would be useful for a teacher managing a group lesson?
    (A) Giving instructions quickly so that no time is wasted
    (B) Keeping interruptions to a minimum after the lesson has begun
    (C) Summarizing only at the end of the lesson
    (D) Having a haphazard seating plan
    (E) Discouraging students' questions about the subject of the lesson

26. Teachers who tend to focus on children who exhibit disruptive behavior in the classroom should watch also for children with
    (A) aggressive behavior
    (B) withdrawn behavior
    (C) high motivation
    (D) few emotional problems
    (E) restless behavior

27. Which of the following are important in helping to motivate students?

    I. Helping them set realistic goals
    II. Providing frequent feedback, both positive and negative
    III. Giving constructive criticism
    IV. Providing challenging situations

    (A) I only
    (B) II only
    (C) III only
    (D) II and IV only
    (E) I, II, III, and IV

28. Which of the following is characteristic of a dyslexic child?
    (A) Mirror writing
    (B) Listlessness
    (C) Below-average intelligence
    (D) Hyperactivity
    (E) Diligence

29. Which of the following is an accurate statement about local school boards?
    (A) They are made up of full-time, paid employees.
    (B) They are made up of teachers in the district, serving on a voluntary basis.
    (C) They are appointed by the governor of each state.
    (D) They are subcommittees of the each state's Department of Education.
    (E) They are usually elected by the citizenry living within the school district.

30. Students with secondary reading problems have normal capacity to read, but are nonreaders because of
    (A) auditory problems
    (B) congenital defects
    (C) visual-acuity impairment
    (D) environmental or emotional factors
    (E) lack of interest

READ THE FOLLOWING DIRECTIONS BEFORE PROCEEDING.

Directions: The following questions contain the word LEAST, NOT, or EXCEPT. Read each question very carefully, then find the answer that applies.

31. Primary reading retardation is presumed to be neurologically based, related to parietal lobe dysfunction. Which of the following behaviors is NOT associated with this dysfunction?
    (A) Inability to relate sounds to letter symbols
    (B) Inadequate auditory information processing
    (C) Left-right directional confusion
    (D) Imprecise articulation
    (E) Speech aphasia

32. In the long run, effective classroom management is NOT achieved through the use of
    (A) a few rules that are enforced inconsistently
    (B) rules with consequences that students accept
    (C) strategies for eliminating distractions
    (D) pupil input to make rules and consequences
    (E) nonpartial enforcement of rules

33. Which of the following behaviors is LEAST likely to be observed in children from father-absent homes in comparison with children from father-present homes?
    (A) A diminished scholastic performance
    (B) A tendency to be absent more frequently
    (C) A desire to receive delayed rewards for performance
    (D) A tendency to show poor personal care
    (E) A tendency to require immediate rewards

TEST OF PROFESSIONAL KNOWLEDGE

34. According to law, a program for a handicapped child must specify all of the following EXCEPT
    (A) the special services to be provided
    (B) the length of tests to be given
    (C) the projected date for beginning individualized instruction, and the duration of the special services
    (D) individualized objectives
    (E) plans for evaluation and for an annual review of the child's progress

35. When compared to parents in other cultures, American parents have similar expectations for their children EXCEPT that
    (A) British parents encourage more independence
    (B) American fathers have little interest in education
    (C) American parents are stricter disciplinarians than western European parents
    (D) European parents spend less time with their children
    (E) American parents encourage more individuality and decision-making by children

S T O P

IF YOU FINISH BEFORE TIME IS CALLED, YOU MAY CHECK YOUR WORK ON THIS SECTION ONLY. DO NOT WORK ON ANY OTHER SECTION IN THE TEST.

MODEL TEST 2
SECTION 2

Time — 30 minutes

Directions: For each question or incomplete statement below, there are five suggested answers or completions. Select the one that *best* answers the question or completes the statement.

1. When dealing with a student who claims to be having a problem with an assignment, the teacher who is well-informed about learning processes is
   (A) likely to conclude that there is no problem
   (B) likely to recognize several causes for the student's difficulty, rather than a single one
   (C) more likely to focus on the difficulty than the student's experience of it
   (D) likely to blame the pupil
   (E) likely to tell the student to "just keep trying"

2. During the learning process the teacher has most control over
   (A) the learner
   (B) the learning environment
   (C) the learning process
   (D) the behavior of the learners
   (E) learner motivations

3. The teachers in a particular school regard learning in a "bifocal" way. This means that they view and interpret classroom activities as
   (A) perceivers   (D) supervisors
   (B) instructors   (E) participant observers
   (C) learners

4. A nonparticipating classroom observer can provide valuable information to a teacher because
   I. The observer is probably less subjective than the teacher.
   II. The observer can spend full time recording observations.
   III. The observer can focus on certain behaviors and systematically code them.

   (A) I only
   (B) II only
   (C) III only
   (D) I and II only
   (E) I, II, and III

5. A teacher is planning an open classroom for her social studies program. Which of the following is unessential in preparing for this method of teaching?
   (A) Placing attractive posters around the area
   (B) Preparing a detailed record-keeping system
   (C) Preparing detailed outlines of each pupil's assignment with the pupil
   (D) Providing a well-stocked library
   (E) Providing materials for students who finish their work early

TEST OF PROFESSIONAL KNOWLEDGE

6. Which of the following conditions interfere with a climate psychologically suited to learning?
   (A) The teacher acts like a "real person."
   (B) The teacher makes all of the decisions about students' learning activities
   (C) The teacher accepts students as they are.
   (D) The teacher shows trust in students' decisions.
   (E) The teacher expresses nonjudgmental understanding of students' personal problems.

7. Which of the following is characteristic of criterion-referenced teaching strategies?
   I. Desired behaviors are specified. For example: "Given 10 sentences containing errors in noun-verb agreement, the student will be able to correct them with 100% accuracy."
   II. Adequate instruction is given to enable students to perform the behaviors that are specified.
   III. Using measures such as tests or specified performance, the teacher makes an analysis of whether objectives are being met.

   (A) I only
   (B) II only
   (C) I and III only
   (D) II and III only
   (E) I, II, and III

8. A teacher tells the senior English class, "You will have to write research papers when you attend college. Tomorrow we will begin to develop techniques for writing one." This is an example of identifying
   (A) psychological needs
   (B) normative needs
   (C) assimilation needs
   (D) instrumental-learning needs
   (E) needs for accommodation

9. Rogers sees teachers as facilitators of learning. According to his findings, significant learning takes place when the teacher does which of the following?
   I. Helps learners clarify their goals
   II. Encourages students to evaluate their learning progress
   III. Helps students modify behavior and attitudes

   (A) I only
   (B) II only
   (C) III only
   (D) I and III only
   (E) I, II, and III

10. During class discussions, a teacher responds with prompting remarks. Select the comment that would further discussion by the pupil to whom it is addressed.
    (A) "That's very interesting, but we have more than enough examples now."
    (B) "I can't understand what you mean. Why can't you explain your ideas more clearly?"
    (C) "Can't you do better than that?"
    (D) "Do you have any other ideas about this problem?"
    (E) "How long have you been keeping such silly notions to yourself?"

MODEL TEST 2

11. Standardized tests for measuring pupil achievement have many advantages over teacher-made tests. Which one of the following is a disadvantage of standardized tests?
    (A) Students are tested under matching conditions.
    (B) Such tests have high reliability.
    (C) Such tests have high validity.
    (D) The norms are based on nation-wide testing.
    (E) Such tests are more costly than teacher-made tests.

12. In emphasizing "mastery learning," studies indicate that, if teachers gave pupils all the time they need,
    (A) only one third would fail in a typical unit of work
    (B) one third would learn something useful
    (C) about one half would turn out to be good students
    (D) about two thirds would pass criterion-referenced tests
    (E) only about 5–10 percent would get grades below A or B

13. The term *reliability* indicates
    (A) meaning   (D) standard deviation
    (B) validity   (E) normal curve
    (C) consistency

14. A teacher likes to use essay questions with his world history class. Students often complain that they know information he does not ask. Another disadvantage of teacher-made tests is
    (A) They are too reliable.
    (B) They are written at appropriate levels of difficulty, which makes it unlikely that students will achieve high scores.
    (C) They may favor the test-taking skills of some students over others.
    (D) They never contain criterion-referenced items.
    (E) They never contain norm-referenced items.

15. The legal basis for compulsory school attendance rests on which of the following?
    (A) Teachers are better at instruction than parents.
    (B) Children, if left uneducated, grow up to be non-productive citizens who may become criminals.
    (C) Illiteracy is illegal.
    (D) Agriculture and industry cannot function without a large number of well-educated employees.
    (E) The state has the authority to enact reasonable laws for the well-being of its citizens.

16. William Glasser advocates the frequent use of classroom meetings, with teacher and students sitting in a small circle. Which one of the following types of discussion would be inappropriate in such a setting?
    (A) An educational-diagnostic conference on the learning weaknesses of individual students.
    (B) An open-ended meeting for the purpose of exploring and discussing students' ideas about the curriculum
    (C) A social-problem-solving meeting to resolve teacher or student problems relating to the school, the class, or any individual member

TEST OF PROFESSIONAL KNOWLEDGE

    (D) A sensitivity-training meeting for the purpose of helping students face their school-related problems and learn how their actions can affect others
    (E) (A) and (C) above

17. Which of the following represents a teacher's contribution to the learning process rather than to the emotional environment of the classroom?
    (A) A strident, compelling voice
    (B) A sustained sense of expectation where student achievement is concerned
    (C) A well-written lesson plan
    (D) A sense of humor in a tense situation
    (E) An instructional tempo that matches the students' pace of learning

18. According to the theory of transactional analysis, full communication is most likely to occur when people maintain certain interaction postures. Which of the following attitudes would be most helpful for teachers to exhibit when communicating with pupils?
    (A) "I'm not OK, you're OK."
    (B) "I'm not OK, you're not OK."
    (C) "I'm OK, you're not OK."
    (D) "I'm OK, you're OK."
    (E) "I'm the parent-figure, you're the child."

19. Habitual set is a deterrent to creative thinking because it is
    (A) Genetic in origin
    (B) Based on convergent thinking
    (C) Accepting of ad hoc solutions
    (D) Flexible in patterns of decision-making
    (E) Open to suggestion

Questions 20–21 are based on the following standardized test results for a student over a four-year period.

Grade — 3.1
Date of Testing — 10/85

Subtest	NUMBER RIGHT	GRADE EQUIV	STANDARD SCORE	NATL PCT
READING Word Attack	23	3.1	142	50
READING Comprehension	46	3.9	154	70
TOTAL READING	69	3.5	148	61
MATHEMATICS Concepts	14	2.5	135	36
MATHEMATICS Computation	20	2.9	145	49
TOTAL MATHEMATICS	34	2.7	140	41
LANGUAGE Vocabulary	39	3.6	147	60
LANGUAGE Usage	55	3.8	153	68
TOTAL LANGUAGE	94	3.7	150	65
SPELLING	30	3.4	147	59
TOTAL BATTERY	227	3.2	150	56

Grade — 4.1
Date of Testing — 10/86

Subtest	NUMBER RIGHT	GRADE EQUIV	STANDARD SCORE	NATL PCT
READING Word Attack	41	4.3	145	56
READING Comprehension	38	5.1	158	75
TOTAL READING	79	4.8	153	67
MATHEMATICS Concepts	33	3.3	132	35
MATHEMATICS Computation	39	3.6	141	45
TOTAL MATHEMATICS	72	3.5	140	42
LANGUAGE Vocabulary	36	4.7	152	65
LANGUAGE Usage	58	4.4	147	60
TOTAL LANGUAGE	94	4.5	148	61
SPELLING	22	4.1	142	50
TOTAL BATTERY	267	4.3	149	54

MODEL TEST 2

Grade — 5.1
Date of Testing — 10/87

Subtest	NUMBER RIGHT	GRADE EQUIV	STANDARD SCORE	NATL PCT
READING Word Attack	52	5.5	148	52
READING Comprehension	41	5.6	153	65
TOTAL READING	93	5.5	150	56
MATHEMATICS Concepts	39	3.9	133	30
MATHEMATICS Computation	30	4.7	138	49
TOTAL MATHEMATICS	69	4.4	136	42
LANGUAGE Vocabulary	21	5.1	143	51
LANGUAGE Usage	36	5.4	153	62
TOTAL LANGUAGE	57	5.3	145	59
SPELLING	30	6.2	159	73
TOTAL BATTERY	249	5.4	151	59

Grade — 6.1
Date of Testing — 10/88

Subtest	NUMBER RIGHT	GRADE EQUIV	STANDARD SCORE	NATL PCT
READING Word Attack	46	5.9	153	48
READING Comprehension	38	6.8	164	74
TOTAL READING	84	6.5	159	62
MATHEMATICS Concepts	24	5.0	144	37
MATHEMATICS Computation	37	6.4	158	56
TOTAL MATHEMATICS	61	5.8	153	44
LANGUAGE Vocabulary	43	6.3	150	57
LANGUAGE Usage	39	6.5	160	60
TOTAL LANGUAGE	82	6.5	159	60
SPELLING	44	6.1	149	50
TOTAL BATTERY	271	6.2	157	58

20. In which skills area is this student's achievement regularly depressed as compared to her/his functioning in other areas?
    - (A) Word attack
    - (B) Reading comprehension
    - (C) Mathematics concepts
    - (D) Mathematics computation
    - (E) Spelling

21. In relation to the group on which these tests were normed, the student's achievement in reading comprehension can be assessed generally as
    - (A) at the upper end of the average range
    - (B) at the upper end of the above average range
    - (C) at the middle of the average range
    - (D) at the lower end of the average range
    - (E) not within the average range

TEST OF PROFESSIONAL KNOWLEDGE

22. Behavior-referenced instruction is an effective educational method in terms of
    (A) the range of behavioral objectives associated with such instruction
    (B) the expectations for performance held out to gifted students
    (C) opportunities for student decision-making
    (D) the accuracy of evaluations possible with such instruction
    (E) opportunities for student input at the planning stages

23. John's first-grade teacher ignores him when he leaves his place once or twice during the period. His teacher is attempting to
    (A) decrease undesirable behavior by ignoring it
    (B) reinforce the desirable behavior of others
    (C) allow time out for undesirable behavior
    (D) prevent other students from engaging in undesirable behavior
    (E) establish who's in control

24. To reduce the probability that a student will repeat undesirable behavior in the future, a teacher should
    (A) reward that student's desirable behavior
    (B) reprimand the student for inattention in class
    (C) make work more interesting for the student
    (D) involve the student's parents in special counseling sessions
    (E) assign busy work to the student

25. Self-control in the classroom can be taught to students by
    (A) encouraging them to penalize themselves for inappropriate behavior
    (B) suggesting forms of self-instruction, such as "Stop, look, and listen" or "Count to 10 before saying anything"
    (C) reprimanding the students on a continuous basis
    (D) encouraging them to criticize one another
    (E) ignoring their presence and contributions until they improve their behavior

26. At varying intervals during the work period, the teacher smiles, nods, or talks to Kim, a child who has difficulty with arithmetic. The teacher will probably find that Kim works for longer periods because of
    (A) the expectation of regular reinforcement
    (B) the surprise element in the reinforcement
    (C) her competitiveness with other students for recognition
    (D) other rewards expected from the teacher
    (E) an increased liking for arithmetic

27. Behaviors learned in Head Start and other preschool programs tend to be
    (A) of permanent value to children
    (B) of little value to children
    (C) lost, unless a "follow-through" program is done at the next level of study
    (D) of decreasing value as children mature
    (E) diluted by other experiences in the child's life

28. A teacher planning to use a criterion-referenced measurement presumably would begin with
    (A) a set of specific objectives for pupil achievement
    (B) varying norms for students of different abilities
    (C) modular scheduling
    (D) a variety of learning experiences to determine student abilities
    (E) pupil-teacher conferences

449

MODEL TEST 2

READ THE FOLLOWING DIRECTIONS BEFORE PROCEEDING.

Directions: The following questions contain the word NOT or EXCEPT. Read each question very carefully, then find the answer that applies.

29. To encourage pupil involvement in the learning situation some teachers use buzz groups. Which of the following statements does NOT reflect the instructional purposes of buzz groups?
    - (A) Buzz groups are useful as "warm-up" devices.
    - (B) Buzz groups help to identify the dominant speaker in each group.
    - (C) Small group discussions can arouse interest in a new subject.
    - (D) Buzz groups extend pupil participation in discussion.
    - (E) Buzz groups are easily initiated by stating a problem in the form of a question.

30. When using objective tests, a teacher will NOT be able to
    - (A) compare students' performances
    - (B) find the mode
    - (C) evaluate students' ability to gather data and derive conclusions
    - (D) do item analysis
    - (E) rank students

31. Educational theory contends that at least 90% of students could reach "mastery level" if appropriate teaching strategies were used. Which of the following would NOT be appropriate advice for a teacher who wants to help underachievers to succeed?
    - (A) Provide more time for slower students to complete a task.
    - (B) Break the curriculum into small steps, teaching incrementally.
    - (C) Determine grades through competitive examinations, giving constant feedback as to comparative performance.
    - (D) Pursue a comprehensive list of performance objectives.
    - (E) Use tutorial help, including cross-age tutoring.

32. Experience-referenced strategies provide quality learning opportunities for pupils. Which of the following would NOT be characterized as an experience-referenced strategy?
    - (A) A student takes a course in baby-sitting.
    - (B) A student develops a project on the 1920s by taping oral histories at a senior citizen home.
    - (C) The editor of the school paper works as an intern on the local newspaper.
    - (D) A student considering a career in design talks to artists whenever she has the opportunity.
    - (E) A student feeds and cares for a guinea pig.

33. A teacher is planning to use diagnostic-prescriptive techniques with his sixth-grade class. Which of the following is NOT likely to be a part of his plan for DPT?
    - (A) sets of behavioral objectives relevant to the unit he will teach
    - (B) tests to determine each student's needs
    - (C) activities designed for remediation of student learning problems
    - (D) improving pupil-pupil interaction
    - (E) class directions for using certain materials

TEST OF PROFESSIONAL KNOWLEDGE

34. Precision teaching is like behavior modification because it is a technique for changing student behavior. Which of the following steps is NOT part of precision teaching?
    (A) Tokens and other extrinsic reinforcers are used.
    (B) Modifications are made as needed in the curriculum, course content, and activities.
    (C) Record-keeping is extensive, and the focus is on having students do it themselves.
    (D) Individual programs are developed for each student.
    (E) Each pupil identifies his or her behaviors that need improvement.

35. Research shows that students who follow the cognitive learning approach manifest all of the following characteristics EXCEPT
    (A) A *global* orientation toward the discovery of new questions and solutions
    (B) An *analytic* mind-set toward new problems
    (C) An *impulsive* habit in drawing conclusions
    (D) A *reflective* manner when examining data
    (E) A *creative* approach to problem-solving

S T O P

IF YOU FINISH BEFORE TIME IS CALLED, YOU MAY CHECK YOUR WORK ON THIS SECTION ONLY. DO NOT WORK ON ANY OTHER SECTION IN THE TEST.

MODEL TEST 2
SECTION 3

Time — 30 minutes

Directions: For each question or incomplete statement below, there are five suggested answers or completions. Select the one that *best* answers the question or completes the statement.

1. According to Mager, instructional objectives should be stated as behavioral objectives. A teacher should specify quantitatively what a student will be able to do, rather than just what he or she should know at the end of a unit or course. Which of the following is the best example of a behavioral objective?
   (A) "The student will explain the reasons for presidential primaries."
   (B) "The student will express himself or herself in class when the subject of primaries is raised."
   (C) "The student will write a research paper on primaries."
   (D) "The student will demonstrate skills for democratic living."
   (E) "The student will list 2 qualifications for each of 5 candidates and will get 8 out of 10 qualifications correct."

2. A mathematics teacher following Gagné's theory of learning believes that
   (A) learning can take place under all conditions
   (B) learning is mainly a matter of accurate discrimination
   (C) learning takes place only when the student is in a receptive state
   (D) learning is reinforced chiefly by classical conditioning
   (E) learning is mainly a matter of linking or chaining ideas

3. A teacher who desires to succeed and to grow should be
   (A) a constant innovator
   (B) a strict disciplinarian
   (C) a flexible, permissive leader
   (D) a model in self-understanding
   (E) a reader and user of educational research applicable to student needs

4. A curriculum committee should consider pupil goals and purposes as
   (A) too immature to be considered in planning course content
   (B) too changeable to be useful
   (C) irrelevant to long-range planning
   (D) significant only for immediate outcomes in daily work
   (E) relevant to the shaping of content and approach

5. Educators today
   (A) differ on the goals of education, but agree on methods
   (B) differ on teaching methods, but agree on goals
   (C) differ on both goals and methods
   (D) agree on methods for teaching reading
   (E) agree on evaluation techniques

TEST OF PROFESSIONAL KNOWLEDGE

6. The teacher who understands the adolescent's need to conform will
   (A) use sarcasm as a disciplinary device
   (B) disregard unique responses in discussions and on examinations
   (C) establish a learning climate that fosters feelings of security
   (D) lecture students on their weaknesses of character
   (E) structure highly competitive learning situations

7. The best public relations agents for a school are the
   (A) pupils
   (B) teachers and pupils
   (C) PTA members
   (D) principals
   (E) athletic coaches

8. The structured curriculum is in decided contrast to the child-centered curriculum, which
   (A) emphasizes fundamental education
   (B) is changeable and is built around student interests and needs
   (C) is oriented to the needs of a democratic society
   (D) utilizes the theory of mental discipline
   (E) emphasizes a particular body of knowledge

9. A teacher has prepared the instructional objectives for his physical education course. What learning outcome does he seek with an objective that begins thus: "Given the question 'What are the requirements for participation in the Olympic games?'"?
   (A) An attitude change
   (B) A verbal association
   (C) Information acquisition and processing
   (D) Signal learning
   (E) A synthesis of information or ideas

10. During the process of learning and comprehending information, pupils experience an *acquisition* phase. The most important processes the pupils use to acquire information are
    (A) motor skills and attitude
    (B) encoding and retrieval
    (C) analysis and evaluation
    (D) decoding and interference
    (E) interference and transference

11. A teacher is doing a task analysis for a science lesson about the honeybee. Which of the following steps is unnecessary in the task-analysis process?
    (A) Describing the learning process to be used
    (B) Specifying educational objectives for the lesson
    (C) Preparing an interest inventory for the students
    (D) Listing prerequisites for the lesson
    (E) Naming the type of performance required for success in the lesson

12. It may seem obvious that the school has a great deal to do with student success. Which of the following statements is disproven by educational research?
    (A) Teachers make a difference in how well students succeed on standardized tests.
    (B) It is possible to measure student achievement with high validity.
    (C) A good curriculum program will turn out academic achievers.
    (D) Students can improve their scores on standardized tests by succeeding in daily classroom work.
    (E) Student achievement is independent of socioeconomic background.

13. A teacher is instructing a beginners' basketball class. If she is to use feedback most effectively, which of the following approaches should she use?
    (A) Put off her comments until 10 minutes before the end of class.
    (B) Provide immediate and informative feedback on an individual basis.
    (C) Comment only when a student fails to make a basket.
    (D) Summarize her observations after each 10-minute interval.
    (E) Criticize individual performances in the hearing of the entire class.

14. Teachers of the handicapped should know the characteristics of common physical disabilities that impair motor function. Which of the following characteristics are NOT correctly matched with a disability?
    (A) *Cerebral palsy:* muscular incoordination and speech disturbance
    (B) *Hemiplegia:* paralysis of one lateral half of the body
    (C) *Diplegia:* paralysis of corresponding parts on both sides of the body, often both legs
    (D) *Muscular dystrophy:* progressive wasting of the skeletal muscles
    (E) *Spina bifida:* curvature of the spine

15. Diabetes mellitus is a metabolic disease related to an insufficiency of
    (A) adrenaline
    (B) insulin
    (C) iodine
    (D) thiamine
    (E) vitamins

16. About 2 percent of the population is affected by epileptic seizures. To assist children with this disorder, a teacher should know the signs that such an attack is occurring. Which of the following describes an epileptic seizure?

    I. An interruption of consciousness with spasmodic convulsions
    II. Apparent daydreaming with twitching eyelids or slight facial movements
    III. Constant "foodless" chewing, purposeless walking, or random hand and arm movements

    (A) I only
    (B) I and III only
    (C) III only
    (D) I, II, and III
    (E) II only

17. All children who suffer a loss through death, divorce, or disability show psychological stress. The grieving process occurs in five successive stages. Which of these stages is the first one out of order in the following list?
    (A) Denial: "If I behave the way I always did, the problem won't bother me."
    (B) Bargaining: "If I do this or you help me do this, the hurt or the problem will go away."
    (C) Anger: "Why did God or my parents or you, my teacher, let this happen to me?"
    (D) Depression: "I feel so bad I don't want to eat or sleep or do anything."
    (E) Acceptance: "I can't run as fast as the other kids, but I can still play ball."

TEST OF PROFESSIONAL KNOWLEDGE

18. If a teacher wants to help his fourth-graders develop social skills, one of the first points he will have to consider with regard to social learning is that
    (A) social roles are learned only in the family
    (B) all role relationships are defined by law
    (C) motor skills are not essential to social behavior
    (D) internalized rules determine personal interaction with others
    (E) social behaviors are unaffected by different social contexts

19. Research on individual learning differences indicates the need for
    (A) the traditonal "lockstep" approach to classroom instruction
    (B) maximizing off-task behaviors
    (C) plenty of free time for each pupil
    (D) the use of the aptitude-treatment-interaction model
    (E) the use of laissez-faire scheduling

20. Students with low achievement levels prefer a classroom learning environment that is
    (A) innovation-oriented
    (B) task-oriented
    (C) well-structured
    (D) competition-oriented
    (E) a combination of (B) and (C) above

21. For a grade placement, which of the following tests would be best to administer to a 10-year-old Puerto Rican boy who does not speak English?
    (A) The Stanford-Binet Intelligence Scale
    (B) The Test of General Ability
    (C) The Otis-Lennon Mental Ability Test
    (D) The Arthur Point Scale of Performance Test
    (E) The Kuhlmann-Anderson Intelligence Test

22. A teacher gave two forms of a standardized test to a class of third-graders. She found that the amount of fluctuation between class scores on both forms was as slight as reported in the test publisher's
    (A) item analysis
    (B) standard deviation
    (C) standard error
    (D) validity proof
    (E) median score

23. A teacher who agrees with Highet that teaching is an art, not a science, will
    (A) focus on learning content
    (B) work on teaching styles rather than on content
    (C) seldom use specific teaching techniques
    (D) maintain that there is more to teaching than content or techniques
    (E) never prepare lesson plans

24. According to federal law, the education of handicapped students
    (A) must be conducted in special classes
    (B) should be done in special schools
    (C) should be done by tutors in the home
    (D) should be a combination of (A) and (B)
    (E) must be done in the "least restrictive environment"

25. According to Bruner, teachers working with young children should
    (A) push the children to maximum cognitive development as rapidly as possible
    (B) present all information verbally so the children will listen well
    (C) present new material from the concrete to the abstract
    (D) present new information from the abstract to the concrete
    (E) use punishment to improve concentration

26. Bruner suggests the use of a spiral curriculum in school planning. This curriculum would be based on
    (A) conservation theories
    (B) pupil-selected learning activities
    (C) appropriate modes of representation
    (D) remediation
    (E) expository learning

27. During class discussions, some high school students tend to be argumentative rather than to listen to another person's viewpoint. The reason for this is their
    (A) egocentric thought process
    (B) use of symbolic thought only
    (C) need for alienation
    (D) Gestalt viewpoint
    (E) inability to use reversability

28. From the educational viewpoint, intelligence is
    (A) an abstract concept
    (B) a trait that can be manipulated
    (C) good judgment
    (D) a form of behavior
    (E) (A) and (D) above

29. A new pupil in a fourth-grade class seems interested in school and is quite verbal, but she cannot read beyond the first-grade level. Before planning work for this child, which of the following should the teacher do?
    (A) Give her individual intelligence and achievement tests.
    (B) Limit her current reading assignments.
    (C) Talk to her parents.
    (D) Request testing by the school psychologist.
    (E) Request placement for her in a third-grade class.

30. Every taxonomy of educational objectives
    (A) describes increasingly difficult learning activities
    (B) describes levels of goals for learner development
    (C) suggests evaluation measures for teacher use
    (D) classifies learning outcomes
    (E) changes broad learning goals to specific goals

READ THE FOLLOWING DIRECTIONS BEFORE PROCEEDING.

Directions: The following questions contain the word LEAST, NOT, or EXCEPT. Read each question very carefully, then seek the answer that applies.

TEST OF PROFESSIONAL KNOWLEDGE

31. Which statement has NOT been borne out by research on children and punishment?
    (A) Some children think they have been punished when the teacher does not give them enough attention.
    (B) Some children are used to punishment in the home and expect it.
    (C) Corporal punishment leads to unpredictable behavior.
    (D) A sharp reprimand is a form of punishment to some children.
    (E) Corporal punishment helps a child learn self-restraint.

32. A teacher is writing new objectives for his social studies class. He wants to advance the cognitive, affective, and psychomotor skills of his students. Which of the following sets of student behaviors would LEAST advance learning?
    (A) Campaigning door-to-door for a mayoral candidate, spelling correctly the names of city officials, joining a walk-a-thon to raise funds
    (B) Sitting in on a press conference, distributing leaflets
    (C) Demonstrating interest in government, painting posters, showing an interest in the lives of the mayoral candidates
    (D) Showing tolerance for differences of opinion, demonstrating the ability to remember issues involved in the mayoral campaign
    (E) Making a scrapbook of campaign speeches

33. According to preliminary research, which of these learning goals in NOT facilitated by the use of classroom word processors?
    (A) The organization of ideas and information
    (B) Accuracy in grammar and punctuation
    (C) The creative process of writing
    (D) Handwriting improvement
    (E) Spelling and word choice

34. According to Vernon Jones, student commitment to accomplishing a learning goal depends on all of the following EXCEPT
    (A) how interesting the goal is
    (B) how likely it seems that the goal can be accomplished
    (C) what degree of challenge the goal presents
    (D) whether the learner will be able to tell if the goal has been accomplished
    (E) whether materials are already assembled for undertaking the goal

35. In talking to teachers about the need for sensitivity toward pupils with behavior problems, a counselor will emphasize all of the following EXCEPT
    (A) awareness of the child's feelings
    (B) empathy for the child
    (C) the need for a variety of affective goals
    (D) the value of reprimands followed by punishment
    (E) the use of reinforcement and warmth

S T O P

IF YOU FINISH BEFORE TIME IS CALLED, YOU MAY CHECK YOUR WORK ON THIS SECTION ONLY. DO NOT WORK ON ANY OTHER SECTION IN THE TEST.

MODEL TEST 2
SECTION 4

Time — 30 minutes

Directions: For each question or incomplete statement below, there are five suggested answers or completions. Select the one that *best* answers the question or completes the statement.

1. A teacher finds that when retarded students and students of normal ability are matched by mental age, both groups of pupils use the same procedures to complete a learning task. This finding corresponds with
   (A) Herbart's theory of intellectual development for all children
   (B) studies that show there is minimal or no advantage in placing retarded students in special classes
   (C) the motivation theory for the development of normal students
   (D) the importance of task-structuring factors in all classrooms
   (E) the concept that learning develops by stages, and that children enter and exit from these stages at varying chronological ages

2. A teacher says that she is planning and implementing success-building strategies in her classes because
   (A) slow learners do not fear failure
   (B) pupils who have repeated successes at school will maintain the motivation to learn and to succeed
   (C) motivation depends less on success than on failure
   (D) this is the current trend in education
   (E) all students should experience failure, since it is a part of life

3. When establishing a teaching strategy plan for Jim who needs to discriminate between the letters *w* and *m*, and the words *was* and *saw*, the teacher plans subtasks, target criteria, reinforcement, and evaluation criteria. If Jim has successive tries without meeting the criteria for discriminating between *was* and *saw* with sentence charts, what should his teacher do next?
   (A) Discontinue the activity and go on to the next step.
   (B) The instruction should be repeated with the same conditions and the same criteria, only the task should be changed.
   (C) If the failure to meet the criteria continues for 8 out of 10 times, for example, an easier task should be selected.
   (D) Reinforcement should be increased in rate after every unsuccessful try.
   (E) The same reinforcement menu should be continued until he meets the criteria.

4. A teacher is having difficulty with discipline in one of his classes and cannot determine the cause. All other things being equal, which of the following suggestions would his supervisor probably make?
   (A) "Become a participant observer."
   (B) "Just ignore the problem."
   (C) "Have a parent conference."
   (D) "Bring in the principal for a couple of hours."
   (E) "Improve your own attitude."

TEST OF PROFESSIONAL KNOWLEDGE

5. Some parents object to the administration of mental maturity (intelligence) tests to their children. Which of the following are the grounds they use to support their objections?

    I. Such tests are inaccurate measurements of ability
    II. Such tests discriminate against children from lower socioeconomic background
    III. The vocabulary in these tests is unfamiliar

    (A) I only
    (B) II only
    (C) III only
    (D) I and II only
    (E) I, II, and III

6. For which group(s) would you expect to have to prepare special motivational materials?

    I. Students with previous experience of failure in a subject
    II. Students from lower socioeconomic households
    III. Students with diagnosed emotional problems
    IV. Students expressing dislike for content or skills areas in the subject

    (A) I only
    (B) II only
    (C) II and III only
    (D) II only
    (E) I, II, III, and IV

7. Children who watch much television during the preschool years often develop a problem that teachers must provide the means to correct. This is a difficulty with
    (A) visual discrimination
    (B) auditory discrimination
    (C) assimilation of ideas
    (D) visual sequencing
    (E) verbal responses

8. A parent met with her child's teacher for a scheduled conference and learned that the teacher had recommended to the principal that the child be retained. The parent requested the reasons for this recommendation and was told that the cumulative record contained a history of test scores indicating academic functioning which was considerably below grade level for several school years. Additionally, she was told that past teachers, as well as the present teacher, had entered information related to the child's inappropriate behavior, lack of interest in school work, and poor attention span. Current and previous information noted on the records indicated that retention would probably be in the best interest of the child. The parent
    (A) had the right to discuss the problem of retention with the principal but could not examine her child's records
    (B) could examine her child's records if she obtained a court order
    (C) could examine her child's records at her request and have inaccurate information removed from them
    (D) must abide by the school's decision to retain her child as it was made by professional educators.
    (E) could require the school to destroy the cumulative records as they might serve to prejudice future teachers

MODEL TEST 2

9. The law stipulates that Janet, who has been classified as mentally retarded, must be evaluated in a "multifaceted" testing program. By definition, which of the following factors must be included in Janet's testing?

   I. Her language and communication skills
   II. Her school achievement, social skills, and activities
   III. Her growth and physical health, as well as her psychological well-being

   (A) I only
   (B) I and II only
   (C) III only
   (D) I and III only
   (E) I, II, and III

10. During a guidance session, a school counselor attempted to bring a student to the point where he would take responsibility for the failure or success of his decisions. When a student can do this, the locus of control is
    (A) internal
    (B) external
    (C) mediated
    (D) neutralized
    (E) phenomenal

11. A teacher's use of rewards and punishment is not working the same way for all pupils. The reason is probably that
    (A) the teacher favors some students over others
    (B) teachers and pupils have different views of what is rewarding
    (C) some pupils don't really care what happens
    (D) some pupils become too anxious
    (E) some pupils mistrust the reward system

12. According to Rosenthal and Jacobson, who researched the "Pygmalion effect," when teachers' expectations of children are raised, these children
    (A) become more restive
    (B) receive higher test scores
    (C) resent the extra work
    (D) become anxious
    (E) become compulsive

13. From their research, Brophy and Good report that during classroom discussions teachers are
    (A) more attentive toward children they consider to be of low ability
    (B) more attentive toward children they consider to be of high ability
    (C) less attentive toward children who seldom say anything
    (D) equally attentive toward children of all ability levels
    (E) overattentive toward children who are shy or apathetic

TEST OF PROFESSIONAL KNOWLEDGE

14. Which of the following is useful for a teacher involved in a "mastery learning" program?

    I. Summative testing over several units
    II. Formative testing during instruction
    III. Diagnostic testing
    IV. Smaller classes and individualized instruction

    (A) I only
    (B) II only
    (C) III only
    (D) III and IV only
    (E) I, II, III, and IV

15. The scope and content of Dewey's curriculum
    (A) emphasize the quantity of experiences, rather than their meaning
    (B) involve interacting, especially with one's peers
    (C) are consistent with the aims of self-realization in a democratic society
    (D) are based on social utility and personal sacrifice
    (E) emphasize the reconstruction of the family, government, and industry

16. A seventh-grade teacher is a firm, autocratic type. The learning climate in his classroom probably would be described by his supervisor as
    (A) competitive
    (B) laissez-faire
    (C) democratic
    (D) purposeful
    (E) self-directed

17. The movement toward accountability in education is significant because it holds
    (A) pupils responsible for their own learning
    (B) parents and pupils responsible for the children's annual progress
    (C) administrators and teachers responsible for students' learning outcomes
    (D) school principals responsible for their students' achievement of national norms
    (E) local boards of education responsible for setting standards for competency testing

18. When constructing a teacher-made test, it is most important for the teacher to
    (A) develop one fourth of the questions at the level of challenge appropriate for the testee
    (B) ask questions based on both factual and conceptual learnings
    (C) ask students to express their point of view
    (D) stress the objectives used during the lesson
    (E) have one essay question to test pupils' integrative abilities

19. When teaching concepts at the elementary grade level, it is most helpful to provide pupils with
    (A) examples and nonexamples of the concept
    (B) a cluster of concepts at one time
    (C) a definition of the concept
    (D) disjunctive concepts
    (E) a story to illustrate the concept

MODEL TEST 2

20. A junior high school principal wants to evaluate the science program. What is the first step she should take?
    (A) Analyze pupil achievement scores.
    (B) Look at national norms for achievement in the sciences.
    (C) Confer with parents.
    (D) Review and, if necessary, revise objectives for the program.
    (E) Give standardized tests.

21. Two classes used the same textbook, had the same assignments, and showed equal intellectual ability and scores on the science pretest. Why did one class score much higher on the final achievement test?
    (A) The successful group had class-supervised study periods.
    (B) The successful group had more students who liked the subject.
    (C) The teacher of the successful group explained the material in more detail.
    (D) Environmental factors in the classroom of the successful group were more conducive to learning.
    (E) The parents of the successful group exerted severe pressure on these students.

22. A teacher is concerned about sixth-grade students who have problems in interpersonal relations. Which of the following devices should she use with these students?
    (A) A sociodrama
    (B) A poetry-writing assignment
    (C) A sociogram
    (D) An interest inventory
    (E) A personality questionnaire

23. In which of the following circumstances can a teacher's employment be terminated?
    (A) Membership in a union
    (B) Membership in a radical political organization
    (C) Pregnancy out of wedlock
    (D) Making public statements, outside of the classroom, on controversial issues not involving employers or co-workers
    (E) Violation of state laws or board policies regulating corporal punishment

24. Interest inventories are valuable for counseling secondary school students because the results are given
    (A) in percentiles
    (B) in the form of career advice
    (C) in the form of a psychological profile
    (D) in stanines scores
    (E) to prospective employers

25. Pupils' creative capabilities can be stimulated through activities. The student who has difficulty expressing himself or herself verbally can write a poem or a story, or construct, draw, or paint an art project. This is a particularly good strategy for disadvantaged children who have
    (A) talent that might be overlooked
    (B) poetic imagination
    (C) poor grammar
    (D) extraordinary experiences
    (E) possibilities listed in (A), (B), and (D)

TEST OF PROFESSIONAL KNOWLEDGE

26. The teacher who shows interest in the way a pupil solves a difficult arithmetic problem is giving attention to the
    (A) affective objectives of education
    (B) pupil's effective work habits
    (C) pupil's maturity
    (D) basis for the student's grade, or score
    (E) mediating processes of learning

27. Instructors often think the intellectually gifted child does not need special attention because such a child
    (A) has more assets than the other children
    (B) should be able to help him- or herself
    (C) probably knows more than the teacher
    (D) usually doesn't want help
    (E) would resent teacher "interference"

28. Under which of the following conditions is a child's IQ more likely to increase?
    (A) If the emotional climate in the classroom improves
    (B) If the child is given a large "research" project
    (C) If the child enjoys problem solving and is given ample opportunity for it
    (D) If all of the above are true
    (E) If (A) and (C) are true

29. The teacher who writes a summative academic evaluation would probably derive the appropriate information from
    (A) a surprise quiz
    (B) a weekly test
    (C) personal observation
    (D) a final examination
    (E) a parent conference

30. High schools that require minimum competency testing for graduation base their pupil evaluation on
    (A) the proficiency levels set for certain courses such as English, social studies, and/or mathematics
    (B) the mean of scores obtained by the upper 10 percent of the class
    (C) the percentile ranking of students in the junior class
    (D) the mean of the scores obtained by the upper half of the senior class
    (E) the student's ability to read at the tenth-grade level

READ THE FOLLOWING DIRECTIONS BEFORE PROCEEDING.

Directions: The following questions contain the word LEAST or NOT. Read each question very carefully, then find the answer that applies.

31. Which one of the following factors is NOT a significant advantage of a standardized test over day-to-day teacher-made tests?
    (A) The standardized test is cost-effective.
    (B) The standardized test is more valid.
    (C) The standardized test is more reliable.
    (D) The standardized test is based on national norms.
    (E) The standardized test provides standard scores and percentile scores.

463

MODEL TEST 2

32. Federal grants for state assistance to schools for the children of migratory workers do NOT provide for
    (A) acquiring school equipment
    (B) construction of school facilities for special needs
    (C) improving existing school programs
    (D) letting the child, with parental consent, continue in the program for up to 7 years
    (E) pre-school educational needs of migrant workers' children

33. When children are denied equal educational opportunity or equal protection under the law involving directly or indirectly the transportation of students, a U.S. court or other agency may set up priorities for the correction of this denial. In that instance, all of the following would apply, but which would have the LEAST priority?
    (A) Establishment or construction of magnet schools
    (B) Revision of attendance zones
    (C) Assignment of students to schools closest to their place of residence, taking into account school capacities and natural physical barriers, and whether the schools have appropriate grade levels
    (D) Assignment of students to schools closest to their residence, taking into account only school capacities
    (E) Permitting students to transfer from a school with a majority of students of their race, color, or national origin to a school where the minority of students are of their race, color, or national origin

34. The knowledge explosion has led to crowding more and more information into curriculum courses. The LEAST likely result is that
    (A) The textbook will no longer be the main instructional medium in many classes.
    (B) The child may spend more time in school.
    (C) The teacher may have to rely more on the use of multimedia materials.
    (D) The teacher will no longer have time to evaluate students.
    (E) Some standardized tests in subject areas such as the sciences will have to be revised more often than was necessary in the past.

35. A teacher wants to use a variety of techniques to appeal to different styles of cognitive learning abilities and interests. Which of the following would be the LEAST effective motivation?
    (A) Making free reading and learning games available for students who complete their projects early
    (B) Canceling a homework assignment
    (C) Penalizing gifted students who fail to reach their potential
    (D) Showing filmstrips
    (E) Offering pupil evaluations on a one-to-one basis

S T O P

IF YOU FINISH BEFORE TIME IS CALLED, YOU MAY CHECK YOUR WORK ON THIS SECTION ONLY. DO NOT WORK ON ANY OTHER SECTION IN THE TEST.

TEST OF PROFESSIONAL KNOWLEDGE

Answer Keys and Explanations—Test of Professional Knowledge

SECTION 1

Answer Key

1.	C	8.	E	15.	D	22.	A	29.	E
2.	D	9.	A	16.	A	23.	B	30.	D
3.	B	10.	B	17.	C	24.	E	31.	E
4.	B	11.	C	18.	A	25.	B	32.	A
5.	A	12.	C	19.	E	26.	B	33.	C
6.	A	13.	A	20.	E	27.	E	34.	B
7.	A	14.	C	21.	C	28.	A	35.	E

Explanations

1. **(C)** Current research shows that heredity and environment interact in a person's development. Certain specific traits are inherited, but whether an individual reaches his or her potential capacity depends on early stimulation and continued positive experiences in a friendly, reinforcing environment.

2. **(D)** Identical twins of normal capability afford the best opportunity to study the influence of heredity. In cases where such children are reared in different home environments by different parents, the researcher can identify common traits that are ascribable to heredity only.

3. **(B)** A major characteristic of the inquiry method is the development of cognitive skills such as these.

4. **(B)** Excessive verbal instructions can become confusing and tedious, especially for children who do not understand the vocabulary used by the teacher when giving directions and explanations. Such students "tune out" the teacher who talks too much.

5. **(A)** Aptitude testing has been refined in recent years.

6. **(A)** According to Maslow, meeting students' survival needs, as well as their intellectual needs, is important.

7. **(A)** The major misbelief about adolescents is that they will learn self-control through autocratic decision-making and punishment given by strict parents. Although some learning and response is acquired through aversive conditioning during adolescence, such a structured environment may encourage rebellion and running away from home.

8. **(E)** In open education, student self-direction is emphasized, as well as success experiences. Both are considered reinforcement for the individual.

9. **(A)** A student with problems in social adjustment will demonstrate all of these behaviors except the combination of isolation and hyperactivity.

465

MODEL TEST 2

10. **(B)** A teacher is required to report suspected abuse. It is not necessary to have proof. Obtaining proof is the function of various child protective services.

11. **(C)** Following Rogers, the emphasis should be on individual experience and growth rather than on competition among pupils for grades.

12. **(C)** The emphasis is on individual experience and progress—not on teacher prescriptions.

13. **(A)** A teacher can observe a child's social skills on a daily basis. If funds are available, standardized scales can be used to add to this information.

14. **(C)** State governments are legally responsible for teacher certification in the United States.

15. **(E)** A child's difficulty with the use of language can affect test outcomes. These three types of tests tend to predict school achievement.

16. **(A)** Individuals should not be evaluated on tests in a language that is not their dominant language and that is based on a culture other than their own. Most IQ tests are not culture-free and, therefore, to some extent assess knowledge of the dominant middle-class culture.

17. **(C)** The percentile is a useful score for showing how a student ranks within a group on the basis of a particular test. This placement is likely to vary from test to test.

18. **(A)** Emotional responses develop over time. Because they are self-reinforcing, they may be difficult to modify.

19. **(E)** The player who emphasizes independent behavior may not be a good team player.

20. **(E)** In shaping, the reinforcement of small steps with frequent feedback gives frequent success experiences to the EMR child. This is essential for his or her self-confidence.

21. **(C)** Children at any level of intellectual ability could be learning-disabled.

22. **(A)** Behavior problems are common among both hyperactive and emotionally disturbed children.

23. **(B)** The reading, writing, and arithmetic skills of EMR children can be improved slowly, according to the ability of each child.

24. **(E)** The use of role-playing elicits class discussion after students observe various behaviors in a "problem situation."

25. **(B)** One of the key elements in a teacher's management of group lessons is the maintenance of a good pace of instruction.

26. **(B)** Children who are withdrawn or moody tend to have more deep-seated problems than those who readily express their emotions.

TEST OF PROFESSIONAL KNOWLEDGE

27. **(E)** In addition to realistic goal-setting, the teacher's feedback, positive criticism, and challenges help to keep students' performance at a high level.

28. **(A)** For some reason, dyslexic children perceive letters and words in reverse—for example, reading *saw* for *was*.

29. **(E)** Local school boards are usually made up of community members who have been elected by voters living within the school district.

30. **(D)** Any number of environmental or emotional factors can, in effect, block a child's reading development and lead him or her to associate reading with failure.

31. **(E)** Speech aphasia is attributed to brain lesion.

32. **(A)** Effective classroom management is laid on the foundation of a few rules that children help to make—rules that are enforced by the teacher consistently for all children. When rules are enforced in this manner, many distractions and arguments are eliminated.

33. **(C)** Children from father-absent homes tend to desire frequent and immediate rewards, as though they need constant reassurance of being worthy and of being loved. Their absence rate is higher than that of children from father-present homes, and they often take poor care of their clothing and show signs of poor personal hygiene habits.

34. **(B)** A program for a handicapped child must be defined clearly, but the teacher has leeway when working within its guidelines.

35. **(E)** The major difference between American parents and parents in other cultures is that American parents permit children more freedom, give them a lot of responsibility, and encourage more individuality and decision-making.

SECTION 2

Answer Key

1.	B	8.	B	15.	E	22.	D	29.	B
2.	B	9.	E	16.	A	23.	A	30.	C
3.	E	10.	D	17.	C	24.	A	31.	C
4.	E	11.	A	18.	D	25.	B	32.	D
5.	A	12.	E	19.	B	26.	B	33.	D
6.	B	13.	C	20.	C	27.	C	34.	E
7.	E	14.	C	21.	A	28.	A	35.	C

Explanations

1. **(B)** Children seldom have just one problem. There tend to be several factors that affect their ability to concentrate, do information-processing, or use cues effectively for problem-solving.

MODEL TEST 2

2. **(B)** The teacher can quickly modify the learning environment, as well as use a variety of orientation techniques. Modification of the habits, skills, and attitudes of individual learners takes much longer to accomplish.

3. **(E)** Teachers often tend to stand apart from the learning situation. The "bifocal" approach requires the teacher to be a participant as well as an observer. This brings the teacher closer to pupils and lets him or her share the learner's experiences.

4. **(E)** An impartial observer who sits in a classroom for a day can give a wealth of valuable information to a teacher because of the time available for observing and recording student behaviors, pupil-teacher interactions, and problems in the areas of discipline, student response-patterns, and the teacher's handling of pupil needs. An impartial observer can focus on either a few pupils or the entire class. Not knowing individual pupils, such an observer is unlikely to have preconceived ideas about any pupil.

5. **(A)** In the open classroom, the library—with its reference books, filmstrips, films, and posters—is most essential for pupil research and reading periods. Posters should be available, with other visual materials, in the library. Planning with students for goals and providing enrichment activities for those who work rapidly are essential.

6. **(B)** An effective learning climate is one in which pupils are encouraged to make daily decisions and choices as they learn the skills of problem-solving. When the teacher makes all the decisions, pupils miss opportunities to initiate learning activities and to evaluate their personal progress.

7. **(E)** Criterion-referenced strategies involve the setting of specific, objective standards and the evaluation of student success against the measure of these standards.

8. **(B)** A normative need is one based on the needs of a group in a certain type of situation. College freshmen are usually required to write themes and research papers. Learning to write a research paper anticipates a normative need for students who plan to attend college.

9. **(E)** Carl Rogers is one of many humanistic educators who emphasize the importance of the learner's initiative, selection of study topics, and self-evaluation. Working with this learner, the teacher is a facilitator who brings acceptance, understanding, and "reality" into the classroom.

10. **(D)** Such a question by the teacher would encourage a pupil's continuance in the presentation of an idea.

11. **(A)** Rote learning, or memorization of information, usually does not involve divergent thinking or creative manipulation of familiar ideas to create new ones.

12. **(E)** Parents expect their children to be good students, but teacher's expectations often are too low. Studies claim that time is a factor in mastery learning and that only 5–10 percent of students would get grades below B if all had the time they needed for a particular learning assignment.

TEST OF PROFESSIONAL KNOWLEDGE

13. **(C)** Reliability is equated with consistency of test scores on a test-retest basis.

14. **(C)** Teacher-made tests of a nonobjective type can be especially problematic. Essay questions tend to cover only a few topics because of the time allotment, and may be no more than a sample of the teacher's favorite topics. Students who have difficulty with spelling and with conceptual formulations may not do well, even when they know the content.

15. **(E)** Under common law the state can make laws to ensure the best interests of its citizens.

16. **(A)** The educational-diagnostic meeting is for the purpose of helping the teacher and the student or the parent understand the learning difficulties of the individual child. The nature of such a discussion requires that it be private and confidential.

17. **(C)** The emotional environment of the classroom can be profoundly affected by a teacher's voice, sense of humor, pacing of instruction, and the sense of confidence he or she exhibits toward each student.

18. **(D)** "I'm OK, you're OK" shows positive teacher reaction and offers a reinforcement of the child's attempts to relate or communicate with others. Such a posture of acceptance encourages the child to continue at the present level, or even to try harder, in order to maintain the teacher's ongoing approval.

19. **(B)** A habitual set toward a certain way of responding would interfere with creative thinking because it is based on acceptable (convergent) responses. It is inflexible as far as decision-making and required solutions are concerned.

20. **(C)** Although it varies somewhat, ranging from a low at the 30%ile at the 5th grade level to a high at the 37%ile at the 6th grade level, this student's percentile ranking in mathematics concepts is considerably below that of her/his ranking in other skill areas. However, functioning in mathematics concepts remains within the average range, although within the lower half.

21. **(A)** The average range extends from the 25%ile to the 75%ile. Since scores in reading comprehension range from the 65%ile to the 75%ile, they are close to the upper limit of this range.

22. **(D)** Before a teacher uses a test a second time as a valid measuring device, a review of objectives, textbooks and other materials is needed and the test itself needs an item analysis.

23. **(A)** Behavior that is not desirable can be extinguished by ignoring it. To get his teacher's attention, John has to engage in desirable behavior, that is, to sit in his seat and attend to his lessons.

24. **(A)** The teacher must provide attention and rewards for desirable behavior to reduce the tension created by undesirable behavior and to indicate appropriate substitutions for release of the student's energies.

25. **(B)** Control of a student's behavior should be transferred from extrinsic sources—in this case, the efforts of a teacher or other pupils—to his or her own powers of self-direction. Self-control is difficult and takes time and patience.

26. **(B)** The use of intermittent reinforcement tends to keep pupils on task for longer periods of time than does regular reinforcement because the child does not know when the teacher will check the work.

27. **(C)** Pupils' gains in any preschool program can be lost unless the same type of work is continued at the next level of study. Neglecting to practice and to use physical, social, or academic learnings can lead to the extinction of such skills, especially in young children.

28. **(A)** Objectives must be established at the outset, so that each pupil knows what is required for a certain grade, what the passing level is, and what the promotional requirements are.

29. **(B)** Buzz groups are used for drawing out the ideas of everyone in the group; for that reason no pupil should be allowed to dominate the discussion.

30. **(C)** Following an objective test, a teacher is able to rank students, find the mode, and locate the most difficult questions by item analysis. But to evaluate students' ability to gather data and develop generalizations, a teacher must use other forms of assessment, such as essay questions.

31. **(C)** Competitive examinations have little place in a mastery program, in which students work at their own pace.

32. **(D)** The notion of a "strategy" implies the existence of specific goals and of the means for evaluating and assessing the pupil's progress. Informal experiences such as occasional interviews could be helpful, but are difficult to evaluate and to incorporate into the overall school program.

33. **(D)** In a diagnostic-prescriptive teaching situation, the teacher attempts to diagnose individual difficulties and to prescribe remediation procedures. Criterion-referenced tests are measures that require a certain level of performance to meet grade standards. Pupil-pupil interaction is irrelevant in DPT.

34. **(E)** The teacher identifies behaviors that need modification. Then programs, content, activities, and reinforcers are developed to meet each pupil's specific needs. Record-keeping is essential for tracking daily progress.

35. **(C)** Impulsive students tend to jump to conclusions without examining all the evidence. They tend to make more errors than students who reflect on the meaning of data and continue to look for new solutions.

TEST OF PROFESSIONAL KNOWLEDGE

SECTION 3

Answer Key

1.	E	8.	B	15.	B	22.	C	29.	D
2.	C	9.	C	16.	D	23.	D	30.	B
3.	E	10.	B	17.	B	24.	E	31.	E
4.	E	11.	C	18.	D	25.	C	32.	E
5.	C	12.	C	19.	D	26.	C	33.	D
6.	C	13.	B	20.	E	27.	A	34.	E
7.	B	14.	E	21.	B	28.	A	35.	D

Explanations

1. **(E)** This objective is the most specific because it indicates exactly what the student must do at the end of the instruction to get a passing grade.

2. **(C)** Gagné believed that because the individual interacts with the environment, learning cannot take place unless the student is in a certain state, or readiness. Thus the teacher must invest time and effort to bring students to the point where they are actively processing signals and stimuli from the environment, discriminating among these, forming and testing rules, and so on.

3. **(E)** Success in teaching derives from many factors. However, a knowledge of research in child psychology and learning theories is basic to success in most situations.

4. **(E)** Pupils are motivated to learn when they see that their own goals and purposes have been considered in planning the learning process.

5. **(C)** Educators base their philosophy both on what they have learned and on what works for them in the classroom—and, in most cases, this is a unique experience. Pragmatic teachers are selective in choosing methods and in setting realistic goals for each of their classes.

6. **(C)** Adolescents have a particular need for affiliation and achievement. They also need firm guidelines, opportunities to make decisions, and time to work together on units and projects. A supportive teacher gives them verbal reinforcement, encouragement, and permission to make choices on topics, reading materials, and research projects.

7. **(B)** Public relations is the responsibility of everyone connected with the school system. Because teachers and pupils are in daily contact with this system, they are its best public-relations agents. Parents hear from their children about school activities and problems. The pupils' enthusiasm or lack of it can affect the outcome of proposals for school taxes.

8. **(B)** The structured curriculum is firmly based on predetermined content and methods. The child-centered curriculum is flexible and is often built around student interests and current needs.

9. **(C)** Information acquisition is the basic goal of this objective. This information may be used in oral communication, perhaps to involve students in discussion after the brief presentation by the pupil who answers the question.

10. **(B)** Encoding, a process that is not well understood, must take place if the memory of some particular information is to be permanent. Encoding seems to involve the physical properties of words (e.g., "a name beginning with B") as well as what we call "verbal associations."

11. **(C)** The characteristics of each student, including his or her interests, are valuable for the teacher to know, but they need not be ascertained before every lesson. What a task analysis must do is anticipate every professional hallmark of a good lesson—objectives, methods, evaluation criteria, and so on.

12. **(C)** According to Squires, Huitt, and Segars, the curriculum package in and of itself doesn't make students successful academically. That goal is the shared responsibility of principal, teacher, and student.

13. **(B)** Feedback that is given immediately and informatively provides the best reinforcement for beginners who are learning motor skills. Teacher encouragement after each try would help to maintain interest and encourage persistence.

14. **(E)** Spina bifida is an abnormality in the closure of the spinal canal, caused by a lack of bony arches in the lumbar region, an undeveloped spinal cord, or a soft tissue mass that covers the lower part of the spine.

15. **(B)** Diabetes mellitus is related to an insufficiency of insulin. It is characterized by excessive thirst, hunger, and weight loss.

16. **(D)** All three are symptomatic of epilepsy. Choice (A) describes a grand mal seizure; choice (B), a petit mal attack; choice (C), a milder form.

17. **(B)** "Bargaining" does not occur until the stage of anger has passed.

18. **(D)** Rules must first be learned and then internalized so that they become a set of values which govern our social interactions.

19. **(D)** Students vary widely in social and academic skills. Research indicates that the teacher should know each pupil's aptitude. Following this, the teacher should structure the classroom to meet the individual student's need for pupil-teacher and pupil-pupil interactions.

20. **(E)** Research shows that pupils who have learning difficulties prefer to work in a structured and task-oriented environment with firm teacher supervision. Their security is based on working in predictable surroundings. Their insecurity with learning tasks increases if the environment becomes uncertain and disruptive.

21. **(B)** For grade placement, the Spanish edition of the Test of General Ability would give the teacher a quick overview of the boy's vocabulary, mathematics skills, and general aptitude.

TEST OF PROFESSIONAL KNOWLEDGE

22. **(C)** The standard error of measurement is an estimate of the range of scores that might be expected if one individual took the test several times. The smaller the standard error of measurement, the more confidence a user can have in the score.

23. **(D)** Effective teachers use style, content, technique, and personality as they interact with pupils. This combination is difficult to define. Some individual teachers have a positive warmth that comes through to pupils regardless of learner differences, content, or classroom environment.

24. **(E)** Plans for teaching handicapped students must look to the "least restrictive environment" whenever possible. Public law requires that the pupil be mainstreamed into the regular classroom rather than be taught in a class for the handicapped.

25. **(C)** According to Bruner, children learn when material is offered in an appropriate mode of representation (enactive, iconic, or symbolic). Young children can work with concrete materials, but not with abstract content.

26. **(C)** The curriculum would be based on the mastery of three successively abstract modes of representation—actions, images, and symbols. The ability to encode information from all three modes is essential to the development of long-term memory.

27. **(A)** Egocentric thought processes occur at several ages. The child aged 2–7 years, according to Piaget, is characterized by egocentrism. In asserting his or her independence, the adolescent often reverts to egocentric mechanisms.

28. **(A)** Intelligence is an abstract concept that, thus far, is difficult to define because it has a multifactor base. Some researchers have found evidence that as many as 100 factors may be involved in mental activity. Guilford's "structure of the intellect" was an attempt to present the multiple factors of intelligence.

29. **(D)** Reading problems seem to have multiple causation. Therefore the teacher should request testing by the school psychologist to determine reasons for the discrepancy between the child's interests and ability to perform.

30. **(B)** Every taxonomy or classification of educational objectives aids teachers in planning strategies and evaluation measures that are appropriate for their students' current and burgeoning skills.

31. **(E)** Children think differently about punishment than adults do. Some of them are so used to it that they try to get attention by disobedience; being punished makes them feel the teacher or parent cares about them. Corporal punishment, however, leads to unpredictable behavior, depending upon the personality and experience of the child.

32. **(E)** Collecting campaign speeches would involve the least experience with live candidates, meetings, and the public.

33. **(D)** Research indicates student improvement in the organization of ideas, speed of completion of writing assignments, awareness of spelling errors, and more enjoyment of creative writing. However, handwriting improvement would not be related because students can work directly on the word processor or computer without copying written materials.

34. **(E)** According to Vernon Jones, the other elements in engaging a student's commitment to a learning goal are the satisfaction or reward associated with completion, and the way in which others relate to the learner throughout the learning process.

35. **(D)** Children who have behavior problems need less punishment and more positive reinforcement, success experiences, and empathy.

SECTION 4

Answer Key

1.	E	8.	C	15.	C	22.	A	29.	D
2.	B	9.	E	16.	D	23.	E	30.	A
3.	C	10.	A	17.	C	24.	A	31.	A
4.	A	11.	B	18.	D	25.	E	32.	D
5.	E	12.	B	19.	A	26.	B	33.	A
6.	E	13.	B	20.	D	27.	B	34.	D
7.	D	14.	E	21.	D	28.	E	35.	C

Explanations

1. **(E)** All children go through stages of behavioral maturation. Retarded children operate at lower stages than their chronological age would indicate.

2. **(B)** Research indicates that experiences of success motivate children to stay on task, try harder, and complete more work.

3. **(C)** Choice (A) would not meet his need to learn one task before going on to the next; (B) would help to some extent, but each task should be purposeful; (D) a reinforcement schedule must meet each child's needs; for some children increasing the number of task requirements leads to more motivation, in others it does not; (E) perhaps the criteria is too difficult and reinforcement would not lead to success experiences. Choice (C) indicates flexibility in meeting special needs.

4. **(A)** As a participant in class projects, a teacher gets involved with the learning process as students see it, and may discover classroom management problems—seating arrangements, for example—that lead to discipline problems. (Presumably, the teacher is always an observer.)

5. **(E)** Parents object to testing on many grounds. Parent–teacher conferences after testing help parents understand the purposes for which the test scores will be used.

TEST OF PROFESSIONAL KNOWLEDGE

6. **(E)** All groups need some special attention, modification of learning tasks, immediate reinforcement, and a wide variety of materials to meet their individual levels of understanding, interest, and performance.

7. **(D)** Children who watch television at the preschool age level, often have difficulty with visual sequencing. Television presentations shift from the future to the past and then back to the present, or go in many other orders. Children do not see the sequencing they need for learning school subjects.

8. **(C)** Federal funds may be withdrawn from any educational institution that fails to provide parents access to their child's educational records. Parents may have information found to be inaccurate or no longer relevant removed from the records.

9. **(E)** The assessment of mentally retarded pupils involves every factor that could affect their academic progress.

10. **(A)** When a student begins to accept his or her own responsibility for making choices, the locus of control for that student's conduct shifts to him or her, away from external influences. In the meantime, the teacher's acceptance and reinforcement of the student's efforts are essential for building confidence and staying on task.

11. **(B)** Children from different life-styles tend to look at rewards and punishment in different ways. For some children punishment is rewarding because it shows that the parent or teacher cares enough to relate to them, even in an angry manner!

12. **(B)** Teacher expectations have a very marked effect on children, who tend to internalize the high (or low) hopes held out for them and perform accordingly.

13. **(B)** Teachers tend to call on children who will know the answers. Thus children who have difficulty mastering communication skills are denied the attention they need.

14. **(E)** Mastery learning requires many kinds of evaluation. Diagnostic, formative, and summative reports are very useful to both the teacher and the pupil as they plan for continuing progress.

15. **(C)** Dewey's emphasis was to prepare learners for living in a democratic environment. Learning by doing things for themselves was Dewey's goal for students.

16. **(D)** Such a teacher would have "purpose" as his goal for all pupils—no time-wasting, no running around the room in aimless activity. Staying on task is a primary feature of an autocratic atmosphere.

17. **(C)** Under "accountability," teachers and administrators are responsible for the learning outcomes in their school. Communities are increasingly concerned about achievement-test scores, placement of seniors on the SAT, and other indices of achievement by their graduates. Some parents have sued teachers or school districts because their children were given diplomas, even though they could not read.

18. **(D)** Every examination should be related to the objectives of the course, unit, or lesson. Otherwise the test results will not be valid.

19. **(A)** Examples and nonexamples help children classify and discriminate as they place objects, ideas, principles, and concepts into categories.

20. **(D)** Local needs may differ from national test emphases, so evaluation of the science program should begin with the needs of pupils in the school. From this, objectives can be set to benefit each and all. Then the national norms should be utilized to determine what is being taught in the sciences and what is appropriate at the local level.

21. **(D)** A warm, reinforcing environment can motivate students to do just a bit more and to stay on learning tasks longer.

22. **(A)** Social learnings are based on examples and experiences. The sociodrama and the roleplay are particularly effective ways to focus such learnings. Children can both participate in and discuss interactions they have experienced in the classroom, home, or playground.

23. **(E)** Reasonable corporal punishment is legal in certain states as a disciplinary technique, but the teacher imposing it must abide by local regulations.

24. **(A)** Interest inventories are useful because they indicate the testee's percentile rank by comparison with occupational and professional groups sharing similar interests. A student's career choice can be aided by such information.

25. **(E)** Children with communication difficulties often have many good ideas and can express themselves creatively, if they are encouraged and are given class time to work on construction projects, stories from their experiences, and poetry or drawings.

26. **(B)** Learning is more than just following directions. Some pupils have wasteful and ineffective work habits that can be discouraging to them. A teacher who helps the child learn how to learn does much to advance his or her overall achievement.

TEST OF PROFESSIONAL KNOWLEDGE

27. **(B)** Gifted children are often neglected because they seem self-directed. They may appear busy, but may not be operating at the level of challenge appropriate to their talents.

28. **(E)** If the emotional climate of the home or the classroom improves, a child's IQ may increase by a few points. Nurturing a child's curiosity and interest in solving problems can have the same effect. In and of itself, though, a research assignment will not spur an increase in IQ.

29. **(D)** A summative report requires more information about the child's productivity than a single test or short quiz can yield.

30. **(A)** The mastery learning concept requires that a child perform according to certain proficiency standards. If these qualifications are not met, he or she cannot go on to the next lesson. Competency testing based on the mastery concept is sometimes used for promotion or graduation requirements.

31. **(A)** In many districts, the cost of standardized tests makes them unaffordable for frequent use as measures of achievement in the content areas. Therefore, teacher-made tests tend to be used on a daily basis.

32. **(D)** Migratory workers' children are permitted, with parental consent, to stay in special programs for up to 5 years.

33. **(A)** Other programs for attendance rule revision and assignment to other schools take precedence over developing or building new schools or magnet schools.

34. **(D)** In some courses, the textbook will play a minor role, and multimedia materials will be used for information, motivation, and pupil interest needs. A longer school day or school year are already being considered in several states. New knowledge is becoming available more rapidly than in the past and is becoming part of the curriculum. Tests will have to reflect this. Planning for individual needs is based on evaluation of pupil progress and learning skills.

35. **(C)** Punishment is not a good motivator because it involves emotional aspects that may affect children's attitudes toward the subject, the teacher, or school in general.

Part V
Specialty Area Tests

Several states require special examinations in subject fields for licensure, certification, or endorsement to teach. These tests are either the National Teacher Examinations (NTE) or a combination of the NTE and the Content Area Performance Assessment (CAPA) tests. In 1986, other states formed a group to prepare a State-Sponsored Testing Program (SSTP) for the content areas not available from the National Teacher Examinations. Applicants for certification should contact their state department of education, division of certification, to obtain complete information about test requirements.

Read all instructions very carefully. Currently, ETS has no penalty for using an educated guess rather than leaving an answer blank. Only the correct answers are counted on the Core Battery and the Specialty Area tests to obtain the score.

Part V provides brief content descriptions and sample questions for 26 of the Specialty Area tests given nationwide. More detailed information and sample questions are available from the Educational Testing Service. Address requests for information to:

    NTE Programs
    Educational Testing Service
    CN6051
    Princeton, NJ 08541-6051

SPECIALTY AREA TESTS

Art Education

The examination in Art Education tests the academic competence of candidates for the teaching of art on the elementary level (nursery through grade six) and the secondary level (grades seven through twelve). Some questions are unrelated to any specific level.

Content and Scope (150 questions, 2-hour test)

The content of the examination covers three main areas:

  I. World Art and Art Analysis
  II. Processes, Materials, Tools, and Techniques
  III. Professional Practices

Test questions are based on the usual art education curricula taught in colleges and departments of education, and cover such media as drawing and painting; crafts; sculpture; photography, motion pictures, and electronic media; architecture; and environmental design.

Sample Questions

Directions: For each question or incomplete statement select the *best* answer or completion from the five choices.

1. John Singleton Copley, a prominent eighteenth-century artist, painted this portrait of a famous fellow American who, himself, demonstrated considerable artistic ability as

   (A) a silversmith
   (B) a print-maker
   (C) an architect
   (D) a landscape painter
   (E) a sculptor

2. The teacher of a high school beginner's art class is introducing the students to different kinds of media for expression. In which one of the following is the artist incorrectly linked to the medium?
   (A) Woodcut—Dürer

ART EDUCATION

(B) American sculpture—Pollack
(C) Chalk drawings—Hans Holbein the Younger
(D) American murals—Ezra Winter
(E) Urban tall buildings—Mies van der Rohe

3. There are no laws and rules governing the expression of art because
   (A) the end product is more important than the creative act
   (B) art is not yet a fully developed skill
   (C) artists do not want to leave their ideas in permanent form
   (D) the creative act is based on the power of individual imagination
   (E) art is the prerogative of great artists

4. In this picture of the Pantheon can be seen a type of construction developed by the Romans that requires special concern and planning by architects and engineers because of its weight and thrust. This form of structure is
   (A) the arch
   (B) the atrium
   (C) the aqueduct
   (D) the dome
   (E) the flying buttress

5. The art instructor tells the elementary class, "Keep your hands moist while working with this material." The project the pupils are working on is
   (A) clay modeling
   (B) making a cork relief
   (C) preparing an eggshell mosaic
   (D) painting a fabric
   (E) making a leaf rubbing

6. When making "pots" or free-standing figures, there are several techniques to be used separately or in combination. Which one of the following is not a viable technique?
   (A) "Pinching"—the fingers are used to pinch or model the clay.
   (B) "Coiling"—lengths of rolled clay are pressed together.
   (C) "Slab pottery"—a flat sheet of clay is cut into lengths, which are then joined together.
   (D) "Firing"—the clay is fired at slightly over 1000°C to form pottery.
   (E) "Selecting"—clay is collected along river beds in the local area.

The Metropolitan Museum of Art

7. The serenity of *Madonna and Child*, which is due in part to the excellent balance of composition, is characteristic of the religious paintings of
    (A) Leonardo
    (B) Urbino
    (C) Perugino
    (D) Raphael
    (E) Doni

8. A student who is concerned about the quality of his or her art work can best be helped by a teacher who
    (A) emphasizes the use of proper techniques
    (B) demonstrates perspective and composition
    (C) uses great artists as models
    (D) urges students to criticize each other's work
    (E) stresses art as a personal search and an individual expression of the wonders of life

9. The table, chair, and highboy shown are evidence of the skill of Colonial America and of the influence of styles and fashions popular at the time in
    (A) England
    (B) Spain
    (C) Germany
    (D) France
    (E) Italy

ART EDUCATION

The Metropolitan Museum of Art

10. Which of the following statements about intaglio line-engraving and etching is INCORRECT?
    (A) It produces a concave effect.
    (B) It is the reverse of cameo.
    (C) Gems can be cut by this method.
    (D) Seals and signet rings usually use intaglio forms.
    (E) It cannot be done on a metal plate.

Kunsthistorisches Museum, Vienna

11. This is a self-portrait of which of the following artists?
    (A) Bruegel
    (B) Rubens
    (C) Titian
    (D) Van Loon
    (E) Rembrandt

483

SPECIALTY AREA TESTS

12. The movement toward abstract art in the United States in the 1940s gained impetus from the use of abstract lines and swirls to communicate emotion, as shown in the works of
    - (A) Kandinsky
    - (B) Orozco
    - (C) Rousseau
    - (D) Miro
    - (E) Masson

13. When the avant-garde style of decorating is used in interior design,
    - (A) the result is symmetric and conventional
    - (B) the past is disregarded and new materials are incorporated
    - (C) antiques are used exclusively
    - (D) Americana—folk art—is stressed
    - (E) an art wall is included for balance

14. In photoengraving, when the line cuts or drawings are in solid black and white only, the photoengraving (etching) is done on
    - (A) a silver plate
    - (B) a metal plate
    - (C) a zinc plate
    - (D) a copper plate
    - (E) a bronze plate

The Metropolitan Museum of Art

15. It is possible to learn about a civilization from its artifacts. For example, this storage jar, showing runners painted in black, not only is typical of a certain style of art work, but also links a contemporary worldwide athletic event to the country where it originated, which was ancient
    - (A) Rome
    - (B) Greece
    - (C) Egypt
    - (D) Persia
    - (E) Phoenicia

Answer Key

1. A	4. D	7. D	10. E	13. B
2. B	5. A	8. E	11. B	14. C
3. D	6. E	9. D	12. A	15. B

BIOLOGY AND GENERAL SCIENCE

Biology and General Science

The examination in Biology and General Science tests the academic competence of candidates for the teaching of these areas of science at the secondary level.

Content and Scope (160 questions, 60 percent on biological sciences, 2-hour test)

The test is broad in scope to assess mastery of factual information and also knowledge of effective teaching processes and techniques.

Three major content areas are covered:
- I. Biological Science
- II. Physical Science (chemistry, physics, earth and space science)
- III. Philosophical and Historical Background, Scientific Methodology, and Science Technology.

Some Topics for Review

1. Basic principles, laws, and concepts
2. Scientific methods and inquiry techniques
3. Current teaching strategies

Sample Questions

Directions: For each question or incomplete statement, select the best from the five choices.

1. Which of the following statements in regard to atoms and energy is NOT true?
   - (A) Most of the weight of an atom is centered in the nucleus.
   - (B) The mass number of any atom indicates the sum of the protons and neutrons.
   - (C) The light energy that is released in small units when the electrons move from outer to inner orbits is called isotopes.
   - (D) High-energy electrons are beta particles.
   - (E) Energy is released when a positron collides with an electron

2. Here are the directions for an experiment: Place 7 grams of iron filings and 4 grams of powdered sulfur on a sheet of paper, and mix them thoroughly. Which one of the following statements is true about this experiment?
   - (A) The iron and the sulfur cannot be separated with a magnet.
   - (B) The iron filings and the sulfur are chemically combined.
   - (C) A catalyst is needed for the formation of an iron–sulfur compound.
   - (D) A compound could be made by heating these two substances in a Pyrex test tube until a black mass is produced.
   - (E) The two substances would not combine if they were heated.

3. Fossil-bearing rocks have been formed most frequently by layers of
   - (A) silicates
   - (B) lava
   - (C) sediment
   - (D) amber
   - (E) minerals and bark

4. Certain bacteria and insects are not destroyed by antibiotics and insecticides; some strains even appear to thrive on them. The best explanation is that
   - (A) the antibiotics or insecticides were too old and had lost their potency
   - (B) they are not the right antibiotics or insecticides
   - (C) the proper dosage was not used
   - (D) the antibiotics or insecticides were not administered long enough
   - (E) because of variation, mutants that survive and mutants that thrive on these substances have come into being

SPECIALTY AREA TESTS

5. During an experiment with fruit flies to determine the effects of radiation, students used three groups of flies. A local radiologist exposed group 2 to 1000 roentgens of radiation and group 3 to 1500 roentgens. Why did he not expose group 1 to radiation also?
   - (A) Group 1 had already been exposed.
   - (B) Group 1 was needed for breeding since the exposed fruit flies might become sterile.
   - (C) Group 1 represented the normal or control group.
   - (D) Group 1 will be exposed after the first batch of offspring is hatched.
   - (E) Mutants are needed for study from Group 1.

6. A ninth-grade class studying the interior of the earth presented a program for social studies students studying the effects of a recent earthquake in Japan. Which one of the student reporters made an error?
   - (A) Reporter 1.: "The thick layer of rock that lies beneath the earth's thin crust is called the mantle."
   - (B) Reporter 2: "The center of the earth is about 6000 miles below the surface."
   - (C) Reporter 3: "Earthquakes are caused by rocks slipping along a fault."
   - (D) Reporter 4: "The P-wave seismic wave is a compression wave."
   - (E) Reporter 5: "Seismographs are used to detect and measure earthquakes. The base of a seismograph is usually fastened to bedrock."

7. Transfer of learning is a basic concern of science teachers. For this reason as many lessons as possible should be brought up to the
   - (A) recall level
   - (B) understanding level
   - (C) association level
   - (D) recognition level
   - (E) experimental level

8. The science instructor must be able to determine why students are having difficulties in applying the scientific method to problems or laboratory lessons. One reason why some students do not understand inductive reasoning processes is that
   - (A) most student are incapable of abstract reasoning
   - (B) most students cannot interpret the evidence they collect
   - (C) many students dislike science and/or the science teacher
   - (D) teachers often give the answers to students before the students work with the facts
   - (E) inductive reasoning is too time consuming to be fully explained in science classes

9. When teaching scientific theories, the science teacher should emphasize that
   - (A) theories have limitations and are open to question
   - (B) almost all theories are eventually accepted by the scientific community
   - (C) theories should be published at once, so that other scientists can work on them
   - (D) theories are not subject to change
   - (E) theories and laws are the same

10. Many organisms require dietary supplements, even though these supplements do not provide energy or perceptible bulk to the cells. Examples of such supplements are
    - (A) molds
    - (B) essential metabolics
    - (C) yeasts
    - (D) enzymes
    - (E) holozoics

BIOLOGY AND GENERAL SCIENCE

11. Certain molds are used in industrial processes and in tissue cell cultures. Which one of the following procedures is NOT necessary for dry-weight measurement?
    (A) Effective washing
    (B) Constant degrees of dehydration
    (C) Complete dehydration
    (D) Membrane filter counts
    (E) Accurate weighing

12. One of the quickest ways of detecting and identifying antigens or antibodies is the
    (A) antigen-antibody reaction in gel method
    (B) *in vitro* method
    (C) fluorescent antibody-staining method
    (D) agglutinin manifestation
    (E) precipitin reaction

13. To apply Robert M. Gagné's concept of learning hierarchies in science classes, the instructor must prepare lessons on the assumption that each level of learning is based on the student's learning of the previous level or of the subcapabilities necessary for the higher level. Which of the following concepts is INCORRECT?
    (A) Signal Learning—concern that the right substances be mixed together in a laboratory experiment
    (B) Chaining—opening the locker door, taking a science book from the shelf, sharpening a pencil before class begins, taking one's seat
    (C) Multiple-Discrimination Learning—distinguishing among compounds, gases, liquids, solids
    (D) Concept Learning—a set of objects fits into a class (flies are insects)
    (E) Principle Learning—sets range from 0 (an empty set) to 7

14. Photosynthesis is a two-step process resulting in the production of glucose. All of the following are true of carbohydrate production EXCEPT
    (A) photolysis ("light splitting") occurs first
    (B) water molecules become separate hydrogen and oxygen
    (C) CO_2 fixation is the second step
    (D) the sequence is noncyclical
    (E) the product of photosynthesis is a monosaccharide

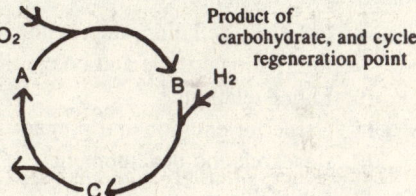

15. The specific information contained within the genes is a set of building instructions to make new DNA from the old and pass it on in succeeding cell generation. Nucleotides are joined together so that one chain is attached by a purine of the chain to a pyrimidine of another as a spiraled double chain of DNA. All of the following are possible sequences EXCEPT
    (A) adenine–desoxyribose–phosphate
    (B) guanine–desoxyribose–phosphate
    (C) thymine–desoxyribose–phosphate
    (D) enzyme–desoxyribose–phosphate
    (E) cytosine–desoxyribose–phosphate

Answer Key

1. C	4. E	7. B	10. B	13. E
2. D	5. C	8. D	11. D	14. D
3. C	6. B	9. A	12. C	15. D

SPECIALTY AREA TESTS

Business Education

The examination in Business Education tests the academic competence of candidates for the teaching of business subjects in such a way that business and economic literacy is emphasized. Areas of specialization are also covered on the test.

Content and Scope

The content of the examination covers three main areas:

    I. Business Information. More than one third of the test questions relate to business mathematics, communications, consumer-related topics, economics, and other detailed business information.

    II. Professional Education for Business. About one fourth of the test covers such topics as career education, teaching strategies, research, and curriculum planning.

    III. Specialization Areas. More than one third of the test is derived from the content of specific business courses, including typewriting, shorthand, accounting, marketing, and data processing.

SOME OF THESE AREAS OF SPECIALIZATION MAY NOT HAVE BEEN STUDIED BY THE CANDIDATE. THEREFORE, NO ONE IS EXPECTED TO ANSWER ALL THE QUESTIONS ON THE TEST.

Some Topics for Review

1. Job requirements, work standards, and ethics
2. The free-enterprise system
3. Finance, banking, credit, and investments
4. Government fiscal and monetary policies
5. Taxation
6. Business law
7. Price systems
8. Inflation, deflation, depression, recession
9. International trade and competition
10. Labor relations
11. Career orientation and preparation
12. Research and development
13. Budgeting
14. Staffing
15. Equipment and facilities
16. Teaching strategies for business education
17. Business organizations, publications, and legislation

Sample Questions

Directions: For each question or incomplete statement, select the *best* answer or completion from the five choices.

1. During the learning of a psychomotor skill such as typewriting, verbal instruction by the teacher is helpful in all of the following ways EXCEPT
   (A) for guiding initial responses
   (B) for eliminating errors
   (C) for strengthening correct responses
   (D) for describing strategies for improving performance
   (E) for acquiring speed and accuracy

BUSINESS EDUCATION

2. A teacher of an advanced accounting class gave daily quizzes to her students but did not return the graded papers for several days. What is the most likely reason that the students showed little improvement on difficult problems?
   (A) They were dull-normal in ability.
   (B) They did not read the teacher's comments on the papers that were returned.
   (C) They disliked accounting.
   (D) They needed frequent information and encouragement to stay on task.
   (E) They disliked learning what their scores were on the quizzes.

3. The rationale for international trade is based on
   (A) the theory of comparative advantage or comparative cost
   (B) the balance of trade concept
   (C) the idea that we can produce at less cost than the nations from which we buy
   (D) a desire to assist developing nations
   (E) the need to support the World Bank and its creditors

4. Mary borrowed $660 for 60 days at 9% to purchase an automobile on sale. How much interest did Mary pay per day on this loan?
   (A) $1.50
   (B) $1.00
   (C) $0.57
   (D) $0.284
   (E) $0.165

5. A student wants to divide 45 by the sum of 5 plus 6. Her computer performs calculations left to right according to the following:
   First: −, minus sign indicating negative numbers
   Second: ↑, exponentiation, left to right
   Third: */, multiplication and division, left to right
   Fourth: + −, addition and subtraction, left to right
   How should she type the problem on her computer?
   (A) 45 / 5 + 6
   (B) ? 45 / 5 + 6
   (C) ? 45 / (5 + 6)
   (D) 6 + 5 / 45
   (E) (45 / 5 + 6)

6. Which of the following statements is NOT true of the Federal Reserve System?
   (A) It is the central banking system of the United States.
   (B) All national banks must belong to the system.
   (C) Each reserve bank is the central bank for its district.
   (D) The system controls the credit market through discount rates and other procedures.
   (E) The Board of Governors is elected by member banks.

7. For balance sheet purposes, change and petty cash funds are
   (A) handled separately at the end of the month
   (B) added to the cash on hand at the end of the month
   (C) deducted from the cash on hand at the end of the month
   (D) added to the cash on hand and in the bank
   (E) classified and counted separately as imprest funds to balance the account

8. The *Nation's Business* is the organ of
   (A) the Better Business Bureau
   (B) Wall Street
   (C) Dun and Bradstreet
   (D) The American Manufacturer's Association
   (E) The U.S. Chamber of Commerce

9. When counseling students about careers in business, all of the following should be given consideration EXCEPT
   (A) the changing job market and women's roles
   (B) economic predictions for the years ahead
   (C) future manufacturing priorities
   (D) the on-the-job training offered in some service fields
   (E) the American political climate

10. The two binary digits used in data processing are
    (A) 0 and 1
    (B) 1 and 2
    (C) 2 and 3
    (D) 3 and 4
    (E) 4 and 5

11. Which one of the following equations used in bookkeeping, as written below, contains an error?
    (A) Assets = Liabilities + Owner's Equity
    (B) Net Sales = Sales − Sales Returns and Allowances
    (C) Cost of Goods Sold = Beginning Inventory + Net Purchases + Ending Inventory
    (D) Gross Profit = Net Sales − Cost of Goods Sold
    (E) Net Income (or Net Loss) = Gross Profit − Total Expenses

12. Sometimes the balance shown on the monthly bank statement is larger than the balance indicated in the depositor's checkbook. The most likely reason for this discrepancy is that
    (A) one or more checks written by the depositor have not yet been presented for payment
    (B) incorrect information was entered into the bank's computer
    (C) the bank forgot to deduct the service charge
    (D) deposits are not recorded the same day they are made at the bank
    (E) the depositor does not keep accurate records

13. Large department stores or public utilities often use *cycle billing* to aid their accounts-receivable systems. Under this system, customers in each subcontrol group are billed
    (A) on the tenth day of each month
    (B) at the end of the month
    (C) at the first of the month
    (D) at different times during the month
    (E) at the fifteenth of the month

14. The chief purpose of the Taft-Hartley Labor Act was to
    (A) uphold the principle of the closed shop
    (B) forbid federal seizure of essential utilities or industries to avert a strike
    (C) curb strikes
    (D) prohibit racial discrimination in hiring where federal contracts were concerned
    (E) set a minimum wage for all workers

15. Retailers and wholesalers who use the cost-plus pricing technique must consider which one of the following kinds of costs?
    (A) Total fixed costs and total variable costs
    (B) Total variable costs only
    (C) Variable freight costs
    (D) Average fixed costs only
    (E) Variable rent costs

Answer Key

1. E	4. E	7. D	10. A	13. D
2. D	5. C	8. E	11. C	14. C
3. A	6. E	9. E	12. A	15. A

Chemistry, Physics, and General Science

The examination in Chemistry, Physics, and General Science tests the academic competence of candidates for the teaching of these subject areas at the junior or senior high school level.

Content and Scope (140 questions, 75 percent on chemistry and physics, 2-hour test)

The content and scope of the examination provides information on the candidate's preparation in one or both of the physical sciences and/or in general science. About 75 percent of the questions are based on chemistry and physics, with equal numbers on each of these areas. Of the remaining questions, half deal with biology and half with the earth and space sciences and oceanography.

Four major content areas are covered:

   I. Major Concepts in Chemistry *and* Physics
  II. Chemistry
 III. Physics
  IV. Astronomy, Biology, Geology, Meteorology, Oceanography

Some Topics for Review

1. Experimental methods in the sciences
2. Mathematics and statistical applications
3. Classroom teaching techniques

Sample Questions

Directions: For each question or incomplete statement select the *best* answer or completion from the five choices.

1. The use of new instrumentation has facilitated the study of the sun and sunspots. In addition, solar eclipses have provided opportunities for the study of
   (A) solar prominences
   (B) the coronal matter
   (C) the sunspot vortex
   (D) the aurora
   (E) clouds of calcium vapor

2. Uranium-235, an isotope, is obtained by the gaseous process known as
   (A) diffusion
   (B) fusion
   (C) fixation
   (D) filtration
   (E) fallout

SPECIALTY AREA TESTS

3. In the following equation which substance is the reducing agent?

$$CuO + H_2 \rightarrow Cu + H_2O$$

   (A) Hydrogen
   (B) Cupric oxide
   (C) Copper
   (D) Water
   (E) Sodium peroxide

4. Soap or detergent decreases the surface tension of a liquid because
   (A) the soap or detergent is lighter than the liquid
   (B) capillary action affects the liquid
   (C) the water is heavier than the soap or detergent
   (D) the cohesive force is equal to the adhesive force
   (E) soap or detergent molecules get between the water molecules and reduce their cohesive ability

5. Since the California naval orange is a seedless mutant, how does it reproduce?
   (A) By bee pollination
   (B) By wind pollination
   (C) By grafting
   (D) By cutting
   (E) By vegetative propagation

Questions 6 and 7

Directions: The questions below are based on a classroom situation. Read the problem and then the students' answers. Select the student—(A), (B), (C), (D), or (E)—in each situation who needs further assistance in understanding the concepts involved in static electricity.

A teacher asked students to investigate how electrons can be detached from an atom by friction.

   Students (A) and (B) rubbed two hard rubber rods with a piece of fur.
   Students (C) and (D) rubbed two glass rods with a piece of silk.
   Student (E) rubbed one hard rubber rod with a piece of fur and a glass rod with a piece of silk.

Then one of the electrified glass rods was suspended so that it could swing freely.

   Student (A) brought a piece of electrified rubber near the suspended rod. The rod moved toward the piece of rubber.
   Student (C) brought the other electrified glass rod toward the suspended rod; the suspended rod moved away.

The teacher then asked, "Why was the suspended rod attracted to the electrified piece of rubber?"

CHEMISTRY, PHYSICS, AND GENERAL SCIENCE

Student (A): "The charge on the rubber is different from that of the rod. That's why they attracted each other."
Student (B): "The rubber gained electrons from the fur because the fur holds electrons more loosely than the rubber does."
Student (C): "The silk gave up electrons to the glass rod; the rod is then positively charged."
Student (D): "The glass rod was positively charged, and the rubber rod was negatively charged."
Student (E): "Like charges repel; unlike charges attract."

6. Which student needs to repeat this experiment with assistance?

Student (A) was asked to bring her two electrified rods close to each other. The teacher then asked, "Why do the electrified rods repel each other?"

Student (A): "They are both positively charged; they lost electrons to the silk."
Student (B): "No, they are not. They did not lose any electrons at all."
Student (C): "Rubbing the glass rods with silk gave the rods the same charge."
Student (D): "Both glass rods gave up electrons to the silk."
Student (E): "Like charges repel; unlike charges attract."

7. Which student needs assistance in understanding how electrons act?

8. The high reactivity of the fluorine atom is due to its
    (A) low electronegativity
    (B) high electronegativity
    (C) atomic weight
    (D) nuclear charge
    (E) noble gas properties

9. What is the genetic makeup of two brown-eyed parents who have a blue-eyed child?
    (A) *BB* and *BB*   (D) *Bb* and *bb*
    (B) *Bb* and *Bb*   (E) *BB* and *bb*
    (C) *BB* and *Bb*

10. If a sonic sounder uses sound waves that travel at a speed of 4800 feet per second, how many seconds will it take to reach a depth of 20,000 feet and return?
    (A) 9.0 seconds   (D) 4.17 seconds
    (B) 10.1 seconds   (E) 3.97 seconds
    (C) 8.33 seconds

Answer Key

| 1. B | 3. A | 5. C | 7. B | 9. B |
| 2. A | 4. E | 6. C | 8. B | 10. C |

SPECIALTY AREA TESTS

Early Childhood Education

The examination in Early Childhood Education tests the academic competence of candidates for the teaching of children aged 3 through 8 years.

Content and Scope (150 questions, 2-hour test)

The test covers two major areas:

    I. Child Development (physical, interpersonal, mental, aesthetic)
   II. Appropriate Teaching Behaviors, Curricula, and Activities

Some Topics for Review

1. Factors influencing child development
2. Management of the learning setting
3. Diagnosing individual pupil needs
4. Evaluating and recording pupil progress
5. Parent-school and community-school relations
6. The teacher's legal responsibilities in regard to pupils
7. Significant curricular theories and practices

Sample Questions

Directions: For each question or incomplete statement select the *best* answer or completion from the five choices.

1. When teaching children to feed themselves, the principle of shaping can be very useful. An example of shaping is
    (A) feeding the reluctant eater
    (B) holding the child while feeding him or her
    (C) giving verbal praise as the child gets food into the mouth
    (D) scolding children who are messy at the table
    (E) removing the food quickly if the child doesn't begin to eat

2. During the nursery school years each child's psychosocial development can be aided by all of the following experiences EXCEPT
    (A) self-selection of activities
    (B) cooperation and conflict with other children
    (C) hurt feelings and frustration during play
    (D) dealing unaided with anger
    (E) trial-and-error success and failure

3. The kindergarten teacher who plans for the daily use of such materials as clay, paints, sand, and wood is providing a variety of experiences that stimulate chiefly
    (A) curiosity
    (B) the tactile senses
    (C) motor responses
    (D) independent play
    (E) left-brain development

4. The lack of definitive long-range results from the Head Start Programs can be attributed chiefly to
    (A) poor teaching
    (B) parental indifference
    (C) insufficient government funds
    (D) inadequate follow-up planning
    (E) the children's lack of motivation

EARLY CHILDHOOD EDUCATION

5. In regard to language development, Annette, a typical 3-year-old in a preschool program, can be expected to do all of the following EXCEPT
   - (A) use "telegraphic" sentences
   - (B) name such body parts as head, legs, arms
   - (C) know the important people in her life by name
   - (D) use plurals and past tenses in conversation
   - (E) understand and use a total of 1500 words

6. When a teacher asks, "Where would the rabbit be if he got out of his cage?" she is using language to help the children
   - (A) see cause-effect relationships
   - (B) categorize events
   - (C) put events into a time frame
   - (D) do sustained sequential thinking
   - (E) look for meanings in language

7. A teacher who wants to apply for a federal child study grant for use with preschoolers should consider all of the following EXCEPT
   - (A) the ratio of children to teachers
   - (B) the percentage of minority children
   - (C) the percentage of nonminority children
   - (D) the number of handicapped children
   - (E) the experience of the instructional staff

8. The teacher of José, a 6-year-old who recently came to the United States from Puerto Rico, decides to have the boy tested by the school psychologist. Which of the following statements about tests is NOT accurate and would NOT be made by the psychologist?
   - (A) The Cattell Culture-Fair Intelligence Test is an oral test.
   - (B) The first level of the Cattell would be suitable for José.
   - (C) The instructions for the Cattell can be given in Spanish.
   - (D) The Raven Progressive Matrices Test requires the use of abstract information.
   - (E) The Raven measures general intelligence.

9. Arnie doesn't share toys or play with other children; he acts as if others don't exist in the kindergarten class. Which of the following would be most helpful in changing Arnie's attitude?
   - (A) "The toys belong to everyone, Arnie. If you don't share, you can't play."
   - (B) "Come on, Arnie. It's time to sit in the corner again!"
   - (C) "Look how nicely Timmy and Joel are playing together. They're building a big block tower."
   - (D) "Be a good boy, Arnie. Give the toy to Chris."
   - (E) "That's a good boy, Arnie; let Timmy have the truck. Now let's ask Bobbie what he is doing."

10. Three-year-old Sarah puts an apron on Carlos and says, "You do the dishes today." Her action represents the use of
    - (A) symbolic play
    - (B) egocentrism
    - (C) mental symbolism
    - (D) operational thought
    - (E) centration

495

SPECIALTY AREA TESTS

11. In a class of hyperactive, distractible children the teacher uses the following procedure in reading class:

    Cue: "Maria, please read your story to the class."
    Behavior: Maria reads slowly, sounding out words and watching for periods and question marks.
    Consequence: "You read the story very well, Maria. I like the way you sounded out the new words and watched the stop and go signs in the story."

    As a result of the teacher's use of reinforcement, Maria is most likely to
    (A) develop self-confidence in attempting new tasks
    (B) place more emphasis on the end result than on the learning process
    (C) place more emphasis on the process to be used than on the answer itself
    (D) show a lack of self-referent labels in class discussions
    (E) wait for teacher approval before attempting new assignments

12. Several children in the first grade demonstrate undesirable behavior—angry outbursts, complaining, telling on others. Which of the following techniques would be LEAST useful in helping these children to improve their behavior?
    (A) The teacher acts as a role model, demonstrating self-control.
    (B) The teacher changes frequently from positive to negative reinforcement.
    (C) The teacher has the children use puppets as they talk about their feelings.
    (D) The teacher introduces games that require the children to tell what happens in certain situations.
    (E) The teacher sometimes stands back and lets the children solve their interpersonal problems.

13. Almost daily a teacher makes comments like the following in the kindergarten class as he initiates observation:

    "Tim has a blue shirt. Who else is wearing something blue?"
    "I have a small block. Who has a big block?"
    "Is this stone rough or smooth?"

    The primary purpose for such comments is to
    (A) help the children to interact with each other
    (B) improve auditory and visual discrimination
    (C) make the children follow directions accurately
    (D) help the children to make comparisons
    (E) make learning a pleasant experience

14. Elena scored highest in her class on the verbal subtests of the WISC, Revised. Evidently she is a child who
    (A) has a talent for visual imagery and tasks with spatial relationships
    (B) has taken the Stanford Achievement test
    (C) processes information easily
    (D) bases her acts on intuition
    (E) is at the formal learning stage

15. Bloom believes that
    (A) age and experience are positively correlated
    (B) intelligence and experience are negatively correlated
    (C) the quality of parenting makes little long-range difference
    (D) emotional growth parallels age
    (E) intellectual development needs early stimulation

EARLY CHILDHOOD EDUCATION

16. The primary distinguishing characteristic of young gifted children is
    (A) early reading
    (B) talking before 1 year of age
    (C) walking by 9 months
    (D) precocious manipulative skills
    (E) extreme curiosity

17. The kindergarten room needs a pleasant atmosphere. All of the following are recommended EXCEPT
    (A) the room temperature should be between 72 and 75 degrees
    (B) the thermostat should be about 45 inches from the floor
    (C) the sink should have automatic tepid water and a disposal-type drain
    (D) formica counters near windows should be provided to work on
    (E) cork walls or bulletin boards should be available to display children's work

18. An infant usually repeats spontaneous vocalizations during the babbling stage because
    (A) the sounds he hears give him pleasure
    (B) he wants to express his thoughts
    (C) he wants to please his mother
    (D) an unknown internal factor makes him babble
    (E) he recognizes a particular sound and wants to repeat it

19. A child in the kindergarten who is advanced in language development is most likely to be
    (A) an only child
    (B) a triplet
    (C) a twin
    (D) a first-born girl with a sibling 3 or more years younger
    (E) a first-born of either sex with a sibling very close in age

20. Lenneberg offered evidence that children move through the same developmental patterns of speech, regardless of cultural environment. To the teacher this means that
    (A) language is a continuous process of imitation
    (B) morphemes are practiced and then combined in imitation of adult language
    (C) language development is not subject to critical periods
    (D) language development is maturational in nature
    (E) early speech is based on a large number of free responses called operants

Answer Key

1. C	6. C	11. A	16. A
2. D	7. E	12. B	17. A
3. B	8. A	13. B	18. A
4. D	9. E	14. C	19. D
5. E	10. C	15. E	20. D

SPECIALTY AREA TESTS

Education in the Elementary School

The examination in Education in the Elementary School tests the academic competence of candidates for teaching grades 1 through 8 in elementary and middle schools.

Content and Scope (150 questions, 2-hour test)

The test covers two major areas:

    I. The Child as the Center of the Teaching-Learning Setting
    II. The Process of Teaching in the Elementary/Middle School

Some Topics for Review

1. Child growth and development (mental, physical, social, individual differences and variations in growth patterns)
2. Children with special needs
3. Teaching techniques, diagnosis of student needs, appraisal of progress, classroom management, teacher decision-making and its philosophical basis

Subject Areas Covered

Mathematics, social studies, and science (about 45% of the test questions)
Language arts and reading (about 33%)
Music, art, and physical education (about 22%)

About one third of the questions are unrelated to a specific grade level, one third relate to grades 1–3, and one third relate to grades 4–8.

Sample Questions

Directions: For each question or incomplete statement, select the *best* answer or completion from the five choices.

1. Of two boys in the classroom, John does well on IQ tests and in daily work; Steve does poorly on both. Which of these factors relating to school performance will be of most use to their teacher in planning individualized instruction packets?
   (A) There are genetic influences on the development of cognitive ability.
   (B) The conceptual styles of the children differ.
   (C) Temperamental characteristics vary from child to child.
   (D) John's IQ is 110 and Steve's is 90.
   (E) Both sets of parents want their sons to succeed in school.

2. Each teacher has been asked to select at least one fifth-grade student who could benefit from an enrichment course to encourage creativity. Which of the following would be the most relevant characteristic for making this choice?
   (A) Average or above-average intelligence
   (B) The ability to do convergent thinking
   (C) The willingness to take risks
   (D) Strong self-confidence
   (E) Lack of anxiety

EDUCATION IN THE ELEMENTARY SCHOOL

3. In regard to teaching arithmetic to third graders, one of the best background experiences for success in the use of addition, subtraction, multiplication, and division is
   (A) learning Roman, as well as Arabic, numerals
   (B) seeing one-to-one relationships
   (C) understanding sets
   (D) counting both forward and backward
   (E) using representative objects

4. A good program for the gifted emphasizes all of the following EXCEPT
   (A) competition for grades
   (B) self-directed learning opportunities
   (C) course work on a higher grade level
   (D) specially designed enrichment or honors courses
   (E) placement in the regular classroom

5. According to Flanders, which of the following teacher statements best illustrates the concept of indirect influence?
   (A) "We should have a science fair this year."
   (B) "When the fourth grade did this project last year, they had the best garden in the school."
   (C) "I like your idea, but we don't have the supplies to do it."
   (D) "Why don't you ask your parents? I think it is a good idea."
   (E) "Jackie, do you mean that we should invite the room mothers to our Lincoln's Birthday party?"

6. A teacher is helping the pupils in science class set up experiments to discover chemical changes. Which one of the following should she reject as INCORRECT?
   (A) Place one painted nail and one iron nail in jars with a little water. (Rust is formed because the air unites with the iron.)
   (B) Put a little sugar in a spoon; then heat the spoon until the white sugar becomes black. Now it does not taste sweet. (The sugar molecules have broken down into water and carbon; the water bubbles away, leaving only the carbon.)
   (C) Take a polished silver spoon, place some cooked egg yolk on it, and leave it for at least an hour. The spoon then has black material on it. (The silver in the spoon and the sulfur in the egg have united to form silver sulfide.)
   (D) Melt some ice cubes in a dish over a candle; then heat the water until it evaporates. (The ice, a solid, becomes liquid; then, after more heating, it becomes a gas.)
   (E) Pass around soda crackers; then tell the children to chew them slowly and to notice that the taste becomes sweet. (The enzymes in the saliva cause a change from starch to sugar—thus the sweet taste.)

7. Planning is essential for teaching locational skills pertinent to social studies. Which of the following skills is LEAST appropriately linked to the grade level suggested for teaching it?
   (A) Constructing graphs—grades 5 and 6
   (B) Finding information in footnotes—grades 5 and 6
   (C) Using an appendix—not later than the middle grades
   (D) Using an atlas—not later than grade 5 or 6
   (E) Using timetables (bus, train, subway, or streetcar)—grade 6

SPECIALTY AREA TESTS

8. Bill, in good physical health, has a higher than average mental age and does well in arithmetic. In spelling and reading, however, Bill gets only average grades. He probably needs the most assistance with
   (A) auditory discrimination
   (B) visual imaging
   (C) reading speed and comprehension
   (D) the blending of consonants
   (E) handwriting skills

9. During the last period of the day, in which reading is taught, pupil disruptiveness frequently increases. To reduce this disturbance, which of the following measures would be most effective?
   I. Moving the reading class to another period
   II. Changing the seating arrangements
   III. Using the last period as a free period
   IV. Increasing teacher movement among the pupils
   V. Scheduling a course with high interest value for the pupils at that time

   (A) I
   (B) I, II
   (C) I, II, III
   (D) IV, V
   (E) III, V

10. Jenny can pronounce words accurately, but often she does not know their meanings. Her basic weakness is likely to be in
    (A) decoding skills
    (B) sight vocabulary
    (C) orientation
    (D) visual discrimination
    (E) encoding skills

11. Tina reads fluently but always mispronounces some words (e.g., she says "tingle" for "twinkle"). In Tina's case all of the following could be weaknesses requiring remedial assistance EXCEPT
    (A) sight vocabulary
    (B) work attack skills for initial consonants and vowels that follow
    (C) vowel and medial consonant difficulties
    (D) visual discrimination
    (E) auditory discrimination

12. When teaching a new song in music class, the neutral syllable *loo* is useful because it helps children maintain full attention on the element of pitch being taught. Which one of the following would NOT ordinarily be used when teaching pitch?
    (A) The teacher indicates the note with a pointer; the class sings the syllable name.
    (B) The teacher speaks the names of the syllables.
    (C) The class responds with the syllables or with *loo* on pitch.
    (D) The teacher sings a group of notes, using *loo*; the class repeats.
    (E) Repetition is continued until each individual sings on pitch.

13. In regard to teaching art to middle-schoolers, research shows that pupils of this age generally
    (A) dislike to experiment with different materials
    (B) require a challenge beyond their usual capabilities
    (C) represent what they visualize mentally, rather than what they actually see, in their projects

500

EDUCATION IN THE ELEMENTARY SCHOOL

(D) should be evaluated according to adult standards of performance
(E) have an interest in and a capacity for working with details

14. Creative children can be distinguished from those who merely like art by the way they work on a project such as pottery-making. The most likely difference in the approach of the creative child to this project will be the
    (A) degree of curiosity
    (B) interest in novel forms of pottery
    (C) excitement about making a piece of pottery
    (D) unpredictability of the project outcome
    (E) persistence in getting answers to questions

15. A popular game of ball that teaches cooperation, competition, muscular coordination, and catching and throwing skills is partially described below:

    Grade level: 3–6
    Number of players: 5–10
    Equipment: 1 playground soccer ball, 4 bases
    A runner may take as many bases, in order, as he or she can or may stay on first base and be advanced by the next kicker.

    This game is called
    (A) dodgeball   (D) kickball
    (B) soccer   (E) lacrosse
    (C) touch football

16. Piaget's studies of moral development in children illustrate how ideas evolve by
    (A) compensation   (D) reaction-formation
    (B) substitution   (E) rationalization
    (C) sublimation

17. When a child gives one reason for a phenomenon and then, under different circumstances, attributes an opposite reason to another form of the same phenomenon, this is called
    (A) intuitive thought
    (B) formal operations
    (C) autistic reasoning
    (D) idiosyncratic cognition
    (E) a perceptual point of view

18. Studies indicate that a child who has become bored with reading will also quickly lose interest in spelling. This is an example of
    (A) inhibition   (D) negative transfer
    (B) satiation   (E) cosatiation
    (C) short attention span

19. The young child beginning to use handwriting concentrates first on
    (A) the spelling of the words he or she is writing
    (B) the movement exclusively of the arm
    (C) his or her grip on the writing instrument
    (D) the finger movements involved in writing
    (E) the natural combination of finger and arm movements

501

SPECIALTY AREA TESTS

20. Which one of the following is NOT emphasized by educators promoting the organismic point of view of cognitive and social growth?
    (A) Helping the child gain impulse control
    (B) Resolution of interpersonal conflicts
    (C) Clarifying the self-concept
    (D) Learning how to function in small groups
    (E) Evolving the stages and schema that guide pupils' progress

21. Bruner feels that a child has to
    (A) develop models that serve as strategies for coping with the environment
    (B) play to organize the brain functions
    (C) have stimulus variety at an early age
    (D) have few sensory restrictions in infancy
    (E) become organized as a result of environmental stimulation

22. Socialization begins to take place
    (A) when the child identifies with a behavior model, either male or female
    (B) when the child "does his or her own thing" and ignores others
    (C) when the child engages in parallel play
    (D) when the child reacts to parental instructions
    (E) when the child constructs puzzles and builds with blocks

23. A teacher using discovery learning in her mathematics class would set up the course so that
    (A) learning would result from children's actions on things
    (B) the emphasis was on general understanding of the structure of mathematics
    (C) children could explore the alternatives before giving a solution
    (D) learning was activated by innate drives
    (E) children worked at the respondent level

24. As children mature, they change from using transfer of learning based on associative learning to transfer based on cognitive learning. This transition usually occurs between the ages of
    (A) 1 to 2 years   (D) 8 to 10 years
    (B) 2 to 4 years   (E) 11 to 13 years
    (C) 5 to 7 years

25. A child who is bilingual is likely to be
    (A) superior in vocabulary in both languages
    (B) deficient in vocabulary in both languages
    (C) handicapped in English but superior in the second language
    (D) proficient in English but handicapped in the second language
    (E) intellectually superior but socially inferior

Answer Key

1. B	6. D	11. C	16. B	21. A
2. C	7. E	12. E	17. E	22. A
3. D	8. B	13. C	18. E	23. C
4. A	9. D	14. D	19. C	24. C
5. E	10. A	15. D	20. E	25. B

Education of Students with Mental Retardation

The examination in Education of Students with Mental Retardation tests the competence of candidates for teaching students with mental retardation. The focus of the test is on mildly retarded (educable), moderately retarded (trainable), and severely and profoundly retarded students; a few questions cover the entire field of exceptional children from the elementary through the secondary levels.

Content and Scope (150 questions, 2-hour test)

The test covers the following content areas:

   I. Principles of Child Development (about 15 questions)
  II. Understanding Exceptional Students Other Than Those with Mental Retardation (about 10 questions)
 III. Understanding Students with Mental Retardation (about 38 questions)
  IV. Knowledge of Assessment Principles and Practices (about 20 questions)
   V. Delivery of Services (about 20 questions)
  VI. Design and Implementation of Instruction (about 37 questions)
 VII. Professional Responsibilities (about 10 questions)

Some Topics for Review

1. Social and adaptive behaviors of Students with Mental Retardation
2. Coping with single or multiple handicaps
3. Classification of handicaps
4. Commercial and teacher-made tests for diagnosis and planning
5. Community programs and resources, consultants, and rehabilitation agencies
6. Ethics
7. Current and past legislation
8. The teacher's legal responsibilities
9. Parent-school and community-school relationships

Sample Questions

Directions: For each question or incomplete statement select the *best* answer or completion from the five choices.

1. Current studies show that, of the total population, the educable mentally retarded comprise
   (A) 2.5 percent
   (B) 9 percent
   (C) 0.4 percent
   (D) 0.1 percent
   (E) 4 percent

SPECIALTY AREA TESTS

2. The causes of mental retardation can be grouped under all of the following headings EXCEPT
   (A) endocrine malfunctioning
   (B) genetic factors
   (C) anorexia nervosa
   (D) blood incompatibilities of parents
   (E) anoxia at birth

3. One misconception about mentally retarded children is that they never grow up, but remain as children all their lives. The educable mentally retarded child grows physically, emotionally, socially, and intellectually; but, in comparison to a normal person,
   (A) his or her rate of development is 1/10 to 1/12 as rapid
   (B) his or her rate of development is 1/5 to 1/6 as rapid
   (C) his or her rate of development is 1/2 to 3/4 as rapid
   (D) he or she is 1 year behind physically
   (E) he or she is 1 year behind mentally

4. According to PL 94-142, the parents of children placed in special instructional programs have all of the following rights EXCEPT
   (A) the right to review all school records related to the child
   (B) the right to examine the tests and procedures that will determine the placement of the child
   (C) the right to withhold consent for the child to be tested or the placement to be changed
   (D) the right to have the test results explained adequately
   (E) the right to give either verbal or written consent for placement

5. The postschool adjustment of the educable mentally retarded person is best served by
   (A) parental emotional support
   (B) school follow-up counseling
   (C) postschool courses
   (D) employment in sheltered workshops
   (E) the retarded person's own initiative

6. The most significant difference between the trainable mentally retarded and the educable mentally retarded is that the educable mentally retarded usually develop
   (A) self-help skills
   (B) language facility
   (C) emotional control
   (D) social adaptation
   (E) auditory discrimination

7. The initial assessment of the retarded child's capabilities should be conducted by
   (A) the school psychologist
   (B) a multidisciplinary team
   (C) the classroom teacher
   (D) an out-of-school agency
   (E) ancillary school personnel

EDUCATION OF STUDENTS WITH MENTAL RETARDATION

8. With respect to adolescents, the term "adaptive behavior" refers to
   - (A) appropriate reasoning and judgment in daily affairs
   - (B) sensory-motor skills
   - (C) communication skills for job application
   - (D) self-help skills for daily living
   - (E) socialization techniques for dating

9. Which of the following intelligence tests can be used for children with language differences or difficulties?

    I. The Raven Progressive Matrices
    II. The Leiter International Intelligence Scale
    III. The Draw-a-Person Test
    IV. The WISC
    V. The Stanford-Binet

   - (A) I, II
   - (B) I, II, IV
   - (C) II, III, IV
   - (D) I, II, III
   - (E) III, IV, V

10. Parents have the right to review their child's test scores. If they are not satisfied with the child's educational assessment, they may
    - (A) require the school to have the child retested
    - (B) initiate a due process hearing
    - (C) take the child out of school for a period not longer than 2 weeks
    - (D) obtain an independent educational evaluation
    - (E) require the school to destroy the records in question

11. An individualized instruction program must include all of the following EXCEPT
    - (A) the projected date for starting the program
    - (B) the specific instructional objectives
    - (C) copies of the testing materials used
    - (D) the date of the annual evaluation-of-progress report
    - (E) the type and duration of special services

12. The following requirement: "The teacher will keep continuous (daily) objective records of the time it takes Sammy to begin work on the arithmetic problems after the explanations have been given" means that one of the educational services to be provided will be
    - (A) removal from the regular classroom
    - (B) behavior management
    - (C) psychological counseling
    - (D) referral to the special education room
    - (E) special help from the teacher's aide

13. Most "learning disabled" children show no
    - (A) neurological signs of brain damage
    - (B) signs of perceptual malfunctions
    - (C) discrepancy gap in ability and performance
    - (D) signs of hypoactivity
    - (E) signs of distraction while on-task

SPECIALTY AREA TESTS

14. When counseling mentally retarded children or their parents several critical steps are involved in the relationship, the problem discussion, and the problem resolution. Which one of the following is NOT included among the basic conditions required for an effective relationship?
    (A) Showing unconditional positive regard for the child
    (B) Refusing to condone or approve deliberately inappropriate behavior by the child
    (C) Maintaining a consistent attitude
    (D) Showing sympathy for the child's dilemma
    (E) Manifesting genuine rather than superficial concern

15. Arousing and maintaining interest is a problem for teachers of the mentally retarded. Which one of the following is NOT an effective technique for this purpose?
    (A) Praising successful attempts
    (B) Exhibiting finished craft projects for the entire school to enjoy
    (C) Giving gold stars or tokens for completing timed tasks correctly
    (D) Inviting parents to see schoolwork during an evening program
    (E) Writing notes to parents about their child's accomplishments

Answer Key

1. A	4. E	7. B	10. D	13. A
2. C	5. B	8. A	11. C	14. D
3. C	6. B	9. D	12. B	15. C

Educational Leadership: Adminstration and Supervision

The examination in Educational Leadership: Administration and Supervision assesses the professional knowledge and responsibilities of a school administrator or supervisor. The test is offered primarily for those who have master's degrees or who are candidates for that degree and are applying for administrative positions.

Content and Scope (145 questions, 2-hour test)

The examination covers three major areas:

   I. Instructional Leadership
   II. Administrative Leadership
   III. Group and Individual Leadership

Some Topics for Review

1. Program Improvement (curricular trends and theories; assessing needs of multicultural populations; decision-making from developmental, national, state, and local perspectives; curriculum objectives, design, and changes; instructional resources; staff needs, development, and evaluation; assessment of objectives and pupil achievement; application of findings)

2. School Management (fiscal requirements and resources; budgeting for program and support services; processing and utilizing data; legal aspects of due process, privacy, affirmative action, and collective bargaining; governance functions of local, state, and federal agencies; other organizations and school governance; pupil personnel services; title requirements; student activities; ancillary services; personnel evaluation structures)

3. Human Relations (coping with motivations and behavior of leaders, parents, staff, and pupils; dynamics of individual and group behavior; developing effective school-community relations and use of resources; communication with verbal and nonverbal cues, oral and written techniques; maintaining a healthy learning climate; sensitivity to human needs and adaptability)

Sample Questions

Directions: For each question or incomplete statement, select the *best* answer or completion from the five choices.

1. The proportion of A grades in mastery-oriented courses, when compared to traditional courses, is
   (A) typically lower.
   (B) about the same.
   (C) higher because of low standards.
   (D) lower because of high standards.
   (E) higher because of student motivation.

SPECIALTY AREA TESTS

2. A widely used definition of learning disabilities, proposed by the National Joint Committee on Learning Disabilities in 1981, does NOT include which of the following?
   (A) Pupils with learning disabilities have a heterogeneous group of disorders.
   (B) Learning disabilities are intrinsic to each child.
   (C) The problems may be related to a dysfunction of the central nervous system.
   (D) The diagnosis of learning disabilities is complex.
   (E) Learning disabilities are the result of other handicapping conditions or influences.

3. Administrators, supervisors, and teachers are placed under pressure to raise students' scores on state examinations in reading, science, and mathematics. Which of the following are true, based on research about student performance?
   I. Student aspiration levels vary with courses.
   II. A student's need to achieve is related to feelings of self-esteem.
   III. Some students give up when they are faced with challenges.
   IV. Some students believe good grades are based on luck.
   V. Every student will try harder because these tests are very important.
   (A) I only
   (B) I, II, and III only
   (C) IV and V only
   (D) I, II, IV, and V only
   (E) I, II, III, IV

4. Educational leadership includes helping teachers and staff set a positive, learning climate in the school. This can be achieved best by
   (A) frequent interruptions in the learning activities when observing in the classroom.
   (B) using parents to patrol halls and restrooms.
   (C) publishing the honor roll monthly.
   (D) encouraging pride in self and school by both teachers and pupils setting expectancy goals.
   (E) having an annual assembly for student awards.

5. Each district, to maintain and encourage a dynamic faculty, must provide for staff development. To obtain the best results, administrators should
   (A) encourage teachers to attend national meetings.
   (B) require in-service workshops.
   (C) try to keep ahead of national trends.
   (D) specify course work in computer technology every two years.
   (E) help teachers meet their needs for individual enrichment and increasing competence to achieve instructional goals.

6. To ensure open communication between the administration and individuals, both within the school and the community, which of the following should be encouraged?
   (A) Administrators should be quickly available for consultation.
   (B) There should be a climate of shared governance, demonstrated leadership, teacher empowerment, and parental input.
   (C) It is understood that information will be filtered and somewhat distorted during discussions.
   (D) Major decisions are made only through committees.
   (E) Frequent meetings are planned with teachers and community leaders with opposing views.

7. Research on the "schools that work" reveals one common characteristic, which is
   (A) a constant but slow acceleration in district financial support.
   (B) a basic commitment of administration and staff to excellence in education.
   (C) the use of area business individuals as mentors for individual students.
   (D) well-paid, highly qualified, motivated teachers.
   (E) teacher and parent participation in long-range school planning.

8. Teachers who are interested in promoting multicultural understanding but who have no established program in the school system, should
   I. be aware that some people oppose multicultural and/or bilingual education.
   II. begin with a limited program of information and activities related to the cultural heritage of children in their classrooms.
   III. assign projects for sharing culture-specific experiences, knowledge, and skills.
   IV. begin with a major program of language, literature, and history of ethnic groups in the school.
   (A) I only
   (B) I, III only
   (C) II, IV only
   (D) I, II, III only
   (E) II, III only

9. Student teachers often dread the first day of their teaching assignments. The first few minutes can set the tone for the whole term. Therefore, which of the following techniques and attitudes should be avoided?
   (A) Be prepared and act confident, but firm.
   (B) Treat students as individuals; begin to learn their names.
   (C) "You helped me write these rules; now I'm going to enforce them!"
   (D) "It's a privilege for you to be here. I will not accept any excuses or careless work in this English class!"
   (E) Present a short lesson, with clear instructions, to be completed by everyone in the class during the period.

10. School-community leaders are cooperating on many antidrug programs for elementary and secondary students. National studies indicate that
    (A) a majority of high school seniors have tried marijuana.
    (B) fewer students use alcohol than other drugs.
    (C) alcohol and drug use declines as students go through high school.
    (D) more than one-third of all students try alcohol before the age of 12.
    (E) the use of cocaine more likely exists among female than male students.

11. Teachers who feel left out of the decision-making process and less than motivated to try cooperative learning and new teaching techniques need administrative interaction because
    (A) they should be motivated from the top leadership.
    (B) they don't fit into committee plans.
    (C) feedback is the major function of upward communication.
    (D) resistance to change is often due to lack of information and/or inexperience.
    (E) adminstrative directives must be accepted by the staff.

12. In 1991 the Council of State School Officers, in a new policy statement, focused on the transition students make from school to work. If responsibility is taken for the student beyond the high school diploma, this could mean
    I. the elimination of the end goal of graduation from the general-education track.

II. better preparation for applying academic courses on the job.
III. expansion of youth apprenticeship programs.
IV. introduction of cooperative education.
V. new state and national educational policies.

(A) I and II only
(B) III and IV only
(C) II only
(D) I, II, III, and IV only
(E) I, II, III, IV and V

13. American parents oppose certain school reforms. One that is controversial and relates to lifestyle is
    (A) year-round schooling.
    (B) technology-based reform.
    (C) teaching study skills to at-risk students.
    (D) more parent and community involvement in education.
    (E) school-industry partnerships in education.

14. The federal government has revised educational block-grant programs several times. Congress, during the Reagan administration, consolidated 28 categorical programs, giving schools more flexibility for spending funds. The result of this action came to be known as
    (A) Chapter 1.
    (B) Chapter 2.
    (C) PL-94-142.
    (D) technology grants.
    (E) bilingual education grants.

15. After a science teacher shortened classroom lectures and added hands-on learning activities based on real-life situations, students became more enthusiastic about science and gained a better understanding of scientific principles and concepts. Which of the following contributed toward the changes in attitude and achievement?
    I. In the discovery environment, students could find their own answers to the problems.
    II. The learning style of convergent thinkers was challenged the most.
    III. Students were free to test their hypotheses.
    IV. Formal laboratory periods involved all the students.
    V. These activities appealed to students with divergent thinking styles.
    (A) I, II only
    (B) I, III, V only
    (C) I, II, III only
    (D) I, II, III, IV, V
    (E) I, II, III, IV only

16. The 1990 census revealed that one out of every four Americans is a member of a minority group. This information can have a positive effect on education if planners consider that
    (A) increasing numbers of students whose first language is not English are attending suburban schools.
    (B) racial tensions are at an all-time high.
    (C) these pupils will achieve lower test scores.
    (D) cultural diversity can provide enriching learning experiences for life in a global society.
    (E) American students rank lower than students from many other countries in mathematics and science.

EDUCATIONAL LEADERSHIP

17. Many factors contribute to school violence; among them are large, impersonal schools and low levels of achievement. Which of the following may help increase performance levels and reduce violence?
    (A) Using tracking systems in senior high school
    (B) Purchasing one computer for every five students
    (C) Teaching learning strategies through a mastery approach
    (D) Using severe punishment for misbehavior
    (E) Having the principal handle all discipline problems

18. Teachers who are involved for the first time in the whole language concept should use peer conferencing to share and learn from others because of the following changes in teaching procedures:
    I. Modifying the use of teacher's manuals and basal textbooks
    II. Having to move frequently from one topic to another as children's interests, ideas, and needs change
    III. Doing daily independent evaluations of each pupil's growth
    IV. Helping children keep notebooks for assignments, review, and creative work.
    V. Preparing pupils to meet standardized test requirements
    (A) I only
    (B) II, III only
    (C) II, III, IV only
    (D) II, III, IV, V only
    (E) I, II, III, IV, V

19. A team of teachers is engaged in planning programs for disadvantaged pupils. Their concern for the most basic educational needs of disadvantaged students should involve
    (A) goal-setting experiences and opportunities for frequent gains in achievement.
    (B) providing for horizontal enrichment.
    (C) contact with several teachers.
    (D) encouraging pupil-pupil teaching-learning experiences.
    (E) participation in vertical enrichment activities.

20. A school district implements site-based management. An appropriate rationale for doing so would be:
    (A) Because their children are the beneficiaries of education, parents have a right to participate in local school planning and decision making.
    (B) Principals and teachers should have more control over school operations because they are in the best position to know about the unique learning needs of their students.
    (C) As more control is given to the local school and community, problem identification and solutions will be more accurate.
    (D) Principals and teachers are in the best position to develop programs to meet the needs of individual students.
    (E) All of the above.

21. Which of the following statements best describes the Reading Recovery program?
    (A) An early instructional intervention strategy that provides one-to-one individualized instruction for first-grade reading students who need help in beginning reading
    (B) A specialized reading program designed to aid in the rehabilitation of stroke victims
    (C) A program tailored for use with nonreading adults
    (D) An interactive, computer-based reading program
    (E) A program for adolescents emphasizing low-level, high-interest reading materials

22. Which of the following is not usually considered a major factor in student achievement?
    (A) Student time spent on a task
    (B) Per-pupil expenditures on books and supplies
    (C) High teacher expectations
    (D) Active student participation in the lesson
    (E) Parental involvement

23. Which of the following behavior characteristics does not provide a supportive climate for working in small groups?
    (A) Empathy   (D) Spontaneity
    (B) Control   (E) Equality
    (C) Problem orientation

24. Which of the following outcomes of conflict situations is MOST likely to lead to a satisfactory and permanent resolution of a problem?
    (A) Avoidance   (D) Win-lose outcome
    (B) Compromise   (E) Lose-lose outcome
    (C) Win-win outcome

25. The term "governmental immunity," as applied to public schools, means that:
    (A) school districts, boards of education, and certain school administrators cannot be held liable for negligence when they are engaged in the exercise or discharge of a governmental function.
    (B) school boards and educators have broad discretion in First-Amendment cases, as long as their actions are reasonably related to legitimate pedagogical concerns.
    (C) students do not surrender their constitutional rights when they enter the school building.
    (D) parents can collect attorney fees when they succeed in overturning an IEP (Individualized Education Program) at the administrative level.
    (E) school districts that rent space to civic groups cannot refuse to rent space to religious organizations.

26. Which of the following behaviors of school principals is least likely to result in an orderly and studious school environment?
    (A) Enforcing discipline personally with students
    (B) Developing a code of conduct that is a list of "dos and don'ts" for students
    (C) Providing support and backup for enforcement of discipline
    (D) Visibility in all areas of the school building
    (E) Providing counseling for students who are consistently disruptive

27. Using the consensus decision-making process has many benefits for school administrators. Which of the following is NOT an advantage of consensus decision-making?
    (A) It requires less time than other methods.
    (B) It generates decisions that are more creative than those arrived at by individuals.
    (C) It provides decisions that people are more committed to because of their involvement.
    (D) It promotes a "team spirit" among employees.
    (E) It improves employee self-esteem because everyone contributes.

EDUCATIONAL LEADERSHIP

28. Which of the following criteria is LEAST likely to be considered by the courts in a teacher dismissal case?
    (A) Teacher knowledge of subject matter
    (B) Teacher ability to impart knowledge effectively
    (C) Teacher ability to maintain discipline
    (D) Teacher dress and appearance
    (E) Physical ability to perform the duties of a teacher

29. Which of the following is the BEST example of participatory governance?
    (A) Parents meet as P.T.A. members and plan the school's fundraising activities.
    (B) Parents are members of the School Improvement Team and contribute to the development of school-improvement goals.
    (C) Parents appear at Board of Education meetings and lobby for equipment needed by their school.
    (D) Parents meet regularly with the building principal and schedule cultural-enrichment activities.
    (E) Parents organize and chaperone field trips.

30. School administrators often serve as team leaders. In order to effect positive team cooperation, team leaders should
    (A) recognize and reward team members for their participation.
    (B) intervene immediately when the team experiences difficulty.
    (C) encourage every team member to become involved in the team process.
    (D) withhold feedback on team progress until the assigned task is completed.
    (E) A and C above.

31. Which of the following statements about peer coaching is incorrect?
    (A) The teachers involved mutually agree to work with one another.
    (B) The focus of the peer-coaching process is the mastery of specific instructional skills.
    (C) Peer coaching normally focuses on a model of teaching and is supported by staff development.
    (D) Peer coaching concludes with the provision of a formal, written evaluation.
    (E) The peer-coaching goal is a classroom-centered improvement.

32. Which of the following statements does NOT describe beneficial teacher evaluation practice?
    (A) Principal assesses goals that were mutually established early in the school year
    (B) Principal provides feedback on classroom-management techniques observed
    (C) Principal assesses the variety of teaching techniques utilized
    (D) Principal evaluates teacher performance based upon student achievement-test results
    (E) Principal provides feedback on clarity of lesson objective

33. Which of the following statements about standardized achievement tests is incorrect?
    (A) Standardized achievement tests do not promote student learning.
    (B) Standardized achievement tests are poor predictors of an individual student's future performance.
    (C) Standardized achievement-test content is often mismatched with the content emphasized in the school's curriculum.

513

(D) Standardized achievement tests may be culturally, racially, and socially biased.
(E) Standardized achievement tests measure all the content and skills in the subject area tested.

34. Which of the following is NOT a characteristic of proper school readiness assessment?
    (A) An ongoing process of observing a child rather than a one-time snapshot
    (B) A group-administered paper-and-pencil test
    (C) Conducting the assessment in a natural setting that is comfortable and non-threatening to the child
    (D) Management of the assessment by someone who is properly trained and can relate well to children
    (E) Scoring that can yield a profile along various readiness dimensions

35. Which of the following is NOT generally considered a correlative of an effective school?
    (A) The school must be safe, orderly, and conducive to learning.
    (B) The school personnel strongly believe that all students can learn at approximately the same rate.
    (C) The school gives top priority to avoiding disruptions in the learning process.
    (D) The school regularly informs parents about educational goals, objectives, and priorities.
    (E) The school principal functions as an educational leader and sets a tone of high expectations among the staff and students.

36. Which of the following is NOT generally considered an effective classroom management technique?
    (A) Moving physically close to students engaged in minor disruptions
    (B) Clearly communicating the behaviors the teacher does or does not want the students to engage in
    (C) Asking the disruptive student a question the teacher knows the student cannot answer
    (D) Touching (gently) the disruptive student on the shoulder
    (E) Pausing for a moment and making eye contact with the disruptive student

37. Which of the following statements about portfolio assessment is incorrect?
    (A) Portfolios contain diverse samples of student work.
    (B) Portfolios provide an opportunity to document student progress over time.
    (C) Portfolio information is generally comprised of paper-and-pencil test results.
    (D) Responsibility for portfolio content is often shared by teacher and student.
    (E) Portfolio information contributes to more comprehensive reporting to parents.

38. Which of the following would NOT contribute to Kindergarten readiness?
    (A) All disadvantaged children have access to high quality and developmentally appropriate preschool programs.
    (B) Every parent is the child's first teacher and devotes time each day helping the preschool child to learn.
    (C) Children receive the nutrition and health care needed to arrive at school with healthy minds and bodies.
    (D) Every parent has access to training and education focusing upon parenting skills.
    (E) All children participate in a highly structured academic prereading program.

EDUCATIONAL LEADERSHIP

39. Frederick Herzberg contributed to the theory of worker motivation by proposing that
- (A) events leading to dissatisfaction are different than events leading to satisfaction.
- (B) the needs of people can be arranged in a hierarchy from life preservation to self-actualization.
- (C) people do not hate work; it is as natural as play.
- (D) the absence of dissatisfiers does not, of itself, cause satisfaction.
- (E) A and D above.

40. Outcomes-Based Education is best described as
- (A) focusing instructional efforts on clearly defined and measurable student outcomes.
- (B) an instructional system that emphasizes early intervention with at-risk students.
- (C) a curriculum focusing on enhanced learning for gifted students.
- (D) a method for teacher intervention with disruptive students.
- (E) a systematic method for determining when students should be promoted to the next grade level.

Answer Key

1.	E	11.	D	26.	B
2.	E	12.	E	27.	A
3.	E	13.	A	28.	D
4.	D	14.	B	29.	B
5.	E	15.	B	30.	E
6.	B	16.	D	31.	D
7.	B	17.	C	32.	D
8.	D	18.	D	33.	E
9.	D	19.	A	34.	B
10.	D	20.	E	35.	B
		21.	A	36.	C
		22.	B	37.	C
		23.	B	38.	E
		24.	C	39.	E
		25.	A	40.	A

SPECIALTY AREA TESTS

English Language and Literature

The examination in English Language and Literature tests the academic competence of candidates for the teaching of English in secondary schools.

Content and Scope (150 questions, 2-hour test)

The emphasis of the test is on three general areas, plus reference materials and the media.

    I. Literature, Mainly English and American, of All Periods
   II. Composition and Rhetoric
  III. Language

Some Topics for Review

1. Major English and American authors of various periods
2. Well-known examples of such literary forms as biography, criticism, drama, essay, novel, poetry, short story
3. The Bible
4. Translations from well-known foreign authors
5. Major themes and literary movements
6. Formal literary devices (e.g., meter, figures of speech)
7. Mechanics of usage and diction
8. Rhetorical devices
9. History of the English language
10. English grammar, both traditional and modern
11. Lexicography
12. Standard reference works

Sample Questions

Directions: For each question or incomplete statement, select the *best* answer or completion from the five choices.

   Questions 1–3 are based on the following poem:

>That orbed maiden with white fire laden
>   Whom mortals call the Moon,
>Glides glimmering o'er my fleece-like feet,
>   By the midnight breezes strewn;

1. The beautiful, melodious language used above in "The Cloud" exemplifies which type of poetry?
  (A) Narrative   (D) Ballad
  (B) Sonnet   (E) Free verse
  (C) Lyric

516

ENGLISH LANGUAGE AND LITERATURE

2. The author of "The Cloud" also wrote "To a Skylark." The appropriate imagery and perfect rhythm are typical of the poems of
   (A) Shelley
   (B) Keats
   (C) Byron
   (D) Landor
   (E) Southey

3. "The Cloud" and "To a Skylark" are good examples of the literary period known as the Age of
   (A) Classicism
   (B) Realism
   (C) Romanticism
   (D) Idealism
   (E) Modernism

4. Which of the following groups of literary works could be used in a unit on the black experience in America?
   (A) *As I Lay Dying, The Naked and the Dead, Crime and Punishment*
   (B) *The Invisible Man, Native Son, Go Tell It on the Mountain*
   (C) *The Just and the Unjust, Darkness at Noon, Of Human Bondage*
   (D) *Giles Goat-Boy, On the Road, You Can't Go Home Again*
   (E) *U.S.A., An American Tragedy, The Trial*

5. The setting is New Orleans, and the theme is the conflict between the old and the new, and between illusion and reality, as personified by Blanche DuBois, on the one hand, and Stanley Kowalski, her brother-in-law, on the other. The play just described was written by
   (A) Eugene O'Neill
   (B) Imamu Amiri Baraka (LeRoi Jones)
   (C) Edward Albee
   (D) Tennessee Williams
   (E) Arthur Miller

Questions 6 and 7 are based on the following sentences:

I. Eileen promised that when she reached the station in Jamaica that she would telephone her boyfriend.
II. Hank was but a mere boy when his father died.
III. Bettina taught him to hope, to work, and that he should never be discouraged.
IV. In 1976 José graduated college, went to work for a large corporation, and married his high school sweetheart.
V. The phenomena studied by the Harvard University professors was the green light seen in the sky during June and July.

6. Which two sentences above could be used as examples of syntactical redundancy?
   (A) I and II
   (B) I and IV
   (C) II and IV
   (D) III and IV
   (E) IV and V

7. Which sentence above could be used as an example of the omission of a grammatically needed word?
   (A) I
   (B) II
   (C) III
   (D) IV
   (E) V

SPECIALTY AREA TESTS

8. Following are five quotations from literary works dating from various periods:
   I. On anginne gesceōp God heofenan and eordan.
   II. Then let not winter's ragged hand deface
       In thee thy summer, ere thou be distill'd
   III. Gif hwā stalie, swā his wīf nyte ond his bearn, geselle lx scillinga tō wīte.
   IV. Loveliest of trees, the cherry now
       Is hung with bloom along the bough
   V. And so befil it that this kyng Arthour
       Hadde in his hous a lusty bacheler

   In which of the following is the quotation INCORRECTLY dated?
   (A) I: Old English
   (B) II: Early Modern English
   (C) III: Old English
   (D) IV: Modern English
   (E) V: Early Modern English

9. The novel begins as follows: "To the red country and part of the gray country of Oklahoma, the last rains came gently, and they did not cut the scarred earth," and recounts the story of the forced migration of the Joads, a Dust Bowl farm family, to California during the Great Depression. The preceding sentence describes the novel
   (A) *The Way West*
   (B) *Of Time and the River*
   (C) *O Pioneers!*
   (D) *The Sun Also Rises*
   (E) *The Grapes of Wrath*

10. Which of the following reference books should be consulted for the answer to this question: Who won the Nobel Prize for literature in 1978?
    (A) *Encyclopaedia Brittanica*
    (B) *Readers' Guide*
    (C) *World Almanac*
    (D) *Who's Who in America*
    (E) *Books in Print*

Questions 11, 12, and 13 are based on the following quotations from plays by William Shakespeare:

   I. We are such stuff
      As dreams are made on, and our little life
      Is rounded with a sleep.
   II. The quality of mercy is not strain'd,
       It droppeth as the gentle rain from heaven
       Upon the place beneath.
   III. Out, damned spot! Out, I say!
        . . .
        Who would have thought the old man
        To have had so much blood in him?
   IV. To be, or not to be: That is the question.
   V. Who steals my purse steals trash; 'tis something, nothing;
      'Twas mine, 'tis his, and has been slave to thousands;
      But he that filches from me my good name
      Robs me of that which not enriches him,
      And makes me poor indeed.

ENGLISH LANGUAGE AND LITERATURE

11. Which of the above is taken from *Othello*?
    (A) I
    (B) II
    (C) III
    (D) IV
    (E) V

12. Which of the above is spoken by a woman in the guise of a judge?
    (A) I
    (B) II
    (C) III
    (D) IV
    (E) V

13. Which of the above is spoken by a grieving son?
    (A) I
    (B) II
    (C) III
    (D) IV
    (E) V

Questions 14 and 15 are based on the following poem:

> Daughters of Time, the hypocritic Days,
> Muffled and dumb like barefoot dervishes,
> And marching single in an endless file,
> Bring diadems and fagots in their hands.
> To each they offer gifts after his will,
> Bread, kingdom, stars, and sky that holds them all.
> I, in my pleached garden, watched the pomp,
> Forgot my morning wishes, hastily
> Took a few herbs and apples, and the Day
> Turned and departed silent. I, too late,
> Under her solemn fillet saw the scorn.
>
> Ralph Waldo Emerson, "Days"

14. Which of the following student summaries best expresses the idea of the poem?
    (A) "Life is made up of an endless procession of days, one following the other."
    (B) "People who strive to reach the stars get more out of life than those who are satisfied with little."
    (C) "Self-betrayal comes when a person settles for less than he or she once aspired to."
    (D) "Some days a great deal can be accomplished, but others are best spent in a quiet pursuit like gardening."
    (E) "It is better to be content with simple things than to strive for the stars and the sky and be rewarded only with scorn."

15. What literary device does the author use at the beginning and the end of the poem?
    (A) Alliteration
    (B) Hyperbole
    (C) Metonymy
    (D) Onomatopoeia
    (E) Personification

Answer Key

1. C
2. A
3. C
4. B
5. D
6. A
7. D
8. E
9. E
10. C
11. E
12. B
13. D
14. C
15. E

SPECIALTY AREA TESTS

Foreign Language

The foreign-language examinations test the academic competence of a candidate planning to teach the language. Answer all questions; there is no penalty for guessing on any of the Specialty Area tests. Native speakers are heard on audio tapes during the test. Practice listening, if possible, to tapes made by people who are fluent in the language.

In addition to the languages described in the next pages with some practice questions (French, German, and Spanish), there are also Specialty Area tests in the following languages:

Italian

Content and Scope (130 questions, 2-hour test)

This test has four sections in Italian: Listening Comprehension (25%); Structure and Written Expression (15%); Reading Comprehension (25%); Culture (25%); Pedagogical and Professional Knowledge (10%). A fifth section is in English.

Japanese

Content and Scope (130 questions, 2-hour test)

This test has two sections: Listening Comprehension (some questions are in English); and Reading Comprehension (includes printed material ranging from short passages to whole paragraphs). The examinee is not required to do any interpretation of the literary materials.

Latin

Content and Scope (130 multiple-choice questions, 2-hour test)

This test has four sections: Grammar (25%); Latin Literature Passages (40%) (the readings are in Latin, the questions in English); Roman Civilization (15%); English Word Study (10%–15%); and Latin Pedagogy (5%–10%). Latin words and expressions, everyday English derived from Latin, and how to teach Latin are measured in this section. All questions are in English.

Russian

Content and Scope (102 questions, 2-hour test)

The test has two sections: Listening Comprehension (of different kinds of passages in Russian) and Reading Comprehension. The examinee is required to understand and analyze short articles and other kinds of information in Russian.

FRENCH

French

The examination in French tests the academic competence of candidates for the teaching of this foreign language.

Content and Scope (160 questions, 2-hour test)

The test consists of five sections:

I. Listening Comprehension
II. Reading Comprehension } All material is in French.
III. Written Expression

IV. Language Learning (methodology) } Most material is in English.
V. Cultural Background

Section I is tape-recorded, using native French speakers.

Some Topics for Review

1. Conversational French—vocabulary, idioms, and sentence structure
2. Written French—grammar, sentence structure, and appropriate styles for various kinds of writing (e.g., formal text, social and business letters, newspaper articles)
3. Linguistic differences between English and French
4. Typical problems encountered in teaching and learning French
5. French culture and civilization (history, geography, literature, the arts), customs, and lifestyles

Sample Questions*

I. Listening Comprehension

In this section you will hear statements or questions, short dialogs, and brief talks or news items.

Directions: You will now hear a series of questions or statements. Next to each number in your test book you will find four sentences, one of which is the most appropriate response to the spoken question or statement. In each case, select the best choice.

1. (You will hear)
   Pourquoi vous arrêtez-vous? C'est encore assez loin.
   (In your test book you will read)
   (A) Je me suis trompé de rue.
   (B) J'ai peur de stationner.
   (C) Je suis d'accord.
   (D) Je suis tout près.

---

*Sample questions selected from *NTE Programs Descriptive Book for the Core Battery and Specialty Area Tests*, Educational Testing Service, 1986. Reprinted by permission.
Permission to reprint the above NTE material does not constitute review or endorsement by Educational Testing Service of this publication as a whole or of any other test questions or testing information it may contain.

SPECIALTY AREA TESTS

II. Reading Comprehension

* *Directions:* Read the following passage carefully for comprehension. It is followed by a number of incomplete statements. Select the completion that is best according to the passage.

Sir Alfred vivait toujours en cette année 1923, mais il avait dépassé l'âge d'être le père de sa femme. On le voyait parfois assis à l'arrière de sa Rolls-Royce arrêtée sur quelque chemin en bordure de la plage. De telles sorties étaient rares, Sir Alfred ne quittant guère le joli manoir où il avait fait installer à grands frais une canalisation qui lui permettait de faire venir l'eau de mer dans sa salle de bains pour y prendre des bains de mer chauds. Nous eûmes longtemps la preuve de ce luxe inouï par la présence de tuyaux rouillés qui montaient de la grève à travers les rochers, jusqu'au manoir.

2. D'après ce passage, on peut affirmer que Sir Alfred était
   - (A) sourd
   - (B) fou
   - (C) avare
   - (D) vieux

3. Le manoir qu'habite Sir Alfred se trouve situé
   - (A) en pleine campagne
   - (B) prés de la côte
   - (C) dans les montagnes
   - (D) au bord d'un lac

III. Written Expression

Part A requires the examinee to select, from the four choices given, the correct word or expression to complete a sentence.

* *Directions:* This part consists of a number of incomplete statements, each having four suggested completions. Select the most appropriate completion and blacken the corresponding space on the answer sheet.

4. Le premier ministre espère qu'aucun incident ne . . . troubler les élections.
   - (A) vienne
   - (B) viendra
   - (C) soit venu
   - (D) venait

In Part B the examinee's knowledge of appropriate style is tested as it applies to a total passage.

* *Directions:* The paragraphs in this part are drawn from various types and styles of written text, such as formal and informal letters, newspaper accounts, and other materials. Each contains numbered blanks, indicating omissions in the text. Following each paragraph are four suggested completions for each numbered blank. All four completions are grammatically correct, but one of them is stylistically INAPPROPRIATE to the paragraph. Read the entire paragraph carefully, and then for each question select the ONE choice that is NOT APPROPRIATE to the style of the paragraph as a whole.

En pratique, l'instructeur ne refusera pas ———— ses étudiants, et notamment il
                                              5
leur fournira le vocabulaire courant qui a trait au sujet de conversation. ———— de
                                                                              6
constater combien les mots qui viennent à l'esprit des étudiants sont en général peu usités ou d'un emploi très spécialisé.

FRENCH

5. (A) de donner la main à
   (B) de venir en aide à
   (C) d'aider
   (D) de seconder

6. (A) Il est en effet curieux
   (B) Il est intéressant
   (C) Il est drôle
   (D) Il est vraiment étonnant

IV. Language Learning Problems

Certain differences between the English and French languages present problems for the learner. The teacher needs to know these areas of difficulty in order to provide effective teaching-learning situations.

* *Directions:* For each question, select the most appropriate answer. In all cases, assume that the students are native speakers of English who have recently begun the study of French.

7. Which of the following might not be understood as a question if the student failed to pronounce *demain* with a rising intonation?
   (A) Vous venez demain?
   (B) Avez-vous l'intention de venir demain?
   (C) Venez-vous demain?
   (D) Est-ce que vous venez demain?

8. For teaching purposes in beginning classes, the presence of a circumflex accent in words such as *arrêt* can be most usefully related to
   (A) written style
   (B) orthographic changes
   (C) levels of language
   (D) phonological convention

V. Cultural Background

* *Directions:* Each of the incomplete statements below is followed by four suggested completions. Select the completion that is best in each case.

9. The revocation of the Edict of Nantes resulted in the
   (A) exile of the Protestants
   (B) religious wars
   (C) Fronde
   (D) crusade against the Albigensians

10. *Le goûter* is most likely to be served at
    (A) 12 h 30   (C) 16 h 30
    (B) 15 h 00   (D) 21 h 00

Answer Key

1. A   3. B   5. A   7. A   9. A
2. D   4. B   6. C   8. B   10. C

SPECIALTY AREA TESTS

German

The examination in German tests the academic competence of candidates for the teaching of this foreign language.

Content and Scope (160 questions, 2-hour test)

The test consists of five sections:

I. Listening Comprehension
II. Reading Comprehension   } All material is in German.
III. Structure and Written Expression

IV. Language Analysis
V. Cultural Background   } Most material is in English.

Section I is tape-recorded, using native German speakers.

Some Topics for Review

1. Conversational German—vocabulary, idioms, and sentence structure
2. Written German—grammar, sentence structure, and diction
3. Linguistic differences between English and German
4. Typical problems encountered in teaching and learning German
5. German culture and civilization (history, geography, literature, the arts), customs, and lifestyles

Sample Questions*

I. Listening Comprehension

In this section you will hear statements or questions, short dialogs, and brief talks or news items.
Directions: For each question in this part you will hear a short conversation between two people and will read a question about the conversation in your test book. From the four choices following each question, choose the most appropriate response.

1. (You will hear)
    (Woman A) Sie können Diktat aufnehmen?
    (Woman B) Ja, deutsche Einheitskurzschrift. Und ich tippe 70 Worte in der Minute.
    (Woman A) Wir haben eine umfangreiche Korrespondenz mit den USA. Ich hoffe, Frau Schmidt, Sie können gut Englisch, denn das ist für uns unbedingt nötig.
    (Woman B) Es tut mir leid, aber Englisch habe ich leider nie gelernt.
    (in your test book you will read)
    Bekommt Frau Schmidt die Stellung?
    (A) Ja, denn sie kann stenographieren.
    (B) Nein, denn sie war nie in Amerika.

---

*Sample questions selected from *NTE Programs Descriptive Book for the Core Battery and Specialty Area Tests*, Educational Testing Service, 1986. Reprinted by permission.
Permission to reprint the above NTE material does not constitute review or endorsement by Educational Testing Service of this publication as a whole or of any other test questions or testing information it may contain.

524

GERMAN

(C) Ja, denn sie schreibt schnell Maschine.
(D) Nein, denn sie kann kein Englisch.

II. Reading Comprehension

Directions: Read the following passage carefully for comprehension. It is followed by a number of incomplete statements. Select the completion that is best according to the passage.

Die junge Generation leidet unter einer schweren Identifikationskrise. Sie lebt, sicherlich recht angenehm, in einem Land, das die Vereinigten Staaten in vielem oft allzu getreu kopiert. Seit zu langer Zeit sieht die Jugend Deutschlands wenige deutsche Filme, hört wenige deutsche Schlager mehr, verbringt die Ferien oft nicht in Deutschland.

Die Jugend Deutschlands empfindet gegenüber den Herausforderungen der modernen Gesellschaft die gleichen Verwirrungen and Ängste wie die Jugend der übrigen Welt. Zum Unterschied von anderen jungen Europäern sind aber deutsche Jugendliche weniger geneigt, sich mit ihren Eltern zu beraten.

2. Der Verfasser scheint zu mißbilligen, daß die deutsche Jugend
   (A) zu gut lebt   (C) keine eigene Kultur hat
   (B) keinen Vorbildern foigt   (D) zu leichtsinnig lebt

3. Die jungen Deutschen unterscheiden sich von anderen jungen Europäern dadurch, daß sie
   (A) eine bessere materielle Existenz haben
   (B) andere soziale Probleme haben
   (C) ähnliche Schwierigkeiten haben wie die jungen Amerikaner
   (D) ein anderes Verhältnis zur älteren Generation haben

III. Structure and Written Expression

Part A requires the examinee to select the correct words or forms to fill the blanks in a sentence or short paragraph.

Directions: The paragraphs below contain blank spaces indicating omissions in the text. Below each blank are four choices. Select the choice that is grammatically correct in the context. Be sure to read the entire paragraph first.

Es kommt oft _____, daß man _____ eine Erfahrung verzichten muß, die schön

        4. (A) daran   5. (A) an
           (B) nach   (B) für
           (C) vor   (C) mit
           (D) davon   (D) auf

_____ wäre.
6. (A) gehabt
   (B) gewesen
   (C) gewollt
   (D) gelassen

In Part B errors in grammar or diction in sentences must be identified.

Directions: Each of the sentences below contains ONE error in grammar or diction. Select the underlined word or phrase that is grammatically or stylistically INCORRECT in the context of the sentence. Note that in this part of the test you are asked to identify an INCORRECT word or phrase.

SPECIALTY AREA TESTS

7. <u>Im diesem</u> Sommer war es <u>in der</u> Schweiz <u>bedeutend</u> wärmer als <u>im</u> Rheinland.
      A   B   C   D

IV. Language Analysis

Certain differences between the English and German languages present problems for the learner. The teacher needs to know these areas of difficulty in order to provide effective teaching-learning situations.

Directions: Each of the questions below is followed by four suggested answers. Select the answer which is best in each case.

8. In which of the following words is the pronunciation of the underlined sound different from that of the other three?
   (A) schließen
   (B) voraus
   (C) Dienstmädchen
   (D) Absatz

V. Cultural Background

*9. Which of the following statements about German customs is INCORRECT?
   (A) Plane and train schedules indicate the hours up to 24 rather than a.m. and p.m.
   (B) In dates, the day always precedes the month.
   (C) In informal letters, the salutation is followed by an exclamation point.
   (D) In addressing a letter, the postal code number always follows the name of the city.

Answer Key

1. D	4. C	7. A
2. C	5. D	8. D
3. D	6. B	9. D

SPANISH

Spanish

The examination in Spanish tests the academic competence of candidates for the teaching of this foreign language.

Content and Scope (160 questions, 2-hour test)

The test consists of five sections:

I. Listening Comprehension
II. Reading Comprehension } All material is in Spanish.
III. Structure and Written Expression

IV. Language Analysis
V. Cultural Background } Most material is in English.

Section I is tape recorded, using native Spanish speakers.

Some Topics for Review

1. Conversational Spanish—vocabulary, idioms, and sentence structure
2. Written Spanish—grammar, sentence structure, and diction
3. Linguistic differences between English and Spanish
4. Typical problems encountered in teaching and learning Spanish
5. Peninsular and Spanish-American culture and civilization (history, geography, literature, the arts), customs, and lifestyles

Sample Questions*

I. Listening Comprehension

In this section you will hear statements or questions, short dialogs, and brief talks or new items.

Directions: For each question in this part you will hear a short conversation between two people and will read a question about the conversation in your test book. From the four choices following each question, choose the most appropriate answer.

1. (You will hear)
   (Woman)   ¿Y en qué otros campos está Ud. preparado además de ventas?
   (Man)   Me gradué en contabilidad y tengo experiencia en asuntos de créditos internacionales.
   (Woman)   Tenemos oficinas en el extrajero y quizás podriamos ubicarlo alli.
   (Man)   No tendria inconveniente en viajar a cualquier parte si Uds. me dieran la oportunidad.
   (In your test book you will read)
   ¿Que quiere el señor?
   (A) Obtener crédito.   (C) Ir de vacaciones.
   (B) Vender casas de campo.   (D) Encontrar trabajo.

---

*Sample questions selected from NTE Programs Descriptive Book for the Core Battery and Specialty Area Tests, Educational Testing Service, 1986. Reprinted by permission.
Permission to reprint the above NTE material does not constitute review or endorsement by Educational Testing Service of this publication as a whole or of any other test questions or testing information it may contain.

SPECIALTY AREA TESTS

II. Reading Comprehension

Directions: Read the following passage carefully for comprehension. It is followed by a number of questions or incomplete statements. Select the answer or completion that is best according to the passage.

Son las tres de la mañana. Noche madrileña en la calle de Alcalá. Cruzan esos taxis que no van a ningún lado, y la vendedora de lotería dando vueltas ofreciendo millones. El ciego del violín, como tiene los ojos cerrados de por vida, no tiene sueño. El perro del ciego, con el platillo entre los dientes, se ha dormido. También se acostó entre nubes la luna.

2. Según este párrafo, ?qué hacen los taxis en Madrid a la hora mencionada?
   (A) Van sin rumbo fijo.
   (B) No aceptan pasajeros.
   (C) Constituyen un peligro público.
   (D) No conducen con ánimo.

3. El que toca el violín parece no tiene sueño porque
   (A) los viejos no duermen mucho
   (B) nunca tiene los ojos abiertos
   (C) ya ha dormido suficiente
   (D) prefiere su propia música

III. Structure and Written Expression

Part A requires the examinee to select the correct words or forms to fill the blanks in a sentence or short paragraph.

* *Directions:* The paragraphs below contain blank spaces indicating omissions in the text. Below each blank are four choices. Select the choice that is grammatically correct in the context. Be sure to read the entire paragraph first.

_____ el trabajo del dia, los obreros cansados no

4. (A) Terminaron
   (B) Terminaba
   (C) Terminando
   (D) Terminado

_____ ganas de comer ni siquiera _____ habian traido de merienda.

5. (A) teniendo
   (B) habian tenido
   (C) tenian
   (D) han tenido

6. (A) lo cual
   (B) lo que
   (C) el cual
   (D) la que

528

SPANISH

Directions: Each of the sentences below contains ONE error in grammar or diction. Select the underlined word or phrase that is grammatically or stylistically INCORRECT in the context of the sentence. Note that in this part of the test you are asked to identify an INCORRECT word or phrase.

7. El àguila solitario de las montañas rocallosas anda buscando el nido
             A   B   C
   del año pasado.
        D

IV. Language Analysis

Certain differences between the English and Spanish languages present difficulties for the learner. The teacher needs to know these areas of difficulty in order to provide effective teaching-learning situations.

Directions: Each of the questions below is followed by four suggested answers. Select the answer which is best in each case.

8. Which of the following has the same pattern in the formation of the future as *poder*?
   (A) perder   (C) haber
   (B) conocer   (D) leer

9. In which of the following words will the *s* most likely be pronounced as an English *z*?
   (A) ca*s*a   (C) ca*s*pa
   (B) cri*s*tiano   (D) fanta*s*ma

V. Cultural Background

Directions: Each of the incomplete statements below is followed by four suggested completions. Select the completion which is best in each case.

10. In the Hispanic world, it is traditional for children to receive presents on
    (A) Christmas eve   (C) New Year's day
    (B) Christmas day   (D) Three Kings' day

Answer Key

1. D   3. B   5. C   7. A   9. D
2. A   4. D   6. B   8. C   10. D

SPECIALTY AREA TESTS

Health Education

The examination in Health Education tests the academic competence of candidates for the teaching of this subject in junior and senior high schools.

Content and Scope (120 questions, 2-hour test)

The test covers five areas:

  I. Health Education as a Discipline (10%*) (objectives, outcomes, organization, and implementation of health programs)
 II. Personal Health Care (34%*) (nutrition, safety and first aid, physical fitness, personal hygiene, drugs and medicines, personal health, mental and emotional health, assessment, changing health care, increasing student responsibility)
III. Community health (10%*) (health agencies, health careers, the environment)
 IV. Family Living and Sex Education (26%*) (reproduction—anatomy and physiology, interpersonal relations of dating, marriage, parenting, the family, social problems and services, aging, death and dying)
  V. Diseases and Disorders (20%*) (misconceptions about diseases, their prevention and treatment; communicable diseases; chronic diseases-diabetes, cardiovascular, cancer, genetic disorders; mental and emotional illnesses; the role of counseling)

Sample Questions

Directions: For each question or incomplete statement, select the *best* answer or completion from the five choices.

1. There is an international search for a vaccine for
   (A) diphtheria
   (B) smallpox
   (C) whooping cough
   (D) AIDS

2. Diabetes, heart disease, and cancer can be related to diet, beginning in childhood and adolescence. In 1988, the First Surgeon General's Report on Nutrition recommended that Americans
     I. increase fiber in their diet by eating peas, dried beans, and whole grains.
    II. reduce their intake of sodium and sugar.
   III. eat less red meat, fish, and poultry.
    IV. eat more fruits and vegetables.
     V. exercise to burn off unneeded calories.
   (A) I and II only
   (B) I, II, III, IV only
   (C) I, II, IV, V only
   (D) I, II, III, IV, V

---

*approximate percentage of test questions

HEALTH EDUCATION

3. Which of the following is an accurate statement about drug addiction and dependence?
   (A) Most of the groups of drugs that can produce physical dependence do not alter mood or behavior.
   (B) The withdrawal from long-term use of tranquilizers may produce such symptoms as a sense of well-being or euphoria because the chemical balance in the body has been changed.
   (C) Withdrawal from alcohol abuse, in some cases can cause delirium tremens (hallucinations), seizures, and even death.
   (D) People who drink excessive amounts of regular coffee, tea, or cola may have such withdrawal symptoms as chills, tremors, and alertness within three hours after the last drink containing caffeine.

4. Students can assist in recycling projects by sorting and taking all of the following to recycling centers EXCEPT
   (A) plastic milk jugs   (C) aluminum pie tins
   (B) waxed cardboard cartons   (D) newspapers

5. After divorce and the breakup of the family, the economic level is
   (A) lowered more for the husband than the wife
   (B) about the same as during the marriage
   (C) stable for wife because she receives the house
   (D) unstable for children because of the child support system

6. Women are most at risk for poor nutrition (aside from pregnancy) during the second decade of life (adolescence). During this period women's diets should have
   (A) increased amounts of vitamins and minerals
   (B) more protein from red meats
   (C) more grains and nuts
   (D) more iron and calcium

7. Which of these factors is most likely to produce feelings of acceptance during acculturative stress?
   (A) Competition with some opportunity for success
   (B) Family reciprocity and friendship
   (C) Strong core values similar to the majority group
   (D) Students of a minority race placed in white students' classrooms

8. All people are responsible for decision-making in the care of their own health. Parents who smoke expose their children to lung irritants and themselves to an increased risk of premature death from all of these ailments EXCEPT
   (A) lung cancer.   (C) cancer of the esophagus.
   (B) cirrhosis of the liver. (D) gastric ulceration.

9. Which of the following will determine the presence of mononucleosis in a student's system?
   (A) Feeling tired and rundown
   (B) A sore throat with white spots and a fever
   (C) A blood test
   (D) Swollen lymph glands

SPECIALTY AREA TESTS

10. Which of the following is most likely to deter adolescents from smoking?
    (A) Parental and school rules
    (B) Cigarette-package warning labels
    (C) Medical television programs
    (D) Peer friendships among nonsmokers

11. When a new teacher begins planning a health instruction program for a junior high school class, the first step should be to determine whether
    (A) parents are conservative on certain issues.
    (B) films and visuals are available.
    (C) the material was introduced in the previous grade.
    (D) there is a graded state model program mandate.

12. Medical research indicates that women who begin their sexual activity in their early teens and have several sexual partners carry an added risk factor for
    (A) breast cancer.   (C) cervical cancer.
    (B) ovarian cancer.   (D) uterine cancer.

13. Anorexia nervosa is characterized by
    (A) unusual weight gain.
    (B) a desire for exotic food.
    (C) a very positive body image.
    (D) anxiety about possible weight gain.

14. Which of the following is the most effective way to prevent sports injuries among youths?
    (A) No competitive sports during the preteen years
    (B) Adequate warmup before practice
    (C) Mandatory athletics for all, beginning in the elementary grades
    (D) Intramural activities for junior high school students only

15. Teenage mothers are most at risk for giving birth to infants with
    (A) Down's syndrome.   (C) low birth weight.
    (B) a cleft palate.   (D) muscular atrophies.

16. It takes several months or even years to place new medications on the market. Which agency has to review research on the safety and utility of each drug?
    (A) American Medical Society   (C) American Cancer Society
    (B) World Health Organization   (D) Food and Drug Administration

17. What is the first function lost after drinking too much alcohol?
    (A) coordination   (C) peripheral vision
    (B) judgment   (D) decreased hearing level

18. If a girl compares her perception of her physical appearance with prevailing female stereotypes, which of the following is likely to occur?
    I. Only a small number of adolescent girls will approximate the role models.
    II. Some girls will begin compulsive dieting leading to bulimia.
    III. Adolescents with atypical characteristics may face psychological problems.
    IV. Students with high self-esteem will ignore these stereotypes.
    (A) I, II, III only

(B) III, IV only
(C) II, III, IV only
(D) II, III only

19. Lead poisoning (plumbism), a chronic disorder, can lead to cognitive defects in children. Sources of lead to which children can be exposed are
    I. chips of old paint
    II. gasoline fumes
    III. metallic objects, such as shot, fishing weights
    IV. glazed ceramic ware, battery casings
    (A) I only
    (B) I and II only
    (C) I, II, III, IV
    (D) II and III only

20. After the onset of the menarche, typically at about 12 or 13 years of age, the U.S. girl's cycle may not become regular for as long as two years. During this time there is an added risk of pregnancy because
    (A) estrogen is not produced by the ovaries.
    (B) ovulation is unpredictable.
    (C) PMS gives false signals.
    (D) the egg can survive for three days in the cervix.

21. Cocaine use causes
    I. the heart muscle to work harder.
    II. a lack of interest in food.
    III. a chemical imbalance in the brain leading to depression.
    IV. construction of blood vessels, thus impeding circulation.
    (A) I, III, IV only
    (B) I, II, III, IV
    (C) II and III only
    (D) III only

22. The HIV virus can be transmitted through
    (A) a blood donation.
    (B) coughing or sneezing.
    (C) an exchange of blood.
    (D) touching someone who has the virus.

23. The Heimlich maneuver is used
    (A) when someone has had an electric shock.
    (B) when the person has injured an arm in a fall.
    (C) to aid a person having a seizure.
    (D) to dislodge an object from the windpipe.

24. Feelings are necessary for wholesome emotional development. Which is the most positive approach to take to reduce stress?
    (A) "I express my feelings whether people like it or not."
    (B) "When people get angry at me, I get angry at them!"
    (C) "My feelings are private; I hide them from everyone."
    (D) "My friends and I share our feelings."

SPECIALTY AREA TESTS

25. Which of the following will most likely be least productive in helping adolescents build self-confidence and self-control?
    (A) Learning to make responsible decisions about the care of their bodies
    (B) Discussing their feelings and concerns with others in small supportive groups
    (C) Providing frequent assignments of moderate difficulty
    (D) Using students as group leaders for health projects

Answer Key

1. D	9. C	17. B
2. C	10. D	18. A
3. C	11. D	19. C
4. B	12. C	20. B
5. D	13. D	21. B
6. D	14. B	22. C
7. C	15. C	23. D
8. B	16. D	24. D
		25. C

Home Economics Education

The examination in Home Economics Education tests the academic competence of candidates for the teaching of home economics.

Content and Scope (150 questions, 2-hour test)

The range of the examination is broad and includes both the content of home economics and the methodology of teaching in a number of programs common to the field. These eight areas are tested:

   I. The Family
  II. Human Development
 III. Theory and Methods of Home Management
  IV. Consumerism—Laws, Rights, Responsibilities, Marketing
   V. Nutrition and Food Preparation and Service
  VI. Clothing—Wardrobe Management and Knowledge of Textiles
 VII. Housing—Types, Purchasing Methods, and Regulations
VIII. Principles and Methods of Teaching Home Economcis

The test emphasizes (a) the individual and the family and (b) decision-making. The questions are divided equally among the eight topics.

Sample Questions

Directions: For each question or incomplete statement, select the *best* answer or completion from the five choices.

1. A young woman decided to set up a small crafts business. To obtain initial financing the wisest course would be to
   (A) rely on her husband's credit rating
   (B) borrow from a family member
   (C) set up a partnership form of business
   (D) sell from her home and buy only the stock for which she has the funds
   (E) establish a credit history in her own name

2. When buying blankets, the size that will fit a full-size double bed is
   (A) 65 x 90 inches
   (B) 80 x 90 inches
   (C) 72 x 90 inches
   (D) 90 x 108 inches
   (E) 90 by 120 inches

3. Which of the following statements is NOT true of the cotton fabric designated?
   (A) *Muslin* sheets have 112–140 threads per inch.
   (B) *Percale* sheeting is smoother than muslin with 180–200 + threads per inch.
   (C) *Sanforized cotton* does not exceed 1 percent shrinkage.
   (D) *Duck* is a durable and tightly woven cotton fabric.
   (E) *Organdy* needs little or no ironing when used for curtains.

SPECIALTY AREA TESTS

4. A man bought a chair for $100, paid $10 down, and made 12 monthly payments of $9 each. What was the true annual interest rate?
   - (A) 12 percent
   - (B) 10 percent
   - (C) 20 percent
   - (D) 32 percent
   - (E) 15 percent

5. The average infant of 12–14 months of age can digest all of the following foods EXCEPT
   - (A) whole grain or enriched cereal with milk
   - (B) applesauce, mashed bananas, stewed fruit
   - (C) baked potato
   - (D) raw apple slices
   - (E) chopped or pureed whole-kernel corn

6. Pile fabrics are pressed best on
   - (A) a seam roll
   - (B) a tailor's ham
   - (C) a press mitt
   - (D) a needle board
   - (E) a dressmaker clapper

7. Sewing machine needles are made in different sizes and types for various fabrics. Which of these needles is best to sew knit fabrics?
   - (A) Sharp-point
   - (B) Ball-point
   - (C) Wedge-point
   - (D) Twin or triple needle
   - (E) Size 9 or 11 regular

8. Which of these electrical appliances is the heaviest user of current?
   - (A) Skillet
   - (B) Waffle iron
   - (C) Roaster
   - (D) Toaster
   - (E) Iron

9. Which of the following are energy-saving options for the home?
   - I. An automatic-defrost refrigerator-freezer
   - II. A microwave oven
   - III. A self-cleaning oven
   - IV. A dimmer switch for all lights in the kitchen
   - V. Twinkle Christmas tree bulbs
   - (A) I and III
   - (B) I and IV
   - (C) II and III
   - (D) II and V
   - (E) III and IV

10. Oxalic acid solution is an agent for the removal of
    - (A) paint stains
    - (B) airplane glue stains
    - (C) rust stains
    - (D) black marks on kitchen towels
    - (E) candle wax

11. Which materials make poor cooking ware in terms of care and heat distribution?
    - I. Copper
    - II. Stainless steel
    - III. Aluminum
    - IV. Enamelware
    - V. Glass-ceramic ware
    - (A) I and II
    - (B) I and III
    - (C) II and III
    - (D) III and V
    - (E) I and IV

536

HOME ECONOMICS EDUCATION

12. Hazardous contaminants can find their way into infant formulas. Cases of fatal infant cyanosis have been traced to the use of water containing
    (A) nitrates
    (B) lactose
    (C) calcium sulfate
    (D) dextrin
    (E) sodium nitrate

13. Preschoolers often show a sense of humor. They tend to laugh most often
    (A) when they are involved in activities
    (B) when they are riding in their car seats
    (C) at incongruities
    (D) at riddles
    (E) when another child is punished

14. One disadvantage of a variable-rate mortgage is that
    (A) the initial down payment required is larger than that for a conventional mortgage
    (B) most banks are reluctant to give such mortgages
    (C) negative amortization of the mortgage may result
    (D) mortgages of this type have to be paid off within 10 years
    (E) the initial interest rate is higher than that on a conventional mortgage

15. Home economics programs often must share space and equipment. Which of the following criteria is LEAST important for an effective program?
    (A) Space should be similar to that of a well-managed home.
    (B) Floors should be easy to clean.
    (C) Adequate storage space should be provided.
    (D) There should be space for individual and small-group activities.
    (E) A separate room should be available for each type of program that is taught.

Answer Key

1. E	4. C	7. B	10. C	13. A
2. C	5. E	8. C	11. E	14. C
3. E	6. D	9. D	12. A	15. E

537

SPECIALTY AREA TESTS

Introduction to the Teaching of Reading

The examination in the Introduction to the Teaching of Reading tests the academic competence of candidates for the teaching of reading. The test is based on the typical course of study in the field and can be taken by any education major.

Content and Scope (150 questions, 2-hour test)

The test covers eight major areas:

    I. The Reading Process (psycholinguistics, metacognition, schema theories)
   II. Specific Reading Skills and Methods of Teaching Them (enlisting parental assistance)
  III. Analyzing Individual Differences (new assessment tools)
  IV. Instructional Theories (interrelatedness of the language arts)
   V. Instructional Methods (high interest level, cooperative learning, computers)
  VI. The Affective Domain (sociological and psychological factors)
 VII. Professional Resources (reading specialists, library media specialists, aides)
VIII. School Organizations for Teaching Reading (RIF and others)

Some Topics for Review

1. Word recognition and word analysis
2. Comprehension
3. Oral and silent reading
4. Study habits and skills
5. Diagnostic testing
6. Developing individual pupil profiles
7. Impact of developmental differences on learning to read
8. Characteristics of the English language
9. Teaching basic sight words and syntax
10. Phonics
11. Linguistics
12. Programmed reading (computers)
13. Experience techniques
14. Motivating pupils to read
15. Teacher-pupil rapport as a factor in learning to read
16. Professional organizations and publications
17. Nongraded, cross-graded, and open classrooms
18. Team teaching
19. Paraprofessionals and their use
20. Systemwide approach to teaching reading

Sample Questions

Directions: For each question or incomplete statement, select the *best* answer or completion from the five choices.

1. José, recently arrived from Puerto Rico, knows only one English word: *I*. What would be the first step in preparing him to learn to read?
   (A) Assign him a specific number of words a day from the basal reader.
   (B) Spend time talking with him during the seatwork period for the regular reading class.
   (C) Place him with the other non-English-speaking students in the same section of reading.
   (D) Assign a "buddy" to stay with him throughout the school day.
   (E) Translate the lesson into Spanish and put it on a cassette.

INTRODUCTION TO THE TEACHING OF READING

2. There are certain aspects of the language-learning process that a teacher must consider when structuring the sequence of presentation of materials. In this connection, which of the following statements is INCORRECT?
   (A) Comprehension precedes repetition (production of language).
   (B) Meaning is developed only within the context of language.
   (C) When children become aware of language as a communication tool, their facility for language use increases.
   (D) A child's instrinsic motivation and natural curiosity have a large impact on learning to read.
   (E) Children, when ready, will learn to read in spite of the teacher.

3. All of the following tests can be used to evaluate individual learning difficulties and to plan remedial programs EXCEPT
   (A) Frostig's Development Test of Visual Perception
   (B) Orton's Test of Motor Response
   (C) Wepman's Auditory Discrimination Test
   (D) Wechsler's Intelligence Scale for Children
   (E) the Illinois Test of Psycholinguistic Abilities

4. Which of the following are consonant digraphs?
   (A) ch, th, sh
   (B) cl, fl, pl
   (C) cr, tr, pr
   (D) sm, st, str
   (E) bl, br, sl

5. A reading class has a short attention span and is easily distracted. Which of the following techniques suggested by different teachers would be LEAST likely to give the desired result of changing the pupils' behavior?
   (A) Ann would use a fixed-ratio and fixed-intervals approach, so that pupils would know when she would smile or say "That's fine" for on-task behavior.
   (B) Ben would comment on a new task every time a pupil tried it, with or without success.
   (C) Deborah would give immediate reinforcement whenever a pupil read a paragraph well aloud, or stayed on task for at least a few minutes.
   (D) George would set up rate and speed goals several times a week, and comment every time a student met one of these goals or approximated it.
   (E) Max would use both distributed and massed practice, for he believes pupils should read under supervision several times a day. Occasionally he would comment favorably, but students wouldn't be able to anticipate his comments.

6. Whenever the reading supervisor visits a classroom, she notices the affective behavior of pupils and the general emotional climate in the classroom. Which classroom described below would benefit the most from her comment, "You should shorten the reading period and use higher interest materials?"
   (A) Pupils listen to records, write on the board, or just wander around the room while the other reading groups have class.
   (B) A few pupils test the rules of the teacher and get punished for not staying in their seats during the reading sections.
   (C) Every day each pupil gets the opportunity to read aloud or answer questions.
   (D) The children seem to wiggle a lot and keep on turning the pages; when asked to read, several have lost the page and lose a turn.
   (E) A few pupils seem to know all the answers. The teacher calls on them, but expects the class to listen intently to their comments.

7. A seatwork assignment contains this question: The words *go* and *going* are alike in some ways and different in some ways; how are they alike and how are they different? The teacher has assigned this problem because pupils have
   (A) word recognition difficulties
   (B) difficulty with consonants
   (C) difficulty with consonant blends
   (D) difficulty with medial vowels
   (E) difficulty with pronouncing and spelling word endings

8. Which of the following is NOT useful for teaching structural analysis of words?
   (A) The teacher pronounces a word of two or more syllables and accents the syllable breaks in the word. The students repeat.
   (B) The teacher breaks words apart on a chart with colored chalk, saying, "Here are two consonants; break at this place (run/ner)." The students listen.
   (C) The teacher says, "A single consonant between two vowels usually goes with the second vowel (ba/con)." The students work on worksheets.
   (D) The teacher says, "Prefixes and suffixes are separate syllables (un/clean/ness)." The students watch a filmstrip.
   (E) The teacher reads a word list. The students raise their hands when they hear matching initial consonant sounds and then repeat the consonant sound.

9. A teacher permits Spanish-speaking pupils to teach some of their language during the reading class. Parents who object to this procedure should be informed that this
   (A) builds the self-confidence of the Spanish-speaking pupils
   (B) is an enrichment activity
   (C) expresses the concept of sharing ideas
   (D) improves auditory discrimination
   (E) increases pupil interest in learning

10. A systemwide approach to the teaching of reading is most productive for pupil growth when
    (A) listening, speaking, and writing skills are integrated
    (B) cross-age tutoring takes the place of adult tutoring
    (C) the reading supervisor spends more time in each classroom
    (D) diagnosis and sequencing begins at the first grade and is continued through the middle school with parental involvement
    (E) the program is developed and evaluated by commercial sources with little teacher or parent involvement

Answer Key

| 1. D | 3. B | 5. A | 7. E | 9. B |
| 2. E | 4. A | 6. D | 8. E | 10. D |

Library Media Specialist

The examination for the Library Media Specialist tests the academic competence of candidates, at either the undergraduate or graduate level, for the position of library media specialist, K–12, in individual schools. It is a test of knowledge and its appropriate application.

Content and Scope (150 questions, 2-hour test)

The test covers five areas:

I. Administration of the Library Media Center (23%–25%) (philosophy, planning, evaluating, budgeting, staffing)
II. Acquisition of Resources (22%–25%) (policy, selection, collections, bibliographic sources, supplies, equipment, audiovisuals, evaluation, classification, circulation, organization)
III. Information and Program Services (20%–25%) (references, statistical formats, online services, interlibrary networks, programmed materials, knowledge of media, standard authors and publications, media presentations)
IV. Availability of Services and Staff (20%–25%) (physical plan of the center, circulation, operations, preparation of materials, pupil orientation, participation with faculty in curriculum planning for special goals, increasing certain skills and attitudes toward learning and use of media)
V. Professional Development (8%–10%) (continuing education, professional associations, legislation, professional literature, trends and issues, ethics, intellectual freedom, accreditation, support)

Sample Questions

Directions: For each question or incomplete statement, select the *best* answer or completion from the five choices.

1. Which one of the following would be least helpful to the library media specialist in the selection of current publications?
   (A) Publishers' and booksellers' catalogs
   (B) *Books in Print*
   (C) *New York Times Book Reviews*
   (D) Local periodicals
   (E) ASLIB'S Book List

2. To facilitate the best use of books and equipment within a limited budget, the most appropriate action a media specialist could take would be to
   (A) purchase new equipment only when it was on sale.
   (B) order computer software after seeing it demonstrated at professional meetings.
   (C) read reviews of each book before ordering it.
   (D) share materials and equipment with other schools when it is cost effective.
   (E) consult curriculum committees to ascertain teachers' needs and objectives.

3. Library automation computer software has programs for all services EXCEPT
   (A) immediate pupil direction.
   (B) circulation.
   (C) data-entry.
   (D) public-access catalogs.
   (E) acquisitions and cardmaking.

SPECIALTY AREA TESTS

4. Booklists are published by such organizations as The National Council of Teachers of English. These lists usually do not
   (A) give the appropriate grade level.
   (B) include the publisher's name.
   (C) constitute an endorsement for books unless so indicated.
   (D) give a short description of the content.
   (E) give any information about the author.

5. Which one of the following could be rented rather than purchased?
   (A) 8mm single concept loops for science classes
   (B) 16mm film for American history class
   (C) transparencies of economic charts and graphs
   (D) graphics for mathematics classes
   (E) a school-made video

6. When teaching elementary children how to use the library, which step should come first?
   (A) showing some interesting parts of a book
   (B) demonstrating several uses of Webster's dictionary
   (C) describing how books are arranged on the shelves
   (D) explaining where the *Encyclopedia Americana* is located
   (E) integrating library use with a classroom subject (such as reading)

7. During a tour of the school library, pupils asked many questions. "Yes" would be your answer to which question?
   (A) "Does Earth have a separate classification number?"
   (B) "Do all books about animals have the same classification number?"
   (C) "Should I always use an encyclopedia when writing a science report?"
   (D) "Can I find the history of my state under the call number for the history of the United States?"
   (E) "Are the Table of Contents and the Index of a book arranged alphabetically?"

8. Before releasing equipment to students or teachers, the media specialist or assistant should check
   I. projection lamps for looseness and dead lamps.
   II. electrical cords for shorts or breaks.
   III. focus controls.
   IV. switches.
   V. lenses and other glass surfaces.
   (A) I and II only
   (B) II only
   (C) II, III only
   (D) I, II, and IV only
   (E) I, II, III, IV, V

9. When teaching students to use equipment, what should be the basic starting point?
   (A) Demonstrate the whole procedure for each piece of equipment.
   (B) Show the simplest equipment first.
   (C) Determine what students already know from experience.
   (D) Tell them that "anybody can run a 16mm projector."
   (E) Let students learn by trial and error.

LIBRARY MEDIA SPECIALIST

10. The most annoying factor for students when watching 16mm educational films is
    (A) the keystone effect.
    (B) that the sound is not synchronized with the picture.
    (C) that students are sitting in the front row.
    (D) that students are seated in the last row.
    (E) that a beaded screen is used.

11. Freshmen students in English classes want to use word processors to prepare their research papers. How should they be taught to use the equipment?
    (A) Students who know how to use it give demonstrations.
    (B) Show a video about the machine.
    (C) Students teach themselves by following the instruction book.
    (D) Use a tutorial floppy disk in the machine.
    (E) Librarians instruct individual students.

12. A library media specialist is assisting teachers in the selection of Spanish books for new students. They are considering selection aids for reluctant readers. Which will be of most assistance to them in making choices?
    (A) Reader appeal includes individual student involvement.
    (B) Many books have attractive illustrations.
    (C) Literature for children in Spanish-speaking countries is largely undeveloped.
    (D) Adventure books are written with male characters.
    (E) Pupils with low-level reading ability need high-interest books.

13. The librarian finds which factor a first priority when attempting to develop a well-rounded collection?
    (A) Books are purchased now that may be used at a later time.
    (B) All areas of the curriculum are represented.
    (C) The classics may be the teachers' favorites.
    (D) The needs and interests of the students are constantly changing.
    (E) Collections become outdated quickly.

14. Building a good working relationship between the media specialist and teachers can be fostered by
    (A) the library specialist giving the impression of knowing everything about learning resources.
    (B) teachers feeling inadequate when using equipment.
    (C) librarians, curriculum specialists, and teachers often discussing needs and goals.
    (D) students frequently asking for library resources that are not available.
    (E) being informed about parents' educational goals.

15. The media specialist can assist teachers in planning alternative lessons if speakers or films are not available. Human interest can be added to an abstract lesson by using any of the following EXCEPT
    I. a video from a collection of educational topics with student narrators.
    II. a class discussion with a filmstrip.
    III. a case study from a vertical files collection.
    IV. a sociodrama on tape.
    V. transparencies from a previous lesson for review.
    (A) I only
    (B) I, II only

(C) II, III, IV only
(D) I, II, III, IV
(E) I, II, III, IV, V

16. When selecting computer software for mathematics and science, coordinate with teachers' skills and proficiency goals; then purchase
    (A) teacher references.
    (B) sample lessons.
    (C) user-friendly programs.
    (D) a vocabulary list.
    (E) single-grade materials.

17. Pupils of all ages waste time while using library resources. Before they begin to write research papers, they should know how to use
    I. the vertical files.
    II. the subject and author card files.
    III. the dictionary and atlas.
    IV. the indexes of books and materials.
    V. the encyclopedias and almanacs.
    (A) I only
    (B) I, II only
    (C) I, II, III only
    (D) II, III, IV, V only
    (E) I, II, III, IV, V

18. The library media specialist can most assist high school students who are doing independent study by
    (A) preparing information sheets and visuals.
    (B) showing media to small groups of students.
    (C) using aids to answer questions.
    (D) giving the class a library tour.
    (E) letting the teacher answer their questions.

19. The least useful way to encourage students and teachers to increase their use of library facilities is to
    (A) place colorful displays in the hallways.
    (B) give information about new books and visuals to teachers.
    (C) have theme weeks with displays in the library.
    (D) encourage students to illustrate stories.
    (E) send notes about the library to parents.

20. One of the quickest ways high school students can access information for indepth research is to use
    (A) Facts on File materials.
    (B) CD-ROM data bases.
    (C) vertical files.
    (D) the Britannica *Book of the Year*.
    (E) the subject card files.

Answer Key

1. D	6. A	11. D	16. C
2. D	7. A	12. E	17. E
3. A	8. E	13. D	18. A
4. C	9. C	14. C	19. E
5. B	10. B	15. D	20. B

Marketing Education

The examination in Marketing Education tests the academic competence of candidates for the teaching of marketing and distributive education at the secondary level.

Content and Scope (120 questions, 2-hour test)

The test covers seven areas:

I. Marketing and Distributive Education (18%) (curriculum, cooperative education programs, career planning)
II. Marketing (18%) (functions, channels, research, business structures, economic concepts)
III. Merchandising (18%) (receiving, marking, pricing, inventory control, customer services, business and consumer credit, business cycles)
IV. Marketing Mathematics (10%) (costs, sales, employee compensation)
V. Communication Theory and Practice (7%) (oral, written, social communication with listening skills)
VI. Advertising and Sales (12%) (sales processes, salespersons, transactions, customers, motivations)
VII. Salesmanship (15%) (salesperson, sales process, product information, transactions, customers, motivations, psychology of buying and selling)

Sample Questions

Directions: For each question or incomplete statement, select the *best* answer or completion from the four choices.

1. Marketing includes which of the following?
    I. Anticipation leading to research
    II. Management involving creating, stimulating, facilitating, and regulating demand
    III. Self-regulation of service and product
    IV. Demarketing a product or service
    (A) I, II
    (B) II only
    (C) I, II, III, IV
    (D) II, III, IV only

2. In order to review production expenses and marketing performance, a profit-and-loss statement consists of all of the following EXCEPT
    (A) gross sales.
    (B) cost of goods.
    (C) gross margin (profit).
    (D) gross margin ratio.

3. Markup is
    (A) the difference between cost and selling price.
    (B) the average variable cost.
    (C) the difference between net price and sale price.
    (D) 5 percent above purchase price.

SPECIALTY AREA TESTS

4. What is the retail markdown percentage for a $15 doll that sold before the sale at $20?
   (A) 5 percent
   (B) 4 percent
   (C) 25 percent
   (D) 33 percent

5. During low consumer demand, reluctant consumers may be motivated to buy
   (A) during half-price sales at the end of the month.
   (B) when an offer is made to sell below any competitor.
   (C) at midnight clearance sales.
   (D) during one-day sales.

6. In which of the following does marketing play an important role?
   (A) Manufacturing technology
   (B) Conforming to government regulations
   (C) The economy
   (D) A target consumer group

7. Marketing myopia refers to
   (A) a broad plan for sales production.
   (B) late feedback evaluation.
   (C) short-sighted observation of consumer needs.
   (D) a lack of advertising.

8. Consumers have different reasons for buying products and services. Psychological research indicates that
   I. a target audience can be influenced by television advertising.
   II. parents are influenced by their children when buying school clothing.
   III. consumers buy products to reduce tension from unfulfilled needs.
   IV. an inner-directed person tries to please people.
   (A) I only
   (B) I, II only
   (C) I, II, III only
   (D) IV only

9. The factor(s) with the least influence on consumer decision-making
   (A) is a social class system.
   (B) are reference groups.
   (C) is the family life cycle.
   (D) is unperceived risk.

10. Sometimes a consumer may experience a feeling that the best product was not purchased. A firm can help to overcome consumer dissatisfaction the least by
    (A) doing careful advertising.
    (B) exchanging the purchase for a product of equal value.
    (C) giving a trial period after purchase on warranty.
    (D) telling the customer that no one else has complained about the product.

11. A store is interested in retailing children's clothing at a discount. The factor(s) the owners should consider as most significant
    (A) is the demographics of the area.
    (B) is the distance from the factory.
    (C) is the available storage space.
    (D) are existing area family retail stores.

MARKETING EDUCATION

12. Distribution costs add to retail prices. Which one of the following costs does not apply to physical distribution?
    (A) Delivery of raw materials to the shoe store
    (B) Moving unfinished materials to and from the manufacturing plant
    (C) Sorting, packaging, and warehousing
    (D) Shipping, trucking, and store location

13. Retail cooperatives are increasing as chain stores dominate certain consumer products and services. A retail cooperative gets goods to the market through
    (A) selling produce through operation and ownership
    (B) its organization of independent stores.
    (C) being a large convenience store.
    (D) its status as a large superstore in a suburban location.

14. Consumers' brand loyalty is demonstrated best by
    (A) consumer buying of basic needs and supplies, year after year, regardless of price.
    (B) unplanned, impulse buying.
    (C) attribute-based decision-making.
    (D) price-based selection.

15. Target pricing requires a specified return on the investment in relation to annual production goals. It is used by capital-intensive firms such as automobile manufacturers. For this concept to work,
    (A) costs rise slowly.
    (B) demand levels off early in the year.
    (C) special incentives are keyed to demand.
    (D) the entire annual volume is sold at the initial set price.

16. Marigail and three friends borrow $10,000 to renovate her garage for use as a craft shop. Two methods can be used to calculate the interest on their loan, the ordinary and the exact. Which of the following statements will lead to saving them money on the interest?
    (A) The ordinary method requires the interest to be paid up-front.
    (B) With the exact method, the lender receives less interest than with the ordinary method.
    (C) If interest is paid at the end of the loan, it is compounded.
    (D) The ordinary method uses a 360-day year.

17. Josh has selected business administration as his career. Communication will be one of his major skills in interpersonal relationships. Select the least appropriate statement.
    (A) Negotiating involves exchanging information, then forcing conflict resolution.
    (B) Persuading is useful for influencing others to buy American products.
    (C) Josh uses speaking/signaling to give directions to others.
    (D) Mentoring involves learning about a person's total personality before giving advice at work.

18. At a sales meeting, production volume and sales volume were discussed. How do these factors affect pricing?
    (A) Per unit variable costs are inconstant when related to a set production volume.
    (B) Total costs per unit remain constant, regardless of volume.
    (C) As production volume increases, per unit average fixed costs increase.
    (D) Fixed costs per unit are paid off at the break-even point.

SPECIALTY AREA TESTS

19. When Appliance Store A advertises its low prices as compared to the same brands at Stores B and C, who is most likely to buy from Store A?
    (A) People who are loyal to stores they know well
    (B) People who live more than one-half hour from the store
    (C) People who find comparable service among the stores and need the product immediately
    (D) People who look for ethics in advertising

20. A manufacturer of word processors was informed through research personnel that consumers were willing to pay $435 for this product. The company's selling expenses, including advertising and profit, will be 28 percent of the selling price. What is the maximum amount the firm can spend to manufacture this product?
    (A) $313.20
    (B) $325.50
    (C) $299.50
    (D) $225.15

Answer Key
1. C
2. D
3. A
4. C
5. B
6. D
7. C
8. C
9. D
10. D
11. A
12. A
13. B
14. A
15. D
16. D
17. A
18. D
19. C
20. A

Mathematics

The examination in Mathematics tests the academic competence of candidates for the teaching of this subject at the secondary level.

Content and Scope (120 questions, 2-hour test)

Two major areas are stressed:
  I. Mathematical Content
  II. Educational Theory of Teaching Mathematics

Some Topics for Review

1. Basic arithmetic
2. Elementary algebra
3. Two- and three-dimensional geometry
4. Trigonometry
5. Advanced placement calculus
6. Finite mathematics
7. Mathematical systems
8. Number theory
9. Statistics and probability
10. Methods and principles of teaching
11. Curriculum development in the field of mathematics
12. History of mathematics education
13. Professional journals and organizations

Sample Questions

Directions: For each question or incomplete statement, select the *best* answer or completion from the five choices.

1. Which of the following is the nearest decimal approximation of $\sqrt{27}$?
   (A) 5.181
   (B) 5.188
   (C) 5.196
   (D) 5.202
   (E) 5.217

2. When the discriminant in a quadratic equation is a perfect square, it indicates that
   (A) the radical can be removed
   (B) the roots of the equation are rational
   (C) the trinomial can be factored
   (D) all of the above
   (E) only (A) and (B) above

3. In imaginary numbers, any integral power of i reduces to one of four quantities. Which of the following is NOT one of the four?
   (A) $\sqrt{-1}$
   (B) $-\sqrt{-1}$
   (C) -1
   (D) $+1$
   (E) $\sqrt{i}$

4. Which of the following expressions is undefined for $x = 3$?
   (A) x^0
   (B) $(0)^x$
   (C) $x - 3$
   (D) $\dfrac{1}{x - 3}$
   (E) $\dfrac{3 - x}{3 + x}$

5. In order to obtain a fractional expression equivalent to $\dfrac{3 + \sqrt{2}}{3 - \sqrt{2}}$ but having a rational denominator, the given expression must be multiplied by
   (A) $\sqrt{2}$
   (B) $3 - \sqrt{2}$
   (C) $3 + \sqrt{2}$
   (D) $\dfrac{3 - \sqrt{2}}{3 + \sqrt{2}}$
   (E) $\dfrac{3 + \sqrt{2}}{3 + \sqrt{2}}$

6. The graph of the equation $xy = 12$ is symmetric with respect to
   (A) the line $y = x$ only
   (B) the line $y = -x$ only
   (C) the x-axis only
   (D) the y-axis only
   (E) both the line $y = x$ and the line $y = -x$

7. The solution set of the equation $\sqrt{x+6} = x$ is
   (A) $\{-2\}$
   (B) $\{3\}$
   (C) $\{-2, 3\}$
   (D) $\{-3, 2\}$
   (E) $\{\ \}$

8. If $\log_b n = x$, then $\log_{b^2} n^2$ is equal to
   (A) x
   (B) x^2
   (C) $\sqrt{x}$
   (D) $2x$
   (E) $x + 2$

9. Test scores obtained by a class fall into a normal distribution having a mean of 78 and a standard deviation of 6.0. Between what limits can 68 percent of the scores be expected to fall?
   (A) 75 to 81
   (B) 66 to 90
   (C) 72 to 84
   (D) 76.5 to 79.5
   (E) $78 \pm 0.68(6.0)$

10. What relation is **NOT** a function?
    (A) $\{(x,y) \mid y = -x\}$
    (B) $\{(x,y) \mid y = 8\}$
    (C) $\{(x,y) \mid x = 8\}$
    (D) $\{(x,y) \mid y = x^2 + 2x + 3\}$
    (E) $\{(x,y) \mid y = \cos x\}$

11. What is the probability that a function chosen at random from the set $\{\sin \theta, \cos \theta, \tan \theta\}$ will be positive if $\frac{\pi}{2} < \theta < \pi$?
    (A) $\frac{1}{3}$
    (B) $\frac{2}{3}$
    (C) $\frac{1}{2}$
    (D) 0
    (E) 1

12. Which of the following expressions represents the area between the curve, $y = -x^2 + x + 2$, and the x-axis?
    (A) $\int_{-1}^{2} (-x^2 + x + 2)\, dx$
    (B) $-\int_{-1}^{2} (-x^2 + x + 2)\, dx$
    (C) $\int_{-2}^{1} (-x^2 + x + 2)\, dx$
    (D) $\int_{0}^{2} (-x^2 + x + 2)\, dx$
    (E) $\int (-x^2 + x + 2)\, dx$

13. How many meters are equivalent to 936 millimeters?
    (A) 9.36
    (B) 93.6
    (C) 936,000
    (D) 0.936
    (E) 0.0936

14. $|x + y| = |x| + |y|$ if and only if
    (A) $x > 0$ and $y > 0$
    (B) $x \geq 0$ and $y \geq 0$
    (C) $x < 0$ and $y < 0$
    (D) $x \leq 0$ and $y \leq 0$
    (E) $x \geq 0$ and $y \geq 0$, or $x \leq 0$ and $y \leq 0$

15. Stress on which of the following would help students avoid the error of reducing $\dfrac{3x^2 + x}{x}$ to $3x$?
    (A) The associative law
    (B) The distributive law
    (C) The commutative law
    (D) The subtraction of exponents in division
    (E) The distinction between a term and a factor

Answer Key

1. C	4. D	7. B	10. C	13. D
2. C	5. E	8. A	11. A	14. E
3. E	6. E	9. C	12. A	15. B

Music Education

The examination in Music Education tests the academic competence of candidates for the teaching of music.

The test is divided into two sections. The first section takes about 40 minutes and uses a single taped excerpt as the basis for 45 questions. These questions relate to the period, composer, style, techniques, structure or form, rhythmic or melodic patterns, mode, meter, and so on of the music excerpt.

The second, nontaped section of the test has 105 questions and takes 80 minutes.

Content and Scope (150 questions, 2-hour test; first 45 questions from taped musical excerpts)

Emphasis is placed on three main areas of content:
  I. Basic Musicianship (history of music, theory of music, performance skills, and listening skills)
  II. Curriculum and Instruction
  III. Professional Information

Questions on area I comprise about 60 percent of the test; the remaining 40 percent is divided between areas II and III.

Some Topics for Review

1. Styles of music
2. Composers
3. Elements—mood, timbre, pitch, dynamics, performance, acoustics
4. Sequence of music courses
5. Content of courses
6. Performance (skills and types)
7. Instructional techniques
8. Evaluation of music program
9. Philosophical and psychological aspects of instruction
10. Music literature
11. Ethical practices
12. Music organizations and publications

Sample Questions for the Taped Section

Directions: Before listening to a particular excerpt, note, next to the number of the question, the characteristic or aspect of the music to which your attention should be directed. *After* listening to the excerpt, select the correct answer from the five choices given.

(You would hear an excerpt from a well-known tragic opera, a favorite medium for colatura sopranos.)

1. NAME OF OPERA   The story concerns Edgar and the woman he loves, whose brother wants her to marry someone else. Thinking that Edgar has wed in France, his beloved marries her brother's choice, only to learn that Edgar still awaits her. Before stabbing himself, Edgar sings of his love:

    This well-known tragic opera is
    (A) *Lucia Di Lammermoor,* Donizetti
    (B) *The Barber of Seville,* Rossini
    (C) *Don Giovanni,* Mozart
    (D) *The Flying Dutchman,* Wagner
    (E) *Otello,* Verdi

SPECIALTY AREA TESTS

(*You would hear a short excerpt from the following piano composition.*)

2. **TECHNIQUE** The pianist plays each note with a similar tonal color. This technique is called
   (A) largo
   (B) portemento
   (C) legato
   (D) andante
   (E) contabile

3. **COMPOSER** The composer of this well-known piece is
   (A) Schubert
   (B) Schumann
   (C) Dvorak
   (D) Haydn
   (E) Strauss

(*You would hear an excerpt from the following symphony.*)

4. **NAME OF SYMPHONY** The theme of this symphony is played softly on the violins until the eighth measure; there a loud crash is heard. This effect identifies the composition as
   (A) Schubert's *Unfinished* Symphony, Movement 1
   (B) Stravinsky's *Symphony in Three Movements*
   (C) Copland's *Symphony No. 3*
   (D) Beethoven's *Fifth Symphony*
   (E) Haydn's *Symphony No. 94 in G Major*

(*You would hear three short excerpts from a single composition.*)

I.

II.

III.

552

5. **FORM** This horizontal interweaving of musical themes is called
   - (A) the instrumental trio
   - (B) homophony for strings
   - (C) orchestral polyphony
   - (D) the flute codetta
   - (E) melodic cadence

Sample Questions for the Nontaped Section

Directions: For each question or incomplete statement below, select the *best* answer or completion from the five choices.

6. When teaching children a rote song by the phrase method, the teacher should do all of the following EXCEPT
   - (A) sing the song through in its entirety
   - (B) sing the first phrase; have the class repeat it
   - (C) sing the second phrase; have the class repeat it
   - (D) sing the third phrase; have the class repeat it
   - (E) have each child sing each phrase alone and repeat it

7. The second theme of the last movement of Beethoven's *Third Symphony* is played by the first violins. The music below is written in intervals of
   - (A) thirds
   - (B) fourths
   - (C) fifths
   - (D) major and minor seconds
   - (E) inverted minor chords

8. In teaching children to sing songs with tonic-chord skips, the preferred technique is to
   - (A) point out that *do* always lies in the first space on the staff
   - (B) show that *mi* and *sol* lie in the third and fourth spaces above *do*
   - (C) use the hand as a staff and have pupils sing the skips beginning with *mi*
   - (D) use the sound of *mi* for the initial teaching of the singing of the tonic chord
   - (E) sing or sound the pitch of *do* and have beginning pupils practice by singing *do*, then *do, mi, sol*

9. When introducing a music class to the structure of melody, the instructor can begin with a familiar song like "America" to demonstrate that all of the following are true EXCEPT
   - (A) the melody can be divided into two halves, called *phrases*
   - (B) two phrases together form a musical *sentence*
   - (C) each phrase has a period of rest or *cadence*
   - (D) a "full" cadence creates a sense of *expectation*
   - (E) the first phrase ends in an upward *inflection*

10. The composer of the blues usually uses a strict musical form. The lyrics, melodies, and harmonies have a specific pattern. The polyphonic texture is given to the music when
    - (A) the singer interprets the melody
    - (B) the instrumentalist uses improvisations behind the vocalist
    - (C) the pianist uses *blue notes*, sharped third, fifth, or seventh notes
    - (D) the chord progressions are played with special consonance
    - (E) the melody is repeated in the second line

SPECIALTY AREA TESTS

11. Millions of Americans enjoy the compositions of Ravel. Ravel and Debussy shared an attraction for the scales used in medieval and exotic music, and they both believed that the main purpose of music was to delight the senses. How does their music differ?
    (A) Debussy's music has a brightness that Ravel's lacks.
    (B) Ravel used crisper harmonies and more decisive rhythms.
    (C) Ravel disliked the use of dissonance in chord progressions.
    (D) Debussy emphasized the whole orchestra rather than a solo instrument.
    (E) Debussy used the steady crescendo, while Ravel seldom reached such a peak.

12. The signature $\frac{12}{8}$, because of its accents, has which of the following notes?
    (A) Quadruple
    (B) Triple
    (C) Sixths
    (D) Double triple
    (E) Eighths

13. The teacher of music groups must be aware of the copyright law, which
    (A) controls the use of recordings in class settings
    (B) limits the use of musical compositions for theory classes
    (C) restricts the use of orchestrations with instructor's arrangements
    (D) controls the type of arrangements that can be reproduced
    (E) forbids the duplication of sheet music for vocal or instrumental groups

14. The underlying purpose of public performance by school music groups should be to
    (A) furnish a vehicle for the talented
    (B) win high ratings at band and choral competitions
    (C) impress the parents of the performers
    (D) demonstrate the instructor's talent
    (E) develop music interest and appreciation among participants and the audience

15. The most stressful problem that teachers of music at the junior high school level experience is
    (A) opposition by other instructors to practice time
    (B) finding interesting literature for choirs
    (C) developing groups to the performance level
    (D) getting parents' consent to field trips
    (E) classroom management during rehearsals

Answer Key

Taped Section

1. A
2. C
3. B
4. E
5. C

Untaped Section

6. E
7. A
8. E
9. D
10. B
11. B
12. A
13. E
14. E
15. E

Physical Education

The examination in Physical Education tests the academic competence of candidates in physical education from kindergarten through high school.

Content and Scope (150 questions, 2-hour test)

The examination covers six areas:

   I. Historical and Philosophical Foundations of Physical Education
  II. Psychological, Sociological, and Biological Foundations
 III. The Curriculum in Physical Education
  IV. Administration of the Physical Education Program
   V. Professional Responsibilities
  VI. Evaluation of the Physical Education Program

Some Topics for Review

1. Goals, objectives, and current trends in physical education, planning, implementation
2. Group and cultural impacts on participation (intramurals, girls' activities, games)
3. Growth and development, human anatomy
4. Perceptual-motor development (human movement)
5. Physiology and importance of exercise and conditioning on physical fitness
6. Planning for individual differences, needs, and interests, including those of the handicapped (writing IEPs)
7. Utilizing personnel and school facilities
8. Maintaining health and safety
9. Legal applications
10. Sports medicine
11. Public relations and school spirit
12. Professional organizations and resources
13. Current issues
14. Ethics
15. Selection and proper use of testing instruments for teaching and evaluation
16. Assessment of individual pupil needs and growth
17. Equipment and rules for sports and games commonly taught with safety factors involved

Sample Questions

Directions: For each question or incomplete statement, select the *best* answer or completion from the five choices.

1. In which one of these tournament types of competition does each team play at least two games before being eliminated?
    (A) Round robin
    (B) Ladder
    (C) Single elimination
    (D) Consolation
    (E) Pyramid

555

SPECIALTY AREA TESTS

2. In badminton, 15 points make a game except in women's singles, where a game consists of
   (A) 14 points
   (B) 13 points
   (C) 12 points
   (D) 11 points
   (E) 10 points

3. In basketball, the individual on offense should obey all of the following guidelines EXCEPT
   (A) shooting only when he or she may score
   (B) always keeping his or her eye on the ball
   (C) keeping in motion with quick stops and starts
   (D) passing when in motion
   (E) constantly watching for feints

4. The Amateur Athletic Union of the United States has promoted physical fitness test standards for boys and girls. At age 14–15 the boys' time for the 100-yard sprint is faster than the girls' time by
   (A) 2 seconds
   (B) 3 seconds
   (C) 4 seconds
   (D) 5 seconds
   (E) 6 seconds

5. A physical fitness test in the U.S. Air Force requires walking and/or running as far as possible in 12 minutes. If just over 1½ miles are covered, the appropriate physical fitness category is
   (A) "Very poor"
   (B) "Poor"
   (C) "Fair"
   (D) "Good"
   (E) "Excellent"

6. The most popular sport in the United States, and the one on which the most money is spent, is
   (A) football
   (B) baseball
   (C) golf
   (D) fishing
   (E) bowling

7. Which one of the following factors has NOT contributed to longevity among Americans today?
   (A) Reduced infant mortality
   (B) Greater muscular strength
   (C) Conquest of many diseases
   (D) Better nutrition
   (E) Active, strenuous exercise

8. In physical education classes hearing-impaired children suffer all of the following additional handicaps EXCEPT
   (A) they isolate themselves
   (B) they feel insecure
   (C) they don't like to move around
   (D) they are limited to individual sports
   (E) they may have poor balance

PHYSICAL EDUCATION

9. For all outdoor track events *except* cross-country running, which type of shoe is essential?
   (A) Canvas with crepe-rubber soles
   (B) Leather with spiked soles
   (C) Canvas with leather soles
   (D) Leather with crepe-rubber soles
   (E) All leather

10. In the pole vault, during the run toward the bar, the vaulter should carry the pole with the tip about
    (A) waist high
    (B) knee high
    (C) hip high
    (D) shoulder high
    (E) head high

11. A foot disturbance the onset of which, caused by pressure on the plantar nerve, is usually sudden and very painful is
    (A) talipes cavus
    (B) metatarsalgia
    (C) hallux valgus
    (D) irritation of the bursa
    (E) tendosynovitis

12. Which one of the minimum score standards on the five athletic items used on a Marine Corps physical readiness test is wrong as given below?
    (A) Chin-up from bar: minimum score = 3
    (B) Pushups from floor: minimum score = 21
    (C) Situps: minimum score = 25 in 2 minutes
    (D) Half-mile run: minimum score = no time limit or stopping
    (E) Standing broad jump: minimum score = 5 feet

13. Which of the following conditioning activities would NOT be used with elementary school children?
    (A) For body coordination: pyramids, stunts, and/or apparatus
    (B) For endurance: running and jumping
    (C) For shoulder and abdominal muscles: chinning and pushups
    (D) For muscles to improve posture: apparatus
    (E) For leg muscles: knee bends and squats

14. The evaluation of the physical education student must begin with
    (A) the pupil's social development
    (B) the defined objectives of the physical education program
    (C) pupil goals and outcomes
    (D) the pupil's physical fitness and skills
    (E) the pupil's scholastic record

15. Which one of these rules would NOT apply to apparatus activities?
    (A) Use mats at the take-off and receiving locations.
    (B) Use apparatus only when you are physically well.
    (C) Do only approved activities.
    (D) Teach others how to use the equipment.
    (E) Wait for the supervisor or instructor before using equipment.

SPECIALTY AREA TESTS

16. Water safety instructors can use the American Red Cross graded sheets for testing for weaknesses and strengths. What is the name of the test item as used with elementary students that is described as follows: "Flutter kick for 20 feet on back or front without use of hands or arms"?
    (A) Prone glide and recovery
    (B) Back float
    (C) Kick glide
    (D) Finning
    (E) Sculling

17. In regard to a pupil's accidental injury, the law of negligence implies all of the following EXCEPT
    (A) a teacher can be held responsible
    (B) the school board is financially liable
    (C) negligence is failure to act to prevent an accident
    (D) teachers should anticipate danger
    (E) teachers can be censored or dismissed for failing to take reasonable care

18. For which one of the following communicable conditions is (are) the symptom(s) given INCORRECT?
    (A) Impetigo: crusty skin sores around mouth and nose
    (B) Infectious hepatitis: pain in upper abdomen, nausea, fatigue
    (C) Geman measles: cold symptoms, fine rash
    (D) Pediculosis: itching scalp, tiny beads (eggs) on hair
    (E) Pinkeye: double vision, headache

19. The first movement of the downswing in golf is
    (A) pulling the club down with the left hand
    (B) turning the left hip to the left
    (C) bending the left elbow and flexing the left wrist
    (D) shifting the weight to the left foot
    (E) raising the head to check the distance to the green

20. In baseball a variety of pitches are available. Which one of the following statements is INCORRECT?
    (A) The curve ball is the main offspeed pitch.
    (B) A curve ball is slower than a fastball.
    (C) A forkball is thrown with a snap of the wrist.
    (D) A slider leaves the fingertips slightly off center.
    (E) A knuckleball usually is not directed by its spin.

Answer Key

1. A	5. D	9. B	13. E	17. B
2. D	6. D	10. E	14. B	18. E
3. E	7. B	11. B	15. D	19. B
4. B	8. C	12. E	16. C	20. C

Social Studies

The examination in Social Studies tests the competence of candidates for the teaching of this subject at the secondary level.

Content and Scope (150 questions, 2-hour test)

The scope is broad and the content includes those subjects usually taught in the social studies, including history, the special inquiry skills of the discipline, and the professional techniques necessary for effective instruction.

The questions cover six areas:

    I. Professional Education
    II. Political Science
    III. Economics
    IV. History
    V. Geography—Cultural Concepts in the World Setting
    VI. Sociology/Anthropology/Psychology

Some Topics for Review

1. Current approaches to the social studies
2. Teaching techniques and strategies (social science inquiry methods)
3. Curriculum design and integration
4. Evaluation of pupil progress
5. Understanding the American political system and the ways in which it works
6. The application of microeconomic and macroeconomic concepts
7. Current problems and issues in the public and private sectors of the American economy
8. American social and political history
9. The roles of minority groups in American history
10. The emerging Third World countries of Africa, Asia, and Latin America
11. Anthropology in the urban setting
12. Current social issues and problems
13. Ethnicity and related special issues

Sample Questions

Directions: For each question or incomplete statement select the *best* answer or completion from the five choices.

1. The building of the Panama Canal was begun during the presidency of
    (A) Abraham Lincoln
    (B) Theodore Roosevelt
    (C) Andrew Jackson
    (D) Grover Cleveland
    (E) Thomas Jefferson

2. According to Gordon Allport, a person's political behavior is
    (A) completely imitative
    (B) largely affective in nature
    (C) indistinguishable from his or her personality as a whole
    (D) based on adolescent experiences
    (E) dependent on the family

3. Which U.S. President had such a high regard for public office that he stated, "Public officials are trustees of the people"?
    (A) George Washington
    (B) John Quincy Adams
    (C) Andrew Jackson
    (D) Abraham Lincoln
    (E) Grover Cleveland

SPECIALTY AREA TESTS

4. Which of the following statements about minorities in the United States is NOT true?
   (A) Black Americans constitute about 11 percent of the population of the United States.
   (B) Black Americans have lived in the New World since the seventeenth century, when they arrived in Virginia as indentured servants.
   (C) Sentiment against slavery first came into focus after the French and Indian War (1754–1763).
   (D) In every state the black population is larger than the Hispanic population.
   (E) The Civil Rights Act of 1875, giving equal rights to blacks in public accommodations and jury duty, was invalidated by the Supreme Court in 1883.

5. The history of political science reveals a change in direction from the study of
   (A) government to politics
   (B) political processes to institutions
   (C) political science as a social science to a separate field of study
   (D) political theory to national government
   (E) comparative government to local government

6. Which one of these statements regarding ideologies is NOT true?
   (A) The ideological symbols of a society are manipulated by the lowest social class.
   (B) Ideologies are challenged by the intelligentsia.
   (C) A well-integrated political system resists outside ideologies.
   (D) New ideologies are readily accepted when groups are divided.
   (E) New ideologies are accepted or rejected by the process of selection.

7. The world climatic classification that applies to Southern California is
   (A) Low or Tropical
   (B) Low Middle or Subtropical
   (C) Mountain
   (D) Middle or Temperate
   (E) High or Subpolar

8. Current events are essential to the social studies program. The LEAST important criterion in selecting events for discussion is
   (A) the national importance of the event
   (B) the persisting or recurring nature of the event
   (C) the relevance of the event to the curriculum
   (D) the students' knowledge of the event
   (E) the contribution of the event to critical thinking

9. By 1825, nationalism was yielding to the growing sentiments for sectionalism. The economic bases of sectionalism were derived from all of the following EXCEPT
   (A) the manufacture of textiles soon became the leading industry of the North
   (B) textile manufacturing was aided by the decline of shipping as a result of the Embargo Act and the War of 1812
   (C) after 1815, farming on a family-sized farm became the leading economic base in the West; it was aided by the liberal government land policy
   (D) after 1815 economic activity in the South was centered on the plantation, where tobacco, rice, and sugar cane became the leading crops
   (E) the West bought its manufactured goods from the North and Great Britain before the Civil War

10. Which of the following is NOT essential for the development of feelings of ethnocentrism?
    (A) Superiority feelings in comparison to other groups
    (B) A common geographical location
    (C) A "traditional ways are the right ways" philosophy
    (D) In-group double standards in relation to other groups
    (E) Personal identification with a group

SOCIAL STUDIES

Questions 11 and 12 refer to the following passage.

In the councils of government, we must guard against the acquisition of unwarranted influence, whether sought or unsought by the military-industrial complex. The potential for the disastrous rise of misplaced power exists and will exist. We must never let the weight of this combination endanger our liberties or democratic processes. We should take nothing for granted. Only an alert and knowledgeable citizenry can compel the proper meshing of the huge industrial and military machinery of defense with our peaceful methods and goals, so that security and liberty may prosper together.

11. Which American president expressed this concern about the influence of the military before leaving office?
    (A) Harry Truman
    (B) Dwight Eisenhower
    (C) Lyndon Johnson
    (D) Richard Nixon
    (E) Jimmy Carter

12. The military-industrial complex referred to in the passage involves all of the following EXCEPT
    (A) the Armed Forces
    (B) organized American veterans
    (C) the U.S. Department of Defense
    (D) industrial firms that supply the military
    (E) subcontractors that manufacture parts for planes, tanks and weapons

13. During a social studies discussion a teacher stated, "Human beings depend on the land surface for most of their survival needs. The land surface, including all continents and islands, constitutes 29.2 percent of the global surface. As much as 90 percent of this area is unsuitable for living, and most of the people live on 3 percent of the global area." Then she asked, "What does this mean to you as an inhabitant of planet Earth? Why should you be concerned about soil erosion or pollution? Why should the government continue to support space exploration?" The instructor was giving the students practice in
    (A) deductive reasoning
    (B) making generalizations
    (C) formulating factual statements
    (D) seeking empirical evidence
    (E) conceptual development

14. At the Equator the period of daylight is the same throughout the year. The daylight period is
    (A) 8 hours long
    (B) 10 hours long
    (C) 12 hours long
    (D) 14 hours long
    (E) 16 hours long

15. During the nineteenth and early twentieth centuries the federal government passed several major laws that gave impetus to the agricultural revolution. The law, still in use today, that provided funds for county agents to bring research information directly to farmers was the
    (A) Rural Credits Act
    (B) Merrill Act
    (C) Hatch Act
    (D) Smith-Lever Act
    (E) Warehouse Act

Answer Key

1. B	4. D	7. B	10. B	13. B
2. C	5. C	8. D	11. B	14. C
3. E	6. A	9. D	12. B	15. D

561

SPECIALTY AREA TESTS

Special Education

The examination in Special Education tests the academic competence of candidates for the teaching of special education. Questions relate to the planning and delivery of instruction for exceptional individuals ages 3 through 21.

Content and Scope (150 questions, 2-hour test)

The test covers five major areas:

  I. Understanding Exceptionalities (about 23 questions)
  II. Legal Issues and Compliance (about 15 questions)
  III. Assessment/Evaluation in Special Education (about 30 questions)
  IV. Service Delivery and Instruction (about 49 questions)
  V. Classroom management (about 33 questions)

Topics for Review

1. Major historical movements and trends in special education
2. Characteristics, prevalence, degrees of severity, and causation of the various types of exceptionalities
3. Research in the field of special education
4. Legal rights involving special education
5. Education for All Handicapped Children Act (PL94–142)
6. Using tests for diagnosis, placement and instruction
7. Procedures for determining students' eligibility for special education programs
8. Components of an individualized education program (IEP)
9. Design of instruction for special education students
10. Nonschool influences on student performance
11. Classroom organization for exceptional students
12. Managing student behavior (including behavior analysis, behavior modification, and discipline techniques)

Sample Questions

Directions: For each question or incomplete statement, select the best answer or completion from the five choices.

1. Mary is a pre-schooler. She does not speak. Which of the following is the LEAST likely contributing factor to her non-verbal behavior?
   (A) Brain injury
   (B) Emotional illness
   (C) Learning disability
   (D) Mental retardation
   (E) Deafness

SPECIAL EDUCATION

2. For assessment purposes, which of the following would be the most helpful for determining a child's visual perception skills?
   (A) Pictorial materials
   (B) Comparison lists of geometric designs
   (C) Alphabetic symbols exercises
   (D) A diagnosis of perceptual errors
   (E) Word forms reading exercises

3. Which of the following best describes the effect of physical or health disabilities on children?
   (A) Children with these handicaps are less likely to have behavior or emotional difficulties than their unimpaired peers.
   (B) Most of these children can learn in special classes independently of their peers.
   (C) Children who have cerebral palsy are mentally retarded.
   (D) Children with progressive muscular dystrophy learn well in the regular classroom if necessary equipment and facilities are provided.
   (E) Children with disorders of the nervous system (epilepsy) should be isolated from their peers.

4. Task-related behavior deficits include all of the following EXCEPT
   (A) visual-auditory discrimination difficulties
   (B) vascillating attention span
   (C) a lack of persistence to bring a task to completion
   (D) requiring more time than their peers to complete a task
   (E) poor quality of output

5. Kent, a fifth-grader, has a visual handicap. Under Public Law 94–142 which provision must be made for his education?
   (A) Home tutoring must be provided, but at his parents' expense.
   (B) He should be placed in a special education room.
   (C) A psychologist must provide an assessment every six months.
   (D) Certain regular courses will not be open to him.
   (E) An IEP must be written for him.

6. Of the following auditory discrimination exercises, which is the LEAST likely to assist the child with auditory difficulties?
   (A) The child learns the concepts of *same* and *different*.
   (B) The teacher uses a pair of phrases, then asks the child to circle *S* or *D*.
   (C) The teacher pronounces words and phrases out of the view of the children.
   (D) Discrimination exercises are used in the group every Friday afternoon.
   (E) No voice fluctuations are given as *S* or *D* clues.

7. Bob reads well at the third grade level, but he is in the fifth grade; Mary won the spelling contest in her school, but she was defeated by a younger girl in the county "spell-off." Jim is a computer whiz kid in the sixth grade, but he has difficulty with penmanship. These cases indicate that it is important to view exceptionality in which of the following ways?
   (A) As a characteristic of all children.
   (B) All children exhibit some behaviors that are inherently inappropriate.
   (C) Exceptionality is a relationship deviation between performance and the level of expectation under specific conditions.

(D) Children should be labeled according to their deficits, and then instructed accordingly.
(E) The consequences of differences in performance are insignificant to children after the third grade.

8. A classification system that is descriptive of the exceptional learning and behavior characteristics of each pupil represents all EXCEPT which of the following?
   (A) A recognition that some behaviors have a transitory nature.
   (B) The intervention efforts will be focused on the characteristics of each child.
   (C) The system uses preconceived assumptions and implications about etiology, prognosis, and treatment.
   (D) Some problems are age, stage, or situation specific.
   (E) One of the uses of this functional classification procedure is to obtain parental involvement for planning the child's educational program.

9. Which of the following does NOT describe findings from studies on exceptionality during the 1970's and the 1980's?
   (A) Long-time cultural deprivations affect generalized cognitive skill development.
   (B) Learning difficulties in the first grade show no relationship to environmental variables.
   (C) Culturally specific learnings can affect social adaptation and skill development.
   (D) Poor school performance can result from a mismatch between incentives and the motivational characteristics of a child.
   (E) The failure to attend to reading task assignments may be a form of avoidance behavior.

10. The coping behavior of a child with a physical disability depends LEAST upon which of the following?
    (A) The age of onset of the disability
    (B) The personal-social characteristics of the child
    (C) The type of disability
    (D) The psychological experiences of the child
    (E) A specially trained teacher in the classroom

11. The handicapped student's motivation to achieve can be increased and sustained the most through which of the following?
    (A) Placement in a regular class
    (B) Facilities to meet the child's special needs
    (C) Home instruction by a qualified teacher
    (D) Cross-age tutoring during school time
    (E) Acceptance of the child by teachers and peers

12. On a continuum of services for exceptional children, the least restrictive environment (LRE) provides for
    (A) placement in a self-contained special education class
    (B) placing the child in a special residential facility
    (C) enrolling the child in a regular class with special equipment and instructional programs
    (D) placing the child in a private day school
    (E) placing the child in a special education resource room for ten hours each week

SPECIAL EDUCATION

13. Which of the following might be most useful for the emotional-social development of Mike, who shows negative behavior toward his peers in kindergarten?
    (A) Placing him on a behavior modification schedule in which appropriate behavior is rewarded
    (B) Removing him from the group in which he has misbehaved and having him sit in the corner until he feels he can play nicely
    (C) Removing him from school until he matures
    (D) Calling his mother whenever misbehavior occurs
    (E) Explaining to him that he may not be promoted to first grade if he continues to demonstrate such childish behaviors

14. Current federal guidelines include the following in the definition of learning disabilities, EXCEPT
    (A) a disorder in the processes for understanding and using spoken or written language
    (B) perceptual dysfunctions
    (C) brain injury or minimal brain dysfunction
    (D) dyslexia
    (E) visual, motor, or hearing handicaps

15. Dick and Janet have superior cognitive abilities. The best learning procedure the teacher can use with them in the eighth grade general science class is to
    (A) provide time and encouragement for them to enter the county science fair with original projects
    (B) let them teach the class twice a month
    (C) require them to keep a scientific journal of observations they make about the environment
    (D) divide the class into two groups and let each one lead a group in an experiment
    (E) give them extra assignments to increase the possibility of their getting a science scholarship eventually

Answer Key

1. C
2. D
3. D
4. A
5. E
6. D
7. C
8. C
9. B
10. E
11. E
12. C
13. A
14. E
15. A

SPECIALTY AREA TESTS

Speech Communication

The examination in Speech Communication tests the academic competence of candidates for the teaching of communication, speech, and theater arts at the high school or college levels.

Content and Scope (150 questions, 2-hour test)

The test covers eight areas:

   I. Interpersonal Communication and the Communication Process
  II. Small-Group Communication Skills (verbal, nonverbal, in intercultural relations)
 III. Public Speaking (forms, styles, purposes, strategies, audiences)
  IV. Mass Communication and the influence of Media (techniques, production)
   V. Play Production (theory, acting, directing, construction, management)
  VI. Oral Interpretation (analysis, aesthetics, techniques)
 VII. Forensics (debate, individual and teamwork, events, evaluation)
VIII. Professional Factors (leadership, responsibility, curriculum, evaluation)

The 150 questions that comprise the test are divided approximately among the eight areas, with slightly less emphasis on areas IV, VII, and VIII. Candidates should not expect to be able to answer all questions.

Some Topics for Review

1. Coding, verbal and nonverbal, in interpersonal communication
2. Perceptual skills in communication
3. Listening skills
4. Problems in intercultural communication
5. Dynamics of group communication
6. Discussions, panels, buzz groups
7. Conflict resolution in group communication
8. Strategies of public speaking
9. Language and delivery
10. Audience involvement and feedback in public speaking
11. Mass media—television, film, and radio
12. Play production—theories and techniques of acting, directing, and stage design
13. Principles of oral interpretation
14. Curricular and cocurricular forensic instruction
15. Copyright laws and legal responsibilities
16. Community resources

Sample Questions

Directions: For each question or incomplete statement select the *best* answer or completion from the five choices.

SPEECH COMMUNICATION

1. The term "ethics of communication" implies that a skilled speaker or writer can assert influence or force on the receiver of the message. Which of the following statements suggests unethical communication techniques?
   (A) The receiver of the message makes a self-determined decision because of compatibility of beliefs and feelings with the speaker.
   (B) The receiver recognizes the alternatives presented and then makes a choice.
   (C) The receiver perceives the communicator's message as giving the only choice possible.
   (D) The receiver senses a freedom to respond or not to respond to the urgency in the message.
   (E) In spite of group pressure, the receiver responds according to his or her own value system.

2. All of the following are descriptive of techniques used in every interview EXCEPT
   (A) opening statements are made by interviewer and interviewee
   (B) the purpose of the interview is revealed in these opening statements
   (C) information representing opinions, beliefs, attitudes, and skills is obtained
   (D) rapport is established through the creation of a positive atmosphere
   (E) the performance is appraised and suggestions are made

3. A speaker who talks about things with which the audience is familiar, shows enthusiasm, makes direct eye contact, and states his or her major goal for the talk is preparing the audience mainly for
   (A) serial communication
   (B) managing conflict
   (C) effective listening
   (D) persuasive motivation
   (E) coping with new ideas

4. Which of the following statements is INCORRECT according to parliamentary procedure?
   (A) An amendment must be seconded before it can be discussed on the floor.
   (B) A substitute motion can be introduced, rather than a motion to amend, while the main motion is on the floor for discussion.
   (C) A group can overrule the chairperson's ruling on the relevancy of an amendment.
   (D) Prior to discussion, once a motion is made and seconded, it cannot be restated.
   (E) A motion cannot be voted on until all second- and first-degree amendments have been acted on.

5. The use of an arena stage differs from other methods of play production in that
   (A) the downstage area is smaller
   (B) body language is less easily interpreted by the audience
   (C) the acoustics are inferior
   (D) the stage is surrounded on all sides by the audience
   (E) the changes of scenery are fewer and less time consuming

6. A speech criticizing the school football team's performance during a game can be presented if it is neither intended nor likely to cause disruptive behavior. The success of the speech, which seeks to change team behavior, will depend most upon which two of the following factors?

567

I. The receiver's beliefs in relation to cognitive inertia
II. The receiver's receptivity to persuasive messages
III. Informal student networks and their strength
IV. The prescribed behavior of the speaker and his or her credibility
V. The attitude of the administration and the faculty

(A) I and IV
(B) II and III
(C) III and IV
(D) II and IV
(E) III and V

7. Recent lawsuits against newspapers and other media have been won by individuals on all of the following grounds EXCEPT
   (A) written agreements were made with the reporter before the interview
   (B) an interview was never granted to the reporter
   (C) the story was in violation of the individual's privacy
   (D) the story was untrue and caused emotional suffering
   (E) information was given but later retracted by the interviewee

8. For a teacher of speech communication who desires to keep discipline problems to a minimum during play production, which of the following is of first importance?
   (A) Making a list of rules and regulations regarding behavior
   (B) Deciding how to reinforce productive behavior
   (C) Choosing well-liked students to assist with equipment and the stage
   (D) Appointing committees to select plays and material for oral interpretation
   (E) Recognizing the impact of nonverbal communication

9. A teacher wants to persuade his best friend to join him in teaching abroad for a year. Which of the following communication techniques would probably be LEAST effective for this purpose?
   (A) Stressing the value of new experiences
   (B) Brainstorming the options available to the friend
   (C) Arguing aggressively in favor of teaching abroad
   (D) Responding directly to the friend's questions and doubts
   (E) Watching for nonverbal cues to the friend's real feelings

10. During a rehearsal for a play the students get into an argument over the correct placement of various parts of the stage set. Communication is relevant to the outcome of conflict situations. Which of the following types of remarks should the teacher use to reduce the conflict?
    (A) Controlling: "Either we place the table and chairs where I put them, or we don't do the play!"
    (B) Accommodating: "Let's try some of the suggestions; then we can see the different effects."
    (C) Defining: "I discussed this matter with you last week. We all agreed then that this was the best placement."
    (D) Forcing: "We don't have all night, you know. We still have the third act to rehearse!"
    (E) Adapting: "It doesn't make any difference to me. I'll go along with the decision of the majority!"

Answer Key

1. C	3. C	5. D	7. E	9. C
2. E	4. D	6. C	8. E	10. B

Teaching Hearing-Impaired Students

The examination in Teaching Hearing-Impaired Students tests the competence of candidates for special education with particular emphasis upon the hearing-impaired students.

Content and Scope (150 questions, 2-hour test)

The test covers four significant areas:

   I. Understanding the Developmental and Special Needs of Students with Hearing Impairment
   II. Resources, Services, and Implementation of Instruction
   III. Legal Regulations, Issues, and Compliance
   IV. The Roles and Relationship of Community Services, School Staff, and the Family

Topics for Review

1. Historical trends and current research for teaching the hearing-impaired students
2. Definitions, degree, and type of loss
3. Causes of hearing loss, prevalence and identification
4. Developmental profiles, language and cognitive development
5. Federal regulations, requirements of PL 94-142, the IEP, parental involvement, the least restrictive environment
6. Current methodology, academic achievement, special needs, multiple handicapping conditions
7. Priorities, assessment of progress, instructional technology, social and personal adjustment
8. The role of audiologists, psychologists, special teachers, administrators, medical personnel, and the family

Sample Questions

Directions: For each question or incomplete statement, select the *best* answer or completion from the four choices.

1. Which factor would not be appropriate for consideration when planning an IEP for a student with severe hearing loss?
   (A) He has not heard any spoken words.
   (B) He was placed in a self-contained special class.
   (C) His speech is difficult to understand.
   (D) His deafness is a progressive congenital disease.

2. Educational adaptations are developed around the degree of hearing loss. The most severe hard-of-hearing loss involves
   (A) speech therapy only
   (B) understanding conversational speech to auditory training only
   (C) preferential seating to speech therapy only
   (D) a condition ranging from hearing loud sounds to being considered deaf

3. Mariko is a prelingual deaf child. On a developmental profile compared to a postlingual child of similar age and ability, she would
   (A) display a greater loss in language development only.
   (B) have no loss in speech development.
   (C) exhibit a greater loss in speech, reading, and spelling.
   (D) achieve the same level of social maturity.

569

SPECIALTY AREA TESTS

4. Students with hearing loss are hampered least by
   (A) those persons who emphasize their deficiencies.
   (B) pupils who treat them as if they had mental retardation.
   (C) teachers who always talk loudly to them.
   (D) school staff who emphasize their strengths.

5. The total communication method is the most common one used with students who have severe or profound hearing loss. It places the most emphasis on
   (A) finger spelling only.
   (B) appropriate aural, oral, and manual expression.
   (C) the SEE I and SEE II.
   (D) the oral method only.

6. The classroom teacher plays an important role in the identification of students with hearing loss who need referral for examinations. Which of the following is NOT the responsibility of the classroom teacher?
   (A) Paying attention to pupils who are reluctant to participate in discussions
   (B) Using simple word lists to check pupils who omit constant sounds
   (C) Obtaining parental permission for audiological testing
   (D) Speaking with students who verbalize, "What?" or "Huh?"

7. High-interest, interactive, individual reading programs should be prepared to aid the cognitive development of pupils with hearing impairment because
   (A) female students with hearing loss score slightly lower than males on reading achievement tests.
   (B) these students need experiences that develop vocabulary and critical thinking, and encourage them to share ideas.
   (C) reading achievement is indirectly related to hearing loss.
   (D) students with one deaf parent score higher on reading tests than those with two deaf parents.

8. CAI has one major weakness for students with special needs. It is that
   (A) typical programs use more new materials than review work.
   (B) insufficient feedback is provided.
   (C) frequent responses are expected.
   (D) numerous motivation devices can become distractors.

9. Students with severe hearing loss or deafness can communicate by telephone if they use an acoustic coupler and typewriter (TDD). The new telephone relay system provides
   (A) for a broader age range of users.
   (B) for sending messages to people without special equipment.
   (C) a lower cost for the equipment.
   (D) for assistance after 8 PM.

10. Students who can read can learn from newscasts, but
    (A) telecaption equipment must be attached to the television set.
    (B) closed-captioned programs are limited to educational subjects.
    (C) closed-captioned programs are not available for home use.
    (D) telecaptions move around too fast and are too difficult to follow.

TEACHING HEARING-IMPAIRED STUDENTS

11. The appropriate teaching procedures for students with hearing loss include
    I. displaying new words in different colors and sizes.
    II. indicating the relationship between information previously learned and new ideas.
    III. stressing meaning in each lesson.
    IV. using chunking and distributed practice for long spelling lists.
    (A) I only
    (B) I, II only
    (C) I, II, III only
    (D) I, II, III, IV only

12. The regular English curriculum has four basic processes: listening, speaking, reading, and writing. For pupils with hearing loss lessons, it should be
    (A) integrated into a whole only at the secondary level.
    (B) based upon learning stimuli created by the teacher.
    (C) based upon the experiences of the learners as they encounter life.
    (D) less functional than for nonhandicapped students.

13. The most enjoyable outcome of the study of literature by students with hearing impairment is
    (A) social sharing of knowledge, ideas, and attitudes.
    (B) growth in understanding literary styles.
    (C) increased ability in critical analysis.
    (D) increased ability to write poetry.

14. Bob is a ninth-grade student with both a hearing impairment and learning disability. The best way to serve his needs is to
    (A) place him in a sheltered workshop.
    (B) coordinate instruction by the teacher of the deaf and the learning-disability specialist.
    (C) have him taught only by the instructor of the deaf.
    (D) have the teacher of the deaf and the learning-disability specialist teach him during alternate six-week periods.

15. Cross aids are used when one ear is substantially better than the other. The purpose of using a microphone on that side to transfer sound to the good ear is
    (A) to double the hearing capacity of the child with a loss.
    (B) to provide true stereophonic sound.
    (C) to replace body hearing aids.
    (D) to keep the sound level up as it travels around the head.

16. The concept of never having to place children into special classes emphasizes the first priority of providing more
    (A) kindergarten teachers.
    (B) reading specialists.
    (C) early diagnosis and intervention in the home.
    (D) individual instruction in the elementary grades.

17. School districts can best meet the needs of secondary students with hearing impairment by
    (A) centralizing their programs and services.
    (B) placing these students in self-contained classes.
    (C) providing tutorial services.
    (D) mainstreaming students with hearing loss into English classes only.

SPECIALTY AREA TESTS

18. One of the most basic problems children with hearing loss face in cognitive development is
    (A) not having enough words in the sign language for expression.
    (B) living with parents who do not sign.
    (C) the predominantly late diagnosis of deafness.
    (D) not having a sharable language until school age or later.

19. The effective use of the computer by a pupil with hearing loss involves all of the following EXCEPT
    (A) having an opportunity to construct a language of her own.
    (B) utilizing interactive language.
    (C) being a passive agent during the lessons.
    (D) using intellectual stimulants to discover language patterns.

20. Language growth programs for the deaf most often fail to provide
    (A) practice in intrasentential construction of words and phrases.
    (B) time for right-wrong answers in daily reading lessons.
    (C) multiple-choice testing experiences.
    (D) language play with pragmatic contexts to create and revise thoughts in intermediate stages.

Answer Key

1. D	8. D	15. D
2. D	9. B	16. C
3. C	10. A	17. A
4. D	11. D	18. D
5. B	12. C	19. C
6. C	13. A	20. D
7. B	14. B	

Teaching Visually Handicapped Students

The examination in Teaching Visually Handicapped Students tests the academic competence of candidates for teaching visually impaired students.

Content and Scope (120 questions, 2-hour test)

The test focuses on these areas:

   I. Special Education Applied to the Visually Impaired Students
  II. Conditions Affecting Students During Their Development
 III. Legal Issues and Professional Ethics
  IV. Lesson Planning and Implementation of Instruction
   V. The Relationship of the Special Education Teacher to Other Teachers and Staff

Sample Questions

Directions: For each question or incomplete statement, select the *best* answer or completion from the four choices.

1. The positive reason for labeling children as exceptional or handicapped is that it
   (A) decreases the possibility of rejection.
   (B) places no stigma on them.
   (C) is an accurate classification.
   (D) increases eligibility for special funding and programs.

2. Students who are least likely to attend regular classes are
   (A) visually handicapped.   (C) mentally retarded.
   (B) learning-disabled.   (D) hard-of-hearing.

3. Brian, a pupil with visual impairment, has been placed in a regular fourth-grade class. Who can assist his teacher in preparing lessons for him?
     I. The special education teacher
    II. The school psychologist
   III. The library media specialist
    IV. His parents
   (A) I only
   (B) II only
   (C) I, II only
   (D) I, II, III, IV

4. A teacher's responsibility to assist in the assessment of a pupil is to furnish to the committee all of the following EXCEPT
   (A) examples of the child's homework.
   (B) test scores and other reports.
   (C) examples of speech or language problems.
   (D) examples of pupil's strengths but not weaknesses.

SPECIALTY AREA TESTS

5. What is the basic determinant of the classification for a visual handicap?
   (A) Severe visual impairment
   (B) Severe visual impairment to total blindness
   (C) Total blindness only
   (D) Wearing glasses for correction of vision

6. Which one of the following statements about visual handicaps is incorrect?
   (A) A legally blind child can see at 20/200 or less, with correction.
   (B) A legally blind child has no visual imagery or sense of light or darkness.
   (C) Educational classifications are: moderate, severe, and profound.
   (D) The main learning channels for a child with profound visual disability are touch and hearing.

7. Learning that requires visual interpretation with detailed tasks
   (A) is a function of the medulla in the brain.
   (B) is based on visual-oral coordination.
   (C) involves light refraction on retinal cells only.
   (D) cannot be performed by pupils with profound visual disability.

8. The human eye has several interrelated parts that can become defective through
   I. heredity.
   II. disease.
   III. an accident.
   IV. other causes.
   (A) I only
   (B) II only
   (C) II, III only
   (D) I, II, III, IV

9. Which statement refers to sensory compensation?
   (A) Children with visual handicaps use more verbalisms with few or no concrete meanings.
   (B) Lack of adequate vision is a primary handicap affecting cognitive development.
   (C) Stimulation during the preschool years helps children integrate learning experiences.
   (D) Research indicates that hearing or touch is not superior in children with visual handicaps.

10. The health agency that has developed several screening tests with the Snellen chart for preschool and school-age children is
    (A) the American Health Association.
    (B) the American Medical Society.
    (C) the National Society for the Prevention of Blindness.
    (D) the American Opthamology Association.

TEACHING VISUALLY HANDICAPPED STUDENTS

11. Under the provisions of PL 94-142, when making pupil assessments, the teacher may be assisted by an interdisciplinary team including
    (A) the school psychologist, classroom teachers, a special education teacher, and a disability specialist.
    (B) the guidance counselor and classroom teacher.
    (C) the school social worker, school psychologist, and parents.
    (D) the speech therapist and/or guidance counselor.

12. In the human eye, when the student looks at an object closer than 20 feet,
    (A) the cornea narrows.
    (B) the ciliary muscles increase the convex curvature of the lens.
    (C) the ciliary muscles decrease the concave curvature of the lens.
    (D) no muscular change is necessary.

13. Social relationships for blind children are limited most by
    (A) their visual impairment.
    (B) their inability to participate in sports.
    (C) their fear of trying new things.
    (D) their feeling of being different.

14. When a student with a visual handicap spends most of the time in a regular classroom, which adaptation may not be required every day?
    (A) Wheels on her chair so she can get close to the chalkboard quickly
    (B) The teacher reading aloud everything put on the chalkboard
    (C) Special boldline paper for written assignments or classnotes
    (D) Requiring the pupil to use very bright lighting

15. The reading efficiency of adolescents who use Braille
    (A) cannot be increased.
    (B) naturally increases with use.
    (C) can be increased by short-term training with the code.
    (D) causes significant anxiety during further training.

16. Mobility is increased by the use of the Sonicguide. It
    (A) emits high frequency sounds reflected from nearby objects.
    (B) gives information about distant objects only.
    (C) is worn on a pair of earphones.
    (D) responds to motion only.

17. Adolescents with multiple handicaps may require which of the following?
    I. Vocational and career counseling
    II. Sheltered workshops
    III. Mobility specialists
    IV. Apprenticeship training
    (A) I only
    (B) II only
    (C) III only
    (D) I, II, III, IV

18. Adaptations that help students overcome feelings of learned helplessness include all of the following EXCEPT
    (A) experiences with space, reaching, touching, listening.
    (B) exposure to sizes, shapes, and textures.
    (C) comparing relationships, similarities, and differences.
    (D) planning long periods of times alone.

19. All but one of these instructional techniques is in widespread use with learners who have visual handicaps. Select the least appropriate method.
    (A) Synthetic speech from a computer; a talking calculator
    (B) An optician
    (C) Tactile maps and charts
    (D) Wooden shapes of different sizes to manipulate

20. Participation in physical education is the most significant experience for adolescents with handicaps because
    (A) it encourages movement in enlarged space.
    (B) new skills can be learned.
    (C) peer respect is often increased.
    (D) orientation is sharpened while independence and obstacle perception are increased.

21. A comprehensive assessment of children with visual handicaps should include which of the following?
    I. An eye examination and visual efficiency tests
    II. A check on mobility and functional living skills
    III. An evaluation of intellectual, cognitive, and perceptual-motor performances
    IV. An evaluation of gross and fine motor development along with the use of social skills
    (A) I and II only
    (B) II, III, IV only
    (C) I, II, III, IV
    (D) I, II, III only

22. One of the new science programs for use in the upper elementary grades is the SAVI—Science Activities for the Visually Impaired units. Which of the following makes these activities most challenging for use in mainstreamed classrooms?
    (A) Object manipulation
    (B) Experiments with everyday things
    (C) The sighted and visually impaired can work together
    (D) Each module has detailed instructions and vocabulary terms

23. The cognitive development of children with visual handicaps is characterized by all of the following EXCEPT
    (A) limits on integrating and interpreting experiences.
    (B) a need for early stimulation, if impaired in infancy.
    (C) a decrease in proprioception with age.
    (D) problems with spatial relationships.

TEACHING VISUALLY HANDICAPPED STUDENTS

24. Robin, a fourth-grade pupil, says geography is her favorite subject; she likes to know about different places where people live. However, she is having difficulty reading tactile maps. Which of the following would be the LEAST helpful to her?
    (A) Developing her own search skills at her own pace with the teacher's praise as the reward
    (B) Readiness skills for map reading, taught with different objects and shapes
    (C) Teaching her cues and details in one area of the classroom at a time.
    (D) Using a tape recording that explains or describes what each part of the tactile map represents

25. Many blind students lag in writing skills. For this reason,
    (A) writing should begin in kindergarten.
    (B) writing is taught first with the braille typewriter.
    (C) reading and writing should be taught as whole language skills.
    (D) writing is taught after reading skills become useful.

Answer Key

1. D	9. D	17. D
2. C	10. C	18. D
3. D	11. A	19. B
4. D	12. B	20. C
5. B	13. C	21. C
6. B	14. D	22. C
7. D	15. C	23. C
8. D	16. A	24. A
		25. D

SPECIALTY AREA TESTS

Technology Education

The examination in Technology Education tests the academic competence of candidates for the teaching of this subject at the middle, junior, or senior high school levels.

Content and Scope (150 questions, 2-hour test)

The test covers basic facts and principles in industrial arts and technology. It has two components, professional and technical, and covers six major areas:

> I. Program Development and Management (about 30 questions)
> II. Professionalism and Professional Growth (about 6 questions)
> III. Communications—includes graphic arts, electricity/electronics, and photography (about 30 questions)
> IV. Construction—includes carpentry, masonry, house wiring, plumbing, heating, and air conditioning (about 21 questions)
> V. Manufacturing—includes woods, metals, plastics, ceramics, and crafts (about 42 questions)
> VI. Transportation/Power/Energy—includes auto mechanics, small engines, power mechanics, and alternate energy (about 21 questions)

Some Topics for Review

1. Manufacturing management
2. Processing
3. Packaging
4. Marketing
5. Servicing and repairing
6. Construction management
7. Exteriors and interiors
8. Substructures and superstructures
9. Installing utilities
10. Selling and transferring property
11. Graphic and electronic communications
12. Energy sources
13. Conversion and storage of energy
14. Transportation systems—control, servicing, repairing
15. Properties of various materials
16. Testing materials
17. SI system of measurement
18. Curriculum development for industrial arts
19. Teaching strategies, including those for handicapped pupils
20. Maintenance of physical facilities
21. Safety considerations
22. Evaluating and reporting pupil progress
23. Professional organizations and journals
24. Interfacing industrial arts with general or vocational education

Sample Questions

Directions: For each question or incomplete statement, select the *best* answer or completion from the five choices.

TECHNOLOGY EDUCATION

1. Industrial tasks have both knowledge and skill components that vary from task to task. Which tasks have the largest requirements of skills and knowledge?
   (A) nonrepetitive work
   (B) single-purpose machine work
   (C) multipurpose machine work
   (D) group machine work
   (E) handwork or handwork with tools

2. What is the chronological order of strokes in a four-cycle engine?
   (A) Compression, power, exhaust, intake
   (B) Intake, compression, power, exhaust
   (C) Power, exhaust, intake, compression
   (D) Intake, power, compression, exhaust
   (E) Compression, power, intake, exhaust

3. An orthographic projection drawing has how many views?
   (A) 3
   (B) 5
   (C) 7
   (D) 8
   (E) 9

4. The correct wiring procedure to use with single-pole switches rated at 30 amperes and above with CU/AL markings would be
   (A) copper or copper-clad aluminum wiring only
   (B) copper wiring only
   (C) copper-clad aluminum wiring only
   (D) copper, copper-clad aluminum, or aluminum wiring only
   (E) aluminum wiring only

5. In the soft soldering operation, flux is used to
   (A) increase the temperature
   (B) strengthen the joint
   (C) clean the metal
   (D) regulate the heat
   (E) counteract the sal ammoniac

6. The architect's scale most commonly used in house construction is
   (A) $\frac{1}{4}'' = 1'0''$
   (B) $\frac{1}{2}'' = 1'0''$
   (C) $1'' = 1'0''$
   (D) $1\frac{1}{4}'' = 1'0''$
   (E) $1\frac{1}{2}'' = 1'0''$

7. Two major types of trowels are used by masons: the London and Philadelphia patterns. Which one of the five parts of a trowel is different in the two types named?
   (A) The toe
   (B) The shank
   (C) The ferrule
   (D) The heel
   (E) The handle

8. Teachers can use several communication strategies to break down learning or performance difficulties. Which one of the following would most likely lead to correct diagnostic solutions of complex problems?
   (A) Continuous prose instructions (oral and/or written)
   (B) Heuristics—trial-and-error or discovery processes
   (C) Algorithims—sets of instructions in a format
   (D) Demonstrations by pupils as they work on the problem
   (E) Decision or logic tables—sets of questions that must be answered

579

SPECIALTY AREA TESTS

9. When quartz crystals are forced between metal plates, electricity is created; the greater the pressure on the crystals, the greater the relative
   (A) voltage
   (B) magnetism
   (C) number of watts
   (D) vibration
   (E) number of ohms

10. In the future, research in industrial arts education will probably develop better processes and objectives for teaching
    (A) "normal" adults
    (B) emotionally disturbed adolescents
    (C) retirees
    (D) blind and other physically handicapped persons
    (E) elementary school teachers

11. The pressure tank in a home water system should turn on when the pressure in the tank falls to
    (A) 25–30 pounds
    (B) 30–35 pounds
    (C) 35–40 pounds
    (D) 40–45 pounds
    (E) 45–50 pounds

12. In woodworking, the simplest boring bit is the
    (A) shell bit
    (B) spoon bit
    (C) centre bit
    (D) rimmer bit
    (E) tape bit

13. A cubic foot of concrete weighs
    (A) 100 pounds
    (B) 180 pounds
    (C) 160 pounds
    (D) 120 pounds
    (E) 140 pounds

14. In the construction of wooden floors, what should be placed on top of the subfloor?
    (A) The joist
    (B) The stud
    (C) The header
    (D) The sole plate
    (E) The sill

15. In regard to painting the exterior of a house, which of the following is an INCORRECT statement?
    (A) Paint should not be applied over wrinkled, blistered, and peeling surfaces
    (B) The first side of the house to be painted is the one that the sun has already passed over.
    (C) The best temperature for exterior painting is about 80°F.
    (D) Paint should be applied only when a temperature of at least 40°F is forecast for the evening and the next morning.
    (E) The brush should be dipped about halfway into the paint, and the excess patted off on the inside of the pail.

Answer Key

1. A	4. D	7. D	10. D	13. E
2. B	5. C	8. E	11. A	14. D
3. A	6. A	9. A	12. C	15. C

Appendix

State Departments of Education

Alabama State Department of Education
Teacher Certification Office
349 State Office Building
Montgomery, Alabama 36130

Alaska Department of Education
Department of Certification
Pouch F, State Office Building
Juneau, Alaska 99811

Arizona Department of Education
Teacher Certification Unit
1535 West Jefferson Street
P.O. Box 25609
Phoenix, Arizona 85007

Arkansas Department of Education
Office of Teacher Certification
State Capitol Mall
Little Rock, Arkansas 72201

State of California
Commission for Teacher Preparation
and Licensing
1812 9th Street
Sacramento, California 94244-2700

State of Colorado
Teacher Certification
Colorado Department of Education
State Office Building
201 East Colfax Avenue
Denver, Colorado 80203

State of Connecticut
Connecticut State Department of Education
Teacher Certification Unit
Box 2219
Hartford, Connecticut 06115

State of Delaware
Department of Public Instruction
Teacher Certification Unit
Dover, Delaware 19901

State of Florida
Dept. of Prof. Regulation
Bureau of Examination Services
1940 N. Monroe Street
Tallahassee, Florida 32399

State of Georgia
Teacher Certification Services
Georgia Department of Education
209 State Office Building
Atlanta, Georgia 30334

State of Hawaii
Department of Education
Office of Personnel Services
Teacher Certification
P.O. Box 2360
Honolulu, Hawaii 96804

State of Idaho
Office of Teacher Certification
State Department of Education
Len B. Jordan Building
Boise, Idaho 83720

Illinois State Board of Education
State Teacher Certification Board
100 North First Street
Springfield, Illinois 62777

State of Indiana
Department of Public Instruction
Division of Teacher Education and
Certification
Room 229, The State House
Indianapolis, Indiana 46204

State of Iowa
Department of Public Instruction
Teacher Education and Certification
Division
Grimes State Office Building
Des Moines, Iowa 50319

State of Kansas
State Department of Education
Certification Section
120 East Tenth Street
Topeka, Kansas 66612-1103

State of Kentucky
Department of Education
Division of Teacher Certification
Capital Plaza Tower
18th Floor
Frankfort, Kentucky 40601

State of Louisiana
Department of Education
Certification Division
P.O. Box 94064
Baton Rouge, Louisiana 70804

State of Maine
Department of Educational and
Cultural Services
Certification and Placement
State House Station No. 23
Augusta, Maine 04333

STATE DEPARTMENTS OF EDUCATION

State of Maryland
Maryland Department of Education
200 West Baltimore Street
Baltimore, Maryland 21201

Commonwealth of Massachusetts
Department of Education
Bureau of Teacher Certification
31 St. James Avenue
Boston, Massachusetts 02116

State of Michigan
Michigan Department of Education
Teacher Preparation and Certification
Services
Box 30008
Lansing, Michigan 48909

State of Minnesota
Education Department
Teacher Licensing and Placement
Capitol Square
St. Paul, Minnesota 55100

State of Mississippi
Division of Instruction
Office of Teacher Education and
Certification
P.O. Box 771
Jackson, Mississippi 39205

State of Missouri
Department of Education
Teacher Certification Section
P.O. Box 480
Jefferson City, Missouri 65102

State of Montana
Office of Public Instruction
Teacher Certification Office
The State Capitol
Helena, Montana 59620

State of Nebraska
Department of Education
Teacher Certification
301 Centennial Mall South
Box 94987
Lincoln, Nebraska 68509

State of Nevada
Nevada Department of Education
Teacher Certification
400 W. King St.
Carson City, Nevada 89710

State of New Hampshire
State Department of Education
Division of Administration
Office of Teacher Education and
Professional Standards
410 State House Annex
Concord, New Hampshire 03301

State of New Jersey
Department of Education
Division of Field Services
Bureau of Teacher Education and
Academic Credentials
CN 503
Trenton, New Jersey 08625-0503

State of New Mexico
Department of Education Building
Teacher Education and Certification
Division
Education Building
Santa Fe, New Mexico 87501

State of New York
State Education Department
Division of Teacher Education and
Certification
Cultural Education Center, Room 5A11
Empire State Plaza
Albany, New York 12230

State of North Carolina
Department of Public Instruction
Division of Standards and Certification
116 W. Edenton Street
Raleigh, North Carolina 27603-1712

State of North Dakota
Department of Public Instruction
Teacher Certification Office
Bismarck, North Dakota 58505

State of Ohio
Department of Public Instruction
Teacher Education and Certification
State Office Building
Columbus, Ohio 43266-0308

STATE DEPARTMENTS OF EDUCATION

State of Rhode Island
State Department of Education
Teacher Certification Division
22 Hayes Street
Providence, Rhode Island 02908

State of South Carolina
Department of Education
Teacher Certification Section
1004 Rutledge Building
1429 Senate Street
Columbia, South Carolina 29201

State of South Dakota
Teacher Certification Office
Division of Elementary and
Secondary Education
Kneip Office Building
Pierre, South Dakota 57501

State of Tennessee
Tennessee Department of Education
Division of Teacher Ed. and Cert.
6th Floor, North Wing
Cordell Hull Building
Nashville, Tennessee 37243-0377

State of Texas
Texas Education Agency
Division of Teacher Certification
201 East Eleventh Street
Austin, Texas 78701

State of Oklahoma
State Department of Education
Section of Teacher Certification
Oliver Hodge Memorial Building, Rm. 232
2500 North Lincoln
Oklahoma City, Oklahoma 73105

State of Oregon
State Department of Education
Teacher Standards and Practices
Commission
580 State St., Room 203
Salem, Oregon 97310-3782

Commonwealth of Pennsylvania
Department of Education
Bureau of Teacher Certification
333 Market Street
P.O. Box 911
Harrisburg, Pennsylvania 17126-0333

Utah State Board of Education
Division of Curriculum and Instruction
Teacher Certification
250 East 500 South
Salt Lake City, Utah 84111

State of Vermont
Department of Education
Teacher Certification Office
State Offices Building
Montpelier, Vermont 05602

State of Virginia
Department of Education
Teacher Certification Office
P.O. Box 60
Richmond, Virginia 23216-2060

State of Washington
Superintendent of Public Instruction
Certification & Licensing Office
7510 Armstrong Street, SW.
Olympia, Washington 98504

State of West Virginia
Department of Education
Educational Personnel Certification
1900 Washington Street East
Charleston, West Virginia 25305

The State of Wisconsin
Department of Public Instruction
Teacher Certification Office
125 South Webster Street — Box 7841
Madison, Wisconsin 53707

The State of Wyoming
State Department of Education
Accreditation Services Unit
Hathaway Building
Cheyenne, Wyoming 82002

District of Columbia
District of Columbia Public Schools
415-12 Street
N.W., Washington, D.C. 20005

Puerto Rico
Certification Officer
Department of Education
Hato Rey
Puerto Rico 00900

Introducing
Barron's Book Notes
The Smart Way to Study Literature

Everything you need for better understanding, better performance in class, better grades! Clear concise, fun to read—Barron's Book Notes make literature come alive.

101 titles to choose from:

THE AENEID
ALL QUIET ON THE WESTERN FRONT
ALL THE KING'S MEN
ANIMAL FARM
ANNA KARENINA
AS I LAY DYING
AS YOU LIKE IT
BABBITT
BEOWULF
BILLY BUDD & TYPEE
BRAVE NEW WORLD
CANDIDE
CANTERBURY TALES
CATCH-22
THE CATCHER IN THE RYE
CRIME AND PUNISHMENT
THE CRUCIBLE
CRY, THE BELOVED COUNTRY
DAISY MILLER &
    TURN OF THE SCREW
DAVID COPPERFIELD
DEATH OF A SALESMAN
THE DIVINE COMEDY: THE INFERNO
DR. FAUSTUS
A DOLL'S HOUSE & HEDDA GABLER
DON QUIXOTE
ETHAN FROME
A FAREWELL TO ARMS
FAUST: PARTS I AND II
FOR WHOM THE BELL TOLLS
THE GLASS MENAGERIE &
    A STREETCAR NAMED DESIRE
THE GOOD EARTH
THE GRAPES OF WRATH
GREAT EXPECTATIONS
THE GREAT GATSBY
GULLIVER'S TRAVELS

HAMLET
HARD TIMES
HEART OF DARKNESS &
    THE SECRET SHARER
HENRY IV: PART I
THE HOUSE OF THE SEVEN GABLES
HUCKLEBERRY FINN
THE ILIAD
INVISIBLE MAN
JANE EYRE
JULIUS CAESAR
THE JUNGLE
KING LEAR
LIGHT IN AUGUST
LORD JIM
LORD OF THE FLIES
THE LORD OF THE RINGS &
    THE HOBBIT
MACBETH
MADAME BOVARY
THE MAYOR OF CASTERBRIDGE
THE MERCHANT OF VENICE
A MIDSUMMER NIGHT'S DREAM
MOBY DICK
MY ANTONIA
NATIVE SON & BLACK BOY
NEW TESTAMENT
1984
THE ODYSSEY
OEDIPUS TRILOGY
OF MICE AND MEN
THE OLD MAN AND THE SEA
OLD TESTAMENT
OLIVER TWIST
ONE FLEW OVER THE
    CUCKOO'S NEST
OTHELLO

OUR TOWN
PARADISE LOST
THE PEARL
PORTRAIT OF THE ARTIST
    AS A YOUNG MAN
PRIDE AND PREJUDICE
THE PRINCE
THE RED BADGE OF COURAGE
THE REPUBLIC
RETURN OF THE NATIVE
RICHARD III
ROMEO AND JULIET
THE SCARLET LETTER
A SEPARATE PEACE
SILAS MARNER
SLAUGHTERHOUSE FIVE
SONS AND LOVERS
THE SOUND AND THE FURY
STEPPENWOLF & SIDDHARTHA
THE STRANGER
THE SUN ALSO RISES
A TALE OF TWO CITIES
THE TAMING OF THE SHREW
THE TEMPEST
TESS OF THE D'URBERVILLES
TO KILL A MOCKINGBIRD
TOM JONES
TOM SAWYER
TWELFTH NIGHT
UNCLE TOM'S CABIN
WALDEN
WHO'S AFRAID OF
    VIRGINIA WOOLF?
WUTHERING HEIGHTS

Priced from $2.50 to $2.95
($3.50 to $3.95 Can.)

On sale at your local bookstore

All prices subject to change without notice. At your bookstore or order direct from Barron's.

Call toll-free 1-800-645-3476.

BARRON'S

Barron's Educational Series, Inc.
250 Wireless Blvd., Hauppauge, NY 11788
In Canada: Georgetown Book Warehouse
34 Armstrong Ave., Georgetown, Ont. L7G 4R9

ASPIRE HIGHER WITH THE POWER... OF WORDS!

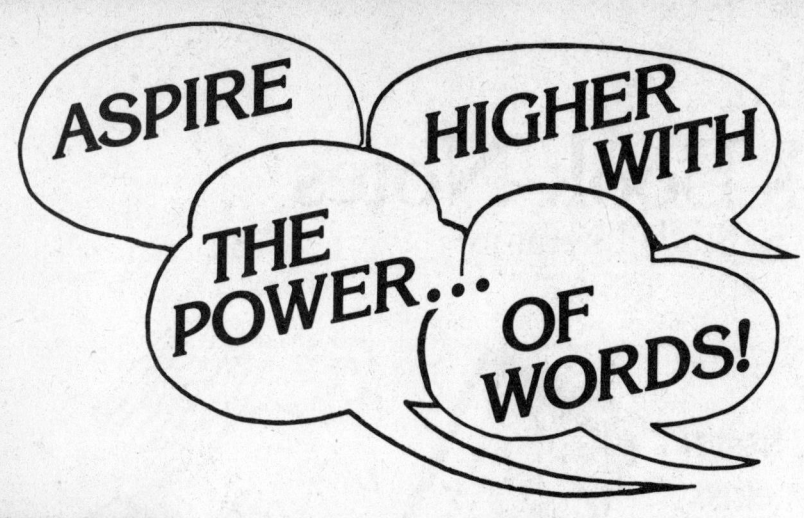

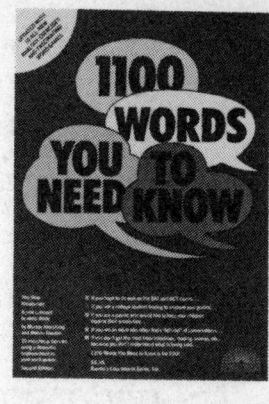

504 ABSOLUTELY ESSENTIAL WORDS
$8.95, Can. $11.95 (3702-2)
Builds practical vocabulary skills through funny stories and cartoons plus practice exercises.

BUILDING AN EFFECTIVE VOCABULARY
$9.95, Can. $13.95 (2041-3)
Covers all the methods of evaluating words to improve communication skills.

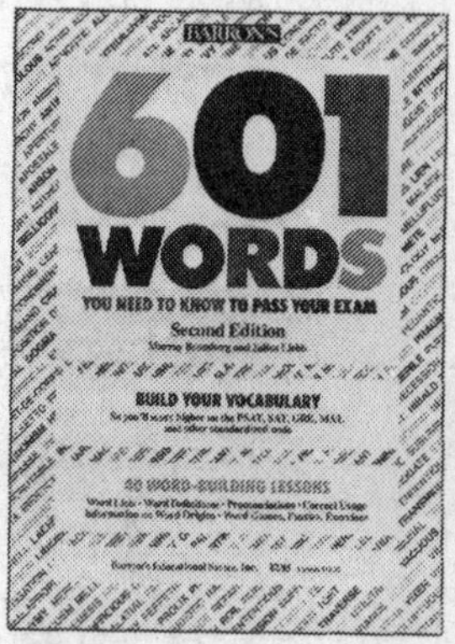

1001 PITFALLS IN ENGLISH GRAMMAR, 3rd Edition $8.95, Can. $11.95 (3719-7)
Examines the most common errors in the English language.

1100 WORDS YOU NEED TO KNOW, 2nd Edition
$7.95, Can. $10.95 (2264-5)
This book is the way to master more than 1100 useful words and idioms taken from the mass media.

601 WORDS YOU NEED TO KNOW TO PASS YOUR EXAM, 2nd Edition
$7.95, Can. $10.95 (4232-8)
Here are 40 updated lessons consisting of word lists, definitions, pronunciations, and notes on word origins and usage.

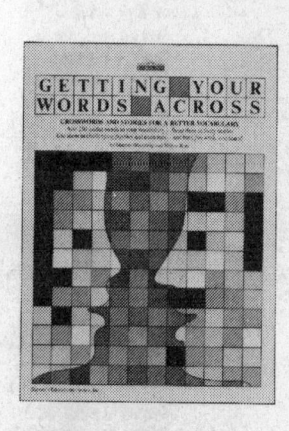

WRITE YOUR WAY INTO COLLEGE
$8.95, Can. $11.95 (2997-6)
A step-by-step guide to writing an effective college application essay. Actual student essays are included with helpful critiques.

GETTING YOUR WORDS ACROSS
$7.95, Can. $10.95 (2082-0)
The unique basic vocabulary book that uses brief articles, exercises and crossword puzzles to build word power.

HANDBOOK OF COMMONLY USED AMERICAN IDIOMS, 2nd $6.95, Can. $9.95 (4614-5)
With 1500 popular idioms, this book will benefit both English-speaking people and those learning English as a second language.

BARRON'S EDUCATIONAL SERIES, INC.
250 Wireless Boulevard
Hauppauge, New York 11788
Canada: Georgetown Book Warehouse
34 Armstrong Avenue
Georgetown, Ontario L7G 4R9

Prices subject to change without notice. Books may be purchased at your bookstore, or by mail from Barron's. Enclose check or money order for total amount plus sales tax where applicable and 10% for postage and handling (minimum charge $1.75, Can. $2.00). All books are paperback editions. ISBN prefix: 0-8120